Introduction to Networking

Wendell Odom

PEARSON IT CERTIFICATION

800 East 96th Street
Indianapolis, Indiana 46240 USA

Introduction to Networking

Copyright © 2013 by Pearson Education, Inc.

ISBN-13: 978-0-7897-4845-4

ISBN-10: 0-7897-4845-2

Library of Congress Cataloging-in-Publication Data:

Odom, Wendell.

  Introduction to networking / Wendell Odom. — ITT version.

    p. cm.

  ISBN-13: 978-0-7897-4845-4 (hardcover)

  ISBN-10: 0-7897-4845-2 (hardcover)

1. Computer networks. I. Title.

  TK5105.5.O327 2013

  004.6—dc23

                              2012023683

Printed in the United States of America

Second Printing: January 2013

Trademarks

Warning and Disclaimer

Bulk Sales

Pearson IT Certification offers excellent discounts on this book when ordered in quantity for bulk purchases or special sales. For more information, please contact

> **U.S. Corporate and Government Sales**
> **1-800-382-3419**
> **corpsales@pearsontechgroup.com**

For sales outside the United States, please contact

> **International Sales**
> **international@pearsoned.com**

Associate Publisher
Dave Dusthimer

Executive Editor
Brett Bartow

Senior Development Editor
Christopher Cleveland

Managing Editor
Sandra Schroeder

Senior Project Editor
Tonya Simpson

Copy Editor
John Edwards

Indexer
Brad Herriman

Proofreader
Sheri Cain

Technical Editors
Dr. Theodor Richardson
Douglas E. Maume

Publishing Coordinator
Vanessa Evans

Interior Designer
Gary Adair

Cover Designer
Alan Clements

Compositor
Studio Galou

Illustrator
Mike Tanamachi

Contents at a Glance

Contents

About the Author

Wendell Odom has helped teach a generation of networkers about LAN switching and IP routing. In addition to writing textbooks, Wendell has long been a widely respected author of Cisco certification books for the Cisco CCENT, CCNA, CCNP, and CCIE certifications. He has also created video learning and simulation software products for those exams. He has worked as a network engineer, consultant, instructor, course developer, and book author. He graduated from the Georgia Institute of Technology, and he has achieved expert-level certification from Cisco Systems (CCIE No. 1624). Wendell connects with readers through blogs, Facebook, and a website, all of which can be found on his company's website (www.certskills.com).

Dedication

For Dr. Oliver Ibe, one of my professors during my undergrad years at Georgia Tech.
Dr. Ibe's enthusiastic lectures in class, his willingness to dig into the details of how things
really work, and his combined industry and theoretical insights when advising me on my senior
project (An Analysis of Ethernet LAN Performance) were some of the big reasons I chose the
field of computer networking. Thanks for all your help and guidance, Dr. Ibe!

Acknowledgments

Like most books, this book acknowledges the author's name on the cover, but writing any textbook such as this book requires a lot of work from a lot of people. An entire team of people contributed in many key roles to make this book and associated materials become a reality. The finished product has much better content and finish because of the work of the entire team.

Thanks to Brett Bartow, executive editor, for continuing to work with me on all my projects with Pearson Education. Brett has a great ability to match the right projects with the right timing and schedule. This book was a joy to write—Brett, thanks for the opportunity to write it.

Chris Cleveland, development editor, developed the book, walking through the manuscript and author review stages. Chris always strikes that balance of helping the book communicate better through following a common-sense application of publishing rules, while knowing when to break the rules to communicate the ideas for some of the more unusual topics. The only sad part about completing the author review stage is that it means Chris has to move on to other books from other authors; thanks for jumping back on board to help me with a book, yet again!

Douglas Maume and Dr. Theodor Richards worked as technical editors, reviewing the manuscript and making comments. Doug was particularly helpful in finding those errors that seem to crop up in any book, and Ted was helpful in making me think about some of the bigger-picture discussions. Both helped make the book better, but as always, responsibility for the accuracy of the final content falls to me.

Mike Tanamachi worked with me on the figures, drawing the figures based on my rough hand-drawn ideas. Mike did a great job of drawing what I meant, rather than what I drew, and improving how well the figures communicated the ideas. And he kept to a pretty aggressive schedule as well. Thanks, Mike—looking forward to working together again down the road.

Laura Robbins, illustrator for Pearson, went above and beyond on this title. Besides her usual work, she also worked with me on a new outside-the-box figure development process along with Mike Tanamachi. Laura, thanks for helping me work out all those niggling little details about figures, color versus grayscale issues, finding the "right" blue, and generally answering any figure question that popped into my head.

Thanks to Gary Adair for the fantastic interior design for the book. The design differs quite a bit from many of my other books, and Gary did a great job seeing how to present the various features of the book in the design. Thanks, Gary!

Most of my work is done when the production team takes the book and runs with it. As usual, thanks to Sandra Schroeder for juggling the production process for countless books while making sure that my project got all the attention it needed, right on time. Thanks to Tonya Simpson, senior project editor, for managing this book through the production maze and through the outside-the-box steps with the new figure process. Thanks to John Edwards, copy editor, for cleaning up my crummy wording, and thanks to Sheri Cain for doing the painstaking task of reading to find all those little errors that spell checkers cannot find. And thanks to Brad Herriman, for adding in all the index codes to create the index—quite a task, given the large amount of terminology, topics, and concepts in this book.

Beyond the book itself, the project includes several other related elements, without which the book would not be complete. All those elements necessarily make use of this text, which requires the other authors to both know the text and write other materials. Specifically, thanks to DeAnnia Clements for creating the Instructor's Guide, Douglas Maume for developing the slide decks for use in class, and Sean Wilkins for creating additional question banks. Also, thanks to Dr. Theodor Richardson for creating the lab guide.

Thanks to readers of my other books, and to those who post on my Facebook page (Facebook.com/WendellOdom), for some surprisingly relevant help. It always amazes me how often a reader comment or perspective from one book helps make another book better.

Thanks go to my family as well. As usual, my wife Kris has been a big support throughout the writing process. For this title, both my wife and daughter Hannah actually helped with the book content on occasion. Thanks in particular for all the opinions on different figures, and for Hannah, the comments on using mind maps more effectively.

Finally, thanks to God for giving me a truly enjoyable time writing this book, turning a long process into what seems like just a brief and enjoyable moment, because of how much fun the work turned out to be.

About the Technical Reviewers

Mr. Douglas E. Maume is the lead instructor for the computer networking program at Centura College Online. He has been conducting new and annual course reviews for both the CN and IT programs since 2006. He also is an adjunct professor for Centura College, teaching computer networking, information technology, and business management courses since 2001. Mr. Maume owned his own business called Wish You Were Here, Personal Postcards, creating digital postcards on location at the Virginia Beach oceanfront. He earned a Bachelor degree in graphic design from Old Dominion University and an Associate in Applied Science degree in graphic design from Tidewater Community College. Mr. Maume is the District Deputy Grand Exalted Ruler for Southeast Virginia in the Benevolent and Protective Order of Elks. He has been actively involved with the Elks since 1999, serving the veterans and youth of the Norfolk community. He also is a member of the Shipps Corner Soccer Club adult men's league and has been playing competitively since 1972.

Theodor D. Richardson is an author, *Choice* magazine book reviewer, online program director, and assistant professor for a private university. He has served as an assistant professor for six years in the area of security and multimedia/web design. Theodor wrote *Secure Software Design* (Jones and Bartlett Learning, 2012) and *Microsoft Office and Beyond* (Mercury Learning and Information, 2011). Theodor earned his Ph.D. degree in computer science and engineering from the University of South Carolina in 2006 with a concentration in multimedia and image processing (Graduate Student of the Year 2005). Theodor received an NSF Graduate Research Fellowship and an NSF GK–12 Graduate/K–12 Teaching Fellowship during his graduate studies. He has earned the NSA Graduate Certificate in Information Assurance and Security from the University of South Carolina.

We Want to Hear from You!

As the reader of this book, *you* are our most important critic and commentator. We value your opinion and want to know what we're doing right, what we could do better, what areas you'd like to see us publish in, and any other words of wisdom you're willing to pass our way.

As the associate publisher for Pearson IT Certification, I welcome your comments. You can email or write me directly to let me know what you did or didn't like about this book—as well as what we can do to make our books better.

Please note that I cannot help you with technical problems related to the topic of this book. We do have a User Services group, however, where I will forward specific technical questions related to the book.

When you write, please be sure to include this book's title and author as well as your name, email address, and phone number. I will carefully review your comments and share them with the author and editors who worked on the book.

Email: feedback@pearsonitcertification.com

Mail: Dave Dusthimer
               Associate Publisher
               Pearson IT Certification
               800 East 96th Street
               Indianapolis, IN 46240 USA

Reader Services

Visit our website and register this book at www.pearsonitcertification.com/register for convenient access to any updates, downloads, or errata that might be available for this book.

Introduction

Computer networking touches most every activity in the world today. While the average person does not need to know about computer networking, every IT job role requires that the IT worker understand something about how computer networks work. And if you decide that networking seems interesting, the world of networking has many networking-focused job roles.

This book acts as a "Networking 101" college textbook. In that role, this book has three major goals: to be easily understood by students with no prior networking knowledge; to uncover the most central and important topics in networking, even if only lightly discussed; and to prepare the student for further studies in networking by emphasizing the most important parts of modern networking.

As with most textbooks, this textbook balances many competing goals. No matter what major you might choose in college, you cannot learn everything about that topic, even by the time you complete a degree program, much less in a single course. As an introductory text, this book tries to balance the following:

- Discuss a broad range of topics, while emphasizing the importance of how all the pieces fit together rather than the importance of any single piece.

- Focus on modern networking topics, while including some less-modern topics when they show why and how modern networks work the way they work.

- Explain important theoretical and conceptual foundations, while limiting those discussions to topics that modern network engineers need to think about in modern computer networks.

Organization of the Text

The book begins with the assumption that students know nothing about how computer networks work. It builds a broad foundation in the first three chapters. The next four chapters focus on how to build networks to move data, both over shorter distances (local-area networks, or LANs) and longer distances (wide-area networks, or WANs). Chapters 8 and 9 move into a vast topic area: how TCP/IP uses those LANs and WANs to create today's corporate TCP/IP networks and the worldwide Internet itself. The final chapter looks at how networking connects the individual piece of software you use—the application—to the matching software that sits somewhere in the vast reaches of the global Internet.

Each chapter has the same basic organization. Each chapter has some short features to begin, followed by the core explanations inside the chapter. The end of the chapter lists various review tools. As you might expect, your instructor might or might not want you to read all sections of the chapter, or to use every review tool, so check your syllabus for information about which parts of the book to use.

Key Pedagogical Features

To begin the chapter:

Each chapter begins with a few features that help direct you as to what the chapter discusses, before getting into the core topics of the chapter:

- **Chapter Introduction** describes the big ideas in the chapter, with perspective on how it fits with the other chapters.
- **Chapter Outline** lists the titles of the (usually three or four) major sections in each chapter, with a short description.
- **Chapter Objectives** list the most important student results from using this chapter as part of a networking course.
- **Key Terms** list the terms for the most important concepts in the chapter. These terms and their related concepts should be the reader's top priority for what to understand and recall from this chapter. As a suggestion, while reading through the chapter, make notes about each of these terms.

In the core of the chapter:

The majority of each chapter, following the chapter introduction, uses text, tables, lists, and figures to explain various networking topics. Along with those descriptions, the core topics also use the following features:

- **Key Terms:** Inside the chapter, the key terms are noted in a **large, bold font** so that they can be easily found.
- **Author's Note:** These notes list topics that the author wants to draw particular attention to, but which you can skip when reading if you want to maintain the flow. Author notes typically list some deeper fact about the current topic or some fact that may be a little off-topic. Read these notes at some point, whether during your first read of the chapter or when reviewing and studying.
- **On the Side:** These notes list topics that add interest to the topic, but which your instructor probably will not require you to know for tests. (Check with your instructor.)

In the chapter-ending Chapter Review section:

The end of each chapter closes with a Chapter Review section, which has tools and activities that you can use to review the reading from inside the chapter:

- **Chapter Summary:** A brief summary of the big points made inside the chapter.
- **Answer These Questions:** Multiple-choice questions that can be used to review the topics in the chapter.
- **Define the Key Terms:** This heading lists the same key terms listed in the beginning of the chapter. This section reminds you of the terms, and suggests an activity where you write the definition for these terms in your own words. You can then compare your definition with the definitions in the glossary.
- **List the Words Inside Acronyms:** As a simple review, take this list of acronyms from the chapter and write out the words represented by the acronym. Then, check the acronyms in the glossary.
- **Create Mind Maps:** This heading suggests a few mind-mapping activities to help you mentally review the chapter.
- **Define Other Terms:** As a simple review, take this list of other terms from the chapter, beyond the list of key terms, and write out a definition for each. You can then compare your definition with the definitions in the glossary.

Other features outside each chapter:

Beyond the features in each chapter, this book comes with other helpful features as well:

- **Complete the Tables and Lists from Memory:** In some cases, the chapter organizes information into tables, both for easier reference and so that you can use the tables when studying. The publisher creates copies of these tables with some information missing as an exercise where you complete these tables when studying to memorize the information. You can find this information as Appendix B, "Memory Tables," and Appendix C, "Memory Tables Answer Key," online at www.pearsonitcertification.com/title/9780789748454.

- **Appendix A:** Numeric Reference Tables: This appendix lists some of the most common information about numbers, as used throughout networking, including a conversion table for 8-bit binary to decimal.

- **Glossary and Index:** The glossary lists the various terms used in the book, with definitions, while the index lists page references for the most common of those terms.

- *Introduction to Networking Lab Manual*: As a separate title, the *Introduction to Networking Lab Manual* offers lab exercises that can be used with each of the chapters in this book.

A Brief Word on Mind Mapping

Mind maps, a type of graphic organizing tool, give learners a visual way to learn, take notes, organize thoughts, and basically think. Each chapter includes some suggested mind-mapping exercises as a way to help you think about the topics in that chapter.

With the mind-mapping exercises in these chapters, the goal is not for you to create the exact same mind map that the author had in mind when making up the activity. Instead, the point of the activity is what happens to your own mind and memory by simply doing the activity:

- Organize the topics in your own mind and your own words.
- Improve your memory of the networking concepts and terms.
- Build a stronger understanding of how networking ideas relate to each other.
- Build a stronger understanding of what topics go together, and which topics differ.

You can create mind maps with software, or just with pen and paper. The main point is that you write something and put a circle (or rectangle, or some shape) around the text. You write another point in words, circle it, and then connect the two if some relationship exists. Then you keep writing ideas and connecting the ideas that relate to each other.

For example, Figure I-1 shows a figure of a mind map created using software. In this case, a student in a PC fundamentals course was given a task to organize what they know about personal computers into two categories: the parts typically found inside the computer, separated from those typically found outside the computer. The figure shows an example mind map that separates the ideas.

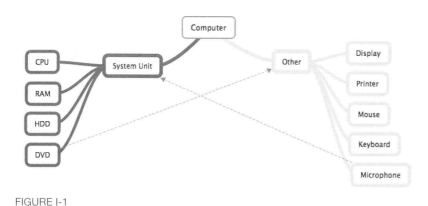

FIGURE I-1

Sample Mind Map

If you just glance at the figure, and see the somewhat basic ideas and terms and stop there, you miss the whole point of the mind-map exercise. First, think about the core idea, listed in the center as "System Unit." Would you use this term for a computer or some other term? The mind map starts with a blank sheet of paper, so you have to choose. What other terms might you use instead of "System Unit"? If you thought of several, you could add a list of synonyms or alternatives to the mind map (not shown), but it gives you the chance to think about what terms to use.

Next, think about the next level of organization, moving to the left for items inside the computer and to the right for items outside the computer. Can you think of others to add to the list? Also, some of these might be inside or outside the computer, so you have to account for putting a device in both lists. (This example just shows a line to the other side of the figure, rather than repeating the term.)

Finally, imagine that the core topic is "computers" and that you include laptops, desktops, tablets, and even smart phones in the list of computers. For some of those, the display and keyboard are part of the device. For some devices, no physical keyboard exists—it just shows up as an image on the display screen.

Or, what about laptop computers or tablet computers? In those cases, the display is integrated into the computer, and for a tablet, the keyboard is typically not even a physical device.

The point of these exercises for this book is not the finished product mind map as much as the process. The mind map might be changed, expand, have items moved, or have lines added and erased. (Using a pencil rather than a pen, or software, really is preferred so that you can make changes.) Each time you write something and see the correct relationship, it reinforces your memory. Each time you write something and start to question it, it helps you uncover where you have questions, and you can then look further.

Author's Book Web Pages

The book author's website includes a microsite for this book. The site, at www.certskills.com/ITN, essentially lists links related to each chapter. For example, the page for the entire book lists some links to mind-mapping software. The web page for Chapter 3, which discusses standards for TCP/IP networks, lists links for websites that let you look at the TCP/IP standards. These pages can be useful for those of you looking for additional information for the topics in each chapter.

Conclusion

Networking moved from its infancy to maturity in the last quarter of the twentieth century and now touches many parts of the everyday life of a large percentage of the world's population. Networking offers a wide variety of career options and many interesting technical areas, and it will likely be important to the world for generations to come. I hope you enjoy learning some of the fundamentals of networking as you work through this text.

Chapter 1

Introduction to Computer Data

When most people think about a computer, they think about a traditional personal computer (PC). It might weigh 10–15 pounds and sit on the floor, with the computer connected to a keyboard, mouse, and display. Or you might think of a laptop computer, which integrates the keyboard/mouse/display with the computer for easy transport.

However, in a much broader sense, computers come in many shapes and sizes. Simply put, computers process data. With that broad definition, your phone is a computer, your tablet (for example, an iPad) is a computer, and so is your MP3 player, your video game system, and your modern digital television. Figure 1-1 shows a few photos of these kinds of devices, for perspective.

FIGURE 1-1

Images of Various Types of Computers/ Computing Devices (© bloomua, © Topix, © James Phelps JR, © ambrits)

Smart Phone   Tablet   Game Console   MP3 Player

In addition to these consumer computers, the world of computers includes many other types of computers as well. Some have a lot more computing power, like servers and supercomputers. Some exist to solve specific problems for specific industries. For example, the networking world relies on many types of specialized computing devices, in particular two types of devices called *routers* and *switches*. (Several later chapters discuss the purpose of both routers and switches.)

The typical consumer does not actually care that these devices act like computers internally. Consumers buy devices because of the features useful to the human: sending text, playing games, surfing the web, listening to tunes, and getting work done for a job or for school.

To understand the world of computer networks, you need to understand computers. What common features make all these devices computers? This basic definition of a **computer** outlines the answer:

> A computer is a device that processes (receives, thinks about, changes, stores, sends out, displays, and prints) data in the form of bits.

This chapter looks at this broad definition of computers and computing, but with a goal in mind—to prepare you to think about computer networks. If a single computer works with "data in the form of bits," a computer network lets that same computer send those bits to another computer.

In short, this chapter focuses on the word *computer* in the term *computer networking*, with the rest of the book focusing on the *networking* part.

Finally, this chapter purposefully keeps the discussion somewhat general. This chapter attempts to give enough information about how computers work so that you can better understand computer networking. This chapter does not, however, try to explain any one topic fully, and it does not attempt to explain everything about computers in this one chapter. Instead, think of the chapter as the foundation from which to then focus on how computers communicate.

Chapter Outline

Introducing Data and Information, Bits and Bytes

Permanent Storage for Bits, Bytes

Input and Output

Chapter Summary

Chapter Review Activities

Objectives

- Define the concepts behind the terms bit and byte.

- Describe in general terms how computers store data in random-access memory (RAM).

- Explain how a computer can represent text characters using the bits held in RAM.

- Explain how a computer file system organizes data.

- Describe in general terms how computers store data in a hard disk drive.

- Explain the general steps that occur when a user presses keys on a computer keyboard.

- Describe the basic information that a mouse sends to a computer so that the computer moves the mouse pointer.

- Explain the concepts behind a computer display's pixel map, and describe how the computer uses bits to represent the color of each pixel.

Key Terms

computer	file	keyboard map
bit	file system	mouse
byte	directory	display
random-access memory (RAM)	hard disk drive	screen resolution
character set	input and output	

Introducing Data and Information, Bits and Bytes

Data exists in a computer as bits. What are these bits? How are they stored? What do they mean? The following sections begin to answer these types of questions, focusing on the concepts of bits and bytes, how a computer stores bits in random-access memory (RAM), and how the data bits actually represent useful information.

Defining Bits, Bytes

To understand one of the most fundamental computing terms—bit—first you need a brief math review.

First, ever since any of us started learning math, we used a base 10 numbering system. That is, 10 decimal digit values exist (0 through 9). If you count upward, you cannot go past 9 without running out of digits of course, so we use multiple digits, with each position in the number representing a power of 10. For example, 321 means "three 100s, two 10s, and one 1."

Base 2 math uses the same logic, but with only two binary digit values: 0 and 1. If you count upward, you cannot go past 1 without using multiple digits. In this case, each digit represents a higher power of 2. For example, 1010 in binary, which is the equivalent of decimal 10, means "one 8, zero 4s, one 2, and zero 1s."

Computers use **bits** to represent the concept of a *binary digit*. Computers cannot write numbers on paper to remember them. Computers record the ideas they work with electronically, as bits, and these bits represent either a value of 0 or 1. So, from one perspective, a computer processes (receives, thinks about, changes, stores, sends out, displays, prints) binary numbers.

A bit is the smallest unit of data that a computer works with. However, just like humans use multidigit decimal numbers every day, computers work with multidigit binary numbers. To make the topic easier to discuss, the computing world has many terms for different-sized groups of bits: nibble, **byte**, word, and double word. Figure 1-2 shows the ideas.

FIGURE 1-2

Nibble, Byte, Word, Double Word

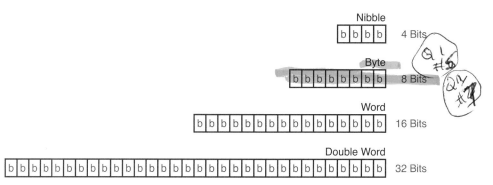

For some tasks, computers work with a few bytes of data, but for other tasks, computers actually organize data into groups of thousands or millions of bytes. Because computers use binary math, however, computers number these large groups based on powers of 2. Table 1-1 lists four of the most common such terms, the literal numbers of bytes meant by each term, and the approximate number of bytes used to estimate size for the term.

TABLE 1-1

Kilobyte, Megabyte, Gigabyte, Terabyte

Term	Size (Bytes)	Size (2^n Bytes)	Rounded Size (Bytes)
Kilobyte	1024	2^{10}	1000
Megabyte	1,048,576	2^{20}	1,000,000
Gigabyte	1,073,741,824	2^{30}	1,000,000,000
Terabyte	1,099,511,627,776	2^{40}	1,000,000,000,000

> **AUTHOR'S NOTE:**
> Frankly, the exact number of bytes associated with each term does not really matter in most cases. However, knowing each of these terms, and the approximate number of bytes, is important.

Random-Access Memory (RAM)

Computers process data in the form of bits, whether it is one bit at a time, one byte at a time, or a megabyte at a time. But how do they process bits? Computers use many methods to store bits depending on what the computer intends to do with the bits. This section looks at one of the most fundamental ways a computer temporarily stores bits: **random-access memory (RAM)**.

RAM physically exists as a set of microchips installed on a plastic card called a *memory module* (shown later in Figure 1-5). The chips and the electronics on the card together create a set of physical locations in which a computer can store and read bits or bytes of data.

The computer's *central processing unit (CPU)* uses RAM like people use a notepad. The CPU often needs to remember a binary value so that the CPU can use it later, so the CPU wants to write (store) the binary value in RAM. Later, the CPU can read the data from RAM to recall the value stored earlier.

To write data to RAM, the CPU must communicate with RAM, telling RAM both the binary value to store as well as the location in RAM. To communicate with RAM, the CPU sends an electrical signal over an electrical pathway called a *bus*. To identify the location in RAM, RAM uses an address for each unique memory location where a byte can be stored. To write (store) a particular value into a byte of RAM, the CPU sends a signal to RAM over the bus, listing two facts: the address in RAM plus the value to be written.

To read from RAM, the CPU uses a similar process, as shown in the example in Figure 1-3. To read the current value of a byte in RAM, the CPU uses the same bus to send a message to RAM. The read request lists the address of that particular byte, asking for its value. The RAM returns the binary value stored at that address.

Figure 1-3 shows the idea of how the CPU can read the byte stored at address 4 in RAM.

FIGURE 1-3

CPU Reads Byte 4 from RAM

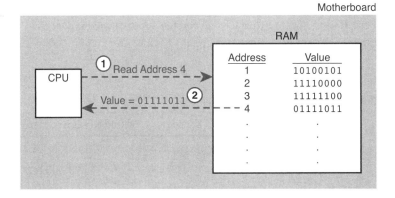

Many different types of RAM chips exist, which also means that many methods to store bits on RAM chips exist. Frankly, to accurately understand the details of how RAM stores bits, you need some understanding of digital electrical engineering, and those topics are beyond the scope of this book. However, understanding some of the electrical concepts can be useful to know at this point, just to get the general idea.

In some types of RAM, the chip stores a 1 or 0 by storing a different electrical charge in a capacitor. A *capacitor* is an electronics part that can store an electrical charge; think of it like a short-lived battery. The RAM chip has a capacitor for each bit. The RAM chip can physically control the capacitor in each bit to either store a full charge, meaning that bit holds a binary 1, or store a partial electrical charge, meaning binary 0.

To control the capacitors in RAM, the RAM circuitry sends a slightly different electrical input to the bits that need to store a 1 versus a 0. Essentially, the RAM chooses one of two inputs to each bit, which results in either a full or partial charge in the capacitor, which in turn represents either a 1 or 0, respectively.

Figure 1-4 shows the general idea. In the figure, Step 1, at the bottom, shows the value that the CPU wants to write to RAM. Step 2 shows the different RAM input values, with the low input signals being sent if the bit value was 0 and the high input values being sent if the bit value was 1. Finally, at Step 3, the various capacitors each store either a partial or full charge to match.

The drawing of the bits in Figure 1-4 might be visible to humans, but the bits on the RAM chips are far too small to see. Each bit is literally microscopic. For example, Figure 1-5 shows a photo of a memory module: a plastic card that happens to hold eight RAM chips. Each of the RAM chips holds 2 gigabits of memory. Working together, the eight chips on the one memory module in the figure hold 2 gigabytes of memory. And the photo as printed in the book is roughly to scale—the entire card fits easily in the palm of my hand.

ON THE SIDE:
Although a single bit is the smallest unit that a CPU can think about, most CPUs read and write data at least one byte at a time, so the RAM addresses identify the location of an entire byte.

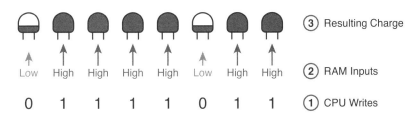

FIGURE 1-4

Writing Individual Bits in Byte 4 of RAM

FIGURE 1-5

Photo of a 1-Gigabyte RAM Card (©Mykola Mazuryk)

Representing Information Using Bytes of Data

In the early days of computing, many people used the term *data processing* to refer to the world of computing. Your job title might be senior data processing specialist, the department might be called the Data Processing Department, and so on. Later, the term *information technology* replaced data processing as the most often used term. Today, many people work in the IT department and have degrees with the word *information* in the title.

While that small history lesson might not sound important, the two core terms— *data* and *information*—have important differences. In the world of computing, these words usually imply the following:

- **Data:** Focused on the bits and bytes
- **Information:** Focused on the meaning and context of what those bits and bytes represent

While working in IT, sometimes you truly only care about the data, in other words, the bits and bytes. At other times, the meaning of those bits might have a large impact on your choices at work. For example, you might be working with a customer order database, knowing that if database access fails for a long period, you might be looking for a new job. You might sometimes think of that database as a bunch of bits and bytes, but most of the time, you will instead think of it as information about customers.

So, just how does a computer take this very basic concept of bits and bytes and represent all this wonderful information? The next two topics show a couple of examples: how a computer uses bits to represent text and how a computer uses bits to represent numbers.

Text Character Sets

If you sit down in front of your computer, open your favorite word processor, start a new document, and start typing, what happens? If you did everything right, text shows up on the display. However, all the computer can do is process bits: 1s and 0s. This section looks at part of the mystery as to how the computer works when you type text that then shows up in a word processor.

Behind the scenes, the computer must interpret user actions and convert those actions into bits. Focus for a moment on what happens starting with the point in which the word processor was ready for the user to type a brand new document. For each letter pressed on the keyboard, hidden to the user, the keyboard sends some bits to the computer, specifically to the CPU. Again hidden, the CPU processes the bits that arrive from the keyboard; the CPU stores those bits in RAM. Additionally, the CPU updates some other bits that represent what the computer displays on the screen and sends the new image (again represented by bits) to the screen. Figure 1-6 shows these actions as three separate steps.

FIGURE 1-6

Process Overview: Typing in a Word Processor

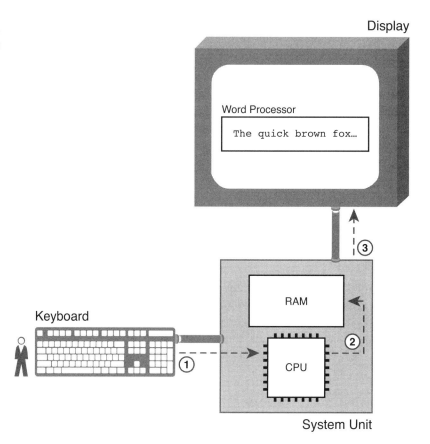

Focus on the bits that the CPU stores in RAM for the purpose of representing the letters the user typed. When the user typed the letter *e*, clearly, the CPU cannot store an *e* in RAM, because *e* is not a binary 1 or 0. All the CPU can do is store an 8-bit value in a byte of RAM, and *e* is not a binary 0 or 1. The solution? Computers use a concept called a *character set*.

A **character set**, sometimes called a *character encoding scheme,* lists all the text characters on the computer with a matching binary value. When the user types one character, the computer CPU looks at the character set and stores the matching (mapped) binary value.

For example, one of the earliest character sets, American Standard Code for Information Interchange (ASCII), used a 7-bit code for each character, with the following binary values associated with the lowercase letters *a*, *b*, and *c*:

> a: 1100001
>
> b: 1100010
>
> c: 1100011

If the word processor happened to be using this same ASCII character set, when the user typed an *a*, at some point, the word processor application, running on the CPU, would store the letter *a* by storing binary 1100001 into RAM. (Note that in this case, the code is only 7 bits long, and because the CPU typically stores data a byte at a time, the computer would probably use an entire 8-bit byte and ignore the extra bit.)

Now that you have seen a few of the details, take a step back from the detail for a moment and just think about any time you have created a document on a computer. Every time, that computer converted what is typed on the keyboard into bits. Each time, the computer stored those bits in RAM. At the same time, those bits represented information you want to be in a document, specifically, the letters you happened to type.

Character sets also play a vitally important role for computer networking. Have you ever sent a copy of a document to a coworker, classmate, or friend? They could probably open the document and see the same words you had originally typed. For both users to see the same letters, both computers must use the same character set. Without a standard character set, you might be able to exchange the document, but the receiving computer would have no idea what the bits meant.

Numeric Values

Computers also need to do math problems on occasion, both on behalf of the user but more frequently for reasons hidden from the user. For example, the user might simply open a calculator application and the computer needs to do the math problem. Additionally, a lot of the background work a CPU does—managing RAM, moving data between RAM and permanent storage, deciding exactly what lights (pixels) to illuminate on the display, and so on—all requires the CPU to do math.

As always, the CPU can store bits and bytes in RAM. But how can the computer store a decimal number in RAM? In this case, rather than using a table of mapped values like a text character set, the computer can represent the decimal number as its equivalent binary number and store that binary number into RAM.

For example, consider the decimal number 123. The computer needs to store that value in RAM after a user has typed that value into a calculator application. For now, assume that the computer will store the value as an 8-bit value. The computer converts the value for decimal 123 to binary.

This book assumes a working knowledge of binary math, but a brief review of how to work with decimal values between 0 and 255, and their 8-bit binary equivalent numbers, can be useful (modern networks happen to use numbers in this range quite a bit).

First, consider 8-bit binary numbers and how to find the equivalent decimal number. Figure 1-7 helps break down the concept while also showing a specific example of converting from a specific 8-bit binary value (01111011) and its decimal equivalent (123).

FIGURE 1-7

Converting Binary 01111011 to Decimal 123

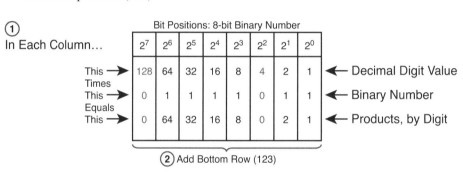

Focus for a moment on the structure and meaning of an 8-bit binary number, as represented at the top of the figure. Each binary digit represents a power of 2. The rightmost digit represents the lowest power of 2 (2^0, or 1). Moving right to left, the next digit represents the next power of 2 (2^1, or 2). Continuing to the left, each digit represents the next power of 2, up through 2^7, or 128. To calculate the decimal equivalent value, you basically add up the decimal values for each bit position for any bits that have a value of 1. More formally, you can follow this two-step process:

1. In each of the eight columns, multiply the decimal digit value times the binary value.

2. Add the eight numbers found in the previous step (the bottom row in the table).

> **AUTHOR'S NOTE:** This textbook assumes that you have a working knowledge of binary math as a prerequisite. However, very little in the book requires you to do any math using binary numbers. Ask your instructor whether you need to be ready to perform binary math procedures, such as converting from binary to decimal, as shown in Figure 1-7.

To convert in the opposite direction, from decimal to binary, usually takes a little more thought. Many different methods exist to find the equivalent binary value. Basically, you have to pick binary values (0 or 1) for each bit position so that the math in the previous figure adds up to the original decimal number.

The following formal process shows just one way to find the equivalent 8-bit binary number when converting decimal numbers from 0 through 255. The process begins with a table with the eight bit positions. It lists the known decimal digit values for each binary digit. It also has a place to keep a value this chapter calls a *countdown* and a place to record the binary result.

For this process, follow these steps for all eight bit positions, beginning at the left and moving to the right:

1. If the countdown is less than the decimal digit value:

   a. Write a 0 for the binary digit.

   b. Copy the countdown, unchanged, to the next bit position.

2. If the countdown is greater than or equal to the decimal digit value:

   a. Write a 1 for the binary digit.

   b. Subtract the decimal digit value from the countdown and place in the next bit position.

Figure 1-8 shows an example using the same decimal number (123) shown in Figure 1-7.

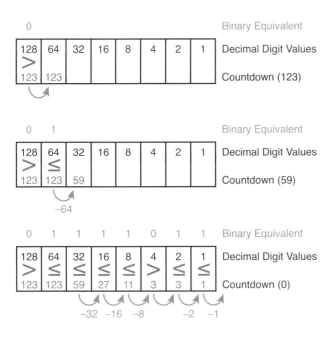

Figure 1-8 has three parts. The top shows the first pass through the process, the middle shows the second pass through the process, and the bottom shows the final six passes through the process.

At the top of the figure, for the first pass, the countdown starts with the original decimal value (123). Each pass compares the countdown of the decimal value for that column, so in this case, the countdown of 123 is less than the decimal digit value of 128. So, per Steps 1a and 1b, the figure shows a bit value of 0, and it just copies the countdown of 123 to the next column.

At the middle of the figure, for the second pass through the process, the countdown (123) is larger than that column's decimal value (64), so Steps 2a and 2b apply. The figure shows this column with a binary value of 1 and the countdown reduced by 64 before copying it to the next column.

The bottom of the figure continues this same logic, until all eight bit values have been set.

While the examples in the last few pages used 8-bit binary numbers, the bigger the decimal number, the more bits the computer needs to store its binary equivalent. For example, if you use just 2 bits, only four possible combinations exist: 00, 01, 10, and 11, representing decimal 0, 1, 2, and 3. With three bits, eight combinations exist: 000, 001, 010, 011, 100, 101, 110, and 111, representing decimal 0 through 7. Basically, a computer can represent 2^n numbers using n bits, namely, decimal values 0 through $2^n - 1$. Table 1-2 lists the typical sizes of RAM used to store nonnegative decimal numbers as binary.

NOTE: Appendix A, "Numeric Reference Tables," includes a table of decimal numbers 0–255, along with their 8-bit binary equivalent values.

TABLE 1-2

Unsigned Integers in Computers, Various Sizes

Size of Storage	Number of Bits	Decimal Range	Range, From 0 to $2n - 1$
Byte	8	0 – 255	$2^8 - 1$
Word	16	0 – 65,535	$2^{16} - 1$
Double word	32	0 – 4,294,967,296	$2^{32} - 1$

Permanent Storage for Bits, Bytes

RAM works well for its intended purpose. RAM sits near the CPU, on the motherboard, and serves as high-speed, short-term memory. RAM has many benefits, and pretty much all computers use RAM. However, RAM has one big negative: It forgets everything when the computer loses power.

Clearly, for computers to be useful, they need a way to store data even when the computer loses power. This section looks at permanent data storage: A place to store data so that the computer will not forget the data when the computer loses power.

First, before thinking about how computers permanently store data, think of the paper you use in your daily life. Some of it is obviously temporary, for example, things you write down quickly on a notepad and toss in the trash that same day. Other paper you will likely keep for the long term: textbooks, other books for fun, photos, financial records, lab books for school, or manuals for computers, just to name a few. In some cases, you might not know how long you will need to keep each item, so you put it somewhere, thinking you will keep it for now at least. (For example, maybe the incoming postal mail keeps stacking up in the kitchen, as if it has a life of its own, growing onto every available flat space.)

Now picture how you personally organize all those papers, books, notebooks, and so on. Do you have a good filing system? Can you easily find the exact information you need? Would your friends say that it's an organized mess? Do you have plenty of filing cabinets, bookshelves, folders, and recycle bins—everything you need to manage all the paper in your life?

When a computer organizes data into permanent storage, that computer has some similar challenges—just multiplied by 10,000 or so. A computer first needs a place to store data so that it does not disappear when the computer loses power; however, just storing the data is not enough. The computer also needs a way to organize the data so that the user and all the applications can find the data that they need.

This second major section of this chapter looks at several major topics. First, it looks at the concept of a file system, which a computer uses to organize the permanently stored data. Just like you would probably not toss all your papers into a single room with no thought as to how to organize the papers, a file system gives a computer a way to organize data. The rest of this section then looks at the devices for long-term storage, focusing on the most commonly used device, the hard disk drive.

File Systems

Computers organize their data into files using a **file system**. The file concept lets the computer treat all the bytes in one document, one song, one video, and so on as one group of bytes that can be referenced by a name. The computer's file system allows the computer to store the bytes of a file in many locations while still keeping track of the location of all the bytes in a file, avoiding the equivalent of a room full of randomly stacked papers.

Most computer operating systems (OS) today have similar file system features, including the concept of files and a directory structure created by the file system. The next few pages take a closer look at these topics.

Files

A computer **file** is a named set of related bytes of data. By naming the file, the OS can more conveniently store the file as a single entity (based on the name) and more easily refer to that data, for example, to copy the file or open the file to work with the data again.

The file concept plays a huge role in how people use computers every day:

- Files have names, for convenient reference, copying, storing, and so on.
- Files keep the bytes in order.
- Files can be stored on any kind of physical computer storage device.
- Files can be sent to other devices and stored there as well.

For example, when writing a short paper using a word processor, you typically save the file. To save the file, you must give it a name: the filename. Later, when you open the file to edit it, you again use that same name.

Saving the file also stores information that keeps all the data together and in the right order. The file contains the important content, of course: the text you typed, plus some formatting information about the fonts you chose, colors, and so on. But parts of the file might not be stored together on the storage device, so the file system keeps track of which parts of the file are in what order. Later, when you open the same file to work on your document some more, the text has not been rearranged into a different order (that would be bad!); the file kept the bytes in the same order.

Additionally, the file concept does not tie the file to a particular kind of physical storage device. You could originally store the file on your computer's hard disk drive. Later, you could have copied the file to a flash drive, which is a second type of permanent storage, one that you can easily remove from your computer and hand to another person. You could hand that flash drive to a classmate, who could plug it into his computer and copy the file to his hard disk drive. Or you could send the file over a network, post it online, and so on. No matter when the file is stored and no matter the type of physical storage, copying the file to any of those types of storage devices does not change the file.

Most OSs use filenames with two parts, formatted as follows: name.type. The user or application that creates the file makes up the filename. The file type, however, identifies to the OS the purpose of the file, so the user should not just make up a file type.

For example, the mp3 file type typically means that the file contains audio, possibly some song. The OS, knowing that fact, would start that computer's default audio-playing software when the user tries to open an mp3 file.

The following list mentions some types of files according to their purpose. It also lists some of the common file types for files of this type, but note that the file type identifiers vary from OS to OS.

- A single song that you can play on an MP3 player (.mp3, .wav)
- A YouTube video (.swf, .mpeg, .avi)
- A text file (.txt, .rtf)
- This chapter of the book, while I was writing it (.doc, .docx)
- A high-resolution image from a space telescope (.png, .jpg)

The Process of Storing Files

Many user applications store data in RAM until you decide to save the data to a file. For example, most computers let you record and save the audio from a microphone, take video from an attached video camera, type text into a word processor, and so on. The application stores the bytes of data in RAM. At some point, you click the right options and tell the application to save your work; only at that point do you create a file.

Figure 1-9 shows just such an example. In this case, the user of a text editor has typed that common typing practice sentence "The quick brown fox jumped over the lazy river." At that point, the application holds the text in RAM, encoded using whatever character set the text editor is using. When the user chooses the option to save this text to a file, the application asks the user for a filename. In this example, the user chooses the name mydoc, and the OS, on behalf of the application, copies the contents of the document from RAM to the disk drive.

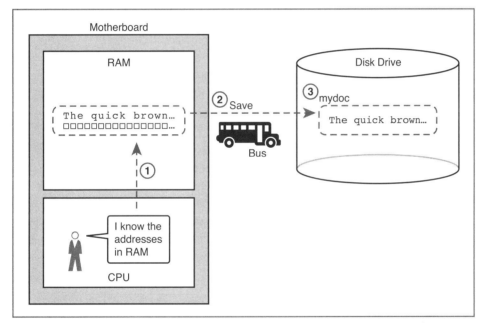

FIGURE 1-9

Creating a File on Disk (Bus icon © Sam)

Following the steps in the figure:

1. The application knows the addresses in RAM that hold the contents of the document.

2. When the user clicks Save and supplies the filename, the OS sends the file contents over the bus to the disk drive.

3. The disk drive stores the file, with the same contents, with the supplied name mydoc.

File Systems and Directories

Computers and computer users face a big challenge in organizing all the files that could exist on a computer. For perspective, consider the simple text document in Figure 1-9, called mydoc, stored on a disk drive. Suppose it required only 1 kilobyte (KB) of storage. In comparison, not long before writing this chapter in 2011, I had just bought a 1-terabyte (TB) drive for less than $100. For perspective, 1,000,000,000 files the size of the mydoc file would fit on that disk drive.

Now think about that file folder at home with this year's bank statements in it—the ones you keep until it is time to do your taxes, or any other small set of papers that you keep in a folder so that you keep the papers together. Instead of having space to store one billion such folders in your house or apartment, imagine that you had a mere 1000 such folders. Would you just pile them up in one stack, and later, search sequentially when it came to finding something? Would you at least store the folders in multiple stacks by related topic: financial, family, by date, bills, hobbies, and so on? Having thousands of folders, completely unorganized, would make it hard to find what you are looking for later.

The computer **file system**, a part of the OS, provides the means by which the OS, applications, and user can organize the files on the computer. File systems let you do the equivalent of keeping similar paper files in the same stack by using directories, or folders. The *directory*, a part of the file system, lets the computer organize files into a hierarchy, keeping similar files together.

For example, the OS itself is software, and the OS exists as many files, in most cases, tens of thousands of files. The people who wrote the OS did not put all the files in one place in the file system; instead, they organized the files into a directory structure (in other words, into folders). When you install the OS, the installation process creates all the same directories (folders) as chosen by the people that created the OS, and the installation process copies the files into the correct folders. The same kind of process happens when you install an application: That process puts the new files in folders, typically as chosen by the people who wrote the application.

Users can also create and use file system directories. The user can create nodes (folders) in the directory structure, choose the names, and copy/move/rename/delete files from those folders, in whatever way makes sense to the user. This is similar to what you might do when organizing your papers at home. For example, a user might create a folder per class if she is in school and keep the work for each class in the folder by that name.

The file system keeps a directory for each permanent storage device. The directory looks like an upside-down tree, with the top literally called the *root*. By convention, the OS identifies the root of the tree for each storage device with a letter. For example, Figure 1-10 shows a sample directory structure on two permanent storage devices: a hard disk drive and a digital video disc (DVD) drive.

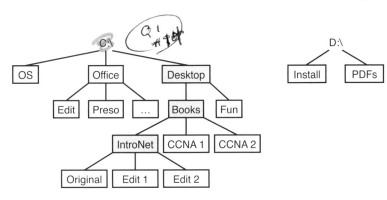

FIGURE 1-10

Directory Structure: Disk Drive (C:) and DVD Drive (D:)

The left side of the figure shows three main branches off the C: drive. Most OSs have a hard disk drive whose root directory is referenced as C:, as shown here. When the OS is installed, it creates a *subdirectory* called Desktop, referenced as C:\ Desktop. The desktop concept gives the user a place to put files as if the files were the user's virtual workspace. The OS installation also creates other subdirectories, for example, maybe the OS subdirectory was created to store the OS's files. As another example, maybe an office application, like Microsoft Office or OpenOffice, was installed in a subdirectory called Office.

The figure shows more subdirectories that might have been created by a user. For example, and as shown in the figure, I could have created a subdirectory called Books to hold all the files for all my books, and then create another subdirectory called IntroNet for this book. Then, because the book goes through many edit passes, I might have additional subdirectories to hold copies of each chapter at each stage in the writing process (original, edit1, edit2).

OSs usually include graphical tools to display the directories and the files contained in them; Figure 1-11 shows the same Books subdirectory as viewed with the Finder application on an Apple Mac.

FIGURE 1-11

Books Subdirectory Example, Using the Apple OS X Finder Application

Mapping Files and Directories to File Content

Next, think back to your imaginary growing problem with too much paper in your house or apartment. You have thousands and thousands of folders holding little pieces of paper, so many that you have a room with nothing but stacks and stacks of folders that hold papers. (In the good ol' USA, we call this problem *hoarding*.) Finding specific papers among stack upon stack of paper could become a problem.

To actually find the papers you keep, it helps to take some kind of notes about where you put different types of papers. Maybe you would keep a list of all the file folders and what is in them. Maybe you would keep that list somewhere handy, somewhere you will remember, and somewhere you would never lose it, maybe right by the door. You could later just walk into the room, grab the list, scan it, and find a reference to the file you need to get. At least you have a chance to find the right file folder!

The OS file system does the same kind of thing on every permanent storage device. The OS, which implements the file system, puts the directory for each storage device in a special place on that storage device. Later, when the user tells the application to save a file to some permanent storage device, not only do the application and OS cooperate to save the file contents, but the OS also updates the directory on that storage device. Those notes include the directory structure, the name of the file, other file statistics (like the date the file was last updated), and importantly, a pointer to where the file actually exists on the storage device.

Figure 1-12 shows the general concept of the information the file system keeps on a disk drive. The top part of the disk drive shows the file information, saved in a reserved part of the disk drive. The arrowed lines represent the idea of a *pointer*: information that tells the OS exactly where each file's contents (bytes) sit on the device.

FIGURE 1-12

**File System with Pointers
to Actual Files**

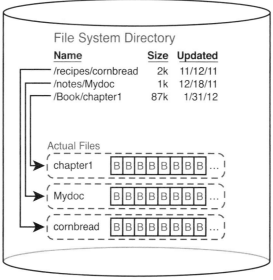

Disk Drive

Because the file system keeps a record of every directory (folder) and file on the disk, the computer can then find the actual contents of the file. For example, imagine that the user decided to open a file that he had created earlier, one that he had stored in the folder called /notes, with the filename mydoc. The user opens a word processor app and asks the app to open the file C:/notes/mydoc, usually by clicking on items from the user interface. Figure 1-13 shows the sequence of events that follows.

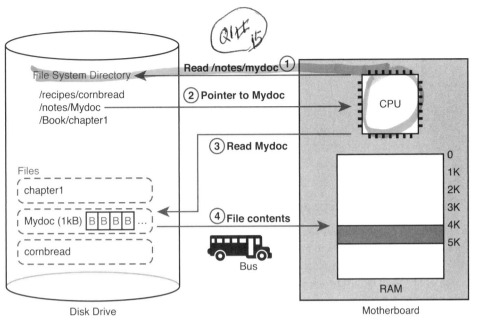

FIGURE 1-13

General Conceptual Steps to Find a File Location and Then Read the File's Contents (Bus Icon © Sam)

Following the steps in the figure:

1. The CPU attempts to read the file called /notes/mydoc, meaning the file in the folder called /notes with name mydoc.

2. The file system supplies the file information from the directory, including a pointer to the location on the disk where the file actually resides.

3. The CPU reads the file's contents from the location discovered in the previous step. This means that the CPU gets a copy of the bytes held at that particular place on the disk.

4. The disk drive transfers the bytes of the entire (small) 1-KB file to the CPU, with the CPU storing the 1-KB file in RAM so that the application can work with it.

File System Miscellany

This section wraps up a few other points about the role of the file system in a computer OS.

First, the file system also lets you secure the data, which can be particularly useful for computers that have multiple users. The OS might be able to assign rights per subdirectory, or even per file. These rights typically give a user the right to read the file, write to the file (to update the file's contents), and/or delete the file. For example, you might make some work files available to be read and written (changed) by coworkers, but for your personal files, you change the settings so that they are readable and writable only by yourself.

Additionally, the OS defines the file system so that the type of physical storage device does not matter. All the file system concepts in this section apply whether the storage device is a small disk drive, a large disk drive, a drive with removable media (for example, a DVD drive or a flash drive), or any other kind of storage media. Why? The OS needs to work, and it needs to store data in permanent storage, no matter what hardware you use to store the data.

Even though the file system works the same way, no matter the type of permanent storage device, it is important to take some time to look more closely at those devices. The next topic looks more closely at hard disk drives, followed by a short look at some other types of storage devices.

Hard Disk Drives

Hard disk drives are the most common long-term computer storage devices today. Why are these so popular? They can store a lot of data, and they do not cost a lot of money. They store so much data that most users can store all the files they need—the OS, all the applications, and all their user data—on one disk drive. The hard disk drive makes the data available all the time, unlike some other types of storage devices that use removable media. Although slower than RAM, hard disk drives run pretty fast, so opening a file might take only a few seconds. And of course, as with all these permanent storage options, the disk does not lose the data when the drive loses power, unlike RAM.

So, you might wonder, why not use hard disk drives instead of RAM? The short answer is speed. RAM reads and writes data much faster than hard disk drives, and that speed difference matters. So computer hardware designers use RAM as high-speed temporary memory, and they often use hard disk drives as the primary long-term higher-volume storage.

Next, the text looks at the disk drive hardware itself, followed by a discussion of the process of how the computer OS stores files on the drive.

Hard Disks Versus Floppy Disks

Back in the 1970s and 1980s, when companies first introduced personal computers into the marketplace as consumer products, computers commonly had two types of permanent storage devices: *floppy disk drives* and *hard disk drives*.

Floppy disk drives used removable media called floppy disks. These removable thin square pieces of plastic were flimsy, about as flimsy as a light piece of cardboard, hence the name *floppy*. Basically, the user could push a floppy disk into a slot in the floppy disk drive, store files on the disk, and then remove the disk.

Those same PCs often had another type of disk drive called a hard disk drive. With a hard disk drive, the disks stayed inside the disk drive; the user did not put a disk into the drive and take it back out again. These disks were hard as opposed to flimsy or floppy. Mainly, these disks became known as hard disks just in comparison to floppy disks. The user could read and write files without having to think about inserting and removing any disks.

ON THE SIDE: With a name like floppy *disk*, you might think they would be round. It was round—but only on the inside. A square outer plastic cover protected an internal round disk, and that disk actually stored the bits.

Early PCs often had both a floppy disk drive and hard disk drive, but over time, floppy disk drives became less popular. The ability to store files, remove the floppy disk, and give someone the floppy disk was a nice feature. Today, more modern options such as CD, DVD, and flash drives all use removable media and have replaced floppy drives; however, modern hard disk drives remain.

Hard Disk Drive Internals

From the outside, a hard disk drive does not show anything of real interest, because it is just a hard plastic case. If you open the plastic case and look inside, however, you can get some nice insight to what the hardware looks like, as seen in Figure 1-14.

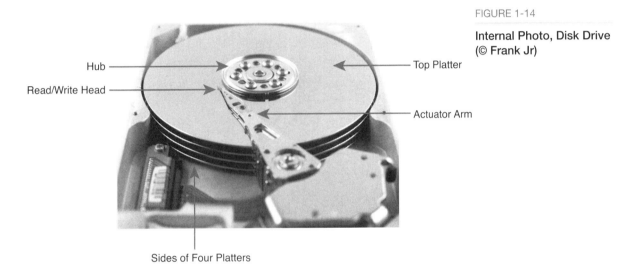

FIGURE 1-14

Internal Photo, Disk Drive (© Frank Jr)

First, focus on the round part at the top of the photo. The term *disk* refers specifically to the round disks, also called *platters*, that sit inside the disk drive. Several of these disks sit stacked on top of each other with just a little space between them; make sure to look at the sides of the platters. These disks look a lot like a compact disc (CD) or digital video disc (DVD).

The word *drive* refers in part to the fact that parts move around inside the disk drive. For example, the disk drive spins the *hub* in the middle of the disks so that the disks rotate. Next, look at the part that looks a bit like a stick that sits over the top disk. The entire part, the *actuator arm*, moves outward from the hub, in toward the hub, and up/down to get between different platters. The arm places the *read/write head* so that it sits near any point on any of the platters.

All the parts and movements work together to allow the drive to record bits as different magnetic charges on the surface of the platters. Hard disk platters are coated with a material that can hold a magnetic charge—not a single charge over the entire disk, but different charges on very small individual parts of each platter. The combination of the spinning of the disks, plus the movement of the actuator arm, can place the read/write head under or over every point on every disk in the drive.

After it is in the right position, the read/write head can either read or write each bit. To write a bit, the read/write head sets the magnetic charge at the location on the disk to either negative or positive—one for binary 0 and the other for binary 1. To read a bit, the head senses the magnetic pull or push from that part of the platter as it passes by the read/write head and interprets those pushes/pulls as 1s or 0s.

Writing Data to Sectors, Tracks

Disk drives organize the storage locations based on platters, tracks, and sectors. Treating an entire modern disk drive as one big bunch of bytes might be difficult to manage. Organizing the storage into parts helps the drive and the file system manage the data.

Figure 1-15 shows a top-down view of a single disk drive platter, with tracks and sectors shown. The platter has many locations that can hold a magnetic charge. Physically, these locations exist in concentric circles, with each circle called a *track*. The term *sector* refers to a subset of a track, as shown in the figure.

FIGURE 1-15

Tracks and Sectors in a Single Disk Drive Platter

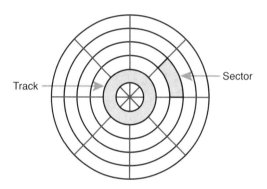

The number of bytes held in each track and sector depends in part on the disk drive. Over the decades-long history of computers and computing, devices have continually gotten smaller while getting better at the same time. Decades ago, disk drives were larger in that they took up more space, but smaller in that they stored fewer bits. Over time, hard disk drives have gotten smaller and smaller, but at the same time, they hold more and more data. So, newer drives can have more platters and more tracks per platter, with the bits literally sitting much closer together on the surface. For example, one disk drive might have 256 bytes per sector, while another might have 512 bytes per sector, with the bits being stored closer together.

A computer takes several steps to write a file to disk. First, the computer identifies some unused sectors, with enough space to hold the entire file. The computer must mark these sectors as used, so the computer does not try to use them to store the contents of some other file. The specific locations—the platter, track, and sectors—have to be recorded and noted as holding the contents of that particular file so that the file contents can be found later. (The details matching the sectors to the file might exist as part of the file system, or they might exist elsewhere.)

Figure 1-16 shows an example. In this case, the OS (running on the CPU) has already discovered four currently unused sectors on a platter of a hard disk. The OS next tells the disk drive to prepare to write the file by reserving those sectors so that no other application or process tries to use those sectors. The CPU then delivers the file contents (1 KB in this case) to be written in those just-reserved sectors. Four sectors of 256 bytes each will hold the entire 1-KB file.

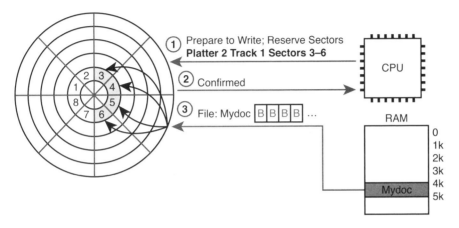

FIGURE 1-16

General Concept: Reserving Sectors and Then Writing a File to Disk

The figure shows specific steps, but keep in mind, the particulars will differ depending on the OS and hardware. In this general example:

1. The CPU prepares the disk drive by telling it to reserve those specific sectors.

2. The drive confirms that those sectors are reserved.

3. The CPU moves the file contents from RAM, over the bus, to the disk drive.

Using a Bus to Communicate

In the real world, if you want to repeatedly move people to and from the same small number of places every day, you set up a bus route and the people ride a bus. In a computer, when you want to repeatedly move bits between a small number of components inside a computer, the computer hardware designer can also use a bus. This section expands the bus concept.

The CPU and RAM can communicate without a bus because they both sit on the motherboard. The CPU is a microchip that sits directly on the motherboard. RAM is also made up of microchips, often on a small plastic board, which is in turn sitting on the motherboard. The motherboard itself contains circuitry that connects the CPU and RAM, creating electrical circuits between the two. The CPU and RAM use these electrical circuits to communicate.

For the CPU to communicate with components that do not also sit on the motherboard, like a hard disk drive, the CPU relies on a cable. The cable creates a bus between the motherboard and devices that connect to the cable. Similar to how the motherboard creates an electrical pathway between the CPU and RAM, the cable creates an electrical pathway between the entire motherboard and the disk drive and other devices.

The term *bus* refers generally to many kinds of electrical pathways between internal components of a computer. For the bus that connects a CPU to a hard disk drive, the bus typically uses different electrical circuits to pass control information versus data. For example, many types of disk buses can transfer an entire byte at a time, as well as send some form of control traffic, similar to the first step back in Figure 1-16.

In its most basic form, a bus creates one or more electrical circuits between the motherboard and the disk drive. To send a bit value of 0, the device varies the electrical current in some predetermined way; to send a bit value of 1, the device varies the electrical current in some other way. This uses the same general idea as does RAM and hard disk drives—do something different to mean a binary 1 than you do to mean a binary 0. In this case, the devices vary something about the electrical signal on the bus, with predetermined rules about what signal means binary 0 and what means binary 1.

Other Permanent Storage Devices

The computer industry has many competing types of permanent storage devices. These different devices use different mechanisms to read and write data. For example, most people have used *digital video discs (DVD)*, at least to watch movies. Computers use DVD drives that can read and write data to DVD discs, to store video or audio or simply to store data. Compared to hard disk drives, these DVD drives use completely different technology to read and write the data on the disc.

ON THE SIDE: The words *disk* and *disc* have the same general meaning in the context of this book. However, when discussing hard disks and floppy disks, the more common spelling is *disk*; when referring to CDs and DVDs, the more common spelling is *disc*.

The user of the permanent storage also sees some outward differences in different permanent storage options in some cases. For example, DVD drives use removable media (DVDs). So, similar to floppy drives, you can put one DVD into a DVD drive, record data on the DVD, remove the DVD, and then insert another blank DVD to record more data. You can easily hand the DVD to a friend, classmate, or coworker. So disk drives with removable media have an advantage.

The big disadvantage with DVD drives? Interestingly, it is the same feature: removable media. When you want to read a file you stored on a DVD, and that DVD is not already in the DVD drive, you have to go find the DVD and put it back into the DVD drive, and only then can you open the file.

You might consider many features when comparing storage options. For perspective, Table 1-3 lists some of the key comparison points to consider when reading this section. Following the table, the text looks at flash drives and then CD/DVD drives.

TABLE 1-3

Key Comparison Points, Permanent Storage

Short Description	Longer Description	Hard Disk Drive (HDD)
Internal or external?	Does the device sit inside the computer, where is stays, or does it connect externally, so that it can be easily moved between computers?	Both
Removable media?	Can you remove the media from the drive and insert new blank media to record more data?	No
Solid state?	Solid state means that the device has no moving parts; moving parts are more likely to break over time.	No
Read/write speed vs. internal HDD	How fast do reads and writes occur compared to an internal hard disk drive (HDD)?	N/A
Price/GB, at publication, compared to HDD	How much does a typical device cost, per gigabyte (GB) of storage, relative to a hard disk drive (HDD)?	N/A

USB Flash Drives

From a user perspective, USB flash drives provide permanent and portable storage. However, instead of using a drive that stays in the computer, with removable media, the entire (somewhat small) USB flash drive can be connected to a computer using a plug on the side of the computer. When the user finishes reading and writing files, the user can disconnect the entire drive, give it to others, plug it into other computers, and use it like any other removable media. Figure 1-17 shows a photo of a USB flash drive.

FIGURE 1-17

Photo of a USB Flash Drive (© Nikolai Sorokin)

After seeing this photo, you might be thinking that you have used these before and just not used the term *flash drive*. These small devices also go by these names: flash drives, jump drives, thumb drives, USB drives, flash sticks, and memory sticks. These small devices, often found for a low price near the cash register at office stores, come in a variety of entertaining shapes and colors.

USB drives make good use of the fact that they use a *Universal Serial Bus (USB)*, which is the most common type of external serial bus used in modern personal computers. Remember, a hard disk drive inside a computer connects to the motherboard using a bus. A USB flash drive connects to a bus as well, but this bus extends from the motherboard to a plug on the side of the computer. The USB drive then plugs into the computer, connecting the drive to the USB bus. After the drive is connected, the general idea of passing commands and data from the motherboard, over the bus, to and from the storage device remains the same, as shown earlier in Figure 1-16.

USB flash drives use flash memory to store the data. To help you get at least a general idea of how flash works, consider one type of flash that works a little like RAM. With RAM, when it loses power, the capacitors for each bit lose their charge, and they all drain to the point where they all have no charge. For example, when the RAM shown in Figure 1-4 loses power, all eight capacitors lose their charge.

Some types of flash physically act like RAM that has been modified so that it does not lose its memory. Continuing the story, now imagine that a mad scientist decides to try and help some RAM not lose its memory. The scientist lovingly takes each bit of RAM and insulates it—not insulation to keep each bit warm at night, but electrical insulation that keeps the bit from losing its electrical charge. The scientist has essentially created one type of flash memory in use today. This type of flash requires different microscopic circuitry to write values into bits, and different hardware to insulate the bits so that they do not lose their electrical charges. Instead of losing the bits when the flash drive is unplugged, the flash memory remembers them for years.

AUTHOR'S NOTE:
As with all the descriptions in this chapter about how bits are stored, the descriptions here omit many details, keeping the concepts simple to make sure that the big concepts are clear.

The user probably does not care how USB flash memory works; she just uses it. If you go to the store, buy a USB flash drive, and plug it into a computer, the computer usually recognizes it. The OS assigns the drive a drive letter. Remember the file system concept, which lets the computer keep track of files, regardless of the type of long-term storage device? The flash drive would be no different. The flash drive would have the information about the file system on the drive. You could add directories, display them, create/copy/move files on/off the flash drive, and then take it with you when you are done.

Table 1-4 summarizes some of the key comparisons between USB flash drives and hard disk drives.

TABLE 1-4

Key Comparison Points, USB Flash and Hard Disk Drives

Short Description	Hard Disk	USB Flash Drive
Internal or external?	Both	External
Removable media?	No	Yes*
Solid state?	No	Yes
Read/write speed vs. internal HDD	N/A	Slower
Price/GB, at publication, vs. HDD	N/A	More expensive

*The media cannot be removed from the drive, but the entire drive can be removed from the computer.

Note that Table 1-4 lists some subjective information, some of which might even change over time. But as of publication, USB flash drives work well for convenience, portability, and low price but are too slow and too small to be used to replace a hard disk drive.

> **ON THE SIDE:** A relatively new type of disk drive, called a solid state disk (SSD), has begun to compete with hard disk drives. These drives use flash memory instead of platters and actuator arms. But they connect over the same buses, and play the same role, as traditional internal hard disk drives (HDD).
>
> The advantages and disadvantages of SSDs, at least around publication time for this book? SSD drives read data much faster than HDDs. I did a brief informal experiment with two Macs, running the same version of the OS, one with an HDD and one with an SSD. The Mac with the SSD actually had a slower processor. (Note that one of the most time-consuming tasks that occur when you turn on a computer is the reading of OS files to load into RAM.) In this informal test, the Mac with the SSD booted in 15 seconds; the one with the HDD, 135 seconds.

CD and DVD Drives

Compact disc (CD) and digital video disc (DVD) drives provide an entirely different class of computer storage as compared with hard disk drives and USB flash drives. But before getting into detail on these devices, first consider a little history about CD and DVD technology outside the world of computers.

For almost the first 100 years of recorded music, the way to record, sell, and buy music was using phonograph records. To play the records, you needed a device called a phonograph or record player. The recording device took a flat vinyl disc (record) and made circular grooves in it. The phonograph placed a needle onto the record, with the record spinning, so that the needle followed the groove. The needle could feel differences in the grooves and play different sounds based on the different grooves.

Although phonograph technology improved over time, eventually people invented newer replacement technologies. Two popular technologies used magnetic tape, encased inside a hard plastic case to protect the fragile tape: the 8-track tape and then the cassette tape.

> **ON THE SIDE:** Ever used the word *groovy*? The word started as a reference to the grooves in a phonograph record.

All these early technologies (records, 8-track tapes, and cassette tapes) used analog technology. That is, the recordings made something *analogous* to the sound waves onto the media, so today we call those kinds of technologies *analog*. These analog music technologies grew up before computers became common as consumer technology.

Continuing this stroll through history, the CD became the first common digital consumer music technology, at least the first one that spread to the masses. Instead of recording an analog signal on the media, digital audio storage, as done with CDs, represents each sound with a bit pattern. For example, to represent a very short time period of sound, with a particular pitch (note), loudness, and so on, the CD simply stores a particular bit pattern. As long as the device that records the CD and the CD player agree about which sounds are represented by which bit patterns, the process should work—much like the idea of using a standard character set so that you can create a document on one computer and open it correctly on another computer.

Figure 1-18 shows a general idea of the timeline for perspective.

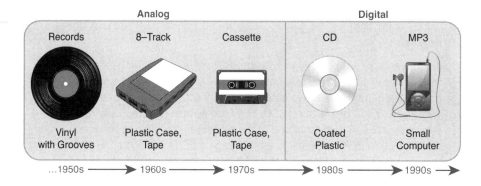

ON THE SIDE: CDs first became popular in the 1980s, before the existence of web browsers and web servers, and even before the Internet could be used to buy and sell things. The web simply did not exist back when audio CDs first hit the market. By the time the Internet allowed websites to sell digital products—products made from bits, like digital music—the music industry had tons of experience working with digital music on CDs. The good news? The music industry could save lots of money: It could sell direct to consumers, without stores, without producing CDs, and without packaging and shipping them. The bad for the industry? It allowed everyone to share music with their friends without paying for it. Those forces led to a complete transformation of the music business.

DVDs followed a similar kind of history as CDs, but with video. One of the first popular formats on which to buy movies to view at home was an analog magnetic tape technology called VHS. Similar to the migration from albums and tapes to CDs, the video world migrated from VHS tapes to video DVDs—essentially the equivalent of CDs, but for movies. DVDs used many of the same ideas as CDs, just with more storage capacity, because video requires many more bytes per second to store as compared to audio.

Although the historical look at CDs and DVDs can be interesting, CDs and DVDs simply store bits. How? They use optics (light). In fact, in comparison to the term *hard disk drives (HDD)*, CD and DVD drives are sometimes called *optical disc drives* (ODD). Figure 1-19 shows a DVD drive with the tray open and a removable DVD visible.

FIGURE 1-19

Photo of USB DVD Drive
(© papa1266)

To best understand generally how ODDs work, first think about how they read data using light and light sensors. (As usual, the details differ depending on many factors, different types of drives, different types of discs, and so on.) The plastic CD and DVD discs have a coating. The drive shines a light on the disc and senses the angle at which the light is reflected. You guessed it—the disc reflects the light differently for a binary 1 as compared to a binary 0.

To appreciate how the writing process works, consider how some of the earliest CD technology worked. The earliest CDs could only be written once, because the process of writing the bits permanently changed the surface of the disc. To make a binary 0 reflect light differently, the writing process used the laser to heat the surface and cause a small bump to raise on the surface of the disc. As you might guess, when reading the bits, light reflects differently on the flat surface (1) as opposed to the bump (0).

Newer CD technology allows multiple writes to the same disc. The disc still reflects light differently to mean a binary 1 versus a 0. However, the process to write makes a different change in the surface of the disc, one that can later be reversed, so it allows the disc to be written to again and again.

Finally, these optical disc drives do have some similarities to a hard disk drive. Both types of drive spin the discs, so there can be some delay waiting on the disc to spin around to the light. (That time is very short to us humans, but it does take time.) However, rather than use an actuator arm that moves in and out over the disc, with ODDs, the light stays still and the drive uses mirrors to reflect the light to the right place on the disc.

Again, the particulars vary for different classes of CD and DVD media, but all use the same basic idea:

- A light (usually a laser) shines on the surface.
- Mirrors make the light shine toward the inside or outside of the disc.
- The disc spins inside the drive, so the drive must wait for the right part of the disc to rotate around to the light.

- When reading previously stored bits, a binary 1 reflects the light differently than does a binary 0.

- When writing bits, the light changes the surface for binary 0s and 1s so that later, the light reflects one way for 1s and a different way for 0s.

Table 1-5 summarizes some of the key comparisons between optical drives, USB flash drives, and hard disk drives.

TABLE 1-5

Key Comparison Points, USB Flash and Hard Disk Drives

Short Description	Hard Disk	USB Flash Drive	Optical Disc
Internal or external?	Both	External	Both
Removable media?	No	Yes[1]	Yes
Solid state?	No	Yes	No
Read/write speed vs. internal HDD	N/A	Slower	Slower
Price/GB, at publication, vs. HDD	N/A	More expensive	N/A[2]

[1] The media cannot be removed from the drive, but the entire drive can be removed from the computer.

[2] See the next paragraph.

That last row of the table brings up one interesting comparison point. A single CD can hold 700 MB of data, with a DVD holding 4.7 GB. Because the discs can be relatively cheap, you could store data for a similar cost per gigabyte compared to storing data on an HDD. However, most people do not bother comparing these options based on price, because if you chose the HDD, all the data would be available to the computer all the time. With CDs and DVDs, you would have to find the right CD or DVD out of the hundreds of discs it would take to store as much data as an HDD.

Input and Output

So far, this chapter has introduced some of the big ideas about how a computer works. The CPU works with bits and bytes, using RAM as temporary high-speed storage. Those bits can be thought of simply as bits and bytes, as data. They can also be thought of as representing information—for example, binary value 1100001 might represent the letter *a* in a document.

Additionally, the CPU can then read and write data on various kinds of permanent storage devices, using various kinds of buses, to store data as files. Thankfully, the file system concept applies to all the permanent storage devices, which lets the user think about files and happily ignore the details of how the devices physically store the data. In short, the CPU can work with information as bits and bytes, store those bytes permanently as files, and later read the contents of those files to use the information once again.

Those bits did not somehow just *appear* in RAM on the computer, however. Something had to happen to create the bits in the first place. And while the CPU can work with the bits, if the user never benefits, never uses the results of the computer's work, there is no point in doing the work in the first place.

For example, most of us listen to music, whether on our phone, a separate MP3 player, a computer, or the radio. In today's world, those songs exist as bits somewhere. But if you think about the history of a single song, at some point, the songwriter had not yet made up the song, and the artist had not recorded the song. How did we get from songwriter inspiration to a bunch of bits that you listen to—bits that sit in your phone, on your MP3 player, or on the player the radio station uses? And how do those bits later get converted into sounds that we can hear?

The short and general answer? **Input and output**, commonly called I/O.

With I/O, the input part refers to creating information in the computer. Some actions involve the user, and some do not. For example:

- A user typing at the keyboard
- A user clicking with a mouse
- A user talking into a computer microphone
- Recordings from a video security camera connected to a computer
- Statistics gathered by a website about how many users looked at a video you posted online
- Sales data from a grocery store clerk who scans your groceries

Similarly, the output side of I/O both presents information to humans and for other purposes as well. For humans, examples include

- The computer display showing an image or some video
- Computer speakers playing sound
- Printers printing images

This final major section of the chapter looks at several common types of I/O in a personal computer. First, you will look at the two most common input devices—keyboards and mice. Following that, you'll take a close look at displays and a brief look at printers.

Keyboard

A computer keyboard gives you two general categories of actions—it allows you to input text and numeric data into an application and it lets you control the computer's actions.

Some keys on the keyboard are designed to tell the computer actions to take. For example, you might press a function key on the keyboard, which tells either the current application or the OS to take an action. Or, with a Microsoft OS, pressing Ctrl-Alt-Delete (at the same time) tells the OS to bring up a particularly important window: a window that lets you reboot or shut down the computer, or to stop specific tasks on the computer.

And of course, to input data, the keyboard lets you type text and numbers for an application. For example, when using an application like a word processor, the keyboard simply lets you type the letters and numbers, and the word processor puts those into the document.

None of these details about keyboards should have surprised you. However, many people might use a keyboard for their entire careers without knowing what actually happens to make the key you press show up as a letter on the screen.

How Keyboards Send Bits to Represent Letters

Consider Figure 1-20, which shows a wired keyboard. The keyboard sits outside the computer system unit, with a cable connecting the two. Internally, the connector on the side of the system unit connects to the motherboard, which in turn has circuitry that connects to various other components, including the CPU.

FIGURE 1-20

Wired Keyboard
Connection to a PC
System Unit

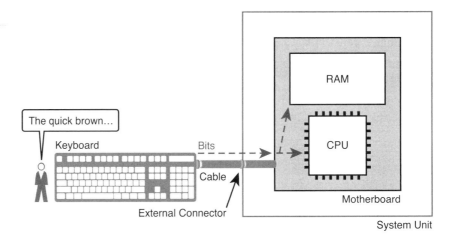

The keyboard cable has two key functions: giving the keyboard electrical power as well as creating a way for the keyboard to send the keystrokes to the computer. By design, the cable has several wires that allow multiple electrical circuits. Typically, one circuit provides power to the keyboard, which is needed because the keyboard needs power to run its small keyboard processor and send data. The cable also supports another electrical circuit that the keyboard uses to send bits to the computer.

To physically send bits to the computer, the keyboard varies the electrical signal over time. It should come as no surprise at this point, but the general idea is the same as the general idea of storing bits on various types of storage: Do something differently over the electrical circuit to represent a binary 0 versus a binary 1. Just to illustrate the concept, to send a binary 1, the keyboard might use a positive voltage (meaning that the current flows in one direction), and to send a 0, use a negative voltage (meaning that the current flows in the opposite direction). As usual, this description avoids the details of exactly how the electrical signal is changed for a 1 or 0, leaving that discussion for physicists and electrical engineers.

So imagine that the user has again opened a text editor and is ready to practice typing, using the sentence "The quick brown fox jumped over the lazy river." What happens when the *T* is pressed—a process that actually requires that you press the Shift and *t* keys? Figure 1-21 shows some of the steps, with an explanation to follow.

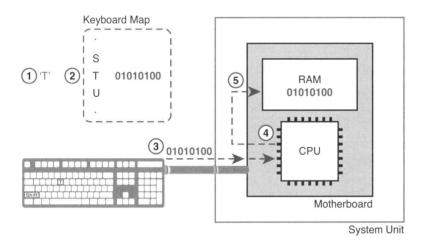

FIGURE 1-21

Keyboard, Character Map, Bit Transmission, and Storing the Typed Character

The keyboard itself uses a small processor and a small amount of memory to hold the *keyboard character map*, or simply **keyboard map**. The keyboard map lists all keys and key combinations (like pressing Shift and *t* at the same time) that the user can press. The keyboard map also lists a matching binary value for each key or key combination that identifies the key.

The figure shows five steps that indicate how the computer CPU and OS can record the binary value that represents the key that was pressed on the keyboard:

1. The user presses the Shift and the *t* character at the same time, for a capital *T*.

2. The keyboard processor looks at its keyboard map, which lists a binary code associated with capital *T*.

3. The keyboard sends the binary code (shown as 01010100, just as an example; the actual code might be different).

4. The CPU (or other specialized processors on the motherboard) processes the input, using the same keyboard map information as the keyboard, so the CPU knows what key was pressed on the keyboard.

5. The CPU stores the newly arrived input character *T* into RAM, ready to give that input to the application that was active when the input was received.

Note that the process shown here ends with the computer OS knowing what key was pressed, but the application has not yet processed the input. In this example, the *T* was intended for the currently active application, a word processor. After Step 5, the application would take over, with the knowledge that the letter *T* had been typed, and using some of the logic discussed earlier in the section "Text Character Sets."

How Keyboards Know What Key(s) You Pressed

For the next part of the keyboard discussion, consider this question—How does the keyboard processor know what key you pressed?

To appreciate the big ideas, first think about what happens with a simple electrical circuit when turning a light on or off. When you turn the light switch on, the light switch closes an electrical circuit, which lets electrical current flow, which lights the light bulb. Flip the light switch off and the switch breaks the circuit, which stops the electricity from flowing, which makes the light bulb go dark.

Now think of every keyboard key as an on/off switch. When you press a key, it closes a circuit, which makes electricity flow, telling the keyboard processor what key you pressed. Press multiple keys, and the processor can notice that multiples of these circuits have current flowing—for example, when you hold the Shift key down and then type a letter. Figure 1-22 shows the idea, assuming that a capital *T* again has been pressed.

FIGURE 1-22

Current Flow from Each Pressed Key to the Keyboard's Processor

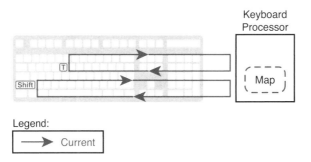

A keyboard basically monitors for pressed keys and then reacts. For any pressed key or key combination, the keyboard processor notices the electrical circuits have a current. The processor determines which circuits have current, implying which keys have been pressed. Then the keyboard processor just sends the binary code for that key, per the keyboard map, to the CPU.

Mouse

A computer **mouse** also lets you control the computer's actions, but in a much different way than the keyboard.

First, the mouse lets the user point at something on the computer display. When the user moves the mouse, the *mouse pointer*—an icon on the computer display—moves in the same direction. The user moves the mouse pointer to essentially tell the computer what the user cares about on the computer desktop.

To tell the computer what action to take, the user does something with the mouse. Mice have different buttons the user can click, bars that can roll, and other mechanisms. The OS has a list of actions to take depending on the mouse action the user does. For example, by default in Microsoft OSs, the following might occur, depending on where you start in the user interface:

- **Single click of the left mouse button:** The OS notes the application window to which the mouse pointer currently points and makes that application active. In other words, that application gets control of the CPU and the OS puts that window in the foreground of the desktop.

- **Double-click of the left mouse button:** If the mouse pointer points at an icon or file, the OS starts the application or opens the file with its default application.

- **Single click of the right mouse button:** The app or OS displays a contextual menu, with the context being different based on where the mouse pointer was when the click occurred.

Wired keyboards and wired mice have many similarities in how they work. They both connect to the computer using a cable. Both rely on the system unit to have internal components that receive and process the input. Both use wires in the cables to create electrical circuits, sending bits by varying the electrical signal to imply a binary 1 or 0. They both send binary codes to the computer using those electrical circuits, and the computer must have a map (like the keyboard map) that shows each code and what it means. Also, both types of devices let the user tell the computer to act.

One of the biggest differences between keyboards and mice relates to the mouse movement and the matching mouse pointer that moves around the screen. To explore those ideas, next look at how mechanical mice recognize movement, turning that movement into numbers on an X,Y graph. Following that, the text looks at how the mouse communicates those X,Y coordinate changes to the CPU in a way that allows a nice, even movement of the mouse pointer on the screen.

Mechanical Mice and How They Sense Movement

A mechanical mouse senses movement using machines: One part moves, which moves another part, and so on. Although most of the mechanical parts are hidden, the user can see part of the mechanism—the mouse ball—that pokes out from the bottom of the mouse. The user moves the mouse with the bottom of the mouse on a flat surface, like a physical desktop (not the computer desktop!), which rolls the mouse ball. (If the user picks up the mouse and moves it, the ball does not roll.)

Internally, the mouse ball triggers other movement. In particular, two different wheels, one aligned front to back on the mouse and the other aligned side to side, touch the edges of the ball. When the ball moves, these internal wheels also move, and they can measure the amount of movement in a line (either front to back or side to side). These wheels connect to other parts and eventually to wires, and collectively, these mechanisms cause the mouse to measure the amount of movement in two directions.

The mouse essentially translates the movement in any direction into movement on an X,Y graph. The internal wheels have a 90-degree separation. The wheel aligned front to back measures movement in the Y axis, and the wheel aligned side to side measures movement in the X axis. Figure 1-23 shows an artist's drawing of the interior of a mouse.

FIGURE 1-23

Mechanical Mouse Internals

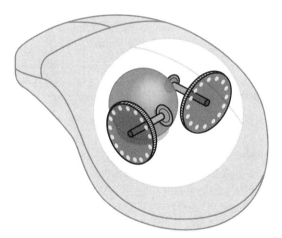

Coordinating Mouse and Mouse Pointer Movements

As you have probably noticed without even pausing to think about it, when you move a mouse, the mouse pointer moves smoothly across the screen. In other words, no matter how fast you move the mouse itself, the mouse pointer does not just sit still while you move the mouse, and a few seconds later, suddenly jump from one side of the screen to the other. While you move the mouse, the mouse pointer immediately mimics the way you moved the mouse. (In fact, I challenge you to move the mouse in a way that you can make the mouse pointer appear to instantly jump to another place!)

Knowing that, now stop and think about the mouse, the CPU, and the display as separate parts of a personal computer. You move the mouse; it senses the movement. However, the computer's OS, running on the CPU, tells the display what to show, including the mouse pointer. Clearly, the mouse must tell the CPU about the movements, and then the CPU, which controls the display, must tell the display to show the mouse pointer in a different location. But all those actions have to happen so that the movement looks smooth, happening at the same time you move the mouse.

To make all that happen, the mouse cannot wait to see where the user stops the mouse and then tell the CPU the ending location when the mouse moves. Instead, the mouse must tell the computer about any movement immediately, as a series of very small movements. The mouse cannot wait and tell the computer the equivalent of "I moved 3 inches left and 2 inches up" because then all the CPU could do would be to make the mouse pointer jump to another location. Instead, when you move the mouse pointer a few inches on the screen, the mouse sends a continuous stream of binary messages that basically mean "I moved this little bit. Now just this little bit. Now this little bit."

To tell the computer to move the mouse pointer, the mouse sends bits to the CPU. The bits together make up a message, with some bits stating how much movement on the X axis (and which direction) and other bits stating how much movement on the Y axis, plus direction.

Figure 1-24 shows the general idea. In this case, the mouse moves from an upper-left position to the right and lower. From an X,Y axis perspective, that movement will be a positive change in the X axis (to the right) and a negative change in the Y axis (downward). For the sake of discussion, the figure shows messages where the mouse tells the CPU that the mouse has moved a positive .1 on the X axis (to the right) and a negative .1 on the Y axis (down) in each message.

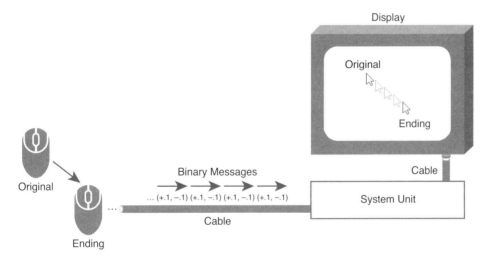

FIGURE 1-24

Mouse Moves, Many Messages, Human Sees Smooth Movement

Other Mice

As with the other computing devices mentioned in this chapter, many other mice options exist.

For example, wireless mice require no cable connected to the mouse itself, which makes using the mouse a little more convenient. Instead of sending bits over the cable, the mouse uses low-power radio waves, typically using a technology called *Bluetooth*; it's the same wireless technology used with many mobile phone wireless headsets.

Wireless mice, similar to wireless keyboards, must have something that connects to the motherboard that can receive their input signals. A wireless mouse product comes with a *wireless receiver*, which has a cable and connects to the system unit. The wireless signals pass from mouse to receiver, and then the receiver uses the cable to send the bits to the system unit. Many vendors also sell wireless keyboard and mice combinations, which use a single receiver for both keyboard and mouse, as shown in Figure 1-25.

FIGURE 1-25

Wireless Keyboard and Mouse Combination

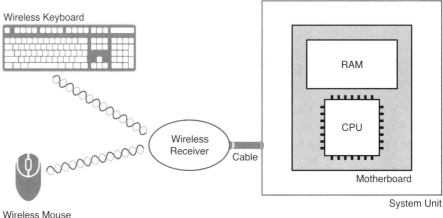

An *optical mouse*, another type of mouse, uses light and light sensors to sense the movement of the mouse, as opposed to how mechanical mice use their internal mechanisms to sense movement. Basically, the mouse shines a light, watches the reflections, and senses the movement. But these mice use the same messages that mechanical mice use to tell the CPU about changes in movement and commands, as shown earlier in Figure 1-24.

Now that you have seen a few details about input devices, the text now looks at the most commonly used output device: the computer display.

Display

Computers provide output in ways that humans can use their senses, primarily sight through the display and printers, and sometimes through hearing with speakers. In terms of volume, most of the computer output that we humans use comes through the computer **display**, also called the computer monitor, or screen.

The display shines light so that the user can see information. The following sections discuss some details of how the computer and display work together to shine the millions of little lights that sit inside the display. These sections also look at how a computer takes the information it holds in memory and converts that to the concept of a bunch of little colored lights sitting on the face of the display.

The Big Picture of How Displays Work

Just like input devices, output devices like displays can do very little without the work done by the components inside the system unit. The display itself sits outside the system unit, connecting to the system using a cable. When the system unit is powered off, the display either shows nothing or maybe some kind of error message telling you that the computer is turned off.

Many components work together to make the display work, but three components—the OS, the display adapter, and applications—play particularly important roles.

First, the OS controls the contents of the display screen. When you boot a computer, you load the OS, and the OS creates a binary representation of the image on the screen—and that is what is displayed. In most modern user OSs, the OS refers to that view into the computer as the *desktop*. When the user moves windows around on the desktop, the OS plays a big role.

The *display adapter*, specialized hardware inside the system unit, controls the display itself. This hardware sits between the motherboard and the display, as you can see in Figure 1-26. So, what does the display adapter adapt? It adapts from the OS's conceptual view of what should be displayed, in binary, to the specific commands that are sent over the cable to the display. Those commands tell the display to illuminate each of its individual tiny lights (called pixels) in the right way to create the image the computer wants to display.

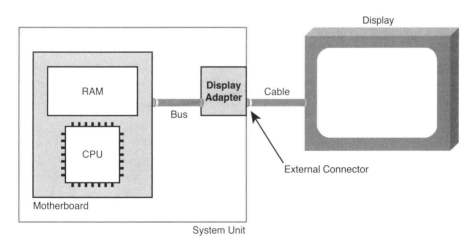

FIGURE 1-26

Key Components in the Basic Operation of a Computer Display

In short, the OS decides what to display. It sends information to the display adapter, and the display adapter sends the specific details about what lights and colors of lights to use on the display to make that image show up on the display.

Finally, applications also play a big role in determining the image on the display. The OS creates a concept called the desktop, and applications carve out a conceptual rectangle of the desktop called a *window*. The application decides on the contents inside its window—the headings, the icons, the visual look and feel, the data, and how it is presented—and saves those details in RAM. When the application changes the contents of the window, the app stores some binary representation of that window in memory. The OS plays the role of managing the windows and updating the entire view of the desktop.

Table 1-6 summarizes these key roles.

TABLE 1-6

Components That Control the Contents of the Computer Display

Component	Location (Internal, External)	Its Job Related to Making an Image Be Displayed on the Display
OS	Internal	Creates desktop, works with app windows, directs display adapter
Display adapter	Internal	Converts binary representation of the screen to commands understood and useful to the display
Display	External	Lights—many lights—with colors as specified by the display adapter
Apps	Internal	Create the contents inside a window

Pixel Grids and Pixel Maps (Frame Buffers)

Imagine that you are back in art class from your younger days. The teacher gives you a piece of paper. The paper has a grid of squares on the right and open space on the left. Your art project for the day: Draw a stick figure on the left, and then draw the same stick figure inside the grid. However, when drawing in the grid, you can only color a square at a time, and you must fill in the entire square. You might end up with something like what is shown in Figure 1-27.

FIGURE 1-27

Art Class Example, with Pixelating

 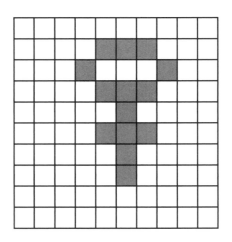

Clearly, the figure on the right is not quite as good as the one on the left. In particular, the head looks funny, because it cannot show the curves correctly, because you have to fill in all of each square.

A computer display works on a concept similar to the grid you see in Figure 1-27; however, you do not see the same rough corners in Figure 1-27 in the output on a computer display. Why no rough edges? Well, the individual squares are very small, so small that to the human eye, the edges are simply too small to see.

Computer displays use a grid of physical lights called *pixels* —short for *picture element*. Each pixel can shine light. The pixels line up in a grid, like the grid in the art project of Figure 1-27. The display defines a maximum **screen resolution**, with the maximum resolution based on the number of pixels that physically exist. This screen resolution lists the pixel width and then the pixel depth. For example, many displays support a screen resolution of 1280 × 1024, meaning that the grid is 1280 pixels wide and 1024 pixels tall.

To control the display, the OS and/or display adapter will build and update a **pixel map** (also called a *frame buffer*). The pixel map lists information about each pixel, whether it should be lit, and what color it should be.

To build an understanding of pixel maps, imagine a very simple display whose pixels do not support different colors—each pixel is either on or off. (For the sake of picturing this display, each pixel is green when lit.) The pixel map could list a single bit per pixel, with a value of 1 meaning on and a value of 0 meaning off. If the pixel map used 1 bit per pixel, it would have enough information to tell the display what to do for every pixel.

Continuing the example, next consider the amount of memory required for the pixel map. For the sake of keeping the math simple, say that the screen was square, with a screen resolution of 1000 × 1000. The matching pixel grid is also 1000 × 1000, for 1,000,000 total pixels, so with 1 bit per pixel, the pixel map would require 1,000,000 bits. With 8 bits per byte, those 1,000,000 bits equal 125,000 bytes, or 125 kilobytes (KB).

Of course, displays support color, and to get color, each pixel can shine light in a variety of colors. In fact, to make the display show realistic color for humans, each pixel can actually shine a large variety of colors. Conceptually, to support eight colors per pixel, you would need 3 bits to describe each pixel, because you can create 2^3 unique numbers using 3 bits. Want 256 unique colors? You need 8 bits to describe each pixel, for 2^8 unique numbers. Typical displays today use 24 bits (3 bytes) or 32 bits (4 bytes) to support many colors.

> **ON THE SIDE:**
> Displays whose pixels have only one color are called *monochrome* displays. Today, most consumer computers use color displays, but in the early days of computing, all displays were monochrome.

> **ON THE SIDE:** Using 24 or 32 bits to represent different colors creates 16 million or 4 billion (or so) colors, respectively, which might seem like overkill. However, the human eye can distinguish fine shades of color. For example, go into a paint store and look at the color charts for white. You'll find 50 or more shades of off-white, and side by side, you can tell the difference. Or, look at the color settings for text or drawings with most any office application. These apps let you change the color setting easily, and even with 1 bit changed in a 24-bit color code, side by side, you can tell the two colors apart.

Printers

To wrap up this chapter's introduction to I/O, this section briefly introduces a few concepts about printers.

Printers give the user a way to put some image onto a piece of paper. The printed image might represent text, the images seen on the display, or images and text sitting in a file on the computer.

Many printers work based on a general concept that resembles the pixel map used by a display. Many printers print by creating a number of dots—circles—onto the paper. The printer organizes these dots into a grid, similar in concept to a pixel grid on a display. In fact, printer makers advertise each printer as supporting a particular number of *dots per inch (DPI)* , which defines how many dots of ink or toner sit in a square inch on the paper. The more dots per inch, the better the quality.

To print, the computer has to translate from its current view of information to a mapping of the dots that can be printed by the printer. For example, a word processor might hold the text "The quick brown fox jumps over the lazy river" as ASCII text, as discussed earlier in the section "Text Character Sets." The app has bytes stored in RAM that represent the characters, but the user does not want a printout of the bits. To print that short document, something—usually software called a *printer driver*—translates. That process, for example, would determine which dots to print on the paper to form the shape of the letter *T*.

Chapter Summary

Computer networking, the main topic for this entire book, provides a way for computers to communicate. To appreciate computer networking, you must first appreciate how computers work, which is the focus of this chapter. So, while this chapter might act as a brief introduction to how computers work, it has a specific purpose: to prepare you so that when you read the rest of the chapters in the book, you know enough about computers to understand how computers use a network.

The single task that makes any device a computer is that the device processes data. The smallest unit of data, a single bit, represents a single-digit binary number. More commonly, computers work with data in bytes (8 bits), words (2 bytes), or double words (4 bytes). However, computer *users* typically do not think in binary. To do all the wonderful and useful things that computers do, the computer must somehow use bits and bytes. For example, users often create and read text, so computers use character maps to represent each text character in a language as a unique binary code.

Computers need a way to work with large amounts of data. To make sense of the volume of data, computer operating systems (OS) use files and file systems. File systems organize the data in ways similar to how humans put papers in folders and folders in filing cabinets, with some index stating where each file sits. Without a file system, the computer could not find the data.

To store the data long term, even if the computer loses power, the computer uses various types of permanent storage devices. All these devices represent a binary 1 differently than a binary 0, and they do so in a way that does not require the device to have electric power all the time. Hard disk drives store data using magnetic charges applied to the surface of a platter. USB flash drives store electrical charges using small electrical components like capacitors. DVD and CD drives store bits on plastic discs by making a physical change to the surface of the disc, which changes how the surface of the disc reflects light.

Finally, computers use input and output (I/O) to communicate with the world outside the computer. The most common input devices are the keyboard and mouse. The keyboard lets the user type characters and numbers, plus control the OS and apps, while the mouse primarily lets the user control the OS and apps. The display and printer are the primary output devices.

All these I/O devices require that a computer translate between the external world and the computer's internal ways to represent information as bits. For example, the keyboard senses that a key was pressed and sends a unique binary code to identify that key to the CPU. As another example, the OS builds a pixel map as binary data. The pixel map describes which pixels to light on the display, and with what colors, and the display lights those colors, showing the user the images and text that the user wants to see.

Chapter Review Activities

Use the features in this section to study and review the topics in this chapter.

Answer These Questions

1. Which of the following is true about 1 bit?

   a. Can represent decimal values 0 through 9

   b. Can be used to represent one character in the lowercase English alphabet

   c. Represents one binary digit

   d. Represents four binary digits

2. Which of the following terms means approximately 106 bytes?

   a. Terabyte

   b. Megabyte

   c. Gigabyte

   d. Kilobyte

3. Which answer lists the correct number of bits associated with each term?

   a. 8 bits per double word

   b. 32 bits per word

   c. 64 bits per quadruple word

   d. 4 bits per byte

4. Which of the following answers are true about random-access memory (RAM) as it is normally used inside a personal computer? (Choose two answers.)

   a. Used for short-term memory

   b. Used for long-term memory

   c. Used to process data

   d. Connects to the CPU over a bus using a cable

   e. Is installed onto the motherboard

5. This chapter describes the concepts behind how a CPU reads the contents from RAM. Which of the following is true about the process of read data, as described in the chapter?

   a. The CPU tells the RAM which address holds the data that the CPU wants to read.

   b. The CPU reads all RAM sequentially, beginning with the first byte, until it happens to read the byte that the CPU wanted to read.

   c. The smallest unit of data that RAM supplies back to the CPU is 1 bit.

   d. The CPU must first find the file in the file system before reading the data.

6. A user has opened a word processor, typed the numbers 123456789, and stored the document as a file called report1. Which of the following determines, in part, what bits the computer stores in the file to represent the text typed into the report?

    a. Keyboard map

    b. Pixel grid

    c. Character set

    d. The binary equivalent of decimal 123456789

7. A user has opened a calculator application, typed the numbers 123456789, and then done some math problem using this number. Which of the following determines, in part, what bits the computer stores in RAM to represent the number 123456789?

    a. Keyboard map

    b. Pixel grid

    c. Character set

    d. The binary equivalent of decimal 123456789

8. Which of the following is not a feature of a file system that might be used with a hard disk drive?

    a. An actuator arm

    b. A directory

    c. A file

    d. A place to keep directory information on the hard disk

9. A student writes a report using a word processor, saving the report in a file called my_report. The student stores the file on his laptop hard disk drive. Later, he posts the file on a file-sharing site for a classmate to review the report. Then, he copies an updated version of the file to a flash drive to submit it to his instructor. Which of the following are some of the important features supplied by files as defined by a computer OS? (Choose three answers.)

    a. Keeps data in order

    b. Provides a convenient way to name a set of data for easier operations like copying and moving

    c. Names give users an easy way to reference the data

    d. Gives the CPU an easy way to identify the data it wants to read from RAM

10. You write some files to a flash drive and then share the drive with a classmate. That classmate opens an application that lists the contents (folders and files) of what is on the flash drive. The classmate sees all the files you had placed onto the flash drive. How does your classmate's computer know what is on the flash drive?

    a. By reading the file system's directory information, which is stored on the storage device

    b. By reading the file system's directory information, which is automatically posted to a centralized online site

    c. By reading the files and autogenerating a directory structure for the files, for use on your classmate's local computer

    d. The flash drive's contents will not be usable by the classmate

11. Which of the following answers best describes how a hard disk drive physically writes a binary 0 or 1?

    a. Using an electrical charge

    b. Using a magnetic charge

    c. Changing the disk's surface so that later the light will reflect differently for 0 or 1

    d. Holding a sound wave in a vacuum

12. Which of the following answers are true about an internal hard disk drive (HDD) as it is normally used inside a personal computer? (Choose two answers.)

    a. Used for short-term memory

    b. Used for long-term memory

    c. Used to process data

    d. Connects to the CPU over a bus using a cable

    e. Is installed onto the motherboard

13. Which of the following are components of an internal hard disk drive (HDD)? (Choose two answers.)

    a. Actuator arm

    b. Laser

    c. Platters

    d. Sliding media tray

14. Which of the following technologies are considered to be solid state? (Choose two answers.)

    a. RAM

    b. Hard disk drive

    c. Optical disc drive

    d. USB flash drive

15. A user has opened a word processor, typed the numbers 123456789, and looked at the number on the screen in the word processor window. The user sits and starts to daydream about how computers work, particularly about what happened from the time before she typed 123456789 until the number showed up on the screen. Which of the following answers lists the first item that the computer will need to consider?

    a. Keyboard map

    b. Pixel grid

    c. Character set

    d. The binary equivalent of decimal 123456789

16. A user presses the a key on a computer keyboard. Which of the following answers best describes how a keyboard knows that the a key was pressed?

   a. By sound that travels through a vacuum in small pathways under the keyboard called keyboard channels

   b. By a change in the magnetic charge in a plate beneath that spot on an underlying metal plate

   c. Using a series of light (on/off) pulses, sent by each key, triggered when the user presses the key

   d. By closing an electrical circuit connected to the key when the key is pressed

17. In a mechanical computer mouse, the mouse, computer, and display work together to move the mouse pointer across the screen. When the mouse signals the computer about how the user has moved the mouse, which of the following answers best describes what the mouse tells the CPU?

   a. One dimension: movement as a single number and single direction on an X,Y graph.

   b. Two dimensions: movement as two numbers: one in the direction of the X axis of an X,Y graph and the other on the Y axis.

   c. Three dimensions: movement as three numbers: one each on the X, Y, and Z axes of an X,Y,Z graph.

   d. None of the other answers is even remotely close to what the mouse tells the CPU.

18. Which of the following answers describes a feature in common between computer mice and computer keyboards?

   a. To store data

   b. Input of user data

   c. Input of commands that control the computer

   d. To output sound from the computer

19. For a particular computer display, the screen resolution is set to 1280×1024. Which of the following is true about the term screen resolution, these two numbers, and what they describe? (Choose two answers.)

   a. 1280 is the number of items top to bottom in a grid on the screen.

   b. The screen resolution is the number of lighted dots per inch (DPI) currently in use on the screen.

   c. The screen is using more than 1 million pixels.

   d. 1024 is the number of items top to bottom in a grid on the screen.

20. Which of the following might be a useful part of a pixel map? (Choose two answers.)

   a. Information that identifies each individual pixel on the computer display

   b. A binary code for each pixel, defining its color

   c. A table of text characters and a unique binary code for each

   d. A directory that lists all folders and files on a hard disk drive

Define the Key Terms

The following key terms include the ideas most important to the big ideas in this chapter. To review, without looking at the book or your notes, write a definition for each term, focusing on the meaning, not the wording. Then, review your definition compared to your notes, this chapter, and the glossary.

Key Terms for Chapter 1

computer	file	mouse
bit	file system	pixel map
byte	directory	display
random-access memory (RAM)	hard disk drive	screen resolution
character set	input and output	
	keyboard map	

List the Words Inside Acronyms

The following are the most common acronyms discussed in this chapter. As a way to review those terms, simply write down the words that each letter represents in each acronym.

Acronyms for Chapter 1

RAM	MB	HDD
OS	GB	ODD
CPU	TB	I/O
KB	USB	DPI

Create Mind Maps

Create a mind map, or multiple smaller mind maps, for the eight categories listed in the mind map shown in Figure 1-28. For each of the these categories, think of any short terms you read in this chapter that could be connected to each term, and just write down the term. For example, for keyboard, you might list terms like keyboard map, keyboard controller, cable, wired keyboard, or anything else that comes to mind. Keep in mind that with all the mind map exercises, the goal is to help you organize thoughts and terms in your own mind to review and remember.

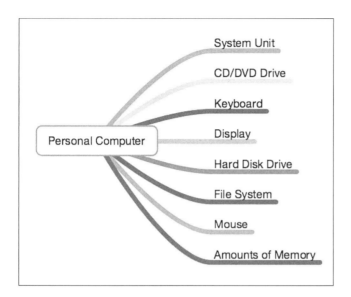

FIGURE 1-28

Main Levels of Mind Map on Left; Beginnings of Reorganization on Right

If you choose to make a single large mind map, also take an additional step to reorganize the eight categories in any way that makes sense to you. For example, a computer mouse and keyboard are both input devices.

Define Other Terms

Define the following additional terms from this chapter, and check your answers in the glossary:

binary digit	information technology	optics
word	drive letter	optical disc drive
double word	folder	mouse pointer
quad word	pointer	wired keyboard
kilobyte	disk (disc) drive	wireless keyboard
megabyte	platter	wired mouse
gigabyte	actuator arm	wireless mouse
terabyte	read/write head	mechanical mouse
ASCII	track	optical mouse
character encoding scheme	sector	screen
	bus	monitor
memory module	DVD	display adapter
system unit	CD	desktop
motherboard	removable media	pixel grid
central processing unit (CPU)	Universal Serial Bus	frame buffer
	USB flash drive	dots per inch
bus	solid state	printer driver
data processing	analog	circuit board

Complete the Tables and Lists from Memory

Print a copy of Appendix B, "Memory Tables" (which you can find online at www.pearsonitcertification.com/title/9780789748454), or at least the section for this chapter, and complete the tables and lists from memory. Appendix C, "Memory Tables Answer Key," also online, includes completed tables and lists to check your work.

Chapter 2

Introduction to Computer Networking

Computer networks use a large variety of components that work together for the purpose of sending bits from one computing device to another. This chapter expands on this basic statement by rewording, by expanding, by introducing terms, and by considering computer networks from different angles. But if you reduce all the complexity to one statement, computer networks move bits from one device to another.

First, consider the term *computing device* in that original simple definition. Devices of course include computers of all shapes and sizes. But they also include many devices people do not think of as computers: game systems, televisions, phones, tablets, GPS navigation systems, watches, and so on. Pretty much any device that uses electricity today has some kind of computing power and some memory that stores bits. Many of those devices communicate. How do they communicate? They use computer networks.

Next, consider the thing that networks copy from device to device: bits. So, what is a bit? If you stop people on the street, what would they tell you? You might actually hear a lot of different answers.

From the perspective of computer networking, a bit is a binary 1 or 0 as used by a computing device. On the computing devices, the bits must somehow physically exist as well—with electrical circuitry in RAM, magnetic charges on hard disk drives, and bumps or other marks on DVD discs, to name a few. However, most computer networking discussions do not care about the particulars of how a computer stores a bit. Instead, computer networking focuses on copying the bits on one device to another device, regardless of how the devices physically store the bits.

When you discuss bits without any context, the bits represent data, but when you discuss the meaning of bits, the bits represent information. Bits might be just 1s and 0s, but what do they represent? This partial list identifies a few items: video games, videos on your computer, videos that you watch from a DVD or Blu-ray disc, a phone call from your cell phone, a phone call from your age-old home telephone, any function on an app on a smart phone, and anything that happens on a traditional computer.

In short, for any electrical device built during the twenty-first century, if it communicates, it uses a computer network. That's why the subtitle of the book states that computer networking enables the modern world.

This chapter takes a basic definition of a computer network and expands it in three major sections:

- The first section, "Defining a Network with User Applications," looks at computer networking from a user perspective by focusing on user applications, or apps.

- The second major section, "A Deeper Look at One Application: World Wide Web," then dives deeply into one app: the World Wide Web (WWW).

- The final of the three sections, "Uncovering the Network Between the Application Endpoints," looks at the hidden world of computer networking: the links and nodes that exist behind the scenes to create a road system over which the bits can move.

AUTHOR'S NOTE:
This book uses the term *app* in its traditional sense as simply a shorter version of *application*. Note that the mobile phone industry has popularized the term *app* to also specifically refer to software that runs on a mobile phone.

Chapter Outline

Objectives

- Define the term *computer networking*.

- Compare the similarities and differences in how several applications send bits: email, voice calls, video downloads, and web browsing.

- Make generalizations about how other networked apps make use of computer networks.

- Sketch how web protocols work so that a user's web browser requests a web page, and describe how the web server responds to supply that web page.

- Explain generally how web server software, running on some computer hardware, uses the network between the computers to send a web page to a user's computer.

- Compare the functions in a computer network to a transportation system (roads and intersections).

- List common terms used to describe networks of different sizes, from small home networks to the worldwide Internet.

- Describe a network topology as a set of nodes and links.

Key Terms

computer networking	web server	enterprise network
computer network	web browser	link
application	web address	node
email	web page	the Internet
voice call	protocol	
video frame	HTTP	

Defining a Network with User Applications

The users of a computer network often do things that use the network without knowing how the network works. For example, if someone sends a text message to another person's phone, and the second person sends back a text message in reply, those text messages used a network. Your posts to a social media website such as Facebook use a network, and your friends use a network to look at what you posted. In fact, some vendors even talk about their networks when they advertise services—for example, many mobile phone companies argue that their network is better than the other guy's network. The evidence of networks exists all around us, whether or not we stop to think about networks.

This first of three major sections in this chapter focuses on parts of the network that most people use: applications. People use phones, watch videos, walk by digital advertising, play video games against people in other places, send text messages, browse websites, post items on social media, send email, and many other things. All these activities use networks.

Computer networking includes a large number of individual topics, so when learning about networks, it helps to ignore some topics. For example, when discussing the latest movie, you do not need to talk about your car that you drove to the movie theatre. When discussing computer networks, people can ignore parts of the network and focus on just some of the topics.

Interestingly, network diagrams sometimes tell us which parts of a network to ignore for a discussion. Diagrams often use a cloud to identify what part of the network to ignore for that particular discussion. In this section, the discussion focuses on end-user devices, so Figure 2-1 shows a typical network figure, with a cloud representing the parts of the network between devices that this section will basically ignore.

FIGURE 2-1

Computer Networks: Cloud Representing Hidden Parts of the Network

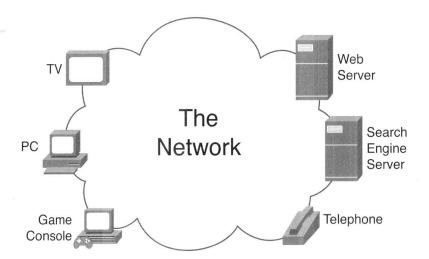

Defining a Network with User Applications 55

An Informal General Definition of a Computer Network

Throughout the chapter, the text will keep adding to and refining this definition of a *computer network*:

> Stuff that works together to send bits from one computer to another

Yes, this book is a textbook on computer networking, and the first definition of computer networking uses the word *stuff*: an incredibly squishy, general, nonspecific term. For the time being, the definition needs to be general, so to avoid implying any specific technical meaning, for now, use the general idea: stuff.

Next, before going further, this text uses the terms **computer network** and **computer networking** as a noun and verb form, respectively, but they are otherwise synonyms. So if you see the "ing" on the end, it is there just to make the English wording correct. A computer network is the stuff that works together (and so on), and computer networking is the process of the stuff working together (and so on).

Two other terms, *telecom* and *datacom*, have almost the same meaning as the term *computer networking*. Both terms actually take two words and put them together into a single word. The second word in both original phrases, *communications*, means the same thing as *send bits* in this section's original definition of networking. The term *telecom* shortens the phrase *telephone communications*, and *datacom* shortens the term *data communications*.

No one owns the right to tell the world exactly what each of these terms truly means. However, the industry generally uses these two terms as follows:

> **datacom:** An older synonym for computer networking
>
> **telecom:** A term similar to computer networking, but with more focus on the role of traditional telephone companies

> **ON THE SIDE:** One of my college professors, from whom I took an entire senior year of networking courses, used to stress the importance of understanding terminology. He tried to convince us that two people would use the same term to mean two different things, or different terms to mean the same thing. And he encouraged us to master both the concepts and terms, because the people who knew the terms and their meaning, and could figure out what people truly meant—those people would have a great chance at being successful in a networking career. Dr. Enslow's advice was right on—so I share it with you these years later, because I think it is still true today.

With that definition in mind, next turn your attention to the user actions and the user devices. Users use PCs, phones, games, TVs, and so on. But why do they use them? For the **applications** or apps. Would you use a phone that did not allow phone calls? Maybe, but what if it also did not allow texting? Or email? Or posting to social media? Or web surfing? Or anything that used a network? The phone would be almost worthless without the network. The applications that happen to use a network are what drives us all to buy them and use them in the first place.

The key common feature for many of these cool apps, on all these different networked devices, is that they all need to send bits. All these apps are part of the networking "stuff" that works together to send bits in this chapter's working definition. The text now takes a look at several example apps: email, voice calls, and video downloads.

Email

Email (electronic mail), one of the oldest applications that uses networking, acts like sending letters through the postal service. To send a paper letter through the postal service (sometimes jokingly called *snail mail*), you put the words on paper, put the paper in an envelope, write the sender and recipient postal addresses on the front, add postage to the front of the envelope, and give it to the postal service. The postal service delivers it to the right address. With email, the same basic process happens, just electronically with bits. You write (type) the email, identify (type) the sender's and receiver's email addresses, and give it to the email service (typically using a mouse click). Then the email service delivers the email to the right email address.

Users typically access email using one of two software options: email software or a web browser. The examples in this section use an email software app. In other words, the user's device uses a software package that gives users a way to create, send, and receive email. And while this is not a complete list by any means, it shows some of the more common email apps:

AUTHOR'S NOTE:
This section's choice
to focus on email
clients, and ignore
the use of web
browsers to send
email, does not mean
that email clients
are better. The email
client examples
just worked better
to make the points
included in this
section.

- Microsoft Outlook
- Microsoft Windows Mail
- Mozilla Thunderbird
- Apple Mail
- Many built-in mail apps on most any phone/tablet

For example, Figure 2-2 shows a sample window created when a user clicked a button in an email client, asking to create a new email. (The figure uses Apple's Mail application.) Of particular importance, note that the window lists the "To" address (the recipient's address, fred@example.com), the "From" address (the sender's address, barney@certskills.com), and the text of the email (both the subject line plus the entire message, at the bottom of the screen).

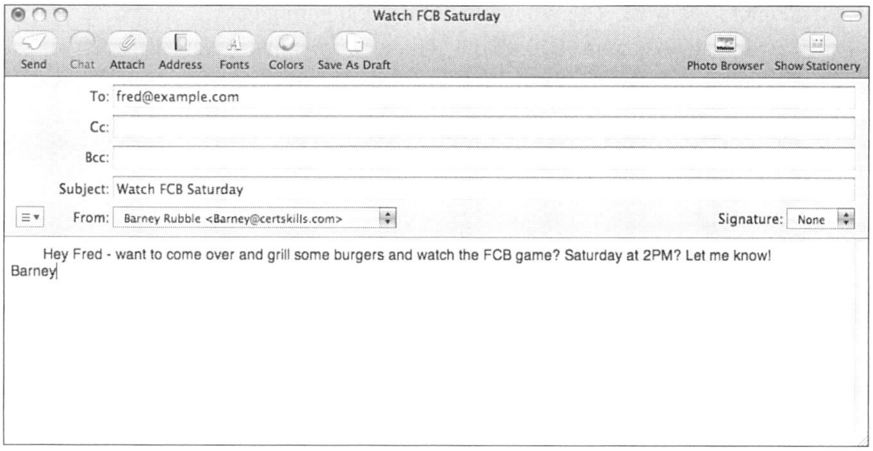

FIGURE 2-2

Sample Window on Email Software: Barney Types Email to Fred

Sending Email: Sender's Computer Perspective

Think more about what happens on Barney's computer. He started the email application and clicked something, maybe a button called New, to cause a window in Figure 2-2 to open. Barney then typed Fred's email address and the text in the email. Next, consider four perspectives about what happens behind the scenes when Barney typed this email.

First, applications store and process data (bits and bytes). Like any other software, the email app keeps the bits temporarily in RAM and stores them permanently as files in some form of permanent memory, like a hard disk drive. What did the email application do in reaction to Barney's typing? At a minimum, it stored some bits in RAM. But most email client apps keep a copy of the emails you send, so the app most likely also stored a copy of the email in a file on the disk drive or other permanent storage on Barney's device.

Second, email apps use some kind of *character set* to represent the text. Chapter 1, "Introduction to Computer Data," introduced this concept in the section titled "Text Character Sets," using the example of what happens when a user types text into a word processor. Computers cannot store the letter *a* as a shape that looks like *a*; instead, the computer uses a known binary value that represents *a*. And how does the computer know what binary value to use for *a* versus *b* or *c*? A character set. The character set lists all the characters that can be added to the email, and a matching binary code. The email client stores the binary values that represent each character in the email based on the character set.

Third, email apps use email addresses. Much like the postal system uses street addresses, emails use email addresses to identify the sender and recipient of the email. In this example, Barney (the human) uses address barney@certskills.com, and Fred (the human) uses email address fred@example.com. The concept mirrors postal addresses: To receive an email and receive a reply email back, both people need a working email address.

ON THE SIDE: Still not sure about email clients and what they look like? Check out the author's book support page for this chapter for links to articles about the most popular email clients.

Finally, email apps work with other parts of the computing device to send the email. The operating system (OS) on the computer typically plays a big role, because every modern OS includes lots of networking features, and the apps rely on the OS to do part of the work. The email client essentially asks the OS to send the email; however, the OS, being software, cannot physically send the bits. So the OS asks for help from the hardware that can physically send the bits, typically called a *network interface card (NIC)*. Figure 2-3 shows the general idea.

FIGURE 2-3

General Process of Sending an Email on Barney's Computer

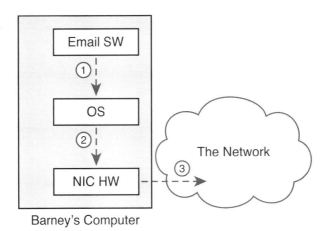

This figure shows a basic example of how many different components work together in a network—in this case, the email application, the OS, and the NIC—to send the bits that make up the email into the network.

Sending Email: Network's Perspective

The network that sits between the user devices must physically move the bits between devices, but the network must do far more than that in some cases. Among other things, networks must provide *services* that help *clients* (the devices that use the network) to do the tasks they want to do. And when someone sends or receives an email with an email app, the network actually has to supply some services to make that all happen.

To better understand how email works, think about what you already know about the postal service for sending letters. Every time you send a letter, you could go to a different post office or different drop box to send the letter to the postal service. More likely, you put your outgoing letters into the same outgoing mailbox or mail drop every time. Why? You just do what is convenient, and dropping the letters at an outgoing mail drop on the way to work, school, or in a box at your house or apartment building is convenient.

Now think about getting paper mail from the postal service. You know the one place you go to get your mail, right? For every postal address, the postal service knows exactly where to leave that mail. Everyone who receives postal mail knows where to go to pick up that mail. For residential addresses, that place can again be the box by your door, in the common area for your apartment complex, or at the end of your driveway. But for each mailing address, both the post office and the people who live at that address know the place: the place where the post office leaves the mail, where the person can go to get the mail.

For example, imagine that Barney sends a paper letter to Fred's postal address:

1. Barney drops the letter in the mailbox for outgoing mail at his apartment complex.
2. The postal service moves the letter toward Fred.
3. Eventually, the postal service leaves the letter in Fred's mailbox.

Then, the letter can sit in Fred's mailbox for a day or two, in case Fred is out of town; whenever Fred next checks his mail, the letter should be there. Figure 2-4 shows the general idea.

ON THE SIDE: The place where the postal service leaves the mail can be most anywhere, as long as everyone knows where that is. For example, there's a town in Georgia called The Rock, so named because the place where the postal service left the mail was a rock in the town.

FIGURE 2-4

Using an Outgoing Mail Drop/Box and an Incoming Mail Box

Barney / Barney's Outgoing Mail– Usual Dropoff / Fred's Incoming Mail Dropoff / Fred

Email works pretty much the same way. To make the email process work, the network must include *email servers*. The servers, which exist as software running on some computer in the network, must be ready to receive, process, and hold emails for email clients. To send email, the email app sends the mail to its outgoing mail server. Before that can happen, the email client must be told the location of that outgoing mail server. Similarly, to receive mail, the email client must get the mail from its incoming mail server; again, the email app must be told the location of the incoming mail server.

Figure 2-5 outlines the email process defined here:

1. Barney begins by sending an email to his outgoing email server.
2. Barney's outgoing email server must know how to find the incoming email server used by Fred—more specifically, the incoming email server used by email address fred@example.com. Only then can this next transaction occur.
3. Fred's incoming email server holds the email for Fred, waiting until Fred next checks his email.

FIGURE 2-5

**Using Outgoing
and Incoming Email
Services**

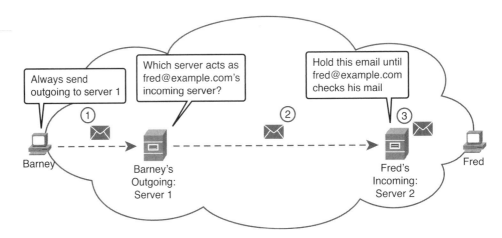

Voice Telephone Calls

Email might be one of the most traditional, commonly used, and most basic
networked computer apps, but the next app was purposefully chosen because it is
very different from email. In fact, many people would not even think of this next
application as an application. The application? Telephone calls, also known as
voice calls.

Making a telephone call is certainly common, and it has been for a long time. At
your home growing up, you probably had a home phone. At your job and at school,
phones were around. Most everyone has a mobile phone these days. And for all
these devices used to make telephone calls, the ability to make a call is just part
of the device; you do not have to download a telephone call app to use your home
phone or to your mobile phone. Making phone calls is just part of the core function
of telephones.

In the twenty-first century world of networking, telephone calls (or voice calls)
send bits. And how do telephone devices send bits? Using a computer network.
Modern computer networks need to be ready to send bits, no matter whether those
bits make up an email or whether they happen to represent voice traffic. The
following sections give a short introduction to voice traffic, again with the goal to
explore the basics of what a computer network is and what it does.

Early Analog Voice Calls

History credits Alexander Graham Bell with the invention of the telephone in the
1870s. The companies that Bell helped start went on to create the telephone system
in the United States, which might have had an even larger impact on the connected
world in which we live. Essentially, the majority of telephone service in the United
States for the first 100 years after the invention of the telephone grew from Bell's
original work and business ventures.

To get the general idea about how home phones worked in the early years of
telephony, up through the middle of the twentieth century, in the United States at

least, look at Figure 2-6. The local *telephone company*, or *telco* as they came to be known as, ran a cable to each home. The cable contained two wires. Inside the rest of the telco network, lots of other equipment existed, and it connected together to create a telephone network. Figure 2-6 shows the idea, with the cloud in the middle helping us focus on the details of what happens between the telco and the home.

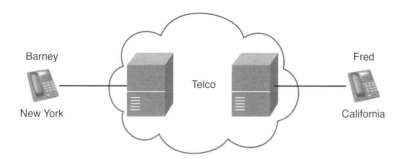

Next, consider what happens when Barney picks up his home phone in New York and calls Fred in California. That phrase *call Fred* really means that Barney somehow tells the telco Fred's phone number, meaning that Barney wants to create a voice call to Fred's phone. Today, we press numbers on a keypad or program the phone to remember phone numbers; in the old days, the phones had a round dial, called a rotary. Regardless, the user, Barney in this case, somehow dialed or pressed keys to tell the telco to make a call to Fred's phone number.

To make Barney's call to Fred work, and to make every other call work, the telco has to know all phone numbers and their matching phone lines. Sound familiar? The idea is a little like the postal service knowing where to leave mail for each postal address, or the email system knowing exactly where to leave mail for each email address. The telco must keep a list of all phone numbers and know which phone line connects to the phone using that phone number. Knowing that information, when a new call occurs, like Barney's call to Fred's phone, the telco knows exactly where the call physically needs to go.

Finally, to create the call, the telco creates an electrical circuit all the way from one phone to the other. Figure 2-7 shows the idea: After the telco creates the call by creating an electrical circuit, the two people can talk.

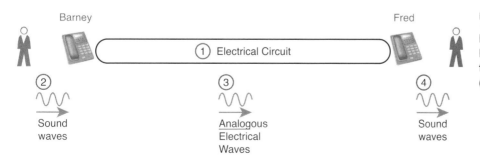

The figure also points out several steps that tell some facts about how the sound travels from left to right in the example. Following the steps in the figure:

1. The telco creates an electrical circuit between the phones because Barney called Fred.

2. Barney (the human) speaks, creating sound waves in the air. When graphed over time, those sound waves go up and down, just like waves in the ocean; the figure shows the graph of the sound waves at Step 2.

3. This step shows the results of the phone converting the sound energy into electrical energy using a key part of the phone: a microphone that sits near the mouth of the speaker. A microphone takes in sound waves and outputs an electrical signal that, when graphed over time, looks very similar to the graph of the sound waves. In other words, the electrical signal's graph is *analogous* to the sound wave graph; the electrical signal is considered an *analog* electrical signal. Barney's phone sends this electrical signal over the circuit to Fred's phone.

4. Fred's phone converts the analog electrical signal back to sound waves using a speaker in the part of the phone near Fred's ear. A speaker takes in the analog electrical signal and vibrates the air, creating sound waves that look like the analog electrical signal. As a result, what Barney speaks, Fred hears.

Digital Voice Calls

The invention of the telephone, and its introduction into normal life around the world, took place far before the computer revolution. The telcos of the world had already created large networks to support analog voice calls long before computers became commonplace in businesses. Later, with the introduction of computers, the telcos began to think about how to use computers to improve their networks. However, computers process digital data (bits), and the telephone network processed analog electricity.

To take advantage of computers and related technology, the telcos eventually replaced their analog telephone network with a digital telephone network by finding a way to change analog voice to digital voice. To do that, the telcos developed a way to take the electrical signal they already worked with (the analog signal) and convert it to a digital signal. That process, called *analog to digital* (A to D, or simply A/D), converted the analog signal to binary digits (bits).

One part of the A/D process for voice breaks the voice into very small time intervals. For example, one of the original A/D processes developed by AT&T, the primary telco in the United States at the time, sampled the voice in a call 8000 times per second, which means that each separate sound was only 0.125 milliseconds long. If you think about all the different sounds the human voice can make, the differences in how different voices sound, and the differences in pitch, the human voice can make a lot of different sounds. However, heard as only very short sounds, there really are not that many different combinations.

A second big part of the voice A/D process assigns a binary value to each unique short sound. The idea works a little like a character map, but instead of mapping text characters to a unique binary code, this mapping matches each unique short sound with a matching binary code. The original A/D conversion process by AT&T used an 8-bit code for each short sample.

Now think back to real life, with a normal home phone. In the United States at least, the home phone still uses analog signals. The telco wanted to make use of computers to make its network more efficient, lower costs, and provide better service. So, the telco added equipment to its network to do an A/D conversion process on each end of each call. Figure 2-8 shows the idea, in which the two home phones create an electrical circuit into the telco, but the analog circuit does not extend from phone to phone.

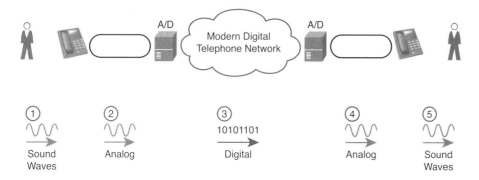

FIGURE 2-8

Analog to the Phones, Digital in the Telco (Phone Icon ©Andrey)

The figure shows what happens after the phone call is set up, again focusing on Barney speaking and Fred listening:

1. Barney speaks, creating sound waves.
2. The phone, as before, creates an analog signal representing the voice, sending it out into the telco network.
3. The telco uses a device that does A/D conversion, creating bits; at that point, the telco's modern network can send those bits.
4. The telco must convert the bits back to the analog signal for transmission to Fred's home phone.
5. Finally, Fred's home phone uses a speaker to convert the analog electrical signal into sound waves.

End-to-End Digital Voice with Business and Mobile Phones

Most of the phone calls from homes in the United States for the last 30–40 years work as illustrated previously in Figure 2-8. In contrast, modern business telephones and mobile phones send voice as bits, rather than using analog signals.

ON THE SIDE:
Generally, the devices that perform the A/D conversion are called coders/decoders, or *codecs* for short. That one original AT&T codec mentioned in this section is today named G.711. At 8000 samples per second of voice, and with 8 bits per sample, voice calls using that codec create 64,000 bits per second.

This short section touches briefly on some of the big concepts, beginning with business phones:

- Most modern business telephones actually connect to the same computer network as the PCs that sit on the same desk at a business.

- Modern business telephones send and receive digital signals (bits) directly, because they have an A/D converter on each phone.

- These phones often have computer-like features built-in. For example, you might have a display with a simple web browser built into the phone.

- Some of these phones essentially have built-in tablet computers that you can remove and take with you.

In short, modern business telephones look more like small computers that have a phone attached, and the voice-calling feature is just one of many features.

Mobile phones have some of the same features as business phones, but with one big and somewhat obvious difference: no cables. *Mobile phones*, sometimes also called *cell phones*, use wireless technologies to send and receive bits, whether the phone sends those bits as part of a voice call or as part of some data application like text messaging.

Summarizing, voice traffic exists as one of the more common types of traffic in computer networks today. Networks not only can support voice, but they typically do, and voice is just one of the many applications that make use of a modern computer network.

Recorded Video

The previous section discussed voice calls that needed to cross the network at a given point in time. In other words, the calls were live, rather than recorded. Networks can also send recorded voice (audio) as well. The network might need to treat the audio differently depending on whether the audio is live or recorded in a file, but this chapter only discussed voice audio as live traffic.

The next topic looks at a third application—recorded video. As with both live and recorded voice applications, networks need to support both live and recorded video. This topic focuses just on recorded video just to give you a little different perspective as compared to live voice calls.

Digital Video Recordings

Modern video cameras actually make digital recordings; in other words, they store the video as bits. The camera itself has optics to take in the light and a microphone to take in the sound. The video camera also has processors to take that input and convert the light and sound into bits, and some form of permanent storage on which to stores the video in a file. At that point, the video exists as bits stored in a file. Later, the user can copy the video to a PC, either by connecting a cable, by removing the memory card (usually some kind of flash memory), or in some cases, by using a network. Figure 2-9 shows the idea.

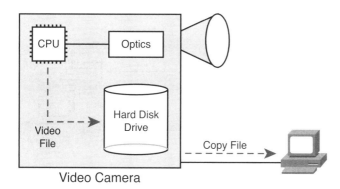

Video Camera

FIGURE 2-9

Video Camera
Components and Moving
the Video Files to a PC

If the user only wanted to view the video on her computer, the discussion could stop with Figure 2-9. However, this section actually focuses more on the story after doing the tasks in Figure 2-9, in which people share a video over a network. Many people today like to post videos on the Internet: on social media sites, on video-sharing sites, on their web pages, and for many reasons. This section looks at some of the interesting facts and things to think about when posting video files for others to download and watch.

Video Files

Digital video revolves around the concept of a single **video frame**. A video frame is a rectangle (width by height) of individual points of light of the video image, as frozen in time. When played back, the video player software shows one frame after another. Because each frame shows only a slight change compared to the previous frame, and the player shows many frames per second, the human brain sees those small changes as movement. (This effect with the human eyes and brain is called *persistence of vision*.)

Computers cannot store a video as points of light, or as motions on a screen, but they can store bits. To store the video as bits, the computer thinks of the video frame as a pixel grid, with a pixel being one very small light that can be lit on the computer display. To represent the color of the pixel, you guessed it, the computer uses a table that lists all the colors and a matching binary code. Conceptually, to store a complete video frame, the video file could list a color code for every pixel. The video file would store a series of video frames.

Video files can become too large, however. As a simple but extreme example, imagine that you made up a new video recording standard for high-definition video, with these specifications:

- Use a 3-byte code to represent the color of each pixel.
- Use a frame size of 1920 (wide) by 1080 (high), to match high-definition (HD) video specifications
- Record 30 frames per second to make sure that the video looks smooth.

Figure 2-10 shows the concepts visually.

FIGURE 2-10

Somewhat Extreme Example of Uncompressed Video

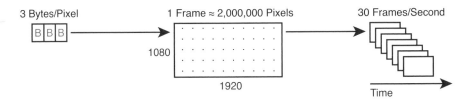

3 Bytes/Pixel

1 Frame ≈ 2,000,000 Pixels

30 Frames/Second

1080

1920

Time

Assuming these approximate values, with no compression, this imaginary video recording standard requires 180 megabytes per second (180 MBps) of video stored in the file: 3 bytes/pixel * 2,000,000 pixels/frame * 30 frames/second. In bits per second, the normal measurement for network speeds, the video requires almost 1.5 gigabits per second (1.5 Gbps).

For comparison, an uncompressed voice call, like those voice calls discussed in the previous section, require only 8 kilobytes for each second of voice (64 kilobits per second), or less than 1/10,000[th] of the number of bytes as this (admittedly extreme) uncompressed video example.

Video Compression

Video products store the videos much more efficiently than the rules shown in the example around Figure 2-10. For example, if the next 40,000 pixels in a video frame are sky blue, the (imaginary) video recording standard in Figure 2-10 would have stored the same 3-byte code 40,000 times in a row. Real-life video-recording standards instead use codes that mean the same thing but use less bytes. For example, a 2-byte code might be used, with the code meaning "the next 40,000 pixels use the same color code," and list that sky blue 3-byte code only once, reducing the size of the video file.

Beyond these common-sense ways to reduce file sizes, video recording standards also use compression. *Compression* takes a video and stores it as a smaller video file. In some cases, the smaller video file, when played back, looks just as good as the original video. In other cases, to make the video file smaller, the compression reduces the quality of the video. However, you cannot expect people to wait hours to download and watch a short video, so compression gives people choices for less quality but much faster downloads.

For example, one type of compression that reduces the quality to some extent is to reduce the number of pixels in each frame. You might take a video that was recorded with a video frame size of 1920 × 1080. The user could choose to shorten the width and height to 1/4 the original width and height, a 480 × 270 video frame, which requires 1/16 the original number of pixels in the frame. And if viewed in a smaller window on someone's computer, rather than viewing it on the entire screen, the video would probably still look pretty good.

ON THE SIDE: The world of video and video compression has many aspects, and it is something you can learn and experience using many tools on a PC. If you find the topic interesting, check out the book *Real World Video Compression*, by Andy Beach.

This discussion of video shows a great example of why the user of networked applications cannot completely ignore the network. If the person producing the video creates a video that requires an hour to download, even over a fast Internet connection, not many people will bother watching the video. However, if the video producer takes the same video and compresses it into a smaller size, the video will likely find more people willing to watch.

Figure 2-11 shows an example of the overall flow, in which the video producer—the person who recorded the video and decided what compressions to use—compressed and posted the file on a video server on the Internet (Steps 1 through 3). Later, at Step 4, video users might actually watch the video because it downloads in a reasonable amount of time.

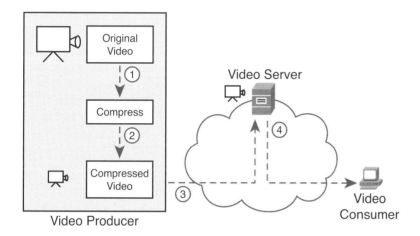

FIGURE 2-11

Producing and Posting Smaller Compressed Video Files

Refining the Definition of a Network

This section began with a very general definition of computer networks:

> Stuff that works together to send bits from one computer to another

Before moving on to the second major section in this chapter, take a moment to expand this definition in your mind. Focus on the word *stuff*, a purposefully general term that can be expanded with almost any term discussed in this first section. For example, computer hardware and computer software work together. The devices that the user uses, plus other devices, like servers or the A/D converter in the voice examples, work together to send bits. And even all the rules and conventions mentioned in this section fit as well, like the rules about using various email servers.

> **AUTHOR'S NOTE:** The section "Create Mind Maps," near the end of this chapter, lists four mind map activities. The second activity relates to this first section of the book, which ends here. It might be a good time to pause and do that activity.

A Deeper Look at One Application: World Wide Web

The *World Wide Web* (*WWW*, or simply *the web*), particularly web browser software with which users access the web, might well be the single most commonly used application in the world. The fact that many of you reading this book have used the web makes it a great example app to use in this book.

The World Wide Web also works well for learning networking because it uses a basic *client-server model*. The user sits at a computer and uses software commonly called a *web browser*, or more formally, a *web client*. The term *client* emphasizes the fact that this software wants to receive some service from another device. In this case, the web client wants to see information that sits on a *web server*.

The web browser (client) and web server cooperate so that the web browser can get a copy of the information on the web server. The server organizes information into pages called web pages. The web browser somehow asks the web server for a web page, and the server sends the web page back to the web browser. Figure 2-12 shows the idea.

FIGURE 2-12

Web Browser Requesting and Receiving a Web Page from a Web Server

The following sections take a closer look at the two big players in the web: the user computer where the web browser sits and the server computer that acts as the web server. Additionally, this section also weaves in a discussion about a set of rules—protocols—that both the client and server must know and follow.

Web Browsers (Web Clients)

A **web browser** is software that allows a user to get and display a copy of a web page from a web server. Figure 2-12 earlier showed the basic concept of a web browser getting the web page. After the web server sends the web page content back to the browser, the browser displays the information correctly.

For example, Figure 2-13 shows the window created by Apple's Safari web browser after loading a web page from the author's website. Note that like most applications, the web browser window has some controls on the outer edges of the window, but the majority of center of the window contains the web page that was received from the server.

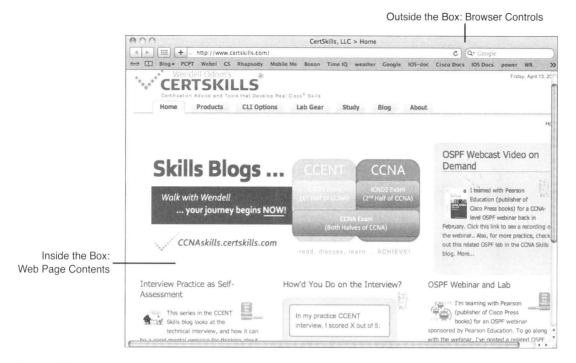

FIGURE 2-13

Window Created by Apple Safari Web Browser

The history of web browsers and web servers dates back to the early 1990s when they were first created. Since that time, many web browsers have been written. As of the original writing of this chapter back in 2011, the more commonly used browsers on personal computers included Microsoft's Internet Explorer, Mozilla's Firefox, Google's Chrome, and Apple's Safari.

Typically, for today's computing devices, if a human user uses it, the device also has a web browser. The series of computer OSs from Microsoft (including Windows 7), Linux, and Mac OSs all support multiple different web browsers. Phones and tablets also typically include a browser, with other browsers that can be downloaded as apps. For example, Apple includes its Safari browser in OS X (the OS that runs on Mac computers) and in iOS, the OS that runs on Apple iPhones and iPads.

All web browsers must follow the same set of known rules. These rules tell a browser how to request a web page from a web server. No matter which browser you use, they all request the web pages in generally the same way. Browsers also work generally the same way in how they divide the work: The browser does some work, but it also relies on the computer OS to do parts of the work as well.

Components on the Client Computer

Web browsers display web pages, but the browser software needs help from other components on the client computer. This section takes a brief look at some of the ways the job of getting and displaying a web page is divided among the components of the client computer.

First, each client computer (the computer on which the web browser sits) needs a way to physically connect to the network. The bits that make up the web page sit on the web server, which is a different computer. To move the bits to and from the network, the client typically uses hardware called a *network interface card* *(NIC)*. Its name actually defines what the NIC does: It provides an interface to the network. The NIC physically connects the computer to the network.

Figure 2-14 shows a traditional NIC used in a PC. The upper part of the figure shows the circuit board with microchips and circuits. The lower light-colored edge shows the part of the NIC that can be seen from outside the computer. In that lower edge, the dark rectangle in the bottom/front of the image is an opening into which a cable can be inserted, with the cable connecting the NIC to the network.

FIGURE 2-14

Photo of Network Interface Card (NIC) (© Mark Jansen)

The term *NIC* might refer to a separate card, but the term can also simply refer to a function on some device. Some NICs do exist as a separate computer expansion card, like the one shown in Figure 2-14. Other devices simply put the same NIC functions onto some other part of the device, making the NIC function simply be part of the device itself. For example, a tablet computer has a wireless NIC function, but physically, the NIC does not exist as a separate card, but rather just as one function of the device itself.

Next, think about the operating system (OS) software on the client computer. The OS already has to control the CPU, RAM, and permanent memory. The OS actually controls other hardware as well, including the NIC. The OS must also manage all the applications and provide services to those applications.

When a user clicks or types something that makes a web browser try to load a new web page, the web browser, OS, and NIC all play a role. Figure 2-15 shows the major steps, with an example in which the user decided to load a web page from the www.example.com web server.

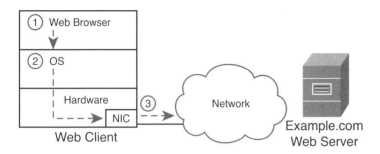

FIGURE 2-15

Three Major Steps on the Client Computer After the User Requests a Web Page

The steps that follow the figure describe what occurs:

1. The browser creates a message (made of bits) to request a web page from the www.example.com web server, but the web browser needs help, including help physically sending the request. So the web browser gives the request to the OS and asks the OS for help.

2. The OS does some work on the request, including locating the web server's address in the network. However, the OS cannot physically send the bits without help from the hardware, so the OS asks the NIC to send the request.

3. The NIC has the job of sending the request (as bits) physically into the network.

The example in Figure 2-15 shows some detail behind what happens when a user requests a web page. The next topic takes a closer look at what happens in Step 1, specifically, how the web browser identifies the web page it wants to load.

Using Web Addresses (URLs)

Every time a web browser displays a new web page, the browser must identify the web page using a web address. Usually, the user already shows some web page, and when he clicks something on that page, the browser loads a new web page. Sometimes, the user just types the web address into a particular place in the web browser window, which tells the browser what web page to display. This section looks at the concept of a web address and its format.

A **web address** identifies the specific web page that the user wants to display. Also referenced by the more formal name *Uniform Resource Locator*, or *URL*, each web address identifies a web page by identifying the web server, and the specific web page on that web server, as follows:

Server name: Identified by the name listed between a // and a / in the URL

Web page: Identified by the name after the / in the URL

ON THE SIDE: The term *URL* goes by the more formal name Uniform Resource Identifier (URI). Also, the *U* in URL is commonly referenced as "Universal" instead of "Uniform." But the concept of how a URL is used is far more important than the actual letters in the acronym.

For example, consider the small network shown in Figure 2-16. The figure shows a web address on the bottom of the figure, as typed by a user into his web browser. Two web servers sit on the top, each with multiple web pages. To display any of those web pages, the user needs to type in a web address in the browser that identifies the correct web server, by name, and then the correct web page, by name. In this case, the URL identifies the server on the left and the web page in the middle (page2).

FIGURE 2-16

Example of Identifying a Web Page Using a Web Address (URL)

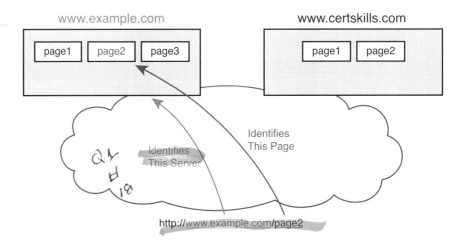

Users might type web addresses occasionally, but most of the time, users click *hyperlinks* to see new web pages. Hyperlinks hide web addresses on a web page. When the user clicks a hyperlinked item on a web page (usually text or a graphic), the web browser loads the web page for the web address listed for that hyperlink. For example, if you go to any website that sells products and search for products, the website will give you a list. The web page does not list a bunch of web addresses, but all the items in the list have hyperlinks. If you want to see more about one of the products, you click on the product and another page appears; that happens because of a hyperlink.

> **ON THE SIDE:** When using a web browser, if you want to see the hidden web address associated with a hyperlink, hover over the link and use the right-click (or equivalent) mouse button. The browser will list a menu that typically shows options to either display the linked web address, or at least copy it, so that you can look at the hyperlinked web address.

Web Servers

Web browsers play an important role, but web browsers would be useless without web servers. **Web servers** store information (text, graphics, video, and audio) that the user wants to see and hear, collecting that information into web pages. The web server then waits to receive requests for those web pages, and the server sends the page back to the browser. The following sections take a closer look at the web server itself, as well as look a little more closely at what a web page includes.

Web Server Hardware and Software

First and foremost, a web server is software. Of course, as software, it must run on some computer hardware, but that hardware and its OS can support many kinds of applications. The web services—storing web pages, listening for requests for web pages, sending web pages in response to those requests—all happen because of web server software.

Many competing web server software options exist in the market, for the same reasons why many web browser options exist. As of the time of the original writing of this chapter, the Apache web server, from open source foundation the Apache Software Foundation, and Microsoft's Internet Information Server (IIS) appear to be two of the most popular web servers.

To create a functioning web server, the web server hardware can literally just be any computer with an OS that supports web server software. Just install the chosen web server software, and start adding web pages. It sounds easy, and it actually is relatively easy to get a simple web server installed and working, just to prove the concept.

However, building a website for a business requires a lot of thought and work. Many people work their entire IT career in web-related jobs, creating websites, managing content, and supporting web servers. Businesses have more serious needs, so instead of just putting web server software on the same kinds of PCs that sit on the employees' desks, they often use specialized server hardware with a server-optimized OS (like Microsoft's Windows Server 2008) for their web services. Businesses have to think about more than just whether the web server responds in a lab when doing a simple test of a single web page. They have to think about the number of users that use the web page at the same time, the number of pages a server must supply per second, the speed of the connection to the network, and many other factors.

Many businesses build or lease space for their physical servers in a special type of room called a *data center (DC)*. The server hardware sits in racks, without displays and keyboards for each server, because the IT staff manages the servers from their offices. However, the servers do have CPUs, RAM, and storage. The DC also typically connects each server to the network using some cables. Figure 2-17 shows a conceptual view of a data center.

FIGURE 2-17

Data Center with Servers in Racks (© Dreaming Andy)

> **ON THE SIDE:** Coincidentally, I wrote this section of the chapter on Cyber Monday 2011. Cyber Monday is the Monday after the Thanksgiving holiday in the United States, traditionally the largest online shopping day of the year. The TV news the next day reported $1.2 billion in online sales (U.S. only) that day. Being ready for events like Cyber Monday certainly requires an IT staff that pays close attention to the hardware used for their web servers.

Figure 2-18 pulls the main ideas about web server components together. The right side of the figure shows the web server concept, with the server software, and web pages it is ready to serve. The web server, just like the web browser, relies on the OS and NIC to play a role as well.

FIGURE 2-18

Three Steps: Web Server Sends Web Page into Network

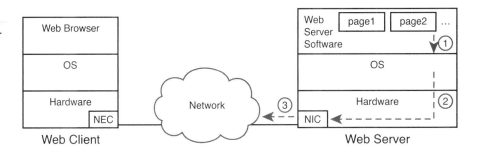

Similar to the steps shown with Figure 2-15, the figure shows what happens inside the server after the server has decided to send a web page out into the network:

1. The server takes the web page that sits in permanent storage and asks the OS to send it out into the network back to the web browser that requested the page.

2. The OS does some work (not detailed here), but the OS cannot physically send the data, so it asks the NIC for help.

3. The NIC has the job of sending the request physically into the network.

Web Sites, Pages, and Objects

Many of you reading this book have used the web, used it a lot, and use web terminology as part of your everyday speech. Many people who reached college in the twenty-first century throw out terms like *web surfing*, *surf the web*, or simply *surf*; *Google it* or *web search*; and *web page*, *website*, *web address*, or even *URL*. Being familiar with all these terms is great, but having used these terms, the danger is that not everyone might use the terms the same way. This section attempts to give everyone a more specific understanding of three specific terms: *website*, *web page*, and *web object*.

The term *website* refers to all the web pages associated with a web server that goes by a particular name. For example, Figure 2-16 shows a user asking for one web page from the example.com web server, and the figure shows that server with three different web pages. In that case, all three web pages are part of the example.com website.

The term **web page** refers to a collection of content (text, images, video, and audio) that web browsers display in a single browser window at one point in time. For example, imagine that you go to your favorite site to buy books, and you search that website. The next page, which lists a bunch of books, is one web page. When you click the name of an interesting book, the web server supplies another web page, this one likely to be a web page about that one book. All the content that shows up in your browser window when you click for the next web page—text, images, and so on—is part of one web page.

Or, for another example, Figure 2-13, earlier in this chapter, shows a web browser window, with a web page inside the window.

Following the same concept, each web page typically contains multiple *web objects*. The web server stores a single web page not as a single file on the web server, but as separate files, called web objects, with links between the objects. For example, if a web page includes text and graphics, the web server actually stores the text in one web object (file) and each graphic in a different file.

Figure 2-19 shows the idea of a simple website, for example.com, with two web pages. Each web page has a main web object that holds the web page text, with each of these files linking to two or three other objects.

FIGURE 2-19

Conceptual View: Website, Web Page, Web Object

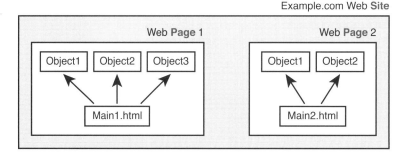

An analogy can help with some of the organization of these terms. Think of a typical small town that has some houses. Depending on what is happening, you might talk about the town, or you might need to talk about someone's specific house. The entire town is like a website, with each house being like an individual web page.

Taking the analogy a step further, most of the time people ignore the building materials in their house. Sure, the house has wood, nails, concrete, roofing shingles, pipes, electrical cabling, and so on. Most of the time, people ignore those details after the house has been built, but sometimes those details matter, for example, when something in the house needs to be repaired. In this analogy, each individual web object is like an individual board, individual pipe, individual shingle on the roof, and so on. And similar to the idea that a house has many pieces of wood, many nails, and so on, each web page might have many web objects of each type.

So, why even think about web objects in particular? As it turns out, and as the next section explains, when a browser gets a new web page, the browser actually gets every individual object in the web page. It's like making a copy of a house by making an exact copy of every wooden board, every nail, every pipe, and so on, and the exact location of each copied part, and then putting the copied parts back together again.

The Process to Get One Web Page

This topic completes this chapter's look at the web traffic by examining how protocols work, in particular, the *Hypertext Transfer Protocol (HTTP)*.

A Protocol Primer

In networking, a **protocol** is a set of rules. That set of rules can be standardized by some standards body (more on standards in the next chapter), or they can just be a set of rules you created for your company. But the rules exist for some reason, and for computer networks, the rules help the devices work together.

For example, think about driving a car in a world with no traffic rules. When you get to an intersection, anyone could drive through at any time. Anyone could drive on any part of the paved road, or the sidewalk, or beside the road for that matter. While it might sound interesting for an experiment, or for a movie, in real life, having no traffic rules would pretty much stop traffic. People would get hurt in accidents, and even without accidents, overall the traffic would be slower—possibly much slower. The roadways would either be filled with cars that could no longer move forward or backward, or at least the system would work poorly overall.

Similarly, networking protocols define rules that make the network work well. Sure, networking includes software, like web browsers, and hardware, like computers and NICs. But those components must also follow networking protocols, which define how the software and hardware should behave when using the network.

Using HTTP to Get the First File for a Web Page

HTTP, the **Hypertext Transfer Protocol**, defines the rules by which a web browser can ask for a web page from a web server, and the rules a web server uses to send the web page back to the web browser.

HTTP defines the idea of a message that lists *requests* and *responses*. The most common of these is the HTTP GET request and response, which, you guessed it, allows a web browser to get a web object (GET request) and the web server to supply the web object (GET response). Figure 2-20 shows the idea.

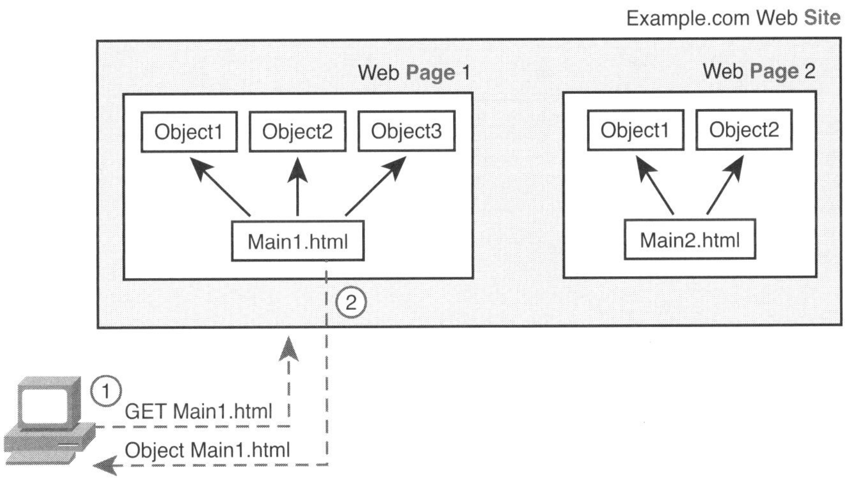

> **ON THE SIDE:**
> The original WWW objects were mainly text that used a format called Hypertext Markup Language (HTML), so the word *Hypertext* in Hypertext Transfer Protocol comes from that original object type.

Example.com Web **Site**

FIGURE 2-20

HTTP GET Request and Response

The figure shows the general idea, with the browser asking for an object at the example.com web server, with filename Main1.html. Essentially, the GET request identifies a file (a web object) on the server, either directly or indirectly. The server reads the file from its permanent storage and sends it back to the web client.

Note that HTTP does not define everything about web browsers and web servers, but it does define rules each must follow. For example, HTTP does not define what the web browser user interface should look like, so competing web browsers have a different look and feel and different menu items to configure different settings.

AUTHOR'S NOTE:
The web addresses
that you see in a web
browser typically
start with *http*
because the letters
before the // identify
the protocol that is
used to transfer the
files.

However, HTTP does define the details important to getting web pages, like the GET request and reply messages, so competing web browsers use the exact same HTTP messages. HTTP also defines the format of web addresses.

Getting All the Files for a Web Page

Users want to get web pages, but the HTTP GET mechanism gets web objects. Each web page contains one or more objects, and today, a web page can include dozens of different objects.

To get an entire web page, the web browser must do multiple HTTP GET requests and then look for instructions in each object. Each web object can include data that tells the browser to get other objects. For example, the first object that the browser gets can include text instructions that tell the web browser to get a web object that contains a photo, and to place that photo on the left side of the web page.

Figure 2-21 shows an example. In this case, the web browser gets the first object, Main1.html. That file contains only text, plus additional instructions to download three other graphical web objects.

FIGURE 2-21

Using Four HTTP GET Requests for One Web Page

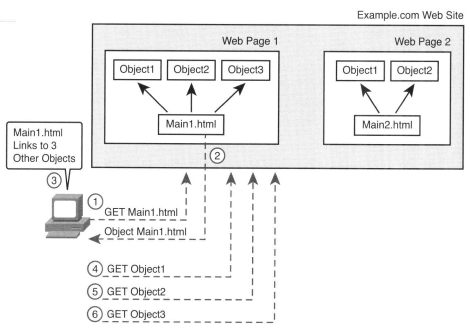

The figure shows the following steps:

1. The web client issues an HTTP GET request for the original object, Main1.html, based on what the user clicked or typed.

2. The web server supplies the web object Main1.html in the HTTP GET reply.

3. The web browser reads the Main1.html file and sees directions that tell the browser to get three other objects on this web page.

4. The web browser issues an HTTP GET request for the first extra object (Object1.jpg).

5. The web browser issues an HTTP GET request for the second extra object (Object2.jpg).

6. The web browser issues an HTTP GET request for the third extra object (Object3.jpg).

Refining the Definition of a Network

As a reminder, this chapter earlier listed this somewhat general definition:

Stuff that works together to send bits from one computer to another

To refine the definition, you can again replace the word *stuff* with most any of the components discussed in this section. The revised definition that follows shows much more detail, and it emphasizes a very important point from this section: In computer networking, no one component does all the work. In fact, many pieces work together. Keeping that in mind, a revised definition of computer networking could be as follows:

Software on client computers (for example, web browsers), software on server computers (for example, web server software), the OS on those computers, some hardware to connect the computers to the network (for example, a network interface card, or NIC), a network that can deliver the bits from one computer to another, and a complete set of protocols (rules) by which the various components can work together to send bits from one computer to another

To help pull it all together visually, consider the seven-step process shown in Figure 2-22. The process in the figure begins when a user clicks a link, resulting in a request to load the page at www.example.com/Main1.html. The steps end at the point at which the web server considers the HTTP GET request.

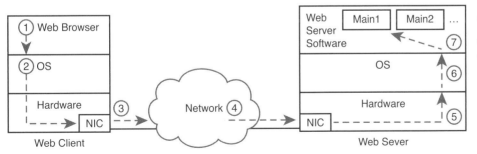

FIGURE 2-22

Demonstration of Web Components Working Together

Following the steps in the figure:

1. The web browser thinks about the user's action (a click of a hyperlink) and creates an HTTP GET request for the web address.

AUTHOR'S NOTE:
The section "Create Mind Maps," near the end of this chapter, lists four mind map activities. The third activity relates to this second section of this book, which ends here. It might be a good time to pause and do that activity.

2. The OS performs some networking tasks that the browser cannot do, like identifying the correct web server's address. The OS then asks the NIC to transmit the bits.

3. The NIC physically transmits the bits representing the HTTP GET request into the network.

4. The network delivers the bits that contain the HTTP GET request to the server.

5. The server's NIC receives the bits and gives them to the OS.

6. The OS processes the data, mainly deciding which application should be given the received data.

7. The web server thinks about the HTTP GET request and prepares to respond.

Uncovering the Network Between the Application Endpoints

No matter what application or device you talk about, including many already discussed in this chapter, if the device/app communicates data to some other device/app, a computer network delivers the data. When someone sends an email or a text message, the sender's device/app converts the typed text into binary data (bits) and sends the data (bits) over the network, and eventually it arrives at the other device/app. When someone talks on a phone, the device converts the sound to electricity, and at some point, that electricity becomes bits—and those pass over a network to the other phone. The act of downloading a video means that a user receives a copy of the digital video file (bits) over a network. And with the client-server model for web traffic, the network must be able to transmit the HTTP messages between client and server, and of course transmit the contents of the web pages.

So far, this chapter has mostly ignored the network that sits between the user devices and servers. This third (and last) major section of this chapter begins to uncover some of the ideas and devices in the network that sits between these devices.

First, the following sections draw some comparisons between computer networks and transportation systems, particularly roads. Computer networks move bits, and transportation systems move people and vehicles. Some of the big concepts in networking act like a transportation system, and we use transportation most every day, so using these analogies make a good place to start when learning.

Following that, the rest of these sections look at four different categories for networks. These range from the Internet, to networks built by companies, to small networks like home networks and networks you build in a lab room in school.

Comparing Computer Networks to Road Systems

Most everyone needs to move around, and even if you do not go far, you might need things that come from afar, like food, clothing, and so on. So governments often plan for the transportation needs of their country, state, province, and so on, to help make sure that it all works. Private industry also plays a big role, for example, with airlines that schedule flights, automobile companies that build vehicles, and construction companies that the government pays to build roads.

The next topic makes comparisons between two example roads and networks. The first case shows a simple country road connecting two houses, and the second shows a road connecting two towns.

Creating a Road (Link) Between Two Places (Devices)

For the first comparison between networks and transportation, think about the cables used in networking and the roads in a transportation system. Networks use cables to physically transmit bits from one device to another, and transportation systems use roads to allow vehicles to physically go from one place to another.

For comparison, imagine that you owned two computers. You wanted to experiment with web services, so you wanted to install web server software on one computer and use a web browser on the other computer. You could literally create a network using one (correct) cable between the two PCs.

Using a single cable between PCs is the transportation equivalent of using a road on private land. Imagine a guy who is now a grandpa, who owns a house on some land in the country. His son grew up, got married, and had some kids of his own. Then his son built a new house on the same property. As part of that construction project, Grandpa gets someone to bring out a bulldozer to make a small dirt road between the two houses—not a very sophisticated road, but it works. Figure 2-23 compares these ideas.

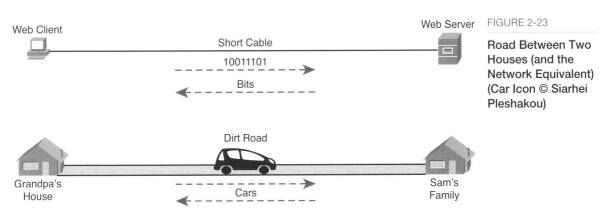

FIGURE 2-23

Road Between Two Houses (and the Network Equivalent) (Car Icon © Siarhei Pleshakou)

Although it is pretty obvious how a car can travel over a road, understanding how bits travel over a cable takes a little more discussion. Chapter 4, "Transmitting Bits," actually discusses the details a bit. For now, consider these basics. A cable looks a little like a thin rope, but the outside is made from plastic. If you take a knife and cut into the cable, the middle holds some copper wires. The cable then connects to the NIC in each device. The two devices can send bits over the wires by sending electricity over the wires, using a different electrical signal to mean binary 1 versus binary 0.

Sometimes, the world of computer networking uses the work *link* to describe a single cable between two devices. In some cases, the specific cable matters, and people use the word *cable*. However, when all you really care about is the idea that the cable allows the two devices to send bits—to be linked together if you will—just use the word *link*.

Sharing Roads (Links) Between Towns (Sites)

Next, think about roads again, this time in two nearby small towns. Each town has a number of houses near to each other, but the towns sit 5 miles apart. For the sake of discussion, each town has 10 houses. Would the local government do what Grandpa did in Figure 2-23, between every pair of houses, even those in different towns? Would the government build a road directly from each house in the first town to each house in the other town? Of course not—it would build one road between the two towns and share the road.

The same general concept occurs in networking. Say that you have two sites in a network, with some computers in each site. The network must have a physical path over which the bits can be sent from each device to every other device. However, the network planners do not need to install a cable between each pair of computers. Instead, the networking world has created a way to let the devices at each site share a single connection between sites, like a road between towns.

To let multiple computers share the use of a single link, computer networks use devices called networking devices. *Networking devices* are essentially specialized computers that provide specific functions to create the network. In this example, a networking device can connect to the link between the two sites, as well as to the computers at each site, knitting the pieces of the network together. The top of Figure 2-24 shows the idea, again comparing the transportation system to the computer network.

The bottom of the figure shows roads, with a traffic light at each intersection to help control the flow of traffic. The people in their cars follow the rules. They drive on the road. They stop at the traffic light if it is red and go when it is green. And these rules help them all avoid having a wreck while sharing the roads.

In the networking equivalent, the networking devices complete the physical path among all the devices while also helping control traffic like a traffic light. Each networking device can receive bits over one cable and send them out again over another cable, which completes the physical path that exists between each pair of devices. The networking devices also make sure that the data from all the devices gets a turn at using the link between the sites.

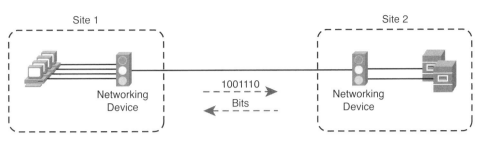

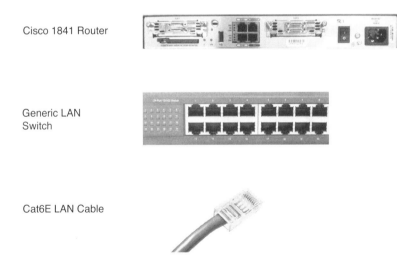

FIGURE 2-24

Sharing a Road Between Towns (and the Network Equivalent) (Car Icon © Siarhei Pleshakou)

Many types of networking devices exist. This book discusses two very common devices in some depth: *switches* and *routers*. For perspective, Figure 2-25 shows a photo that includes a router and a switch, plus a networking cable.

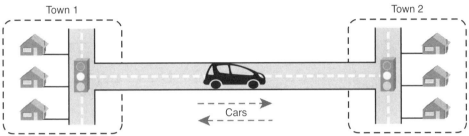

Cisco 1841 Router

Generic LAN Switch

Cat6E LAN Cable

FIGURE 2-25

Photos of a Router, Switch, and LAN Networking Cable (Cat6E LAN Cable © Mikko Pitkänen)

Networking Topologies with Links and Nodes

Because networking includes so many topics, in some conversations, you can ignore parts of the network, and in others, you need to discuss all the details. Sometimes, a networking discussion can completely ignore the details, showing the network between the devices as a cloud. In other cases, the discussion can be more detailed and needs to list the specific cables and each specific networking device. In other cases, the discussion focuses on the general ideas of the cables and networking devices by discussing the *network topology*.

The network topology shows each networking device as a node and each cable between pairs of devices as a link, but with little or no detail about the type of device or cable. Essentially, **link** refers to any cable between two devices, and **node** refers to any device. The link acts like a road between two towns, and the node acts like an intersection. Figure 2-26 shows the idea, with links as straight lines and nodes as circles.

FIGURE 2-26

Network Nodes (Like Intersections) and Links (Like Roads)

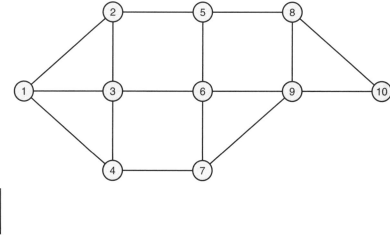

Legend

○ Node
— Link

The network topology in Figure 2-26 looks a lot like a simple road map, with towns for the nodes and roads for the links. However, one big difference exists in terms of getting around on the roads versus bits getting around a computer network: On the roads, the person in the car makes the decision. In a computer network, the node makes the decision.

To carry the road analogy one final step further for comparison, computer networks act like a road system in which you have to listen to a policeman at every intersection. You get in your car and write down your final destination on a sign. You drive to the next town and hold up the sign. The policeman at the intersection points: left, right, or go straight. For example, imagine that you are in a car and you put "node 10" on your sign. You just drove up to node 1. Figure 2-27 shows the process, with your arrival at node 1 as the first step.

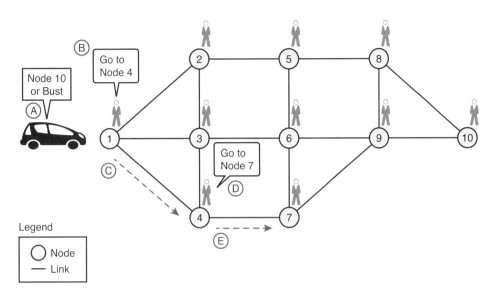

FIGURE 2-27

Road Network with Policemen at Every Intersection (Node) (Car icon © Siarhei Pleshakou)

Following the steps in the figure:

- **A.** You arrive at node 1, with "node 10" on your sign.
- **B.** The policeman for node 1 tells you to take the lower path.
- **C.** You travel over the link to node 4.
- **D.** The node 4 policeman tells you to take the link toward node 7.
- **E.** You travel over the link to node 7.

Fundamentally, the preceding process happens for every set of bits that flow in a network. The bits go over a link to a node, the node makes a choice, and the node sends the bits over the next link. By working together, and making the right decisions, the links and nodes deliver the bits to the correct destination.

> **AUTHOR'S NOTE:** Chapter 4 discusses more detail about how devices can transmit bits over cables (and wirelessly using radio signals). Chapters 5 through 8 include discussions of how and why different types of devices make choices to send bits a particular direction through the network topology.

The following sections examine a few different general categories of networks to give you some different perspectives for comparison.

Small Lab Networks

Each computer or other device that uses a network has some common components. These devices each have apps. Each uses some OS that controls the hardware and creates an environment for the apps to run. Each has some kind of network interface card (NIC) or equivalent hardware that allows the device to connect to the network either using a cable or using wireless radio signals.

In a lab, at school or work, the devices typically all sit in the same room. The network does not need to be sophisticated at all. In fact, with just two computers, just connect the two computers by connecting a cable to the NIC in each computer, as represented in Figure 2-28.

FIGURE 2-28

Simple Lab Network: One Cable

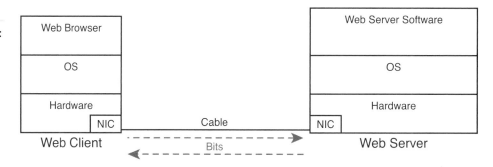

If a lab network grows past two devices, however, the network must expand. For example, every time a new device is added to the lab, the lab technician could cable each device to each other device with a cable. That requires more cables, and for each link to another computer, each PC actually needs another NIC, so it has another place to connect the cable.

A more convenient way to connect multiple devices into the same small network uses a device called a *local-area network (LAN) switch*. The term *local-area network* simply refers to the idea that the computers sit near each other (local). To create this kind of small network, connect each computer's NIC to a cable and connect the other end of the cable to the LAN switch. Figure 2-29 shows an example, with four end-user PCs and two servers.

FIGURE 2-29

Simple Lab Network: All Computers Connect to One Switch (Node)

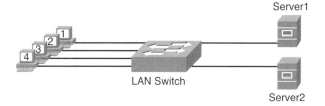

As with any network topology, at a very basic conceptual level, the nodes decide where to forward the bits, and the links pass the bits to the next device. For example, PC1 might send an HTTP GET request to Server1 to get a web page. When PC1 (a node) chooses to send those bits out its NIC, they travel over the link to the LAN switch. The switch (a node) receives the bits and makes a choice of where to send the bits next, similar to the traffic policeman in the earlier roadway example in Figure 2-27. In this case, the LAN switch would choose to send the bits out the link that connects to Server1.

Home Networks

Many of you reading this book use it as a textbook for a college class, typically as part of an IT-related degree program. If you care enough about IT to pursue a related degree, you probably have at least one computer at home. It might be a traditional laptop or desktop computer. It might be a tablet computer, like an Apple iPad. It might be a game system that lets you compete with other players on the Internet. In fact, today, many people have multiple such devices at home: some that stay at home and some mobile devices as well.

Some of the home-based devices, particularly those that do not move around, can connect to a network in the home using cables. The concept works just like the small lab network in the previous section—connect each user device to the LAN switch using a cable and they can communicate.

For other devices, using a cable can be a problem. Some devices, like mobile phones and tablet computers, cannot be tied to a cable, because people want to be connected to the Internet while moving around with these devices. In fact, these devices typically do not even have a place to connect a networking cable. Other devices might be able to support and use a LAN cable, but the user might just prefer to connect to the network without using cables.

Wireless networking refers to the idea of using radio waves to communicate. (For learning, a better choice of terms might have been *cableless networking*, just to compare it to networking that uses cables.) Basically, with wireless, the device has a *wireless NIC* or equivalent hardware. The wireless NIC, instead of sending and receiving bits over a cable, sends and receives bits through space using radio waves.

> **AUTHOR'S NOTE:**
> For comparison, networks that use cables are sometimes referred to as *wired networks*, in reference to the wires over which the bits flow.

For a home-based network with multiple user devices, each device creates a link to a switch, either using a cable or using wireless. The devices using cables (wires) and the devices using no wires (wireless) can send bits to each other by first sending the bits to the switch. More importantly, the network also typically connects to the Internet, which allows all the devices to connect to other services: web surfing, texting, downloading songs and video, joining in multiplayer games, watching television shows on a networked television, and so on. Figure 2-30 shows the idea.

FIGURE 2-30

**Home Network Using
Wired (Cabled) and
Wireless**

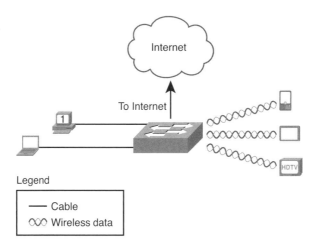

SMB and Enterprise Networks

Most every company today, certainly most every company that uses computers, has a network to support those computers. That network allows the computers inside the company to communicate. Often, that company network can also communicate with other networks, particularly the Internet. And when people talk about that network, they might call it the company network, the corporate network, or some other similar term.

People who study how companies work, and how they build their corporate networks, notice that smaller companies typically build their networks differently than do larger companies. As a result, the IT industry, and the business world as a whole, often calls a company either a small or large company based on the size. The literal dividing line is typically 1000 employees or less being in the small category.

However, whether a company looks like a small or large company has a lot more to do with how the company builds its network, rather than the literal number of employees. For example, a company with 900 employees might have business needs closer to a much larger company, while a company with 2000 employees might actually operate more like a small business. So, keep in mind that this idea of small- and large-company networks is a general idea, with plenty of exceptions.

Regardless, the two main terms IT uses to distinguish companies and their networks, based on their size, are as follows:

> **Small/medium business (SMB):** (Also called *commercial*) small businesses.
>
> **Enterprise:** Businesses larger than an SMB.

Because of these two general categories, the more likely terms to see when reading about different companies' networks will be the terms *SMB*, *SMB network*, *enterprise*, and *enterprise network*.

An SMB network supports fewer devices in total, fewer per site, and probably many fewer sites. For example, a typical SMB might have a few hundred employees at a main manufacturing plant, with four or five remote sales or distribution sites. Each site needs a network, and each site's network needs to connect to all the other sites. These companies often use less-expensive networking devices, sometimes the same consumer-grade networking devices you can buy at the local office supply store.

In comparison, enterprises would be larger than SMBs, and in some cases, the companies are household names. If you think about where you shop for food and clothes, and where you bank, how many sites do you think each company has? For example, grocery store companies often have a lot of stores, and banks have a lot of stores and a lot of standalone cash machines. All those sites connect to each company's network. These types of companies often have thousands of sites in their enterprise network. These companies often use networking devices built for enterprises, with more features, but are usually more expensive than the devices used by SMBs.

For example, imagine an enterprise network for a bank. The bank leases the bottom five floors of a building in a downtown area, and it also leases space on the very top of the building for a big sign advertising the name of the bank. Each floor has 100 PCs. The IT staff decides to use cables; however, rather than pull all the cables to one place in the building, they use a design as shown in Figure 2-31.

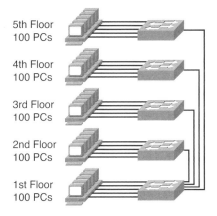

5th Floor
100 PCs

4th Floor
100 PCs

3rd Floor
100 PCs

2nd Floor
100 PCs

1st Floor
100 PCs

FIGURE 2-31

Single Site in an Enterprise with LAN Switches

The network topology in Figure 2-31 shows most of the cables sitting on a single floor, with only a few cables running between floors. That saves a little on the cabling cost, both in the cost of the cables and in the cost to install the cables. It also makes the cabling a little more manageable. And it works: A path exists from each PC to every other PC through the links and nodes in the figure.

Enterprise networks typically use *LAN switches* at each site as the devices to which to connect user devices using a cable. In fact, LAN switches are designed to be the right type of networking devices to which to connect nearby user devices to the network using a cable. (You will learn more about why a network designer chooses switches as you work through the entire book.) As a result, each site in the enterprise network will have one or more switches, with devices connected to the switches.

Additionally, enterprise networks use *wide-area networks (WAN)* to connect the various remote sites together, and network designers prefer *routers* to connect sites using a WAN. WANs provide a link between far-away sites, and routers can connect to both WAN links and LAN switches. You will learn the basics of why routers work well for connecting to WANs throughout several more chapters of this book.

Figure 2-32 shows more of the enterprise network for that same bank. The bank has 1000 branch offices, with three branches shown as examples on the right of the figure. Each branch has computers connected to a LAN switch, the switch connected to a router, and the router connected to a WAN link. The WAN link connects to the bank's Miami headquarters site, the same LAN shown earlier in Figure 2-31.

FIGURE 2-32

Multiple Sites in an Enterprise with Routers

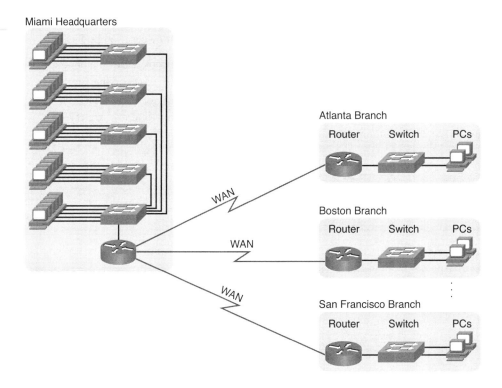

Just to complete the point, even though this figure shows the largest network in this chapter so far, a physical path (node – link – node – link and so on) exists between each pair of endpoints. For example, a loan officer in the Boston branch might need to send a query to a server that sits at the Miami headquarters. The loan officer can type a customer's account number in her PC as part of a query about a loan. The bits that represent the customer account number would flow over the LAN link to the Boston switch, then over the LAN link to the Boston router, then over the WAN link to the headquarters router, then over the short LAN link to the headquarters' first-floor switch, and so on.

The Internet

The Internet is the global network that connects physically to most parts of the planet Earth. Whenever you use terms like *connect to the net*, *surf the web*, *Google it*, *check something online*, or *surf for it*, often you are using the Internet. It is not an exaggeration to say that the Internet is the crowning achievement of the networking industry.

The reach of the Internet spans much of the worldwide population. According to statistics published by the *International Telecommunications Union (ITU)*, more than 70 percent of the population in developed countries uses the Internet. The percentage of the population using the Internet keeps growing, both in developed and undeveloped nations.

The term **Internet** actually helps define itself, because the term Internet simply shortens the phrase *interconnected networks*. Take a step back and think about every home in the world that has computers that want to connect to the Internet. Then think of every business with a corporate network, no matter whether it is small or large. What if you put one network in the middle, and then every other network connected to that one network? Then a path would exist from each network to each other network. Every device in the world would have a path to send bits to every other device. The result is a supernetwork of networks, a meganetwork, a really big network of networks: the Internet.

Drawing the Internet can be a challenge; it is, after all, pretty big. But to get the general idea of a small portion of one of its structures, Figure 2-33 provides a conceptual view, with a couple of enterprise networks, a network at a coffee shop, several homes, and a few mobile phones. Some use cables (WAN links), and the phones in this figure use wireless (radio).

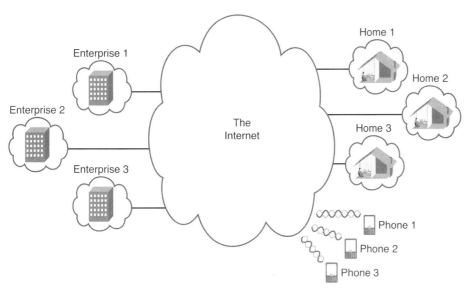

FIGURE 2-33

All Who Care to Use the Internet Connect to the Internet

Everything in the figure makes up the Internet. The Internet includes all the networks, big and small, company and personal, that connect together. The Internet also includes the network in the middle of the figure, the network to which each company and home network connects so that they can be a part of the Internet: the Internet core.

The *Internet core* itself looks like one big network, at least in Figure 2-33, but it is not. Instead, the Internet core exists as many networks itself, some actually quite large. Companies called *Internet service providers (ISP)* build the networks that combine to create the Internet core. Why? So that they can make money by charging individuals and companies money to connect their networks to the Internet.

Figure 2-34 shows a revised view of the Internet, with more insight into the Internet core. This figure simply adds detail to the Internet core as compared to Figure 2-33. The Internet core now shows three ISPs, each of which builds a network with switches, routers, and other devices. It also shows a mobile phone company's network, which besides offering voice services, must also provide Internet services so that users can use their phone to connect to the Internet.

FIGURE 2-34

Internet Core: Three ISPs and One Mobile Service Provider

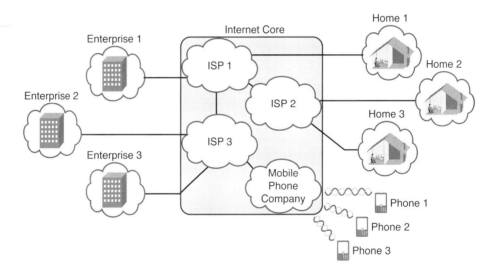

The figure shows a conceptual view of the Internet, but it does not show the size. The Internet is huge. Some ISPs have thousands of sites, with many network devices at each site. Worldwide, thousands of ISPs (of different sizes) exist. Millions of business customers connect to these ISPs, and billions of individuals connect as well. So while this figure shows some of the core concepts of how the Internet works, do not forget about its massive size as well.

Refining the Definition of a Network One More Time

In this third of the three major sections in this chapter, the topics focused on the network that sits between the end-user devices, or between the client device and the server that holds the data. With that general theme in mind, you can again add to and refine that general definition of computer networking with which this chapter began: *stuff that works together to send bits from one computer to another.*

If your instructor asked you to define computer networking right now, after reading this chapter, you would have a lot of terminology and concepts to add to the definition instead of using the word *stuff* (*stuff* that works together...). In fact, the rest of the book keeps adding to that list. More importantly, networks also require that the pieces work together. Computer networking is a world with many components, both small and large, and the challenge and joy of working with networking is to discover how all the pieces fit and work together. If you like to know how things work, discovering how all this networking stuff fits together can be very interesting indeed.

Chapter Summary

Computer networking includes many concepts and technologies, some of which people see every day and some of which most people never know about. To help you learn this new topic, this chapter begins by focusing on the parts of networking that the average person uses: apps on typical consumer electronics and computing devices. Along the way, the chapter introduces the hidden concepts and terms of networking while using those familiar topics to ease the process.

Many user apps show an obvious need for a network because the app relies on information moving from device to device, but other hidden networking components must also work together to make the obvious parts happen. For example, emails and text messages clearly go from one user device to another, but both require some hidden servers in the network that receive and process the messages. Sometimes the idea of a server is more obvious to the casual user, as with web browsers and web servers. Most people that use computers understand the idea of a website, with the general idea that when they browse a website, they actually communicate with a web server. And no matter whether the device is a more modern user device like a smart phone, television, tablet computer, or game system, or even a simple telephone, if it communicates, it uses a network, and that network probably includes some hidden pieces that help make that communication happen.

Networks rely on many cooperating pieces to work together. Networks rely on the endpoint devices, many devices in between, and cabling. Each device uses software of various kinds, including apps and an OS, plus hardware to connect to the network. Some of the pieces need to work together to create a functional network by following the same set of rules called a protocol. For example, the various pieces in the WWW application use a protocol called HTTP, which tells the web browser and web server the format of web addresses and the messages that they both use to exchange those objects.

Finally, this chapter closed with some discussion about the hidden network that sits between user devices and other user devices and other servers. That network can be viewed as links and nodes that act much like roads and intersections. In networking, many devices either function as a link or as a node, so to learn about new networking features, you will learn more about how a new type of link works, or more about how a new type of node does its work. And no matter whether the network has a single cable or thousands of sites like a larger corporate enterprise network, or whether the network is the worldwide Internet with literally billions of connected devices, the path from end to end reduces to simple logic: Go from this node, out this link, to the next node, out the next link, and so on.

Chapter Review Activities

Use the features in this section to study and review the topics from this chapter.

Answer These Questions

1. Which of the following terms is the closest synonym to the term computer networking?

    a. Telecom

    b. Protocol

    c. Datacom

    d. Stuff

2. Ann uses her email address, me@here.com, to send an email to Bob, whose email address is you@there.com. The message contains a few paragraphs of text. Which of the following will be important to the process of making sure that Bob receives this email?

    a. Ann's incoming email server

    b. Bob's incoming email server

    c. Bob's outgoing email server

    d. Ann's compression algorithm

    e. The A/D converter near Ann

3. According to this chapter, which of the following concepts happens in a modern-day, end-to-end voice call between two business telephones sitting in the same office building in the United States? (Choose two answers.)

    a. The call uses only analog electrical signals.

    b. The call uses only digital electrical signals.

    c. The call uses both analog and digital electrical signals.

    d. The call represents short sounds as a unique set of bits.

    e. The call represents each spoken word as a unique set of bits.

4. According to this chapter, which of the following concepts happens in a modern-day, end-to-end voice call between two home telephones in the United States? (Choose two answers.)

    a. The call uses only analog electrical signals.

    b. The call uses only digital electrical signals.

    c. The call uses both analog and digital electrical signals.

    d. The call represents short sounds as a unique set of bits.

    e. The call represents each spoken word as a unique set of bits.

5. A student makes a video recording of a professor teaching a class. The student posts the video to a website. The answers list information that the student used or chose on the computer on which he was processing the video. Which of the following answers is the least likely to impact the size of the video file?

   a. A character set

   b. A per-pixel color code

   c. A video frame of a particular size

   d. A choice for the number of frames per second

6. A student records a video of a professor teaching a class. The student plans to later post the video online on a website. Which of the following answers lists something discussed in this chapter that the student could do to improve the chances that other students will watch the video?

   a. Store the video on a flash drive

   b. Use an incoming video server

   c. Use an A/D converter

   d. Compress the video

7. A PC user opens his Internet Explorer web browser, types the **www.certskills.com/books** web address, and presses Enter. The browser displays a new web page. What part of the web address most directly identifies the web page that shows up in the window?

   a. http

   b. www.certskills.com

   c. books

   d. None of the answers is correct.

8. A user on a tablet computer opens her web browser, taps the **www.certskills.com/books** web address, and then taps the button to load the page. The user then sees a web page that lists text plus several different graphics images. The web server actually stored the web page as one text file and several graphics files (objects). What happens to cause all the text and images to arrive back at the web browser?

   a. The web browser asks for each file individually.

   b. The web browser asks for the one object identified by the web address, and the web server automatically sends the rest of the objects to the browser.

   c. The web server sees the request for the web address, dynamically creates a single graphical image of the entire web page, and sends that one graphical image to the web browser.

   d. None of the answers is correct.

9. Comparing the terms web object, website, and web page, which of the following answers list a true statement about these terms? (Choose three answers.)

   a. A website typically contains many web objects.

   b. A web object typically contains many web pages.

c. A web page typically contains many web objects.

d. A website typically contains many web pages.

e. A web object typically contains many websites.

10. A PC user opens her Internet Explorer web browser, types the **www.certskills.com/books** web address, and presses Enter. The web browser acting alone cannot send a request for that web address directly; it needs help. Which of the following components on that user's PC likely help the web browser? (Choose two answers.)

a. The PC's hard disk drive

b. The web server software

c. The operating system on the PC

d. The PC's NIC

11. A user grabs his smart phone, opens a web browser, taps the **www.certskills.com/books** web address, and taps the button to load this web page. The web page at that web address is an HTML file that includes instructions that link to 15 other web objects; those instructions state that to load this web page, these other 15 objects must be loaded as well. Which of the following best describes how the phone's web browser gets all the contents of this web page?

a. 16 HTTP GET request messages with 16 matching HTTP GET reply messages

b. 1 HTTP GET request messages, with 16 HTTP GET reply messages

c. 1 HTTP GET request message, plus 1 HTTP GETMANY request message, with HTTP GET reply messages from the server

d. None of the answers is correct.

12. Which of the following are defined by the HTTP protocol? (Choose two answers.)

a. Web browsers

b. Web addresses

c. Web servers

d. The GET request

13. A PC user opens her Internet Explorer web browser, types the **www.certskills.com/books** web address, and presses Enter. The browser displays a new web page. What part of the web address most directly identifies the web server from which the web page will be retrieved?

a. http

b. www.certskills.com

c. books

d. None of the answers is correct.

14. Using the terminology introduced in this chapter, think about network topologies. Which of these terms lists a network component that acts the most like a policeman directing traffic in an intersection by directing the bits through the network?

    a. Protocol

    b. Link

    c. Node

    d. Hyperlink

15. Which of the following types of devices typically act as a node in a network topology? (Choose two answers.)

    a. Router

    b. Cable

    c. Protocol

    d. Switch

16. Fred started a mining company as a young lad. The company has grown, now with three mines and an administrative office in town, with 100 employees. The company has a network that connects all the computers at all four sites. Which of the following terms best describes Fred's company network?

    a. The Internet

    b. Enterprise network

    c. Home network

    d. SMB network

17. A company builds a network that connects its 1000 branch offices with about ten employees each, plus three other sites with over 2000 employees each. Most of the end-user devices connect to the network using cables. Which of the following is the most likely device at the other end of the cable connected to each end-user device?

    a. Router

    b. Access point

    c. A/D converter

    d. Switch

18. A student got distracted in class for a while and was not paying attention. He looks up, and the professor has a drawing on the screen, with phones, PCs, and tablet computers all on the edge of a cloud. The professor then happens to move on to the next slide. What did the cloud represent?

    a. A WAN

    b. A LAN

    c. A part of the network whose details were not important to the discussion

    d. The Internet

19. The acronym ISP, as used in networking, stands for which of the following?

    a. Internet service provider

    b. Internet Services Protocol

    c. Internet solution provider

    d. Internet Solutions Protocol

20. To connect to the Internet, a large enterprise network typically connects its network through some link to which of the following?

    a. Any other enterprise network

    b. Any ISP's network

    c. Any network at all

    d. None of the answers is correct.

Define the Key Terms

The following key terms include the ideas most important to the big ideas in this chapter. To review, without looking at the book or your notes, write a definition for each term, focusing on the meaning, not the wording. Then review your definition compared to your notes, this chapter, and the glossary.

Key Terms for Chapter 2

computer networking	web server	enterprise network
computer network	web browser	link
application	web address	node
email	web page	Internet/the Internet
voice call	protocol	
video frame	HTTP	

List the Words Inside Acronyms

The following are the most common acronyms discussed in this chapter. As a way to review those terms, simply write down the words that each letter represents in each acronym.

Acronyms for Chapter 2

A/D	KBps	OS
DC	Kbps	telco
fps	LAN	URL
GBps	MBps	WAN
Gbps	Mbps	WWW
HTTP	NIC	

Create Mind Maps

For this chapter, consider making four different sets of mind maps: The first is general, and the next three each relate to one of the major sections in the chapter.

As usual, the goal of these exercises is to get your brain to organize the new information in this chapter into what your brain already knows about networking. As usual, list only short terms and phrases. For ideas that require more words, leave them out for this exercise, or make up some abbreviation. Also, you can list ideas mentioned in the chapter, plus ideas you already knew; just note which is which. If you are using mind map software, use blue for the ideas and terms mentioned in this chapter and some other color for items you already knew before reading this chapter.

Also, if the mind map software or concept gets in the way, feel free to just make notes. The mind map concept is a tool, but the real goal is to let your brain work through the concepts to make connections between each concept and term.

1. Create a mind map that captures the most important big ideas from the entire chapter. List up to 10 items, but no more; the goal with this mind map is to sift the entire chapter to find the biggest, most important concepts. Note that your list does not have to be just a list of terms from the chapter. For example, you could choose cooperation as a brief reminder that all the pieces of a network need to work together to send bits.

2. Create a mind map for the first major section, "Defining a Network from the User's Perspective." For this mind map, focus on all terms and concepts that might replace or fit into the word *stuff* in the definition for computer networks at the beginning of that section. You can add terms and concepts not in the book, but keep this mind map within the scope of the three major user activities in that section: email, live voice calls, and recorded video.

3. Create mind maps for the topics in the second major heading, "A Deeper Look at One Application: World Wide Web." For these mind maps, separate your ideas into three categories: the web client, the web server, and the protocol rules used by both. You can use either one or three mind maps, whichever works best for you. The most important goal with this exercise is to help you think about the interactions between the client and server that includes details defined by HTTP.

4. For the last of the three sections in the chapter, "Uncovering the Network Between the Application Endpoints," focus on the big-picture concepts of *link* and *node* by creating a mind map with each of these terms as the key concept. Then add items to each mind map, based on whether it is a link or a node. If you see a way to organize the terms in each map, do so, but the more important task for these mind maps is to list all terms and ideas related to the big ideas: *link* and *node*.

Define Other Terms

Define the following additional terms from this chapter, and check your answers in the glossary:

analog electrical signal

analog to digital

app

bandwidth

cable

cell phone

character set

client-server

codec

commercial business

compression

Cyber Monday

data communications (datacom)

download

email server

email system

enterprise

game console

HTTP GET reply

HTTP GET request

Hyperlink

Hypertext Transfer Protocol

incoming email server

Internet service provider

local-area network

mobile phone

network servers

network topology

networking device

outgoing email server

router

search engine

Skype

small/medium business

sound wave

speaker

standard

switch

telco

telecom

telephone

telephone company

the web

topology

Uniform Resource Locator (URL)

video compression

web client

web link

web object

wide-area network

World Wide Web

Complete the Tables and Lists from Memory

This chapter does not have any memory tables.

Chapter 3

TCP/IP Networks

Chapter 2, "Introduction to Computer Networking," began a broad introduction to computer networking as a whole. That chapter focused on applications that drive the network, creating the bits that flow through the network. Chapter 2 also introduced the ideas behind the network that sits between the applications, acting like a road system: as a series of links (roads) and nodes (intersections).

This chapter completes the broad introduction to networking by introducing some of the most important ideas about TCP/IP networks. The Internet uses TCP/IP, most every corporate network uses TCP/IP, and home networks use TCP/IP. TCP/IP defines a group of standards so that when networks use the TCP/IP standards, the computers can pass data between computers, much like a car can deliver people between two locations. To know networking today, you must know TCP/IP, and you must know it well.

This chapter examines the various aspects of TCP/IP in three major sections:

- This chapter begins in the first section, "Defining the Rules for a TCP/IP Network," by looking at TCP/IP as an end to itself. What is TCP/IP? What is the TCP/IP model? How does the world get networking standards? The first of three major sections in this chapter looks at all the big questions related to TCP/IP, which is a set of networking standards.

- The second major section of this chapter, "Comparing the TCP/IP and OSI Models," compares TCP/IP to other networking models. Today, TCP/IP dominates as the primary networking model used worldwide, but most companies used other networking models besides TCP/IP in the recent past. This second major section looks at that history, including terminology that is still important today, especially the terminology from one model in particular: OSI.

- The third and largest major section of this chapter, "Understanding How a TCP/IP Network Works," examines the pieces of a TCP/IP network. Those pieces include LANs, like Ethernet, and WANs, like leased lines, each of which defines how to move data over physical links. It includes IP, which defines how to move data over any link, no matter what type of physical link it is. Plus, this section introduces the TCP and UDP protocols.

By the end of this chapter, this book will have introduced the more important ideas in a computer network. The applications send data to each other, and the various network components play some role in delivering the data from one application to an app on the other side of the network.

After this chapter, the rest of the chapters of this book each takes a topic already introduced in the first three chapters and dives into more detail: Chapter 4 with physical transmission details, Chapters 5–7 with how to control those physical links in the LAN and WAN, Chapters 8 and 9 about how IP delivers data across any TCP/IP network of any size, and Chapter 10 closes by showing the final connections between applications using the transport layer protocols.

Chapter Outline

Defining the Rules for a TCP/IP Network

Comparing the TCP/IP and OSI Models

Understanding How a TCP/IP Network Works

Chapter Summary

Chapter Review Activities

Objectives

- Distinguish among the key terms related to networking standards, including standard, protocol, and model.

- List the layers of the TCP/IP model.

- Explain the purpose of the TCP/IP model.

- Name other standards organizations on which the TCP/IP model relies.

- Briefly compare the history of the OSI and TCP/IP models.

- Classify the layers of the OSI and TCP/IP layers in comparison to each other.

- Summarize the key functions of Ethernet LANs.

- Summarize the key functions of leased-line WANs.

- Explain how IP addressing and IP routing work together.

- Label different headers shown with data moving in a network.

- List two transport layer protocols.

Key Terms

computer networking

computer network

application

email

voice call

video frame

web server

web browser

web address

web page

protocol

HTTP

enterprise network

link

node

the Internet

Defining the Rules for a TCP/IP Network

When anyone builds a computer network today, the network is almost always a TCP/IP network. This first of three major sections in this chapter defines the basics of what it means to be a **TCP/IP network**.

TCP/IP defines standards for networking products and rules to follow when building a network using those products. To build a TCP/IP network means that you purchase products that use the TCP/IP standards. It means that when you build the network, the people use rules standardized by TCP/IP. The general idea is like a house builder: He has to buy products that meet building standards, and if he does not follow the required building codes, the house might fall down, the plumbing might not work, and so on. To build a TCP/IP network, network engineers use TCP/IP products and TCP/IP rules.

TCP/IP defines all these standards (rules), and anyone can download and read them. In fact, the name TCP/IP is formed from the names of two standard protocols: Transmission Control Protocol (TCP) and Internet Protocol (IP). TCP/IP lists each standard as a separate document called a Request for Comments (RFC), a term that refers to the fact that at some point in the life of that document, it was passed around for people to comment and improve the ideas.

Most computer networks today, including the Internet, are TCP/IP networks. But the idea of a *TCP/IP network*, versus simply a *network*, might make you wonder: Are there other types of networks? Historically, have other types of networks existed? The short answer is yes. But for the most part, you can ignore those other types of networks and still understand modern networking, because modern networking means TCP/IP.

In this first of three major sections in this chapter, the text will first revisit that basic definition of computer network from Chapter 2, but with a slant toward TCP/IP. Then the text looks at the concept of a networking standard, and then how TCP/IP creates a large group of related standards into a concept called the TCP/IP model. This section closes with a few words about the organizations that make these standards happen.

Our Current Working Definition for Network

Chapter 2 used a basic definition of computer network:

> Stuff that works together to send bits from one computer to another

After first introducing this definition, Chapter 2 then introduced many items that could be added to this definition as stuff, and other items that define how items worked together. For example, the *stuff* included many devices: phones, game systems, televisions, tablets, and of course, computers. The stuff also included software and hardware, plus cables and networking devices.

The *working together* part of the definition described how different hardware and software worked together: For example, the application software asked the operating system (OS) for help sending data, and the OS asked the hardware for help. Different computers also work together using protocols. For example, Hypertext Transfer Protocol (HTTP) defines web addresses and how web browsers request web pages from a web server.

In a **TCP/IP network**, TCP/IP identifies both the stuff and how the stuff works together. TCP/IP defines the HTTP protocol, which defines how a web browser and web server use a TCP/IP network. TCP/IP defines the concepts of local-area networks (LAN) and wide-area networks (WAN). It defines the concept of links and nodes, and the functions done by networking devices like routers and switches.

TCP/IP does not just give the general idea, but lists enough detail, in clear language, so that people can build products. Do you have programming skills? You could literally create your own brand-new web browser software, because TCP/IP publishes all the communications details, for free. Just put down this book, search the Internet for a minute or two, and find a website that lists all the TCP/IP standards. Search for HTTP (look for a document named RFC 2616), start reading, and you can start writing your new web browser.

The people who work on TCP/IP also save time and effort by using other standards when possible. If some other group has created a networking standard useful to TCP/IP, the people working on TCP/IP just note that the other standard works well, rather than waste time defining the same thing. For example, the IEEE defines all the wired and wireless LAN standards in networks today. However, TCP/IP defines how to best use these LAN standards as part of a TCP/IP network.

In summary, the following revises our more general definition of a computer network into a more specific definition of a *TCP/IP network*—a network built using TCP/IP standards and rules—with emphasis on TCP/IP's role:

> Stuff *defined or referenced by TCP/IP*, that works together *in ways defined or referenced by TCP/IP*, to send bits from one computer to another

Standards, Protocols, Conventions, and Other Terms

Thinking about our working definition of a network, TCP/IP defines lots of different stuff and lots of different rules about working together (protocols). In this next topic, the text looks at some of the reasons why standards exist, and the terms the IT world uses to discuss those terms. But first, consider this imaginary but realistic story about how new ideas blossom in computer networking.

A Story: Taking an Idea in a Lab to Worldwide Acceptance

Picture a lone person, late at night, sitting in the computer lab where he works and studies at college. He has been working trying to make two computers do something that has never been done before. (The particular something is unimportant to the story.) Finally, inspiration happens, and he makes a mental breakthrough and finds a good way to make it work. He has created something new that solves a problem.

Inspired by his breakthrough, our hero works on writing software, or making hardware, and making sure that all the pieces work together. He talks with classmates and coworkers, and a few of them join in the fun of creating something new. They sometimes disagree on particulars, and misunderstand each other, but they are friends, the work is fun, they work it all out, and write down the details of their choices on a dry erase board on the wall. Eventually, it works, and they all get the satisfaction of knowing that they created something new.

Now fast-forward ten years. The new something that our hero and friends created (whatever it was) was a huge success. More than 1 billion people use it every day, most without even knowing it exists. Millions of IT professionals worldwide learned about these ideas in school or by reading books like this one. Hundreds of companies created products that use this new idea, the idea that started with those few folks in the basement computer lab.

The history of computer networking has plenty of stories like this. For example, web browsers and web servers, and the HTTP protocol they use, did not exist until the early 1990s, and now everyone uses them. Humans make up all these new things that computers do, and it starts in someone's head. (Check out this link for a brief history on web browsers and servers, from the guy who made it all up, Tim Berners-Lee: http://bit.ly/vd0pWE.)

Standards: The Bridge from Creation to Worldwide Acceptance

A journey from a great idea in a lab to acceptance and being part of networks worldwide requires standards. **Networking standards** record the details of exactly what a new networking technology does, and how it does what it does. Networks do not work if the pieces do not work together, and standards help everyone agree on how something works so that it works well within the network.

Getting agreement for a standard accepted in one country, or worldwide, takes work. Why? Well, getting our hero and his three friends to agree in the story might be easy. What happens when dozens, or hundreds, of competing vendors need to agree? What happens when the documentation does not say anything about a particular part of how things work, and one vendor—for example, based in Japan—makes a different choice than a vendor in the United States? Just the simple mechanics of getting agreement when companies have different goals, or when the engineers speak different languages in different time zones, means that getting agreement takes time.

Every standard has two important features on which this book will focus. First, a standard documents ideas. Those ideas are the ideas that matter to anyone creating products to put in a network, or ideas that matter to people building a network. For example, HTTP began life as an idea. But before those ideas could be implemented in many competing web browsers, and many competing web servers, the details of how HTTP worked had to be written down and shared. That document answered questions like this:

- What byte values does a browser send to mean HTTP GET?

- What byte values does a server send to mean HTTP REPLY?

    (See the section, "Using HTTP to Get the First File for a Web Page" in Chapter 2 for more information about HTTP commands.)

- Is it required or optional to list the // before the name of the server in a web address?

- How does the server tell the browser when it simply cannot supply a particular web object?

- How does the server tell the browser where the object's bytes begin and end?

The standard answers these questions and many others.

Beyond the ideas in a standard, people must agree to a particular version of the document. When the work on a standard begins, the standard document can change a lot. It might leave out necessary details, or the people doing the work might add new interesting features. It might be changed to make it clearer. At some point, the people doing the detailed work announce that they think they are done, and present a particular version of the documentation as the proposed standard. At that point, some kind of approval process (oftentimes with a vote) occurs, and the document can become a standard.

Standards apply to both hardware and software. For example, computers use a network interface card (NIC) or equivalent to connect to a wired network. That NIC has a hole (socket) into which a cable connects. If no standard existed for that socket, or for the connector on the end of the cable, you might buy a cable, but it would not fit in the NIC. Or you might buy a new computer, but the NIC built into the computer does not fit your network's cables.

Of course, the size and shape of connectors and sockets used in networking gear follow standards. Pause for a moment, and look for a connector and plug like those found in Figure 3-1. The cable shows an RJ-45 connector on the end; RJ-45 is the name of the standard for the connector. The NIC has an RJ-45 socket of the same size. If you have a moment and sit near some computers, wall outlets, or network devices, look around for RJ-45 connectors and sockets in the room.

FIGURE 3-1

Example of Physical
Standard: RJ-45
Connector (on Cable)
and Socket (on NIC) (RJ-
45 Connector © Mikko
Pitkänen; Ethernet NIC
© Mark Jansen)

Types of Standards

Not all standards are equal. Standards can be created by different groups. Some standards might go through a long process with reviews, comments, revisions, and so on, while others might not. Some standards might require votes from various government agencies, requiring a more formal approval process.

Because different standards might have been through so many different processes, the standards world uses many different terms to describe standards. All these terms refer to written documents that define some technology, some rules, or some detail of how to create products that meet these rules. However, each of the terms in the following list differs in some way related to how a standard comes to be considered to be a standard:

Standard: A document that has been agreed upon by a known group of people, beyond the original creators of the technology or ideas.

National standard: A standard approved by a nation. In practice, a nation's government typically creates or appoints some organization to oversee standards for the nation. That organization either creates standards or chooses already-known standards, and uses an approval process to bless certain standards as national standards. For example, in most countries, all the electrical power outlets have the same size, shape, and electrical current and voltage, all as a result of the national standard for residential power outlets.

International standard: A standard approved by a group of nations. It is the same idea as a national standard, except the approval process includes many countries. The standards typically relate to functions that benefit from being consistent between countries.

Vendor standard: Also called a *proprietary standard*, a standard approved by a single vendor. In some cases, the vendor might not want to give control of a technology to a standards organization, but it does want to share the details with other companies so that the technology works with other products. Vendor standards allow vendors to keep control, and other vendors to learn the details.

Vendor group standard: A standard approved by a group of vendors. (A vendor group can also be called a *vendor consortium*, *vendor alliance*, or *vendor forum*.) Vendor groups typically want their standards to become national and international standards—they just want to move more quickly than the standards groups. These vendor groups work to get compatible products to market more quickly than would otherwise happen, while also working with the formal standards groups.

De facto standard: A standard that exists because it is what already happens. For example, if all computers do the same task the same way, even if it is not written down, that convention is a de facto standard.

> **ON THE SIDE:**
> The American National Standards Institute (ANSI, ansi.org), a nonprofit organization, oversees voluntary standardization processes across many industries in the United States.

Depending on the conversation, these small differences in the meaning of the word *standard*, and the types of standards, might or might not matter. Most of the time, the word *standard* just reminds us that some people wrote it down in a document for all to use the same details. Other times, not only does the type of standard matter, but some people might also even disagree with some of the definitions in the list (just before this paragraph). For example, if talking about formal standards processes, someone might argue that a vendor standard is not a standard at all, and that to be a standard, the document must have been approved by some government-appointed agency.

Standards Versus Protocols Versus Hardware Specifications

A standard exists as some written document. In some cases, the networking industry uses other terms—*protocols* and *hardware specifications*—to focus more on what the standard does, rather than the fact that the document has been standardized.

The term *networking protocol*, or simply *protocol*, refers to a set of rules and messages that do something useful for a network. Protocols typically define how software on different devices communicates. To communicate, they have to send each other messages, made up of bytes of data. If both devices agree as to the meaning of the messages, plus they agree to some other rules, they can get some work accomplished.

For example, as a networking protocol, HTTP defines both the messages used by web browsers and web servers, as well as the rules for how to use those messages. (Chapter 2 discusses in some detail the ideas behind the HTTP protocol in the section "The Process to Get One Web Page.") HTTP defines the exact binary value of the messages called HTTP GET request and HTTP GET reply. HTTP also defines rules about how the web browser uses the GET request to ask for a web object, and how the server uses the GET reply to send the object back to the browser.

A *hardware specification*, or *hardware spec* ("speck"), details information about the physical world of networking. Those details include the size and shape of connectors, like those seen earlier in Figure 3-1. Hardware specs also include electrical details, details about the materials used to make cables, mechanisms that actually move, or anything to do with the physical world.

Figure 3-2 captures the comparison of these three terms, along with a reminder that not all protocols and hardware specs might be standardized; however, most protocols and hardware specs used today happen to be standards.

FIGURE 3-2

Networking Standards Compared to Protocols and Hardware Specs

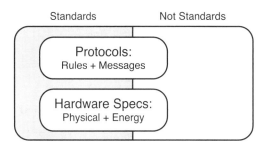

Standards   Not Standards

Protocols:
Rules + Messages

Hardware Specs:
Physical + Energy

The TCP/IP Model

To build a safe and useful house, building professionals follow hundreds of building standards. They cannot just use any concrete for the foundation, or it might crumble under the weight. They cannot use just any wood for the frame, because it might crack under the weight. They cannot just nail the wooden frame together in a random way, or the entire house might literally fall over on its side. They cannot ignore electrical standards or risk having the house burn down. They must follow standards that tell the builder what kinds of power outlets to install; otherwise, the homeowners will not be able to plug in any of their appliances. To make it all work well, the builder has to know all these standards and follow them.

To build a safe and useful computer network, IT professionals follow hundreds of standards defined in the TCP/IP model. The **TCP/IP model** defines a large set of standards, which, when implemented together, create a safe and useful network.

The name *TCP/IP model* has many variations, all of which refer to the same idea. First, the name itself comes from two of the more important standard protocols: IP and TCP. Instead of TCP/IP model, many people call it *TCP/IP network architecture*, *TCP/IP architecture*, *TCP/IP networking model*, *TCP/IP model*, *TCP/IP networking blueprint*, or simply *TCP/IP blueprint*. Or, you can just forget all these variations and call it simply *TCP/IP*.

The TCP/IP model organizes its standards into layers. The layers make TCP/IP easier for humans to understand what TCP/IP does. It also makes it easier to divide the work among different products.

Figure 3-3 shows two versions of the TCP/IP model. The left side shows the TCP/IP model as formally defined in RFC 1122, with the four layer names (application, transport, Internet, and link) taken directly from the RFC. It also shows several other terms used for the lowest of these four layers.

TCP/IP Model (Per RFC 1122)
Application
Transport
Internet
Link (Media Access, Network Access, Network Interface)

TCP/IP Model (Common)
Application
Transport
Network
Data Link
Physical

FIGURE 3-3

TCP/IP Model

The right side of the figure shows the more commonly used TCP/IP model. In the years following the formal model defined by RFC 1122, people expanded the lowest original layer (the link layer) into two layers: data link and physical. These new lower layers better matched the real protocols and physical standards, making this newer version of the TCP/IP model more useful and more practical. The model on the right does not change the functions at the upper three layers, but it does rename the Internet layer to instead be the network layer. (It also borrows the layer names from the OSI model, which is discussed later in the section "Open Networking Models: TCP/IP and OSI".)

Which of the two models should you know and use? The answer depends on your goals. The four-layer model is more correct from a theoretical perspective. The model on the right has more practical use because it better matches the actual lower-layer standards in practice. Both give you a useful tool to think about and discuss the many TCP/IP protocols.

Note that I mostly use the five-layer TCP/IP model on the right side of the figure for the remainder of the book.

No matter which version of the TCP/IP model you think about, each layer of the TCP/IP model defines different types of functions. For example, the physical layer unsurprisingly defines how to physically transmit bits. Therefore, a LAN NIC, which transmits bits, must follow some standards defined at the physical layer. The application layer defines how applications use the network; therefore, the HTTP protocol is considered to be an application layer protocol. The majority of the rest of this book discusses various TCP/IP features, and all those features follow standards defined at specific layers in the TCP/IP model.

ON THE SIDE: The model on the left side of Figure 3-3 came to be known as the DoD model, in reference to the U.S. Department of Defense, which paid for many of the early research projects that resulted in the TCP/IP model.

Standards Organizations Useful to TCP/IP

TCP/IP includes standards created for TCP/IP, but it also uses standards created by other standards groups. This section introduces the most important standards groups related to TCP/IP.

First, to define a few terms, this section will use the term *standards group* as a generic term for any group that works on standards. These groups might be called simply a standards group, but they can also be a *standards body*, *standards organization*, or *consortium* or *alliance* if more focused on vendors and less focused on national or international standards.

Next, no matter the type of standards group, each follows some kind of standards process. That process includes repeated experimentation, documentation, review, comments, and so on. At some point, people vote whether to make that document a standard.

A standards group works a little like a company, but instead of producing a product to sell, it produces standards. Often, the standards group works as a not-for-profit company, getting funding from the governments that want the standards. (For example, the TCP/IP standards began through research projects funded by the U.S. government, but over the years, they have been primarily developed by volunteers.) Also, the organization of the standards group helps make for fairer final standards, as a result of using a nonprofit organization with a mostly volunteer workforce.

The Internet Engineering Task Force (IETF) acts as the primary standards group for the TCP/IP model. That is, the IETF, through its volunteer workforce, creates TCP/IP standards. The IETF also looks for other standards that TCP/IP could use, rather than creating a whole new standard. As a result, the TCP/IP model actually includes standards created by the IETF, and standards created by other standards groups. Figure 3-4 shows the general idea.

FIGURE 3-4

Sources of Standards in the TCP/IP Model

TCP/IP Model

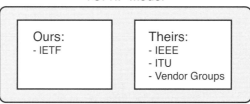

The following sections provide some background on several of these standards groups.

IETF

The Internet Engineering Task Force (IETF, www.ietf.org) works as the standards group for TCP/IP. The IETF decides what existing parts of TCP/IP need to be updated because of changes in the networking world. It decides what new technologies to add to TCP/IP by defining new standards. And the IETF decides which standards created by other standards groups need to work with TCP/IP, publishing details of how to make these other standards work well in TCP/IP networks.

As with most standards groups, the end product of the work is a set of documents. The IETF calls one such document a *Request for Comment (RFC)*. Simply put, one RFC defines the details of one standard. All the RFCs put together make up TCP/IP as we know it. (You can find RFCs on the Internet on many websites, including www.rfc-editor.org.)

The IETF organizes its work around the concept of a *working group*. When the IETF decides to work on a technology, it forms a working group, made up of volunteers willing to do the work. The working group documents the potential new standard in a document called an *Internet draft*. The working group then experiments, changes the details, improves how the new technology works, and shares its changes with the world. The rest of the world can comment to the working group.

The IETF purposefully allows some documents to go through a more demanding process to become a standard RFC, while others can be published with a less-demanding review process. When the working group thinks that its Internet draft is ready, the working group can submit the document into the standards process. It takes time, with several additional steps. If the group chooses to not submit it as a standard, the document can become another type of RFC, typically either an informational RFC or experimental RFC. Both allow people to read and use it, but they have less weight and importance than an RFC on the standards track. Figure 3-5 shows the overall process.

ON THE SIDE: You can volunteer with the IETF, online, with no expense. Just check out the Getting Started in IETF link on the IETF web page.

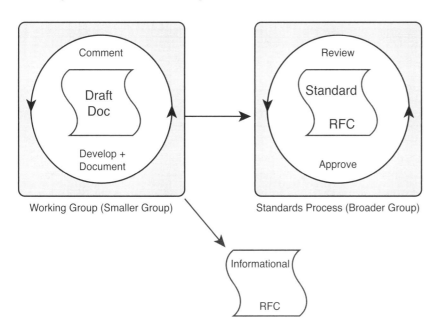

FIGURE 3-5

Standard and Nonstandard TCP/IP RFCs

IEEE

The Institute of Electrical and Electronics Engineers (IEEE) plays a huge role in networking today, and for TCP/IP in general.

First, according to its website (www.ieee.org), the Institute of Electrical and Electronics Engineers (IEEE; "I triple E") is the world's largest professional organization. That is, the IEEE has members; you could indeed join the IEEE. While based in the United States, the IEEE has members and participants from across the globe. Their work includes many activities: publications, conferences, and of course, standards work.

IEEE standards work includes a wide variety of topics, but for TCP/IP, the IEEE plays a huge role with local-area networks (LAN). The IEEE took proprietary vendor-created LAN technologies in the early 1980s and standardized those technologies, which in part helped create the networking boom in the latter part of the twentieth century. Those IEEE standards include what the IT world today calls Ethernet, the primary wired LAN technology used worldwide. The IEEE also standardizes wireless LAN standards.

As a standards body, the IEEE does not function as an agency of any particular government or government organization. However, governments can and do use IEEE standards. For example, the U.S. government appoints ANSI to manage U.S. standards across industries. ANSI certifies different standards in part by certifying other standards groups, and ANSI chooses the IEEE as the source for LAN standards considered to be the standards for the United States, for example.

> **ON THE SIDE:** Many wireless consumer electronic devices mention the IEEE wireless standards they use. You might have seen packages with the terms 802.11b, 802.11g, or 802.11n: all IEEE standards.

The TCP/IP model refers to the IEEE standards, rather than redefining the same concepts. TCP/IP networks make use of IEEE-defined LAN technologies every day. The IETF did not bother to create a working group to create a competing LAN standard; instead, they just cooperate. As a result, the TCP/IP model's RFCs do not include RFCs that define LANs. However, the TCP/IP model does include RFCs that define how TCP/IP networks interact and work with IEEE LANs.

ITU

The International Telecommunications Union (ITU) acts solely as an international standards body. As for geography, the ITU has a global standards focus because it is chartered as an agency of the United Nations. As for technology, the ITU focuses on standards for information communications (in other words, networking), but with emphasis on telecom. As for standards creation, like other standards bodies, the ITU both creates standards and certifies standards created by other groups.

The ITU has created many commonly used standards in its over 100 years as an organization, with some emphasis on telco and WAN technologies. For example, ITU standards define two common Internet access technologies: dialup and

DSL. ITU standards define the international country codes used when making international phone calls: the short digits you dial to identify the country you want to call. By doing so, the ITU enables global communications among all the telephone companies in the world. And the ITU enables worldwide digital voice communications by standardizing voice codecs, the same codecs mentioned back in Chapter 2's section "Digital Voice Calls."

The TCP/IP model uses ITU standards for the same general reasons that TCP/IP uses IEEE standards.

> **ON THE SIDE:**
> Look for a link to a YouTube video, on the author's study page for this chapter, which gives a nice synopsis of ITU activities.

Vendor Consortia and Other Groups

One vendor can work alone to come out with a new technology, some new feature for its customers, and its customers might like it. That happens pretty often. However, because so many applications use networks, and because people use so many different types of devices, vendors typically want new features and new technology to work on as many devices as possible, and soon.

Vendors that want quick and broad acceptance in the marketplace of some new technology, faster than they could manage by themselves, often team up with other vendors. One way to team up is to create a vendor group, also called a vendor consortium.

With a vendor group, instead of just one vendor pushing its idea, or worse, competing with four other companies each with very similar ideas, a dozen vendors might join together. They essentially agree to a standard version of the new technology, even though no standards group has standardized the technology yet. They all get to market quickly, and maybe those who join in sell more products than those who did not join the group. And it allows the companies to move quickly, without waiting on the slower (and sometimes political) formal standards processes.

For example, the Wi-Fi Alliance (www.wi-fi.org) is a great example of the positive effect of a vendor group. Simply put, the Wi-Fi Alliance has helped vendors get new wireless technology to market much more quickly than if the vendors had waited on the formal IEEE standards process. Essentially, the Wi-Fi Alliance defined prestandard rules based on the big ideas of upcoming IEEE standards—documents that had not passed the IEEE standards process, but documents that all vendors tried to live by when making products. Then, the Wi-Fi Alliance tested those products to certify (confirm) that the products all worked together using those prestandard rules. That process allowed vendors to bring products to market more quickly, and to brand a product as Wi-Fi certified. And by cooperating with the IEEE, this group actually helped the overall standards process.

Figure 3-6 shows the overall process: No matter whether a person with good ideas works through the Wi-Fi Alliance or IEEE, those two groups cooperate, products get to market sooner, and the standards still happen as well.

FIGURE 3-6

Vendor Groups' Impact on Speed to Market (Light bulb icon © Mr_Vector)

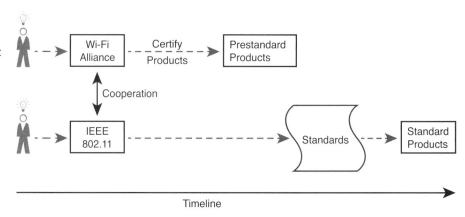

> **ON THE SIDE:** Next time you go to a store that sells computer supplies, stop and look for wireless LAN products. Look for the little black-and-white Wi-Fi logo. Almost every wireless LAN product also shows this kind of logo to indicate that it has been certified by the Wi-Fi Alliance.

The TCP/IP Model: LAN and WAN Standards

As mentioned earlier, the TCP/IP model both defines standards and refers to standards from other groups. But a large amount of the borrowing of standards relates to the bottom two TCP/IP layers, and those layers define LAN and WAN technologies. In particular, most of the LAN standards, which define details that match TCP/IP's bottom two layers, come from the IEEE, with some early wireless LAN standards coming from vendor groups like the Wi-Fi Alliance. Most WAN standards come from the ITU, again with early standards coming from vendor groups. Figure 3-7 summarizes these facts.

FIGURE 3-7

TCP/IP Using Other Standards for LAN and WAN

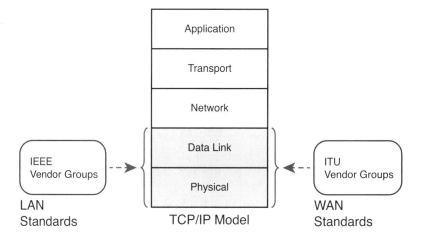

Based on all this perspective on standards with TCP/IP, the definition of a computer network, revised for TCP/IP, could now be as follows:

> Stuff *defined by the TCP/IP model, or referenced by TCP/IP (typically from the IEEE, ITU, or vendor groups)*, that works together to send bits from one computer to another

Comparing TCP/IP to Other Networking Models

Networks require that devices work together, and standards give networking products a reasonable chance to work together—even if the people that create the products have never met. For example, many vendors and open source groups create web browsers, and the people from those different companies and groups might never talk with each other. All those browsers can pull web pages from web servers that use the popular Apache web server software—again without ever having a conversation or email with the people that wrote the web server software. How is that possible? They all use and follow the HTTP standard, part of TCP/IP, which lists all the details about how the browser and server communicate; anyone can get the standard and read it.

For another example, many vendors make wireless LAN NICs that you can put in your PC, and they all work when you go to a wireless hotspot. Most coffee shops offer wireless LAN service. A single coffee shop might have hundreds of customers a day that connect to its wireless LAN, using wireless hardware from dozens of vendors. All those wireless NICs work correctly with the wireless equipment installed at the coffee shop. What makes all these devices work together? Standards, from IEEE, with early work on those standards done by the Wi-Fi Alliance.

While a single standard typically focuses on one protocol or hardware spec, the TCP/IP model collects all the standards needed to do everything required to make a complete modern network. Each device in the network, and each component, follows a subset of the TCP/IP standards, depending on each device's role. Similar to how a builder follows standards for electrical, plumbing, framing, roofing, foundations, and so on when building a house, a network engineer follows the standards in the TCP/IP model when building a TCP/IP network. Figure 3-8 shows the concept, using imaginary standards at each layer just to show the concept.

FIGURE 3-8

Conceptual View of
TCP/IP Model

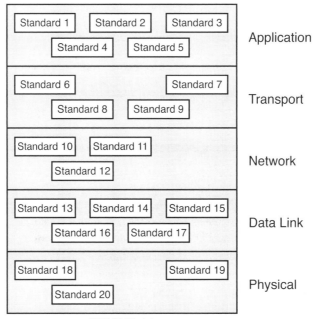

TCP/IP Model

Like every networking model, the TCP/IP model categorizes standards by layer. Each layer defines a general category for the functions done by the standards at that layer. For example, the physical layer defines the most obvious functions: anything you can touch or see, plus the energy (like electricity) that flows over the cable.

Each standard then fits into the category defined by a layer. For example, the standard for the shape of a connector on an Ethernet LAN cable, called RJ-45, is one physical layer standard. Another wireless LAN standard that defines how to use radio signals between wireless NICs would be another physical layer standard.

Networking models other than TCP/IP have existed in the past. All these networking models use the concept of a layered model, with each layer defining a category of functions, and with individual standards falling into one of the layers. For the most part, those models do not matter today, with one exception: the OSI model. This second of three major sections in this chapter begins with a brief look at the history of networking models. After that, it looks at the OSI model and describes how the OSI model is still used today to describe the TCP/IP model.

A History of Networking Models

In the earliest days of computing, there were no networks. The first commercial computers, called mainframes, sat in large rooms with lots of air conditioning to keep them cool. These first hit the market in the 1950s and became more common in larger companies by the 1960s. (For perspective, personal computers did not hit the market until the late 1970s, and they did not become common until the 1980s.)

These original computers did not have a network to use; networks simply did not exist yet. This brief historical look at networking models takes us from a world of no networks to a world in which every company has a network and many people connect to the global Internet.

The First Networks Using Proprietary Vendor Networking Models

The original mainframe computers did not use networks, but eventually, computer vendors saw the need to create a network between the computers. In those days, say in the 1960s, personal computers did not exist yet, and most large companies might own just a few dozen computers. However, those computers needed to share data, so the computers that did exist needed to be connected.

Individual computer vendors created their own networking products so that their loyal customers could have and use networks. In those earliest days of computers, most customers bought computers from one computer vendor, or at most two. So, when those vendors first created their networking products, vendors focused on supporting only their own computers, ignoring computers from other vendors.

When creating their early networking products, most vendors also created their own proprietary **vendor networking models**. A vendor networking model helped that vendor create new networking products that worked with the other networking products from that same company. For example, if your company owned IBM computers, you used IBM's networking model (called SNA). When IBM came out with new networking products, it followed the SNA networking model. If you owned DEC computers, you used products that followed DEC's networking model (called DECnet), with future networking products from DEC also following that same DECnet networking model.

Each networking model helped in the development of networking products from one vendor, but these proprietary networking models did not solve one large problem—allowing interoperability between computers from different vendors. For example, if one company bought computers from both IBM and DEC, it had to build a network using IBM's SNA products and another network using DEC's DECnet products.

Because the IT world had only proprietary vendor networking models by the 1980s, a company had as many networks as it had computer vendors. Although these networks could be connected, essentially translating from one networking model to the other, connecting the networks required more hardware, more software, more effort, and more money. Figure 3-9 shows three typical enterprise networks from the 1980s: one that used only the IBM networking model, one that used only the DEC networking model, and one that used multiple models, connecting them together.

ON THE SIDE: Some of the more common vendor networking models included IBM's SNA, DEC's DECnet, Apple's Appletalk, Novell's NetWare, Xerox's XNS, and Banyan's Vines.

AUTHOR'S NOTE: IBM and DEC were the largest and second largest computer makers in the world, respectively, in the 1970s.

FIGURE 3-9

Typical Mix of Corporate
Networks over Three
Decades

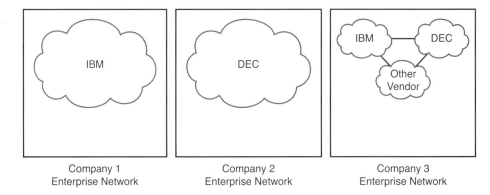

Company 1
Enterprise Network
Company 2
Enterprise Network
Company 3
Enterprise Network

From Multiple-Vendor Networking Models to One Open Model: TCP/IP

By the 1980s, the IT industry saw the huge benefits of networks and also the huge negatives of using only incompatible vendor networking models. Why not get all the vendors to use one single networking model? And if the vendors cannot agree to use one of the existing vendor networking models, because that would give one vendor an unfair advantage, how about they all use an open networking model created by a standards group? Those were the questions asked and answered, and the answer was for all computers to start using the TCP/IP model.

TCP/IP began its life in the 1970s through research projects sponsored by the U.S. government's Department of Defense (DoD). TCP/IP grew and matured in the 1980s, with a many more researchers working on individual standards and protocols. By the end of the 1980s, vendors started offering TCP/IP products for most OSs. So the timing worked well: When the IT industry really needed an open standardized networking model, TCP/IP was ready.

Figure 3-10 shows what happened in typical enterprise networks from the 1980s into the early twenty-first century. On the left, the figure shows a typical 1980s-style enterprise network, with only closed vendor network models in use. By the 1990s, companies started adding TCP/IP networks. They could not migrate all devices to TCP/IP instantly, so they added TCP/IP and migrated to TCP/IP over time. By the year 2000, many companies had completed the migration to use only TCP/IP, as shown on the right side of the figure.

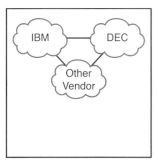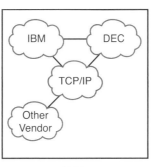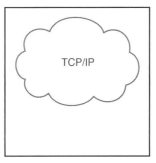

1980s   1990s   2000s

FIGURE 3-10

Typical Migration of Enterprise Networks from Vendor Models to TCP/IP

> **ON THE SIDE:** For those of you interested in business and finance, Cisco Systems, today the largest vendor of networking products in the world, shipped its first product in 1986. Cisco made its name selling products to help connect those multivendor networks and the TCP/IP networks shown in the left and center blocks of Figure 3-10.

Open Networking Models: TCP/IP and OSI

TCP/IP serves as the one primary open networking model today. In the old days, vendors owned their vendor networking models, so these models were considered *closed*. Vendors could change the standards, and prevent other companies from using those standards, by simply not sharing the details of those standards. An **open networking model** like TCP/IP purposefully shares the details so that any vendor can make products using those standards. As a result, the marketplace gets the benefits of better competition, a wider range of products, lower prices, and so on.

The closed nature of vendor networking models caused some problems, and the problem could be solved by migrating to one open networking model. The world needed one workable open networking model, but actually two such models were created around the same time frame, from the 1970s into the 1990s: TCP/IP and the **Open Systems Interconnection (OSI) model**.

An international standards organization called the *International Organization for Standardization (ISO)* set out with a noble goal to create an open networking model. The goal: It must be open, it must be standardized across the globe, and it must include any type of computer, from any vendor. Also, this model must allow the computer equivalent of the worldwide telephone network: a global network to which every computing device on the planet can connect and communicate.

ISO began work on the OSI model, following a timeline that was somewhat close to TCP/IP's time. It started in the 1970s, with a lot of progress on individual standards in the 1980s, and with vendor products appearing by the early 1990s. And of course, OSI organized its standards around a layered model design, which is shown in Figure 3-11.

FIGURE 3-11

OSI Model

OSI Model

Comparing OSI and TCP/IP

OSI differed from TCP/IP on many detailed technical points, but it had many similarities. As networking models, both listed standards and organized the standards by categories called layers. Both were open, so both standards groups published their standards for anyone to use. Both models tried to allow any device to participate. Both made use of existing accepted standards, for example, they both included Ethernet LANs as standardized by the IEEE.

As for the technical points, both models performed the same kinds of tasks, but used different details. For example, both used addresses to identify each computer so that data could be delivered to the correct computer. However, each model used different numbers of bytes for the addresses, with different formats, so the two would not work together.

Both TCP/IP and OSI used different models, with different layer names and different numbers of layers. In fact, as noted earlier, TCP/IP used a four-layer formal model, but many people further divided the model into five layers. OSI used seven layers.

Thankfully, many of the functions defined by an OSI layer matched closely to just one layer of the TCP/IP models, so you could compare the models, find where a function in OSI would be defined in TCP/IP, and vice versa. Figure 3-12 compares those layers, showing which layers in each model defined similar functions.

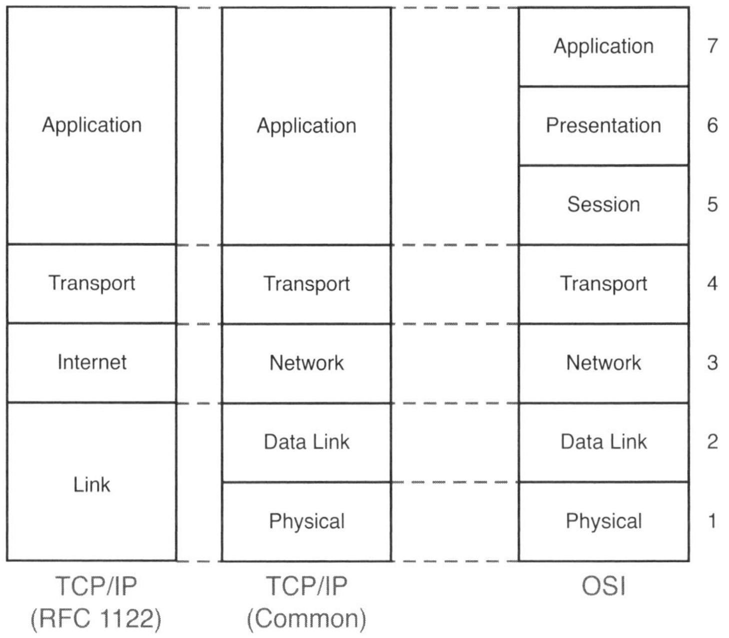

FIGURE 3-12

Mapping the Layers of the TCP/IP and OSI Models

The bottom four layers of both models match up pretty well. A standard that works as a TCP/IP physical layer standard would match the OSI model's physical layer. Likewise, the data link layers match in terms of what they define. These two OSI layers combined match the original TCP/IP model's link layer, shown on the left side of the figure. Finally, OSI Layers 3 and 4 match directly to TCP/IP layers: the network/Internet layer and the transport layer, respectively.

The biggest differences between these models exist at the top. Essentially, the TCP/IP model defines many functions as part of the application layer, and OSI split those functions into multiple layers. Today, there is no real benefit to thinking about exactly what functions the TCP/IP model would put in the OSI session and presentation layers. In fact, most experienced network engineers could not give you a good answer about those OSI layers, mainly because it does not matter to real networks. Just know that the top layer of TCP/IP (application) maps to the top three layers of the OSI model, but think of these three layers as a group.

The ISO and the IETF continued their work on their respective models through the 1980s and into the 1990s, but eventually, it became clear that TCP/IP had won the race. The OSI networking model faded away, and no one uses the OSI model to build networks today.

> **ON THE SIDE:** OSI was a real contender to win the battle to become the world's most popular networking model. As an example, the U.S. government passed federal law in the early 1990s requiring that all future computers sold to the U.S. government must support OSI, in a law popularly called the Government OSI Profile (GOSIP). The law was later changed to no longer require OSI and to allow TCP/IP.

Using OSI Terminology in a TCP/IP World

OSI still matters to the IT world today. That might seem odd at first thought, because you just read that the OSI model faded away by the 1990s. The story goes like this: The IT world saw the OSI model coming in the 1980s, as a solution to the problems caused by the closed nature of vendor networking models. Before OSI products even made it to market, the IT world expected OSI development to continue, that vendors would eventually offer products, and that eventually the world would migrate to OSI. Another problem with all these vendor networking models was that they all used different terminology, so IT pros started using OSI terminology as a kind of common lingo to describe every vendor network model, just to have a common set of terms. Those terms became common in the networking world.

The IT world adopted some OSI terms but eventually left OSI behind, instead choosing TCP/IP. But the OSI terms did not disappear, and even today, OSI terms are still used every day instead of TCP/IP terms.

One way the networking industry uses OSI terms is that when speaking about layers in the models, people refer to the layers based on the OSI layer names and OSI layer numbers, even when talking about TCP/IP. When you think about a single TCP/IP standard (hardware spec or protocol), you should think about it with the TCP/IP model. However, when you talk about it, use layer names and numbers from the OSI model. That might sound crazy—use the terms from an old unused networking model? However, it is the reality.

As an example, consider three TCP/IP standards either defined by or referenced by TCP/IP: HTTP, IP, and RJ-45. HTTP defines a protocol that fits in the TCP/IP application layer, IP defines a protocol that fits in the TCP/IP Internet (formal) or network (common) layer, and RJ-45 defines a hardware spec that fits within the TCP/IP link (formal) or physical (common) layer. Figure 3-13 shows all three examples, with a left-to-right flow, with the right side showing the phrase you might speak when talking about each standard.

First, look at the HTTP standard at the top of the figure. HTTP happens to be a TCP/IP application layer protocol. The TCP/IP application layer maps to the top three layers of the OSI model, but by convention, ignores OSI Layers 5 and 6. As a result, when discussing HTTP, use phrases like "HTTP is an application layer protocol." No problem there—both the TCP/IP models and the OSI model use the word *application*. However, when referring to the layers by number—which is common—refer to Layer 7, with phrases like "HTTP is a Layer 7 protocol."

Next, think about IP. With the original TCP/IP model per RFC 1122, IP sits at the Internet layer, which would be Layer 2 counting from bottom to top. The more commonly used TCP/IP matches the OSI model terms more closely, with the exact same names and layer numbers for the lower four layers. So, when discussing IP, IT pros say "network layer," using phrases like "IP is a network layer protocol," using the OSI terms and numbers.

Example

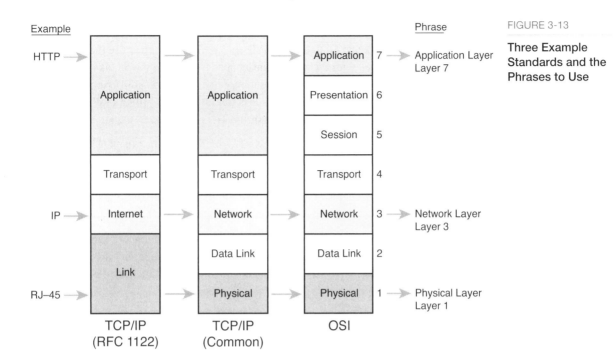

FIGURE 3-13

Three Example Standards and the Phrases to Use

Understanding How a TCP/IP Network Works

All modern networks are TCP/IP networks because they use products that follow the standards in the TCP/IP model. The earlier parts of this chapter focused on the TCP/IP model itself. The following sections focus on some of the specific standards and protocols in TCP/IP and describe how they work together to create a TCP/IP network.

These sections start by looking at LANs and then at WANs. Both these categories of networking technology match TCP/IP's lower two layers. The LAN section focuses on the most popular LAN technology today (Ethernet), with the WAN section focusing on the most basic WAN technology (leased lines). Following that, the text discusses Internet Protocol (IP), probably the most important single standard in a TCP/IP network, and the sections end with some brief comments about the TCP/IP transport and application layers.

Ethernet LANs in TCP/IP Networks

LANs define standards that match both the physical and data link layers in TCP/IP. Before discussing LANs in particular, this topic first discusses the terms *LAN* and *WAN* in relation to the TCP/IP model. Then, the following sections break Ethernet LAN technology down to match the TCP/IP model's lower two layers.

LANs and WANs Compared to the Physical and Data Link Layers

Network pros think and talk about TCP/IP on a daily basis. They use the layer names and numbers, with those terms influenced by the OSI model, as mentioned earlier in the section "Using OSI Terminology in a TCP/IP World." Network pros also use the terms local-area network (LAN) and wide-area network (WAN), each of which refers to the lower two layers of the TCP/IP model.

LANs get their name, particularly the word *local*, from the fact that LANs connect devices that sit relatively near each other. Of course, that begs the question: How near? Generally, devices on the same floor of the same building, in the same building, or in the same campus office park can be connected to the same LAN. Literally, a LAN can be hundreds of meters long, or even a few thousand meters.

WANs get their name from the fact that the devices can sit far apart, separated by a "wide" distance. That description again begs the same question, but the answer can be subjective. However, WANs can connect devices that sit literally thousands of miles apart.

A more objective way to classify a physical network as either a LAN or WAN is that companies often own their LAN and lease their WAN. LANs exist in small enough spaces so that a company owns the right to install cables between all the devices, so that employees can buy cables and devices and create a LAN that the company owns. As you will see later, WANs often require links that go between company sites, and the cables have to pass through land owned by other people and public land owned by the government. As a result, companies must lease these WAN links from a telephone company (telco).

Summarizing, when you think of the terms *LAN* and *WAN*, always think of the lower two layers of the TCP/IP model. Then think about them generally as local versus remote, and also as owned versus leased. Figure 3-14 also summarizes these ideas.

FIGURE 3-14

Terms LAN and WAN in the TCP/IP Model

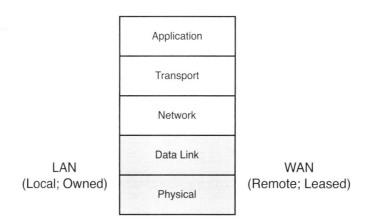

Ethernet LAN Physical Links

The physical layer of the TCP/IP model defines anything that can be seen or touched that matters to the process of sending bits. For example, Figure 3-1, earlier in the chapter, shows a cable that can be used for Ethernet LANs, along with an Ethernet network interface card (NIC). Both exist in the physical world, and both play a role in communicating bits, so Ethernet physical layer standards define both.

The TCP/IP physical layer also defines what energy must flow over the physical parts during the process of sending bits. Ethernet has standards that define how to send bits using electricity over copper wires, and other standards that define how to send bits using light over glass fibers. This section discusses how Ethernet uses wires inside a cable to create a loop (circuit), put electricity onto that loop, and change the electricity over time to communicate sets of 0s and 1s.

The devices on the end of a LAN cable create a circuit using the wires inside the cable, connectors on the end of the cable, and electronics in the device. The cable itself has plastic on the outside but copper wires on the inside. The ends of the wires sit in the connectors on the ends of the cable. Once inserted into the devices, typically in a NIC or similar hardware, the electronics on the NIC can connect the wires, as shown in Figure 3-15. By connecting electronics to the same two wires, a loop exists.

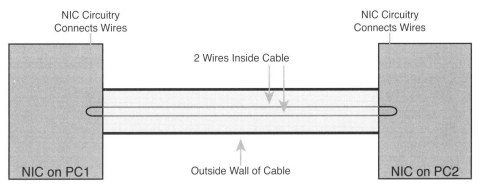

FIGURE 3-15

NICs on Both Ends of a Cable, Creating a Loop

Both the sender and receiver must agree on the rules of how to use the electrical circuit. Using the loop, the NIC sending the bits creates the electrical signal. The sender varies the signal over time to encode different bits. The NIC receiving the bits must know what rules the sender uses to choose how to change the electricity; knowing those rules, the receiving NIC can interpret the changes into the correct 0s and 1s.

As an analogy, think about what happens when people talk. When you speak words in some language, your voice changes over time to make different words. The people around you hear you make different sounds. However, if the other people do not speak your same language, they have no idea what you meant by all those sounds. To communicate, both the speaker and listener must be close enough to hear, and they must use the same language.

The **encoding** standard creates something like a spoken language that uses electricity. The device sending the data, called a *coder* or *encoder*, uses the encoding standard. The encoder changes the electrical signal over time based on the encoding standard. The encoding rules state exactly how to change the electricity to mean 0 or 1: possibly a different voltage, current, or some other electrical feature.

Of course, the receiver must use the same encoding standard as well, just like the person listening to you needs to understand the language you speak. On the receiving side, the *decoder* senses the electrical signals, and using the same rules, interprets the electrical signals back into bits.

Beyond the encoding rules, several other physical layer pieces must be standardized. For example, the cable must meet certain standards. Also, the cables must have a connector on the ends, of a size and shape that fit the sockets on the NICs. (See Figure 3-1 for photos of RJ-45 connectors and sockets.) All these details follow standards, with those standards fitting the TCP/IP model's physical layer.

Ethernet LAN Physical Layer Nodes: LAN Switches

As mentioned in Chapter 2, networks exist as a set of links and nodes. Ethernet LANs create links using cables. Ethernet uses several types of devices as nodes, but the most common today is a networking device called a *LAN switch*. Chapter 2 introduced the concept briefly, showing a photo of a LAN switch in Figure 2-25.

Physically, the LAN switch makes cabling more organized. Every Ethernet LAN device connects to the LAN using a cable. The cable installers run a cable from each device to a central place on that one floor, usually in a locked closet called a *wiring closet*. The LAN switch sits in the closet. By connecting all the cables to the LAN switch, all the devices connect to the LAN. Figure 3-16 shows the physical cabling layout of a small LAN with a single LAN switch.

FIGURE 3-16

Using a LAN Switch to Physically Connect Devices to a LAN

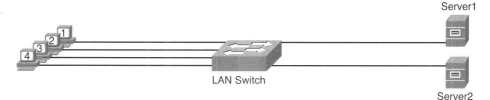

The network in Figure 3-16 shows a single LAN that has multiple physical links. To make it work, the LAN switch must receive data in one link, make a decision of where to send the data, and send the data out another physical link. This forwarding logic uses some data link layer concepts; the next section looks at the data link layer of TCP/IP and explains the basics of how the LAN switch forwards data.

> **AUTHOR'S NOTE:** To summarize, the TCP/IP physical layer includes all standards related to something you can touch or see—something physical—that sends and receives bits. It also includes encoding standards that define how to use electricity, light, and radio waves to send data over physical links.

Ethernet LAN Data Link Layer

The Ethernet data link layer, like other data-link standards, defines the rules (protocols) that tell the devices how and when to use the Ethernet physical layer. In short, the TCP/IP data link layer essentially answer this question:

> What *rules* must be followed to successfully send data between the devices in an Ethernet LAN?

For example, consider a couple of examples that use analogies. For the first example, imagine a single-lane bridge that spans a river. You drive up to the bridge, but a car is coming the other way. You have the physical ability to start across the bridge, but with only one lane, you decide to wait until the other car gets across the bridge, and then you cross.

Sometimes, Ethernet LANs must control links that act like a one-lane bridge. To do that, the Ethernet data-link standards define the rules about how to decide who gets to send its data next. If both devices on the link use the same rules, they can effectively take turns, but it means that one device will need to wait before sending.

For the second example and analogy, think about people and their names. You are hanging out at a party, and maybe a dozen people can hear each other talking. If you want to say something specifically to one person in the group, you say their name first; otherwise, they might not know you were talking to them.

Now think about the LAN diagram in Figure 3-16, the one with a LAN switch. To send data to a particular device on the LAN, Ethernet data-link standards define an address that acts like a name, because it identifies that device on the LAN. When sending data to a specific device, the sender lists the destination device's address, sort of like saying someone's name when you talk to him.

Many data link layer protocols use a **data link layer address** that identifies each device connected to the link. When sending data to another device on the same LAN, the sender must add the destination device's data-link address to the data. Then, the switch can look at the address to decide where to send the data. Also, the destination device knows that the data was meant for that device.

Ethernet data-link standards define a *Media Access Control (MAC)* address that identifies each NIC physically attached to the LAN. Ethernet defines the MAC address as a 48-bit number, written as 12 hexadecimal numbers to make the addresses shorter to type and write.

To show the idea, Figure 3-17 repeats the same LAN as shown in Figure 3-16, but this time showing data sent by Server1 to PC1. In this example, PC1's MAC address is 1111.1111.1111 (the periods just break up the hex numbers to make the MAC address easier to read).

> **AUTHOR'S NOTE:** In networking, the idea that you have only one sender on the link at a time is called *half duplex*, and the ability to let both sides send at the same time is called *full duplex*.

FIGURE 3-17

**Using an Address to
Send Data to the Right
LAN Device**

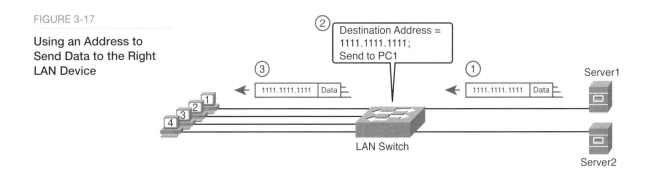

Following the steps in the figure:

1. The server sends the data over the physical link, but only after the server adds the destination Ethernet address of 1111.1111.1111 to the data.

2. The switch sees the destination address of 1111.1111.1111 and decides to send the data to PC1, and PC1 only.

3. The address and data arrive at PC1. PC1 knows that the data was meant for PC1, because PC1 knows its MAC address is 1111.1111.1111.

Data link layer standards, including Ethernet, typically define protocols, and protocols in turn define rules and messages. Figure 3-17 shows some of the rules: the concept of an Ethernet MAC address, its size (48 bits), and its format when written on paper (hexadecimal). Ethernet also defines a place to store a message in front of the data. In Figure 3-17, Ethernet used that space to list the destination MAC address.

Many protocols define a **header** and/or **trailer** as a place to store a message that needs to flow through the network with the user data. Both the header and trailer list bytes of information useful to the protocol. The header simply comes before the data as the message flows over the network, and the trailer comes after the data.

Headers and trailers work like adding a sticky note to the data as it passes through the network. A sticky note (or Post-it note to use the name brand from 3M) is note paper with a little light glue along one edge of the page so that you can attach the note and easily remove it later. Before sending the data into the network, the device puts the equivalent of a sticky note in front of the data. Data-link protocols typically add both a header and trailer, like a sticky note on both sides of the data, as shown in Figure 3-18.

FIGURE 3-18

**Data Link Header and
Trailer, Like a Couple of
Sticky Notes**

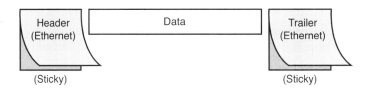

To summarize, the TCP/IP data link layer defines mostly protocols. Those protocols list rules that devices must follow when using a physical link, like rules about when the device can send and when it should not send. These protocols also typically define messages that go through the network, with the data to help the devices use the links. These messages sit inside headers and trailers defined by the protocol.

WANs in TCP/IP Networks

Like LANs, wide-area network (WAN) standards also define details at both the physical and data link layers of TCP/IP. Like LANs, WAN physical layer standards define details about the physical cabling, connectors, and the energy (electricity, light, and radio) used to send data over the physical network. Like LANs, WAN data-link standards control how to use the physical links. The following sections look at a few example WAN options so that you can see the general ideas. Later, Chapter 7, "Wide-Area Networks," looks at a many more WAN options.

WANs Versus LANs, Wide Versus Local, Lease Versus Buy

WAN physical links are created by a service provider company, typically a telephone company (telco), to be used by another company in their corporate network.

To understand the WAN business model, with a telco providing the physical link, first think about this story. Imagine that Fred buys a house, and his best friend Barney also builds one, three miles away. Many other people own the land between their houses. Because they spend a lot of time together, especially because Barney has a bowling alley in his house, Fred decides to build a road to Barney's house. Fred asks the dozens of landowners between the two building lots whether he could buy the right to build a road through all their backyards.

Realistically, Fred will not get everyone to say yes. The neighbors would simply would not want you taking a big chunk of their backyards away.

Of course, a solution to the problem already exists: public roads built by the government. The government knows that everyone needs to move around, so the government sets aside some land for roads. When anyone buys a piece of property, he must make sure that he can connect to at least one government road, and you can take those roads to any destination. Figure 3-19 shows the general idea, with Fred and Barney sitting three miles apart.

ON THE SIDE: To see some actual Ethernet MAC addresses, look at the network setting on any device using the GUI interface. Or, from the command line, try commands like these: **getmac**, **ipconfig**, and **ifconfig**.

FIGURE 3-19

Government Roads Provide a Path to All Private Properties

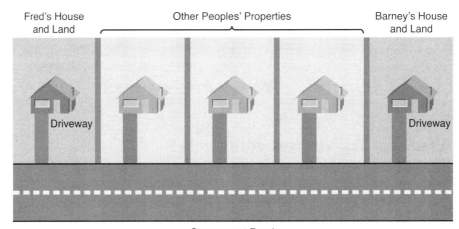

Government Road

How does this government road story matter to networking? WANs are network connections that rely on physical connections built and owned by someone else, similar to how people rely on roads built by someone else.

WANs create a link between parts of a corporate network when the company would not be able to run a cable between the sites themselves. For example, imagine two sites in a single company, three miles apart. Ethernet LAN standards actually allow a three-mile-long cable to connect LAN switches at both sites. However, that company cannot legally put that cable over all the other people's land in between the sites. The company cannot dig up the streets between the sites to bury the cable—most places have laws to prevent just anyone from digging up someone else's land and planting cables underneath. So that company cannot install a cable between sites, much like Fred could not build a private road to Barney's house.

The solution: A few companies have the right to run cables near the existing roads, creating physical networking links, and those links can be leased (rented) to whatever company needs to connect sites. These companies, often also telcos, can connect cables to any and every property—each house, apartment building, office building, and so on. Utility companies do this kind of work already: The telco has a phone line into most houses, the electric company has power lines into most buildings, the cable TV company has cable lines into most buildings, and so on. So the government lets the telco and maybe a few other companies dig up the road to install cables, or to hang cables from poles above ground. Figure 3-20 shows the general idea, this time with cables strung across poles, just because they are easier to visualize compared to buried cables.

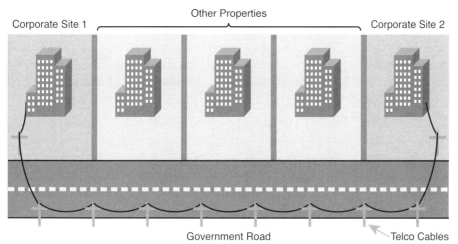

FIGURE 3-20

Big Idea of WAN Service: Telco Connects Two Remote Sites

Finally, the WAN business model works like a lease. Companies pay the WAN service provider a monthly fee for each WAN link. The enterprise that leases the WAN link did not have to buy the cabling between sites, install gear between sites, hire construction crews to dig up the streets to install the cables, and so on. The WAN provider does this kind of work and makes its money back over time by charging rent on use of the cables and devices that it installs.

In contrast, when building a LAN, companies buy the cables, buy the LAN switches, and so on. So, generally speaking, companies own LANs and lease WANs.

Leased-Line WAN Physical Layer

A WAN **leased line** creates the equivalent of a cable directly between two remote sites. The enterprise that wants to connect the sites cannot do so, for various reasons: local law, no equipment with which to dig up the road, the distance is too far, it would cost to much, and so on. To solve the problem, the telco leases the enterprise a link between sites called a leased line.

A WAN leased line creates a two-way path to transmit data, at a predetermined speed, between two sites across a WAN. When data needs to be sent, the leased line can be used. When no data needs to be sent, the leased line sits there, unused, much like a private road would sit unused most of the time. Basically, a leased line acts like a cable between two sites.

Physically, the telco does not just install a cable between two sites. Instead, long before the enterprise asked for a new leased line, the telco had already installed a lot of cables. The telco had built a large network, with lots of extra capacity. The telco probably already had installed cables from each office building to the telco's nearest building, generally called a telco *central office* (CO). In short, the telco already had plenty of cables installed.

AUTHOR'S NOTE:
Leased lines give us a great way to first learn about WANs. In some ways, leased lines are very simple. However, behind the scenes, leased lines use the complexity of the large hidden telco network, which gives us an opportunity to learn more about networking. For now, the discussion focuses on the basics.

When an enterprise orders a new leased line from a telco, the telco chooses some unused cables and unused capacity from the telco network, and creates the equivalent of a cable between the sites. The enterprise knows very little about how the telco builds the leased line, however. All the enterprise knows is that physically, the telco identifies the cable on each end of the leased line (usually in a wiring closet chosen by the enterprise) and that the cable connects to some nearby telco CO. The rest of the picture is vague. Figure 3-21 shows the idea.

FIGURE 3-21

Physical Cabling of a Leased Line, from Each Customer Site to Central Office (CO)

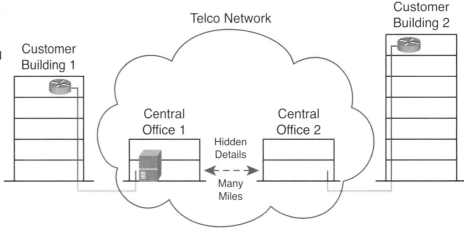

While a telco leased line creates one type of WAN link, networks use nodes called routers to connect to the WAN leased line at each site. The telco identifies the ends of the leased line in the customer (enterprise) wiring closet at each site, as shown in Figure 3-21. The connector on the end of the leased line can connect directly into a WAN interface on the router.

The router also plays a big role in connecting the network together because it can connect to both LAN and WAN links. Typically, each site has a router that connects to the WAN links and to the LAN. The result is that devices on the LANs at both sites can communicate, and the router does the work to actually send the data over the WAN link.

Figure 3-22 shows the general idea, with two leased lines: one connecting Miami to Atlanta and one connecting Miami to Boston.

The figure shows a couple of important conventions in networking. First, the jagged lines that look like lightning bolts represent leased lines, mostly when the physical details of the leased line do not matter. Second, the drawing says nothing about the length of the leased line—each could literally run across the street in a city or for thousands of miles.

Miami Headquarters

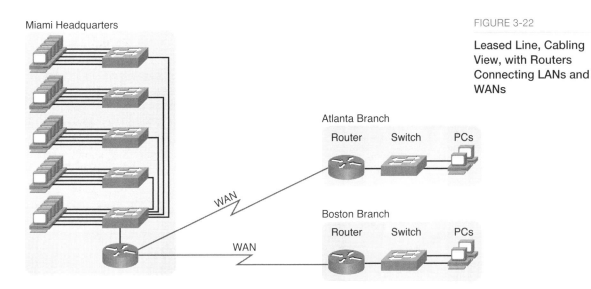

FIGURE 3-22

Leased Line, Cabling View, with Routers Connecting LANs and WANs

HDLC and PPP as the TCP/IP Data Link Layer

LAN and WAN data-link standards have many similarities. Both define mostly protocols, and those protocols define rules about when and how to use the physical links. These protocols define both a header and trailer, for the usual purpose of giving the data-link protocol a place to list messages for the devices on the link.

Leased-line WANs differ from Ethernet LANs a little in that leased lines allow the person who leases the leased line to choose a data-link protocol from several options. Over the history of leased lines, several alternative protocols have emerged and fallen away. Today, physical leased lines typically use one of two data-link protocols: *High-level Data Link Control* (HDLC, standardized by ISO) or *Point-to-Point Protocol* (PPP, defined by TCP/IP in RFC 1661).

Like LAN data-link protocols, both HDLC and PPP define an address in the header to identify the devices on the physical link. However, because leased lines use a point-to-point topology, addresses are boring. For example, if you sit at a coffee shop at a table with one friend only, you do not have to keep saying that friend's name every time you speak; it is obvious to whom you are talking. Likewise, when a router sends data over a leased line, the data can only go to the router on the other end of the link. So, while these protocols define addresses, most people ignore the addresses.

Encapsulation in Headers and Trailers

Every data-link protocol focuses on a particular physical layer technology. That is, the data-link protocols defined for Ethernet LANs focus on Ethernet LANs. If you take that thought one step further, the Ethernet header and trailer also focus on Ethernet LANs. Similarly, on leased lines that use PPP, PPP focuses on getting data over that leased line, and the PPP header and trailer focus on getting data over a leased line.

Keeping those thoughts in mind, the headers and trailers only have a use in a subset of the network. For example, an Ethernet header/trailer cannot help devices send data over a leased line, and a PPP header/trailer cannot help devices send data over an Ethernet LAN. From this perspective, data-link headers and trailers have a limited focus.

Routers typically sit at the border between different data links, so routers remove old data-link headers that are no longer needed, and replace them with the new data-link headers needed for the next leg of the journey. Figure 3-23 shows the idea. In this case, PC Fred, on the left, sends data to Barney, on the right.

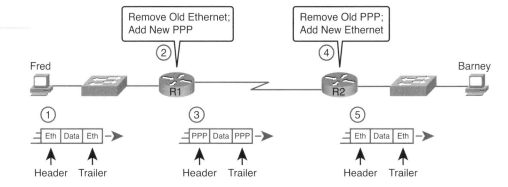

FIGURE 3-23

Encapsulation and Deencapsulation

AUTHOR'S NOTE:
In networking, the process of adding headers (and trailers) is called *encapsulation*; the process of removing them is called *deencapsulation*.

The figure shows five steps, as follows:

1. Fred adds the Ethernet header and trailer to the data, as normal, before sending. The header/trailer remains with the data as it crosses the Ethernet, until it reaches Router R1.
2. R1, the last device connected to the Ethernet on left, removes the old Ethernet data-link header, because it is no longer needed, and adds a PPP header and trailer to the header to send the data over a WAN link.
3. R1 sends the data, with PPP header and trailer, over the WAN leased line.
4. R2, the last device connected to the leased line, discards the PPP header and trailer, because it is no longer needed, and adds a new (different) Ethernet header and trailer, which is useful on the LAN on the right.
5. R2 sends the data, with Ethernet header and trailer, over the LAN to Barney.

This idea of data-link headers and trailers being useful for only part of the data's trip across a network works a little like what happens when you take a long trip. Maybe you start by taking a subway train to the airport. Then you take a plane to another city, where you rent a car. Finally, you drive the car to your final destination. In this case, you used three different vehicles (train, plane, and car), but none of the vehicles took you the entire trip from start to finish.

Similarly, routers separate a TCP/IP network into different physical networks, somewhat like different physical vehicles on a long trip. The data-link protocol for each physical network defines the rules to use in each case. For example, in the same small TCP/IP network shown in Figure 3-23, three separate physical networks exist: two Ethernet LANs and a leased line. Each is considered to be a separate data link, as shown in Figure 3-24.

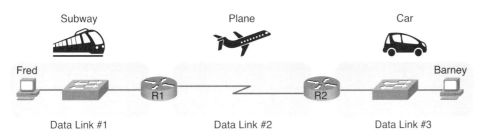

FIGURE 3-24

Routers Separate a Network into Separate Data Links (Subway, Plane, Car Icons © Siarhei Pleshakou)

Using the ideas in Figure 3-24, a data-link protocol helps move data over a single data link. The next topic shows the logic at the network layer that moves the data from endpoint device to endpoint device in a TCP/IP network.

IP as the TCP/IP Network Layer

TCP/IP network layer protocols, especially the **Internet Protocol (IP)**, list the rules so that the network can forward data from end to end through the entire TCP/IP network. Data-link protocols act to control that movement across individual physical links. IP connects all those links together by defining how routers choose where to send data next. The data can pass over many links and nodes (routers), eventually getting to the destination device.

IP uses logic that sounds a little like what most people think about when they plan to take a long trip. When you first plan a trip, do you first stop and think about how to pave roads? Or how to fly a plane? Or traffic laws? Of course not. You think about the bigger questions. You think about where you plan to go. You might get the postal address, so that you can search for some driving directions, or plug the address into your GPS device. If the trip requires a plane ticket, you might start searching for airports near your destination, and start looking for cheap flights. Eventually, you come up with a plan: Take this transportation to one place, another mode of transport to the next place, and so on, until you arrive at the destination.

Summarizing, when you plan a long trip, you find the best way to get from where you are (point A) to the destination (point B), choosing from all available options. In a TCP/IP network, IP defines the rules so that the network can forward data from the sending device (point A) to the destination device on the other side of the network (point B), picking from all available paths through the network.

IP defines two important ideas for TCP/IP networks: IP addresses and IP routing. IP addresses identify the device to the IP network. IP also defines the concept of routing, which defines how *routers* make a choice of where to send the data packet next so that the data arrives at the correct destination address.

The following sections introduce IP addressing and routing, along with a few related topics. Chapters 8, "The Internet Protocol (IP)," and 9, "The Internet," both look at IP in more detail as well.

IP Addressing

A device's **IP address** identifies that device in a TCP/IP network. Remember, computer networks, including TCP/IP networks, need to deliver bits from one device to another. To do that work, the network must somehow be able to look at data as it flows through a network and determine the device that should receive the data. In TCP/IP networks, every device must have an IP address. To forward data to a particular device, the data must be addressed to that device's IP address.

In other words, the idea basically works like a postal address: To send a letter to someone, you send it to his or her postal address.

To process of sending data from the sending device to the receiving device requires cooperation between the endpoint devices and the devices in the TCP/IP network. The sending device must learn the destination device's IP address. The sender must then add the destination device's IP address to an *IP header* and send that header along with the data. After they are inside the TCP/IP network, network devices called *routers* route (forward) the data through the TCP/IP network to the destination device. To do so, the routers must know information about the location of each device, based on its IP address.

> **AUTHOR'S NOTE:** IP calls any device that has an IP address an *IP host*, or simply *host*, as generic terms. These terms allow network pros to talk about TCP/IP without having to use long phrases to refer to all devices that can use IP, like PCs, minicomputers, mainframes, phones, tablets, game systems, TVs, and so on.

Each IP address has 32 bits, usually written using a format called *dotted-decimal notation (DDN)*. The 32-bit format works well for computers, but the IP standard also defines DDN format so humans would have a more convenient decimal-based format. But whether you look at the address as 32 bits or as a DDN number, it still represents a 32-bit number. For example, the following is an IP address, 32 bits long, with some space between each set of 8 bits for better readability:

00000001 00000010 00000011 00000100

The DDN format treats the 32-bit binary IP address as four sets of 8 bits, converts each set of 8 bits to the decimal equivalent, and places a dot (period) between each decimal number. Each set of 8 bits is called an octet. To convert from binary to DDN, take the first octet and convert that 8-bit number to decimal. (Or, simply look up the 8-bit binary number in the table in Appendix A, "Numeric Reference Tables," in the back of the book. Appendix A includes a table of all 256 binary values for an 8-bit number and the decimal equivalent values.) Then, place a dot (period) between each number.

For example, the binary IP address listed just a few paragraphs back converts to DDN address 1.2.3.4. The first octet is binary 00000001, which converts to decimal 1. The second octet is 00000010, which converts to 2. The third and fourth octets convert to 3 and 4, so the DDN format, with dots between each octet, is 1.2.3.4. Table 3-1 lists a few more examples for comparison; if the idea is not clear, work through the math on your own to confirm the numbers in the table.

TABLE 3-1

Example IP Addresses, Binary and DDN Formats

Binary IP Address	Equivalent DDN IP Address
00000001 00001000 00010000 00100000	1.8.16.32
01010101 10101010 00001111 11110000	85.170.15.240
00001010 00000101 00011010 00010101	10.5.26.21
01111110 10000001 01010101 11111000	126.129.85.248
00100001 01000001 10000001 00010001	33.65.129.17

The network engineers at a company decide the IP addresses to use in the corporate network. The network engineer picks a valid IP address for each part of the TCP/IP network. Then the engineer either assigns the addresses to each device or the devices learn their IP addresses dynamically. For example, Figure 3-25 shows a sample network, with IP hosts on the outer edge. In this case, four hosts exist: two PCs on the left and two on the right.

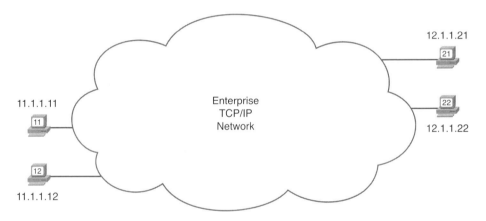

FIGURE 3-25

IP Addresses in a Network Diagram

12.1.1.21

11.1.1.11

Enterprise
TCP/IP
Network

12.1.1.22

11.1.1.12

> **AUTHOR'S NOTE:** Data-link protocols define addresses specific to different types of physical networks, so those addresses are often called *physical addresses*. In contrast, IP defines addresses completely independently from the physical network, so IP addressing is sometimes called *logical addressing*, a term that simply means that the addresses are not physical.

The figure shows one IP address per PC, with one connection into the TCP/IP network per PC. However, in reality, IP requires one address per connection into the TCP/IP network. For example, a PC with a wired Ethernet LAN connection, plus a wireless LAN connection, would actually have two IP addresses—one per connection into the network.

Routers play a big role with the IP protocol in that they route (forward) data based on the destination IP address. To do that routing, a router must connect using multiple interfaces to multiple data links. And because IP tells us to give each interface connected to the TCP/IP network an IP address, routers actually have multiple IP addresses. Figure 3-26 shows an example, which expands on the TCP/IP addressing shown earlier in Figure 3-25.

FIGURE 3-26

Routers: Multiple Interfaces, Multiple IP Addresses

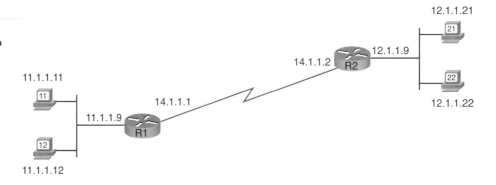

IP Address Grouping

To make IP routing work well, IP tells everyone to group IP addresses together using certain rules. Basically, hosts on the same physical network (data link) need to have similar IP addresses; those similar addresses mean that the addresses sit in the same group. The idea works somewhat like a postal code (ZIP code in the United States), where every address in the same area uses the exact same postal code.

IP defines how to group addresses in a couple of ways. First, IP defines an idea called *classful networks*, which will be used in the upcoming examples in this section. IP also defines a grouping concept called *IP subnetting*. These rules give the network engineer some flexibility in how he assigns addresses, but still let IP routing work well.

ON THE SIDE: If you decide to focus your IT career on networking, IP addressing rules will be one of the more important topics to master early in your career. And mastering IP addressing, and IP subnetting in particular, can be very useful before going for that first job interview.

Next, consider an example that uses classful network rules. With classful networks, all IP addresses that begin with 11 in the first octet are in one *IP network*. IP allows us to represent this network with the number 11.0.0.0. Likewise, all addresses that begin with 12 are in one IP network, represented by the number 12.0.0.0. However, the classful IP network 11.0.0.0 is a different classful IP network than classful IP network 12.0.0.0. That is, one network is the network whose addresses begin with 11, and another is the network whose addresses begin with 12.

If using only the classful network rules from IP, all IP addresses on a single LAN or WAN must be in a single classful IP network. IP addresses in a different LAN or WAN must be in a different classful IP network. Figure 3-27 shows how the IP address assignments would work when following these rules.

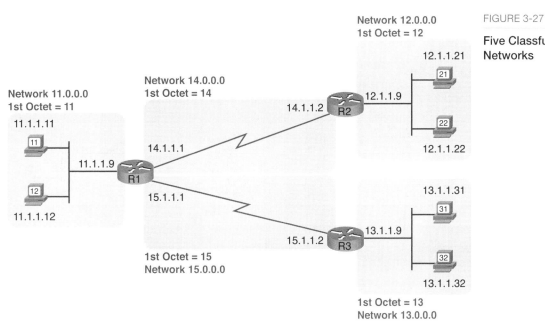

FIGURE 3-27

Five Classful IP Networks

The IP addressing conventions also tell the network engineer about what IP addresses to use for new devices. For example, imagine that new devices need to be added to each LAN. For new devices on the left, the IP addresses must begin with 11. For devices on the other LANs on the right, the IP addresses must begin with 12 or 13, respectively.

IP Routing

Chapter 2 introduced links and nodes, and described how networks forward data over links and nodes. In that model, the data crosses a link and arrives at a node. The node makes a choice of where to send the data next, forwarding the data out the next link. (See Chapter 2's Figure 2-27, and the surrounding text, for that general description.)

IP routing defines exactly how routers makes their choices of how to forward data in a TCP/IP network. To act as a node, each router connects to multiple physical links. To do so, a router typically has multiple physical *interfaces* into which cables can be connected. A router also needs some rules to follow that tell the router how to make its decision of how to forward, or *route*, the data.

IP routing relies on two ideas that work together: The sender addresses the data, and the routers forward the data based on the IP address as supplied by the sending device.

First, IP routing relies on the sending host to identify the destination host. When a host wants to send an IP packet to another host, the sender must put the destination host's IP address into an IP header. The sending host adds that IP header to the data, so the sender has identified the exact IP address to which the packet should be sent.

For example, Figure 3-28 shows PC11 sending an IP packet to PC21. In that case, PC11 adds an IP header to the data. That header includes the source address (PC11's IP address of 11.1.1.11) and a destination IP address (12.1.1.21, PC21's IP address).

FIGURE 3-28

Web Client Host PC11 Puts 12.1.1.21 into the IP Header Destination IP Address Field

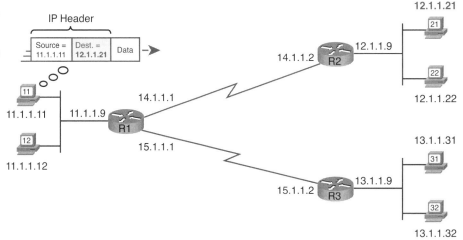

AUTHOR'S NOTE: The term *IP packet*, or simply *packet*, refers to the IP header, along with any other headers that follow the IP header, as shown in the upper part of Figure 3-28.

Additionally, IP routing relies on *IP routers* to forward the data to the correct destination host. To prepare, the routers must talk to each other (using other protocols) to learn about all the IP addresses in the TCP/IP network. The routers then list information about the location of the IP addresses, typically listed by address groups like classful IP networks. The router also keeps notes of how to forward data to those destinations. Routers keep all this forwarding information in RAM in the router, in a table called an *IP routing table*.

For example, Figure 3-29 shows the concept behind one routing table entry for Routers R1 and R2 in a small enterprise network. To be ready to forward the IP packet shown earlier in Figure 3-28, both routers learned a good route for classful network 12.0.0.0. The route shown on each router lists the information each router needs to forward packets to IP network 12.0.0.0, which includes all IP addresses that begin with 12.

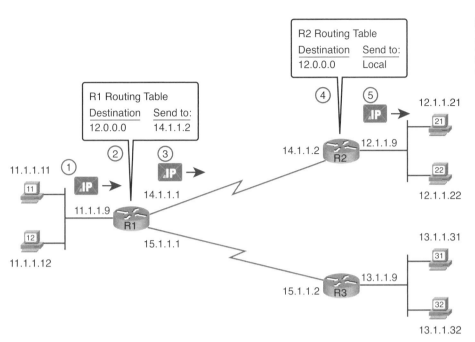

FIGURE 3-29

Routing Tables on R1 and R2, for Network 12.0.0.0

The figure shows five steps, beginning with the sending host (PC11), then R1, and finally R2:

1. PC11 sends the data, destination address 12.1.1.21 (PC21), to the nearby Router R1.

2. R1 compares the destination IP address (12.1.1.21) listed in the IP header with its routing table. R1 acts on the matched routing table entry, which tells R1 to send the data to IP address 14.1.1.2, which is an address on Router R2.

3. R1 sends the packet to Router R2.

4. R2 uses the same overall logic as R1. R2's routing table says that network 12.0.0.0 is local, meaning that R2 should forward the data directly to PC21.

5. R2 forwards the packet over the LAN to PC21.

As you can see, IP routing relies heavily on IP addressing, and IP addressing rules exist to aid IP routing.

IP Routing Forwards IP Packets

Earlier, the section "Encapsulation in Headers and Trailers" made several points about how encapsulation worked with data-link protocols, and how the data-link header and trailer encapsulate the user data (the data sent by the user). IP also creates and adds an IP header to the user data. This section looks at how those pieces fit together, along with some terminology.

First, the sending host adds all the headers and trailers before sending the data into the TCP/IP network. The sending host creates the IP header (network layer) along with a data link layer header/trailer based on the physical link used by that host. The IP header sits after the data-link header, as shown in Figure 3-30.

FIGURE 3-30

Encapsulation on the Sending Host: Frame and Packet

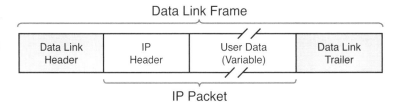

The figure also lists two very important terms in networking: **frame** and **packet**. The term *frame* specifically refers to encapsulated data that includes the data-link header and trailer, plus everything in between—including the IP header. The term *packet* refers to what sits between the data-link header and trailer, but not including the data-link header and trailer.

Sometimes the small difference in meaning between the words *frame* and a *packet* matters, and sometimes it does not. At first glance, especially for someone new to networking, it might seem like such a minor difference. However, to briefly get a coworker to focus on the data-link header details, use the word *frame*. To briefly get a coworker to focus on the IP header details, use the word *packet*. And if you work with networks, you will use these terms often.

Why introduce these specific terms now? Because TCP/IP networks forward IP packets, and not frames, from the source host to the destination host.

When routers forward data, they do not forward the entire received frame, but they extract the IP packet from the frame. First, as a reminder, the earlier section "Encapsulation in Headers and Trailers" showed that each router discards data-link headers and trailers and builds new ones. When a router receives a frame, the router discards the data-link header and trailer, leaving the IP packet. Before forwarding the IP packet, the router encapsulates the packet in a new data-link header and trailer. The routing process eventually delivers the IP packet to the destination host.

Figure 3-31 shows an example of the routing process, and describes how it forwards IP packets, but not frames. It shows the same network topology as the earlier Figure 3-23, which showed each of the two routers deencapsulating and encapsulating data. However, now that you have the basics of IP routing, and a few more terms, Figure 3-31 shows the routing process more exactly.

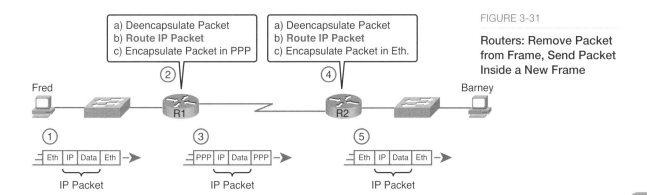

FIGURE 3-31

Routers: Remove Packet from Frame, Send Packet Inside a New Frame

Just to be clear, the steps in the figure show the following:

1. The sending host, Fred, creates and sends an Ethernet frame to Router R1, with the frame holding the original IP packet.

2. R1 uses these steps:

   a. Removes the IP packet from inside the received frame, discarding the old data-link header and trailer

   b. Makes a routing decision to forward the IP packet to R2 next

   c. Encapsulates the packet in a new PPP frame before sending the PPP frame across the leased line

3. The new PPP frame, holding the original IP packet, crosses the leased line to Router R2.

4. R2 repeats the same three steps:

   a. Removes the IP packet from inside the received frame, discarding the old data-link header and trailer

   b. Makes a routing decision to forward the IP packet out the LAN to Barney

   c. Encapsulates the packet in a new Ethernet frame before sending

5. The new Ethernet frame, holding the original IP packet, crosses the LAN and arrives at PC Barney.

TCP and UDP as the TCP/IP Transport Layer

Before getting into the details in this section about the TCP/IP transport layer, take a moment to think about the topics so far in this section. This third (and longest) major section of this chapter has started at the bottom of the TCP/IP model and moved up through the bottom three layers. As it turns out, those bottom three layers do all the work to move bits from one device to another. This chapter could end now if the only goal was to move bits from one device to another.

Moving up the TCP/IP model, each layer supported a wider and wider path across the TCP/IP network. The physical layer (Layer 1) standards focused on how to transmit bits over a single physical connection; Figure 3-32 shows the physical links in that TCP/IP network as L1, for Layer 1. The data link layer (Layer 2) defines frames and the rules to deliver frames over one link or multiple links of the same type, as shown in the figure as L2 (for Layer 2). The network layer (Layer 3) defines the widest range of the lower layers, defining IP packets that flow from source host to destination host, as shown in the figure as L3.

FIGURE 3-32

Widening Scope of Higher TCP/IP Layers

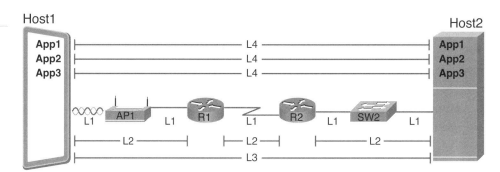

The TCP/IP transport layer, the next layer up in the TCP/IP model, takes the process one step wider than the network layer by connecting the applications. While the work that IP does to deliver IP packets to a host can be important, the host might run dozens of apps. The transport layer protocols provide the connection to the apps as well, as shown with the L4 notations in Figure 3-32.

To send data to the correct app, the transport layer protocols identify the destination app with a number called a *port number*. If a computer has 10 networked apps running, it would use (at least) ten different port numbers. For example, maybe it uses port numbers 2001 through 2010. To send data that will eventually be given to the app using port number 2001, the sender lists a destination port number of 2001 in the transport protocol's header.

TCP/IP defines several transport layer protocols, but two protocols are used far more than the others: *Transmission Control Protocol (TCP)* and *User Datagram Protocol (UDP)*. Both use the concept of port numbers to connect applications, creating the transport layer concept of connecting applications to each other. TCP also does several other useful services, like error recovery, while UDP provides almost no other services. Think of TCP as a premium service at the transport layer, with UDP as a basic service. However, UDP requires less work, with a shorter 8-byte header, versus TCP's 20-byte header.

When building a TCP/IP network, the IT staff does not have the option to sit back and choose the transport layer protocols to use. Instead, they build the TCP/IP network, and the IT staff and the users choose applications to put on the various devices in the network. At some point in the past, the app vendor chose a particular application layer protocol. Before that happened, some other people had created the application layer protocol, which in turn had listed the choice of whether to use TCP, UDP, or some other transport layer protocol. Because the IT staff does not choose the transport layer options, it helps to understand all the options.

Summarizing the TCP/IP Roles

A useful TCP/IP network not only delivers bits from one device to another, but from one application to another. Those applications run on various devices, or hosts. The application vendors follow the rules in application layer protocols, and those protocols let the app communicate well through the network. For example, web browser vendors write their web browsers to use the HTTP application layer protocol.

Application layer protocols rely on transport layer protocols to connect the sending app to the destination app, and possibly to perform other services. The application protocol's creator, not the user, chooses whether to use TCP, UDP, or some other less-common options. TCP and UDP each add a header, which they both use in part to identify the destination app using a destination port number. The choice of transport protocol tells us a lot about what the application protocol expects, because TCP provides several additional features, like error recovery, while UDP provides no other practical function beyond connecting the endpoint applications.

The transport layer protocols rely on IP to deliver IP packets from the sending host (device) to the destination host. The sending host adds the IP header, including the destination IP address. Each router reacts to the destination IP address, making a routing choice and forwarding the IP packet based on that choice. IP defines the details to make all those pieces happen, including logical IP addressing and IP routing.

IP relies on the data link and physical layers to deliver frames, which hold IP packets, from host to router, router to router, and router to host. The physical layer defines how to encode bits over a cable, or even through space using radio waves. The data link layer defines how to best use the physical link, including the data-link header and trailer to use. The ideas work much like a road system, with physical roads (like the physical layer) and traffic laws to make good use of the roads (like data-link protocols).

For study and reference, Table 3-2 lists the five layers of the TCP/IP model, along with some key facts.

TABLE 3-2
TCP/IP Model Summary

Layer Name	Key Functions	Focus: Host or Network	Device Focus
Physical	Physical parts that communicate and energy over those parts (electricity, light, radio)	Network	Cables, radio
Data Link	Rules about when to use physical links; addressing specific to the physical links	Network	LAN switch
Network (Internet)	Logical addressing (addressing independent of the physical links); routing	Network	Router
Transport	Communications functions useful to apps, but likely useful to many apps	Host	Any endpoint device
Application	Communications functions specific to a particular app	Host	Any endpoint device

Chapter Summary

Modern corporate networks are TCP/IP networks, and TCP/IP networks follow the TCP/IP model. Following the TCP/IP model simply means that the people that create products read and use the standards listed as part of the TCP/IP model, so that when IT pros at a company buy those products and use them as intended, all the networking components together follow TCP/IP rules. The TCP/IP model includes standards defined for TCP/IP by the IETF, and other standards from other standards groups, including the ITU and IEEE.

In the roughly 50-year history of computer networking, corporate networks have used many competing networking models. Those models include many vendor-proprietary models, typically one from each major computer vendor. The TCP/IP and OSI models offered open alternatives that used public standards, so the networking world migrated away from vendor models to an open model over time. Although the marketplace chose TCP/IP products over OSI products, some OSI terminology lingers even today, which requires network pros to know something about OSI.

The TCP/IP model organizes its standards into layers based on the major functions. The physical and data link layers define standards that most people today refer to as LANs and WANs. Those standards define how to send bits over a physical link by encoding some energy signal onto the link. The data link layer defines headers and trailers, plus rules, which together let the devices attached to those links send the data over one or more similar physical links. Examples include an Ethernet LAN or a leased-line WAN.

The Internet Protocol (IP) plays an important role in TCP/IP networks. First, IP routes data packets from any host to any other host (any device to any other device). Second, IP uses the same logic regardless of the physical links used by the devices or the physical links used in the TCP/IP network. Finally, IP defines addresses that allow each and every host to be identified in the TCP/IP network, much like a postal address.

Finally, the TCP/IP transport layer protocols, mainly TCP and UDP, do several functions related to what happens on the endpoint hosts. For example, while IP delivers packets from one host to another, the transport layer protocols deliver the data from the right sending application to the right receiving application.

3

Chapter Review Activities

Use the features in this section to study and review the topics in this chapter.

Answer These Questions

1. Which of the following is true about a TCP/IP network?

    a. The network uses only standards defined in TCP/IP RFCs.

    b. The network uses standards defined in TCP/IP RFCs, plus other standards.

    c. The IT personnel must choose to use TCP or IP.

    d. The network must use only LANs, but no WANs.

2. Which of the following terms is *not* a common synonym for TCP/IP model? (Choose two answers.)

    a. TCP/IP architecture

    b. TCP/IP

    c. Ethernet

    d. TCP/IP mapping

3. Think generically about the idea of a networking standard, ignoring any particular standard or standards group. Which of the following is typically true of a standard? (Choose two answers.)

    a. It exists as a written document.

    b. It exists as a deployed network device, which people can visit on the Internet.

    c. It has been passed through some form of review and approval or certification process.

    d. In the United States, it requires a vote by an elected politician.

4. Contrast an international standard as compared to a de facto standard. (Choose two answers.)

    a. De facto standard documents have been reviewed more thoroughly.

    b. International standard documents have been reviewed more thoroughly.

    c. De facto standards typically mean that the standards group has been authorized by many countries to create standards that apply to multiple countries.

    d. International standards typically mean that the standards group has been authorized by many countries to create standards that apply to multiple countries.

5. Which of the following are true about the commonly used version of the TCP/IP model as shown in this chapter? (Choose two answers.)

    a. The application layer sits immediately above the network layer.

    b. The data link layer sits lower in the model than the transport layer.

    c. The physical layer sits just below the data link layer.

    d. The network layer sits in the middle of the five layers.

6. The TCP/IP model refers to standards other than those the IETF defines in RFCs. Which of these standards groups is typically the source of external LAN standards? (Choose two answers.)

   a. ITU

   b. IEEE

   c. Vendor groups

   d. ANSI

7. Which of the following is *not* a typical reason for a group of ten companies to start a vendor group, for the purpose of pushing a new networking technology?

   a. To get products that use this technology to market more quickly

   b. To increase overall acceptance of the technology by having more vendors that support the technology

   c. To improve the chances that the technology will be standardized

   d. To keep intellectual property rights to the technology inside the company

8. The TCP/IP and OSI models have some obvious differences, like the number of layers. Think about the more commonly used version of the TCP/IP model discussed in this chapter, and then think about how to talk about TCP/IP using OSI terms. Which of the following is a correctly phrased statement for how to use OSI terminology?

   a. HTTP is a Layer 5 protocol.

   b. IP is a network layer protocol.

   c. TCP is a Layer 2 protocol.

   d. Leased lines are Layer 7 standards.

9. Historically, which of the following models were the earliest models used in corporate networks?

   a. Vendor models

   b. TCP/IP

   c. OSI

   d. ATM

10. Which of the following statements is true when comparing the OSI and the TCP/IP model as defined in RFC 1122?

   a. Two layer names match.

   b. The lower four layers of TCP/IP define the same kinds of functions as the matching layer numbers from OSI.

   c. The TCP/IP five-layer model is old and has been replaced by the seven-layer OSI model.

   d. The TCP/IP application layer defines functions that match closely to only two OSI layers (application and presentation).

11. A network engineer connects two PCs (PC1 and PC2) using Ethernet NICs and an Ethernet cable that has copper wires inside. The two PCs communicate successfully. Which of the following happens when PC1 sends bits to PC2?

   a. PC1's NIC uses its decoder.

   b. The PCs use one wire to create a circuit to send data from PC1 to PC2.

   c. The PCs use two wires to create a circuit to send data from PC1 to PC2.

   d. PC1 converts the bits to sound waves, and the NIC uses an A/D converter to send the data over the cable.

12. A TCP/IP network includes an Ethernet LAN with 10 PCs uses a LAN switch. PC1 sends data intended for an app running on PC2. Which of the following mechanisms does Ethernet define so that PC2 receives and processes the data?

   a. The Ethernet header lists PC2's MAC address so that PC2 will realize that the data is meant for PC2.

   b. Ethernet defines MAC addresses, but when used in a TCP/IP network, it does not use the addresses, instead relying on IP addresses.

   c. Ethernet works as a broadcast network, with no data-link addresses, so all devices (including PC2) receive the data.

   d. PC1 cannot send data directly to PC2 in this network.

13. Two network pros are having a conversation about some issues in a network. They discuss some issues related to how PPP forwards data, so they happen to be discussing the data structure that includes the PPP header and trailer. Which of the following terms do they use?

   a. Segment

   b. Packet

   c. Frame

   d. Datagram

14. Which of the following are true facts about IP addresses? (Choose two answers.)

   a. 48 bits in length

   b. Can be written in DDN format

   c. Are listed in the data-link trailer

   d. Used by routers to make a forwarding decision

15. Which of the following answers is true about Ethernet MAC addresses?

   a. 48 bits in length

   b. Can be written in DDN format

   c. Is listed in the data-link trailer

   d. Used by routers to make a forwarding decision

16. Which of the following statements is true comparing LANs and WANs? (Choose two answers.)

    a. LANs generally connect devices that are nearer to each other, compared to WANs.

    b. WANs are purchased, and LANs are leased.

    c. WANs generally connect devices that are nearer to each other, compared to LANs.

    d. LANs are purchased, and WANs are leased.

17. Which of the following answers list true facts about the data link layer of TCP/IP? (Choose two answers.)

    a. It focuses mostly on the endpoint devices, rather than the network that sits between the endpoints.

    b. Two TCP/IP data-link protocols are Ethernet and PPP.

    c. Data-link protocols define addresses that identify devices connected to the underlying physical link.

    d. None of the answers is correct.

18. Which of the following answers list true facts about the network layer of TCP/IP? (Choose two answers.)

    a. It focuses mostly on the network between endpoints, rather than the endpoints.

    b. The two primary protocols are TCP and IP.

    c. IP provides logical addressing and routing services.

    d. None of the answers is correct.

19. Which of the following answers lists true facts about the transport layer of TCP/IP?

    a. It focuses mostly on the network between endpoints, rather than the endpoints.

    b. The two primary protocol options are TCP and IP.

    c. TCP provides error recovery services to application layer protocols that use TCP.

    d. None of the answers is correct.

20. A PC user opens a web browser and sends a request to a web server to load a new web page. Three routers forward the data as it passes from client to server. Consider the data plus all headers and trailers that go from the web client to the web server. Which of the following headers go all the way from the web client to the web server? (Choose three answers.)

    a. Data-link header

    b. Network layer header

    c. Transport layer header

    d. Application layer header

Define the Key Terms

The following key terms include the ideas most important to the big ideas in this chapter. To review, without looking at the book or your notes, write a definition for each term, focusing on the meaning, not the wording. Then review your definition compared to your notes, this chapter, and the glossary.

Key Terms for Chapter 3

TCP/IP network	encoding	IP routing
networking standard	header	frame
TCP/IP model	trailer	packet
open networking model	leased line	
Open Systems Interconnection (OSI) model	Internet Protocol (IP)	
	IP address	

List the Words Inside Acronyms

The following are the most common acronyms discussed in this chapter. As a way to review those terms, simply write down the words that each letter represents in each acronym.

Acronyms for Chapter 3

TCP/IP	LAN	RFC
TCP	WAN	OSI
IP	IEEE	DDN
HTTP	ITU	CO

Create Mind Maps

For this chapter, create two similar styles of mind maps, as follows:

1. Create one mind map each for the three upper layers of the TCP/IP model. In each map, list any descriptive term you think relates to that layer on the left, and specific standards from that layer on the right. As always, use as few words as possible. The goal is not to describe the idea but to list enough to remind you of the idea, to help build connections in your brain.

   You can list terms not mentioned in this chapter, but note those in your mind map was well.

   For example, for the network layer's mind map, on the left, list "Internet," because it is the name used for this same layer in the original TCP/IP model, and list "IP routing," because the network layer defines routing. On the right, list "IP" because IP is a TCP/IP network layer protocol.

2. Create one similar mind map for the combined bottom two layers of TCP/IP, because some standards span both Layer 1 and Layer 2. Again, list descriptive terms on the left and specific standards on the right. Also, list LAN information in the upper part of the map and WAN-specific information at the bottom. Figure 3-33 shows the organization of the information in this mind map.

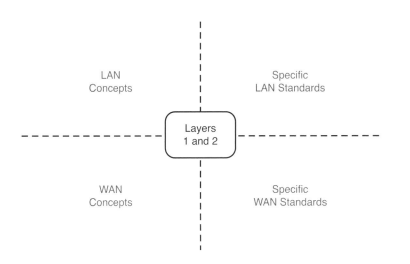

FIGURE 3-33

Mind Map Organization

Define Other Terms

Define the following additional terms from this chapter, and check your answers in the glossary:

central office

coder

coding rule

de facto standard

decode

deencapsulation

dotted-decimal notation (DDN)

encapsulation

encode

error recovery

hardware spec

informational RFC

Institute of Electrical and Electronic Engineers

interface

international standard

International Telecommunications Union

Internet Protocol (IP)

interoperable

IP packet

IP router

IP routing

IP routing table

International Organization for Standardization

LAN switch

layer

local-area network

MAC address

national standard

prestandard

protocol

Request for Comments

standard

standard RFC

standards body

Transmission Control Protocol

vendor group standard

vendor group/vendor consortium

vendor standard

Wi-Fi Alliance

wide-area network

wiring closet

working group

vendor networking model

networking model

Complete the Tables and Lists from Memory

Print a copy of Appendix B, "Memory Tables" (which you can find online at www.pearsonitcertification.com/title/9780789748454), or at least the section for this chapter, and complete the tables and lists from memory. Appendix C, "Memory Tables Answer Key," also online, includes completed tables and lists to check your work.

Chapter 4

Transmitting Bits

When two friends talk, one talks and the other listens and understands. Thinking about what happens in that simple communication can give you some perspectives about this chapter. First, one person speaks using his mouth. The sound travels through the air, and the listener uses his ears to hear those sounds. Also, those sounds have no meaning unless each person uses his brain as well. The talker must first think of the right words to say, using a particular language, and the listener must use his brain to interpret those sounds as words and ideas.

In computer networks, neighboring network nodes send data to each other over a link, with a process similar in some ways to those two friends talking. The sending node acts like the person talking, and the receiving node acts like the person who is listening. Instead of speaking sound waves, the sending node transmits some other kind of energy, usually electricity, light, or radio waves. The energy passes either through the air, similar to sound waves, or over a cable. The receiving node of course does not have ears, but it has the equivalent: hardware to sense the energy to interpret that energy as a bunch of bits.

The nodes on the links have to use their brains (processors), using rules about what the energy means, similar to how humans have to use their brains to interpret sounds as part of some language. The sending node must use its processors to choose what energy to send to represent a set of bits. The listening mode must do the reverse, interpreting the received energy to mean the exact same original bits. And if the two nodes do not agree to the rules, they cannot communicate, just like when two people try to speak when they do not know the same language.

This chapter focuses only on how to move bits over a single link; however, before getting into those details, it helps to remember some key facts about the goal of the network.

Figure 4-1 shows the general idea of how, in a TCP/IP network, the nodes forward IP packets from one host to another. The nodes (routers in this example) in the network each make a choice of where to send the packet next so that the data arrives at the correct destination. So while this chapter focuses on how to move bits over a single physical link, always keep the big goal of the network in mind: delivering data from one computer to another.

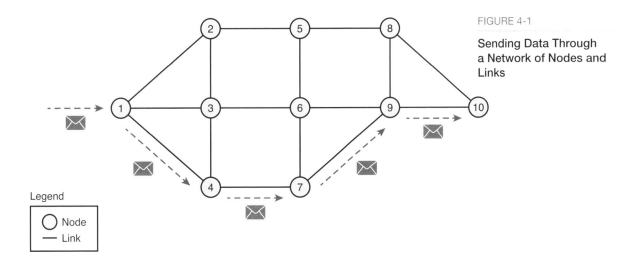

FIGURE 4-1

Sending Data Through a Network of Nodes and Links

Legend

○ Node
— Link

This chapter focuses on three different types of individual physical links, with one section for each type:

- The first section, "Sending Bits with Electricity and Copper Wires," focuses on links that use electricity and copper wires, while also discussing matter to the other types of links as well.

- The second section, "Sending Bits with Light and Fiber-Optic Cables," focuses on optical links, which send data by shining light down thin strands of glass inside a cable.

- The third and final major section of this chapter, "Sending Bits with Radio Waves and No Cables," looks at wireless links, which use radio waves to transmit bits without using a cable.

Chapter Outline

Sending Bits with Electricity and Copper Wires

Sending Bits with Light and Fiber-Optic Cables

Sending Bits with Radio Waves and No Cables

Chapter Summary

Chapter Review Activities

Objectives

- Draw simple examples of how to transmit data using a different frequency, amplitude, or phase in an electrical signal.

- Explain how networking nodes create electrical circuits using NICs, switch ports, and cables.

- Show the basic relationship of network encoding, bit rate, and bit time.

- Describe half-duplex and full-duplex concepts on network links that use either one or two electrical circuits between two nodes.

- Describe the parts of a UTP cable and connector that support a 10BASE-T link.

- Draw the Ethernet 10BASE-T cabling pinouts used between a PC NIC and an Ethernet switch port.

- Describe the two innermost parts of a fiber-optic cable, and show their roles in allowing light to pass through the cable.

- Compare and contrast the two common types of fiber-optic transmitters and two general categories of fiber-optic cables.

Objectives continued

- List common reasons for using fiber-optic cables instead of copper cables in networks.
- Draw a diagram of the relationships between mobile phones, mobile phone radio towers, the mobile network, the worldwide telephone network, the Internet, home telephones, and web servers in the Internet.

- Compare and contrast mobile phones, mobile company radio towers, wireless LAN NICs, and wireless LAN access points.
- Create an example demonstrating how devices share a wireless LAN using CSMA/CA.

Key Terms

electrical circuit

frequency

amplitude

phase

bit time

encoding scheme

unshielded twisted-pair (UTP)

core

cladding

radio waves

wireless WAN

wireless LAN

access point

Sending Bits with Electricity and Copper Wires

LANs and WANs make use of electricity and copper wires to send data. Today, most LANs follow Ethernet standards, and Ethernet allows both copper cables and fiber-optic (glass) cables. In terms of popularity, most Ethernet LAN links use copper cables instead of fiber-optic cable. Chapter 3, "TCP/IP Networks," already introduced several basic concepts of how Ethernet LANs use copper cables, as seen in Figure 3-15.

WANs also use a mix of copper and fiber cables, but many links between telcos and their customers use copper cabling. For example, a leased line acts like an electrical circuit between two endpoints, but physically it exists as a shorter cable from the telco central office (CO) near each site connected to each customer site. (See Chapter 3's Figure 3-21 for a reminder.) The telco typically uses copper cabling from the CO to the customer site.

The first major section of this chapter expands Chapter 3's discussion of copper physical links. The following sections look at some basic facts about electricity, including how the electricity can be described and measured. It goes on to show how networking devices use the electricity to communicate, by changing the electrical signal over time, with the receiving device listening for those changes.

The first two topics in these sections do not show any one specific standard; instead, these topics use simpler electrical examples that keep the focus on the big ideas related to sending bits in networks. These sections end with some specifics about a couple of Ethernet LAN standards.

Fundamentals of Electrical Circuits

To send data over a link using electricity, nodes vary the electrical signal sent over a link over time. But how does that work? How can a node send electricity to another node? The following sections answer these and other basic questions about electricity and electrical circuits.

In particular, this topic looks at the basics of two types of electrical circuits: *direct current (DC)* circuits and *alternating current (AC)* circuits. In those discussions, the text focuses on the electrical features that nodes can change over time to encode data over the link. These sections also show how nodes physically create a loop (circuit) using network cabling.

Direct Current Electrical Circuits

An **electrical circuit** must first exist as a complete loop of material over which electricity can flow. For example, with copper wire, you cannot create an electrical flow over one wire with its ends connected to nothing. If you put it into a complete loop, electricity can flow.

The material used to create the loop (circuit), for example, copper wire, cannot be just any material; it must be a good electrical *conductor*. When electricity flows over a circuit, the electrons in the molecules of the material actually move out of one molecule and into another. This process moves the electrical current around the circuit. Some materials, like copper, work well for these moving electrons, so those materials make good electrical conductors. (Materials that resist electrons moving, like rubber, are called electrical *insulators*; they also have important uses as well.)

An electrical circuit also needs a source of electricity. For example, a battery stores chemicals that, when connected to a circuit, convert the chemical energy into electrical power. That causes an electrical current to flow around the circuit. Figure 4-2 shows the idea, with a battery as the power source, a copper wire as the conductor, and the wire connected to the leads of the battery to complete the loop.

FIGURE 4-2

Simple Direct Current Circuit Using a Battery

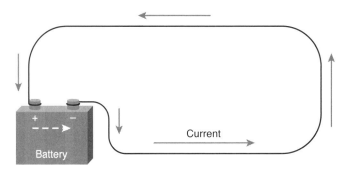

The figure shows the battery, the wire, and some arrows to show the direction in which the electrical current flows. First, the knobs on top of the battery shape in the drawing provide a good place to connect the wires to make a loop. Those knobs on top of the battery are the same kind of positive (+) and negative (–) leads you see on the batteries you can buy at the store. Also, note that the wire does not literally touch end to end, but the inside of the battery completes the circuit.

Although the circuit in Figure 4-2 does nothing useful, most electrical circuits exist for some purpose. For example, maybe you need some light, so you could literally connect a light bulb to that same circuit and the light bulb would illuminate. Figure 4-3 shows the idea.

FIGURE 4-3

Powering a Light Bulb with a DC Circuit (Light Bulb Icon © Mr_Vector)

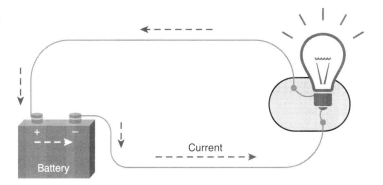

The circuits in the last two figures show a measurable electrical current flowing in a particular direction. *Electrical current* is the amount of electricity that flows past a single point on the circuit. In some ways, you can think of current as the amount of electron flow in the circuit. The current always flows away from the negative (–) lead on the battery in the circuit and toward the positive (+) lead.

The circuit also has a measurable electrical *voltage* when the current is flowing. Also called *electromotive force*, the voltage represents the difference in electrical force between two points. That definition of voltage sounds formal, but the basic concept can be understood in a couple of ways.

First, think back to science classes, and the fact that like charges repel and unlike charges attract. In this case, the negative (–) lead on the battery pushes the electrons (which are negative). So the negative lead pushes current flow away from the negative lead. The positive lead on the battery attracts electrons, so the positive lead pulls current toward the positive lead. Voltage is the total effect of that pushing and pulling of current around the circuit. The higher the voltage, the bigger the electrical force.

An analogy from the world of sports can help. Think about any sport where the players push each other; American football is a great example. When two players push each other with the same force, neither moves. When one player pushes with more force, the players move in the direction of that greater force. The movement stops only when the players again apply equal force, or when they simply stop pushing each other. Voltage is electrical force, and the electrical current moves in the direction from the greater force toward the lesser force.

The examples so far in this section all used *direct current (DC)*. With DC, the current flows in one direction around the circuit, all the time. Most devices that use batteries create a DC circuit, and many computing and networking devices use DC power to run the electronics. The next section looks at a different type of electrical circuit, with alternating current (AC).

Alternating Current: Frequency, Amplitude, and Phase

Both direct current (DC) and alternating current (AC) circuits have many uses today. DC circuits power many devices, particularly those that use batteries. Many computing and networking devices use DC power to run the electronics. On the other hand, the electrical power grid in many countries, including the United States, uses AC circuits. As a result, most light bulbs in lamps and light fixtures run on AC circuits. And most importantly, networking devices often use AC circuits to communicate over links.

The big obvious difference between AC and DC is that in DC circuits, the current flows in one direction only, but in AC circuits, the current changes (alternates) direction over time. With an AC circuit, the device that creates the electricity on the circuit (usually not a battery) can change the polarity on its leads. In other words, it can change its negative lead to positive and vice versa, changing the direction it pushes and pulls the current around the loop.

ON THE SIDE:
Figure 4-3 shows the equivalent of the wiring of a flashlight. You can try the same thing at home with a battery, light bulb, and metal paper clips.

AC circuits change the current to the opposite direction, but the process takes a small amount of time. As a result, when you graph the voltage over time, the graph of an AC current shows a continuously changing voltage, while a graph of a DC circuit shows a constant voltage.

Figure 4-4 shows two example graphs, with a DC circuit on the left and an AC circuit on the right. Both use 1 volt. The DC graph on the left shows a constant +1 volt signal. The graph on the right shows the AC circuit slowly rising to +1 volt, falling to 0, and falling to –1 volt (which simply means 1 volt, but in the opposite direction), repeating itself over time. The resulting wave on the right is a *sine wave*.

FIGURE 4-4

Graphs of 1 Volt (Y Axis) Over Time: DC (Left) Versus AC (Right)

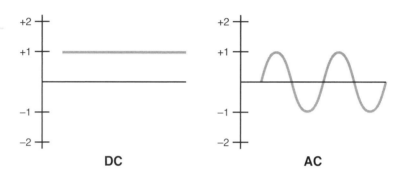

To send data, different networking physical layer standards can change the *amplitude*, *frequency*, *phase*, *period*, and *wavelength* of the AC electrical signal. Figure 4-5 shows a graph that begins to define some of these terms.

FIGURE 4-5

Graphs of AC Circuit: Amplitude, Period, Frequency

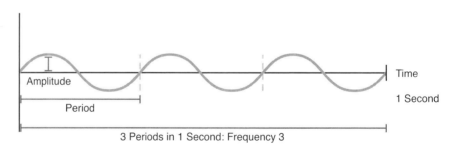

ON THE SIDE: An *oscilloscope* is an electronic testing device that graphs electrical signals with graphs similar to those shown in Figure 4-4.

First, just to be clear about the graph itself, the graph shows voltage on the Y axis and time on the X axis. Over time, the voltage ranges from some maximum positive voltage (meaning the current flows in one direction) to the maximum negative voltage (meaning the current has alternated to the other direction).

The word **amplitude**, a term from the math world, refers to the height of the curve above the centerline (the X axis). With a graph that shows voltage over time, the amplitude is the maximum voltage.

Next, the term **frequency** refers to the number of times the entire repeating wave happens in 1 second. First, note the light dashed vertical lines; these show the end of one complete wave and the beginning of the next. Figure 4-5 shows three complete waves (three cycles). The graph also shows a 1-second marker at the end of the third cycle. So, in this case, three complete waves happen in 1 second, for a frequency of three cycles per second, also known as 3 *hertz*.

Finally, the term *period* (short for time period) refers to the time, in seconds, to complete one cycle. In this case, the period is 1/3 seconds. (Note that the period = 1/frequency, and frequency = 1/period.)

Networking standards use AC circuits to send data in part because the nodes can easily control and change the amplitude, frequency, period, and other facts about the AC signal. To send bits, networking standards must define rules that basically state that one electrical signal means binary 0 and another different signal means binary 1. The people who create these physical layer standards have many AC circuit characteristics that can be used to represent bit values as different electrical signals.

> **AUTHOR'S NOTE:**
> The physical layer standard that defines what energy signal means binary 0 and what signal means binary 1 is called an *encoding scheme*.

Figure 4-6 shows the AC signal features most commonly used in networking encoding schemes. Each box in the figure shows two sample signals. One could be used by an encoding scheme to mean binary 0, and the other could mean binary 1.

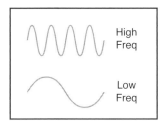
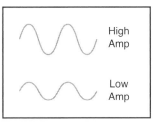
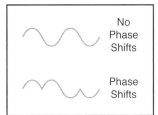

Frequency Shift   **Amplitude Shift**   **Phase Shift**

FIGURE 4-6

Encoding Options: Frequency, Amplitude, and Phase Shifts

The left box in the figure shows frequency, which refers to the number of times the sine wave repeats per second. Electronic devices can easily control the frequency, changing from a higher frequency (more repeats of the cycle) to a lower frequency (less repeats of the cycle). The encoding scheme could assign one signal as binary 0 and the other as binary 1.

The center box shows the amplitude shifting or changing to encode data. The electronic devices can also change the amount of voltage in the circuit, which changes the amplitude. Over time, the voltage could be varied to one of two values, with each representing either 0 or 1.

Finally, the box on the right of Figure 4-6 introduces a feature of AC circuits not yet discussed in this chapter: the phase of the signal. The **phase** refers to different places on the sine-wave curve. Normally, the graph of voltage over time changes with a predictable sine wave, as shown at the top part of the right box. Electronic devices can change the signal so that the graph jumps to another point in the curve. This jump, or shift, to another phase of the curve is called a *phase shift*; encoding schemes can then use different phase shifts to encode data. For example, in the right side of Figure 4-6, the encoding scheme could send the top signal for 0 (no phase shifts) with the bottom signal (two phase shifts) to mean binary 1. (This process is typically known as *phase shift keying*.)

While this topic has focused on the basic concept of how to encode data using frequency, amplitude, and phase, you will likely see two other words as part of the terminology related to encoding: *shift* and *modulation*. Depending on the specific physical layer standard, the scheme on the left of Figure 4-6 might be called *frequency modulation (FM)* or *frequency shift keying (FSK)*. In the center, the terms might be *amplitude modulation (AM)* or *amplitude shift keying (ASK)*. Plus, you will see many variations, but the terms *modulation* and *shift* in this case are just a reminder that something changes in the signal to encode bits.

Table 4-1 summarizes the definition of some of these key features of an AC signal's graph that network encoding schemes use to send data.

TABLE 4-1
Common Features Used by Encoding Schemes

Wave Feature	Definition of the Graph	Electrical Feature It Represents
Amplitude	Maximum height of the curve over the centerline	Voltage
Frequency	The number of complete waves (cycles) per second (in hertz)	Speed with which current alternates directions
Phase	A single location in the repeating wave	Voltage jumps, which make the signal graph jump to a new phase
Period	The time (width on the X axis) for one complete wave to complete	The time for the voltage to change from the maximum positive voltage back to the same point again

Creating Electrical Circuits Using Network Cabling

Before a node can send data by changing the frequency, amplitude, or phase, first the node needs to create a circuit or loop between itself and the neighboring node. To do so, the engineer working on the network connects a cable to the two nodes. The cable has an outer plastic cover, called a *jacket*, which holds all the wires, called *conductors*. The two nodes can use a pair of wires and connect their ends together to create a loop.

Although most people only see the outer part of the cable (the outer jacket), most networking discussions focus on the wires inside the cables. First, the thin copper metal wires are brittle. Also, each wire inside a cable needs to be easily identified. To help solve both problems, each wire has flexible plastic coding to help protect the wire, but with a different color for each wire. The color coding lets the cable technicians look at a cable and easily identify a particular wire on both ends of the cable. Figure 4-7 shows a photo of the wires inside a cable used with Ethernet LANs.

FIGURE 4-7

Photo of Wires Inside a Networking Cable (© Sergey Minaev)

The connectors on the ends of the cable also play a big role. The connectors make for an easy connection to the node, because the node will have a matching opening called a *socket*.

Unfortunately, the networking world uses many different terms to refer to the same basic hardware part and concept: a place where a networking cable connects to the networking device. For example, PCs use *network interface cards (NIC)*. LAN switches often use the word *port*, with each socket on the side of a switch acting like a separate NIC with a separate socket. Routers typically use the term *interface* for this same physical socket. (This chapter keeps the wording generic by just referring to the node as a whole in most cases.)

Beyond connecting a networking cable to two nodes, the two nodes must agree to use the same pair of wires to create a circuit. In many cases, the networking cable has many wires, and sometimes the cable has more wires than the nodes need to use. Figure 4-8 shows the idea. In this case, the cable has four wires, two used and two unused. The hardware for each node must agree which two wires to use and which two to ignore. Then, for the two wires they choose to use, the nodes loop the ends of the two chosen wires together to create a circuit.

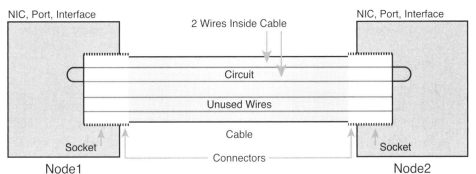

FIGURE 4-8

Physical Components to Create an Electrical Circuit Between Two Nodes

Finally, the loop or circuit shown in Figure 4-8 cannot alone create an electrical circuit: Something has to create an electrical current. The node that needs to transmit data creates the electrical signal, changing the signal over time to encode different bit values. The other device receives the data by sensing the electrical signal, watching for changes in electricity over time, to interpret those changes as bits. The part of the node that sends the data is called a *transmitter*, and the part that listens for the signal to receive the bits is called the *receiver*. Figure 4-9 shows the terms and idea with a single circuit.

FIGURE 4-9

Transmitter Generating a Current to Send; Receiver Sensing a Current to Receive

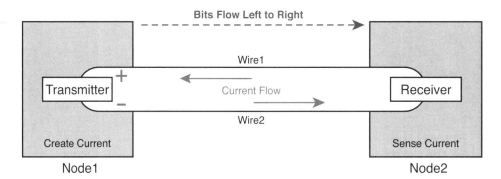

Sending Data Over Electrical Circuits

The topics under this heading take a deeper look at several issues related to how nodes send data. First, the neighboring nodes must agree to the speed or bit rate at which the bits are sent. They must also agree to and use the same encoding scheme. Additionally, they might need to use multiple electrical circuits. And all these actions happen in a world in which all the energy around the cables can actually interfere with sending data over the cables.

Bit Rates Over One Circuit

The **bit rate** (or *link speed*) defines the number of bits sent over the link per second. Different standards define different bit rates. For example, Ethernet LANs include standards for bit rates of 10 million bits per second (10 Mbps), 100 Mbps, 1000 Mbps (also known as 1 gigabit per second, or 1 Gbps), and even higher speeds. Whatever the type of link, the link has a known bit rate.

The bit rate has an impact on how nodes send data over an electrical circuit. Sure, the encoding scheme tells the sender and receiver what electrical signals represent a binary 0 and 1. However, the bit rate tells the encoding scheme how quickly to change the signal to represent the next bit.

The following example shows how bit rate and encoding scheme work together. In this example, the bit rate is 10 bits per second (10 bps). The encoding scheme states that a binary 1 should be shown as a +2 volts and a binary 0 as +1 volt. With a need to send 10 bits per second, the encoder must make a choice every 1/10 of a second. Figure 4-10 shows an example of sending 10 bits: 1010011001. The figure shows a graph of the voltage levels over time.

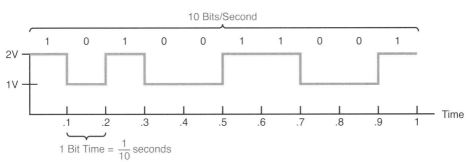

FIGURE 4-10

Example Where the Encoder Changes the Signal Every Bit Time

The example shows two key concepts: the *bit rate* and the *bit time*. The bit rate lists the number of bits sent during 1 second. The bit time is the time that passes while the sender encodes 1 bit onto the circuit. The two numbers are related, unsurprisingly: The bit time is the inverse of the bit rate. For example, to send 10 bps, the encoder should send the electrical signal for 1/10 of a second for each bit. To send at 100 bps, the encoder sends a signal for the bit time 1/100 of a second for each bit.

While the encoding scheme tells the sender exactly what electrical signal to use for a 0 or 1, the bit time tells the encoder how often to change that signal for the next bit. For example, in Figure 4-10, the first 4 bits were 1010. The sender started with +2 volts, to encode a binary 1. After one bit time (1/10 of a second in this example), the sender had a choice: Stay at 2 volts for another binary 1 or change to 1 volt for a binary 0. It changed to 1 volt to send a 0 in the second bit time.

The bit rate not only impacts the sender, but the sender and receiver must also agree to the bit rate as well. In fact, the sender and receiver must agree to use the same bit rate, or the link simply will not pass bits correctly. If the sender sends at 10 bps, and therefore can change the signal every 1/10 of a second, the receiver better also sample the incoming signal every 1/10 of a second, so it receives at 10 bps.

For an example of what might happen with a speed mismatch, imagine that a sending node sends bits at 1000 bps, with a bit time of 1/1000 of a second. If the receiving node processed the electrical signal as if only 100 bps were being sent, the receiver would process the incoming signal for a new bit every 1/100 of a second. After a single second, the sender would think it had sent 1000 bits, but the receiver would think it had received only 100 bits.

Encoding Bits Over One Circuit

An **encoding scheme** works like a language. When you need to communicate with someone standing beside you, you do not just make whatever random noises come to mind and hope the person next to you understands. You say something in a language, and if the other person knows that language, the communication works. In networking, the encoding scheme defines the electrical equivalent: the electricity that means a 1 or a 0.

ON THE SIDE:
The bit rate and encoding scheme are purposefully simplistic in this example to keep the focus on how they work together; no real networking standard uses 10 bps or this encoding scheme.

ON THE SIDE: If you pursue networking as a focus area, you will learn of encoding schemes that send more than 1 bit for each unique energy signal. This section's description of encoding and bit time assumes that the encoder sends 1 bit per signal.

The various encoding schemes used on electrical links take advantage of many different electrical characteristics on the link. For example, Figure 4-10 already shows one encoding scheme that simply uses a higher voltage to mean 1 and a lower voltage to mean 0. (The voltage changes make a change to the amplitude of the graph, so it is a form of amplitude modulation or amplitude shift keying.) The sender changes (or modulates or shifts) to the correct voltage at the beginning of each new bit time, and the receiver senses the voltage at each bit time, interpreting the voltage level as either a binary 1 or 0.

Encoding schemes can also use frequency changes in the AC signal to encode bits. Earlier, Figure 4-5 showed the idea of an AC signal that changes over time, and with the number of times that wave completes in 1 second being the frequency. The encoding scheme can use different frequencies, one to represent binary 1 and another to represent binary 0. Figure 4-11 shows just such an example, sending 1010, with the lower frequency representing binary 1 and the higher frequency for binary 0.

FIGURE 4-11

Frequency Shift Keying: Low Frequency = 1, High Frequency = 0

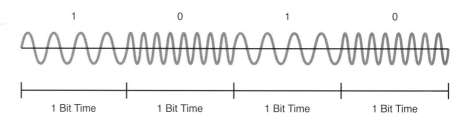

> **ON THE SIDE:** The examples in Figures 4-10 and 4-11 show the basics of digital amplitude modulation (AM) and frequency modulation (FM), respectively. AM and FM radio stations use similar concepts to transmit sound as represented with radio waves.

Before leaving the topic of encoding schemes, look at one more example encoding scheme, one used on some of the early Ethernet standards: *Manchester encoding*. Manchester encoding does not choose one electrical signal at the beginning of the bit time but plans to change the signal in the middle of the bit time. The Manchester encoding rules follow this logic:

- **To encode 0:** Start high and transition low in the middle of the bit time
- **To encode 1:** Start low and transition high in the middle of the bit time

Figure 4-12 shows an example in which the sender transmits bits 101000.

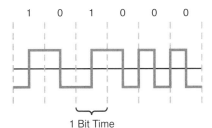

FIGURE 4-12

Manchester Encoding: 0 = High to Low, 1 = Low to High

To interpret the figure, think about each bit separately inside each bit time. The dashed lines show the six bit times in this example. For the 2 bits noted as binary 1s, note that the signal begins its bit time in a lower voltage state and moves in the middle of the bit time to the higher voltage. For the four binary 0s, the signal starts in the higher state and moves to the lower state. Also, note that on the last few bits, at the end of the bit time, the signal had to transition from the low to the high voltage state to be ready for the next bit time.

Sending Bits Over Multiple Circuits

The two nodes connected to the same link typically need to send data in both directions. Some encoding schemes allow the nodes to use a single electrical circuit, and both nodes can send and receive at the same time. However, some encoding schemes get confused when trying to speak and listen at the same time over the same electrical circuit, similar to how humans get confused when two people try to talk at the same time.

In networking, if the encoding scheme works in only one direction at a time (on a single circuit), two solutions typically exist: Take turns using that one circuit, or use different circuits for each direction.

Taking turns, called *half duplex* in the networking world, works well. Node1 sends while node2 listens. After node1 is finished, node2 sends and node1 listens. The physical layer standard has to define the method the nodes use to decide who speaks next. The good news is that it works, and it only requires a single electrical circuit, and therefore a single pair of wires, as seen earlier in Figure 4-9.

Half duplex does not perform as well as the alternative: full duplex. With *full duplex*, both endpoints can send at the same time, enabled because the endpoints use multiple wire pairs. Using multiple pairs allows multiple electrical circuits, so the encoders/decoders do not get confused. It works like a 2-lane road: one lane for each direction. Figure 4-13 shows the idea, with the top circuit in the figure for sending data left to right and the bottom circuit for sending data right to left.

FIGURE 4-13

**Full Duplex Using
Two Pairs, One for
Each Direction**

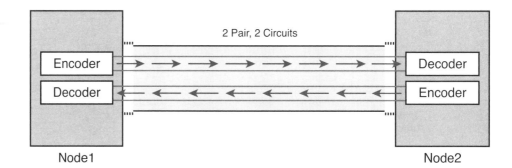

Full duplex works faster because neither side has to wait to send data. Half duplex tended to be used in earlier days, when some physical links only had one pair of wires or when equipment required only one device to send at a time. Today, modern LAN and WAN standards typically expect the cables to have enough wire pairs to support full duplex. For example, the leased lines introduced in Chapter 2, "Introduction to Computer Networking," typically use two pairs in the cable, as do many Ethernet LAN standards.

Possible Problems When Sending Data Using Electricity

Many different kinds of problems can occur to keep those wired links from passing data. This section looks at two of the biggest problems: distance and noise.

By way of analogy, think about sound for a moment. Imagine that you are sitting in a coffee shop one morning with a good friend. You can probably hear each other talking just fine; there is little extra noise around, and the distance between you is short.

Next, you leave the coffee shop, and you take off running, but your friend stands still. Within a minute or two, even if your friend is yelling at the top of his lungs, you cannot hear him anymore. Why? Distance. The sound waves attenuate (fade away) over distances, to the point where you cannot hear the sound.

Finally, that night, you and the same friend go to a rock concert. You might be sitting even closer than you were at the coffee shop, so distance is not a problem, but you cannot hear a word he says. Why? Noise. The sound from the concert is far stronger than your voices.

Network links suffer from similar distance, noise, and other problems. For example, many Ethernet standards limit copper Ethernet links to 100 meters, partly based on the fact that electrical signals attenuate (fade). In other words, the link from a PC to an Ethernet LAN switch, with a copper cable, can be no more than 100 meters. Other links can connect that switch to other devices, and the total length can be more than 100 meters, but no one copper Ethernet cable could be more than 100 meters long (using those standards). Other standards for other technologies have other distance restrictions. So, when planning a network, you have to be aware of distance limitations.

Network links also suffer from electrical noise. Anyone who has used electronic devices has probably experienced the effects of electrical noise: poor images on the TV, poor reception on a phone, noise on a music player, and so on.

One common source of electrical noise for networking links is called *electromagnetic interference (EMI)*. Any electrical current in a circuit creates magnetic energy outside the electrical circuit. Then, that magnetic energy, when it goes through any material that conducts electricity, creates another electrical current. EMI acts as if the electricity jumps from one conductor to the next.

Networking cables help prevent the noisy effects of EMI in many ways, including using *shielding*. Shielded cables have extra material that acts to stop EMI effects. Shielded cables have more material, and take more time to make, so they cost more than unshielded cables.

Using *twisted-pair* cabling also helps stop EMI effects. Remember, a single cable typically has enough wires to support multiple electrical circuits inside the one cable, so EMI can also happen between circuits inside the same cable. Because of the physics of how EMI works, if the two wires used in one circuit are twisted together, it cancels out most of the EMI given off by that wire pair. Most copper networking cables today use twisted-pair cabling.

ON THE SIDE: Most national governments have regulations for products that use electricity so that the products do not cause too much EMI.

Using Ethernet LANs as an Example

So far, this chapter has shown a lot of ideas about sending data using copper wires, but it has not listed a specific networking standard. This next topic looks at two specific Ethernet standards, called 10BASE-T and 100BASE-T, so that you can see examples of standards you will see in real networks.

The term *Ethernet* includes many related standards from the IEEE. Those standards use many different encoding schemes, many different bit rates, with many different kinds of cabling. The two standards that this section examines—10BASE-T and 100BASE-T—also use different encoding and speeds compared to each other. They were both introduced in the 1990s, both became very common in the market, and both actually matter in real networks even today. So these two standards make a good pair of standards to use as an example to move the discussion from theory to specific standards.

AUTHOR'S NOTE: Because this section discusses only some of the many Ethernet standards, but not all, the statements throughout this section do not apply to all Ethernet standards, but only to these two standards, unless otherwise noted.

Ethernet UTP Cables

10BASE-T and 100BASE-T use the same kind of cabling: **unshielded twisted-pair (UTP)**. The word *unshielded* refers to the fact that UTP cables have no added shielding materials to prevent EMI problems. The name also refers to the fact that the cable contains twisted pairs, and the twisting does reduce EMI effects between the twisted pair in the same cable (or in nearby cables). The lack of shielding makes the cables less expensive than shielded cables, lighter, and easier to install, and they work. Figure 4-7, earlier in the chapter, shows a photo of a UTP cable with four twisted pairs.

AUTHOR'S NOTE: Cables that have twisted pairs but also have shielding are called *shielded twisted-pair (STP)* cables.

Both 10BASE-T and 100BASE-T use two wire pairs in UTP cables, with one pair to transmit in each direction, as shown earlier in Figure 4-13.

Bit Rate and Encoding

Ethernet has a long history that spans from the 1970s to today. The IEEE standardized Ethernet in the 802.3 standard back in the early 1980s. Since that time, the IEEE has added many more Ethernet standards. All those standards have some common features, particularly the data link layer header details, that make all the standards be part of the Ethernet family. At the same time, many new Ethernet standards improved Ethernet versus older Ethernet standards, with faster speeds, different cabling, and different maximum cabling distances.

Figure 4-14 shows the progression of some of those Ethernet standards, using the common names rather than the less-used Ethernet standard names. The timeline shows the approximate dates in which the IEEE finalized the standards; in reality, each standard then took years to grow in the market and eventually drive prices down. (Also, note that 100BASE-T is part of the *Fast Ethernet* family listed in the figure.)

FIGURE 4-14

Timeline of the Introduction of Ethernet Standards

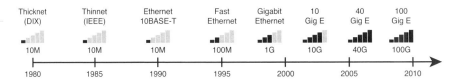

As you can see from the figure, 10BASE-T runs at 10 Mbps, and 100BASE-T runs at 100 Mbps.

> **AUTHOR'S NOTE:** The IEEE standard for 10BASE-T is 802.3i, and the standard for 100BASE-T is 802.3u. Most of the time, people use jargon like 10BASE-T and 100BASE-T more so than the formal standard numbers.

ON THE SIDE: Originally, 100BASE-T referred to a set of UTP-based 100-Mbps Ethernet standards, with the term 100BASE-Tx referring to one of those standards. Because 100BASE-Tx became the most popular of all the options, the term 100BASE-T today often refers to the popular 100BASE-Tx standard.

Over time, each time the IEEE creates new standards in the Ethernet family, each new standard uses a new encoding scheme. For example, 10BASE-T uses a Manchester encoding scheme like the one shown in Figure 4-12. Later, when the IEEE standardized 100BASE-T, it created a completely different encoding scheme.

Although the speed and encoding are related (different Ethernet speeds typically use different encoding), practically speaking, network engineers ignore Ethernet encoding and think about speed. Many Ethernet products (NICs, LAN switches, and routers) support multiple Ethernet standards that run at different speeds.

Network engineers must think about link speeds to be ready for the traffic loads in the network. However, they pretty much ignore the encoding used with various types of Ethernet: It simply works.

RJ-45 Connectors and Sockets

Those same Ethernet standards allow the use of RJ-45 connectors on the ends of the cable, with matching RJ-45 sockets on the NICs, switch ports, and other devices that use these two Ethernet standards.

The RJ-45 connectors give all wires in the cable specific places, called *pin positions*, in which to sit and connect to the nodes to which the cable connects. The RJ-45 connector has eight pin positions (or simply *pins*), which creates locations or lanes in the connector into which the wires in the cable align. At some point, when someone physically attaches the RJ-45 connector to the ends of a cable, he puts each wire into one of these standardized pin positions in the connector. Then the devices (nodes) on the end of the link, knowing those same standards and the literal physical location of each pin position, know exactly which wires sit in which pin positions in the connector.

Figure 4-15 shows a few examples of RJ-45 connectors and sockets (ports). Also, if you can find an Ethernet cable nearby, take a moment to look at the RJ-45 connector as well.

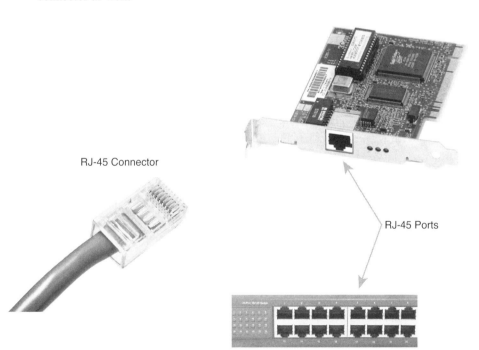

RJ-45 Connector

RJ-45 Ports

FIGURE 4-15

Example RJ-45 Connectors and Sockets (Ethernet NIC © Mark Jansen; LAN Switch © dbvirago; RJ-45 Connector © Mikko Pitkänen)

Ethernet Cabling Pinouts

Imagine that you just flew to a country that you have never been to before. You rent a car, and as you drive off the rental car lot, you realize that you do not know the traffic rules. Should you drive on the left or on the right? (You better figure out the answer before driving too far!)

The two Ethernet standards discussed in this section have a similar dilemma. The UTP cables and RJ-45 connectors support eight wires (four twisted pairs); some Ethernet standards (like Gigabit Ethernet) actually use all four pairs. For 10BASE-T and 100BASE-T, which two pairs do you use if the cable has four pairs? Where are the wires for those pairs, or asked differently, in which lanes of the connector, or which pins, are those wires? Unsurprisingly, Ethernet standards answer these questions.

The term *pinouts*, or *cabling pinouts*, refers to the entire answer of how each wire should be connected to each pin in a cable so that the Ethernet standards can use the right twisted pair to send in each direction.

To understand how pinouts work, use an example with a single link between two nodes: a PC and a switch. Figure 4-16 shows the general idea on the top of the figure. The bottom of the figure shows a representation of the RJ-45 socket on each device and the RJ-45 connector on each cable end, with the numbers that identify each pin.

FIGURE 4-16

Wires, Connector Pin Numbers, and Socket Pin Numbers

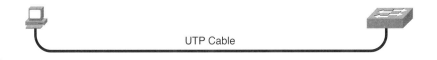

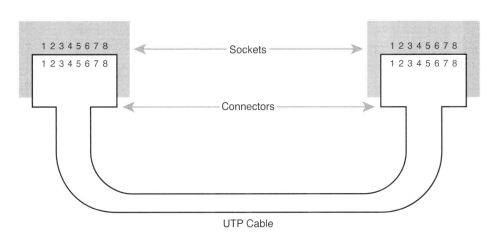

First, the pin numbers on each socket and matching connector always match. The PC socket on the left shows pins 1 through 8, left to right. The cable connector on that end of the cable also has pins 1 through 8, listed left to right. So when defining standards, and talking about pins, any one RJ-45 socket (in the node) matches the pin numbers on the connector (on the cable).

However, the cable itself can be made with any wire connected to any of the pin positions on opposite ends of the cable—even to different pins. For example, if the blue wire is connected to pin 1 on one side of the cable, it might be connected to pin 3 on the other end. Nothing prevents the person who makes the cable from putting the wrong wire into a particular pin position.

Ethernet standards solve the pin problem by defining a straight-through cabling pinout for links like the one in Figure 4-16. *Straight-through* means that each wire connects to the same pin number on both ends of the cable. That is, one wire connects to pin 1 on one side and also to pin 1 on the other side; another wire connects to pin 2 on both sides; and so on. Figure 4-17 shows the idea.

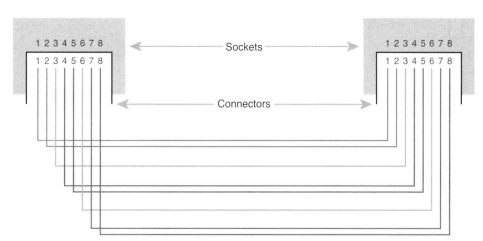

FIGURE 4-17

Conceptual Drawing of a Straight-Through Cable

Ethernet uses cabling standards from the Telecommunications Industry Association (TIA) to define the specific wires to use for cable pinouts. Ethernet UTP cables include up to four pairs, with each pair using a different color: green, blue, orange, and brown. Each pair uses one main color: One wire has a solid color, and the other has that same color with a white stripe. For example, for the green pair, one wire is solid green and the other is green-and-white striped. The TIA has several pinout standards, with each standard defining exactly which color wires go in which pin positions.

To create a straight-through cable, both ends of the cable just need to use the same TIA pinout standard. Figure 4-18 shows a common standard, T568A, which shows notes about the wires that should be in each pin position.

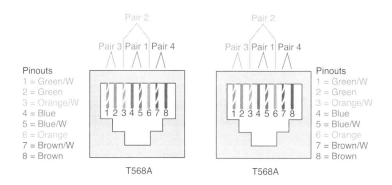

FIGURE 4-18

TIA Cable Pinouts: T568A on Each End Creates a Straight-Through Cable

Finally, how does Ethernet use these wires? A UTP cable with four pairs (8 wires) can support four circuits, but the 10BASE-T and 100BASE-T rules only use two pairs. As it turns out, Ethernet uses the following rules for these two standards:

- Use one pair at pins 1 and 2.
- Use one pair at pins 3 and 6.
- The PC sends, and the switch receives, on the pair at pins 1 and 2.
- The PC receives, and the switch sends, on the pair at pins 3 and 6.

Figure 4-19 shows the idea.

FIGURE 4-19

PC NIC Transmitting on Pair at 1,2 and Receiving on Pair 3,6

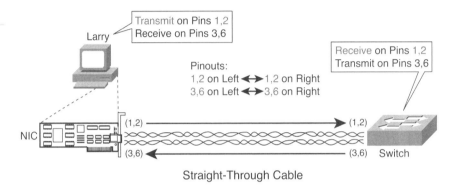

Straight-Through Cable

In summary, 10BASE-T and 100BASE-T use many similar concepts in how they send data. Both use UTP cabling with RJ-45 connectors. Both use the same cabling pinouts. When connecting a NIC to a LAN switch, both expect straight-through pinouts, and the NICs transmit on the pair at pins 1,2 and receive on the pair at pins 3,6. And although they use different speeds and different encoding, for practical purposes, you can ignore the encoding details and focus on the speed.

Sending Bits with Light and Fiber-Optic Cables

The first networks used copper cabling as the networking media. Over time, the networking industry added an alternative type of cabling: fiber-optic cabling. These cables create a dark tunnel in the middle of the cable, made from a very thin strand of glass, over which light can flow. As usual, the sender changes the light to send a 1 or 0, and the receiver watches for those changes to decide what bits were sent.

Fiber-optic cabling gives networks some big advantages, but with some negatives as well. First, fiber-optic cables typically support longer cabling distances than do copper cables; in some cases, a copper cable simply cannot be used because the distance is too long. Fiber-optic cables do not create EMI effects, and are not affected by them, so they work much better in places with lots of electrical noise.

However, fiber-optic cables, and the equipment on the nodes, typically cost more money than comparable copper cables and equipment.

Fiber-optic cables and the related devices play a big role in networks today. This second of three major sections of this chapter looks at how fiber-optic cabling works in a network. In particular, the following sections look at the basic mechanics of how nodes can encode and decode bits using light that shines through the middle of a fiber-optic cable. Then, these sections examine the parts of a cable, and then the text discusses the light transmitters on the ends of the cable. The final part of these sections looks at some examples of how both WANs and LANs use fiber optics.

> **AUTHOR'S NOTE:**
> Fiber-optic cabling can also go by these other names: *fiber*, *fiber cable*, *optical fiber*, and *optical cable*.

The Basics of Optical Transmission Using Fiber Optics

Imagine that your teacher gave you an at-home project to find a way to transmit bits using light. For your project, you and your friend use a flashlight and agree to send data to each other while standing on two hills 100 meters apart. Before going to the different hills, you agree to some rules. Every second, your friend will either have his flashlight on or off. Every second, you will look for the light. Every second, if you see a light, you will write down a 1; if you see no light, you will write down a 0.

Your test works well for a while, but then it does not. At first, the sky has storm clouds, but with no rain, so you can actually easily see the flashlight's light. The experiment works! But in a few minutes, the sun comes out, so it is a little more difficult to see the light.

Optical transmission using fiber-optic cables uses some of the same principles in this class experiment example. The sending node has a light. Both nodes connect to a fiber-optic cable, which is a cable over which light can pass. The two endpoints agree to use the same speed. And they use some basic encoding scheme, for example, with the sender illuminating the light to mean binary 1 and the sender turning off the light to mean binary 0. And the cable creates a nice dark tunnel, so it does not matter how cloudy or bright it is outside the cable, so to speak.

Figure 4-20 shows the idea of how the sender's light looks at every bit time when sending the bits 01011001. At each bit time, the sender either has the light on or off, depending on which bit value the sender wants to transmit. In this case, the encoding scheme states that the light being on means a binary 1.

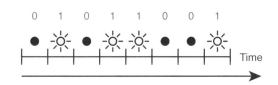

Encoding Bits Using Light On/Off

With this model, one node (the device sending data) uses some form of *optical transmitter*, while the other node (the device receiving data) uses some form of *optical receiver*. The transmitter uses either a *light emitting diode (LED)* or a *laser*. The receiving device senses the light using a device that acts a little like the human eye, typically called a *photodiode*.

Fiber-Optic Cables

Fiber-optic cables contain several parts that wrap around the glass fiber core in the center of the cable. The thin core, about as thin as a human hair, would easily break without some support. The cable has several layers that wrap around the core, essentially tubes of material, as shown in Figure 4-21.

FIGURE 4-21

Components of a Fiber-Optic Cable

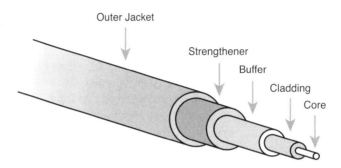

Outer Jacket
Strengthener
Buffer
Cladding
Core

Of all the parts of a fiber-optic cable, the **core** and **cladding** have a direct effect on how the light travels down the cable. The light source (the optical transmitter) on one end of the cable shines light into the core. Like the glass in window panes, the light can shine through the glass in the core. The cladding surrounds the core, for the entire length of the cable, and reflects the light into the core. The light waves reflect off the cladding, back into the core, until the light waves reach the other end of the cable. Figure 4-22 shows the idea.

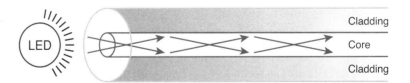

LED

Cladding
Core
Cladding

Fiber-optic cables work well to send light in one direction at a time, but not for two directions. The cable acts like a dark tunnel so that the nodes can easily see the light coming through the cable. If both ends were to try and shine a light down the cable, and look for light coming down the cable at the same time, the optical devices might not be able to tell whether the light was coming from the local node or the remote node.

Instead of using one fiber cable and enforcing half-duplex logic, most fiber links use a pair of cables, one for each direction. Each fiber NIC, port, interface, and so on has an interface that has two sockets: one for the transmit cable and one for the receive cable. When connecting the two devices, just make sure that each node's transmit socket connects to the same cable as the other node's receive socket, and vice versa. Figure 4-23 shows the idea; note that the transmit (Tx) side on one end connects to the receive (Rx) side on the other, for both cables.

FIGURE 4-23

Two Fiber-Optic Cables, with Connectors

> **ON THE SIDE:** In addition to sending data using light sent over fiber-optic cables, the networking world also includes free-space optics, which send the light through the air between two devices with no cable required. Free-space optics require a line of sight between the two devices.

AUTHOR'S NOTE: The world of fiber cabling includes many different cable connectors that can be attached to the ends of the cable. However, each connector has a place for both the transmit and receive fiber.

Fiber-Optic Transmitters

To transmit data over fiber-optic cables, the hardware on the nodes typically has one of two types of light sources: a light emitting diode (LED) or a laser.

LEDs have many applications today. Many electronic devices have status LEDs that light up to tell you whether the device is working. Household appliances have LEDs to tell you whether the power is on. Plus, LEDs cost very little to make, in part because of their relative simplicity and in part because of the popularity and volume of LEDs made.

Lasers have many industrial uses. Beyond being used in networks, lasers can be used in manufacturing to cut materials precisely. They can even be used in laser pointers, devices that shine light on the wall when you make a presentation.

One key technical difference between LEDs and lasers for networking is that LEDs shine light in multiple directions, and lasers shine light in a single direction. Each type of transmitter sits at the end of a fiber cable, and some of the light from the transmitter needs to shine into the core. When using an LED, the core needs to be a little bigger so that at least some of the light waves from the LED shine into the core. With a laser, with much better control over the direction of the light, the core can be much smaller, and the laser light can still shine right down the middle of the cable. Figure 4-24 shows the idea, with an LED on the top and a laser on the bottom.

LEDs with Multiple Modes (Angles) and Lasers with a Single Mode (Angle)

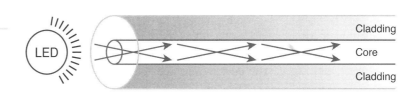

ON THE SIDE:
Although this section so far has avoided specific standards, for perspective, Ethernet standards at 1 gigabit per second (1 Gbps) support maximum distances using MM fiber with LEDs of 550 meters, and a maximum distance using SM fiber with lasers of 10 kilometers.

To match the needs for multiple modes of light (LED) or a single mode of light (laser), fiber cables come in two major categories: *multimode fiber (MM)* and *single-mode fiber (SM)*. Multimode fiber cables have larger-diameter cores and work best with LED transmitters. Single-mode fiber cables have smaller-diameter cores and work best with laser transmitters.

When designing networks, the network designer thinks about the cost, as well as the distances supported, when choosing between LED-based transmitters and laser transmitters. Light generated by a laser simply travels farther. When designing a network, oftentimes a network engineer looks at each link, looks at the standards and equipment available, and starts by asking whether copper links will work. If not, then he asks whether cheaper fiber-optic gear, using MM fiber and cheaper LED-based transmitters, will work at the required length. If not, the engineer looks at the more expensive options that use laser transmitters and SM fiber.

Fiber Optics in Ethernet LANs

Fiber optics give network engineers a different option compared to using copper cables. First, fiber-optic cables do not create EMI, and as a result, fiber-optic links are more secure. Also, fiber-optic cables support longer distances than copper wires, from just a few hundred meters longer with multimode fiber to tens of kilometers with single-mode fiber. However, fiber-optic cables and equipment tend to cost more than copper cables and equipment, and fiber cables require more skill and effort to install.

While this introductory textbook cannot touch on all the trade-offs, this list summarizes the major decision points when a network engineer thinks about building a LAN:

- When distances and electrical conditions allow, use copper cabling.
- If not, use multimode if distance allows.
- If not, use single-mode cabling, and look for specific standards (among many) that use lasers, looking for the standard that best matches the distance requirements for a link.

For example, imagine a typical campus LAN in which a company has employees in two buildings in an office park. The two buildings sit 150 meters apart. As it turns out, Ethernet standards for copper cabling limit the length of a link to 100 meters, but many Ethernet standards allow multimode links to stretch past 200 meters. So, the network engineer avoids trying to use copper between buildings, but he does choose to use multimode rather than single-mode fiber. He contracts with a cabling company to install multimode cables between a wiring closet in the first floor of each of the two buildings.

Figure 4-25 shows the resulting network diagram. All the LAN links inside a building use copper. The links between buildings use multimode fiber.

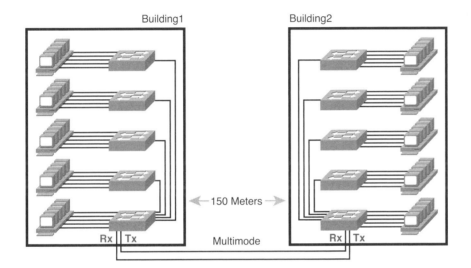

FIGURE 4-25

Typical Use of Fiber Optics in a LAN: Links Between Neighboring Buildings

4

Note that the figure shows two lines between buildings as a reminder that you need two fibers: one to transmit in each direction.

> **ON THE SIDE:** Because the labor cost to install longer cable runs often far exceeds the cost of the cables, many companies install a bundle with many fibers when installing fiber cabling. At first, many of these sit idle (called *dark fiber* because it has no light). Later, when the company needs to add links to the network, it already has cables available.

Fiber Optics in the WAN

The telcos and ISPs that create the networks that support WAN services use fiber optics as well. Their business models require that they connect customers that sit far apart. To do that, a telco or ISP must have a link from the customer to the telco CO (or ISP equivalent, called a *point of presence [POP]*). Then, all the COs or POPs must connect. And that network can span entire countries, or the entire world, so the distances will drive the telco or ISP toward using fiber links to support longer distances.

Telcos and ISPs also need to support much higher speeds than enterprises. For example, imagine that one enterprise paid for 100 leased lines from a telco. Each leased line, called T1, runs at around 1.5 Mbps. The telco's network has to be able to pass 100 times 1.5 Mbps worth of bits to support that one customer. Additionally, the telco might have 1,000 customers just like that first customer. If you add up all the links, that totals to 150 gigabits per second (150 Gbps) total traffic from all those customers. The telco's network, the part hidden from its customers, needs to support at least that much traffic volume to support those customers.

For perspective, think back to the simple point-to-point leased line introduced in Chapter 3. From one perspective, it might look like a link between two routers, completely ignoring the telco network. From another, you might recall the short physical link from the router to the nearby CO, with the hidden telco network existing, but with the details hidden. Figure 4-26 shows both ideas, on the top and the bottom, respectively.

FIGURE 4-26

Two Perspectives on a Leased Line

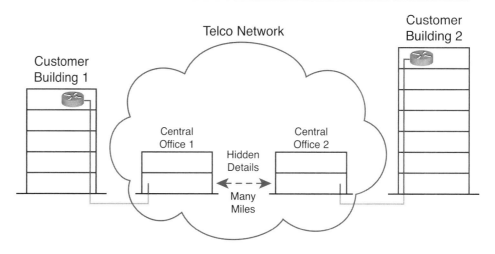

Next, consider a third perspective in Figure 4-27 that shows some insight into the telco network. The figure shows fiber that connects the equipment in the CO to other telco sites, called *core* sites. The COs sit at the *edge* sites of the telco network, with links to the core sites. The physical locations are simply office buildings with computer rooms, with plenty of air conditioning. The rooms hold network nodes, and these devices connect to the fiber links, creating the telco network. The bits that make up the leased line in Figure 4-26 actually flow through the links in the core of the telco network, as shown in Figure 4-27.

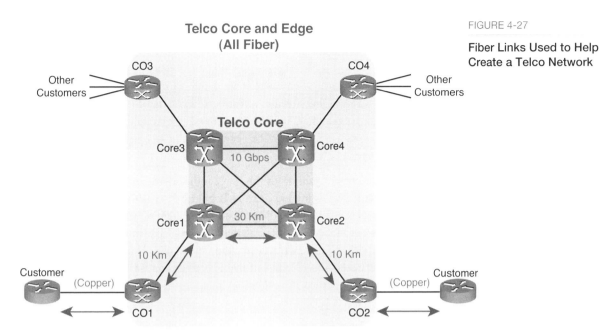

FIGURE 4-27

**Fiber Links Used to Help
Create a Telco Network**

In this figure, all the links use fiber, except the links from the CO to the customer router, which use copper. The links in the core all happen to reach 30 km each; you can think of these nodes as equipment in buildings in different cities. The COs sit another 10 km from the core sites. The distances are imaginary, but just show the point that although the link can be thought of as a single physical link, as in Figure 4-26, the fiber cabling and nodes in the telco core enable the longer distances.

Finally, the links and nodes in the core must also follow some standards. One of the longer-established standards for these links follows a family of standards called Synchronous Optical Network (SONET) . SONET defines a series of physical layer standards for sending bits over optical links, with a hierarchy of speeds that are multiples of the base speed (51.84 Mbps) plus some overhead. Table 4-2 lists some of the SONET optical carrier (OC) link names and their approximate speeds; any of the links between nodes in the telco network of Figure 4-27 could use these standards.

TABLE 4-2
SONET Optical Carrier (OC) Names and (Rounded) Line Speeds

Name	(Rounded) Line Speed
OC-1	52 Mbps
OC-3	155 Mbps
OC-12	622 Mbps
OC-24	1244 Mbps
OC-48	2488 Mbps
OC-96	4976 Mbps
OC-192	9952 Mbps

Sending Bits with Radio Waves and No Cables

When you hear the word *radio*, most people think of listening to music. A radio station broadcasts music into the air, and anyone with a radio can tune in to that radio station and listen to the music. And of course, the radio does not require a cable between the radio station and the person listening—a particularly helpful fact if you want to listen to a car radio.

This third of three major sections of this chapter discusses how networks use radio waves to send data. The following sections begin by discussing a few facts about how radio stations work when sending music to car radio players, just to define some terms and big concepts. Following that, the text looks at mobile phone networks, or wireless WANs, which use radio (and similar electromagnetic waves) to send both voice and data. The rest of these sections look at wireless LANs (WLAN), which again use radio technology to send data without cables.

Radio Basics

Imagine that you hop in your car on a warm Saturday night and start cruising around town. You roll down the windows, and of course, you tune the radio to your favorite station and crank up the volume. Particularly in the US of A, cruising around in a car, listening to tunes, and bumping into friends (old and new) is simply a fun part of the culture.

But how does the radio work?

A car radio works for many reasons, but they all revolve around how radio waves—a type of electromagnetic energy—flows from the radio station to the car radio. First, the radio station plays some music, either from a CD player or from a computer that holds lots of digital music. The music player connects to a large *radio antenna*, which is a device that converts electricity into radio waves. Radio waves pass through things (the Earth's atmosphere, trees, buildings, car roofs) and eventually hit an antenna on the car. The car antenna receives the radio waves and converts them back to electricity. The radio player in the car (car stereo) converts the electricity into music.

Radio stations broadcast their signals so that anyone near enough to the radio station's large antenna (radio tower) can hear the radio station. The radio tower sends electricity through the antenna to create the radio waves; the more electrical power, the stronger the radio waves, and the longer distances. Also, the radio tower sends the signals upward because radio waves happen to bounce off the *ionosphere*, one of the layers of Earth's atmosphere. By bouncing the radio waves off the ionosphere, the radio waves can reach a wider area and more car radios, as shown in Figure 4-28.

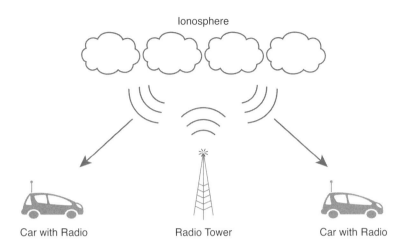

Ionosphere

Car with Radio   Radio Tower   Car with Radio

FIGURE 4-28

Radio Station
Broadcasting a Radio
Signal to a Car Radio (Car
Icon © Sergey Minaev)

The physical universe in which we live happens to have many types of energy called *electromagnetic radiation*. To help make sense of all this energy, scientists describe the types of energy using a conceptual model called the *electromagnetic spectrum*. Because these types of energy travel as waves, they have a wavelength, so the spectrum categorizes energy based on the wavelength. *Radio waves* make up one of those categories in the EM spectrum. Other parts of the EM spectrum include *visible light*, *X-rays*, and *microwaves*.

Radio waves work well for networking because as a waveform, radio waves can be changed (modulated) over time to send data. The following three facts summarize the key points about why radio can be used to wirelessly send data.

- Radio waves have an energy level that moves up and down over time, so when graphed, the waves look like a sine wave.

- Like other energy waveforms, radio waves can be changed and sensed by networking devices, including changes to the frequency, amplitude, phase, period, and wavelength of the radio waves. (See Figure 4-6 for a reminder of the meaning of these terms.)

- EM energy like radio waves does not need a physical medium in which to move.

In fact, radio stations in the United States modulate either the frequency or amplitude of the radio waves when broadcasting music. FM radio stations change the frequency over time to encode the music, with FM meaning *frequency modulation*. As you might guess, AM radio stations change the amplitude of the radio waves to encode the music, with AM meaning *amplitude modulation*.

Because FM stations need to change the frequency over time, they do not use a single frequency, but a range of frequencies. For example, say that you listen to a station called 96.5 FM. The "96.5" stands for 96.5 MHz, meaning megahertz, or millions of cycles of the waveform per second. But this FM radio station does not use only 96.5 MHz, instead using frequencies between 96.4 MHz and 96.6 MHz. The radio station changes frequencies constantly, encoding the different sound as

ON THE SIDE: Have you ever been driving in a car, listening to the radio, and the radio station sound got worse? Or even faded completely? That happens because the radio signal is not strong enough to go to where you have driven, or because the radio waves have to pass through too much material, like hills or tunnels.

different radio frequencies. The radio player listens for all the radio waves from 96.4 to 96.6 MHz and interprets the different-frequency radio waves into different-frequency sounds.

Wireless WANs

The networking industry includes both wireless LAN and wireless WAN technologies. Both use radio waves, and both use no cables (no wires). The next topic looks at some of the options for wireless networking technology in the WAN, followed by wireless in the LAN.

Most of you reading this book already use wireless WANs every day when you use a mobile phone. In effect, mobile phone companies provide a wireless WAN service, and their networks are wireless WANs.

Before thinking about how wireless WANs work, think about the WAN business model for a moment. To be a WAN service, a service provider offers some service that delivers bits between devices for a fee, usually a monthly fee. Additionally, the service provider's customer does not own the service provider's network, essentially leasing the right to some part or capacity of that network. Mobile phone companies use those same ideas, charging a (typically) monthly fee for anyone using its phone service, and the customer does not own the mobile phone network.

Although a mobile phone company's network can act like a wireless WAN service, few people actually use the term **wireless WAN**. Actually, many names exist for these networks. Some names include the word *phone*, because phone companies first built wireless WANs to support mobile phones. Some names include the word *cellular* or the shorter word *cell*, because one of the earliest mobile phone technologies was called cellular. Oftentimes, mainly because of TV advertising, people refer to the mobile networks by the name of the telco. The following list shows a few of the more common terms you will hear for the kind of mobile phone networks:

ON THE SIDE: The list could continue to list every mobile phone provider in the world, but it lists only the three largest U.S. mobile phone companies (as of publication), just as examples.

- Mobile phone network/mobile network
- Cell phone network/cell network
- Cellular phone network/cellular network
- The AT&T network
- The Sprint network
- The Verizon network

For consistency, this section uses the more generic term *mobile network*.

Connecting Mobile Phones to the Rest of the World

To support phone calls and text messages between the phones of their own customers, and only those customers, a single mobile network provider only needs to create its own mobile network. The phones have radio technology, including an antenna. The mobile company installs tall radio towers, with antennas on top of the towers. The customers of that telco can use radio technology to communicate through the mobile network. With that network, the customers of that one mobile phone company can talk to each other.

However, most phone users want to communicate with more phones than just those that happen to use the same mobile company. For example, you might want to make phone calls to the rest of the telephone networks of the world, generally called the *public switched telephone network (PSTN)*. You might want to connect to data services, for example, searching using Google or connecting to social media websites like Facebook. To make that work, the mobile network cannot sit by itself as an island, but it must connect to the other networks of the world, as shown in Figure 4-29.

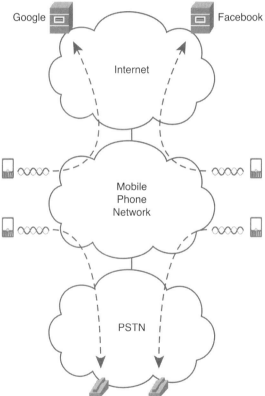

FIGURE 4-29

Major Components in the Mobile Phone Network Model

Figure 4-29 shows what happens, but not how it happens. The next few pages show the basics of how mobile phones communicate through a mobile network.

Sending Voice from Mobile Phones Through the Wireless WAN

Most modern mobile phones act as digital phones, instead of acting like the analog phones found connected to the local home telephone lines in most people's homes. As a digital phone, these mobile phones send and receive digits (bits) that represent the voice traffic. As discussed back in Chapter 2's section "Voice Telephone Calls," when someone speaks, the mobile phone converts the voice into bits. When receiving the bits, the phone converts the bits into sound.

To actually transmit the bits, the phones of course do not have a copper or fiber cable, so they use wireless radio technology. The phone sends the bits encoded as radio waves, talking to a nearby radio antenna on a radio tower owned by the mobile phone company. Figure 4-30 shows the topology for a typical mobile phone call, with the steps showing someone speaking on the left.

FIGURE 4-30

Connecting a Mobile Phone Call Through a Radio Tower to the Telco Network

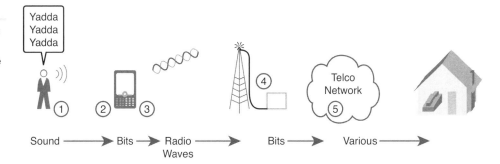

Although this chapter focuses on physical layer details, this particular topic might be better understood by looking at the entire end-to-end path. Focus on Steps 3 and 4 from the figure, which show the physical layer process of sending bits using radio waves. (After looking at these steps, if you want a reminder about how voice basics work, refer to Chapter 2's Figure 2-8 and the surrounding text.)

1. The human speaks, creating sound waves (as usual).

2. The phone converts the sound waves into bits (the usual process for digital phones).

3. The phone sends (encodes) the bits as radio waves, sent through the air toward the cell tower.

4. The radio equipment at the tower receives (decodes) the radio waves back into the original bits.

5. The rest of the trip for the voice uses various technologies; the details are not included here.

The example of Figure 4-30 shows a classic case of a network with nodes that send data over a link. The mobile phone acts as one node, with the radio tower and gear connected to it acting as the other node. The link exists as the space between the two, with the radio waves communicating the bits. In this example, the user's application happened to be voice, but the radio link simply forwarded bits. The next topic looks at using that same radio link to send bits for traditional data applications.

Sending Data from Mobile Phones Through the Wireless WAN

Phones today might still be called *phones*, but most of the interesting phone features today require Internet access. Phones act more like an Internet-connected handheld computer than a traditional phone. In fact, most young people use their phones more for the apps (text, social media, music, and so on) rather than to talk to people. Smart phones, like Apple iPhones and any phones that use Google's Android OS, have revolutionized the electronics and computer market, and many of those apps require a connection to the Internet. Even when using a less expensive not-as-smart phone, most every mobile phone today supports texting, email, and web browsing, and the web browsing in particular requires Internet access.

The radio link on the phone works the same way to support data as it does for voice. When sending or receiving data for an app, the phone just passes bits using radio waves between itself and the radio tower. On the endpoints, data applications already start with the data as bits, so all the phone needs to do is encapsulate the data, as discussed throughout Chapter 3.

The mobile network must act differently, however, based on whether the bits sent by the phone happen to be part of a voice call versus being data from an application. To support data applications, the mobile network simply needs to connect to the Internet and to any other networks that support the various data apps. Then the mobile network can forward the data to the correct destination on the Internet, or the other networks, and not into the PSTN. Figure 4-31 shows the idea.

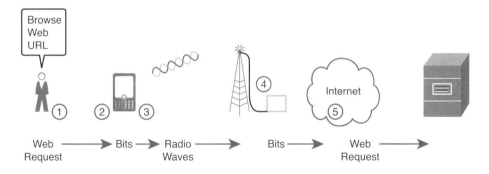

FIGURE 4-31

Smart Phone: Using Radio to Forward Bits to the Tower and Then to the Internet

Just to be clear, the steps in the figure are as follows:

1. The human types a URL or taps a hyperlink.
2. The phone encapsulates the HTTP request into an IP packet and then a data link layer frame, as discussed in Chapter 3, using the appropriate headers and trailers.
3. The phone sends (encodes) the frame's bits as radio waves through the air toward the cell tower.
4. The radio equipment at the tower receives (decodes) the radio waves back into the original bits.
5. The equipment near the cell tower forwards the bits onto the Internet, as it would for any other IP packet.

Sending Bits from Nonphone Devices Through the Wireless WAN

Although mobile networks started life as networks to support mobile phones, today these networks fill the main role of any network: moving bits from device to device. A phone can create those bits as part of a voice call. A phone can also create those bits as part of some app. In fact, the device does not even have to be a phone. It simply needs to be a device that uses a radio to send bits to and from the mobile phone network, using the same standards as the phone.

For example, imagine that you work in a job in which you almost never go to the office because you call on customers all day, driving around from place to place. You have both a laptop and a tablet computer, both of which can connect to a wireless LAN, like at a wireless LAN hotspot you find at most coffee shops. However, you often have only 15–30 minutes between appointments—not enough time to find a coffee shop with any time left to check email, surf, and so on.

With wireless WAN technology, you can connect your laptop and tablet to the same mobile network as your phone. With a laptop, you typically need a *wireless WAN NIC*. Tablet computers have an integrated mobile wireless WAN NIC, assuming that you bought the model with that option. Those hardware components give you the radio with which to connect to the mobile network's radio towers. You also need a contract with a mobile provider. After being configured, you have connectivity from anywhere that you also have connectivity from your mobile phone. Figure 4-32 shows the idea.

FIGURE 4-32

Using the Wireless WAN (Mobile Network) from Computers Instead of Phones

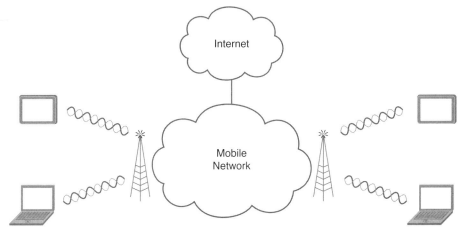

Mobile Phone Network Terminology

This book focuses more on wireless LANs than wireless WANs; Chapter 6, "Wireless LANs," discusses nothing but wireless LANs. This section of Chapter 4 happens to be the only real discussion of wireless WANs in this book. Although the book does not look at specific wireless WAN standards, this brief topic about mobile phone network terminology introduces some of the specific standards terms so that, when you begin to learn more about consumer wireless WAN products on your own, you have some knowledge that can help you fit the pieces together.

Table 4-3 lists some of the standards and terms related to mobile wireless (wireless WANs). The first and third columns list the most likely terms you will see when shopping for wireless WAN products. The rest of the columns in the table fill out other details that your instructor might care to discuss.

TABLE 4-3

Mobile Wireless Standards and Terms

Generation	Umbrella Standard	Other Terms Related to a Generation	Standards Body
2G	GSM (Global System for Mobile Communications)	TDMA, CDMA	ETSI
3G	IMT-2000 (International Mobile Telecommunications-2000)	UTMS	ITU
4G	IMT-Advanced (International Mobile Telecommunications - Advanced)	LTE, WiMax	ITU, ETSI, IEEE

The first column of the table lists terms that categorize wireless WAN technologies into some very broad categories. Over time, as mobile wireless standards have progressed, groups of standards have become known as 2G, 3G, and now 4G, for second generation, third generation, and fourth generation. Worldwide, many wireless companies still support and use 2G technologies. However, mobile companies mostly discuss and advertise 4G technologies, which are the leading-edge technologies with the fastest speeds.

Second, because of the mobile industry's focus on 4G today, you will likely see more and more about the two main components of 4G: *LTE (Long-Term Evolution)* and *WiMax*. However, as of the time of publication of this book, it looked as if most mobile providers prefer LTE over WiMax, so you might see most 4G references mention only LTE.

Wireless LANs

The mobile networks described in the previous few pages meet the basic definition of a wireless WAN. They use no wires (cables), meeting the one literal requirement to be a wireless network. They also charge a monthly fee for sending data through their network, as is the case with typical WAN services.

The following sections next examine **wireless LANs**, or WLANs. WLANs do not use cables and do use radio waves to send data. However, you can own all the gear to make the WLAN and not have to pay a monthly fee. Also, the distances between devices tend to be much shorter than in wireless WANs: a few hundred feet versus a few miles for a typical wireless WAN transmission.

These sections introduce WLANs, focusing on several physical layer topics. First, this topic looks at the devices and topology used to create a WLAN. Then, the text looks at how to transmit data in a WLAN using radio waves. The final topic looks at how WLANs require the devices to take turns when sending data.

Wireless LAN Devices and Topology

In a wireless LAN, every device that connects to the LAN needs a WLAN network interface card (NIC) or equivalent. As with Ethernet NICs, a wireless NIC gives a PC the ability to connect to the WLAN. Unlike an Ethernet NIC, a wireless NIC does not need a socket that allows the connection of a cable. Instead, it has a radio antenna, with which the NIC can send and receive data.

Most WLANs use a small device that in some ways acts like a smaller version of the radio tower in the wireless WAN. Most WLANs use this wireless node, called a WLAN **access point (AP)**, and all the user devices communicate only through the AP, as shown in Figure 4-33.

FIGURE 4-33

Small Wireless LAN with One Access Point (AP)

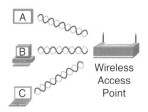

Wireless
Access
Point

ON THE SIDE:
WLANs include other options beyond a BSS. One option, an *ad hoc network*, enables two devices to send data directly to each other, with no AP.

A WLAN with one AP creates a WLAN *Basic Service Set (BSS)*. In a BSS, all communications happen with the AP, much like they do in the wireless WAN model. For example, if device A needed to send data to device B in the figure, A would send the bits to the AP and the AP would then send the bits to B.

The WLAN in Figure 4-33 works for those nearby devices, but it is of little use without being connected to other networks. Wireless WANs must overcome the same problem, as shown back in Figure 4-29: Each wireless WAN provider connects to both the PSTN (for voice) and the Internet (for data). WLANs also connect to voice and data networks as needed.

WLANs connect to other networks using a basic wired Ethernet LAN connection on the AP. Essentially, the AP has an integrated Ethernet NIC. Logically, the AP has a split personality: a WLAN side and a wired Ethernet side. The AP forwards data from the WLAN side to the Ethernet side and vice versa, as shown in Figure 4-34.

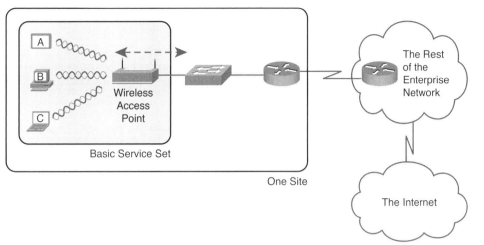

FIGURE 4-34

WLAN AP Bridges Between the WLAN and an Ethernet LAN

Sending Data in WLANs

WLAN devices use antennas to send data, with the encoding scheme defining how to send the data. When a device has data to send, that data exists as bits. The sending device must think about the encoding to determine the radio waves to create. Then, as with other radio technology, the device runs an electric current through the antenna, which gives off radio waves.

The receiving device uses its antenna to receive any incoming radio waves, and it uses the same encoding rules to decode the radio waves back into the original bits.

For most WLAN standards, the encoding scheme uses some form of *amplitude shift keying* or *phase shift keying*, which changes the amplitude or phase (respectively) to represent a 0 or 1. However, to be honest, the details of encoding on WLANs can be fairly complex, beyond the needs of this introductory text. But just to give you the general idea, when using amplitude, the encoding might use a radio wave with some amplitude for 0 and twice that amplitude for 1. Or, it might use a sine wave that begins at the phase going up from the centerline (at the beginning of a bit time) for 0 and the phase that goes down from the centerline (at the beginning of a bit time) for 1. Figure 4-35 shows an example of each, showing the transmission of 010101.

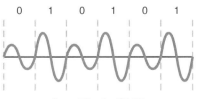

Amplitude Shift

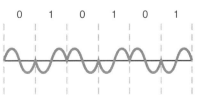

Phase Shift

FIGURE 4-35

Amplitude and Phase Shift Basic Examples

Possible Problems When Sending Data Using Radio Waves

WLANs must overcome the problems related to radio noise between the two devices that send and receive data. Networking links that use cables create a relatively quiet environment in which the energy can travel. However, WLANs, and any link that uses radio, has no media (cable) to use. As a result, the wireless environment can be very noisy.

A brief analogy might help put the issue in perspective. You can think of a link that uses electricity over copper wires as if it were a quiet restaurant, but with some other diners as well, where you and a friend sit for a relaxing meal. For links with fiber cabling, imagine that you were at the same restaurant, but the place was deserted, and you and your friend were the only people there. By comparison, WLANs have noise more like a busy nightclub on a Saturday night. WLANs do not have a cable to keep out other noises, and the world in which we live simply has lots of sources of radio noise that might impact the wireless signal.

Besides sources of noise, WLANs can also have problems because of stuff. Not *stuff* meaning something undefined, but stuff meaning things you can see, touch, and feel: anything made of matter. Radio waves go through the relative vacuum of outer space very easily. They pass through the air in the Earth's atmosphere relatively easily as well, with some loss. However, the amount of matter that radio waves need to pass through, and the type of matter, can reduce, slow, absorb, and reflect the radio waves.

For example, have you ever been in a building and not been able to get a wireless signal on your phone? Typically, that happens because of the amount and type of material (stuff) between you and the cell phone tower.

When building a small WLAN, you might just install the gear, but for enterprise WLANs, the network engineer often performs a wireless site survey before installing the gear. In a *site survey*, the engineer looks at the layout of the building, looking at distances, known sources of radio interference, materials that might cause problems (like lots of metal or concrete walls), and other issues. The site survey often includes a walkabout with wireless testing tools to measure the amount of interference.

Figure 4-36 shows some of the typical problems that might be found when doing a site survey for an existing WLAN. In this case, the AP sits under a metal desk (radio waves do not pass through metal very well). The AP sits next to other equipment and cables, which might interfere. The AP also sits on the other side of the interior wall as compared to the end-user devices. In this case, the WLAN might not work at all or it might not work as well as it could.

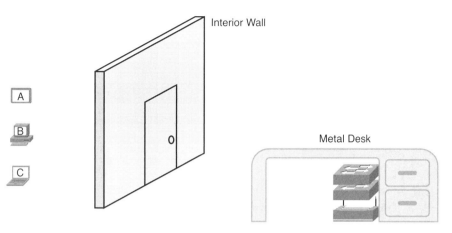

FIGURE 4-36

WLAN with Possible Sources of Interference

Taking Turns to Transmit in Each Direction

Using radios for sending data requires the devices to take turns. When two radios transmit at the same frequency, at the same time, the radio waves collide. When they collide, the other devices receiving those waves cannot decode the original bits from either device. The same kind of thing happens in a meeting when two people talk and neither will stop talking: No one can tell what either one of them is saying.

You have probably seen examples in real life or on television where people use a two-way radio to talk. Done right, one person has to somehow tell the other person when he has finished speaking, to give the other person a turn. For example, police and other emergency workers use two-way radios in their cars. When they speak, they end each phrase with some words that make it sound like they are finished. The following dialogue might happen between a police car and the dispatcher at the police station just before a dinner break:

> "Car 88 to base, **over**."
>
> "Base to 88, **over**."
>
> "Smith and Jones going to the diner for some chow, **over**."
>
> "10-4, enjoy, over and **out**."

Note that each phrase ends with *over* or *out*, letting the other person know that he now has a turn to talk.

Wireless LANs take turns by using some rules called *carrier sense multiple access collision avoidance,* or *CSMA/CA*. The term might seem intimidating, but the rules actually make a lot of sense. First, devices only send radio waves when sending data, so when no devices are sending data, that frequency is silent. When any device decides to send data, it confirms that no other device is sending right now, based on the fact that the frequency is silent. Then, instead of sending data immediately, the device starts its own random wait time to wait before sending.

Why wait, and why a random time? To avoid having multiple devices hear the silence and immediately start sending. The device whose random wait timer pops first gets to send next; Figure 4-37 shows an example.

FIGURE 4-37

CSMA/CA Process

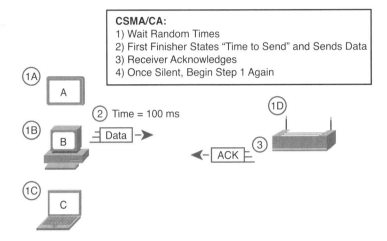

The figure shows a few other details about CSMA/CA. At Step 1 (shown as Steps 1A–1D), all devices use an independent random wait time, and only if they happen to have data to send.

At Step 2, some device (host B in this case) completes its wait timer first, so it sends. However, the sender must list the time it expects to need to send the data (in this case, 100 milliseconds). That lets the other devices know how long it will be before the WLAN might be silent again.

Step 3 shows a required acknowledgment, where the device to which the data was sent must confirm that the data was received.

That acknowledgment has to happen before the WLAN is considered silent again (Step 4).

IEEE WLAN Standards and Speeds

Just like the history of IEEE Ethernet standards shows repeated new standards with faster speeds over the years, the history of IEEE wireless LAN standards shows a similar progression. IEEE standardizes WLANs, with the first standard being 802.11. (IEEE Ethernet LAN standards all begin with 802.3.) The more common standards today are 802.11a, 802.11b, 802.11g, and 802.11n. Each of these standards created new options and generally increased the maximum possible speeds.

Each of these standards has a maximum transmission speed, as well as general guidelines for maximum distance, but the actual distance and speed that actually occur in a WLAN can differ quite a bit. By way of comparison, you might own a sports car that can travel over 200 miles per hour on a racetrack, but you cannot go that fast in rush-hour traffic or off-road. WLANs suffer from the same kinds of problems. As it turns out, if the sender slows to make a transmission work during bad conditions, the bits have a much better chance of getting to the other node.

In WLANs, two common events that make a WLAN slow down are distance and noise. With radio signals, the farther the distance, the weaker the signal, and the more difficult it is to interpret the received signal. Also, the noisier the environment, the more difficult it is to interpret the received signal. So, if the sender slows, it might be able to overcome the distance and noise problems, and at least get some data through, rather than none. WLAN standards specify that nodes can (and should) send more slowly if conditions require it.

Table 4-4 shows a list of the IEEE WLAN standards, along with some notes about the maximum transmission rates. The table lists the standards in the order in which they reached standards status. As you might expect, over time, the newer standards support faster speeds.

TABLE 4-4
WLAN Standards and Speeds

IEEE WLAN Standard	Maximum Stream Rate (Mbps)	Frequency Range (GHz)	Number of Nonoverlapping Channels
802.11b	11	2.4	3
802.11a	54	5	23
802.11g	54	2.4	3
802.11n	72	5	21
802.11n*	150	5	9

* When using a bonded 40-MHz channel, instead of the 20-MHz channel used by the other rows in the table.

Note that the table lists two speeds for 802.11n. One speed shows a more direct comparison to the other (older) standards, while the 150-Mbps speed shows the literal maximum for a single transmission. 802.11n also allows multiple concurrent streams from one device, so many 802.11n products will list a maximum speed of 300 Mbps (implying two 150-Mbps streams) or 450 Mbps (implying three streams).

ON THE SIDE: Most network engineers, when speaking about WLAN standards, leave off the *802*. For example, for 802.11n, they might say "dot eleven n."

ON THE SIDE: By the time this book went to press, products using prestandard versions of 802.11ac, which promises gigabit speeds (with multiple streams) have begun to hit the market. In comparison, 802.11n has a theoretical maximum of four 150-Mbps streams, for a combined rate of at most 600 Mbps.

Example Enterprise LAN with Copper, Fiber, Wireless

Most corporate LANs today use copper, fiber, and wireless in the same campus LAN. To close this chapter, this section shows an example of the topology of a campus LAN that uses all three.

First, imagine a typical office complex with several buildings of a few stories each. If one company leases space in two of the buildings, it typically connects the LANs. Oftentimes, the links between buildings use fiber-optic cables, both for longer distances and to avoid issues with electrical noise.

Most campus LANs use copper cabling to desktop computers and desktop phones. Given a choice between copper and fiber, the copper cabling and NICs typically cost less, and they work very well inside a building.

Finally, some devices require WLANs, and some users prefer WLAN connections instead of wired. Most smart phones and tablet computers require wireless, either a wireless WAN or wireless LAN. And although most laptops can connect to the wired Ethernet LAN, users might prefer to not have to use a cable.

Based on all these requirements, many corporate campus LANs today have both wired and wireless LAN support on each floor. Each cubicle or desk area has connections to the wired LAN, while at the same time, the WLAN coverage extends to those same areas. The WLAN connects to the same Ethernet network, which allows the devices in the two building to communicate. Figure 4-38 shows the topology of just such a campus LAN.

FIGURE 4-38

Campus LAN: Wireless Devices, Wired Desktops, and Fiber Trunks

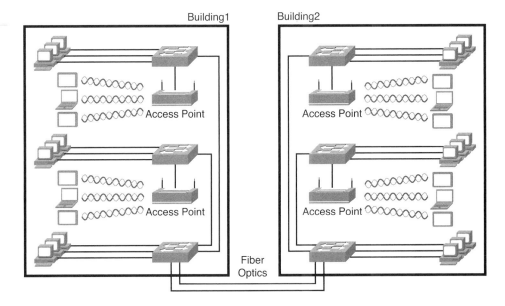

Chapter Summary

This chapter looks at the details of how to move bits from one node to the next node in a network. Although this chapter shows diagrams of an entire network on several occasions, just to give context, the chapter focuses on moving bits over a single link. Those bits can take many such hops, but this chapter discusses the particulars of the jump from one node to the next.

The first and largest of the three major sections of this chapter looks at how to move bits using copper wires and electricity. The general idea can be somewhat simple: Make a circuit between the nodes, and send two different electrical signals (different voltages, frequencies, and so on) to mean 0 or 1. This section explains the fundamentals of how electricity can be graphed and how those graphs show features that can be changed by the sender and sensed by the receiver, so that nodes can use those features to encode data.

Besides the fundamental ideas of how to use electricity to send data, the first section gets into the particulars of how to use those tools for networks. For example, this section shows that some standards require two circuits, with one for each direction. It also discusses how circuits can actually interfere with each other, and what might be done to reduce the effects of this electromagnetic interference (EMI), including the use of twisted-pair cabling. The first section goes on to show specifically how Ethernet LANs use copper UTP cabling, RJ-45 connectors, specific pinouts, and all the specifics needed to make an actual Ethernet link work.

The second major section of the chapter discusses fiber optics. These links use light to transmit data, often using an encoding with the light off meaning 0 and the light on meaning 1. These cables allow relatively longer distances as compared with copper, with no EMI, so network engineers often use them for longer links. In LANs, these links often connect switches in different buildings; in WANs, they often connect different sites inside the telco or ISP network.

The last major section of the chapter looked at wireless technologies that use radio to send bits. These links include the same wireless technology many of us use every day with our mobile phones. These phones connect to mobile networks, which connect the phones to the rest of the world's networks, both for voice and data. The radio part of that overall picture requires the phone and radio tower to encode data using radio waves, often with encoding that uses amplitude or phase shifts.

Finally, this chapter concluded by introducing the basics of wireless LANs. This section introduced the Basic Service Set (BSS), with one wireless access point (AP), and the convention where all transmissions go to/from the AP. It also showed how the physical layer must manage the timing to make the devices take turns using CSMA/CA logic, which lets the devices avoid talking at the same time.

Chapter Review Activities

Use the features in this section to study and review the topics in this chapter.

Answer These Questions

1. You have created a simple electrical circuit with a battery, wires, and a light bulb. Which of the following is true about this circuit? (Choose two answers.)

    a. The battery's positive lead pushes current away from that lead.

    b. The battery's positive lead pulls current toward that lead.

    c. The circuit creates a direct current.

    d. The circuit creates an alternating current.

2. A PC NIC and a switch port create one electrical circuit to use when sending data. The sender creates a (maximum) 1-volt electrical signal with a frequency of 1000 hertz. Which of the following facts are also true? (Choose two answers.)

    a. The period is 1/1000 of a second.

    b. The phase changes over time.

    c. The amplitude changes over time.

    d. The amplitude is 1 volt.

3. A PC NIC and a switch port create one electrical circuit to use when sending data from the PC to the switch. Which of the following tasks is a function done by the transmitter? (Choose two answers.)

    a. Completes the electrical circuit by looping two wires together on its end

    b. Senses current on the circuit

    c. Creates current on the circuit

    d. Removes noise from the circuit

4. A PC NIC and a switch port create one electrical circuit to use when sending data from the PC to the switch. The transmitter uses a simple encoding scheme that uses a higher amplitude to encode 1 and a lower amplitude to encode 0, sending 1 bit in each bit time. The bit rate is 2000 bits per second (2000 bps). Which of the following is true on this circuit?

    a. The bit time is .001 seconds.

    b. The bit time is .0002 seconds.

    c. The transmitter must change the amplitude 2000 times per second.

    d. The transmitter can change the amplitude 2000 times per second.

5. Two nodes use an encoding scheme that cannot use one circuit to both send and receive data at the same time. The link physically contains two wires. Which of the following is a possible option to allow both nodes to send data?

   a. Create two circuits, one using one wire and one using the other.

   b. Create one circuit, and take turns sending over that circuit.

   c. Create one circuit, and hope it works.

   d. None of the answers is correct.

6. UTP cables can have up to eight wires inside the cables. Which of the following is the most likely reason why EMI from one wire does not affect the electrical behavior of another wire inside the same cable?

   a. The shorter the cable length, the less EMI

   b. Twisting the pairs together

   c. Shielding each wire in plastic coating

   d. Converting to glass fiber UTP cabling

7. Which of the following facts are in common between both of the Ethernet standards discussed in this chapter, 10BASE-T and 100BASE-T? (Choose two answers.)

   a. The number of wire pairs used (2)

   b. The cabling pinouts used

   c. The speed

   d. The encoding scheme

8. Which of the following answers best describes the definition of a cabling pinout?

   a. The information about the pin numbers on a connector and its matching socket

   b. The color of the wires and the pin numbers to which they connect on one end of a cable

   c. The color of the wires and the pin numbers to which they connect on both ends of a cable

   d. The physical cable-making act of making the wire stick out of the end of the connector, creating pins

9. A PC NIC connects to a switch port using 100BASE-T. Which of the following is true about what happens on that link?

   a. The switch receives data on a circuit that includes the wire at the switch's pin 2.

   b. The PC receives data on a circuit that includes the wire at the PC's pin 7.

   c. The switch sends data on a circuit that includes the wire at the switch's pin 4.

   d. The PC sends data on a circuit that includes the wire at the PC's pin 3.

10. With a fiber-optic cable, the core of the cable, through which light passes, is made of which of the following?

    a. A mix of gases

    b. Nothing (it's a vacuum)

    c. Glass

    d. Cloth fibers

11. Which of the following is the type of transmitter used on fiber-optic links that provides the longest maximum distances?

    a. Antenna

    b. LED

    c. Laser

    d. Inducer

12. Which one answer lists the most likely place to find a fiber-optic link in a campus Ethernet LAN?

    a. Between a PC and a LAN switch

    b. Between two switches on the same floor

    c. Between two switches on different floors (floors 1 and 2)

    d. Between two switches in different buildings in the same office park

13. This chapter describes SONET, a family of physical layer standards used in telco networks over the last few decades. Which of the following are true about the slow and fast end of the optical carrier (OC) standards mentioned in this book: OC-1 and OC-192? (Choose two answers.)

    a. OC-1 runs at approximately 52 Mbps.

    b. OC-1 runs at approximately 620 Mbps.

    c. OC-192 runs at approximately 19.2 times the speed of OC-1.

    d. OC-192 runs at approximately 10,000 Mbps (10 Gbps).

14. What physical medium/media do radio waves need to move from one place to another?

    a. Air

    b. The Earth's ionosphere

    c. Nothing (no material/matter at all)

    d. None of the answers is correct.

15. Fred has a smart phone and a contract with SlateRock mobile. He uses his smart phone to call his friend Barney, on Barney's home telephone. The call works. Which of the following are not a part of the story of what happens between when Fred speaks and when Barney hears what Fred said? (Choose two answers.)

    a. SlateRock's network sends the voice through the Internet.

    b. SlateRock's network sends the voice to the public switched telephone network.

    c. Fred's phone encodes sound waves onto a radio signal to send to the SlateRock cell tower.

    d. The SlateRock cell tower receives Fred's radio signal and converts it back to bits.

16. Fred has a smart phone and a contract with SlateRock mobile. He uses his smart phone to send a text to his friend Barney's smart phone. Barney uses another mobile company. Barney gets the text and sends a text back to Fred. Which of the following is not a part of the story of what happens between when Fred sends the text and Barney sees the text?

    a. SlateRock's network sends the text (as bits) through the Internet or some other data network.

    b. SlateRock's network sends the text, as bits, into the PSTN.

    c. Fred's phone encodes the text, as bits, onto a radio signal to send to the SlateRock cell tower.

    d. The SlateRock cell tower receives Fred's radio signal and converts it back to bits.

17. If comparing a wireless WAN to a wireless LAN, which of the components of a wireless WAN most closely matches the role and purpose of a wireless LAN access point?

    a. A mobile phone

    b. A radio tower

    c. The mobile company's network

    d. All the other answers combined

18. In a WLAN Basic Service Set (BSS), four user devices exist, labeled A, B, C, and D. A has data that it wants to send to B. Thinking of the specific steps, which of the following happens in this WLAN as part of the successful delivery of data from A to B? (Choose two answers.)

    a. A sends the data to the AP.

    b. A sends the data directly to B.

    c. A receives an acknowledgment from B.

    d. A receives an acknowledgment from the AP.

19. A device on a WLAN just created data that it needs to send using the WLAN. Which of the following is its next step as part of the CSMA/CA algorithm used in WLANs to share a frequency?

    a. Listen, and if silent, send.

    b. Listen, and if silent, wait for 100 milliseconds.

    c. Listen, and if silent, wait for a random wait time.

    d. Do not listen, but wait for a random wait time.

20. Which of the following are IEEE WLAN standards? (Choose three answers.)

    a. 802.3u

    b. 802.11n

    c. 802.11g

    d. 802.11a

Define the Key Terms

The following key terms include the ideas most important to the big ideas in this chapter. To review, without looking at the book or your notes, write a definition for each term, focusing on the meaning, not the wording. Then review your definition compared to your notes, this chapter, and the glossary.

Key Terms for Chapter 4

electrical circuit	encoding scheme	radio waves
frequency	unshielded twisted-pair (UTP)	wireless WAN
amplitude		wireless LAN
phase	core	access point
bit time	cladding	

List the Words Inside Acronyms

The following are the most common acronyms discussed in this chapter. As a way to review those terms, simply write down the words that each letter represents in each acronym.

Acronyms for Chapter 4

AC	EMI	STP
AM	FM	TIA
AP	FSK	UTP
ASK	LED	WLAN
BSS	PSK	2G
CSMA/CA	PSTN	3G
DC	SONET	4G

Create Mind Maps

This chapter suggests two mind maps. The first one gives you a chance to remember and organize a relatively large volume of terms related to sending data over electrical circuits and with sending data using energy that uses waves. The goal of this exercise is not to have everyone finish with the exact same mind map, but rather to give your brain a chance to sift through the terms and organize them in your own mind.

For this first mind map, think of any terms that come to mind related to how networks send data over copper links. List the terms anywhere on your mind map. When you start to see some terms that fit into a category, or seem to be related, move them around into some grouping. If doing this as an in-class exercise, trade with a classmate, review his, trade back, and adjust if that review gave you any ideas.

For the second mind map, organize all the concepts you learned in this chapter about copper and fiber media, including categories for the physical parts of the cables and the different types of cables. This task should probably have 20 or less items.

As always, keep the individual nodes in the mind map to just a few words at most; the goal is not to define the terms, but to organize how they fit with each other.

Define Other Terms

Define the following additional terms from this chapter, and check your answers in the glossary:

100BASE-T	direct current	noise
100BASE-Tx	electromagnetic interference (EMI)	period
10BASE-T		phase shift keying (PSK)
2G	electromagnetic radiation	pin position
3G	Ethernet	pinout
4G	fiber optics	port
802.11	frequency shift keying (FSK)	public switched telephone network (PSTN)
alternating current		
amplitude shift keying (ASK)	full duplex	receiver
	half duplex	shielded twisted-pair (STP)
antenna	hertz	
Basic Service Set (BSS)	laser	single-mode fiber
bit rate	LED	site survey
bit time	Manchester encoding	Synchronous Optical Network (SONET)
conductor	medium (media)	
CSMA/CA	mobile phone network	transmitter
current	multimode fiber	twisted-pair
		voltage

Complete the Tables and Lists from Memory

Print a copy of Appendix B, "Memory Tables" (which you can find online at www.pearsonitcertification.com/title/9780789748454), or at least the section for this chapter, and complete the tables and lists from memory. Appendix C, "Memory Tables Answer Key," also online, includes completed tables and lists to check your work.

Chapter 5

Ethernet LANs

By this point in the book, you have already learned many facts about Ethernet LANs. These LANs connect nearby devices using copper UTP or fiber-optic cables. End-user devices need a network interface card (NIC) to connect to the Ethernet LAN, and the cables connect those NICs to a network device called a LAN switch. The LAN switches can forward data between devices on the LAN, oftentimes from a user device to some nearby router.

This chapter pulls those earlier concepts together, expands on the concepts, adds detail, and completes this book's discussion of Ethernet as an end to itself. The earlier chapters laid the foundation to understand many networking technologies, including Ethernet; this chapter completes the Ethernet story.

This chapter explains many specifics about Ethernet LAN technologies using three major sections:

- The first section, "Defining Ethernet LANs," compares Ethernet LANs to many other parts of networking: WANs, old types of LANs, and wireless LANs. This first section also introduces new Ethernet features among the many Ethernet standards, making comparisons between those standards as well.

- The second major section, "Building Ethernet LANs," continues to explain additional Ethernet features with a group of topics that matter most when an engineer actually builds a LAN for one site in an enterprise network.

- The third and final major section of this chapter, "Exploring Ethernet Data-Link Features," discusses two very important Ethernet features that connect all Ethernet standards together—Ethernet frames and Ethernet LAN switching.

Chapter Outline

Objectives

- List major differences between WAN technologies and Ethernet LAN technologies.

- Distinguish between Ethernet features that are different or the same across the 10-Mbps, 100-Mbps, and 1000-Mbps Ethernet standards.

- Give examples of some of the former and current competing technologies to Ethernet technologies in the LAN market.

- List the different speeds supported by Ethernet standards.

- Explain what functions the IEEE autonegotiation process chooses, and describe how that helps campus LANs support multiple Ethernet standards.

- Draw the UTP cabling pinouts for straight-through and crossover cables to support 10-, 100-, and 1000-Mbps Ethernet.

- Draw a diagram of an Ethernet frame, naming all header and trailer fields.

- Describe the process of how the IEEE ensures that universal MAC addresses are not duplicated.

- Give an example of how a switch forwards a unicast Ethernet frame when a switch has a full MAC address table.

- Give an example of how a switch forwards a unicast Ethernet frame when a switch has a full MAC address table.

- Give an example of how a switch learns the entries in its MAC address table.

Key Terms

Ethernet LANs

802.3

Fast Ethernet

Gigabit Ethernet

autonegotiation

Ethernet frame

MAC address

MAC address table

Defining Ethernet LANs

Ethernet has been a constant force in the world of LANs since LANs were first created. Ethernet began life as a creation by Xerox Corporation around the time of the creation of small personal-use computers back in the 1970s. Ethernet competed against several LAN technologies as the LAN market matured in the 1980s and 1990s, eventually winning the war against those technologies. Today, Ethernet LANs dominate the world of wired LANs.

This first of three major sections in this chapter sets out to further define **Ethernet LANs** by comparing Ethernet LANs to other parts of computer networking. In a series of comparisons, the following sections show what Ethernet includes and what it does not. That story includes some history that helps give some context to the timeline of the many Ethernet standards. These sections also compare Ethernet to itself, because Ethernet includes a wide variety of standards that have some common features but some different features as well. By comparing the entire Ethernet family, and comparing them in different ways, you can see how network engineers think about Ethernet and how they use Ethernet in real campus networks today.

These sections follow a progression of comparisons: first with WANs, then with older types of wired LANs, then with modern wireless LANs, and finally comparing Ethernet to itself.

Comparing Ethernet LANs to WANs

Ethernet began life as a LAN technology and remained a LAN technology for a few decades. As a LAN technology, Ethernet LANs connected end-user devices in one site, with the devices relatively close to each other. Each LAN at each site connected to a WAN, typically using a router, with the router forwarding traffic (in the form of IP packets) between the sites.

Interestingly, as time went on, Ethernet actually grew to support both LAN and WAN technology. The Ethernet standards kept growing to support faster and faster speeds, with longer and longer cabling distances. In the past, the word *Ethernet* always implied that you were talking about LANs, but today, the word might be referring to LANs or WANs. So, before moving too far into this chapter, a quick review of LAN and WAN concepts makes sense, with some comments about this chapter's focus on Ethernet LANs.

First, companies generally own their own LANs, and after they are bought, companies do not have to pay additional fees. The company buys Ethernet LAN NICs, cables, and LAN switches. The company installs the devices and cables, and the devices work. As long as nothing changes and nothing breaks, the network does not require any monthly fees.

WANs, of course, use a different business model. The company that needs to use a WAN (some enterprise, for example) leases WAN capacity from a service provider like a telco. The telco buys some cables, network devices, and so on to create its own network. The enterprise then pays a fee (usually monthly) to use some of the telco network's capacity.

When a network uses an older, more traditional WAN technology, like a point-to-point leased line, the dividing line between an Ethernet LAN and the WAN can be easily found because the WAN uses a different technology. Additionally, routers typically sit at the edge between each LAN and the WAN, because the major roles for routers is to connect LANs to the WAN. (See Chapter 3, "TCP/IP Networks," Figures 3-22, 3-23, and 3-24 for examples that show LANs and simple WANs.)

Many telcos today offer WAN services called *Metro Ethernet*, or *MetroE*, in which the cable from the telco to the customer site uses an Ethernet standard. The LANs at each site can still use Ethernet, but the WAN links also use Ethernet. Figure 5-1 illustrates this idea.

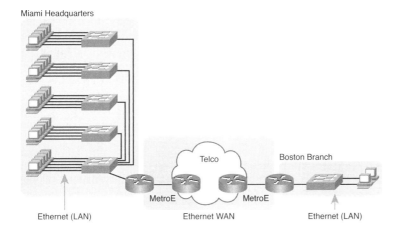

FIGURE 5-1

Ethernet LAN Versus Ethernet WAN

While the use of Ethernet as a WAN technology is interesting, this chapter focuses on Ethernet as a LAN technology, as in the two example sites (Miami and Boston) in Figure 5-1.

Comparing Ethernet LANs to Other Types of Wired LANs

Today, two broad types of LAN technologies exist: Ethernet LANs and wireless LANs. Ethernet LANs, defined by the IEEE 802.3 standards, use wires (cables), and wireless LANs, defined by the IEEE 802.11 standards, do not. However, in years past, many other types of wired LAN technologies existed. This section looks back at that history, in part for perspective, and in part to introduce some terminology.

LANs began as inventions created by researchers working for computer companies. For example, Ethernet started from the work by Dr. Robert Metcalfe, working for Xerox Corporation in the early 1970s. That work grew out of a need to connect a new kind of computer, one of the first personal-use computers, to a network of other computers and printers. Later, Xerox teamed with Intel and Digital

ON THE SIDE:
Metro Ethernet goes by many names: Metropolitan Ethernet, MetroE, Virtual Private LAN Service (VPLS), and Virtual Private Wire Service (VPWS).

ON THE SIDE: Intel and Xerox still exist today. DEC was acquired by Compaq, which was later acquired by Hewlett-Packard Corp. (HP).

Equipment Corporation (DEC) to further the work on Ethernet. The earliest published Ethernet prestandard documents became known as *DIX Ethernet*, named after these three companies.

Token Ring, the biggest early Ethernet competitor, began life as a creation of IBM around the same time frame. During the 1970s and 1980s, IBM and DEC competed in many parts of the computer market, including the LAN product market. DEC and Xerox led the charge with Ethernet technologies, and IBM led with Token Ring technologies.

By the close of the 1970s, the vendors realized that standardized LANs would be better for all vendors and customers, rather than using proprietary specifications from companies like DEC, Xerox, and IBM. In early 1980, these companies essentially passed the work of Ethernet, Token Ring, and a related LAN (Token Bus) over to the IEEE. The IEEE formed new working groups to work on these LAN standards, all beginning with the number 802. These same companies that had worked on the early proprietary LANs typically volunteered to work on the IEEE working groups so that those same companies could continue to mold the future of LAN standards. Table 5-1 lists three of the more important standards from the original IEEE LAN standards groups.

TABLE 5-1

Key Original IEEE 802 LAN Standards

Working Group	Common Reference	Purpose
802.2	Logical Link Control	Defines features in common across Ethernet, Token Ring, and others
802.3	Ethernet	Defines features specific to Ethernet
802.5	Token Ring	Defines features specific to Token Ring

ON THE SIDE: In a small piece of trivia, coincidentally, the IEEE 802 working group initial meeting happened in the second month of 1980, making it a little easier to remember the starting date.

The history of personal computers also follows the same general timeline as LANs, partly because these two technologies each made the other technology more useful. LANs gave PCs a way to connect to a network to work together and to connect to other computers. As people found more and more uses for PCs, more and more companies created LANs, while increasing the need for better and faster LAN technology.

Figure 5-2 shows a timeline of some of the facts related to the development of both PCs and LANs. Vendors created both PCs and LANs in the 1970s. In the 1980s, the computing world moved from networks with practically no PCs to networks with PCs on most desktops. During that same decade, the IEEE finalized and improved LAN standards. Open standards drive down prices, and PCs could use LANs, so the 1980s also saw networks move toward using the newer LAN technology. The left and center boxes in Figure 5-2 show the progression through the 1970s and 1980s.

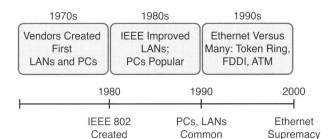

FIGURE 5-2

Timeline Perspectives:
LANs from Creation to
Ethernet Supremacy

Continuing down this historical march, Ethernet competed against several other LAN technologies during the 1990s, with each competitor eventually falling away. First, many enterprises used Token Ring in the 1980s and 1990s. It was one of the original IEEE LAN types, and it ran at both 4 Mbps and 16 Mbps.

Some newer types of LAN came along in the 1990s as well: *Fiber Distributed Data Interface (FDDI)* and *Asynchronous Transfer Mode (ATM)*. Both cost noticeably more money, in part because of their fast speeds (at the time) and their use of fiber cabling for longer distances. Many companies used products based on these LAN standards as well. These newer types of LANs gave network designers different options based on speed, distance, and cost, with many different vendors offering products for each.

The decade of the 1990s saw an interesting series of battles between LAN technologies and LAN vendors, but Ethernet eventually won the war. The 1990s saw a lot of improvement in both Ethernet standards and Ethernet products. Ethernet products were generally cheaper than the competing LAN types. When the newer FDDI and ATM standards emerged, Ethernet standards followed with new standards for faster speeds and longer distances using fiber optics as well.

By the year 2000, most enterprise networks had either migrated to Ethernet as their only LAN technology, or they knew that the next time they upgraded LAN hardware, Ethernet would be the obvious choice. Engineers no longer needed to refer to the type of LAN as a Token Ring LAN, ATM LAN, or Ethernet LAN; the word *LAN* became synonymous with *Ethernet LAN*.

The decade of the 2000s also saw great improvement in Ethernet speeds and distances. Ethernet grew from 1 gigabit per second (1 Gbps) to 100 Gbps, with distances approaching 80 km. Those longer distances, plus other standards, made Ethernet a viable WAN technology. Not only was Ethernet the leader in LANs, but it was also becoming a force in the WAN as well.

AUTHOR'S NOTE:
The dates in Figure 5-2 are approximate to give you the general idea. For example, not every company had LANs by 1990, but most would have claimed to be planning to add LANs as time and money permitted.

Comparing 802.3 Ethernet LANs to 802.11 Wireless LANs

Wireless LANs began life as a way to connect devices that could not connect using a cable. For example, you cannot expect someone to walk around a grocery store with a specialized product scanner with a cable connected to it, tripping every shopper that happens by. Wireless LANs (WLAN) solve that problem by giving any device a way to communicate without a cable.

> **AUTHOR'S NOTE:** Some people make the honest mistake of thinking of wireless LANs as *wireless Ethernet*, or *wireless Ethernet LANs*. Wireless LANs (defined by IEEE in 802.11 standards) are not Ethernet LANs (defined by IEEE in 802.3 standards); all Ethernet LANs use some form of cabling. One campus LAN can combine both, as shown in Figure 5-3.

While WLANs solve mobility problems, WLAN technology has matured enough so that it competes with Ethernet as a LAN technology. The IEEE made several improvements to 802.11 WLANs throughout the 2000s, including the completion of the 802.11n standard. The improvements continued into the decade of the 2010s, with new standards that approach gigabit speeds.

Today, Ethernet LAN has one competing LAN technology: WLANs. LAN designers have a choice of how to connect end-user devices: Use unshielded twisted-pair (UTP) cables to connect to the Ethernet LAN, or use wireless to connect to the wireless LAN. Figure 5-3 shows the competing options, with the typical combined wired/wireless LAN on the left and the wireless-only LAN edge alternative on the right.

FIGURE 5-3

Comparing the Combined Wired/ Wireless LAN to a Wireless-Only LAN Edge

Wired and Wireless LAN Edge   **Wireless Only LAN Edge**

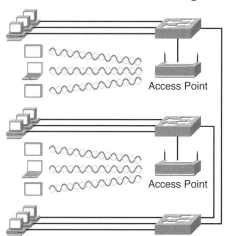

Access Point

Access Point

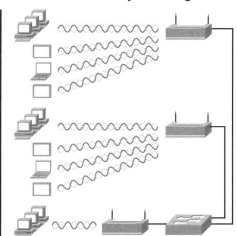

The WLAN-only LAN edge model on the right has some obvious benefits and some negatives as well. It uses no cables, which saves money. Today, with the number of wireless-only devices, most companies already plan on covering all spaces with a WLAN anyway so that the WLAN will already be available. However, WLANs typically require more attention and more skill to troubleshoot and monitor, and those unknowns might cause management to stay with the combined wired/wireless model on the left side of the figure.

As of the time of publication of this book, no one can tell whether the left side of Figure 5-3 or the right side will be more likely in enterprise LANs in the future. Watch for articles on this battle as you work through the class. Figure 5-4 completes the timeline, showing the impact of the progress of the 802.11 WLAN standards.

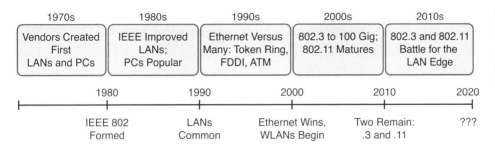

FIGURE 5-4

Timeline Perspectives: LANs from Creation to the 802.3-Versus-802.11 LAN Edge Battle

Comparing Ethernet to Itself

The word *Ethernet* refers to many different LAN standards that all exist as part of one family. Just like brothers and sisters can have some similar habits, while being very different in other ways, these Ethernet standards have some similarities and differences. The following sections look at Ethernet as a whole by examining what is the same and what differs among different Ethernet standards.

In particular, when reading through this topic, look for the following topics, which are typically the same for different Ethernet standards:

- A common topology
- A common data link layer header and trailer
- Common rules for how LAN switches forward data

In comparison, also watch for these key differences between different Ethernet standards:

- Different speeds
- Different cabling types
- Different maximum cable lengths

Ethernet Bit Rates (Speeds)

Ethernet standards have seen a vast improvement since the IEEE first took over the Ethernet standardization process in 1980.

The earliest improvements to Ethernet, in the 1980s, focused on cabling and topology. The original standard (10BASE5) used a thicker coaxial cabling (called Thicknet) with a bus topology. The IEEE followed that with a standard (10BASE2, also called Thinnet) that used a thinner coaxial cable, but with the same bus topology. The next new Ethernet standard, the 1990 10BASE-T standard, used a star topology and UTP cabling.

Each of these first few improvements lowered the cost of Ethernet and made other improvements, but all these early standards ran at 10 Mbps.

The next wave of 1990s standards saw a 100-fold increase in Ethernet speeds, plus the addition of fiber-optic cabling. The IEEE added the 100-Mbps *Fast Ethernet* standard in 1995 and the 1000-Mbps (1-Gbps) *Gigabit Ethernet* standards later in the 90s. Figure 5-5 shows the timeline depicting the evolution of Ethernet.

FIGURE 5-5

Ethernet Standards Dates, Speeds, and Common Names

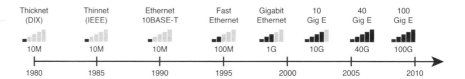

The first decade of the twenty-first century also saw a 100-fold increase in Ethernet speeds, from 1 Gbps (generally called Gigabit Ethernet, or 1 GbE) to 100 Gigabit Ethernet (100 GbE). The IEEE created new standards for each increase in speed, oftentimes multiple standards. Typically, the standards for fiber cabling came before the standards for UTP and were split into different standards documents.

Next, take a moment to think about the bigger picture of the entire Ethernet LAN as well as each individual link. Each individual link must follow a particular standard at a particular speed. A single Ethernet LAN typically has more than one link, however, and those links can all use different standards and different speeds. Each physical link acts independently from the other links, and the LAN switches deal with the differences.

Figure 5-6 shows an example of an Ethernet LAN with eight links that use six different combinations of speed and cable type.

FIGURE 5-6

One Ethernet LAN, Many Different Speeds and Cable Types

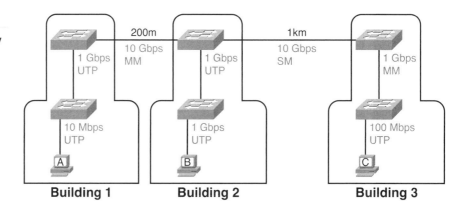

Key:

MM – Multimode Fiber
SM – Single-Mode Fiber
UTP – Unshielded Twisted Pair

The fact that each link works independently allows engineers to upgrade and grow Ethernet LANs much more easily. When any individual link appears to be overloaded with too much traffic, the engineer can upgrade to the next faster type of Ethernet. Often, switch vendors make their switches to allow easier upgrades, with a mix of port types and with removable cards to facilitate an upgrade from one standard/speed to another. The idea works very much like the Department of Transportation widening roads before they get too congested; network engineers can increase the bit rates on links before they get too congested as well.

Ethernet Distances

Another key difference in the Ethernet physical layer standards is the maximum length of the cable. Each physical layer standard defines cable limitations for one or more types of cables. The limits start with some relatively short distances for specialized media, to typically 100 meters for UTP cable, and to several hundred meters for multimode (MM) fiber and several kilometers for single-mode (SM) fiber.

Memorizing the various Ethernet standards and their maximum cable lengths serves no good purpose for this introductory book, but knowing some key comparison numbers can help give you some good idea of where to start thinking.

First, Ethernet UTP cables have a maximum cable length of 100 meters. Each time the IEEE sets out to define a new faster standard that uses UTP, it maintains the same 100-meter maximum. By keeping a consistent maximum cable length for UTP, companies have a chance to use their already-installed UTP cabling when upgrading to use a new Ethernet UTP standard. If the new standard supported a shorter maximum cable length, that shorter length restriction might require a move to use fiber-optic cables and prevent the use of the old installed UTP cabling.

Second, comparing the maximum cable length for a set of standards that use the same speed can give you some good perspective. Network engineers usually first choose the speeds for each link, and then they think about what cabling supports the length of each link at that speed.

For example, Table 5-2 lists details about different parts of the specific Gigabit Ethernet standards. The IEEE 802.3z standard defines Gigabit Ethernet using fiber links, including both MM and SM fiber. Another standard, IEEE 802.3ab, defines Gigabit Ethernet using UTP cabling. These standards also define the maximum cable lengths, as listed in the table.

TABLE 5-2

Gigabit Ethernet Standards and Cable Lengths

Standard	Shortcut Family Name	Specific Shortcut Name	Year Standardized	Cabling	Maximum Length*
802.3z	1000BASE-X	1000BASE-LX	1998	MM	550 m
802.3z	1000BASE-X	1000BASE-SX	1998	SM	5 km*
802.3ab	1000BASE-T	1000BASE-T	1999	UTP (4 pair)	100 m

* The 1000BASE-SX standard was later improved with 1000BASE-SX10 to allow a 10-km link.

ON THE SIDE: Some
Ethernet standards
extend the maximum
fiber-optic cable
length of a single link
to 80 km.

Generally, the network designer uses the least expensive cabling type that supports the required length of the cable. UTP costs the least, MM fiber a little more, and SM fiber the most. The costs include the cost of the cable plus the cost of the hardware in each node (NICs and switch ports) to connect to the link.

Ethernet Star Topology and Point-to-Point Links

Modern Ethernet LANs use a *star topology*. Generally, the word *topology* refers to the shape of the network. In a simple Ethernet LAN, all the devices connect to a single LAN switch. If you spread the devices out to all points on the compass and look at the shape, it looks a little like how a child might draw a star or the sun. So, network topologies that connect links to a single point are called star topologies. Figure 5-7 shows an example.

FIGURE 5-7

Star Topology in an
Ethernet LAN Compared
to a Drawing of a Sun
(Star)

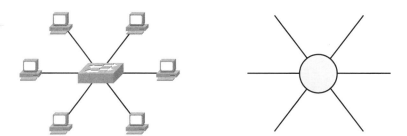

Even in larger campus LANs with many switches, the LAN is still considered to have a star topology. Visually, a diagram of a complex large campus LAN does not actually look like a child's drawing of a star. However, each switch still has links going out from the switch, so people still call the topology a star topology.

Modern Ethernet LAN topologies also use only *point-to-point links*. In other words, each link connects two points or nodes; no links connect to more than two points (nodes). The nodes on an Ethernet link can be a PC and a LAN switch, as shown in Figure 5-7, two switches, or other combinations.

> **ON THE SIDE:** Some older Ethernet standards that came before 10BASE-T used another topology, called a *bus topology*. With a bus topology, the network looked like a bus route with many stops on a single street, because the LAN existed as a cable with a part of the cable connected to each user device. A single link connected to more than two devices.

Data-Link Framing and Forwarding

All the Ethernet standards use the same consistent Ethernet headers and trailers. That consistency allows one Ethernet LAN to use physical links that use many different Ethernet standards, while still delivering data over all those links.

The idea of using one standard header and trailer, but many standards for physical links, works a little like using your car to travel on different roads. If you own a car, you can drive on 1-lane dirt roads, skinny 2-lane country roads, nicely paved 2-lane roads, 4-lane roads, and 12-lane superhighways, all with your one car. With Ethernet, an Ethernet frame—which starts with an Ethernet header and ends with an Ethernet trailer—can travel over any type of physical Ethernet link, like a car driving over many types of roads.

Figure 5-8 shows a conceptual example of how an Ethernet frame flows in an Ethernet LAN. The figure repeats the exact same topology as the earlier Figure 5-6. In this case, host A sends an Ethernet frame to host C. The frame travels over six links, using four different speeds, using UTP, MM fiber, and SM fiber. Over all these links and through all these switches, the Ethernet frame remains intact and unchanged over the entire journey.

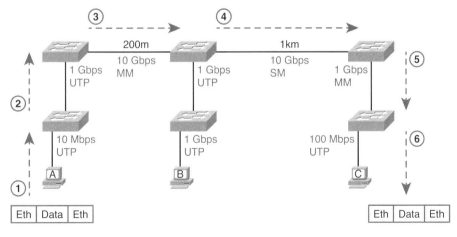

FIGURE 5-8

Forwarding One Ethernet Frame Over Six Different Types of Ethernet Links

The third major section of this chapter, "Exploring the Ethernet Data-Link Features," discusses in detail the Ethernet header and trailer, plus the forwarding logic used by the switches.

Names of Ethernet Standards

In some cases when discussing Ethernet, people need to refer to Ethernet as a whole, so they refer to all of Ethernet as simply *Ethernet*. In other cases, however, the discussion needs to point out a particular part of Ethernet: a particular standard, a particular speed, a particular cabling type, or some other part of Ethernet. Unfortunately, Ethernet uses several types of names, and Ethernet includes many standards, so figuring out the correct names can be quite a chore.

This short topic gives some insight into the naming of Ethernet standards, while avoiding listing every single Ethernet standard. This topic teaches you enough to recognize the more common Ethernet standards by their various names. It should also give you enough knowledge of how the Ethernet naming works so that you can predict the meaning of the name of an Ethernet standard that you have never seen before.

IEEE Ethernet standards can be referenced by their informal names, by an IEEE standard, or by an IEEE shorthand name. This section explains all three, in order.

First, the *informal names* refer to various Ethernet standards using names that many people in the industry use, but the standards might not actually use the terms. These informal names typically focus on the speed and mostly ignore the cabling types. Figure 5-5, earlier in this chapter, referenced the Ethernet standards with their informal names.

For example, the 1990 IEEE standard, formally known as 802.3i and also known as 10BASE-T, defines 10-Mbps Ethernet using UTP cabling. Informally, the industry tends to call this particular standard *Ethernet*. Five years after that standard came out, the next big Ethernet standard was introduced, and it ran at 100 Mbps. So, the informal name became *Fast Ethernet* because it was the first Ethernet standard to run faster than 10 Mbps; formally, it was known as standard 802.3u. By the time the next Ethernet standards came out, the industry just started using informal names that referred to the speed. Table 5-3 lists some of the informal names.

TABLE 5-3

Informal Ethernet Names Based on Speeds

Speed	Informal Name	Other Common Informal Names
10 Mbps	Ethernet	—
100 Mbps	Fast Ethernet	Fast E
1 Gbps	Gigabit Ethernet	Gig E, 1 GbE
10 Gbps	10 Gig E	10 GbE
40 Gbps	40 Gig E	40 GbE
100 Gbps	100 Gig E	100 GbE

Of course, the IEEE has a formal name for each standard. The IEEE formally identifies each standard by its IEEE *project number*. When the IEEE starts work on a potential new standard, it starts a new project with a new number. If the project results in a standard, the standard uses the number created for the project when the project started. But no one refers to the words *project number*, instead just referring to the project number as the standard.

IEEE standards (project numbers) for Ethernet LANs all begin with 802.3, with a suffix that follows. For example, the IEEE first standardized fiber Gigabit Ethernet, identified as 802.3z. Not long after that, the IEEE standardized UTP Gigabit Ethernet as 802.3ab.

In addition to the informal names and the project numbers, the IEEE also defines more descriptive *shorthand names*. The shorthand names list the speed as part of the name, which helps in remembering the right name. The shorthand names also imply something about the type of cabling. Because these shorthand names have more obvious meaning than the formal standards numbers, most people ignore the formal standards numbers and use either the informal name or these shorthand names.

Anyone who sees an IEEE shorthand name and wants to know with confidence exactly to what standard the name refers should refer to the IEEE website. However, anyone can interpret the meaning of the most common shorthand names by just following a few basic rules.

To interpret IEEE shorthand names, first break the name into parts, as shown in Figure 5-9. Every shorthand name discussed in this book has the word *BASE-* or *GBASE-* in the middle. Treat that word as a way to separate a prefix and suffix for the term, and then use the rules that follow the figure.

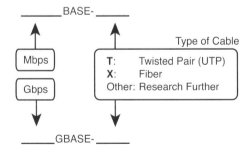

FIGURE 5-9

Structure of IEEE Shorthand Ethernet Names

To interpret any such shorthand Ethernet name, use these general rules:

- Mentally separate the term into a prefix and suffix, based on what comes before and after the word *BASE-* or *GBASE-*.

- The prefix lists the speed:

    - The speed is in Mbps if the middle lists *BASE-* (without a G).

    - The speed is in Gbps if the middle lists *GBASE-*.

- The suffix lists the cabling type:
    - *T* refers to twisted-pair (UTP) standards.
    - *X* somewhere in the suffix refers to fiber-optic standards.
- Other values require more research.

In a networking job working with a real network, most of the time you can use much easier informal wording or informal names, or describe what you mean. In some cases, particularly when ordering products or researching for new LANs, you will likely need to remember some of this more formal terminology. Table 5-4 lists the names of the more common Ethernet LAN standards for reference.

TABLE 5-4
Ethernet Naming Summary

Original IEEE Standard ID	IEEE Shorthand Name	Informal Name(s)	Speed	Typical Cabling Type
802.3i	10BASE-T	Ethernet	10 Mbps	UTP
802.3u	100BASE-T	Fast Ethernet (Fast E)	100 Mbps	UTP
802.3z	1000BASE-X	Gigabit Ethernet (Gig E, GbE)	1000 Mbps	Fiber
802.3ab	1000BASE-T	Gigabit Ethernet (Gig E, GbE)	1000 Mbps	UTP
802.3ae	10GBASE-X	10 GbE	10 Gbps	Fiber
802.3an	10GBASE-T	10 GbE	10 Gbps	UTP
802.3ba	40GBASE-X	40 GbE (40 GigE)	40 Gbps	Fiber
802.3ba	100GBASE-X	100 GbE (100 GigE)	100 Gbps	Fiber

Building Ethernet LANs

The earlier chapters of this book, plus the first major section of this chapter, have combined to describe Ethernet physical layer concepts pretty well already. However, those earlier topics did not touch on a few issues that come up when you build an Ethernet LAN larger than a small office LAN.

This second of three major sections of this chapter looks at several points that come up in conversations when building and growing an enterprise campus LAN over time. Engineers not only have to think about link speeds and distances, which have already been discussed in this book, but the engineers must also consider the cost of those links. The following sections discuss the cost trends over time. Next, these sections look at some issues related to how to move devices from older Ethernet standards to newer standards, taking advantage of IEEE autonegotiation. These sections end by reviewing the pinouts used on UTP straight-through cables, plus introducing another important cabling pinout—the crossover cabling pinout.

Trade-offs of Speed Versus Pricing

Unsurprisingly, when the IEEE creates new, faster Ethernet standards, and vendors start offering new faster Ethernet products, the price for older, slower products starts to fall. Before looking at the pricing trends, it helps to look at the timeline for UTP and fiber Ethernet standards for perspective.

Ethernet standards began with a 10-Mbps bit rate from the earliest published standards from Digital, Intel, and Xerox, called DIX Ethernet, back in 1980. The IEEE standards continued to use the same 10-Mbps speed up through the 1990 10BASE-T standard. Eventually, the IEEE increased the speed by a factor of 10 with the standardization of Fast Ethernet (802.3u) in 1995. (See Figure 5-5, earlier in this chapter, for a reminder of the timeline.)

In most cases, when the IEEE introduces a faster version of Ethernet, the standards split out the UTP cabling from other standards. The first such bump in speed, 802.3u Fast Ethernet, was the exception, defining both UTP and fiber details in one standard. Since that time, each new increase in speed used one standard for fiber and another later standard for UTP. It just so happens that the UTP work has traditionally required more time. After Fast Ethernet, the IEEE introduced newer standards using fiber cabling first, with a different UTP-based standard coming later.

Figure 5-10 shows the timeline for the current standards as of publication, from Fast Ethernet up through 100 GbE.

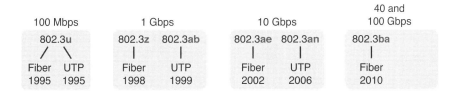

FIGURE 5-10

IEEE Standards—Dates and Cable Types

Ethernet Pricing Trends

Over time, the price of a device that uses a particular Ethernet standard goes lower—much lower. This section discusses the two main reasons.

First, the prices of all computer technology fall over time. Computer technology requires some expensive research to develop. It often requires new microchips, and new microchips require a large up-front cost. However, after investing large amounts of money to make the first chips and other parts for some new technology, the cost to make more is relatively low. Over time, competitors see that low ongoing cost, so they lower prices, hoping to beat the competition on price. In short, the high up-front cost, but lower ongoing costs, helps computer technology prices fall in the long run.

Second, for Ethernet LANs, new products that use the new faster Ethernet standards push the old slower product prices lower. No one wants last year's model of anything, and the market usually wants faster, stronger, more powerful products when possible. As a result, the demand falls for the older products, which drives down the prices.

Third, new fiber Ethernet standards usually only lower the price of older fiber-based products, and new UTP Ethernet standards usually lower the price of older UTP-based products. For example, 1000BASE-T helped drive down the prices for 100BASE-T.

The combination of these reasons, plus others, means that the prices of Ethernet NICs and LAN switch ports have fallen over time for most every specific type of Ethernet. When the new standard comes out, the prices remain high for products that use that standard. Eventually, the prices start to fall, because of time in the market and normal technology pricing trends, and when the replacement newer standard comes out, the prices fall further.

Figure 5-11 shows the flow of pricing trends, representing the relative price of UTP Ethernet NICs over time. The graphs show prices for UTP NICs that support four speeds, from 10 Mbps through 10 Gbps.

FIGURE 5-11

**Ethernet LAN NIC
Relative Price History**

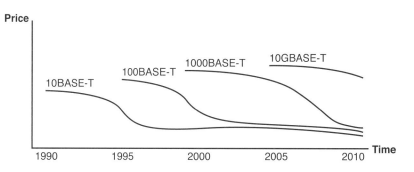

The Impact of Pricing on Campus LANs

Enterprise campus LANs could use the fastest possible type of Ethernet on every switch port and NIC. However, because of the price differences, network engineers typically have to pick and choose where to use the newer, more expensive options and where to use the older, much less expensive options.

To think about the issues, think about a design for a campus LAN in one building to support 1000 users. This LAN uses 40 *edge switches*, each of which connects to an average of 25 end-user devices. Each of these edge switches connects to a centralized switch called a *distribution switch*, which distributes data frames to the rest of the LAN. Figure 5-12 shows the topology.

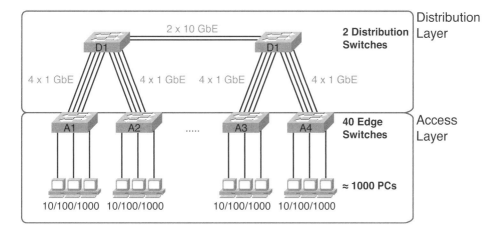

FIGURE 5-12

1000-User Campus LAN, with Speed Versus Cost Choices

First, think about the links at the edge of the LAN, at the bottom of the figure. The edge of the LAN, where all the user devices sit, makes up the majority of the cabling and switch ports. To keep the cost down, these links should use the least expensive cabling possible: UTP. At press time (2012), 1000BASE-T prices had fallen pretty low but 10GBASE-T prices had not. So most LANs in 2012 would use 1-GbE links at the edge, or more likely, NICs and ports that could autonegotiate to run at 10, 100, or 1000 Mbps. (These NICs and ports, called 10/100/1000 NICs and ports, are discussed further in the next section.)

The links from the edge switches into the rest of the LAN could use newer or older standards. These links, typically called *uplinks* or *trunks*, could have been faster (and more expensive) 10-GbE links in this design. However, Figure 5-12 shows the older and cheaper 1-GbE uplinks to help make a point about balancing the cost.

In this case, for the uplinks, the engineer designing this LAN might decide that the uplink from switch A1 to switch D1 needs to be faster than 1 GbE. The 10-GbE LAN switch ports, however, might cost more than the hardware and cables to support the four 1-GbE links in the figure. So the engineer made a trade-off between speed and cost, creating a combined 4-Gbps uplink from each edge switch into the distribution switches.

Finally, the design in Figure 5-12 does show two 10-GbE links between the two distribution switches. In this case, the two links provide a total of 20 Gbps capacity. From a cost perspective, the hardware might be more expensive than slower Ethernet speeds (at least until prices fall over the years). However, the number of these more expensive links is low, and the capacity might well be needed.

ON THE SIDE: Often, newer Ethernet standards are first used for those higher-speed trunks in the core of the campus LAN, as shown in Figure 5-12, and they slowly migrate out toward the LAN edge as pricing falls over the years.

Migration Issues and Autonegotiation

When building enterprise campus LANs, the company does not install the LAN all at once with the expectation that the LAN will never change again. LANs change over time—end-user devices are upgraded to new hardware, individual people and their devices move to new locations, whole departments move, leases run out requiring moves to entirely new facilities, and the load on networks always goes up over time; this can require upgrades to the speeds and capacities of the campus LAN. In a smaller LAN, the LAN might not change often, but in a larger campus LAN, things change.

Most of the changes in an enterprise LAN occur on the edge of the LAN. The *LAN edge*, also called the *LAN access layer* by LAN designers, is where the end-user device connects to a LAN switch.

Both Ethernet nodes on a single link must use the same speed; if not, the link simply cannot pass data. However, the LAN edge sees lot of changes and lots of moving devices, with devices that support different speeds. So, Ethernet standards have to deal with these changes so that the LAN still works. Thankfully, those issues can be easily overcome using an IEEE Ethernet feature called autonegotiation, as discussed in the sections that follow.

Autonegotiation of Speed

Imagine that you went back in time to the mid-1990s, just before Fast Ethernet products entered the market. You have a LAN with thousands of PCs, all with 10BASE-T NICs. Then the new 100BASE-T standard comes out. You decide that you want to migrate to the new standard during the weekend change window, when you are allowed to make changes to the LAN. However, you only get three hours, from 2 a.m. to 5 a.m. Sunday morning, to make all your changes. How do you do the migration?

To help companies migrate to new Ethernet technologies that use faster speeds, the IEEE created a feature called **autonegotiation**. First, vendors made products (NICs and switch ports) that supported both the new and the old standard. Then the nodes on a link could use autonegotiation to automatically decide the best speed that both nodes on the link support. If both nodes support the faster speed, great; they use the faster speed. If not, they at least work using the slower speed. Later, when the hardware on both ends of the link supports the faster speed, autonegotiation lets the nodes choose to use the newer and faster speed.

Figure 5-13 shows an example of how autonegotiation can be used to migrate from 10BASE-T to 100BASE-T with switches. The left side of the figure shows a typical LAN that uses only 10BASE-T. Then, as depicted on the right side of the figure, the engineer replaces the left switch (SW1) with a 10/100 switch, which means that this new switch's ports can negotiate to run at either 10 Mbps or 100 Mbps. Similarly, the engineer updated the NICs in PCs B and D to use 10/100 NICs, which can run at either speed, and negotiate to use the best speed supported by both nodes.

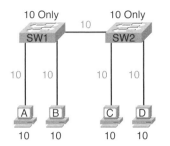
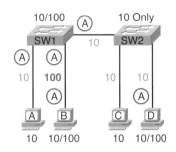

FIGURE 5-13

Using Autonegotiation to Migrate from 10 Mbps to 100 Mbps

Before looking at the specific example shown in the figure, first read about the IEEE autonegotiation rules that a port follows:

- If both nodes send autonegotiation messages, both state their supported speeds in a list. The nodes choose the fastest speed in both their own list and the other node's list.

- If the local node sends autonegotiation messages, but does not receive any messages from the other node, to be safe, the local node uses its slowest supported speed (usually 10 Mbps).

The small LAN on the right side of Figure 5-13 shows the speed that the nodes use beside each link. In this example, three devices will attempt autonegotiation: switch SW1, PC B, and PC D. In the case of SW1, all its ports are 10/100 ports and support autonegotiation. The following list details why each link runs at the speeds listed in the figure:

SW1 – PC A: In this case, SW1 sends autonegotiation messages, but it hears nothing from PC A. SW1 therefore chooses its slowest speed. PC A, with a 10-Mbps-only NIC, also uses 10 Mbps, so the link works, at 10 Mbps.

SW1 – PC B: In this case, both SW1 and PC B send autonegotiation messages, and both list speeds of 10 and 100 Mbps. Both choose the fastest supported speed (100 Mbps).

SW1 – SW2: This case works just like the SW1–to–PC A case, so both SW1 and SW2 use 10 Mbps.

SW2 – PC C: Neither SW2 nor PC C supports autonegotiation. Both support only 10 Mbps, so both use 10 Mbps.

SW2 – PC D: PC D sends autonegotiation messages, but it hears nothing from SW2. PC D therefore chooses its slowest speed, 10 Mbps. SW2, with ports that support only 10 Mbps, also uses 10 Mbps.

Autonegotiation helps a LAN change over time with an easy migration to new speeds at the edge of a LAN. First, a switch needs to be upgraded to use switch ports that support multiple speeds. (Most ports on most switches today support multiple speeds and autonegotiation.) At that point, when any device upgrades to a new NIC, the device is replaced with a device with a faster NIC, or the device moves to a new location and new switch port, the end-user device and the switch can always negotiate to use the faster speed.

> **AUTHOR'S NOTE:** NICs and switch ports that support multiple speeds list the speeds with a / between them. For example, a 10/100 NIC (spoken as "a ten one-hundred NIC") supports 10- and 100-Mbps speeds, and a 10/100/1000 NIC supports 10-, 100-, and 1000-Mbps speeds.

Today, many PC NICs and switch ports can autonegotiate to use 10, 100, or 1000 Mbps. These 10/100/1000 NICs often cost very little, for the same reasons discussed around Figure 5-11.

Autonegotiation of Duplex

In networking, the duplex setting on a single link determines whether the nodes can or cannot send at the same time. With half duplex, the nodes must take turns; with full duplex, the nodes can send at any time.

Because of some historical reasons, NICs and switch ports must be ready to support both half and full duplex. Full duplex works better than half duplex, so nodes should use full duplex if possible. All Ethernet LAN physical links discussed in this book allow full duplex; however, one older type of networking node, called a LAN hub, does not support full duplex. So, in modern Ethernet LANs, the NICs and switches must be ready to use half duplex when connecting to a hub.

To understand a little more about LAN hubs, consider this brief walk through a little more Ethernet history. In the very earliest days of Ethernet, before 10BASE-T, the LAN did not use a networking device like a switch. The Ethernet LAN had NICs, with all the NICs connected to the same physical link but with no other device, as shown on the left side of Figure 5-14. When the IEEE introduced 10BASE-T, it introduced UTP cabling, with a star topology, with all the NICs cabled to a centralized device. When 10BASE-T was first introduced, that device was called a hub, as seen in the center of Figure 5-14.

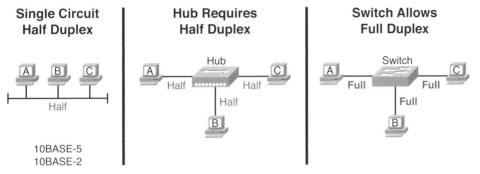

FIGURE 5-14

History of Half and
Full Duplex

To finish this brief history of duplex, look at the three parts of the figure, from left
to right. The earliest Ethernet standards used coaxial cabling and created a single
circuit. The devices used half-duplex logic to share the one circuit, taking turns.
In the middle, 10BASE-T with hubs had cabling with two circuits in each cable,
which physically allowed full duplex, but the hub could not handle all devices
sending at once. So the NICs had to keep using half-duplex logic, taking turns.
Finally, vendors started offering LAN switches that allowed full duplex.

Each node needs to choose the correct duplex setting, so the IEEE allows devices to
negotiate duplex using autonegotiation. In a modern LAN, most links will use full
duplex, but when an old hub still exists, the autonegotiation process will cause the
nodes to fall back to use half duplex. The rules are

- If both nodes send autonegotiation messages, each node states whether it
  supports both full and half duplex, or only half duplex. If both nodes support
  full duplex, both use full duplex; if not, both use half duplex.

- If the local node sends autonegotiation messages, but does not receive any
  messages from the other node, to be safe, the local node uses half duplex.

A couple of examples can help. Using the center part of Figure 5-14, when host A
performs autonegotiation, the hub pays no attention and sends no autonegotiation
messages. So host A uses half duplex, which works well, because the hub expects
the hosts connected to it to use half duplex.

As another example, on the right side of Figure 5-14, when host C sends
autonegotiation messages, the switch port also sends messages. Both devices claim
to support both full and half duplex, so they choose to use full duplex.

> **ON THE SIDE:** When a node uses half duplex, it uses the carrier sense
> multiple access collision detect (CSMA/CD) algorithm to limit when it sends
> data. When it uses full duplex, the node disables CSMA/CD, sending data
> whenever it has data to send.

Distances Using Fiber Optics Versus UTP

When building an enterprise campus LAN, the engineer thinks about many factors. He thinks about the speeds needed for each device and the speeds needed to connect the switches together. He thinks about the cost of the hardware and the links. And as mentioned several times in Chapter 4, "Transmitting Bits," he thinks about the length of each link, which tells the engineer which cabling options can support each link.

The book purposefully avoids listing the specific maximum distances for every possible Ethernet standard. For the purposes of this book, the big ideas for Ethernet link distance planning are this:

- UTP links can be up to 100 meters.
- Multimode links can run several hundred meters.
- Single-mode links can run several kilometers, sometimes tens of kilometers.

In real life, the engineer would check the standards and the vendor's documentation to make sure that the length requirements would work.

For a review of the maximum cable lengths with Gigabit Ethernet, look back to Table 5-2.

Ethernet Cabling Pinouts

Any physical layer standard that uses copper wires needs to define the correct cabling pinouts. Pinouts, as explained in Chapter 4's section "Ethernet Cabling Pinouts," defines which wires connect to which pin positions on the connectors, on both ends of a cable. Both nodes on a link expect specific wires to be in each pin position. By knowing the pinouts, the nodes can use specific pairs of wires to create each circuit, and specific circuits to send in each direction.

Chapter 4 showed the specific pinouts for a straight-through cable used for both 10BASE-T and 100BASE-T. The following sections review those concepts, add more about the correct straight-through pinouts to support Gigabit Ethernet, and then discuss the need for another cabling pinout—the crossover cable.

Straight-Through Cables

To understand why a straight-through cable works for 10BASE-T and 100BASE-T links, focus on the logic used by the nodes on a link. A PC NIC sends on the pair at pins 1,2; however, a switch uses pins 1,2 to receive data. For a link that connects a PC to a switch port, the wires at pins 1,2 on the PC must connect to pins 1,2 on the switch port as well so that the PC transmit logic connects to the same electrical circuit as the switch port's receive logic.

The logic for the other direction works the same way. A switch sends on the pair at pins 3,6, and a PC NIC uses pins 3,6 to receive data. Again, pins 3,6 on each end must be connected so that the switch port's transmit logic connects to the same electrical circuit as the PC's receive logic.

Figure 5-15 shows the PC and switch port logic, along with the straight-through cable logic.

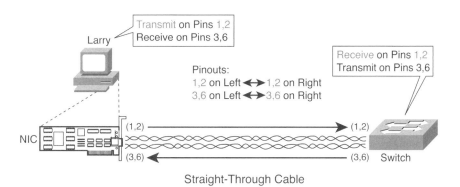

FIGURE 5-15

100BASE-T Transmit and Receive Logic, PC to Switch, with Straight Through Cable

1000BASE-T also uses a straight-through cable, but the cable differs slightly because 1000BASE-T uses four pairs. The same concepts apply, however. The 1000BASE-T straight-through cable begins with the same pinouts as a 10BASE-T or 100BASE-T cable, with two more pairs: another pair at pins 4,5 on both ends and the final pair at pins 7,8 on both ends.

With four pairs, you might assume that 1000BASE-T uses two pairs to send in each direction, but it does not. Instead, 1000BASE-T uses all four pairs, in both directions, at the same time. When the IEEE created 1000BASE-T, the encoding allowed two-way sending at the same time on the same circuit—a feature not supported by the earlier Ethernet encoding schemes. Essentially, each 1000BASE-T node sends 250 Mbps over each of the four circuits, for a total of 1000 Mbps, or 1 Gbps.

Crossover Cables

The 10BASE-T and 100BASE-T straight-through cable works because the PC NIC and the switch port use opposite pairs to send. The PC NIC sends on the twisted pair at pins 1,2, and the switch port sends on the twisted pair at pins 3,6.

When a UTP cable connects two nodes that use the same pin pair to send data, the cable must swap the wire pair. For example, most campus LANs have multiple LAN switches, with cables between the switches. When using UTP at 10 or 100 Mbps, the switch still tries to receive using the pair at pins 1,2, and it tries to send on the pair at pins 3,6; however, both switches on the link use that same logic. If the cable has a straight-through cable pinout, the link does not work.

A crossover cable pinout solves the problem. The crossover cable crosses the two pairs, as shown in Figure 5-16. The two like devices, which each want to send on the same pins, can continue to send on the same pins (3,6). The crossover cable connects the wires at pins 3,6 to the receive pins (1,2) on the other end of the cable.

FIGURE 5-16

Crossover Cable
for 10BASE-T and
100BASE-T

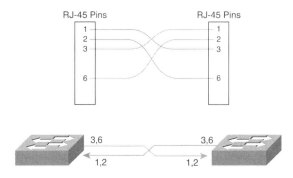

AUTHOR'S NOTE:
10GBASE-T uses
the same four-pair
pinouts as does
1000BASE-T.

1000BASE-T also uses a crossover cable, but with four wire pairs. It uses the same wiring as shown in Figure 5-16, plus with the pair at pins 4,5 crossed with the pair at pins 7,8.

Finally, the TIA cabling standards specify exactly which color pair to put in each position in the connectors on each end. To make the correct pairs cross, use TIA wiring standard T568A on one end and T568B on the other. Figure 5-17 shows the pinouts for each standard. If you compare the colors listed for each pin, you will see that these standards will cross the wires shown conceptually in Figure 5-16.

FIGURE 5-17

TIA Pinout Standards
T568A and T568B Used
to Create a Crossover
Cable

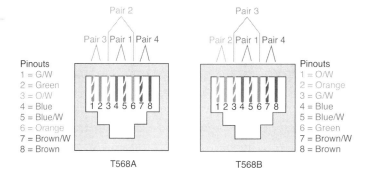

Exploring Ethernet Data-Link Features

Ethernet defines standards at both the physical layer and data link layer of the OSI model. The Ethernet physical layer standards give Ethernet many options for speed, types of cables, and cabling distances. The Ethernet data link layer standards make those different types of links work together. The work of the Ethernet data link layer enables one LAN, with many types of physical links, to pass data among all the devices.

This last of the three major sections in this chapter examines two particularly important data link layer topics. First, the following sections look at Ethernet frames. These frames include the Ethernet header and trailer, plus data supplied to the Ethernet data link layer by the higher-layer protocols. The frame defines many details, most importantly, Ethernet addresses.

The second part of these sections discuss LAN switching. In a single Ethernet LAN, an Ethernet frame can flow over several Ethernet links, with the frames forwarded by Ethernet switches. The logic used on those switches plays an important role in how Ethernet LANs work.

Ethernet Frames and Addresses

The IEEE 802.3 standard defines the **Ethernet frame**. An Ethernet frame includes the Ethernet data link layer header and the Ethernet data link layer trailer, plus the data and other higher-layer headers that need to be sent through the LAN.

Each Ethernet LAN has a basic job—deliver Ethernet frames from one device on the LAN to another device on the same LAN. If you step back and think about the entire network, of which one Ethernet LAN is just a subset of the network, the network delivers bits from one user device to another. The Ethernet LAN does part of that work. For a single Ethernet, the Ethernet delivers data, in the form of an Ethernet frame, from one Ethernet-connected device to another Ethernet-connected device. In short, Ethernet LANs deliver Ethernet frames from one Ethernet device to another. (Refer to Figure 5-8 for an example of an Ethernet LAN delivering a frame between two devices.)

This topic describes the details of the Ethernet frame, with emphasis on the Ethernet MAC addresses in the Ethernet header.

The Ethernet MAC Header and Trailer

The IEEE defines the header and trailer as a part of the 802.3 standard called *Media Access Control (MAC)*. The name itself, taken literally, helps define the purpose of the header and trailer: to control how Ethernet devices access (use) the physical media. An Ethernet frame holds a MAC header, data, and a MAC trailer. (The header and trailer can also be called an *Ethernet header* and *Ethernet trailer*, or simply a header and trailer.)

Before looking at the specific parts of the header and trailer, a brief analogy can help bring the broader idea of the Ethernet MAC header and trailer to life. Think about all the paved roads near your home, all as built by the local government Department of Transportation (DoT) or equivalent. The DoT builds the roads expecting only certain types of vehicles, of certain sizes, that go certain speeds. For example, in the United States, you cannot drive your tractor at 10 miles per hour on an 8-lane superhighway. You cannot drive a car that is 50 feet wide on the roads, because the DoT makes the lanes in the road much narrower than 50 feet. You cannot (legally) race your friends at hundreds of miles per hour to see who has the fastest car. The DoT builds the roads expecting that the vehicles that use the roads must follow the rules of the road.

For Ethernet LANs, the physical layer standards define the equivalent of the physical roads for cars, and the Ethernet data-link standards define the rules of the road (LAN). Ethernet does not allow the nodes to just send any bits onto the link. Instead, the bits must begin with a valid Ethernet header. The bits must end with a valid Ethernet trailer. Other rules apply as well, but most importantly, you can think of the Ethernet header and trailer as making the data legal for the LAN.

The Ethernet MAC header and trailer include several *fields*. Each field has some different purpose, so to understand the purpose of the header and trailer, you need to understand each field. Figure 5-18 shows the format of an Ethernet frame, with the individual fields.

FIGURE 5-18

Ethernet Frame Format

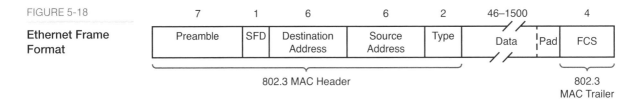

> **AUTHOR'S NOTE:** Ethernet supports an alternate frame format that uses a 2-byte length field instead of the 2-byte type field, followed by an 802.2 logical link control (LLC) header. The LLC header has a field that takes the place of the Type field in Figure 5-18. This text focuses only on the format shown in Figure 5-18.

Table 5-5 lists the Ethernet header and trailer fields, plus a brief description of the purpose for each. It also lists a shorthand phrase to help you remember each field. The text following the table gives a little more detailed description.

TABLE 5-5

Ethernet Header and Trailer Fields

Field	Description	Shorthand Reminder
Preamble	7 bytes of repeating binary 10, so that all devices can synchronize at the physical layer.	Get ready…
SFD	Start Frame Delimiter: basically 1 more byte of preamble, but ending with binary 11 instead of 10, to signal that the destination address follows next.	…last byte before addresses!
Destination MAC Address	The 6-byte address that identifies the Ethernet device to which this frame should be delivered.	To there
Source MAC Address	The 6-byte address that identifies the sending node.	From here
Type	A 2-byte code that identifies the type of data in the data field; often refers to an IPv4 packet today.	The type of data
Data	The data from Ethernet's perspective that includes all headers from upper layers, plus user data.	The actual data
Pad	Extra bytes used to lengthen short frames so that they meet the minimum frame length requirements.	Shortie
FCS	Frame Check Sequence. A field used to determine whether any bits changed during transmission. If so, the receiver should discard the frame.	Check for errors

The Ethernet Header Fields Explained

The *Preamble* and *SFD* fields work together to give the other nodes on the link a warning that a new frame is coming down the link. These fields work a little like when a song starts, with a drummer first laying down a beat while the other players wait on a cue from the drummer or bandleader to join in. These two fields essentially tell the other node to get ready for the more meaningful fields that follow. These two fields repeat binary 10 for most of the combined 8 bytes, but with the last 2 bits of the SFD of 11, to let the other node know that the end of the SFD has arrived.

The *Destination MAC Address* field identifies the MAC address of the device to which the frame should be sent. LAN switches forward the frame so that it arrives at this destination.

The *Source MAC Address* field identifies the sending device. LAN switches use the source MAC address to learn the topology of the LAN. (More discussion about how LAN switches use the MAC addresses follows later, in the section "LAN Switching.")

The *Type* field identifies the type of data held in the next field, the *Data* field. You might recall from Chapter 3's section "A History of Networking Models" that, at one point in the history of networking, networks supported many Layer 3 protocols. At that time, one Ethernet frame might carry an IP packet, while the next might carry an IBM SNA packet, and the next might carry a DEC DECnet packet. To support these different types of Layer 3 packets, Ethernet needed a way to identify the type of packet inside the Ethernet Data field. The Ethernet Type field uses a different number to identify each type of Layer 3 packet that could be in the Data field.

The *Data* field holds the data as supplied by the layer above Ethernet. For example, imagine that the PC user on the left side of Figure 5-19 opens a web browser and types in a URL for a web server, so the PC builds an HTTP GET request. That GET request sits in a TCP segment, which sits in an IP header, forming an IP packet. The PC needs to send that packet to the nearby router in the figure. To send the IP packet over the Ethernet, the PC encapsulates the IP packet inside an Ethernet frame. The data field of the frame holds the IP packet, and the Ethernet Type field lists a number that notes that the data is an IP version 4 (IPv4) packet.

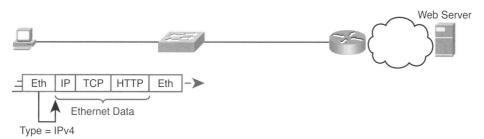

FIGURE 5-19

Ethernet Data Field with IP, TCP, and HTTP Header Included

Finally, the *Pad* field completes the Data field if it is too short. The data + pad must be at least 46 bytes to meet the minimum Ethernet frame size requirements (64 bytes when ignoring the preamble and SFD). The Pad field makes the frame long enough; when the destination receives the frame, it simply discards the pad bytes.

The Ethernet Trailer FCS Explained

Finally, the Ethernet trailer has a single field: the *Frame Check Sequence (FCS)* field. The FCS field plays a key role in how Ethernet nodes detect errors.

Each Ethernet node performs a process called *error detection* when it receives a frame. When a frame arrives, the node separates the FCS from the rest of the frame. The FCS allows the receiving node to tell whether any of the other bits changed values during transmission. As you might expect, if bits changed, an error has occurred; the receiving node should then discard the Ethernet frame.

The error-detection process relies on the FCS field. Essentially, the sending node and receiving node run the frame through a math formula, and if they both get the same answer, the frame did not change while being transmitted. The process works like this:

The sending node:

1. Prepares the entire frame except for the FCS field
2. Inputs the frame (without the FCS field) into a math formula, with a 32-bit result
3. Copies the 32-bit math result into the FCS field
4. Sends the frame

The receiving node:

1. Receives the frame and sets aside the FCS.
2. Inputs the received frame (without the FCS field) into the same math formula as the sender, with a 32-bit result.
3. Compares the new 32-bit result with the received FCS.
4. If equal, no errors occurred. If unequal, errors occurred, so discard the frame!

ON THE SIDE: Most devices actually have specialized circuitry to do the FCS math, just so it happens quickly.

This process happens for each link for each frame. That is, if a frame crosses multiple Ethernet links in a single Ethernet LAN, each switch that receives the frame uses the FCS field to check for errors.

Ethernet MAC Addresses Explained

Of all the parts of an Ethernet header and trailer, network engineers think about the two MAC address fields the most. The devices in the network make use of all the fields, but in the daily work to operate and troubleshoot a network, engineers simply have more reasons to think about the MAC addresses. This topic explains a variety of details about MAC addresses. In particular, it touches on the format of MAC addresses and their use in Ethernet headers, the types of MAC addresses, and the need for unique unicast MAC addresses in an Ethernet LAN.

MAC Address Formats and Types

To begin, first look at the format of the actual MAC addresses. The IEEE defines MAC addresses as 48-bit numbers, but they are usually written in hexadecimal (hex). Each hex digit represents 4 bits, so a hex MAC address is 12 hex digits long, which is still pretty long to read and remember. Because a 12-digit hex number is long, most documents and user interfaces format the MAC addresses with periods for better readability.

For example, the following numbers represent the same MAC address value:

```
00000010 00010010 00110100 01010110 01111000 10011010

02123456789A

0212.3456.789A

02.12.34.56.78.9A
```

The first shows the value in binary. Frankly, you will almost never see MAC addresses written in binary, partly because they would be too difficult to work with. The other three examples show hex versions of that same MAC address, both with and without periods. (There is no required standard for whether periods should be used, or how many, when writing MAC addresses.)

Next, think about the most common type of Ethernet MAC address, called a *unicast MAC address*. The term might sound a little scary, but the idea is relatively simple: A unicast MAC address represents one and only one device on the LAN.

Most of the frames in an Ethernet LAN typically go to a single device, so they go to a unicast destination MAC address. One device creates the frame, and that device puts its own unicast MAC address into the header as the source MAC address. The sender then puts the destination device's unicast MAC address into the destination address field in the Ethernet header and sends the frame. The Ethernet network, mainly the LAN switches, delivers the frame to the correct destination device: the device that uses the unicast MAC address listed in the Ethernet header.

Finally, note that while every device on an Ethernet has a unicast MAC address, two other types of MAC addresses exist as well: broadcast and multicast. The *Ethernet broadcast address*, FFFF.FFFF.FFFF, represents all devices; a frame sent to this address should be delivered to all the devices on the Ethernet. The third category, *multicast MAC addresses*, allows one MAC address to be used by multiple devices so that one frame sent to that multicast address will be sent to all those devices.

Universally Unique MAC Addresses

Each unicast MAC address needs to be unique compared to all other unicast MAC addresses in the same LAN. Why? Switches forward frames based on their destination MAC address. If more than one NIC in the same LAN had the same MAC address, the switches would be confused about which NIC should get the frame.

The IEEE takes a universal approach to making sure that all MAC addresses in a LAN are unique. In fact, the IEEE created a process so that all Ethernet MAC addresses in the world will have a unique unicast MAC address. If the IEEE meets this goal, in your Ethernet LAN, all the devices will have unique MAC addresses as well.

The IEEE created the process, but the process requires cooperation from Ethernet vendors. This list describes the general idea:

- For all Ethernet devices made by a vendor, for each NIC, switch port, router Ethernet interface, and so on, the vendor assigns a permanent MAC address that the device can remember and use.
- The permanent MAC address is a called a *universal MAC address*, because it should be unique across the entire Earth/universe.

The universal MAC address uses a two-part format:

- **Organizationally Unique Identifier (OUI):** A code registered to the vendor and only used by that vendor
- **Vendor assigned:** The second half is a number chosen by the vendor that the vendor never uses again for any other Ethernet product.

If each vendor creates universal MAC addresses that use only their own OUI, it cannot possibly duplicate addresses compared to other vendors. Then, if a single vendor never reuses a vendor-assigned value, that vendor will never create a duplicate among all its products. If everyone follows the rules, all MAC addresses should be unique across the planet.

Figure 5-20 shows the breakdown of the two halves of Ethernet universal addresses, with a few reminders about Ethernet MAC addresses. Following the figure, the text gives an analogy and an example of how the IEEE assigns universal MAC addresses.

FIGURE 5-20

IEEE Organizationally
Unique Identifier (OUI)
and Unique MAC
Addresses

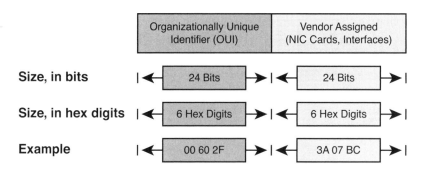

First, for the analogy, my last name is Odom. Say that my friend's last name is McCave, and we want to avoid naming our kids the same name. If we both like the name Dave, my friend's kid can be Dave McCave and mine can be Dave Odom, without duplicating the names. If I had another kid, to keep the names unique, I might name him Sunny Jim Odom, so again, the names are unique: All I had to do was pick a first name other than Dave. If my friend ended up with 23 kids, he could have named them all Dave McCave, which would have obviously failed at the goal of making all the names unique.

Now think about this example specific to Ethernet. Vendor X has contacted the IEEE and registered a new unique OUI: ABCDEF. Vendor X plans to manufacture Ethernet NICs, so the first NIC might have a MAC address of AB.CD.EF.00.00.01. Note that it begins with the OUI, with 000001 as the vendor-assigned code. The next NIC might be AB.CD.EF.00.00.02, the next AB.CD.EF.00.00.03, and so on. As long as vendor X begins all its MAC addresses with the OUI ABCDEF, and as long as the company does not use the same vendor code over again, its MAC addresses will not be duplicated.

> **ON THE SIDE:** Credit for inspiration for the names goes to Dr. Seuss, "Too Many Daves."

> **ON THE SIDE:** Universal addresses used to be called *burned-in addresses (BIA)*. The MAC addresses were stored using older memory technology called PROM. This memory required the data to be written over and over, essentially burning the binary values into the storage material to store the bits.

LAN Switching

The early chapters of this book defined a network's role as delivering bits from one user device to another. To deliver the data, the network exists as a set of nodes and links. Then the nodes deliver the data by sending data over a link to another node, until the data crosses the entire network.

The final topic in this chapter focuses on how one particular type of network node, an Ethernet LAN switch, makes its decisions of how to forward data.

In particular, this topic breaks that LAN switch logic into three pieces. The first piece looks at the switch's logic when it knows how to forward a particular frame. The second part looks at the flooding process: the logic a switch uses when it does not know how to forward a particular frame. The last piece of this section looks at how LAN switches learn the information they need so that they can avoid the less efficient flooding process and forward Ethernet frames more efficiently.

Ethernet LAN Switch Forwarding

In an Ethernet LAN, the NIC in an end-user device has no real decision to make. When an end-user device needs to send data, the PC and its NIC work together to build the Ethernet frame. At that point, the NIC simply sends the frame. The NIC expects the other devices in the LAN, like LAN switches, to forward the frame to the correct destination based on the destination MAC address.

In an Ethernet LAN, the LAN switches must together deliver frames to their correct destinations. Each LAN switch must make a choice every time it receives a frame. Each LAN switch typically has many options of where to forward a frame. LAN switches have multiple ports, many have dozens of ports, and some even have hundreds of ports. Each switch in a LAN must choose to forward a frame out the correct port, so that together, all the switches can deliver the frame to the right destination.

All LAN switches make their forwarding decisions by comparing the frame's destination MAC address to a table called the switch's **MAC address table**. The MAC address table lists MAC addresses, and for each address, the table lists the port out which to forward frames going to that address. To forward a frame, a switch simply compares the destination MAC of the frame to the table, finds the matching entry, and forwards the frame out that port.

> **AUTHOR'S NOTE:** LAN switches must use some identifier for each switch port. Usually, each port has a type, based on the fastest Ethernet speed supported by a port, and then just a sequential number for each port of that type. The examples in this section refer to switch ports as G1, G2, and so on, for the 10/100/1000 ports on these switches.

Figure 5-21 shows an example of how a switch forwards frames. The figure shows four PCs: A, B, C, and D. PC A sends a frame destined for PC D's MAC address (0000.DDDD.DDDD). The figure also shows the single switch's port identifiers along with the switch's MAC address table.

FIGURE 5-21

Switch Forwarding Decision: Single Switch

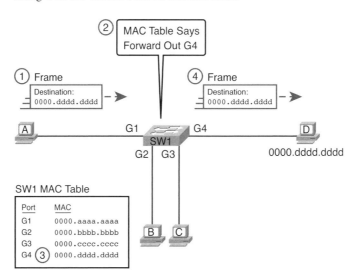

Following the circled reference numbers in the figure:

1. PC A's NIC builds a frame, destination address 0000.DDDD.DDDD, and sends the frame.

2. SW1 receives the frame, compares the destination address to the MAC table, matching an entry that lists G4 as the outgoing port.

3. This number just notes the matching SW1 MAC table entry.

4. SW1 forwards the unchanged Ethernet frame out its G4 port (toward D).

Note that the forwarding logic ignores the type of physical links. The links could have been any speed, any standard, with any cable, and the process works the same. The same frame format works, and the same switch forwarding logic works, regardless of the physical media.

Additionally, each LAN switch works independently from each other. Each switch makes its own forwarding decision, using its own MAC address table, which lists its own local switch ports as outgoing interfaces.

To see how switches work independently, Figure 5-22 shows a second example of LAN switch forwarding. The figure shows the same four PCs, with the same MAC addresses, but this time with a pair of switches. Again, PC A sends a frame to PC D, but now two switches must forward the frame.

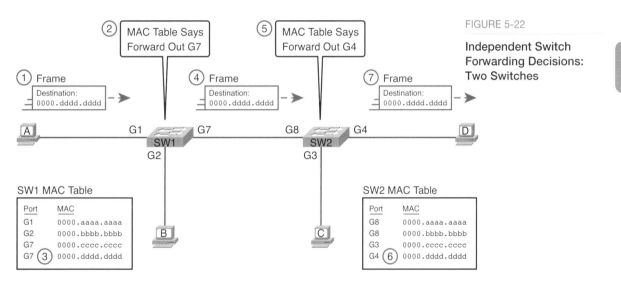

FIGURE 5-22

Independent Switch Forwarding Decisions: Two Switches

Again, following the circled reference numbers in the figure:

1. Just like with Figure 5-21, PC A's NIC builds a frame, destination address 0000.DDDD.DDDD, and sends the frame.

2. SW1 uses the same forwarding logic, but now SW1's MAC address table entry happens to list SW1's outgoing interface as G7.

3. This number just notes the matching SW1 MAC table entry.

4. SW1 forwards the unchanged Ethernet frame out its G7 port (the link to SW2).

5. SW2 matches the frame's destination MAC address (0000.DDDD.DDDD) to SW2's MAC address table, finding port G4 as the outgoing interface.

6. This number just notes the matching SW2 MAC table entry.

7. SW2 forwards the frame out its port G4 to PC D.

The forwarding logic works because the MAC tables have correct information. As it turns out, when switches first power on, their MAC address tables are empty; over time, they learn the correct MAC table entries. The following sections discuss what forwarding decisions a switch makes before learning the correct information, and the process switches use to learn the correct information.

Ethernet LAN Switch Flooding

In some cases, switches do not forward a frame out a single outbound port, instead flooding the frame. *Flooding* means that the switch forwards a copy of the frame out all ports, except the port in which the frame arrived. Flooding delivers a copy of the frame to all devices in a LAN.

Switches use flooding in two different cases, as follows:

> **Unknown unicast frame:** When a switch tries to forward a frame destined to some unicast MAC address, but the switch does not list that destination MAC in its MAC table, the frame is considered an *unknown unicast frame*, and the switch floods the frame.
>
> **Broadcast frame:** Any frames with destination MAC address FFFF.FFFF. FFFF (the Ethernet broadcast address) is a broadcast frame; switches flood broadcast frames.

Figure 5-23 shows an example of flooding for an unknown unicast frame. This figure repeats the example in Figure 5-21, with one change—SW1 has an empty MAC address table. PC A again sends a frame to PC D's MAC address, but because switch SW1 does not have a matching MAC table entry, switch SW1 considers the frame to be an unknown unicast frame, so SW1 floods the frame.

FIGURE 5-23

Flooding an Unknown Unicast Frame

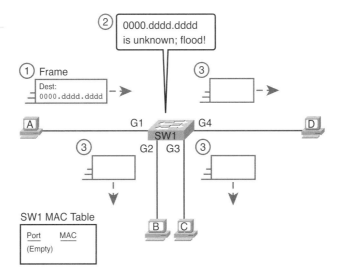

Following the circled reference numbers in the figure:

1. Just like the previous two figures, PC A's NIC builds a frame, destination address 0000.DDDD.DDDD, and sends the frame.

2. SW1 receives the frame, compares the destination address to the MAC table, and does not find a match.

3. SW1 floods the frame, sending copies of the frame out ports G2, G3, and G4; it does not flood the frame out the original incoming port (G1).

Flooding works, but it does cause a few small negative effects. First, think about all the PCs in Figure 5-23. PC D received the frame, which is good. However, PCs B and C also received the frame, so they at least have to spend some time deciding whether to process the frame or ignore it (they should ignore it). So flooding wastes some small amount of processing power on the other devices. Also, the extra frames take up some of the LAN's capacity. However, these small problems are just that—small. The flooding still helps the LAN achieve its goal—delivering LAN frames to other devices in the LAN.

As mentioned earlier, switches also flood broadcast frames. Broadcast frames—frames sent to Ethernet broadcast address FFFF.FFFF.FFFF—should be sent to all devices in the LAN, and flooding does that. Figure 5-24 shows an example, with the same LAN as Figure 5-23, this time with PC A sending a broadcast frame.

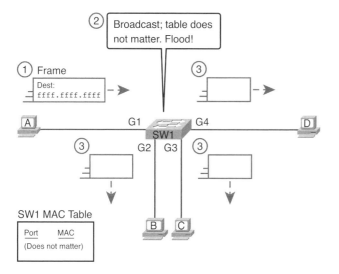

FIGURE 5-24

Flooding Broadcast Frames

As usual, following the circled reference numbers in the figure:

1. PC A's NIC builds a frame, destination address FFFF.FFFF.FFFF, and sends the frame.

2. SW1 receives the frame, sees the broadcast destination address, and ignores the MAC address table.

3. SW1 floods the broadcast frame, sending copies of the frame out ports G2, G3, and G4; it does not flood the frame out the original incoming port (G1).

> **AUTHOR'S NOTE:** Ethernet broadcast frames do not happen randomly or by accident. Higher-layer protocols typically need to do some function, and that function requires a message to all hosts on the LAN, which causes an Ethernet broadcast frame. For an example, see Chapter 8's discussion of the Address Resolution Protocol (ARP).

Ideally, a switch would know all the MAC addresses for all devices in an Ethernet LAN so that the switch would only flood broadcasts. Switches actually learn and build their MAC address tables relatively quickly. The next topic discusses how switches learn the correct table entries.

Ethernet LAN Switch Learning

Switches forward unicast frames. If the switch lists the destination MAC in its MAC address table, the frame is a *known unicast frame* and the switch forwards the frame out only one outgoing port. With unknown unicast frames, the switch has to flood the frame, which is less efficient.

LAN switches can learn their MAC address tables two ways:

- The engineer can type the details to give the MAC address table information to the switch.
- The switch can learn the information by reading the frames that pass through the switch.

To tell the switch what to put in its MAC table, the engineer *configures* the switch. To configure a switch, the engineer uses a PC or other user device. The engineer uses an app, usually either a web browser or a terminal emulator application. (A terminal emulator app lets the user type text, with the app sending the text to another device, in this case, the LAN switch.) The app connects to the switch and the engineer types the information that needs to be in the MAC address table. At that point, the switch knows its MAC address table.

While configuring a switch's MAC address table is useful in some cases, most switches dynamically learn their MAC table entries. You can literally take a brand-new LAN switch out of its box, plug in the devices and cables, and power it on, and the LAN works. The switch not only forwards frames, but it also automatically learns the correct entries for its MAC address table.

LAN switches dynamically learn the entries in their MAC address table by reading the source MAC address field of incoming frames. When a switch first powers on, it has no entries in its MAC address table. The switch then looks at every frame that comes in every port and looks at the source MAC address. Then the switch adds a table entry—the source MAC address and the incoming port number.

To better understand switch learning, think about the next example in Figure 5-25.
The one switch (SW1) has just powered on, so its MAC address table is empty.
Then PC A sends a frame that arrives in SW1's G1 port. Where is PC A compared
to SW1? Connected to SW1's port G1. In this case, SW1 adds PC A's MAC
address of 0000.AAAA.AAAA, with port G1, to its MAC address table.

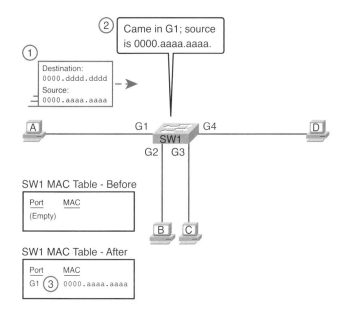

FIGURE 5-25

**SW1 Learns the MAC
Address of PC A**

After the process in Figure 5-25 has completed, the switch is ready to forward
frames to PC A. If SW1 receives a frame destined for PC A, SW1 knows to
forward the frame out its port G1.

Summarizing the concept, when a switch receives a frame—source MAC address
X with incoming port Y—the best way for that switch to later send frames to
MAC address X is to send the frames out port Y. So switches build their MAC
address tables by looking at the incoming frames' source MAC addresses and their
associated incoming interfaces.

Figure 5-26 shows a final example of switch learning, this time with two switches.
Like the forwarding decision, switches independently learn MAC table entries.
For this example, PC A again sends a frame to PC D. (Note that the frame will
be flooded in this case, but only the frames at Steps 1 and 4 matter to the switch
learning process.)

FIGURE 5-26

SW1 and SW2 Learn MAC Table Entries for PC A

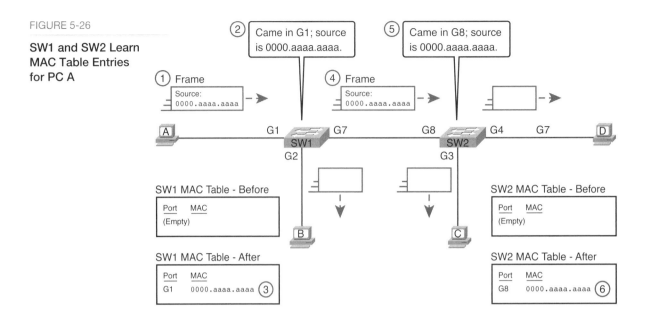

Again, following the circled reference numbers in the figure:

1. PC A sends a frame, source MAC 0000.AAAA.AAAA, destination 0000. DDDD.DDDD.
2. Switch SW1 notes the source MAC and SW1's local incoming interface (0000.AAAA.AAAA, G1).
3. SW1 adds the new entry to its MAC address table.
4. SW1 floods the frame, including one that goes to switch SW2.
5. Switch SW2 notes the source MAC and SW2's local incoming interface (0000.AAAA.AAAA, G8).
6. SW2 adds the new entry to its MAC address table.

Chapter Summary

Modern networks can be broken down into two major parts—LANs and WANs. The LANs can then be further subdivided into wired LANs and wireless LANs. For wired LANs, in years past, many other types of LANs competed with Ethernet. Today, the only type of wired LAN that exists in most networks is an Ethernet LAN, as discussed in this chapter. LANs as a whole usually contain parts that are Ethernet 802.3 LANs and parts that are IEEE 802.11 wireless LANs (WLAN).

The word *Ethernet* refers to a group of standards; some apply to LANs, some apply to WANs, and some might be used for either. The Ethernet LAN standards discussed in this chapter include many different standards for different types of physical links, with different speeds, cabling types, and different maximum cable lengths. The common threads that make all these standards part of Ethernet include the common star topology, with point-to-point links between nodes, and the switching logic that forwards standard Ethernet frames over any type of Ethernet physical link.

This chapter introduces a few details that typically come up in conversation only when it comes time to buy and install the devices in an Ethernet LAN. For example, while the newest and fastest Ethernet LAN standards look great, any network design in the real world must consider the cost, so this chapter discussed some of the cost-versus-speed trade-offs network engineers must consider. To aid the migration of devices to newer Ethernet standards over time, many NICs and switch ports support autonegotiation of speed and duplex, which lets the devices negotiate to use the currently best options that both nodes on a link support. Finally, the UTP links must use the correct cabling pinouts, including straight-through and crossover pinouts—with two-pair-only cabling used for the older 10BASE-T and 100BASE-T standards and four-pair cabling for the newer standards.

Ethernet framing, and its consistency across different Ethernet physical layer standards, makes an Ethernet LAN with multiple types of physical links possible. All NICs and switch ports, no matter the speed or cabling type, pass these same frames. The frames define many fields for various purposes, most importantly, the destination and source MAC address fields.

Ethernet LAN switching defines how a single switch makes its choices of how to forward frames. A single switch forwards a frame either out a single port, if the frame has a known unicast destination MAC address, or the switch floods the frame out all ports, if the frame has an unknown destination MAC address. To make the process work better, switches quickly learn the MAC addresses by looking at the source MAC address of received frames. Collectively, all switches forward a frame toward the destination so that eventually an Ethernet frame goes from one side of the Ethernet LAN to the other.

Chapter Review Activities

Use the features in this section to study and review the topics in this chapter.

Answer These Questions

1. Which of the following types of LANs was a competitor of Ethernet LANs from the earliest days of wired LANs in the 1980s and into the 1990s?

   a. ATM

   b. FDDI

   c. Token Ring

   d. Metro Ethernet

2. Which of the following types of LANs is the strongest competitive option to be used instead of Ethernet LANs today?

   a. ATM

   b. FDDI

   c. Token Ring

   d. 802.11 LANs

3. Which of the following speeds are *not* defined as a speed by some Ethernet LAN standard?

   a. 1 Gbps

   b. 4 Gbps

   c. 10 Gbps

   d. 40 Gbps

4. Think back to the information listed for Gigabit Ethernet for maximum cabling distances. Which of the answers matches the correct standard with the cabling type and maximum cable length?

   a. 1000BASE-LX, MM fiber, 550 meters

   b. 1000BASE-T, UTP, 55 meters

   c. 1000BASE-SX, MM, 5000 meters

   d. 1000BASE-T, UTP, 550 meters

5. A campus LAN drawing shows hundreds of user devices cabled to LAN switches on various floors of a building. The per-floor edge switches have a cable connected to other switches that sit on the first floor of the building. All the links from the edge switches to the end-user devices use 100BASE-T. A PC on floor 2 sends an Ethernet frame to a PC on floor 3, with the frame passing through the switches on the first floor as part of the journey. Which of the following statements is true about the links between the switches in this Ethernet LAN?

a. The links must all use 100BASE-T.

b. The links could use any Ethernet LAN standard.

c. The links could use any UTP-based Ethernet LAN standard.

d. The links could use any Ethernet LAN standard from 1 Gbps speeds and faster.

6. Which of the following shortcut names defines an IEEE standard that runs at 10,000,000,000 bits per second, and includes some fiber cabling options?

a. 10GBASE-T

b. 10000BASE-X

c. 1000BASE-X

d. 10BASE-X

e. None of the answers is correct.

7. Which of the following is the formal IEEE standard for 1-Gbps Ethernet using UTP cabling?

a. 802.3ab

b. 802.3ae

c. 802.3u

d. 802.3z

8. Imagine that you looked back at the history of prices for Ethernet NICs. You looked at typical prices for 100BASE-T NICs over time. Which of the following answers, according to this chapter, had the strongest impact to lower the prices of the 100BASE-T NICs? (Choose two answers.)

a. Overall downward trend for computer technology prices over time

b. The introduction of 1000BASE-X products into the market

c. The introduction of 1000BASE-T products into the market

d. A decrease in prices of fiber-optic cabling

9. PC A has a 10/100 NIC that supports autonegotiation, and PC B has a 10-Mbps NIC that does not support autonegotiation. Both PCs connect to a LAN switch using a UTP cable. Both switch ports are 10/100/1000 ports that also support IEEE autonegotiation. Which of the following are true about autonegotiation in this small network? (Choose two answers.)

a. Autonegotiation works on the switch–to–PC A link, causing PC A to run at 100 Mbps.

b. Autonegotiation fails to work on the switch–to–PC B link, causing the switch to run at 1 Gbps.

c. Autonegotiation fails to work on the switch–to–PC B link, causing the switch to run at 10 Mbps.

d. Autonegotiation works on the switch–to–PC A link, causing PC A to run at 10 Mbps.

10. PC A and PC B both have 10/100 NICs that support autonegotiation, and both connect to a LAN switch's ports G1 and G2 using a UTP cable. Both switch ports are 10/100/1000 ports. Both PC NICs and all the switch ports support autonegotiation, but the user of PC B has chosen to both disable autonegotiation and to only use full duplex by making some configuration choices on the PC. Which of the following are true regarding the different device's choices of whether to use half duplex or full duplex? (Choose two answers.)

   a. PC A uses full duplex as the result of the autonegotiation process working.

   b. The switch port G1 uses half duplex as a result of the autonegotiation process working.

   c. Switch port G2 uses half duplex because autonegotiation fails, making the switch use the default duplex setting.

   d. Switch port G2 uses full duplex because autonegotiation works and detects that PC B only supports full duplex.

11. Think about the various Ethernet standards for a given general category of cabling: UTP, multi-mode (MM) fiber, and single-mode (SM) fiber. Comparing the standards for one type of cable, for various new standards of various speeds over the years, think about the maximum cabling distances. Which of the following best describes the most consistent maximum cabling length across a cabling category?

   a. SM fiber typically supports a maximum cable length of 5 km across all SM standards at all speeds.

   b. MM fiber typically supports a maximum cable length of 550 meters across all MM standards at all speeds.

   c. UTP typically supports a maximum cable length of 100 meters across all UTP standards at all speeds.

   d. All maximum cable distances vary from speed to speed, even for a single category of cable.

12. A network engineer is planning the cabling for a new Ethernet LAN at a new office building. She needs to create an engineering diagram as to which links use straight-through cable pinouts and which use crossover cable pinouts. Which of the following combinations should be marked for crossover pinouts? (Choose two answers.)

   a. A UTP link from a PC to a switch

   b. A UTP link from an edge switch to a distribution switch

   c. A UTP link between two distribution switches

   d. A fiber link between two distribution switches

13. PC A sits at a branch office Ethernet LAN. The LAN includes a router, which in turn connects through a WAN to the rest of a large enterprise network. The user at PC A opens a web browser and types in a URL, which eventually causes PC A to send an Ethernet frame. This frame arrives at the router in that same branch office as part of its journey into the rest of the enterprise network. Which of the following statements is true about this Ethernet frame as it passes over the branch office Ethernet LAN?

a. The Data field in the frame holds user data only.

b. The FCS field sits at the end of the Ethernet header.

c. The Type field identifies the data as an IP packet.

d. The Preamble field lists the length of the frame in bytes.

14. PC A sits at a branch office Ethernet LAN. The LAN includes a router, which in turn connects through a WAN to the rest of a large enterprise network. The user at PC A opens a web browser and types in a URL, which eventually causes PC A to send an Ethernet frame. This frame arrives at the router in that same branch office as part of its journey into the rest of the enterprise network. Which of the following statements are true about this Ethernet frame as it passes over the branch office Ethernet LAN? (Choose two answers.)

a. Any nodes in the branch LAN that receive this frame use the FCS field to help detect errors.

b. The switches in the branch LAN use the source MAC address to help them choose where to forward this one frame.

c. The Preamble and SFD fields both come before the Destination Address field in the header.

d. The trailer lists the Type and FCS fields.

15. Which of the following is true about IEEE Ethernet MAC addresses?

a. 48 bits in length

b. Can be written in DDN format

c. Typically written as 6 hex digits

d. Address field(s) in the Ethernet header use a total of 12 bytes

16. Which of the following entities play a role in helping ensure that universal MAC addresses are unique among all universal MAC addresses in the universe? (Choose two answers.)

a. The IEEE

b. Ethernet vendors

c. Customers that implement Ethernet products

d. None of the answers is correct.

17. In a universal MAC address, which part of the MAC address uses a unique code that identifies the vendor that made the Ethernet product?

a. The vendor-assigned code

b. The first 2 bytes of the MAC address

c. The last 3 bytes of the MAC address

d. The OUI

18. Switch SW1 has four ports: G1, G2, G3, and G4. A frame arrives in port G3. The frame has a destination MAC address of 0000.1234.5678, and the MAC address table lists port G4 as being associated with that MAC address. What action does SW1 take?

    a. Floods the frame out ports G1, G2, and G4

    b. Floods the frame out ports G1, G2, G3, and G4

    c. Forwards the frame out port G4 only

    d. Ignores the frame

19. Switch SW1 has four ports: G1, G2, G3, and G4. A frame arrives in port G3. The frame has a destination MAC address of FFFF.FFFF.FFFF. What action does SW1 take?

    a. Floods the frame out ports G1, G2, and G4

    b. Floods the frame out ports G1, G2, G3, and G4

    c. Forwards the frame out port G4 only

    d. Ignores the frame

20. Switch SW1 has four ports: G1, G2, G3, and G4. A frame arrives in port G3. The frame has a source MAC address of 0000.3333.3333 and destination MAC address of 0000.1234.5678, and the MAC address table lists port G4 as being associated with that MAC address. Which of the following most likely happened before this frame arrived at SW1?

    a. SW1 received a frame sent to MAC address 0000.3333.3333 in port G3.

    b. SW1 received a frame sent to MAC address 0000.1234.5678 in port G4.

    c. SW1 has received no frames from any devices yet.

    d. SW1 received a frame sent to MAC address 0000.1234.5678 in port G3.

Define the Key Terms

The following key terms include the ideas most important to the big ideas in this chapter. To review, without looking at the book or your notes, write a definition for each term, focusing on the meaning, not the wording. Then review your definition compared to your notes, this chapter, and the glossary.

Key Terms for Chapter 5

Ethernet LANs	Gigabit Ethernet	MAC address
802.3	autonegotiation	MAC address table
Fast Ethernet	Ethernet frame	

List the Words Inside Acronyms

The following are the most common acronyms discussed in this chapter. As a way to review those terms, simply write down the words that each letter represents in each acronym.

Acronyms for Chapter 5

VPWS	SFD	MAC
VPLS	FCS	Metro E
DIX		

Create Mind Maps

Create two mind maps for this chapter. For the first, organize all the Ethernet standards you can recall from this chapter. First categorize them by speed. At the next level, categorize them by cable type (UTP or fiber), and finally, list standards. Include the formal standards names, shortcut names, and informal names. When you begin, try to do as much of this exercise as you can from memory, and then refer back to the chapter to fill in the gaps.

For the second mind map, draw out the major pieces of LAN switch logic mentioned in this chapter. Topics should include switch forwarding, learning, and autonegotiation, but can include any function you can remember that an Ethernet LAN switch does. As usual, use as few words as possible. The goal of each node in the mind map is a reminder of the topic, not a full description of the logic. For example, for a switch using the autonegotiation default of 10 Mbps, when the other node does not do autonegotiation, a note like "auto-n default: slowest" is plenty of detail.

Define Other Terms

Define the following additional terms from this chapter, and check your answers in the glossary:

wired LAN	wired/wireless LAN edge	Media Access Control
wireless LAN	shorthand name (IEEE)	error detection
star topology	edge switch	Ethernet broadcast address
Ethernet frame	duplex	
10BASE-T	half duplex	flooding
100BASE-T	full duplex	forwarding
1000BASE-T	straight-through cable	learning
10GBASE-T	crossover cable	unknown unicast frame
Metro Ethernet	Ethernet header	broadcast frame
Token Ring	Ethernet trailer	known unicast frame
LAN Edge	destination MAC address	universal MAC address
wireless-only LAN edge	source MAC address	

Complete the Tables and Lists from Memory

Print a copy of Appendix B, "Memory Tables" (which you can find online at www.pearsonitcertification.com/title/9780789748454), or at least the section for this chapter, and complete the tables and lists from memory. Appendix C, "Memory Tables Answer Key," also online, includes completed tables and lists to check your work.

Chapter | 6

Wireless LANs

By this point in the book, you have already learned many facts about wireless LANs (WLAN). These WLANs connect end-user devices to a WLAN access point (AP), and the AP in turn connects to some computer network. End-user devices use a WLAN network interface card (NIC)—which is often integrated into the device— to send and receive bits with the AP. The WLAN AP enables all the user devices to communicate with the rest of the enterprise network and with the Internet.

This chapter continues to build a story across a wide range of networking topics. Chapter 1, "Introduction to Computer Data," through Chapter 3, "TCP/ IP Networks," laid a broad foundation of networking concepts, while Chapter 4, "Transmitting Bits," focused on the physical layer details of how to send bits over one particular link. Chapter 5, "Ethernet LANs," then completes the rest of this book's story about how one type of LAN (an Ethernet LAN) works. This chapter completes the rest of this book's story of how another type of LAN, a wireless LAN, works.

This chapter, which completes this book's introduction to wireless LAN technology, follows the same general plan as did Chapter 5, breaking the topics into three major sections:

- The first section, "Defining Wireless LANs," defines wireless LANs, building on two foundations: the earlier discussions of wireless in Chapter 4 and the discussion of Ethernet wired LANs in Chapter 5. This first major section shows the similarities and differences, and defines the key terms and standards in the wireless LAN world.

- The second major section, "Exploring WLAN Physical Layer Features," looks at several physical layer features. WLAN physical layer standards go beyond the transmission of bits using radio waves. This section looks at some of those features, including WLAN topologies, coverage areas, bit rates, and frequency channels.

- The last of the three major sections of this chapter, "Exploring WLAN Common Features," looks at a few WLAN features that happen to work the same way regardless of which 802.11 transmission standard happens to be used. For the most part, these features relate to OSI Layer 2 functions. In particular, this last section looks at the 802.11 LAN frame (header and trailer), some overhead work that happens before a WLAN client can send data frames, and some logic used by APs that works somewhat like an Ethernet LAN switch.

Chapter Outline

Defining Wireless LANs

Exploring WLAN Physical Layer Features

Exploring WLAN Common Features

Chapter Summary

Chapter Review Activities

Objectives

- Given a to-scale drawing of a wired and wireless LAN, compare the distance and coverage limitations of user devices connected through both wired UTP Ethernet and wireless 802.11 standards.

- Given a to-scale drawing of a wired and wireless LAN, compare the maximum bit rates of user devices connected through both wired UTP Ethernet and wireless 802.11 standards.

- Explain the difference in the capacity to send bits in two LANs, each with the same number of user devices, one with an Ethernet switch and one with a wireless AP.

- List IEEE 802.11 wireless LAN standards and their ratification order.

- Make simple line drawings with basic descriptions of three to four typical use cases for wireless LANs.

- List and illustrate the most important difference between three WLAN topologies: IBSS, BSS, and ESS.

- Explain the concept of nonoverlapping wireless LAN channels and the importance of these channels in WLAN operation and design.

- List three 802.11 frame fields with the same size, format, and purpose as an 802.3 frame.

- Paraphrase the process that a WLAN client device goes through when a user moves to a new WLAN to discover and start using a new WLAN.

- List three functions performed by WLAN APs under normal operating conditions when the AP connects to both a wireless LAN and wired LAN.

Key Terms

coverage area

shared bandwidth

Wi-Fi

LAN edge

WLAN hotspot

Basic Service Set

Extended Service Set

unlicensed frequency band

nonoverlapping channels

management and control frames

Service Set ID (SSID)

Defining Wireless LANs

This first of three major sections of this chapter introduces wireless LANs (WLAN) by collecting the small pieces of information about WLANs from earlier chapters and putting them together into a complete story. This story reviews the IEEE 802.11 wireless LAN standards and the typical roles of wireless LANs—in the campus LAN, in the home office and small office, as well as in public spaces with WLAN hotspots.

This first major section begins with a set of comparisons to Ethernet. Ethernet LANs and WLANs can be used for the same general reasons, and Chapter 5 discussed Ethernet in detail. Comparing Ethernet to WLANs helps you see some of the reasons why network engineers use WLANs today, rather than just understanding how the WLANs work.

Comparing Wireless LANs to Wired LANs

This topic compares wired and wireless LANs. However, rather than making a long list of similarities and differences to memorize, this topic instead discusses the most important differences, along with a few of the similarities.

First, wired and wireless LANs have one very obvious difference: One uses wires (cables), and one does not. That difference results in many other important related differences. For example, WLANs allow mobility so that devices can move around and still use the network. The following sections take on a few such differences, but first, this topic looks at some of the similarities.

Similarities with Wired and Wireless LANs

Some of the biggest similarities happen to be pretty obvious. First, the term *local-area network* tells us that both types of LANs typically support devices that are nearby, with "nearby" being a little subjective.

As another similarity, both wired and wireless LANs provide a LAN edge connection in an enterprise LAN. The term *LAN edge* refers to the part of any network where the user devices sit, at the edge of the network. Typically, the LAN edge includes each user device and each device's link to the network, along with the network device on the other end of that link (usually a wired LAN switch or wireless LAN access point [AP]). Figure 6-1 shows a sample wired and wireless LAN, with the LAN edge on the left.

> **ON THE SIDE:** Engineers who design LANs also call the LAN edge the *access layer*, with switches that connect the access layer switches together called the *distribution layer*.

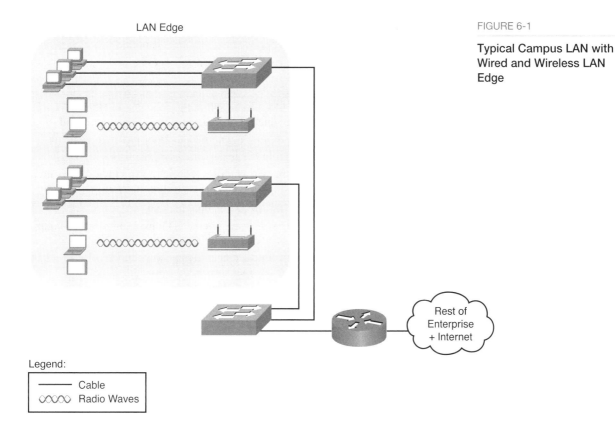

LAN Edge

FIGURE 6-1

Typical Campus LAN with Wired and Wireless LAN Edge

Rest of Enterprise + Internet

Legend:
——— Cable
∿∿∿ Radio Waves

Finally, wired and wireless LAN MAC addresses share the same format and meaning. Those similarities allow combined wired and wireless LANs as shown in Figure 6-1. Even though WLAN headers differ from Ethernet LAN headers, they both use the same MAC addresses with the same format and size, As a result, a combined wired and wireless LAN can be thought of as a single LAN. To make it all work, the AP can translate the header/trailer to forward frames between the wired and wireless parts of the network, as discussed later in this chapter in the section, "Translating 802.3 and 802.11 Data Frames."

In summary, wired and wireless LANs play the same role at the LAN edge, and the two types of LANs play well together. The next topics look at the key differences.

Distance from User Device to Switch or AP

Some LANs exist in smaller spaces, so network engineers do not need to worry about either wired or wireless distance limitations. For example, in a small office or home office, two devices at opposite corners of the house might be only 15–20 meters apart, so the distance might not matter a lot. In these smaller spaces, you can just ignore the distance limitations: Buy the gear and install it, and it typically works.

Other LANs exist in larger spaces, and in these cases, network engineers do need to plan the LAN based on the distances supported by the various types of LANs. For Ethernet 802.3 LANs, each physical layer standard, for each type of cabling, defines a maximum cable length. Wireless 802.11 LANs uses a concept called the **coverage area**, which defines the space around the access point (AP) in which the AP should be able to communicate with other devices. (The coverage area can also be referred to as the AP's *range*.)

To compare Ethernet maximum cable lengths and a WLAN AP's coverage area, look at the example in Figure 6-2, which shows the equipment on one floor of a long, skinny building about 100 meters in length. This floor has a convenient wiring closet on one end of the building. The network engineer wants to put a LAN switch and a WLAN AP in the wiring closet (on the right), but he knows that the PCs at the extreme other end of that floor will be close to the 100-meter UTP cabling limitation. For the sake of this example, imagine that the longest cables happen to be slightly shorter, at 90 meters, within the UTP maximum cable length.

Floor: 25 x 100 Meters

FIGURE 6-2

UTP 100-Meter Maximum Length Versus WLAN Range/Coverage Area

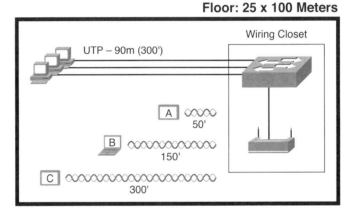

When the network engineer planning for this new LAN asks a WLAN expert for some advice on the WLAN range or coverage area that might work for this new WLAN, the answer might well be the most common answer to questions about WLANs: It depends.

The rules for planning the allowed distances in wired Ethernet LANs are much more objective than the rules used for WLANs. Ethernet LAN standards supply a convenient number for planning—a maximum cable length for every Ethernet LAN standard and for every cable type. The relatively controlled environment inside the cable allows the Ethernet standards to state the maximum cable length. WLANs send data through a mostly uncontrolled space between devices, so the range depends on too many outside factors. So, will device A in Figure 6-2 work well, at 50 feet from the AP? It depends. Will device B work well, at 150 feet? It depends.

To truly answer the question of the range for a particular WLAN, the network engineer needs to do some testing called a *wireless site survey*. The theoretical answer to the question of coverage area depends on many factors. A site survey bypasses some of the theory and simply tests to find out where the WLAN works and where it does not.

In a site survey, essentially the engineer would install the AP in the wiring closet, and walk around to the different locations with some wireless testing tool. (That tool can be as simple as a laptop with a WLAN card and some software.) In that site survey, the engineer can determine how well the WLAN is working with the following kinds of observations:

- When walking around inside conference room 1, wireless works great.
- When walking around inside conference room 2, wireless fails to work.
- When sitting at user A's cubicle, wireless works great.
- When sitting at user B's cubicle, wireless works, but it's a little slow.
- When sitting at user C's cubicle, wireless fails.

> **ON THE SIDE:** A site survey works a little like this story. Imagine that a physics teacher asks the students to calculate how far they can throw a ball today, on a particularly rainy and windy day. While the rest start writing and using their calculators, one clever student grabs a ball and tape measure from his backpack and heads outside to just do the experiment.

While planning for Ethernet LAN distances might be a relatively neat process on paper, planning for WLAN range simply requires a little more work, a little more planning, and maybe a little more money to create the right coverage area. For example, maybe one AP on one end of a long floor of a building, as shown in Figure 6-2, does not create enough WLAN coverage. After testing, the network engineer might add a second AP, somewhere nearer to the other end of the building. With a building with a width of around 300 feet, most devices would be within around 100 feet of an AP. Figure 6-3 shows the idea.

Floor: 25 x 100 Meters

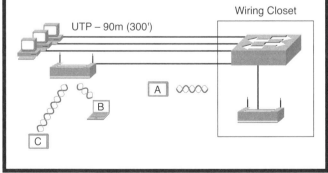

FIGURE 6-3

Increasing WLAN Coverage with an Additional Access Point

To summarize, wired LANs give us objective known cable lengths based on standards, making the LAN planning process easy in comparison to WLANs. WLAN distances (range) for small sites might not require much thought, but for larger sites, planning the range of the WLAN requires some engineering and testing effort with a site survey.

Maximum Bit Rates (Speeds)

The next point of comparison examines the speed of a single transmission in wired and wireless LANs. With wired Ethernet LANs, the standards define the literal bit rate (speed)—in fact, the shorthand name for each standard lists the speed. WLANs each have a literal maximum transmission speed that depends on the WLAN standard. After you get past the maximum bit rate comparison, however, WLANs have many more variables that can change the bit rate. The next several pages of this chapter walk through the discussion of the bit rates and some of those variables.

First, with a purely theoretical comparison of the bit rates, on paper, Ethernet speeds far exceed those of WLANs. As a reminder, Ethernet supports the following bit rates in ratified standards as of the publication of this book: 10 Mbps, 100 Mbps, 1 Gbps, 10 Gbps, 40 Gbps, and 100 Gbps. The fastest WLAN ratified as of the publication of this standard sits at 600 Mbps as a theoretical maximum.

To soften that sheer speed comparison a little, next think about the Ethernet speeds used at the edge of the LAN, where end-user devices sit. Most Ethernet LAN edge devices use 1-Gbps or slower speeds, as discussed in Chapter 5's section "Ethernet Pricing Trends." As time moves forward from the time this book was published, an Ethernet LAN's edge might one day move up to use 10-Gbps NICs, particularly when 10GBASE-T prices fall. However, today, while it sounds impressive to say that Ethernet's fastest speed is over 100 times faster than the fastest WLAN standard, because WLANs mainly sit at the LAN edge, an 802.11n WLAN with stated speeds of 450 Mbps or 600 Mbps has a speed pretty close to the 1-Gbps speed of the fastest likely Ethernet devices at the LAN edge.

With WLANs, the maximum speed tracks to each standard. For the earliest WLAN standards, each standard had one maximum speed. A more recent standard, 802.11n, actually defines multiple maximum speeds, depending on a couple of different options. Table 6-1 lists those speeds.

> **AUTHOR'S NOTE:**
> The chapter discusses the WLAN speeds in various places, but the 600-Mbps number comes from the 802.11n standard, at 150 Mbps per stream, with four streams; more on these topics in the coming pages.

TABLE 6-1

WLAN Standards and Speeds

IEEE WLAN Standard	IEEE Standard Ratified in This Year	Maximum Stream Rate (Mbps)	Maximum Theoretical Rate, One Device, Maximum Streams
802.11b	1999	11	N/A
802.11a	1999	54	N/A
802.11g	2003	54	N/A
802.11n (20 MHz)	2009	72	288
802.11n (40 MHz)*	2009	150	600

* 802.11n allows the use of either a single 20-MHz channel, or two channels bonded together (40-MHz channel). Using two bonded channels allows a faster speed.

First, just compare the first three standards in the table: .11a, .11b, and .11g. The .11a and .11b standards emerged around the same time, with the standards being ratified the same year. At first glance, you might think that no one would use .11b because of its speed (11 Mbps) versus 802.11a (54 Mbps). Interestingly, 802.11b actually became more popular than 802.11a in the market for a variety of reasons, including some other technical advantages and some business advantages. For example, 802.11b supported a wider coverage area than 802.11a.

The most recently ratified standard, 802.11n, competes much better based on speed, as noted in the column labeled "Maximum Stream Rate (Mbps)." First, 802.11n improves the base rate to 72 Mbps using a single wireless channel. Additionally, using an optional feature, devices can use a wider frequency range—two wireless channels instead of one—increasing the speed of a single transmission to 150 Mbps. This 150-Mbps speed almost triples the speed compared to the older WLAN standards.

> **ON THE SIDE:** The packages and web pages for 802.11n WLAN products often list speeds of 150 Mbps, 300 Mbps, 450 Mbps, or 600 Mbps. These speeds reflect the faster single-stream speed (150 Mbps), with either one, two, three, or four streams.

802.11n also increased the speed in another way using a feature called Multiple Input Multiple Output (MIMO) and streams. Instead of having just one antenna, a NIC or AP could have up to four antennas. Theoretically, a device could send at four times the speed using this technology.

One of the big dangers when first learning about WLANs, particularly WLAN speeds, is to see the listed maximum speed and stop there. Be honest: Did you see that 600 Mbps as the fastest WLAN speed back in Table 6-1, and think that it was pretty close (60 percent) to the speedy 1-Gbps speed of 1000BASE-T Ethernet? For the amount of detail discussed so far in this chapter, that comparison is reasonable. However, that comparison is only a starting point to talk about what really happens in a WLAN versus a wired LAN.

> **ON THE SIDE:** At press time, vendors had begun to offer prestandard products using the proposed new IEEE standard 802.11ac, which supports a single-stream rate of 433 Mbps, with multiple streams pushing it past 1 Gbps.

The next few pages discuss two other major factors that impact the speed and capacity of WLANs. First, WLANs do not always run at their maximum speed. Second, WLANs, because of their half-duplex logic, have a smaller capacity to send bits than similar wired Ethernet LANs. So, you cannot simply stop the comparison between WLANs and wired Ethernet at the literal maximum speeds, so the next few pages discuss these other related ideas.

Bit Rate Variations Over Time

After an individual Ethernet link comes up and works, it runs at one speed, and one speed only. The bits in every frame flow at that bit rate. The speed does not change from moment to moment, frame to frame, and so on. It could change over the long term, if one device upgraded to support a faster speed, but when the link came back up again, and both nodes autonegotiated to use a specific speed, Ethernet standards require that both nodes use that one speed for all transmissions.

A single WLAN, with a single AP, still uses multiple speeds. Each WLAN standard defines a maximum speed, but many other slower speeds as well. Literally, in a single wireless LAN, even with a single device, the device can send one frame at the maximum speed and the next frame at a slower speed. Why? Because the slower speeds might work when the faster speeds do not.

Before looking at the WLAN details further, think about this analogy with talking and sound. Say that you get to a party early, with you and two friends sitting in a room, talking. The music is not very loud, and you can all hear each other with no problem. Two hours later, the room is full of people, everyone has taken a turn at bumping up the volume on the music, and now you try to talk to someone. When you speak, he might or might not hear you. When you speak, he might give a blank stare or respond in some way that tells you that he had absolutely no clue what you just said.

In the noisy party environment, if you want to be heard, what do you do? You yell. You lean in close to shorten the distance. The listener turns his ear toward your mouth. Maybe you slow down a little, making sure that you speak each word more clearly.

WLAN standards use similar ideas as with this analogy about being at a party, including the idea of using different speeds to deal with radio noise in the WLAN. In a WLAN, each frame transmission should be followed by an acknowledgment that it was received. When a sender does not receive an acknowledgment, it is like getting a blank stare from someone at a party—the listener just did not receive the frame. So, the sending node resends the frame. However, instead of repeating the frame in exactly the same way, the sender slows down and sends the frame at a slower bit rate. As it turns out, the slower the bit rate, the easier it is for the listener to receive and decode the incoming radio signal.

Figure 6-4 shows an example. Devices A and C both sit within range of the WLAN AP; however, some radio noise exists between device C and the AP, resulting in some lost frames. The figure shows the speeds of the most recent transmissions— device A sent at the maximum speed for 802.11b, 11 Mbps, and device C slowed to 2 Mbps to overcome the radio noise.

FIGURE 6-4

Example of Using Speeds Slower Than the Maximum, 802.11b

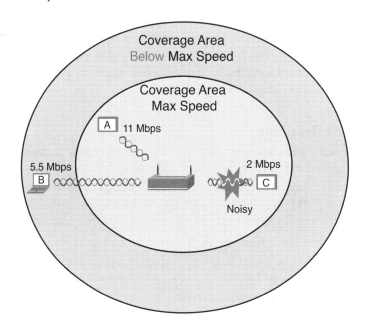

The distance from the AP also affects the speed. In a WLAN, the faster the bit rate, the smaller the coverage area (range). So while the AP might try to send data at the maximum rate, only the devices that sit nearer to the AP will be able to understand that signal. If the AP does not get an acknowledgment to the frame, the AP can then send the data again, with a slower speed. Devices farther away from the AP can receive and understand these slower radio transmissions.

Figure 6-4 shows an example of a slower transmission because of distance. The figure shows a circle that represents the AP's coverage area for the fastest possible speed. Device A sits in the AP's coverage area that works at the maximum rate. Device B sits outside the coverage area for the maximum speed but within the coverage area for the next slower 802.11b speed, 5.5 Mbps, so at least host B can communicate in the WLAN at this slower speed.

Now that you know a little more about WLANs, particularly their coverage areas and speeds, you should have a better idea why some questions about WLANs can be answered with "It depends." How fast is a WLAN? It depends on the standard, which defines the maximum possible speeds for one transmission. It depends on the products and how they have been configured. It depends on the current radio noise, which causes a device to slow down. And it depends on how far away the users roam with their devices.

Shared Bandwidth Versus Dedicated Bandwidth

The next topic looks at one final comparison related to the speeds of wired and wireless LANs—the concept of shared bandwidth versus dedicated bandwidth.

First, the word *bandwidth* can mean several different ideas in networking, but most of the time today, bandwidth refers to the speed (bit rate) of a link. In the past, this term literally referred to the range (band) of frequencies used to communicate, with a wider-frequency band meaning that you could send more data—the higher the bandwidth, the faster the bit rate.

Next, think about each individual Ethernet link, and that for each Ethernet link between two nodes, the bandwidth is either shared or dedicated. If the two nodes use half-duplex logic (using the carrier sense multiple access with collision detection [CSMA/CD] algorithm), they basically take turns sending, so they share the capability to send bits over the link. In this case, the bandwidth would be *shared bandwidth*. When using full duplex, the switch can even use that speed at any time, without waiting, which is called *dedicated bandwidth*.

The capacity of a wired Ethernet LAN to send bits can be measured by adding all the bandwidth on each port. Because the switch ports act independently, it does not matter whether each port uses half duplex or full duplex, but to keep the discussion more obvious, just think about Ethernet switches in which every port uses full duplex. In that case, every switch port can send at its speed, at the same time. If you add up all those speeds, that total tells you the number of bits per second that switch could send. That total defines the capacity of the Ethernet LAN.

For example, the example at the top of Figure 6-5 shows the results of dedicated bandwidth in an Ethernet LAN. In this case, 20 end-user devices all use 1000BASE-T and full duplex. Device 1 sends frames to device 2, and device 2 sends frames back to device 1, both as fast as they can go, and at the same time. Certainly both devices send a combined 2 Gbps of traffic (1 Gbps in each direction). Likewise, if the rest of the Ethernet LAN devices happened to be sending to each other in pairs at the same time, the 20 devices would send data at a cumulative 20 Gbps capacity.

FIGURE 6-5

Dedicated Bandwidth and Shared Bandwidth and the Effect on LAN Capacity

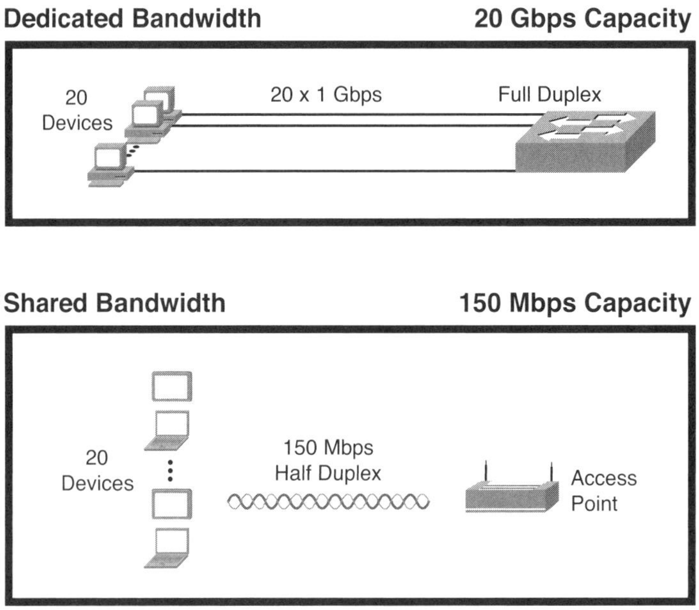

A WLAN uses **shared bandwidth**. All the devices that use a single AP, such as those in the lower half of Figure 6-5, share the right to send through that WLAN. Only one device, including the AP, can send at any one point in time. So while every device might be capable of sending bits at 150 Mbps (in this example, using 802.11n, with one stream), only one is allowed to do so at a time. The networking world refers to the logic as *half duplex*. The networking world calls the overall effect of sharing the ability to send *shared bandwidth*.

> **ON THE SIDE:** A more memorable way to think of shared bandwidth is to think of this imaginary family. The family has 20 kids who are old enough to drive. The (rich) dad built a private racetrack in the backyard, and then he buys all 20 kids a Ferrari. Shared bandwidth is like what happens when the dad puts up a schedule, and each kid can only drive his Ferrari every 20th day or so. So on any one day, 19 Ferraris sit in the garage. (Some garage, huh?) Dedicated bandwidth is like what happens when the kids can drive their Ferraris anytime they want.

In Figure 6-5, the capacity of the WLAN happens to be 150 Mbps. Because only one transmission can happen at a time because the bandwidth is shared, the WLAN's capacity is simply equal to the maximum speed of any one transmission. (This example just happened to use a combination of 802.11n settings that results in a maximum speed of 150 Mbps.)

Figure 6-5 shows a somewhat extreme example (on purpose), to show the differences in capacity for the dedicated bandwidth in an Ethernet LAN and the shared bandwidth in a wireless LAN. In this example, the wired LAN has 1000 times the capacity of the WLAN. However, WLANs as a whole can be designed so that more than one device sends at the same instant. The limitation is that with the set of devices communicating with one AP, only one can send at a time.

Figure 6-6 shows one other example of shared bandwidth that improves the capacity of the WLAN. The WLAN in Figure 6-6 replaces the WLAN at the bottom of Figure 6-5. The new WLAN in Figure 6-6 has the same 20 end-user devices, but it has four APs placed around the floor of a building. As a result, four devices can send or receive data with a nearby AP, at the same time, without interfering with each other.

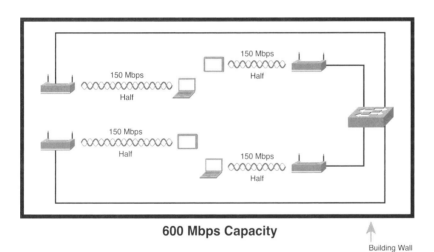

600 Mbps Capacity

Building Wall

FIGURE 6-6

Increasing Capacity 4X by Using Four Access Points

Each AP, configured properly, creates a separate domain of shared bandwidth. Each AP and its associated devices must still share the frequency and use CSMA collision avoidance (CSMA/CA). Four instances of the shared bandwidth now exist, however, so this WLAN's capacity moves up to 600 Mbps (4 x 150 Mbps).

Summary of Comparisons

Summarizing the key points, generally speaking, Ethernet LANs have a few more absolute facts that apply regardless of the particular LAN, while WLAN requires that the engineer think more about applying WLAN concepts to a particular WLAN. Wired LAN standards have clearer cable distance guidelines, while WLANs have no literal preset size limits. The WLAN coverage area simply requires more planning and testing. Wired LAN speeds vary greatly across many

AUTHOR'S NOTE:
The examples in this section focus on the technical differences so that the differences are clear. Please do not take these examples as meant to favor or lobby for wired or wireless LANs, and do not take these as examples as great designs for an effective wired or wireless LAN. The goal is to help you see the differences.

standards, but each standard supports a single speed. WLAN speeds vary—not only across the standards, but also within a single WLAN standard, and even from frame to frame in an actual WLAN. Finally, the dedicated bandwidth in wired LANs gives them a capacity advantage over the shared bandwidth in WLANs, but with proper WLAN design, WLAN capacity can be improved as well.

Table 6-2 summarizes the comparison points brought up in this section, for easier reference.

TABLE 6-2

Comparing 802.3 Wired LANs with 802.11 Wireless LANs

Topic	Wired	Wireless
Uses cables.	Yes	No
UTP cable distance / wireless range is defined by the standard and not significantly affected by local site conditions.	Yes	No
A single LAN standard specifies a single speed, rather than a set of allowed speeds.	Yes	No
Allows full duplex on each link, rather than sharing bandwidth among all devices using half duplex.	Yes	No

Wireless LAN Standards

The IEEE standardizes WLANs, but two other groups also play big roles:

- The vendors who create WLAN products
- A powerful vendor alliance called the Wi-Fi Alliance

The following sections look at the IEEE standards as well as describe how the IEEE, Wi-Fi Alliance, and vendors work together.

IEEE WLAN Standards

The history of WLAN standards follows a story similar to Ethernet. Before WLAN standards existed, vendors created products. Eventually, the IEEE formed the 802.11 working group to create WLAN standards. The 802.11 working group ratified its first standard, simply called 802.11, in 1997. This WLAN standard used frequencies around 2.4 GHz and a maximum speed of 2 Mbps.

Unsurprisingly, since the time of the original 802.11 standard, the 802.11 working group has ratified many other WLAN physical layer transmission standards. Those four newer standards improved the range, speed, and other transmission details. Similar to the naming of IEEE 802.3 Ethernet standards, the names of each 802.11 standard begin with 802.11, with suffix letters that identify the specific standard. Figure 6-7 shows the formal names of the IEEE WLAN transmission standards, along with the ratification dates. It also lists the fastest speed for each standard for a single stream, for reference.

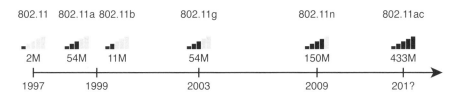

FIGURE 6-7

Timeline of IEEE 802.11 WLAN Standards and Max Single-Stream Bit Rates

Each transmission standard in Figure 6-7 defines a maximum speed, but it also defines a large number of other features. Most of the rest of this chapter describes different WLAN features, some of which differ depending on the 802.11 transmission standard. Table 6-4, later in this chapter, summarizes the differences. For now, know that the speeds have gotten generally faster over time, and that the range (distance between the device and AP) has increased with 802.11n as well.

The Wi-Fi Alliance

The Wi-Fi Alliance works to make the wireless LAN industry a success. According to its website, this vendor alliance has over 300 members; most every company whose wireless LAN products sit on the shelf in the local stores is a part of the Wi-Fi Alliance. The Wi-Fi Alliance is one of the most effective vendor alliances in the history of networking.

Rather than list all the work of the Wi-Fi Alliance, this section mentions a few roles: testing and certification. For example, vendors that use the Wi-Fi Alliance product testing service prove that their products work well with other WLAN products, and they can advertise that fact as being certified by the Wi-Fi Alliance. The process runs something like this:

1. The vendor develops a new wireless LAN product.

2. Before selling the product, the vendor sends the product to the Wi-Fi Alliance for testing.

3. The Wi-Fi Alliance puts the product through a predefined set of tests.

4. The Wi-Fi Alliance tests whether the new product works with other wireless products that have already passed the tests.

5. After the product passes, the Wi-Fi Alliance certifies the product as having passed. The vendor can claim it is certified and use Wi-Fi Alliance logos on the product packaging and advertising.

Besides the testing and certification process, the Wi-Fi Alliance has also worked to establish some recognizable brands and logos to go along with the certifications. For example, while this book has been using the term *WLAN* as a generic term for a wireless LAN, the Wi-Fi Alliance long ago started using the term *Wi-Fi*. It registered trademarks that use the term *Wi-Fi*. In fact, many people who use WLANs or buy consumer WLAN products know those products as "Wi-Fi" products as part of the branding work by the Wi-Fi Alliance.

ON THE SIDE:
The term *Wi-Fi* even made it into the Merriam-Webster dictionary.

Cooperation and Interoperability

Consumers enjoy a wireless world in which you can buy WLAN products from most any vendor and they work well together. In fact, the products work together so well that, most of the time, consumers do not even worry about whether a particular WLAN device will work. People do not think, "My WLAN access point is from vendor X, so I better get my WLAN NICs from vendor X as well." Instead, you have a phone from one vendor, a tablet from another, a laptop from another, a WLAN NIC for a desktop computer from yet another vendor, APs from other vendors, and so on—and it all works.

That amazing degree of *interoperability* in the networking world happens in part because of the cooperation between vendors, the IEEE, and the Wi-Fi Alliance.

First, think about the interoperability challenge from the AP vendor's perspective. That vendor wants its AP to work with every NIC. If you think about every different NIC made by every vendor, the number of different models of NICs numbers at least into the hundreds, if not thousands. To make sure that all those NICs work, the AP vendor needs to test—and potentially test every new NIC that every vendor brings to market. That testing proves which products interoperate with the vendor's AP.

The Wi-Fi Alliance helps the vendors deal with the product testing task. The Wi-Fi Alliance builds a formal set of interoperability tests. All the vendors that participate in the Wi-Fi Alliance—the AP vendor, all the NIC vendors, and so on—send products to the Wi-Fi Alliance for testing. The Wi-Fi Alliance's approved test labs run the tests; some products pass, and some do not. (When a product does not pass, the vendor can change the product and have it tested again until it passes.) Products that pass are certified by the Wi-Fi Alliance as interoperable.

The process between the Wi-Fi Alliance and the vendors has several important results. First, the market has a large set of products to choose from, all of which have been proven to work together in a lab. From a vendor perspective, the vendor does not have to do all that same testing work, with every vendor and all its products, making the testing process more efficient. And when a vendor gets a phone call from a customer, saying that she cannot connect using another vendor's WLAN NIC, the conversation can start with this: "Is the other product Wi-Fi certified?" Today, if a vendor wants to sell WLAN products, the products almost have to be Wi-Fi certified to have any chance of success in the market.

In addition to working with the Wi-Fi Alliance, vendors also cooperate with the IEEE as well. As usual, the IEEE's working groups use a mostly volunteer workforce. Unsurprisingly, a lot of the 802.11 volunteers also work on WLAN products for their respective companies. Oftentimes, that helps the standards process. Sometimes, having volunteers from competing companies might cause some arguments on particular technical points for a particular standard. Regardless, the vendors donate some labor, and the IEEE creates some standards.

Finally, the IEEE and Wi-Fi Alliance cooperate quite a bit as well. The Wi-Fi Alliance wants Wi-Fi vendors to be successful—after all, it is an alliance of wireless LAN vendors. The more successful the wireless LAN industry is as a whole, the better the marketplace for all vendors to sell their products. And open standards happen to be one key to the long-term health of any segment of the networking world.

Figure 6-8 summarizes the key roles of vendors, the IEEE, and the Wi-Fi Alliance, and some of the benefits to those of us who then buy wireless LAN (Wi-Fi) products.

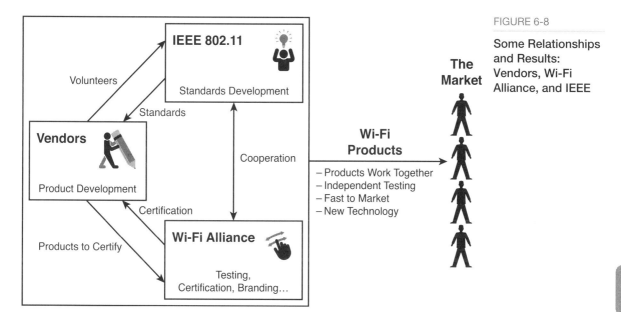

FIGURE 6-8

Some Relationships and Results: Vendors, Wi-Fi Alliance, and IEEE

WLAN Roles

WLANs have several advantages, but the strongest advantages are that WLANs do not require cables and that they allow users to move around (mobility). Stop and think about those two strengths, and then think about a typical enterprise network: lots of smaller remote sites, a couple of main sites with hundreds or thousands of users, some connections to the Internet, and so on. Then, consider these two questions:

- What parts of that enterprise network would make the best use of mobility?
- What parts of the enterprise network, which has no mobile devices, would benefit most from not having to use cables?

The short answer for both questions is the same—the LAN edge. Mobility means that end users will want to move around with their tablets, laptops, or even their smart phones connected to a WLAN. So, modern networks need to support mobile devices (devices that move around). For static devices that do not move, WLANs can simply reduce the cost of cabling for new LAN installations. And where do most of the cables exist in a typical enterprise network? At the LAN edge, where all the end-user devices sit. So, the most natural place to use the WLAN is in any part of the network where user devices exist.

To complete the first major section of this chapter, the final topic looks at a few examples of where modern networks use wireless LANs. The next few pages give some examples of WLANs and their use in a larger corporate network.

WLAN-Only LAN Edge

For the first example, imagine any business that has a large number of small remote offices, plus a small number of large sites. For example, banks have lots of branches, typically with five to ten people working in each branch, but with some large sites to process work such as monthly bank statements, processing all the paper checks and deposits, and so on. For another example, insurance companies often have a small sales office in every town in their geography, but some large sites where they handle the core operations to writing policies, handling claims, and so on.

At both the small offices and the large main sites, these companies could use a wireless-only LAN edge, as shown in Figure 6-9. All user devices use WLAN technology to connect to the enterprise network, even devices that never move, like desktop computers and printers. To communicate with other sites, the network uses the full TCP/IP protocol suite, with routers at each site forwarding IP packets between sites.

FIGURE 6-9

Enterprise Branch Office with Wireless LAN Edge

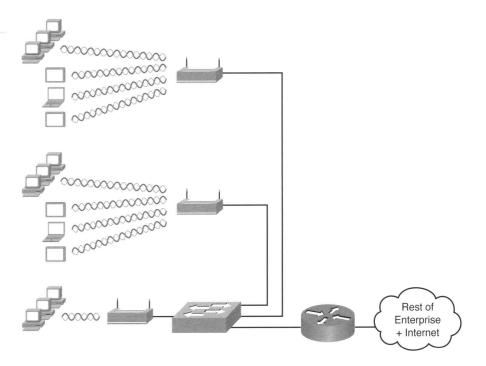

Wired and Wireless LAN Edge

Those same companies—the ones with enterprise networks, small remote offices, and a few larger sites—could use a combined wired and wireless LAN edge. Essentially, the company creates a wired Ethernet LAN for every location where a device might need to connect to the network. The design also creates WLAN coverage for the exact same space, and possibly some spaces the Ethernet cables cannot reach. Figure 6-10 shows the idea.

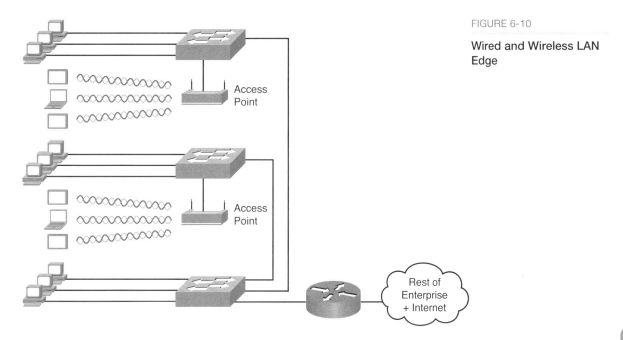

FIGURE 6-10

Wired and Wireless LAN Edge

This design takes advantage of only one of the two primary strengths of WLANs mentioned in the beginning of this topic (mobility). This strategy still requires the company to install UTP cables, so the WLAN does not save the company any cabling effort or expense. However, it allows mobile devices to connect to the WLAN and move around in that space.

Small Office/Home Office WLANs

Many people work from their homes today, whether they work at home all the time or just occasionally. The employee typically has a small home office network, which also has a connection to the Internet, allowing the employee to work at home almost as if he was at work.

The networking industry uses the term *small office/home office (SOHO)* to refer to smaller sites that use the types of technology and devices that you might find at someone's home office. For such a small site, you might have only three or four devices, plus a connection to the Internet. Figure 6-11 shows three different sample SOHO sites on the left, each for a different employee of the same company. Each can communicate with the company's network through his or her Internet connection.

FIGURE 6-11

Wired-Only Versus
WLAN-Only Small Office,
with Combined Devices

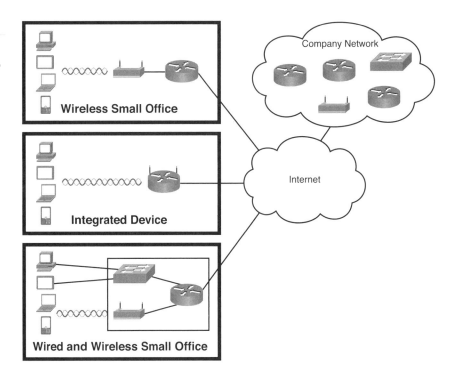

Each SOHO site can use wired, wireless, or both. For example, the figure shows
a wireless-only site at the upper left and a combined wired and wireless SOHO
network at the lower left.

SOHO networks often use *integrated networking devices*. An integrated networking
device performs the same functions as multiple standalone networking devices,
but in a single device. For example, the upper-left example in Figure 6-11 shows
a separate router and AP. Instead of two separate devices, you can buy a wireless
router (as shown in the middle example in the figure), which essentially combines
the functions of an IP router and a wireless LAN AP into a single device. Some
integrated networking devices combine a wired Ethernet switch as well. For
example, the lower-left part of Figure 6-12 shows three devices in a separate box,
but all three functions could exist as a single integrated device.

> **AUTHOR'S NOTE:** The next time you happen by the local office supply store,
> stop in the technology section and look for the wireless products. Then look
> for wireless routers, find a couple, and read the packaging. You should find
> support for an Internet connection. Most consumer-oriented wireless routers
> have the functions of an IP router, a port to connect to the Internet, at least
> one wired Ethernet port, possibly a small built-in Ethernet switch, and possibly
> a wireless AP.

Single-Site Networks and Public WLAN Hotspots

Besides using wireless LANs in corporate networks, many small businesses that
have a single site use WLANs as well.

Many small businesses that have just a single site still need a network, and they often use WLANs today. WLANs have been somewhat common for over ten years, with many people being comfortable using WLANs. When a small business moves into a new space, the idea of buying an inexpensive wireless router, and avoiding the cost of running Ethernet cables, makes a wireless-only option seem very attractive.

For retailers who want their customers to spend more time in the store, the *wireless hotspot* concept has become pretty popular as well. The retailer—for example, a coffee shop or bookstore—installs the same kind of WLAN a small single-site company would install, along with a connection to the Internet. Users can sit, have a snack or coffee, surf the web, stick around, and hopefully spend more money.

The single-site company and wireless hotspots use the same technology and the same kinds of Internet connections, but they have one important difference—the hotspot allows strangers to use the network, and the small company network should not. A policy whereby anyone who happens by can use the hotspot's Internet connection (through the hotspot's WLAN) makes the service work. Most of the time today, the user at least has to click on a web page button to agree to some *acceptable use policy*, in which the user agrees to not use the WLAN for illegal activities and so on.

Figure 6-12 shows a couple of examples for comparison. In this case, three businesses have space in the same office park: one coffee-and-sandwich shop that mostly serves people from the office park, and two single-site businesses. All three use the same model of wireless router, and all have a connection to the Internet.

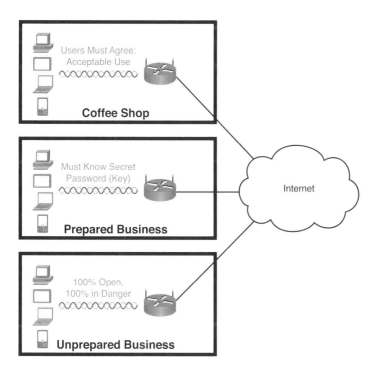

FIGURE 6-12

Single-Site WLANs (Protected and Unprotected) and Public Hotspot

The figure does provide a good example from which to make one important point about WLAN coverage areas, particularly for smaller businesses in office parks—coverage areas can, and often do, cross over into the spaces of nearby businesses. In this figure, a user sitting in the coffee shop might be within range of the WLANs of these other two small businesses. If the unprepared business did not set up proper WLAN security on its wireless router, people in the coffee shop could connect to the WLAN of the unprepared business. The person in the coffee shop can use its Internet connection and attempt to steal data.

Exploring WLAN Physical Layer Features

Wired Ethernet LAN standards give us many plain and specific answers to important questions about how Ethernet LANs work. For example, Ethernet defines that each user device has a cable that can connect to a LAN switch, so it is obvious where the user device sends its data (out the cable to the switch). Also, each standard defines one bit rate, so when using that standard, all bits flow at that one speed. Also, for a given standard and cabling type, the standards define the maximum cable length, defining the maximum distance between nodes.

Wireless LAN standards do not give us as many plain answers because of how wireless works. For example, end-user devices do not have a cable, so where does the user device send the data? WLAN standards allow several options, so WLAN requires more thought as compared to Ethernet. As another example, while Ethernet lists specific speeds for every standard, WLAN standards list maximum speeds, but they actually use a variety of slower speeds in practice. When you use a WLAN today, your device might actually send data at several different speeds at different times over a single minute in time, for example. So, for WLANs, many seemingly basic questions actually require you to think about several related topics before you can understand the answer to the original question.

This second of three major sections of the chapter looks at three parts of the WLAN world that require more than a single simple answer. The following sections begin by looking at WLAN topologies. The topology defines the idea of which device a WLAN client currently sends a frame to whenever the client sends a frame. Next, these sections look again at the coverage area and speed issues, discussing some of the design options for an enterprise WLAN. These sections close with a look at the frequency bands reserved for use by devices like WLAN nodes, and the frequency channels they use to send data.

WLAN Topologies

With Ethernet LANs, the idea of the LAN's topology can be thought of as the cabling and the devices as drawn on paper. Each link connects two nodes. If you take a single edge switch, and put all the end-user devices spread around the switch, the design looks a little like a kid's drawing of a star, as seen back in Chapter 5's Figure 5-7. As a result, the networking world describes modern Ethernet LANs as using a *star topology*, or at least that the physical Ethernet LAN has a star topology.

A wireless LAN also has topologies, but you cannot just look at the cables and devices to describe its shape, because of course, a WLAN does not use cables. Instead, WLAN topologies help us understand how the end-user device (the wireless client) connects to and uses a WLAN. The next topic discusses the three common WLAN topologies, from simplest to most complex.

Independent Basic Service Set (Ad Hoc)

The first topology, called an *ad hoc wireless LAN*, provides very basic WLAN service. An ad hoc topology lets two (or more) WLAN devices send data directly, without needing a wireless access point. You have a device and so does someone else, so you connect with your WLAN NICs, and then you can send data to one another. Figure 6-13 shows the simple concept.

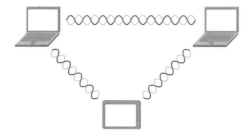

FIGURE 6-13

Ad Hoc Wireless LAN: Independent Basic Service Set (IBSS)

An ad hoc WLAN, also known formally as an *Independent Basic Service Set (IBSS)*, gives users flexibility. To use an AP, someone must have prepared beforehand by buying an AP and installing it. Plus, the users must know the correct password if the AP has been properly secured. An ad hoc wireless LAN lets the user devices communicate directly without an AP.

The downside of using an ad hoc WLAN is that you lose the benefits of connecting to an AP, in particular, you lose the connection the AP normally has to some other network. As a result, most people who use ad hoc WLANs use them for just short time periods.

Basic Service Set

The next topology, called a **Basic Service Set (BSS)**, does exactly what its name says: basic wireless service. With a BSS, one and only one AP creates the wireless LAN. Then, each wireless client that wants to use that WLAN connects through that one AP. The AP controls the BSS, with all wireless frames flowing either to the AP from the user devices or from the AP back to a user device. Figure 6-14 shows an example BSS.

FIGURE 6-14

Single AP Wireless LAN:
Basic Service Set (BSS)

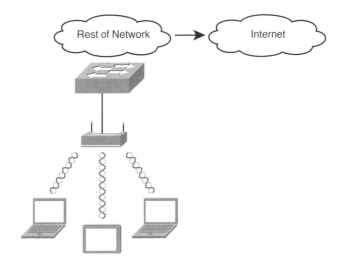

Besides being the central device for all wireless frames, the AP in a BSS WLAN provides another important function—a connection to some other network. Most people do not just want wireless; they want wireless so that they can get access to other services. Those services typically exist on the Internet and on the corporate networks, and often do not connect directly to the same WLAN as the end user. In a BSS, the AP both controls the wireless part of the network and connects the wireless LAN to the wired network, so that users can get to the data in the rest of the world.

Extended Service Set

The third WLAN topology, the **Extended Service Set (ESS)**, extends the wireless functions of a BSS. The big difference? A BSS uses one AP to create one wireless LAN, while an ESS uses more than one AP to create one wireless LAN.

Both BSS and ESS topologies provide the same important services. Both give clients an AP with which to send frames. All frames flow from the wireless client to/from an AP. And the AP(s) connect to some other network, to give the wireless clients connections to the rest of the corporate network and/or the Internet.

An ESS extends the services on the wireless side of the AP in a couple of ways. First, the multiple APs combine to create more coverage area than a BSS. Designed well, the ESS creates more WLAN capacity; the upcoming section, "Increasing Capacity with Nonoverlapping Channels," discusses the details. Furthermore, the ESS allows roaming, in which the wireless client moves around within the ESS coverage area and still works, but in actual practice, switches from using one AP to using another AP. Figure 6-15 shows an ESS WLAN, with an example of roaming.

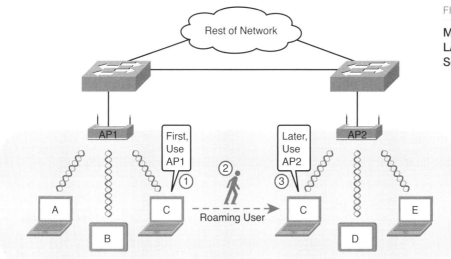

FIGURE 6-15

Multiple-AP Wireless LAN: Extended Service Set (ESS)

SSID = ABC_WLAN

Each BSS and ESS defines a WLAN name, formally called the *Service Set Identifier (SSID)*. In the case of a BSS, the one and only AP defines the SSID, but in an ESS, all the APs use the same SSID and cooperate to create the one WLAN that goes by a single SSID (WLAN name).

For example, in Figure 6-15, all the wireless clients connect to the same WLAN called ABC_WLAN. Every client sends/receives frames to/from one AP at any one point in time. In this case, the user of laptop C walked down the hall (with laptop C) to a meeting, and his device, sensing that a better AP was now closer, automatically switched from using AP1 to start using AP2.

Table 6-3 summarizes the key points in this section that differentiate among the three WLAN topologies.

> **AUTHOR'S NOTE:**
> The idea of what is included in "one wireless LAN" is tied to the definition of a BSS and ESS. One ESS includes all the APs in the ESS, plus all wireless clients that connect (are associated) with that WLAN by name, regardless of which AP through which they currently communicate.

TABLE 6-3

Comparisons of Wireless LAN Topologies

Feature	IBSS (Ad Hoc)	BSS	ESS
Number of APs used	0	1	>1
Data frame flow	Device to device	Device to AP	Device to AP
Connects clients to some other network?	No	Yes	Yes
Allows roaming?	No	No	Yes

Coverage Areas and Speed

Imagine that you and your best friend are having a conversation. Can you hear each other pretty well? Can you understand each and every word? While in your mind's eye you might picture you and your friend in the same room, the answer to whether you can hear each other well depends on a lot of factors. How close together are you? What stuff is between you: a thin wall, a piece of glass, an entire building, or more? You also have to consider the amount of noise—are you chilling at home or at a concert?

In WLANs, both the coverage area and speed depend on a variety of factors as well. If no other factors change, the farther a device moves away from the AP, the more likely the device will have to send at a slower rate. If no other factors differ, the more stuff that's in the planned coverage area of an AP, the more likely the coverage area will be smaller or have dead spots. If no other factors differ, the more radio noise that gets added into the planned coverage area, the smaller the coverage area, and the slower the transmission speeds.

Some factors harm both speed and coverage area, but speed and coverage area also compete with each other directly. Simply put, for a single AP, the farther away from the AP the client sits, the more likely the AP and device will have to use slower speeds to make the transmission work.

The following sections look at some of the facts related to the trade-offs of coverage area and speed.

Coverage and Speed with an Omnidirectional Antenna

Although this chapter expects that you remember the details from Chapter 4 about WLANs sending data using radios, a brief review of the basics can help at this point. To send data, each device has a radio with an antenna. When the device creates an electrical current in the antenna, the antenna radiates radio waves. Other antennas can sense those radio waves, converting the radio waves back into electrical signals. The receiver then interprets the electrical signals as 1s and 0s.

Most NICs and APs use an *omnidirectional antenna*. In other words, when the antenna sends out its radio waves, it sends them in all directions with equal strength. The pattern looks like the waves you see if you drop a brick(?) into a still pond: The waves go out from the center, in all directions, and look like a circle.

As the radio waves travel out from the sender's antenna, the radio waves get weaker. The same idea applies to sound waves: When you speak in a normal voice, someone beside you can hear you just fine, but if he starts walking away, eventually he gets far enough away that the sound waves just fade away too much, and he cannot hear you anymore. The same effect (called attenuation) happens with radio waves.

The coverage area of an AP with an omnidirectional antenna creates a layered coverage area. The closer parts of the coverage area can run at faster transmission speeds and still work, because the signal strength is higher. The farther-away parts of the coverage area require a slower speed. With an omnidirectional antenna, the coverage area looks like a set of concentric circles, as shown in Figure 6-16—the larger the circle, the weaker the signal and the slower the bit rate. (The figure shows the speeds used by the 802.11b standard.)

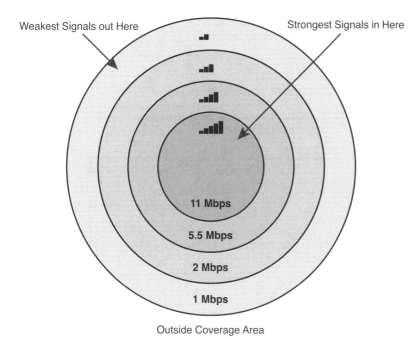

Outside Coverage Area

FIGURE 6-16

Coverage Area for an Omnidirectional Wireless LAN AP

Every 802.11 LAN transmission standard defines a list of speeds that devices can use. When a wireless device senses a lower signal strength, the device can choose to run at a slower speed in hope that the transmission will still work. But do not think of the slower speeds as a penalty—it is better to let the wireless devices work a little slower rather than to not let them work at all.

Now that you understand the theory of the basic trade-off between coverage versus speed, now think about the trade-off for a real company in a new building. If you worked there, and you got to pick your desk's location in the new office space, what location would you pick? If you knew where the APs would be installed, would you be tempted to pick an office location close to one of the APs, hoping to be in a fast part of the WLAN coverage area? Many people would.

When planning for any ESS WLAN, a network engineer must think about coverage, as well as maximizing the coverage areas that run at the faster speeds.

For example, Figure 6-17 shows two competing designs for a new WLAN for a floor in a building. The top design shows an inexpensive design that relies on the maximum width of the coverage area for two APs. The figure shows two coverage area circles for each AP: The inner circle shows the coverage for the maximum speed, and the outer circle shows the far edge of the coverage area at the slowest speed. The top design uses only two APs, which saves money, and it covers about 80 percent of the space on that floor. However, only about 20 percent of the floor sits inside the highest-speed coverage areas.

ON THE SIDE:
The bar charts in Figure 6-16 look like the charts shown on many wireless devices that show signal strength; these graphs typically show the strength of the signal, with the fewer bars meaning a weaker signal.

FIGURE 6-17

Coverage by Design

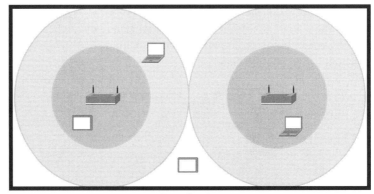

Design Option 1

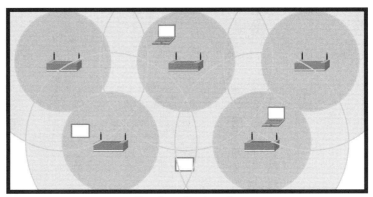

Design Option 2

Legend

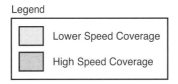

	Lower Speed Coverage
	High Speed Coverage

Design option 2 costs more money, with five APs, but unsurprisingly increases the highest-speed coverage and the total coverage area. In this design, the shaded high-speed areas cover about 50 percent of the space—an improvement over the 20 percent high-speed coverage of design 1.

In a real-life ESS WLAN—that is, a WLAN with multiple APs used to create one WLAN—the design process must deal with the issues of covering all the spaces at the desired speeds.

Antenna Gain (Power) and Direction

As you have probably noticed by now, radio communication has more than a few similarities compared to how humans communicate with sound. This next topic mentions two more similarities, both of which impact the size of a coverage area: the power (gain) of the radio signal and the direction.

First, think about how we as humans deal with trying to talk over longer distances when speaking in person. When someone is far away from you, say a few hundred feet, you have to shout. You might also cup your hands around your mouth when you shout, which helps the sound go toward the person to which you are shouting.

In wireless LANs, NICs and APs can increase the power (gain) of the radio signal, which has much the same effect as shouting. The waves can travel farther than they would otherwise, all other variables being unchanged.

Unfortunately, increasing the gain might not be an easy solution for a couple of reasons. First, some devices, particularly NICs, do not have a setting to boost the gain. Even for APs, on which you can boost the gain on the radio signal, you have to follow national regulations. Every country regulates the amount of electromagnetic (EM) radiation that devices can use when sending data; in the United States, the Federal Communications Commission (FCC) sets those regulations. And the FCC does not just let you bump up the gain on your WLAN to some arbitrarily large setting, because your WLAN would then interfere with the WLAN next door. The regulations help protect us all from the neighbors becoming too noisy.

WLAN devices can also direct their radio signals in a particular direction by using a directional antenna. Most consumer APs that you buy at a store come with an omnidirectional antenna. For example, Figure 6-18 shows a consumer wireless router, with three antennas, all of which happen to be omnidirectional. But some APs, particularly APs intended for use in corporate networks, allow network engineers to replace the antennas with other antennas.

FIGURE 6-18

Generic Router with Wireless Access Point with Three Antennas (© Scanrail)

AUTHOR'S NOTE: The wireless router in Figure 6-18 has three antennas because it supports the 802.11n feature to allow multiple streams at the same time; to do that, the AP needs multiple antennas, one per stream.

Typically, the larger the WLAN, the greater the need to perform a site survey, the greater the need to design for good coverage, and the greater the need to make use of options like using directional antennas. A directional antenna does not create a circular coverage pattern, but it creates some other pattern—for example, the pattern might be close to a semicircle or a quarter circle. By directing the power in a particular direction, the signal travels farther, which increases the coverage area in that direction.

As an example, Figure 6-19 shows a third alternate design compared to the two WLAN designs shown in Figure 6-17. In this case, four APs sit in the corners of the floor, each using a directional antenna that sends out a radio signal for 90 degrees (a quarter circle). Note that these quarter-circle patterns extend farther away from the AP than would a circular coverage pattern from an omnidirectional antenna. Then, in the middle of the floor, along the walls, two APs each use antennas with a 180-degree pattern.

FIGURE 6-19

Four 90-Degree and Two 180-Degree Directional Antennas Cover the Floor

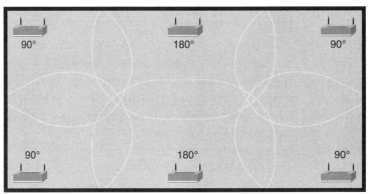

Design Option 3
100% Coverage at Highest Speed

The design in Figure 6-19 has some advantages and disadvantages compared to the designs in Figure 6-17. Comparing design 3 to design 2 (Figure 6-17), design 3 covers literally the entire floor, whereas design 2 did not cover parts of the corners. (The corners in office buildings typically have offices for the bosses, so covering the corners can be important.) Design 3 also shows the entire floor as being covered with the maximum speed, while design 2 provides the highest speeds only for about half the floor.

Design 2 (Figure 6-17) has a couple of advantages over design 3. It uses less hardware, so it costs less. It also uses omnidirectional antennas, which are common in consumer-grade wireless APs that you buy at the local store, so the APs might be cheaper than those used in design 3. Design 3 requires the purchase of the directional antennas, and it also requires more thought and planning from the IT staff.

Wireless LAN Radio Frequencies

As you probably recall from the discussions in Chapter 4, radio waves can be described based on their waveforms. Energy can be measured, with the graph of the energy looking like a repeating wave. The wave has an amplitude: the height of the wave over the midpoint, which typically represents the strength of the signal. The energy has a frequency: the number of times the waveform repeats in 1 second. It even has a wavelength: the length in meters of one complete waveform as it moves.

WLAN product vendors must follow rules about the waveforms that its WLAN products send. First, the products must follow regulations defined by the national government. To sell a product in a particular country, that vendor has to make sure that the product follows the rules of that country, including rules about the energy that the product creates. The products must also follow the rules in the IEEE standards as well.

As a consumer of WLAN products, you do not have to worry about whether a vendor followed the rules. If you plan to work with wireless LANs, however— to install, troubleshoot, and support those WLANs—you need to know some facts about the rules of WLAN frequencies. After you know the basics, you can understand some concepts related to choosing to use something called *nonoverlapping frequency channels* (discussed later in the section, "Increasing Capacity with Nonoverlapping Channels"), which make a WLAN work better.

Electromagnetic Spectrum

Electronic devices give off EM energy—it just happens because of the way the physical world works. When electricity flows over any type of electrical conductor, that process creates some EM energy as a side effect.

Although some electronic devices (for example, WLAN devices) create EM energy on purpose, most electronic devices do not need to give off EM energy. For most electronic devices, the emitted EM energy has no useful purpose; all it does is create noise for devices that do use EM energy for some purpose. All electronic devices give off this extra EM energy, creating noise that can interfere with devices like WLAN clients and APs.

The *electromagnetic spectrum (EM spectrum)* describes all the possible frequencies and wavelengths of EM energy. Basically, over time, scientists discovered and studied energy in all its forms, and they noticed that certain big groups of EM energy frequencies had similar characteristics. So, some types of energy worked well for different purposes. For example, X-rays work well to sense things inside a solid object, while radio waves work well for sending music by bouncing the waves off the Earth's upper atmosphere.

Figure 6-20 lists a brief view of part of the EM spectrum. The EM spectrum works as an initial guide to EM energy, giving names to large sections of the EM spectrum. It also lists the literal frequency and wavelengths for each category in the EM spectrum. The spectrum also typically shows the frequencies from lowest frequency to highest, as shown in Figure 6-20.

FIGURE 6-20

Partial Electromagnetic Spectrum, for Perspective

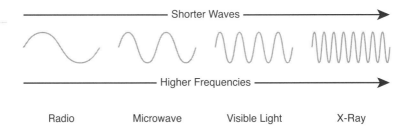

ON THE SIDE: The wavelength, which is the length of one complete waveform, relates to the speed of light and to the frequency. The higher the frequency, the more waves that must fit inside 1 second, so one complete wave takes up less width. The calculations assume that the energy flows at the speed of light, so the formula for wavelength is Wavelength = Speed of light / Frequency.

Frequency Bands and Government Regulation

AUTHOR'S NOTE: In the United States, the Federal Communications Commission (FCC) regulates communications for television, radio, wires, satellite, and cable. This text mentions specific regulations from the U.S. FCC only, just to make some points, rather than attempting to point out small differences in regulations from country to country.

Every national government regulates the EM emissions for electronic products sold in that nation. Why? All electronic products give off EM energy, and if no rules existed, the devices would give off so much energy, the world would be too full of EM noise. If a country's laws allowed electronic devices to create all this EM noise, most communications devices that use EM energy would work poorly, or not at all. So, for the good of all the people, and in particular, to make communications work better, national governments regulate EM emissions.

Regulations like those from the FCC help everyone who wants to communicate get along a little better. In particular, they set aside some frequency bands for specific types of communication. (The generic term *frequency band* refers to a range of frequencies.) Then the FCC defines some rules that apply to all vendors that make devices that use those frequency bands.

The FCC creates some *licensed frequency bands* and some *unlicensed frequency bands*. In a **licensed frequency band**, the FCC creates regulations so that no one can use these frequencies without getting permission (a license). The FCC then slices the licensed frequency band into smaller subsets, called *frequency channels* or *frequency spectrum*, and sells a license for these channels to anyone who wants to buy them. The license allows that one company, and only that one company, to use that particular frequency channel in a particular location.

As an example, think about FM radio stations. The FCC reserves the frequency band from about 87 GHz to about 108 GHz for FM radio stations. When a company wants to start a radio station (for example, in Atlanta), it buys an FCC license for a small part (200-MHz) channel of the FM radio band. The FCC might assign this new company the channel from 96.0 to 96.2 GHz. Based on that license, that one company would be the only company, in the Atlanta area, that could legally generate EM energy from 96.0 to 96.2 GHz.

Without these rules, competitors could cause serious problems. For example, a competitor could put up a radio tower a few miles away and transmit at the same frequencies as the company that bought the FCC license. The new radio signals would ruin the radio signal of the company that paid for the license.

The FCC (and others) also defines some **unlicensed frequency bands**. Like all FCC frequency bands, unlicensed bands contain a set of nearby frequencies; however, anyone can use these unlicensed frequencies without having to pay for a license. However, the world essentially shares those frequencies, because anyone can use them. So, the FCC creates rules to help everyone get along while using the same frequencies, like defining rules about how strong the EM energy can be.

Unlicensed frequency bands work a little like life in an apartment building, especially on the weekends, where everyone owns a stereo. If everyone plays her stereo at a reasonable volume, everyone can hear her own music and not be bothered by her neighbors. But if a few people turn up the volume very high, others cannot hear their music any more. In unlicensed frequency bands, the FCC (and others) tell the people to use the frequencies but to keep the power (gain) down, to not cause too much noise in your neighbor's apartment, house, or office space.

The FCC and other national regulators across the globe define two major unlicensed frequency bands used for WLAN communications:

- Industrial, Scientific, and Medical (ISM) (around 2.4 GHz)
- Unlicensed National Information Infrastructure (UNII) (around 5 GHz)

Each 802.11 standard defines which of these two unlicensed frequency band(s) the standard uses. Most product documentation simply refers to these two unlicensed bands by the rounded frequency number—2.4 GHz (ISM) or 5 GHz (UNII)—rather than the literal low- and high-end frequencies in the range. Figure 6-21 lists the two unlicensed bands used by today's WLAN standards, along with the standards that can use each. Note that 802.11n can use either frequency band.

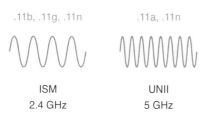

.11b, .11g, .11n   .11a, .11n

ISM   UNII
2.4 GHz   5 GHz

ON THE SIDE: Mobile wireless technology—that is, the technology used between mobile phones and the mobile telco networks, as discussed in Chapter 4—also uses licensed frequencies.

AUTHOR'S NOTE: One reason why WLAN coverage areas extend a few hundred feet, and mobile phone coverage areas extend several miles, is that WLANs use unlicensed frequency bands, which require lower power, to avoid disturbing other nearby devices that might be using the same channel.

FIGURE 6-21

Unlicensed Radio Frequency Bands Used for WLANs

ON THE SIDE: The world of networking uses the term *bandwidth* to mean a couple of ideas. A frequency band is a range of consecutive frequencies, so you can think of the range as a width; so people call the width or range of frequencies the bandwidth. With some technologies, a wider number of frequencies (a wider bandwidth) meant a faster bit rate. As a result, the word *bandwidth* today often refers to the speed of a link, regardless of the literal frequency used when sending the data.

Frequency Channels

When a WLAN device sends data, it uses a wireless *frequency channel*. Like a frequency band defined by an agency like the FCC, a frequency channel is a set of consecutive frequencies. Unlike a frequency *band*, a frequency *channel* is a subset of the frequency band defined by the regulators. Basically, for the United States, the FCC defines one wider range of frequencies (the frequency band), and the wireless device sends using a smaller range of frequencies (a frequency channel).

Figure 6-22 shows a comparison of the ISM frequency band, per FCC regulations, compared to the frequency channels defined by 802.11 standards. The ISM frequency band lists frequencies around 2.4 GHz, with a total frequency range of about 70 MHz. Some 802.11 standards use a 22-MHz frequency channel for transmissions in the ISM band, as shown in the figure.

FIGURE 6-22

Government-Regulated Frequency Bands Compared to 802.11 Transmission Channels

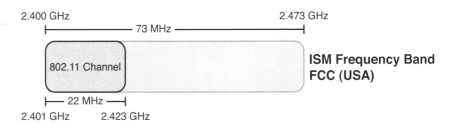

The IEEE 802.11 standards do not allow WLAN devices to use just any 22-MHz subset of the ISM frequency band. Instead, the IEEE standards define specific frequency channels. For example, 802.11b and 802.11g use a channel width of 22 MHz, and they all define 11 channels, such channels that fit into the FCC's definition of the ISM frequency band. Each of the 11 channels has a defined low- and high-end frequency, as represented in Figure 6-23.

FIGURE 6-23

802.11b and 802.11g Frequency Channels

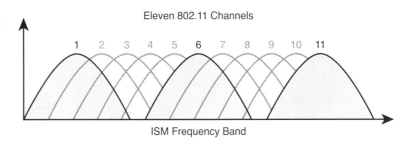

AUTHOR'S NOTE: The width of the frequency channel depends on the physical layer standard used. 802.11b and 802.11g use Direct Sequence Spread Spectrum (DSSS), which uses a bandwidth of 22 MHz. 802.11a and 802.11n use Orthogonal Frequency Division Multiplexing (OFDM), which uses a 20-MHz bandwidth.

Increasing Capacity with Nonoverlapping Channels

If you work in a job where you implement WLANs, you will need to think about which frequency channels to use for each AP. As it turns out, of the 11 channels shown in Figure 6-23, three channels do not overlap. Figure 6-23 uses gray highlights for these channels, numbered 1, 6, and 11.

First, to make sure that the concept of nonoverlapping channels makes sense, look at Figure 6-24. In the United States, the FCC sets aside 73 MHz of bandwidth for the ISM frequency band. Some IEEE standards use a 22-MHz channel for a transmission, so three of these channels, for a total of 66 MHz worth of frequencies, should fit within 73 MHz, with just a little space left over.

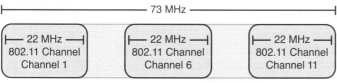

ISM Frequency Band: FCC (USA)

FIGURE 6-24

Three Nonoverlapping 22-Mhz 802.11 Channels Inside the 73-MHz ISM Band

These nonoverlapped channels can be used to increase the capacity of a wireless LAN, because of the following fact:

> Two different pairs of WLAN devices can communicate without interfering with each other—at the same time and in the same space—if using different nonoverlapping frequency channels.

To understand the benefit, first consider an example with a single 802.11g WLAN, with a single AP. That one WLAN has a maximum capacity of 54 Mbps, because the fastest transmission rate for 802.11g is 54 Mbps. If 20 user devices exist in that WLAN, the capacity still cannot exceed 54 Mbps, because the devices must take turns using the CSMA/CA algorithm. In other words, the WLAN uses shared bandwidth.

With multiple APs in the same space, multiple transmissions can occur at the same time, however. For example, look at the design in Figure 6-25, with three APs. The coverage areas do overlap, but each AP uses a different nonoverlapping channel. As a result, even though the coverage areas overlap quite a bit, each AP can send or receive at the same time as the other two APs. If again using the 802.11g standard, the capacity of the WLAN increases to 3 * 54 Mbps = 162 Mbps.

FIGURE 6-25

Using Nonoverlapping 802.11 Channels to Increase Capacity, Performance, and Coverage

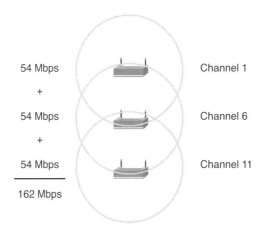

The UNII frequency band has a much wider range of frequencies. As a result, the 802.11a and 802.11n standards, which can use the UNII band, support a larger number of nonoverlapping channels: 23 channels for 802.11a and 21 channels for 802.11n (with a 20-MHz-wide channel).

Summarizing Key Differences in 802.11 Standards

From the topics mentioned in this chapter so far, Table 6-4 summarizes the topics that differ from standard to standard.

TABLE 6-4

Summary of 802.11 Standards and Differences

	802.11a	802.11b	802.11g	802.11n	802.11n[1]
Year ratified	1999	1999	2003	2009	2009
Channel width (MHz)	20	22	22	20	40
Encoding class	OFDM	DSSS	DSSS	OFDM	OFDM
Frequency band (ISM at 2.4 GHz, UNII at 5 GHz)	UNII	ISM	ISM	Both	Both
Nonoverlapping channels, USA (FCC)	23	3	3	21[2]	9[2]
Maximum bit rate, one stream (Mbps)	54	11	54	72	150
Supports up to four streams on one device[2]	No	No	No	Yes	Yes

1. 802.11n can use a standard 20-MHz-wide channel or combine two channels to create a bonded 40-MHz channel. The rightmost column assumes a 40-MHz channel.

2. Assumes transmission in the UNII frequency band, which is wider and therefore supports more nonoverlapping channels.

Exploring WLAN Common Features

This third and final major section of the chapter looks at a few WLAN features that work the same way regardless of which 802.11 standard is used. First, the following sections look at the 802.11 frames that wireless clients and APs send in a wireless LAN. Following that, the text discusses some overhead processes and frames that must happen before a wireless client can send/receive data frames with the AP in a WLAN. Finally, these sections end with a look at how APs work, with some comparisons between WLAN APs and Ethernet LAN switches.

WLAN Frames and Addresses

The 802.11 standard defines a frame format used across all 802.11 physical layer standards. No matter whether the WLAN uses 802.11a, .11b, .11g, or any other 802.11 physical layer standard, the frames that flow over those wireless links use the same format.

The frame format for an 802.11 data frame follows the same general ideas as an 802.3 frame, but with several differences. Some fields have the same meaning, size, and format as the same field in an 802.3 frame. Other frame fields that exist in 802.11 do not exist in 802.3 and vice versa. For example, the 802.11 frame format does not include a Preamble or SFD field.

To be ready to understand the AP functions discussed later in this chapter, however, you just need to know a few facts about several 802.11 fields that work the same way as in 802.3. In particular:

- Both have a 6-byte destination MAC address in the header.
- Both have a 6-byte source MAC address field in the header.
- Both have a 4-byte FCS field in the trailer.

Figure 6-26 shows these three common fields; refer to Chapter 5's Figure 5-18 for a reminder of the 802.3 Ethernet frame format.

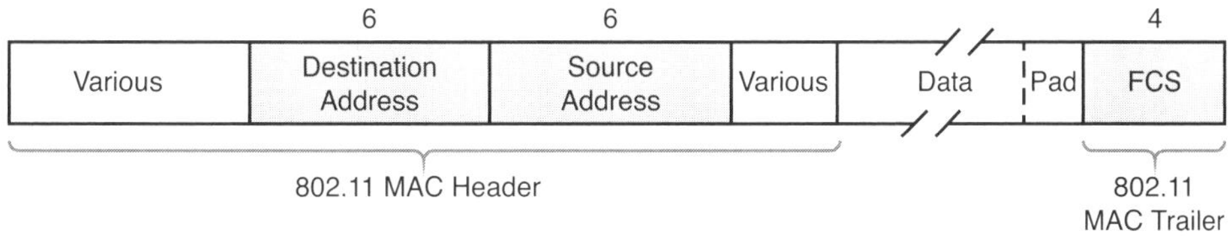

FIGURE 6-26

IEEE 802.11 Frame Format

> **ON THE SIDE:** The idea of using the same frame format for all physical layer LAN standards should sound familiar—the IEEE 802.3 standard uses the same Ethernet frame format over all types of physical Ethernet links.

The IEEE also makes sure that all the WLAN NICs have unique MAC addresses. To make that happen, the IEEE uses the same *universal MAC address* strategy and process that it uses with 802.3 MAC addresses. With universal MAC addresses, every device in the universe that uses a MAC address can have a unique MAC address. The IEEE applies the same process to both 802.11 and 802.3 LANs, so WLAN MAC addresses and wired Ethernet MAC addresses should be unique.

Associating with an Access Point

In a wired 802.3 Ethernet LAN, an obvious connection exists between the user device and a LAN switch. To be a part of an Ethernet LAN, the user device needs to connect to the Ethernet using a cable. When the user device sends data frames and receives data frames, the frames go to/from the Ethernet switch on the other end of the cable. In fact, this connection, or association, between the user device and the local LAN switch is so obvious that most people do not even stop to think or talk about it.

So why even talk about a somewhat obvious wired Ethernet concept in a chapter about wireless LANs? For the sake of comparison. In a WLAN, the wireless client does not have an obvious or implied connection to any one AP. In fact, even after the wireless client chooses an AP with which to communicate, the client can change its mind. So, to understand how WLANs work, you need to understand more about how and why a client chooses to use a particular AP through a process called *association*.

Take a moment to think about life from the wireless client perspective, particularly when the client moves around. Say that a client, a tablet of some kind, arrives at some office. The tablet can only connect through a wireless LAN: It has no Ethernet NIC, and it has no wireless WAN capabilities. The tablet must communicate through some WLAN AP. But which AP? How does the tablet even discover the existence of the nearby APs? How does the client choose one to use? None of these questions exist in a wired Ethernet LAN, because the choice of where to connect the cable actually answers those questions. For a WLAN, many things must happen to answer these questions.

Management and Control Frames

WLAN clients use 802.11 **management and control frames** to help answer some of these questions. These frames do not carry user data, but instead, they perform functions important to the wireless LAN. The 802.11 standard defines many different frames to do different kinds of work.

The best way to get an idea for the purpose of these management and control frames is to see examples. First, think back to Chapter 4 and the CSMA/CA process. That process requires the WLAN devices to send messages to each other to decide who sends next, to announce how long the next transmission will take, and to acknowledge that a frame was received. The actual messages are 802.11 management and control frames.

Another series of 802.11 management and control frames takes a new wireless client from the time it arrives at a new site until it can use the WLAN. WLAN devices must *associate* with an AP before the device can send and receive data frames to/from the AP. To associate, the wireless clients follow a process that uses several management and control frames. During this association process, the client discovers all nearby APs, decides which one to use, passes any security processes, and gets the chosen AP to agree to allow the WLAN client to use the AP. The next few pages outline the process, along with the related management and control frames.

Discovering Existing Wireless LANs

The WLAN association process begins with discovery, and the discovery process typically uses *beacon frames*. APs send beacon frames to announce the AP's existence. That announcement includes the name of the wireless LAN, called the **Service Set ID (SSID)**. A client listens for beacon frames all the time, learning of new APs and new WLANs as a result.

Focusing on the discovery process, consider the example in Figure 6-27, where two companies sit in a small office building. Both have wireless routers that serve as APs, and both have different wireless LAN names (SSIDs) for their WLANs. Both APs send beacon frames to announce their WLAN SSIDs. The coverage areas of the two WLANs happen to overlap, as is typical in most small offices, so all the WLAN clients in both locations discover the SSID of both wireless LANs.

Leased Space, Coffee Shop (Panera Bread)

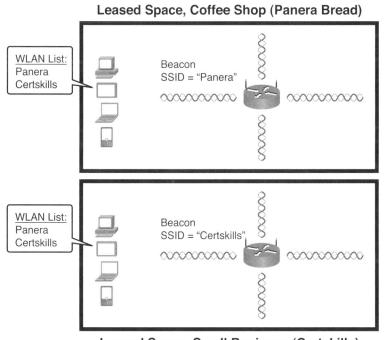

Leased Space, Small Business (Certskills)

FIGURE 6-27

Learning About Multiple
WLANs Through 802.11
Beacon Frames

At this point in the process, the operating system (OS) on each user device typically takes one of two actions: 1) connect to a preferred WLAN by name (SSID) or 2) require the user to choose the WLAN to which to connect. Most devices can be set up to always connect to a WLAN to which it has connected before. The user can also simply pick a WLAN from the list. For example, Figure 6-28 shows a screen shot from the list of WLANs reachable from the author's favorite table at the local coffee shop.

FIGURE 6-28

Example of Discovered WLAN List (Mac OS X)

> **AUTHOR'S NOTE:** The WLANs listed by the client OS were learned from the beacon frames; they are the SSIDs as advertised by the access points.

Associating with an Access Point

After the user has chosen which WLAN to use, the client then has a couple more steps to complete before sending data frames (frames that hold user data). If the WLAN happens to be an ESS, the client might have learned of several APs advertising the same SSID, so the client has to choose which AP is best. For a BSS, the wireless client just has to associate with the one AP.

When a wireless client needs to choose among several APs in an ESS, the client sends out probe frames, with each AP sending a probe response. The client uses the responses to pick the currently best AP for the client to use. At that point, the client must pass some security authentication checks, and finally, the client associates with the AP.

Figure 6-29 shows the overall process with a single ESS with two APs. In this case, the user has just chosen to use the Certskills wireless LAN.

FIGURE 6-29

Example of Probe, Authenticate, Associate

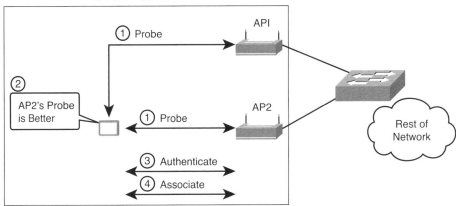

Following the steps in the figure:

1. **Probe request and response:** The device sends probe frames, with each AP in the WLAN responding. In an ESS (a WLAN with more than one AP), the probe responses let the user device pick the best AP to use right now.

2. **Determine the better AP:** The user device looks at the probe responses and picks the better AP to use right now.

3. **Authentication request and response:** The device sends frames with any required password-related values. The AP either allows the process to continue or not, depending on the values sent by the user device.

4. **Association Request and Response:** The device completes the process by asking to associate with the AP; the AP sends a response. Now the AP will accept frames from the device and send frames to the device.

> **AUTHOR'S NOTE:**
> Although this chapter does not discuss WLAN security, as mentioned at Step 2, the topic is important for real-world WLANs. Make sure to enable security; do not allow the general public to happen by and use your wireless LAN!

Access Point Operation

After the client has associated with a single AP, the client can send and receive data frames. The term *data frame* refers to WLAN frames that hold data from the upper layers, like IP packets, instead of management and control frames like beacon frames and Associate frames. This next topic examines what actions the AP takes to process these data frames.

The main function of the AP is to forward data frames. When one WLAN device sends a frame to another WLAN device, the AP sends the frame back onto the WLAN. When a WLAN client sends a frame to a destination on the Ethernet side of the AP, the AP forwards the frame onto the Ethernet.

This next topic discusses a few details of how an AP forwards data frames. In particular, this topic looks at how the AP translates data frames from the 802.11 format to the 802.3 format, how the AP deals with the CSMA/CA sharing logic on the WLAN side, and how the AP makes forwarding decisions using a MAC address table like an Ethernet LAN switch.

Translating 802.3 and 802.11 Data Frames

While it is possible to use an AP to create a WLAN that has no connection to a wired network, most APs connect a WLAN to a wired network. That wired network typically connects to the Internet, either directly or indirectly through a wired Ethernet connection into a corporate network.

If you think about these facts from the AP's perspective, you can think of the world as having two halves: the wireless side of the AP and the wired side of the AP. An AP takes data frames in from one side, forwards them out the other side, and vice versa. That is, when the AP receives a wireless 802.11 data frame, it might forward the frame out its wired Ethernet side. Likewise, when an Ethernet frame arrives on its wired side, the AP might then need to forward the frame out its WLAN side.

As part of the process of forwarding data frames, the AP must actually translate between the 802.11 and 802.3 frame formats. The 802.11 and 802.3 frame headers and trailers have a lot in common—enough so that the translation does not require a lot of work. For example, both frame formats have 6-byte source and destination MAC addresses. The frame formats do have differences, however, so the AP must translate between the two. Figure 6-30 shows the idea, with a frame moving from the WLAN to the wired LAN.

FIGURE 6-30

Conceptual Drawing of WLAN AP Translating from 802.11 Frame to 802.3 Frame

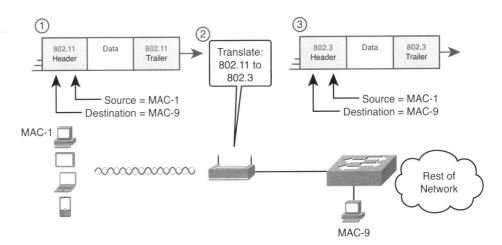

The figure shows a couple of MAC addresses in shorthand form for easier reference. Following the steps in the figure:

1. The device that uses MAC address MAC-1 sends a frame, source MAC address MAC-1, with destination MAC address MAC-9.

2. The AP translates the 802.11 header and trailer into an equivalent 802.3 header and trailer. The source and destination MAC addresses remain as MAC-1 and MAC-9, respectively.

3. The AP forwards the 802.3 Ethernet frame out the Ethernet link into the campus LAN.

Queuing and Buffering

Almost every device that acts as a node in a network has the capability to store messages temporarily and then forward the messages. Why store the messages temporarily? The node might have to wait before sending the message. Many messages might arrive around the same time, all of which need to go out the same outgoing interface. Across the history of networking devices, any device that thinks about processing messages (frames, packets, and so on) can temporarily hold those messages until the right time to forward the messages. That process of holding the messages temporarily is typically called *queuing* or *buffering*.

WLAN APs also need to queue LAN frames for several reasons, and the CSMA/
CA logic happens to be one of those reasons.

First, to review the concepts, a single AP, plus the clients associated with that AP,
act as a group for the purposes of sharing in a WLAN. For example, imagine one
AP with 20 wireless clients associated with it. Only one of these 21 devices (the
AP plus the 20 clients) can send at a point in time. In short, the CSMA/CA sharing
concept applies to a single AP and its associated clients.

When an AP needs to forward a frame out either its WLAN side or its Ethernet
side, when sending the frame, the AP must follow whatever rules apply to that side.
When forwarding a frame out the wired Ethernet interface, the AP must follow
Ethernet standards. When forwarding frames out the wireless 802.11 side, the AP
must follow 802.11 rules, including CSMA/CA rules.

The AP needs to be able to buffer or queue frames going in both directions, but the
need to queue frames typically happens more for frames being sent onto the WLAN.
First, the Ethernet side often runs at a faster transmission rate than the WLAN side.
Second, the AP has to wait its turn to send with CSMA/CA on the WLAN side,
while it likely uses full duplex on the Ethernet side, which does not require the AP
to wait.

Figure 6-31 shows an example of queuing happening on an AP as data frames go
from its Ethernet side to its WLAN side.

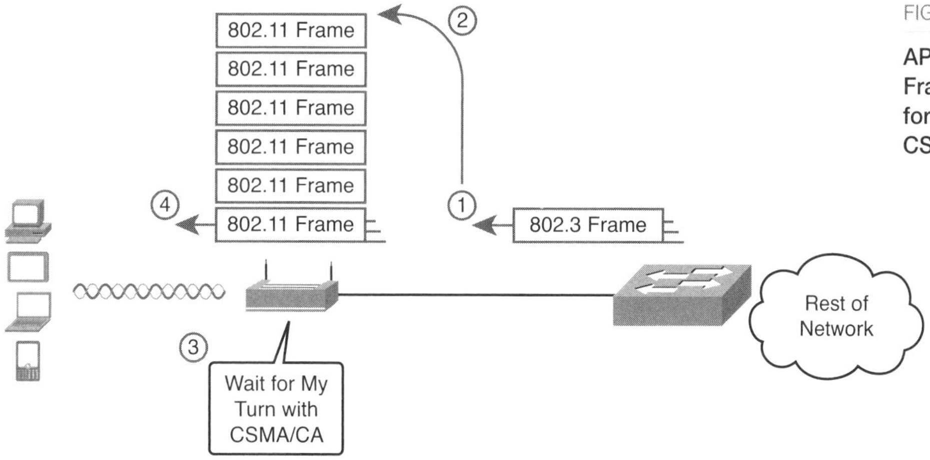

> **AUTHOR'S NOTE:**
> The world of
> networking has
> sometimes used the
> term *packet switching*
> to refer to the idea
> of a node receiving
> a message (packet),
> queuing the packet
> for later transmission,
> and then forwarding
> the packet.

FIGURE 6-31

AP Queuing 802.11
Frames While Waiting
for a Turn to Send with
CSMA/CA

Following the steps in the figure:

1. Frames arrive at the AP, coming in the wired Ethernet side.

2. The AP logic at this point knows that it already has other frames waiting
   to be sent out on the WLAN side, so the AP adds the new data frame to the
   queue (after translating it to 802.11).

3. The AP processes CSMA/CA logic, waiting its turn to send a frame.

4. The AP gets a turn, so it sends the next 802.11 frame waiting in the queue.

AP Switching Logic

Like Ethernet LAN switches, WLAN APs need to make a forwarding decision when they receive a frame. And the decision does not default to simply sending frames that come in the WLAN side out onto the Ethernet side, or vice versa. Sometimes the frame comes in the WLAN side, and the AP needs to send it back out the WLAN interface. Sometimes a frame comes in the Ethernet side, and the AP actually should ignore the frame. So the AP needs more logic than a simple idea of "if it comes in the WLAN, send it out the Ethernet, and vice versa."

To make good forwarding decisions, an AP acts like an Ethernet LAN switch. How? The AP learns MAC addresses, just like an Ethernet switch, on both the WLAN and wired sides. Those learned addresses give the AP some idea where a MAC address sits—either on the WLAN side of the AP or the wired side of the AP. The AP also makes forwarding decisions like an Ethernet switch: Forward known unicasts based on the MAC table, and flood unknown unicasts and LAN broadcasts.

Figure 6-32 shows a sample MAC address table on an AP. The AP has four WLAN devices associated with the AP, with shorthand MAC addresses for easier reference. The AP has also learned the MAC addresses of two wired Ethernet devices as well.

FIGURE 6-32

AP MAC Address Table

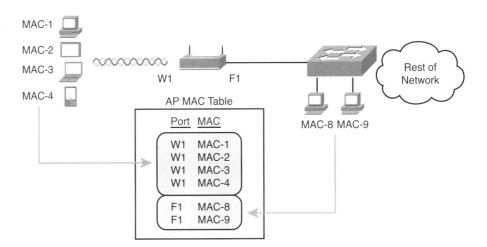

Chapter Summary

Wireless LANs and wired Ethernet LANs have many similarities and differences. The differences give both types of LANs an advantage for different uses of LAN technology. Most notably, Ethernet has faster speeds and longer supported distances, while WLANs support mobile users at solid speeds for the typical use of WLANs. As time passes, the LAN market overall will continue to see shifts in how companies best use both wired and wireless LAN technology.

WLANs mostly exist in small office/home office (SOHO) environments, wireless hotspots, and at the LAN edge for corporate networks. The smaller WLANs can rely on a single AP (a BSS) and require little or no planning because of the size of the WLAN. The larger WLANs require much more planning, in part because so many factors impact the speeds the clients can effectively use, the coverage areas of the WLANs, and the capacity in the WLAN. Building these larger WLANs requires more theoretical knowledge, as well as a willingness to be practical. How big is the coverage area, for example? Go use wireless testing tools to measure it as part of a wireless site survey, and then you will know.

A single WLAN has a speed, capacity to forward bits, and coverage area, all of which can change over time based on some controllable factors and some less controllable factors. The WLAN has a maximum theoretical speed for a given transmission, based on the standard. It has a coverage area, with different transmission speeds used depending on where the devices sit in the coverage pattern. The coverage area can be designed and affected by many choices—the type of antenna, the power (gain) used on the devices, and the location and number of APs. It can also be affected by radio noise, both from unrelated devices as well as from other WLANs.

All clients, regardless of the 802.11 physical transmission standards they use, follow the same processes to discover a wireless LAN and associate with it. The process makes use of 802.11 management and control frames, which, unlike data frames, do not hold an upper-layer packet like an IP packet. Instead, the client and AP use these overhead frames to control other processes, like discovering all WLANs by listening for their beacon frames and associating with a single AP by using Associate frames.

Chapter Review Activities

Use the features in this section to study and review the topics in this chapter.

Answer These Questions

1. An enterprise campus LAN uses wired UTP Ethernet and wireless 802.11 LANs at the edge of the LAN. Looking at a particular floor in a particular building, all the devices connect to either a single Ethernet switch or single wireless access point, both of which sit in a wiring closet in the middle of the space. Which of the following is true about the distance limitations in this LAN?

   a. All user devices, wired and wireless, can be up to 100 meters away, but no farther.

   b. All Ethernet user devices can be up to 100 meters away (but no farther), while WLAN devices can typically be farther away than 100 meters.

   c. All Ethernet user devices can be up to 100 meters away (but no farther), while WLAN devices must typically be closer than 100 meters.

   d. The Ethernet distances must be decreased to match the maximum distance supported by the wireless LAN.

2. IEEE 802.11 standards define a maximum speed for an individual transmission, with some variables that affect 802.11n speeds. Assuming that 802.11n uses the narrower 20-MHz channel and a single stream, which of the following answers matches a particular standard to its maximum bit rate?

   a. 802.11g: 54 Mbps

   b. 802.11b: 54 Mbps

   c. 802.11a: 72 Mbps

   d. 802.11n: 150 Mbps

3. An enterprise campus LAN uses wired UTP Ethernet and wireless 802.11 LANs at the edge of the LAN. A network engineer uses a WLAN testing tool to view the frames moving through the WLAN, and he notes the speeds of the various frames in a single WLAN that uses a single access point. Which of the following answers list a condition that could have affected the speeds that the engineer observed when testing the WLAN? (Choose two answers.)

   a. None. The speed must be the same for every frame transmission with the same WLAN and same AP.

   b. The current radio noise.

   c. Whether the AP uses CSMA/CA.

   d. The distance between the client device and the AP.

4. An enterprise campus WLAN uses a single 802.11n AP, with 20 clients that all use 802.11n. The AP uses only a single stream, but it does use a double-wide channel, with a maximum data rate for a single transmission of 150 Mbps. The same floor has an Ethernet LAN, with 20 PCs

connected using 10BASE-T, UTP cabling. The Ethernet switch and AP both connect to the rest of the network using a Gigabit Ethernet interface. Which of the following statements are true when comparing the wired and wireless LANs on this floor? (Choose two answers.)

   a. The wired LAN has a larger capacity.

   b. The wireless LAN has a larger capacity.

   c. The wired and wireless LAN capacity cannot be compared.

   d. A single transmission from the AP to a WLAN user device goes faster than the transmission from the Ethernet switch to a wired user device.

5. A network engineer is designing a campus LAN, both wired and wireless. When planning the wireless LAN, the engineer looks at a scale drawing of the space for each floor and draws the coverage area associated with each AP. Which of the following answers describes the most accurate method the engineer can use to determine the coverage area?

   a. Do a wireless site survey.

   b. Read the IEEE standard for the specific 802.11 standard the engineer plans to use for each AP, and find the coverage area maximum distances.

   c. Read the coverage area guaranteed distances from the AP vendor's documentation.

   d. None of the answers is correct.

6. Many groups have a positive impact on the development of wireless LAN standards. Which of the following plays the biggest role in testing and certifying products to prove that they work with other products that have already been certified?

   a. ITU

   b. IEEE

   c. Wi-Fi Alliance

   d. The vendor that made the new product

7. Which of the following answers define a wireless LAN physical layer standard that was originally ratified by the IEEE before the year 2000? (Choose two answers.)

   a. 802.11a

   b. 802.11b

   c. 802.11c

   d. 802.11g

8. Which of the following locations is the least likely place to find a wireless LAN?

   a. In a coffee shop to provide Internet access as a WLAN hotspot

   b. As a link between two Ethernet switches on two different floors of the same building

   c. In someone's home

   d. At the edge of a campus LAN (where the user devices sit)

9. Which of the following wireless LAN topologies use at least one wireless access point? (Choose two answers.)

    a. BSS

    b. ESS

    c. IBSS

    d. SSID

10. Which of the following is true of an ESS WLAN topology but not a BSS WLAN topology?

    a. Clients sends frames to/from the access point and not directly to/from each other.

    b. The wireless LAN uses only IEEE 802.11g and more recent standards.

    c. The wireless LAN has at least two access points.

    d. The wireless LAN has a minimum coverage area of 300 feet.

11. An IT worker buys an AP at the local office supply store and installs it. He then gets out a tape measure and measures the distance from the AP to the cubicles used by Amy (20 feet), Bob (50 feet), and Chuck (150 feet). Each user uses his or her tablet computer from a cubicle. The WLAN uses the 802.11g standard, with a 54-Mbps maximum speed. Which answer is most likely to be true about how these user's tablets work?

    a. Chuck's tablet will either work at 54 Mbps or not work at all.

    b. Chuck's and Bob's tablets never use 54 Mbps to send frames because they sit more than 65 feet from the AP (802.11g's maximum distance for maximum speed).

    c. Chuck's tablet is more likely to work at a slower speed than Alice's tablet.

    d. All three tablets will have no trouble sending at 54 Mbps because they sit within the 802.11 maximum distance of 100 meters (330 feet).

12. An IT worker installs a wireless AP, but then realizes through testing that the coverage area does not cover the entire floor of the building. The building is in the shape of a long, skinny rectangle. Which of the following could be used to help change the shape of the coverage area so that it reaches all parts of that floor? (Choose two answers.)

    a. Increase gain.

    b. Replace the antenna with an omnidirectional antenna.

    c. Replace the antenna with a directional antenna.

    d. Lower the value of the SSID.

13. In the IEEE 802.11g standard, how many nonoverlapping frequency channels exist?

    a. 1

    b. 2

    c. 3

    d. 4

14. Which of the following types of energy are not part of the electromagnetic spectrum? (Choose two answers.)

   a. Thermal

   b. Gamma radiation

   c. Visible light

   d. High-pitched sounds

15. Which of the following are true about the frequency bands used by WLANs, but not true about the frequency channels used by wireless LANs? (Choose two answers.)

   a. Defines a set of consecutive frequencies

   b. Regulated by the FCC in the United States

   c. Defined by IEEE standards

   d. Applies to devices that have nothing to do with wireless LANs

16. Which of the following fields in an 802.11 frame have the same format and meaning as a field in an 802.3 frame? (Choose three answers.)

   a. Destination MAC Address

   b. Sender MAC Address

   c. Preamble

   d. Frame Check Sequence

17. A user brings his tablet computer into the office where a wireless LAN exists. When the user turns on the tablet, the tablet detects two wireless LANs. Which of the following 802.11 frames or processes plays a key role in the tablet discovering the presence of these wireless LANs?

   a. Autonegotiation (process)

   b. Beacon (frame)

   c. Discover (frame)

   d. Associate (frame)

18. A user brings his tablet computer into the office where a wireless LAN exists. The client discovers three nearby APs that make up the Certskills wireless LAN. The client connects to the Certskills WLAN successfully and starts surfing the web. Assuming that the APs are named AP1, AP2, and AP3, which of the following is true about how the client uses this WLAN?

   a. The client sends data only through the AP from which it received the first beacon.

   b. The client sends data only through the AP with which it exchanged Associate frames.

   c. The client sends a frame, and all three APs receive the frame and negotiate as to which one forwards the frame.

   d. The client load-balances frames by sending one frame to AP1, the next to AP2, then AP3, repeating the process.

19. A wireless client has started using a WLAN, sending all its frames through an AP named AP1. The client sends an 802.11 data frame to the AP. The frame's destination MAC address is in the same wireless LAN. Which of the following will the AP do when processing this data frame received from the wireless client? (Choose two answers.)

  a. The AP will discard the frame, expecting that the destination client will have overheard the frame anyway.

  b. The AP will translate the 802.11 header into an 802.3 header.

  c. The AP will look for the frame's destination MAC address in its MAC address table.

  d. The AP can queue the frame temporarily, waiting for the AP's turn to send data over the WLAN.

20. A wireless client has started using a WLAN, sending all its frames through an AP named AP1. The client sends an 802.11 data frame to the AP. The frame's destination MAC address is on the Ethernet LAN that sits on the other side of the AP. Which of the following will the AP do when processing this data frame received from the wireless client? (Choose two answers.)

  a. The AP will forward the frame to a router, because routers work well at connecting different types of LANs and WANs.

  b. The AP will translate the 802.11 header into an 802.3 header.

  c. The AP will look for the frame's destination MAC address in its MAC address table.

  d. The AP can queue the frame temporarily, waiting for the AP's turn to send data over the WLAN.

Define the Key Terms

The following key terms include the ideas most important to the big ideas in this chapter. To review, without looking at the book or your notes, write a definition for each term, focusing on the meaning, not the wording. Then review your definition compared to your notes, this chapter, and the glossary.

Key Terms for Chapter 6

coverage area	WLAN hotspot	nonoverlapping channels
shared bandwidth	Basic Service Set	management and control frames
Wi-Fi	Extended Service Set	Service Set ID (SSID)
LAN edge	unlicensed frequency band	

List the Words Inside Acronyms

The following are the most common acronyms discussed in this chapter. As a way to review those terms, simply write down the words that each letter represents in each acronym.

Acronyms for Chapter 6

WLAN	ESS	UNII
SOHO	FCC	SSID
IBSS	CSMA/CA	
BSS	ISM	

Create Mind Maps

Create one mind map the lists "802.3 Ethernet" on the left and "802.11 Wireless" on the right. Then think of any fact that you can that can be compared between the two types of LANs. Put facts unique to Ethernet LANs on the left, unique to wireless LANs on the right, and facts that apply to both in the center, between the two main headings.

Create a second mind map with the main nodes of "Bit Rate," "Coverage Area," and "Capacity." Then think about topics from the chapter that affect each. For items that improve the primary topic, place it above that topic. For items that make the primary topic worse, place it below the primary topic. For example, for bit rate, you could place "use a newer standard" above "bit rate," because newer standards happen to support faster transmission speeds.

Define Other Terms

Define the following additional terms from this chapter, and check your answers in the glossary:

802.11	CSMA/CA	noise
802.11a	data frame	omnidirectional antenna
802.11b	directional antenna	probe
802.11g	electromagnetic spectrum	queuing
802.11n	Federal Communications Commission	range
antenna		site survey
associate	frequency band	small office/home office
Associate (request and response)	frequency channel	stream
	gain	dedicated bandwidth
association process	Wi-Fi hotspot	Wi-Fi Alliance
authenticate	Independent Basic Service Set	wireless client
bandwidth		wireless LAN
beacon	LAN capacity	WLAN name
management and control frame	LAN edge	
	licensed frequency band	

Complete the Tables and Lists from Memory

Print a copy of Appendix B, "Memory Tables" (which you can find online at www.pearsonitcertification.com/title/9780789748454), or at least the section for this chapter, and complete the tables and lists from memory. Appendix C, "Memory Tables Answer Key," also online, includes completed tables and lists to check your work.

Chapter 7

Wide-Area Networks

Wide-area networks (WAN) have some similarities to LANs. Both deliver data between devices. Both define Layer 1 and Layer 2 standards to deliver that data. Both act as a delivery vehicle for Layer 3 protocols like IP, delivering IP packets between user devices and routers, and between routers.

WANs, of course, have many differences compared to LANs, and those differences go far beyond the technology. Sure, from a technology perspective, WANs must work at much longer distances than LANs. WAN technology must also work at a much larger scale; some of these technologies can touch tens of millions of WAN customers. The economics of telcos play a big role as well. New WAN services might take years or decades to install and make available to all customers, just because of the size of the telcos, so the telco investment in new WAN technology can be very expensive.

Another big difference between LANs and WANs is that while the LAN market has settled into two major options, the WAN market has not. Chapter 5, "Ethernet LANs," and Chapter 6, "Wireless LANs," together tell the story of how many types of LANs existed, but today, *LAN* typically means with 802.3 Ethernet and 802.11 wireless LANs. In the WAN world, for a variety of reasons, some of the oldest WAN technology still matters to networks today. From a learning perspective, most of the more modern services happen to be much more complex, plus they often use parts of the older WAN technology.

Given the long history of WAN technology, and how much the older technology matters to the newer technology, this chapter discusses the basics of several of these older technologies: switched circuits, dedicated circuits, circuit switching, and packet switching. In particular, this chapter has three major sections:

- The first section, "Introducing Wide-Area Networks," introduces WANs, first from a telco or service provider (SP) perspective, and then from the customer perspective.

- The second section, "Understanding Leased-Line WAN Links," takes a long look at how telcos created leased-line WAN connections. This section discusses what happens on the ends of the leased lines, in the parts that the customer can see, plus what happens inside the telco network, with technology called time-division multiplexing (TDM) and the T-carrier system.

- The final section, "Understanding Packet Switching and Multiaccess WANs," moves to a different kind of WAN service, called packet switching, by discussing one such service—Frame Relay.

Chapter Outline

Objectives

- Compare switched circuits as used for a typical home telephone call with two computers sending data over a similar switched circuit using modems.

- Explain the basic differences between a circuit-switching WAN service and a packet-switching WAN service from the customer's perspective.

- Illustrate the reasons why IP routers work well at forwarding data between different types of LANs and WANs.

- Draw common WAN topologies.

- Draw and contrast the different customer-site cabling for a leased-line WAN installed between two routers.

- List the types of physical links in the U.S. T-carrier hierarchy, their approximate speeds, and the specific number of slow-speed channels that fit in the next higher-speed line.

- Explain how telcos use CSU/DSUs to match a leased-line speed to a physical DS1 line, using an example of a 768-Kbps fractional T1 leased line between two routers.

- Compare and contrast the HDLC and PPP standards.

- Explain the differences between packet switching and circuit switching from the telco perspective.

- Using an example network, explain how with Frame Relay, a router can have one physical link connected to the WAN, but send data to many other destination routers.

- List the other WAN packet-switching services, and show whether they were introduced before or after Frame Relay.

Key Terms

switched circuit

dedicated circuit

circuit switching

packet switching

leased line

time-division multiplexing

T-carrier system

DS0

DS1

Frame Relay

Introducing Wide-Area Networks

Telephones, and the telephone systems created by telcos around the world starting in the late 1800s, revolutionized communications. By the time computers were invented, telcos often had large networks to support voice traffic, had large staffs, and had a lot of experience in how to deal with the many different local governments when they needed to install more cables in a town. Historically speaking, when the need for WANs finally occurred—the need for computers to communicate across some distance—telcos were the absolutely perfect type of company to provide WAN services.

The type of company that provides WAN services can go by several different names. More generally, many people call these companies WAN service providers, or simply service providers (SP). Many people just use the old name—telcos—which is just short for *telephone company*. This chapter uses the terms telco, WAN service provider, and service provider as the same idea.

This first major section looks at three different topics in succession:

- The WAN services telcos have offered over the years, with some focus on the history behind those offerings
- How typical modern telco customers connect routers to the telco WAN, to send IP packets over that WAN
- Different WAN topologies, both to compare them to LAN topologies and to introduce some WAN terms

Basic Telco Services

The history of computer networking might seem long, but the history of telcos reaches back further, to the late 1800s. Alexander Graham Bell invented the telephone, filing the first U.S. patents in 1876. Bell and others started the companies that turned into the first U.S.-based telcos around that same time.

The history of the telephone, telcos, and the companies that grew from Bell's original companies (called the *Bell System*) has many interesting turns and moves. Many of the events in this long history do not matter to today's computer networks, but some parts of that history do have some lingering effect on how WANs work today. This entire chapter weaves parts of telco history into the story to give some perspective on why today's WAN services use specific conventions.

First, keep in mind that the early telephone companies focused on voice telephone services, not on WAN services. Bell's famous invention happened roughly 60 years before the invention of the first programmable computer, as shown in Figure 7-1. (Moving pictures—movies—existed long before computers as well.) Telcos built huge networks to support voice traffic, long before computers could have possibly been used to create and send bits.

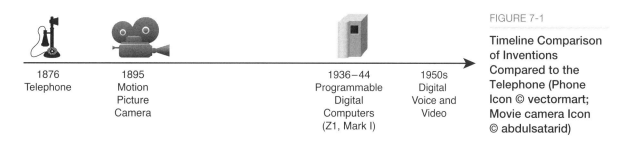

FIGURE 7-1

Timeline Comparison of Inventions Compared to the Telephone (Phone Icon © vectormart; Movie camera Icon © abdulsatarid)

Before the mid 1900s, the telcos in the United States (and in many other parts of the world) built huge networks focused on voice, simply because computers did not yet exist. So, when computers finally came along, and they wanted to send data through the telco network, the telcos sent the data using the voice network. Over time, the telcos created data services that better matched the computers' digital (binary) data. This topic looks at three WAN services—analog voice circuits, digital circuits, and packet switching—and their progression over time as the telcos changed their networks.

Switched Analog Circuits for Voice and Data

In the early days of telephones and voice, a voice call required one analog electrical circuit between the two phones. To make that happen, the telco installed a 2-wire cable into each home, called a *local loop*, with the other end connected equipment sitting in a nearby telco office called the *central office (CO)*. Then, when the user called another number, the telco created one electrical circuit that flowed from one telephone to the other, as shown in Figure 7-2.

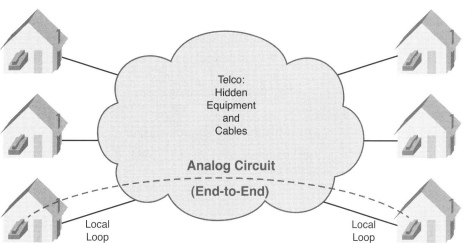

FIGURE 7-2

Early Voice: Telco Creates One Analog Electrical Circuit Between Phones

The 2-wire local loop allowed a single electrical circuit into the home, which worked well for voice. The voice signal for both directions had to be sent over the same electrical circuit, so the signals overlapped each other. Although the voice signals overlapped, when both people talk at the same time, they notice, and one stops talking. So, in most conversations, only one person talks at a time anyway, so a single circuit between phones worked well.

When computers came on the scene by the middle of the twentieth century, the telcos of the world still made most of their money from telephone customers. To create some of the first WAN connections, early computing devices had to act like telephones. One computer device would essentially make a phone call to the other computer, encoding its bits using analog electrical signals. In other words, the computers made the bits look like voice so that it could pass through the telco voice network. Figure 7-3 shows a drawing of the concept.

FIGURE 7-3

Early Computers Using an Analog Circuit to Communicate

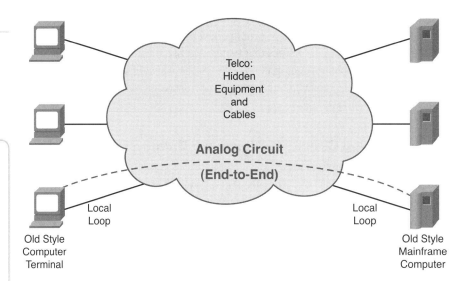

ON THE SIDE: The figure shows icons for some older computing devices. The devices on the left are *terminals*, which have just a keyboard, display, and the ability to send, receive, and display text. The computer on the right is a *mainframe computer*, which did all the data processing.

Although Figure 7-3 shows an example network that would have been common back in the 1960s, 1970s, and 1980s, the modern TCP/IP networks of the twenty-first century still make use of those same analog telco circuits. Why? The telcos of the world support these analog voice circuits to most every part of their networks, so customers know that at least that can connect two sites with an analog circuit. Also, the cost is pretty low.

For example, many people still use analog voice circuits to access the Internet, as shown in Figure 7-4. To make that work, each end of the circuit must use a device called a modem, as explained after the figure.

FIGURE 7-4

Connecting from a PC to an ISP, Using Modems and an Analog Telco Circuit

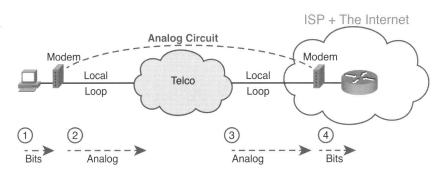

Modems allow computers to send digital data over analog electrical circuits. To make that happen, the modems translate from binary data (bits) to an analog signal or vice versa. The PC and ISP's router need to exchange bits, so the user calls the ISP's phone number to set up an analog electrical circuit. Following the left-to-right example in the figure:

1. The PC sends bits over a (short) cable to the modem.

2. The modem converts the bits into analog electrical signals, with an encoding scheme that represents bits over time as different analog electrical signals (usually a different frequency).

3. The analog signals arrives at the far side of the circuit, where:

4. The modem translates back to a digital signal (bits).

> **AUTHOR'S NOTE:** The word *modem* comes from two terms: *modulate* and *demodulate*. The term *modulate* refers to the changing of the analog electrical signal to represent binary values (in other words, to encode the bits). The term *demodulate* refers to the opposite, interpreting the changing incoming analog signal as bits.

Using analog circuits to send data had both some positive and some negative results. On the positive side, it worked earlier in history when there were no other options. Also, it still works today. Telcos support analog circuits for voice to pretty much all parts of their networks, so you can also send data to pretty much anywhere as well, using analog circuits and modems. On the negative side, although the bit rates were fast enough for the old days, the bit rates for modems over analog circuits remain very slow relative to today's other WAN alternatives.

> **ON THE SIDE:** Most people refer to switched circuits by their more common name: *dialup*.

Digital Circuits and Leased Lines

Before computers existed, telcos kept growing, supporting more and more customers. Most telcos had a monopoly for phone service for a particular part of their country, with a responsibility to install a local loop line to each home and business.

> **ON THE SIDE:** In some countries, but not the United States, the phone company was not a private company, but a part of the government, more like the postal service. Such organizations were typically called Postal, Telephone, and Telegraph (PTT) companies.

Over time, particularly from the middle of the twentieth century onward, many events happened that transformed telcos. In particular:

- **The invention of and commercialization of computers:** The world started with just a few programmable digital computers as rare and unusual devices, and moved to a world in which most companies owned computers.

■ **The migration from telcos as government monopolies to free-market competition:** Governments in some countries started removing the monopoly status from different parts of the telcos' business, eventually removing the monopoly, so that telcos competed for much of their business.

■ **The computerization of the telco's own network:** The computer revolution also revolutionized how the telco could build its own internal network, to create better services at lower cost, which helped in a world with less monopolies and more competition.

For these reasons and more, telcos started offering a service that used a digital circuit between the customer devices. With this new digital circuit concept, the endpoints still had a circuit between them. However, the endpoints could encode the signal using digital encoding rules, as discussed back in Chapter 4, "Transmitting Bits," to encode bits as different electrical signals. Figure 7-5 shows the idea, this time with two routers connected through a leased line.

FIGURE 7-5

More Modern Routers Using a Digital Leased Line

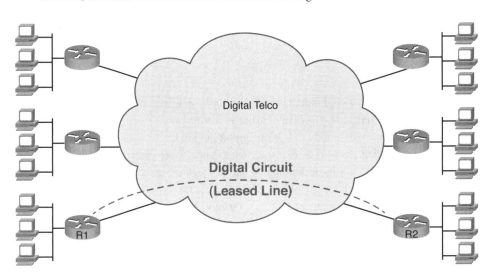

With a digital circuit, the telco typically creates the circuit as a permanent circuit, rather than expecting the endpoints to dial a phone number. From a business perspective, the customer basically leases the digital circuit on a monthly basis, so the telco calls these permanent circuits either a *leased circuit* or a *leased line*. With the leased line in Figure 7-5, R1 can send to R2 at any time and vice versa.

The new leased lines solved some problems, but they did not replace analog circuits completely. On the positive side, the digital leased circuits supported much faster bit rates than the analog circuits. The always-on leased lines also matched the business model for many businesses that wanted to have the WAN working all the time.

Digital circuits did have some negatives compared to analog switched circuits, however. The telcos had a lot of work to do to support leased lines when they first came out, but that was years ago. Today, leased lines typically cost more than a phone line, so for some uses, keeping an extra phone line and using modems for some WAN applications make more sense than using digital leased lines.

Switched Circuits and Circuit Switching

If you stop and think about what the telco does in the last few figures, you will see that the telco spends a lot of time creating a circuit between two endpoints. As a result, the terms used to describe telco networks, and WAN services, uses several terms with the word *circuit*. This short topic introduces a few of those terms to connect the terms to the concepts.

The telco calls each circuit either a *switched circuit* or a *dedicated circuit*, depending on how long the circuit should be up and working. Imagine that you make five phone calls to five different phone numbers. To make that happen, the telco switches from one circuit, to another, to another. So these circuits created when the customer dials a number, and the telco sets up a new circuit to some destination, is called a **switched circuit**, because the telco expects to break that circuit later and then switch to another circuit the next time you make a call.

A **dedicated circuit** exists between two endpoints, and remains, without switching, because the telco creates the circuit to be there permanently. For example, a leased line is a dedicated circuit.

In addition to these terms, the term *circuit switching* refers to how the devices in the telco think in regard to forwarding the electrical signals inside the telco network. To create an end-to-end circuit, the telco uses a series of devices called *circuit switches*. To create an end-to-end circuit, the telco connects each local loop to a trunk (a link between the circuit switches). The combination of connections creates an end-to-end path for the circuit, which remains in place while the circuit is needed.

Figure 7-6 shows an example of circuit switching. In this case, the phone user on the left called 555-2222, creating a switched circuit to the phone on the right. When the user calls a phone number, the various circuit switches connect a circuit on both sides of the switch, as shown with the arrowed lines in the figure. The circuit switches create the effect of an end-to-end circuit by switching or connecting the circuits on the various links, as shown in the figure.

FIGURE 7-6

Circuit Switching

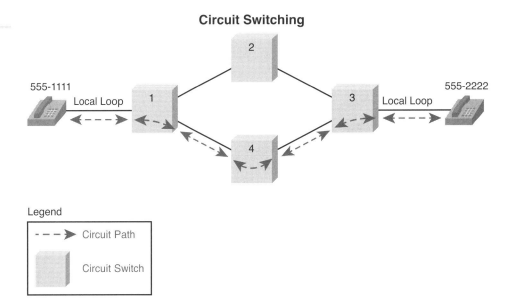

Circuit Switching

To create switched circuits, circuit switches and customer devices (telephones and modems) use *signaling* to set up and take down the circuit. When the telephone user types a phone number, the phone sends the digits as sounds. The circuit switch interprets those sounds into the phone number. Then, the circuit switches, which are actually computers built for the purpose of switching calls, send overhead messages to one another, with the phone number listed in the signaling messages. Those signaling messages allow the switches to choose which switch-to-switch links (called *trunks*) to use for that particular call. The switches set up the switching logic to connect one circuit segment to the next. (The signaling all happens in seconds, while you wait for the phone to ring.)

To create dedicated circuits, the telco essentially programs the circuit switches with the correct switching logic from one circuit segment to the next. The section "Understanding Leased-Line WAN Links," later in this chapter, shows other examples of how circuit switching works with dedicated circuits in the discussion of time-division multiplexing (TDM).

ON THE SIDE: U.S.-based telcos historically used large computers, built specifically to be circuit switches, to act as these circuit-switching nodes. Called an Electronic Switching System (ESS), the ESS products went through several product generations, with the last generation being the 5ESS switch, also informally called a *class 5 switch*.

The following list summarizes some of these concepts and terms related to circuits.

Circuit: A communication path between two endpoints.

Circuit switching: The logic used by the telco network, and the individual telco devices called circuit switches, in which they switch circuits in and out of different physical trunks to create an end-to-end circuit through the telco network.

Switched circuit: An end-to-end circuit through a telco that can and does change over time, because the user calls a number, hangs up, calls another number, and so on.

Dedicated circuit: A leased line. A circuit between two specific devices that the telco never takes down.

The Content-Aware Telco: Packet Switching

When the telco creates a circuit, whether dedicated or switched, the telco does not care about the meaning of the bits. The telco network uses circuit switching to switch the circuit through from end to end, from one customer device to the other, as shown in Figure 7-6. With circuit switching, the telco switches did not care what the analog or digital signals meant; the telco only needed to deliver the signal from end to end.

Continuing on the journey through history, telcos next started offering **packet-switching** WAN services. First, Figure 7-7 places these new packet-switching services into a timeline for perspective.

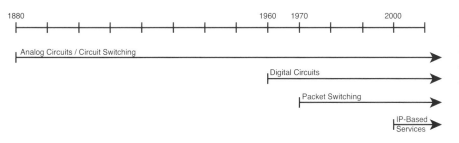

FIGURE 7-7

General Timeline: Circuit Switching, Digital Circuits, and Packet Switching

Telcos have offered many different packet-switching services over the years, by many names, but they all have these basic facts in common:

1. All customer devices that need a direct connection to the WAN connect through a circuit to the packet-switching service, instead of a circuit to another customer device.

2. For a single telco customer, all of that customer's devices can send data to every other device connected to the packet-switched service.

3. The telco (service provider) must look at the meaning of the bits in the headers, as sent by the customer, and make a forwarding decision per packet.

The fact that the packet-switching service makes a choice for each packet that comes over one link, rather than making the choice to send all bits from that link in a single direction, makes the packet-switching service work a lot like an Ethernet LAN switch in concept. With a packet-switching service, the customer device sends data with a particular header. The packet-switching service looks at the header to choose where to send the customer's message. When the customer sends three packets in a row, the packets might have three different addresses, and the packet-switching service sends them to three different customer devices. The same thing would happen on a LAN if a PC sent three Ethernet frames with three different destination MAC addresses (of course, the details of protocols and addresses differ quite a bit between packet switching and Ethernet).

Figure 7-8 shows a conceptual drawing of how the packet-switching process works. In this case, six routers connect to the same telco packet-switching service. Each router physically connects using a leased line, with a telco device called a *packet switch* on the other end of the link.

FIGURE 7-8

Example of a Packet-Switching Service

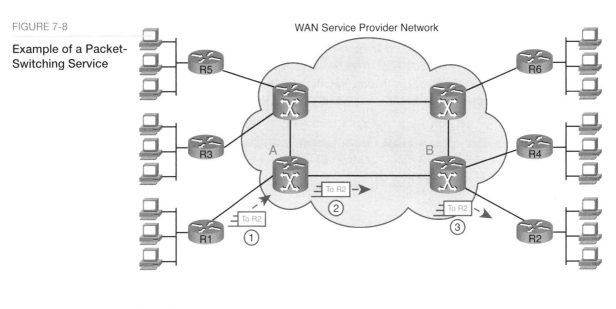

For this example, the following steps occur:

1. Router R1 (owned by the customer) sends a message, with a header that lists R2 as the destination address.

2. Packet switch A (owned by the WAN service provider) makes a choice to forward the message to packet switch B.

3. Packet switch B (owned by the WAN service provider) makes a choice to forward the message to R2.

Packet-switching services give telcos and their customers some big advantages over leased lines and the underlying circuit switching. Some of those advantages will not be as clear until you learn more about at least one packet-switching service (this chapter later looks at Frame Relay). For now, some of the summary points as to why packet-switching services can be better than (digital) leased lines are as follows:

- Packet switching connects more than two sites.
- Packet switching typically costs less per month to get the same number of bits per second between the sites.
- Packet switching typically has a lower installation cost.

Modern networks still use all the WAN services introduced so far in this chapter, plus several others. You can still connect computers using modems and analog switched circuits. In fact, many people use this technology as a low-cost way to access the Internet. You can still use leased lines between routers, with the common term *leased line* meaning the same idea as a *dedicated digital circuit*. And many companies still use packet-switching WAN services, one of which is discussed later in this chapter (Frame Relay).

Using Routers to Send IP Packets over WANs

So far, this chapter has looked at WAN services with a little more focus on the WAN provider (telco) perspective on the services rather than the WAN customer perspective. This next topic turns that perspective around. Hopefully, this topic helps give you some perspective on the bigger picture of how corporate TCP/IP networks work with this brief discussion about what the telco customer is trying to accomplish over the WAN.

From a business perspective, most companies and other organizations do not sit back and decide that they need a WAN as a goal unto itself. Instead, companies and other organizations have missions and goals, and to accomplish those goals, they often need a network. In fact, it is hard to think of a company that could survive today without a network. The users might exist in multiple locations, some far apart, which requires a WAN. But most WAN customers do not sit around talking about their business model with the primary goal being "we need a WAN"—the WAN just helps them build the network, which helps them do the work, which lets them accomplish their goals.

From a technical perspective, the people responsible for the corporate network need a WAN, specifically to move IP packets from one site to another. Almost every corporate network today uses the TCP/IP model. TCP/IP networks use routers, a type of networking device, to connect to WANs and LANs. The routers receive packets from the devices on the LAN, and the routers forward the packets to other devices—sometimes over the LAN and sometimes over the WAN. So when a telco customer thinks about WANs, he thinks of the WAN as a way to move IP packets between his IP routers.

To give you some context about how WAN customers intend to use their WAN connections today, this topic reviews and explains a few concepts about how routers work when connected to WANs.

Routers Connect LANs to WANs

Routers focus on forwarding IP packets to the right destination. IP, a Layer 3 protocol as compared to the OSI model, defines a header, with a source and destination IP address. IP hosts (end-user devices) send their packets to a nearby router. Routers then look at the destination IP address and forward the IP packet to the next router, or to the destination IP host. For a single packet, that process continues until the IP packet arrives at the destination host. (See the section, "IP as the TCP/IP Network Layer," in Chapter 3, "TCP/IP Networks," for a review and for more details about the IP forwarding process.)

IP happens to be a Layer 3 protocol, so it relies on the layers below it for help. LAN standards define Layer 1 and 2 details for LANs. WAN standards also define Layer 1 and 2 details for WAN services of all kinds as well. From an IP perspective, each LAN or WAN acts as a way to move the IP packet from one host or router to the next. Figure 7-9 shows the idea.

FIGURE 7-9

Layer 3 IP Forwarding Logic

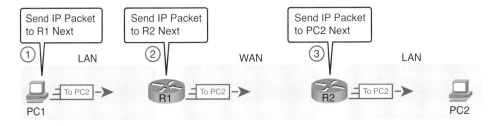

Following the steps in the figure:

1. PC1's IP logic tells it to send the IP packet to the nearby router (R1).

2. R1's IP logic tells it to make a routing decision, based on the destination IP address; that decision is to forward the IP packet over the WAN to Router R2.

3. R2's IP logic tells it to make a routing decision, based on the destination IP address; that decision is to forward the IP packet over the LAN to host PC2.

Routers connect LANs to WANs so that the routers can forward IP packets end to end through an IP network. So, from the perspective of the IP logic used in a typical modern network, the WAN acts like some sort of delivery vehicle—a subway, a truck, a car, a plane, and so on. All the router needs the WAN to do in this case is to deliver the IP packet to the next router on the other side of the WAN.

While it might be useful to think about IP, and only IP, as shown in Figure 7-9, each LAN and WAN requires some thought as well. For example, a LAN might be a simple Ethernet-only LAN, like the one in the upper-left part of Figure 7-10. It might be a simple 802.11 WLAN, as shown at the lower left of the figure. It might even be a more complex campus LAN, with both wired and wireless LANs, as shown on the right.

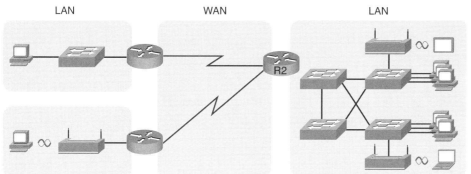

FIGURE 7-10

Example Enterprise Network, with LAN and WAN Details Revealed

Note that the figure also shows the WAN with the traditional drawing of a leased line, but without any physical details of how the telco implements the leased line. The telco customer usually does not care about the details of how the telco creates the leased line. Instead, the telco customer has more of this perspective:

> WANs exist between my routers to deliver my IP packets from one router to the other.

Encapsulation and Deencapsulation

Routers play many roles in an IP network, with one of the more obvious roles being to connect different types of physical links. Routers connect to LANs of many different types, with many different physical connectors. They also connect to many different types of WANs as well.

Routers do a good job connecting different physical links as a side effect of IP's Layer 3 encapsulation and deencapsulation logic. To understand what happens, think about the data-link encapsulation that happens at the same time as the IP packet-forwarding process described around Figure 7-9. The IP packet needs to be forwarded end to end. The IP packet does not need to change because of the type of physical link; however, the data-link header and trailer do change depending on the type of link. The IP packet-forwarding process only uses those data-link headers/ trailers for part of the trip.

Figure 7-11 shows an example of how routers deencapsulate and encapsulate IP packets. When a host sends an IP packet to a router, the host adds a data-link header and trailer to encapsulate the IP packet. However, when the router processes a packet, before forwarding the IP packet to the next router, that router discards the old data-link header and trailer, and puts a new header and trailer around the packet.

FIGURE 7-11

Encapsulation That Happens During the IP Packet-Forwarding Process

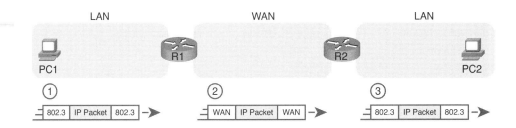

Following the steps in the figure:

1. PC1 sends an IP packet, inside an 802.3 frame, to R1.

2. R1 strips off the 802.3 header and trailer, adds a WAN header and trailer, and forwards the frame over the WAN to R2.

3. R2 strips off the WAN header and trailer, adds a new (different) 802.3 header and trailer, and sends the frame to PC2.

The use of the data-link headers and trailers to just get across a single LAN or WAN works a little like what happens when you take a long trip. Maybe you start by taking a subway train to the airport. Then you take a plane to another city, where you rent a car. Finally, you drive the car to your final destination. In this case, you used three different vehicles (subway train, plane, and car), but none of the vehicles took you through the entire trip from start to finish. Likewise, the IP packet flows end to end through the TCP/IP network, but the data-link headers act like the individual vehicles that get you over one part of the trip.

As you work through this chapter, you will learn about several WAN data-link protocols. Those topics focus on the WAN features. However, whenever you learn about a WAN data-link protocol and its headers/trailers, keep the following WAN customer perspective in mind:

> The WAN data-link header and trailer exist to encapsulate an IP packet, to move it from one customer router to the other.

WAN and LAN Topologies

This book has already listed the key comparison points between LANs and WANs in several places. To summarize:

- WANs connect devices generally far away; LANs connect devices generally closer together.

- WAN cabling connects locations of one company with those locations separated by land owned by others. The cables therefore must run through government-regulated spaces, like with other utility companies (the cable system, the electrical grid, and the phone company's voice network).

- The user of WAN services leases the service from a service provider, usually paying a monthly fee, whereas the user of a LAN buys everything and has no ongoing monthly fees.

This book has listed those comparison points many times before, so rather than discuss them yet again, this next topic compares LANs and WANs in a slightly different way—by comparing topologies. In particular, the following sections look at three common WAN topologies—point-to-point, hub-and-spoke, and multipoint.

Point-to-Point Topologies

So far, this chapter has used several terms for a WAN link between two routers, like the ones shown in Figure 7-10:

- Leased line
- Leased circuit
- Dedicated circuit
- Digital circuit

These terms refer to the same type of WAN service and also tell us something about the service. The term *leased* refers to the idea that the service is leased, so it is more permanent than a typical phone call, which is temporary. The term *dedicated* also refers to the permanent connection. The word *circuit* refers to an electrical circuit, and it also gives us a reminder that this service differs from a packet-switched service. Finally, the word *digital* refers to the fact that the customer devices can encode digital signals, instead of analog, which happens to support faster speeds for the customer.

The term *point-to-point link*, yet another term for this same leased line, gives yet another view of this basic WAN service. This term mentions the topology (point-to-point) in the name; the word *link* is just the same old generic word for a communications medium.

From many perspectives, the logic on the WAN point-to-point link works just like the Ethernet LAN point-to-point link. A modern WAN point-to-point link uses a 2-pair (4-wire) circuit; each router can use one pair to send data and one pair to receive data. On a LAN that uses 10BASE-T or 100BASE-T, the cable also has 2-pair, with one pair for sending data in each direction. So both topologies allow full-duplex operation, and neither the WAN nor the LAN link in Figure 7-12 has to use any kind of an algorithm to share the link.

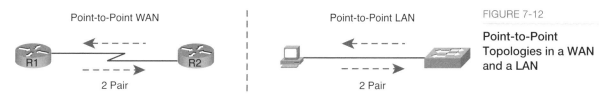

Point-to-Point WAN | Point-to-Point LAN

2 Pair | 2 Pair

FIGURE 7-12

Point-to-Point Topologies in a WAN and a LAN

Hub-and-Spoke Topologies

Many enterprise networks (larger corporate networks) need to connect a large number of sites, and leased lines might not work as well as other WAN options. First, although leased lines work, they connect only two routers. Telcos price leased-line charges based on the length (the distance between the sites). For a large company, some sites probably sit hundreds (or thousands) of miles apart, so for a large enterprise, connecting all routers using leased lines might cost a lot.

Using leased lines can also be a problem if the design requires that all routers be able to send packets directly to all other routers. To meet this requirement with leased lines, you need a leased line between each pair of routers, which can require a surprisingly large number of leased lines. For example, to meet this requirement with only three routers, you need three leased lines. With four routers, you need six leased lines.

For perspective, Table 7-1 shows some examples of the number of routers in an enterprise network, with the resulting number of leased lines required to connect every router to every other router.

TABLE 7-1
Number of Leased Lines to Connect Every Pair of Routers

Number of Routers	Number of Leased Lines	Formula: N(N×1)/2
20	190	(20 × 19) / 2
40	780	(40 × 39) / 2
60	1770	(60 × 59) / 2
80	3160	(80 × 79) / 2
100	4950	(100 × 99) / 2

Because of the math in Table 7-1, and the cost of all those links, large-enterprise WANs do not attempt to connect every pair of sites directly with a separate physical leased line. Clearly, the number of leased lines to connect every site to every other site would be much too large and too expensive compared to some other alternatives.

A *hub-and-spoke* WAN design, using leased lines, reduces the number of leased lines, while still providing a way for packets to reach all sites. This topology connects one router, the hub router, to all other routers using a leased line. If drawn with the hub router in the center, and the other routers spread around in a circle, the drawing looks something like a bicycle wheel. Figure 7-13 shows an example.

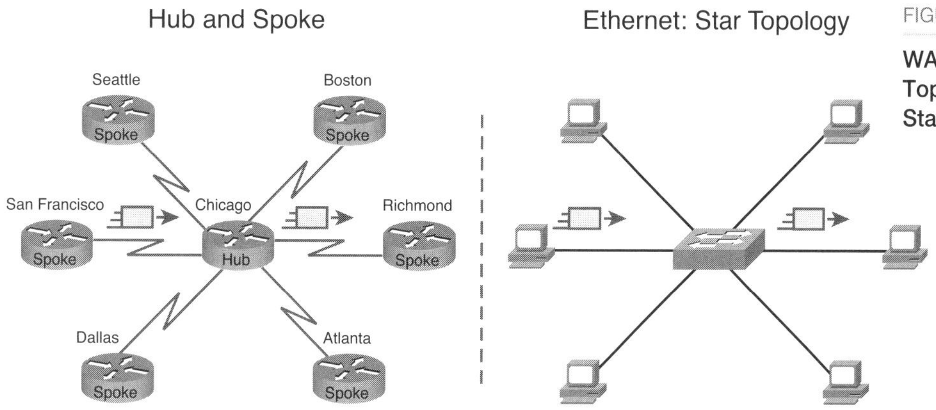

Hub and Spoke   Ethernet: Star Topology

FIGURE 7-13

WAN Hub-and-Spoke Topology Versus a LAN Star Topology

The hub-and-spoke design works; however, it does require some packets to cross two WAN links. Any packets that go from one of the spoke sites to another, like the packet shown going from San Fran to Richmond in the figure, must cross two WAN links.

The hub-and-spoke design does greatly reduce the required number of leased lines as compared to a full mesh between all seven routers. This hub-and-spoke design uses only *six* leased lines, while a full mesh of leased lines between every pair of routers, with seven routers, would require 21 leased lines.

> **AUTHOR'S NOTE:**
> The hub-and-spoke design looks very much like the Ethernet star topology, as noted in the figure, but simply uses a different name.

> **ON THE SIDE:** Not sure about how a full mesh with seven routers requires 21 leased lines? Draw seven routers in a circle, and draw a line between each pair, and you will end up with 21 lines. Or, just use this formula N(N-1)/2, where N is the number of routers.

Multipoint Topologies

The hub-and-spoke topology works, and it works much better than connecting all sites together with leased lines; however, it has two drawbacks:

- It still uses leased lines that might have to run hundreds or thousands of miles, at large expense.

- Packets that go from one spoke site to another spoke site have to cross multiple WAN links.

Packet-switched services create the possibility of a different topology called a *multipoint* WAN topology, which solves some of the problems of building a large WAN with leased lines. In this topology, each customer router connects to the WAN packet-switching service through a relatively short dedicated circuit. For example, a router in Boston would connect to a telco packet-switching service in Boston, a customer router in Richmond would connect to a telco packet-switching device in Richmond, and so on. So all the links from the customer to the telco remain short. Figure 7-14 shows the idea.

FIGURE 7-14

WAN Multipoint Topology

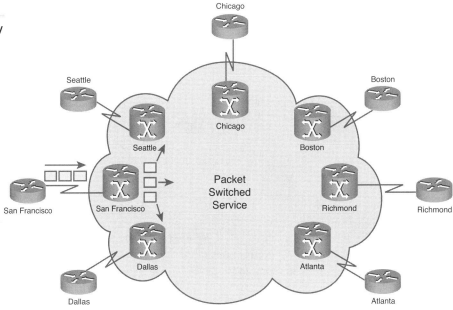

Legend

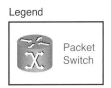

Packet
Switch

The figure shows some of the benefits of a multipoint topology as created by a
packet-switched service. First, with seven customer routers, only seven links exist
between customer sites and the WAN provider. Although you cannot tell from the
figure, the links only have to run a relatively short distance within a metropolitan
area, so the physical links remain short, which costs less money. Finally, from a
customer perspective, an IP packet only goes through the WAN once to reach any
of the remote sites, providing any-to-any connectivity.

Understanding Leased-Line WAN Links

Understanding leased lines from the customer perspective takes only a small
amount of effort. The endpoints, usually routers, have a link between them, and
both routers can send at any time (full duplex). The cables the customer must install
require a little planning, but they typically sit inside the same room, so connecting
the cables, after being ordered, is pretty easy. And the data-link protocols have little
work to do, with simple headers and trailers.

The complexity with leased lines sits inside the telco network. The part of the leased line closest to the customer, from the telco CO to the customer site, follows several different related standards. Each of those standards fits into the bigger world of how telcos first created a digital network to support voice. Understanding some of those details can be helpful in understanding what the leased line offering is, and what it is not.

This second major section of the chapter breaks down the discussion of leased-line WAN links into four parts:

- **Customer perspective:** Ignoring many details inside the telco, this section looks at leased lines from a customer perspective: distances, speeds, cabling, and how to connect a leased line to a router.

- **Telco perspective:** The next topic continues the story by uncovering some of what the telco does to create a leased line. This discussion includes how the telco sets up circuit switches that use time-division multiplexing (TDM) and the T-carrier system to create the digital circuit for a leased line.

- **T1 and CSU/DSU:** The third topic drills down on the physical layer details about one particular type of telco link: a T1 line. In particular, it looks at T1 lines (a part of the T-carrier system) and a customer-site device called a CSU/DSU, which the customer needs to use for the leased line to work correctly.

- **Data link:** This last topic is a short discussion of data link layer protocols that routers use for leased lines.

The Customer Perspective on Physical Leased Lines

When a telco customer decides to use a **leased line**, he expects to get a basic service—the ability to send bits—between two devices (typically routers). Basically, the customer buys the right to send X bits per second, in both directions, all the time, between two sites, as represented in Figure 7-15.

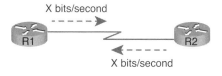

FIGURE 7-15

Leased Line in Concept

The next few pages break down the reality of some of what a telco customer can lease from a telco today in the United States. In particular, this topic looks at the distance limitations for leased lines, the speeds available, and the devices and cables required at the customer site to make it all work, with a closer look then at the underlying Layer 1 technology, called the T-carrier system.

Distance Limitations

Chapters 5 and 6 often mentioned distance limitations when discussing wired and wireless LAN technologies. With WAN leased lines, the discussion can be short and sweet—there is no absolute limit for the distance of a leased line. You can literally have a leased line that stretches for hundreds or even thousands of miles.

The more interesting topic relates to why a leased line can be so long. Basically, while a leased line acts like a pair of circuits between two routers, one for each direction, physically no single circuit extends the entire distance between the two customer routers. Instead, a series of circuits exist, with some kind of circuit switch connecting the circuits, as shown in Figure 7-16.

FIGURE 7-16

Leased Line: Shorter Electrical Circuits, Knitted Together

Actual 20-Mile Leased Line

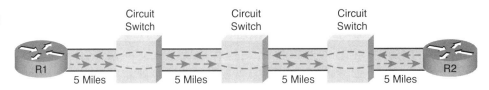

Conceptual View, Same Leased Line

Although no single circuit stretches more than five miles, the entire leased line in this figure stretches to 20 miles. The circuit switch hardware works at Layer 1 to interpret the signals as bits, and then it sends those same bits over the next circuit to the next node. Because no single circuit has to stretch too far, the end-to-end leased line can stretch for thousands of miles. All that the telco has to do is program more connections into more circuit switches to connect circuits from one customer site to the other.

Speeds

The telco can build a leased line to support a large variety of speeds, but not just any speed you choose. Instead, the speeds must be a multiple of some specific number.

Today, for slower-speed lines, telcos in the United States offer leased lines with speeds in multiples of 64 Kbps. In other words, the speeds can be 64 Kbps, 128 Kbps, 192 Kbps, 256 Kbps, and so on. The speed can go up to 24 times 64 Kbps, which is 1.536 Mbps. (Note that the telco also adds some bits to the leased line for management, so the leased line at this higher speed actually runs 8 Kbps faster, or 1.544 Mbps.)

For speeds above the 1.5-Mbps range, the telco then offers leased lines in multiples of the 1.544-Mbps speed, up to 28 times that speed (around 44 Mbps). (The telco also adds management bits on these lines as well.) Table 7-2 lists the speeds for leased lines in the United States.

TABLE 7-2

Leased-Line Speed Options, United States

Incremental Speed Value Based on...	Speed Increment	Up to This Many Increments	Speed Range
DS0	64 Kbps	24	64 – 1536 Kbps
DS1 (T1)	1.536 Mbps	28	1.536 – 43.008 Mbps

These speeds might seem strange at first, but they all make sense when you understand how the telco built its networks to support digital transmission of voice back in the middle of the twentieth century. Those earlier standards used a 64-Kbps building block called a *digital signal level 0 (DS0)*. Each telephone call required a DS0, or the equivalent, for the digital part of the call between two phones.

The telcos also combined the bits from slower-speed links into a single higher-speed physical link using multiplexing, as defined in more detail in the section "Making Efficient Use of Trunks with Time-Division Multiplexing," later in this chapter. For example, telcos combined the bits from 24 DS0s, plus some overhead, into a single physical link called a *digital signal level 1* (DS1, also called a T1). They also created physical links that combined the bits from 28 DS1s, plus overhead, into a DS3 (also called a T3). Figure 7-17 shows the comparison of these three parts of the telco network. (Note that the speeds shown in the figure include the overhead bits.)

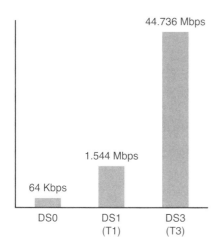

FIGURE 7-17

Visual Comparison of Speeds: DS0, DS1, DS3

Cabling

Learning about LAN cabling can be easier than learning about WAN cabling because you can usually find LAN cabling at home, school, or work. If you care about IT enough to study IT in school, you probably use several user devices every day, and they all connect to a network. Some of those devices probably use an Ethernet LAN, so when learning about Ethernet, you can usually look around, find an Ethernet cable and Ethernet NIC, and get some idea about what LAN devices look like.

Unfortunately, when learning about WAN cabling, you seldom have a chance to go look at the cabling for a real WAN link. You might have some routers in the lab at school, and you probably have seen consumer-grade routers at home for your connection to the Internet. But at a company that uses a leased line between sites, the routers and leased-line cables typically sit in a restricted space, away from the end users, and you would not be able to see the leased-line cabling unless you already had a job working on the network. To overcome some of the challenges, this topic discusses the leased-line cabling and device details at the customer site.

First, a leased line has many physical parts. The telco installs a physical cable between the equipment in the telco CO and the customer site. The 2-pair cable typically runs underground, and then runs up inside customer buildings in the hidden spaces where most electrical, plumbing, and other utilities run, with the cable ending near the router. Figure 7-18 shows the idea.

FIGURE 7-18

Cables in a Relatively Short Leased Line

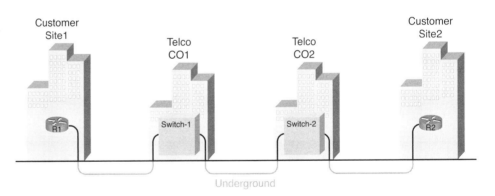

The telco customer needs to plan for the cabling at the end of the cable at each end of the leased line. Figure 7-19 shows a more detailed version of one customer site. It shows the router to which the leased line will connect and the cable installed by the telco.

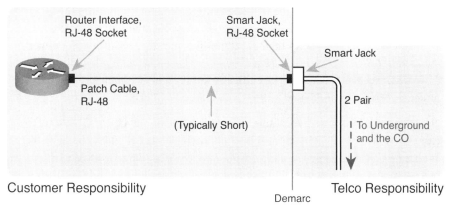

FIGURE 7-19

Components and Responsibilities on One Side of a Leased Line

First, think about the router shown on the left of the figure. Routers connect to many types of LANs and WANs using physical connections called *interfaces*. To connect to a leased line, routers need a particular type of interface called a *serial interface*. And because routers, by their very nature, connect to many types of LANs and WANs, routers support many options for physical connectors on the interfaces. In this case, the router uses a socket called an RJ-48 socket that happens to have the same shape and size as the RJ-45 socket used for Ethernet.

Next, look at the telco cabling. The telco physically installs the cable, with the end connecting to a device called a *smart jack*. It is a small electronic device that also has a connector, oftentimes an RJ-48 connector. The telco owns and installs the smart jack. All the customer has to do is plug a short patch cable from the router interface into the smart jack, and the router is connected to the leased line. Do the equivalent on the other end, and the customer part of the physical installation is complete.

Figure 7-19 also shows a good example with which to introduce an important telco term—*demarc*. First, think about the business model for leased lines. It's 3 months after the installation; the leased line worked great until this morning, but now it does not work anymore. What parts of the cabling does the telco have responsibility for? What does the customer have responsibility for? In telco speak, the exact line between "telco responsibility" and "customer responsibility" is spelled out in the paperwork, and that conceptual line is called the demarc (short for demarcation line).

Channel Service Unit / Data Service Unit

Every leased line physically requires a channel service unit/data service unit (CSU/DSU) on each end. The CSU/DSU function can be a part of the router serial interface card, or it might be part of an external CSU/DSU that sits outside the routers. Whether internal or external to the router, this function goes by the name of the original external device: a *channel service unit/data service unit (CSU/DSU)*.

First, before discussing what the CSU/DSU does, first think about where the CSU/DSU function exists at each customer site. Each leased line has a CSU/DSU function on each side of the line, at the customer site. Each site uses either an *internal CSU/DSU* or an *external CSU/DSU*. As the name implies, the internal CSU/DSU sits inside the router, specifically as part of the serial interface card. The router shown earlier in Figure 7-19 uses an internal CSU/DSU.

Next, Figure 7-20 shows the cabling when using an external CSU/DSU. In this case, the router serial interface card does not perform the CSU/DSU functionality. Without a CSU/DSU, the leased line would not work, so the network engineer purchases a separate external CSU/DSU device. To make the cabling work, the router serial interface connects through a short cable to the external CSU/DSU, with the telco cable connected to the CSU/DSU.

FIGURE 7-20

Customer Equipment and Cabling with External CSU/DSU

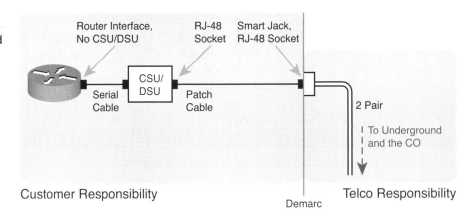

Several different parts exist at the customer site when using an external CSU/DSU versus an internal CSU/DSU. The router serial interface card is a different card, one that usually costs less, because it does not have the CSU/DSU built in. However, you also need to buy the external CSU/DSU. Additionally, the router serial interface card has a connector, and the CSU/DSU has a (different) connector, so you need to buy a cable that connects those two devices. For the purposes of this book, just know that using an external CSU/DSU takes an extra planning step to find out the connector used by the router interface and the connector used by the CSU/DSU, and then find the correct *serial cable* to connect the two. Figure 7-21 shows drawings of several cables, with the connectors shown.

AUTHOR'S NOTE: The serial cables shown in the figure are usually a few feet long—just long enough to connect the router to the CSU/DSU. They both normally sit in the same room in the same equipment rack.

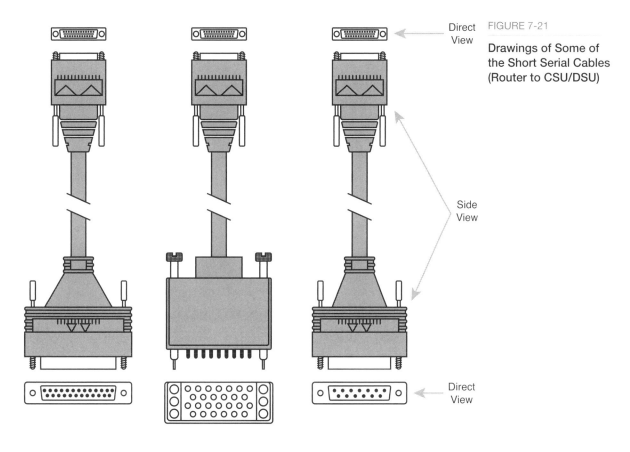

FIGURE 7-21

Drawings of Some of the Short Serial Cables (Router to CSU/DSU)

Summary of the Customer Ends of a Leased Line

Figure 7-22 completes the tour of the physical parts of the leased line at a single site. The figure shows a photo of a Cisco router that you would typically find in a corporate remote office. This particular model has two slots for removable router interface cards. This particular router has two identical 2-port serial cards, each of which requires an external CSU/DSU.

Cisco Systems 1841 Router

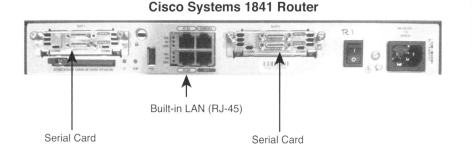

FIGURE 7-22

Photos of Router and Removable WAN Cards

The last few pages have mentioned many small short topics about how to physically install a leased line on the customer ends of the line. The following list summarizes the key steps for reference:

1. Order the leased line from the telco; the order lists the speed and connectors on the ends of the cable. It also lists the details of the exact location where the cable should be installed on each end of the link (street address, floor, and identifying information as to exactly what room).

2. Choose and purchase a router as needed.

3. Choose and purchase a serial interface card for the router, as needed.

4. If the chosen serial interface card does not have an internal CSU/DSU, choose and purchase a CSU/DSU and the matching serial cable.

5. Physically connect all the parts at both sites.

6. Configure the devices (beyond the scope of this book).

The T-Carrier System and TDM

To create a leased line for a customer, a telco can use many different technologies. The line from a CO to a customer physically uses 2-pair copper cabling and uses either the DS0, DS1, or DS3 standards for line rate and encoding, depending on what speed leased line the customer ordered. Telcos have used many different technologies inside the telco network to create the leased line, however.

The companies of the Bell System in the United States invented and used the first DS0, DS1, and DS3 leased lines. To make these new types of digital leased lines work, long ago these same companies invented the equipment and standards to create DS0, DS1, and DS3 leased lines. They also created new types of telco switches that used a new type of logic called *time-division multiplexing (TDM)*. The Bell System named the entire set of products and services the **T-carrier system**; the system used DS0, DS1, and DS3 lines both to customer sites and between COs.

This topic looks at some of the growth challenges in the telcos that led to the need for TDM, and then the following sections show how the Bell System's T-carrier system used TDM to create leased lines for customers.

The Challenge: Too Many Trunks Between Sites

Every leased line takes up some capacity in the physical telco network between the endpoints on the leased line. The telco does not just run a new cable from one customer site to the other to create a new leased line. The telco does need to move the bits from one customer site to the other, however, so there has to be a physical path from end to end over which the bits flow. Every leased line uses some of the capacity of the telco network. Over time, as a telco grows, and customers want more and more service, the telco has to be ready to add more and more equipment, plus more cables between sites, to support the added customer traffic.

First, think about three different leased-line customers (A, B, and C) of a local telco. These three companies happen to have offices in the same two towns, about 15 miles apart, and all three companies have a DS1, or T1, leased line between each site. Figure 7-23 shows the conceptual view of these three leased lines.

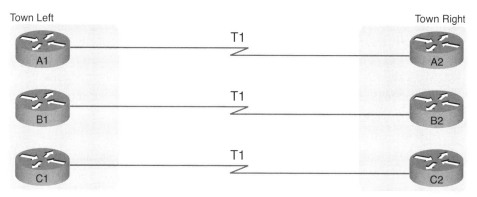

FIGURE 7-23

Conceptual View, Three T1 Leased Lines, Three Customers (A, B, C)

Next, think about the telco network and the local central office (CO) in each town. For the purpose of this example, the routers in each town happen to be near the same CO, respectively, as shown in Figure 7-24. To support sending bits between the two COs, the telco could also install three additional T1 lines, called *T1 trunks*, between the CO switches, as shown in the figure.

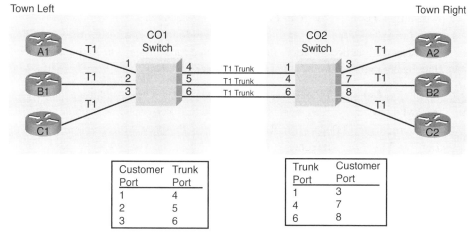

FIGURE 7-24

Telco Switching Connecting Incoming Customer T1s to T1 Trunks

To see how the pieces work together in this example, focus on company A's leased line. To create that one leased line, both CO switches connect to two physical T1 lines. The circuit-switching logic in the switches works like this:

CO1: All bits that come in my customer port 1 (connected to Router A1) send those bits out my trunk port 4 (and vice versa, for the other direction).

CO2: All bits that come in my customer port 3 (connected to Router A2) send those bits out my trunk port 1 (and vice versa, for the other direction)

Both switches, acting as circuit switches, switch the bits coming in one port to go out the other port. With the right linkages configured in each switch, the bits that Router A1 sends go to Router A2, and vice versa.

The telco has a growth problem if the telco actually had to do what this example shows. In the example shown in Figure 7-24, for every new T1 line, the telco had to use another T1 trunk line between COs. That would use up lots of cabling, and running cables for miles, under city streets, digging up the sidewalks and repaving, all costs money. Also, Figure 7-24 shows a relatively short leased line, with only two CO switches. A long leased line would run through several switches, maybe dozens, using up a T1 trunk line between every pair of COs.

Making Efficient Use of Trunks with Time-Division Multiplexing

The telcos solved part of the growth problem by using faster trunks and then sending the bits from many slower leased lines over a single faster trunk. The idea works a little like why we use buses to bring kids to school: Lots of kids need to go to the school, so rather than using a lot of little cars with only a few seats each, you use one bus, with much more seating capacity. In the telco, lots of bits need to move from one CO to the next, so the telco uses trunks with a much higher capacity because of their higher speed. The trick then is to find a way to move the bits from lines that run at a slower speed onto the link that runs at the higher speed.

TDM solves this problem by taking multiple slower-speed serial bit streams, like T1 lines, and sending their bits over a single higher-speed line, like a T3 line. Basically, a TDM switch gives every slower-speed channel a turn to send its bits over the higher-speed link. And the name **time-division multiplexing** itself describes the function: *dividing* the *time* allowed for sending data on the high-speed link, by combining (plex) *multiple* slower-speed channels.

ON THE SIDE: The suffix *plex*, of Latin origin, means to divide into a specific number of parts. One popular use today? Movie theaters, like a Cineplex 24 with 24 screens.

To support customer T1 leased lines, the CO TDM switches could use a single T3 trunk. To physically create and use a T3 trunk, the telco connects a cable using a T3 card in each telco TDM switch. That link runs at T3 speed, 43.736 Mbps, which is 28 times T1 speed (plus some overhead bits). Figure 7-25 shows a new version of Figure 7-24, this time with a T3 trunk instead of three T1 trunks.

FIGURE 7-25

CO Switches Multiplexing T1 Bits onto a Faster T3 Circuit

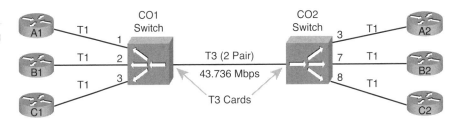

Figure 7-25 shows the new single T3 trunk, but it does not show how TDM logic works. Figure 7-26 begins the story of how TDM works in these switches, for bits flowing from left to right in the figure. The figure represents the same figure shown in Figure 7-25, but with the figure separated into three parts, to focus on three different parts of the process.

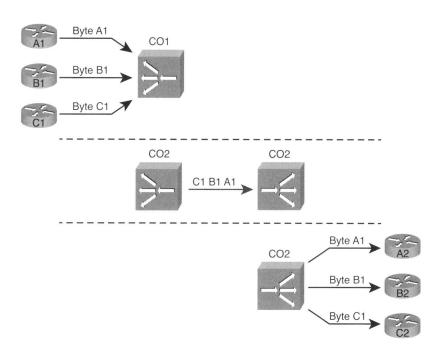

FIGURE 7-26

Three-Part Drawing of the TDM Example

The figure shows three steps, from top to bottom, as follows:

Top: All three routers on the left continually send bits; the top shows the next 1 byte's worth of bits arriving at switch CO1 for all three T1s.

Middle: Switch CO1 has combined ("plexed") these bytes onto a single T3 for transmission, sending A1's byte first, then B1's byte, and then C1's byte. The T3's speed (28 times T1 speed) leaves plenty of time to send bits for all three T1s.

Bottom: Switch CO2 demultiplexes the incoming faster signal back into the original bit streams, sending the bits for customer A's T1 to Router A2, and likewise for the T1s for companies B and C.

ON THE SIDE: Most people call devices that do TDM a *mux* (pronounced *mucks*). The function on the left of Figure 7-26 is called mux, with the function of splitting the bits back out, as done by switch CO2 in Figure 7-26, called demux.

The entire telco system of using many TDM switches, many trunks, with many customer leased lines does not create a traffic jam of bits trying to move around. Each incoming line into the TDM switch has enough capacity reserved for it on the trunk on the other side of the switch. For example, with a single T3 trunk between two CO switches, the telco can choose to send bits for up to 28 T1s over that trunk. Each of those 28 T1s has an allotted time slot, as managed by the TDM switch. By design, the telco does not even try to send the bits for a 29th T1 across the T3 trunk, because a T3 only has capacity to support 28 T1s (plus some overhead).

The link types in the T-carrier system (DS0, DS1, and DS3) define the timing of when a TDM switch can send bits over the link. Those standards define the idea of a time slot called a channel. Figure 7-27 shows the general idea. Again focusing on customer A's T1, the TDM switches give A's traffic a turn on the T3 on a regular basis. As long as the total number of bits allocated to A's traffic totals 1.544 million for every second, the TDM switch can send all the traffic for A's T1.

FIGURE 7-27

View into a Longer Time Period over a T3 Link

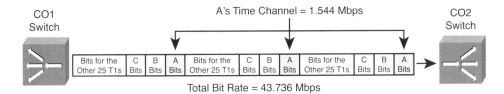

TDM Switches and Mapping T1s to T3 Channels

The last few figures show the general idea of how T3 channels worked and how TDM switches can multiplex T1s into those channels. However, it can help you learn TDM by thinking about how the linkages inside the TDM switch's logic work, as described here in the next page or two.

The TDM switch thinks about the T3 trunk as a physical serial link but logically as 28 T1 channels (plus overhead). Physically, a T3 line uses 2-pair cable, and it sends and receives bits serially (one after the other), at 43.736 Mbps. For the TDM switch's logic, however, the switch views the T3 as 28 T1 channels numbered 1 through 28.

The TDM switching logic maps the physical T1 ports connected to the customer routers to the logical T1 channels inside the single T3 trunk. Figure 7-28 shows an example, with the same three customer T1s, but now with three T1 channels (3, 4, and 5) being programmed into the TDM switches to be used for the three customer T1s used in the last several figures.

FIGURE 7-28

Matching TDM T3 Port and T1 Logical Channel on Both Ends of the T3 Trunk

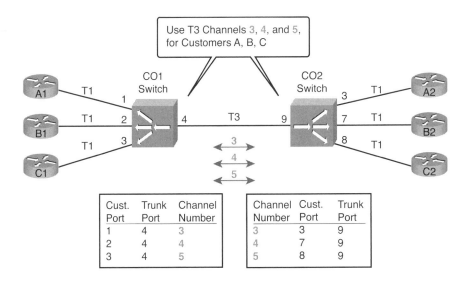

The T-carrier system also defines how to multiplex 24 physical DS0 lines onto the 24 channels of a physical DS1 (T1) line. The concept, to the depth discussed in this chapter, works the same as when multiplexing 28 DS1 lines onto a DS3 line. In the case of DS0 lines being multiplexed onto one DS1 line, the 1.544-Mbps DS1 speed includes 24 DS0 channels at 64 Kbps each, plus 8 Kbps of overhead.

T1 and the Role of the CSU/DSU

So far in this second major section ("Understanding Leased-Line WAN Links"), you have seen how to physically connect the leased line at the customer site, and you have learned how the telco could use its original TDM technology and the T-carrier system to create the leased line service—even without a literal cable from end to end through the telco. This next topic uncovers some surprising details of what happens at Layer 1 on a leased line: The routers use a different bit rate than the CSU/DSU uses when the CSU/DSU sends bits over the cable connected to the phone company.

The CSU/DSU sits at the customer end of each leased line to do several required functions. Routers simply cannot use a leased line based on the T-carrier system— that is, a leased line based on DS0, DS1, and DS3 technology—without using a CSU/DSU at the ends of the link.

> **AUTHOR'S NOTE:** Because routers and CSU/DSUs have different jobs to do on a leased line, it helps to think about the CSU/DSU as an external device. Leased lines used external CSU/DSUs from the earliest days, for several decades, with internal CSU/DSUs coming later. To help the learning process, all the examples for this topic show external CSU/DSUs.

This topic looks at the role of the CSU/DSU, as a separate function from the router, with much attention to these bit rate differences. To understand CSU/DSUs, you need a deeper understanding of T1 technology, including a look at the 24 DS0 time channels logically created inside each T1. This topic walks through the bit rate differences and describes how T1 channels and framing allow the CSU/DSU to adapt between the two different speeds. This topic also shows the differences in how a CSU/DSU works with a leased line that runs at full T1 speed versus a slower link, called a fractional T1.

Different Views of Bit Rates: Routers Versus CSU/DSU

Take a step back and think about telcos, leased lines, and the technology and business needs together. First, on the technology side, the Bell System companies invested heavily and created the ability to send bits over long distances using 2-pair copper cabling. For a variety of reasons, they ended up with three physical line types: **DS0**, **DS1**, and **DS3**. The bit rates on these lines are as follows:

DS0: 64 Kbps

DS1: 1.544 Mbps

DS3: 43.736 Mbps

From a business perspective, the Bell companies and their customers wanted many more speed options in between these speeds. Unsurprisingly, the telco pricing model charged a higher price for higher-bit-rate leased lines. However, the bump in speed from 64 Kbps to 1.5 Mbps required a steep jump in price, as did a jump from 1.5 Mbps to 43 Mbps.

Comparing the technology and the business needs, the people in the Bell System that created TDM and T-carrier technology could have just made lots more types of lines at different speeds. However, each new standard would require more time, effort, and money. They wanted to offer a large variety of speeds to their customers, but they had to keep the cost (and prices) as low as they could.

The technical solution was to still use these same three physical line standards (DS0, DS1, and DS3), but to create a slower speed, restrict the customer to only use a subset of the bits that cross that physical line. To make that work, the lines use a CSU/DSU, which deals with the speed of the physical line from the telco versus the speed the customer has paid to use that line.

For example, imagine that a customer ordered a leased line with a bit rate of 768 Kbps. 768 Kbps is basically half the speed of a DS1 line, requiring 12 DS0 channel's worth of bandwidth (12 × 64 Kbps = 768 Kbps). Physically, the telco installs a T1 line to each site. The bits cross that line at T1 speed; however, the customer router sends data at only 768 Kbps. Figure 7-29 shows the idea.

FIGURE 7-29

Speed Differences on a 768-Kbps Leased-Line WAN

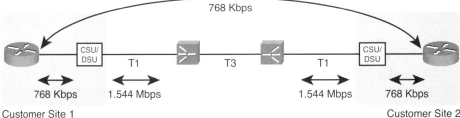

The CSU/DSU makes these two different speeds on the link work correctly. On the telco side, the CSU/DSU understands the T1 Layer 1 standards. Those standards include details called *T1 framing*, as discussed in the next few pages. On the router side, the CSU/DSU uses a concept called *clocking*, where the CSU/DSU acts as the master and the router as the slave. The router sends or receives bits at the speed clocked by the CSU/DSU. In this case, the CSU/DSU would clock the router at 768 Kbps.

To truly understand what is happening, you need to learn more about the standards for DS1s, framing, and channels, as well as see some examples. The following sections walk through those details.

DS1 (T1) and the T1 Frame

The ANSI T1 standard, which grew out of the original work by the Bell System companies, defines a structure for the bits that go over a T1 line. The bits physically flow serially over the line—in other words, they flow one after the other. However, if you take the 1,544,000 bits that flow during the course of a single second, the T1 standards give structure and meaning to those bits, rather than just viewing the bits as a bunch of bits.

The T1 standards call the structure a *frame*. (The word *frame* means something different than how the data link layer uses the term.) The word frame in the T1 world refers to a set of 193 bits that flow over the link. As humans, if you could view all the bits that flow over a T1 in 1 second, and you knew the T1 standards very well, you could look at the bits and identify the beginning and end of every 193-bit frame. The devices on the ends of the T1 line—the telco switch and the CSU/DSU—can also find the edges of the frames and interpret each frame of 193 bits as being separate from the others.

The T1 frame lets the endpoints on the T1 line interpret the bits as 24 separate DS0 channels, plus overhead. Physically, the cable still has two pairs, one for sending in each direction. The bits still flow serially. But the CSU/DSU and the telco switch can identify and view those bits as belonging to different frames, with each frame holding bits from 24 different DS0 channels. Over time, each DS0 channel gets 64 Kbps of the capacity of the T1.

The 193-bit size of the T1 frame makes much more sense when you think about it holding 24 DS0 channels, plus overhead. Each 193-bit frame holds 1 byte for each of 24 channels; this adds up to 192 of the 193 bits in a frame. The T1 equipment uses the data in the extra 193rd bit for several functions, including *framing* —the function of finding the beginning of a frame in the serial stream of bits. Figure 7-30 shows the format of a T1 frame.

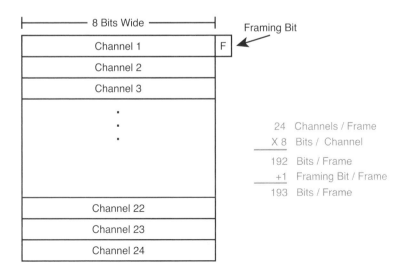

FIGURE 7-30

193-Bit T1 Frame

While the devices on the end of the T1 line—the telco switch in the local CO and the CSU/DSU at the customer site—view the bits as frames, the bits still flow serially. Figure 7-31 shows another view of the T1 frame, as if the frame's bits were flowing from left to right over a link.

FIGURE 7-31

T1 Frame, Shown as Being Sent Serially over a T1

1 Byte Per Channel

| 24 | 23 | 22 | 21 | 20 | 19 | 18 | 17 | 16 | 15 | 14 | 13 | 12 | 11 | 10 | 9 | 8 | 7 | 6 | 5 | 4 | 3 | 2 | 1 |

8000 Frames Per Second

Adjusting the Speed Using a CSU/DSU

The CSU/DSU must adjust the speeds on each side of the CSU/DSU to match the physical line rate of the line from the telco, with the bits allowed to be used by the customer device (usually a router). Now that you know the basics of T1 framing, and how it breaks the serial stream into DS0 channels, you can understand how the CSU/DSU can match the speeds.

First, think about what happens when the customer asks for a leased line that runs at T1 speed or slower. First, the telco physically installs a T1 line between the CO and the customer site. The CSU/DSU knows T1 standards, knows T1 framing, sees the frames, and sees the channels. The CSU/DSU handles the physical layer encoding on the line, at exactly 1.544 Mbps.

The CSU/DSU looks at the T1 line as if it were 24 DS0 channels plus the overhead bits (framing), as shown in Figure 7-32. From a very short-term view, every 1/8000 of a second, each frame gets to send and receive 1 byte of data. From a longer-term view, each DS0 channel gets 64 Kbps of the capacity of the T1.

FIGURE 7-32

CSU/DSU Channel View of the T1 Line from Customer to Local CO

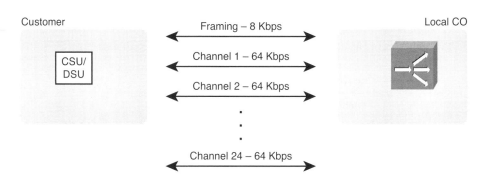

Customer

CSU/ DSU

Framing – 8 Kbps

Channel 1 – 64 Kbps

Channel 2 – 64 Kbps

Channel 24 – 64 Kbps

Local CO

Although the physical T1 line runs at T1 speed (1.544 Mbps), the CSU/DSU controls the number of customer bits per second sent over the line by using a subset of the DS0 channels. When ordering the leased line, the customer cannot order just any speed, but for speeds up to T1 speed, the speed must be a multiple of 64 Kbps. Why? Because the CSU/DSU and the telco switch will agree to use specific DS0 channels for that leased line. For example:

- If ordering a leased line of speed of 4 × 64 Kbps (256 Kbps), the CSU/DSU will use four DS0 channels.

- If ordering a leased line of speed of 8 × 64 Kbps (512 Kbps), the CSU/DSU will use eight DS0 channels.

- If ordering a leased line of speed of 12 × 64 Kbps (1024 Kbps), the CSU/DSU will use 12 DS0 channels.

- If ordering a leased line of speed of 24 × 64 Kbps (1536 Kbps), the CSU/DSU will use 24 DS0 channels.

On the router side of the CSU/DSU, the CSU/DSU uses a feature called *clocking* to control the speed of the router serial interface. The router must send and receive bits at the same speed as the combined DS0 channels on the leased line. For example, if the customer ordered a leased line to run at 256 Kbps (4 × 64 Kbps), the CSU/DSU must use clocking to make the router send and receive bits at 256 Kbps.

The external CSU/DSU does clocking using the serial cable between the CSU/DSU and the router. The serial cable has many wires, with some set aside for clocking. The CSU/DSU signals the router on those leads, and the router only sends and receives a bit when the CSU/DSU signals it. If the CSU/DSU has been configured to make the router run at 768 Kbps, the CSU/DSU sends the right clock signal 768,000 times per second. If configured to make the router run at 256 Kbps, the CSU/DSU sends the right clock signal 256,000 times per second. Figure 7-33 shows the idea.

Customer Site

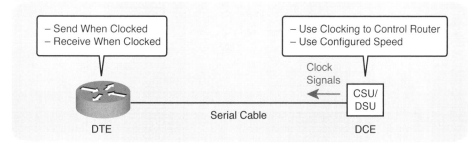

FIGURE 7-33

CSU/DSU View of Serial Cable and Router, with Clocking

The clocking concept works a little like the following game a dad might play with his son. The son needs to throw a ball to the dad from a big bin of balls. However, the kid can only throw a ball when the dad says "beep." If the dad says beep every minute, the son throws only 1 ball per minute (bpm). If the dad beeps every 5 seconds, the rate moves up to 12 bpm. At once per second, the son probably cannot keep up, but if so, the speed is up to 60 bpm. But the entire time, the son reacts to the beeps from the dad. The same process happens on the serial cable: The CSU/DSU beeps by using a particular electrical signal on a clocking circuit, and only then does the router send and receive a bit.

The next few pages show two examples—one with a full T1 leased line and one with a fractional T1 leased line running at 256 Kbps. These examples will show how the CSU/DSU completes the story by matching the speed at which the router sends bits to the channels inside the T1.

The Router and CSU/DSU on a Full T1 Leased Line

Now take a common example for leased lines in which the telco customer orders a T1 leased line between two sites. To make that work, the telco installs a physical T1 from the local CO to each customer site. The customer gets to use 1.536 Mbps of the T1 between the two routers, in other words, the full capacity of 24 DS0 channels. So, the CSU/DSU must clock the router at the slightly slower rate of 1.536 Mbps, as noted in Figure 7-34.

FIGURE 7-34

Full T1 with CSU/ DSU: 1.536 Mbps to the Router, 1.544 Mbps to the CSU/ DSU

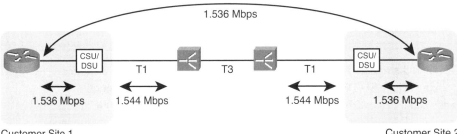

The CSU/DSU makes the small speed difference work by matching the router's 1.536-Mbps bit stream to the 24 DS0 channels in the T1. Those 24 DS0 channels add up to 1.536 Mbps of capacity. When taking data from the router, the CSU/ DSU must fit those bits into the 24 DS0 channels in a T1 frame, avoiding using that 193rd framing bit, because it is reserved for overhead framing. When taking bits in from the T1 to send to the router, the CSU/DSU must remove the framing bit, because the router has no concept of T1 framing. Figure 7-35 shows the idea for the router on the left sending data.

FIGURE 7-35

Role of the CSU/DSU in a Full T1 Leased Line

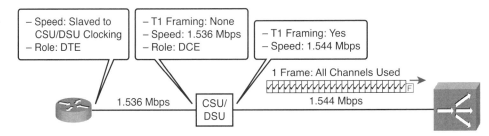

The Router and CSU/DSU on a Fractional T1 Leased Line

When you order a leased line that uses some multiple of 64 Kbps, but less than the full 24 DS0 channels in a full T1, the network engineer has a little more work to do. The CSU/DSU still has to match the speeds. To make it work, the CSU/DSU and local CO switch must agree to use the same DS0 channels and essentially ignore the same DS0 channels. The network engineer needs to configure the CSU/DSU to know the correct DS0 channels, matching the telco's configuration on the telco switch.

For example, imagine that a customer orders a 256-Kbps leased line between two sites. The telco installs a T1 line between each telco switch and each site, using a T1 port on the telco switch. However, to run at only 256 Kbps, which is four times the 64-Kbps speed of a DS0 channel, the telco chooses four DS0 channels to use on the T1 line, as shown in Figure 7-36.

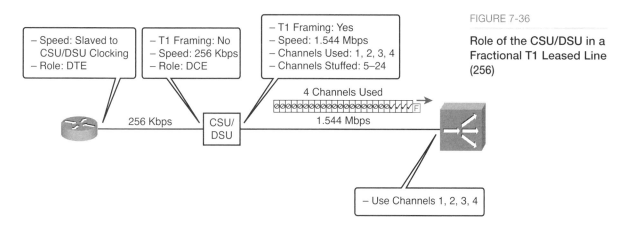

FIGURE 7-36

Role of the CSU/DSU in a Fractional T1 Leased Line (256)

Note that in this example, the telco switch and CSU/DSU use channel numbers 1, 2, 3, and 4. The actual channels do not matter, as long as both devices choose to use the same channels, because both the CSU/DSU and the telco switch need to know where to look in the frame. Both devices must ignore the same 20 of the 24 DS0 channels as well.

On the router side, the CSU/DSU still controls the bit rate with the router. Because only 256 Kbps of capacity exists on the T1 side, the CSU/DSU clocks the router at 256 Kbps to match the same speed. Then the CSU/DSU fits the bits from the router into the working DS0 channels in the T1 frame.

AUTHOR'S NOTE:
Using a part or fraction of a T1's capacity, as shown in the figure, is often called a *fractional T1*.

Worldwide Variations on T-Carrier Lines

This chapter uses examples from the U.S. standards for T-carrier lines. However, some countries happen to have chosen other standards for similar kinds of links. These other standards do use the 64-Kbps DS0 concept as the basis for the links, but they vary as compared with the U.S.-based T-carrier standards.

The two most popular variations from the U.S. standards exist in Europe and in Japan. The European shorthand names use the letter *E* in the names, and the Japanese names use the letter *J*. Table 7-3 summarizes some of the standards from the United States, as well as two other major different sets of standards. The table lists the common names of the standards, as well as the cumulative speeds and the supported number of channels in each.

TABLE 7-3

Summary of Carrier TDM Line Standards

Type of Line	Geography	Speed	Number of Channels
DS0	United States	64 Kbps	N/A
DS1 (T1)	United States	1.544 Mbps	24 DS0
DS3 (T3)	United States	43.736 Mbps	28 DS1
E0	Europe	64 Kbps	N/A
E1	Europe	2.048 Mbps	32* E0
E3	Europe	34.368 Mbps	16 E1
J0	Japan	64 Kbps	N/A
J1	Japan	1.544 Mbps	24 J0
J3	Japan	32.064 Mbps	20 J1

* 30 E0 channels are available for customer data; 2 E0 channels are for other functions.

Controlling Leased Lines with Data-Link Protocols

As discussed early in this chapter, routers focus on Layer 3 tasks, delivering IP packets to the correct destination device in a TCP/IP network. Routers use serial leased lines to forward IP packets from one router to the other. So far, this chapter has only touched on the OSI Layer 1 details of these WAN links. This final short leased-line topic looks at the data-link protocols routers use on leased lines.

Interestingly, data-link protocols for a modern point-to-point leased line have less work to do than LAN data-link protocols. Leased-line data-link protocols do not have to negotiate which router gets to send next, because these links allow full duplex. These protocols define a data-link address, but in a point-to-point topology, the addressing does not matter, because the intended destination is obvious.

An analogy can help to understand why these serial link data-link protocols might not need an address. Imagine that you are sitting beside a friend, and you are the only two people around. Each time you speak, you start with your friend's name. "Hey Fred, what about…." "Hey Fred, did you see…." It would almost get irritating after a while, saying Fred's name every time you speak, because with only two people around, both people know who is talking to whom. The same logic happens on a point-to-point serial link: When one router sends, the data is obviously meant for the other router on the link.

Next, Figure 7-37 reviews the concepts of how hosts and routers use data-link headers and trailers to deliver packets. Essentially, when a node needs to send an IP packet to the next node—a host sending to a router, a router to another router, or the final router to the final host—the sending node adds the data-link header and trailer. Routers connect to leased lines, so routers happen to do the work to add and remove the WAN data-link headers.

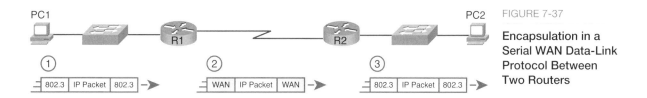

FIGURE 7-37

Encapsulation in a Serial WAN Data-Link Protocol Between Two Routers

Following the steps in the figure:

1. PC1 has an IP packet to send to Router R1, so PC1 encapsulates the IP packet in an Ethernet frame and sends it over the Ethernet to R1.

2. R1 receives the Ethernet frame, removes the header and trailer, and makes a decision to send the packet to R2. At that point, R1 adds a header and trailer based on the WAN data-link protocol used on that link.

3. R2 receives the WAN frame, removes the header and trailer, and makes a decision to send the packet to host PC2. At that point, R2 adds an Ethernet header and trailer so that the frame arrives at PC2.

The figure shows a generic WAN data-link header and trailer, but there are mainly two options available today:

- High-Level Data Link Control (HDLC)
- Point-to-Point Protocol (PPP)

The next few pages discuss a few details of each.

HDLC

High-Level Data Link Control (HDLC) has had a long history. It grew out of an IBM-proprietary protocol (SDLC), with HDLC standardized by the ISO back in the 1970s. That older WAN world actually required HDLC to support many more functions than it needs to support for today's simple point-to-point leased lines. This section points out what is important about HDLC today: making two routers send data over a point-to-point leased line.

The HDLC protocol, and particularly the HDLC header and trailer, has two main purposes:

- To deliver the encapsulated data from the sender to the correct receiver
- To perform error detection, so that if a receiving node receives an HDLC frame that changed during transmission, the receiver can discard the frame

As with most protocols, HDLC uses a header and trailer to do its work, as seen in Figure 7-38.

FIGURE 7-38

HDLC Frame Format

Standard HDLC (No Type Field)

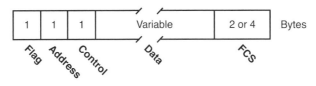

Of the fields shown in the HDLC frame, the Flag and FCS matter most to how two routers use HDLC today. The Flag field signals the beginning of a new frame, much like the Ethernet Preamble and SFD fields together signal a new Ethernet frame. The Frame Check Sequence (FCS) field has the same purpose as the Ethernet FCS field: error detection. The other two fields exist in the header, but these fields have little importance for a pair of routers on a leased line. Table 7-4 summarizes the meaning of each field, with a comparison to Ethernet.

TABLE 7-4

HDLC Header and Trailer Fields

Field	Description	Shorthand Reminder	Similar to Ethernet...
Flag	1-byte (7E) that a frame is beginning.	Here comes the frame!	Preamble + SFD
Address	Identifies the destination device; typically FF ("all stations") between routers, which works well on the point-to-point topology.	To there	Destination MAC
Control	Defines many subfields used by older devices in decades past.	Old; ignore	N/A
Data	The data, including all headers from upper layers, plus user data.	The actual data	Data
FCS	Frame Check Sequence. A field used to determine whether any bits changed during transmission. If so, the receiver should discard the frame.	Check for errors	FCS

AUTHOR'S NOTE:
As a reminder, *error detection* means that the receiving device notices the error and discards the frame if an error did occur. However, the term *error detection* does not include the *error recovery* function—the process of the receiving node asking that the data be resent.

Point-to-Point Protocol (PPP)

HDLC and PPP have some common features, and given their histories, you can almost think of PPP as one of HDLC's grandchildren. IBM's proprietary SDLC was followed by the standardized HDLC in the 1970s, with both being used in many networks throughout the 1970s into the 1990s. As WAN services changed and improved through the years, other WAN data-link protocols emerged, many beginning with the letters *LAP* (LAPB, LAPD, LAPF). When TCP/IP started to blossom, moving from research labs and universities into the rest of the world, yet another WAN data-link protocol was created: PPP. The creators of this new protocol, the Point-to-Point Protocol (PPP), designed PPP to be used by TCP/IP networks and the multiprotocol routers used to create networks that supported TCP/IP and other networking protocols.

PPP emerged as a standard in RFCs 1661 and 1662. These RFCs reached standards status in 1994, which was around the time frame that most companies were marching away from proprietary networking models and migrating toward using TCP/IP. In those years, most companies started using routers because they supported many Layer 3 protocols—usually TCP/IP, plus whatever proprietary Layer 3 protocols a company had used in years past. To make all these Layer 3 protocols work, and let all those Layer 3 protocols flow over the same leased line, the routers needed a data-link protocol with a Type field, like Ethernet's Type field, that identified the type of Layer 3 packet inside the frame. PPP filled that need, with a standard Type field, as shown in Figure 7-39.

> **ON THE SIDE:** If you are wondering where that bit on the history of networking models is from earlier in this book, look for the section "The History of Networking Models" in Chapter 3.

Standard PPP (Type Field)

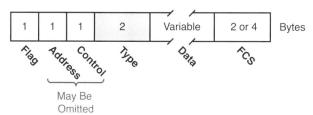

FIGURE 7-39

PPP Frame Format

PPP uses almost identical header and trailer options as compared to HDLC, but with a few twists. First, it has a standard Type field, as already mentioned. Second, the routers might not even bother to send the address and control fields. You might recall that even with HDLC between two routers, the address and control fields had little or no meaning. PPP defines an address and control field, but the routers can negotiate to simply not bother including those two fields. If sent, the fields have the same value in all frames.

> **AUTHOR'S NOTE:** Although HDLC standards do not include a Type field, most router vendors support HDLC, and they added a proprietary Type field to their implementation of HDLC. By doing so, the router vendors gave their customers a way to use HDLC to support packets from many different networking models.

Understanding Packet Switching and Multiaccess WANs

Historically speaking, telcos have created WAN services—the ability to send data over distances—in many ways. Telcos started with analog circuits and modems to send data, using the same circuits the telco used for voice. Analog circuits worked, and they met the need. Next, the telcos created digital circuits, using digital circuit switches, TDM, and the T-carrier system. These faster digital circuits worked better for customers, and also made more efficient use of the trunk lines between sites.

Packet switching was one of the next major steps in the progression of WAN services from telcos and other WAN service providers. Packet switching created more ways for the telco to grow and expand its networks, keeping costs down, while offering better services to customers.

This last of the three major sections of this chapter focuses on packet switching. It starts with a look at the big concepts, with a discussion of how packet switching changed the telco network compared to the T-carrier system and circuit switching. It then discusses one packet-switching system in detail as an example—Frame Relay.

Packet Switching Versus TDM

Circuit switching, with TDM and the telco T-carrier system, worked well. However, as with any technology, time passed, requirements changed, user needs changed, and technology improved. As time went on, packet switching solved some problems for telcos compared to circuit switching and TDM. In particular, packet switching gave the telcos a way to install less cable over long distances, reduce cost in several ways, and therefore give better prices to their customers.

To understand some of the cost savings with packet switching, first think about the fact that with TDM, the telco reserves the channels in a trunk for a particular leased line. After the channels are reserved, those bits cannot be shared with other customers.

For example, say that a customer has a T1 leased line between two routers, but the two sites have zero IP packets to send for the next 10 minutes. However, the telco TDM circuit switches have a T1 channel reserved from one site to the other to create that leased line. The telco has reserved a T1's worth of the T-carrier system for that T1, but for that 10 minutes, the two customer routers did not use it.

To see the TDM reservation concept more clearly, consider the example in Figure 7-40. In this case, a telco has installed 28 T1 leased lines for some customers near two COs. The telco has mapped each T1 to one of the 28 T1 channels in a T3 trunk between the COs. As a result, all 28 channels of the T3 have been used; the T3 is full.

FIGURE 7-40

Single T3 Trunk Consumed by Supporting 28 Customer T1s

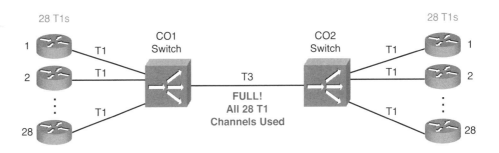

The T3 trunk between CO TDM switches has been fully reserved and allocated for all those T1s. If all the routers coincidentally had no IP packets to forward for the next 10 minutes, the T3 could not be used for other purposes. The telco could not install a 29th T1 off these two COs and use any of the capacity of the T3 to support the new T1; that new T1 would need to be supported on another trunk between the two COs.

With only two nearby COs, the waste shown in Figure 7-40 might sound bad, but not that bad. However, a leased line reserves a channel from one end of the telco network to the other. For example, in Figure 7-41, 28 customer T1 leased lines happen to stretch from two COs that are farther apart than the previous figure. In this case, the leased lines run through a total of four TDM switches and a total of three T3 trunks. These 28 T1s take up all the capacity on all three TDM trunks.

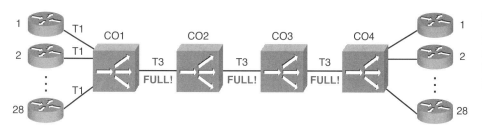

FIGURE 7-41

Multiple T3 Trunks Completely Used by Supporting 28 Customer T1s

Packet switching recovers a lot of the wasted capacity on the trunks that happens when customer devices sit idle. To do that, the telco network changes how the telco equipment works, from a focus of connecting a circuit from end to end and leaving it there forever, to a focus of forwarding a packet to the right destination. Compared to the TDM world, the packet-switching world, the following happens to create a packet-switched world:

- The physical links could remain the same (DS0, DS1, DS3).
- The customer devices use a different protocol, with addresses that the telco will use.
- The telco changes its network to no longer use a TDM circuit switch, to instead use a device called a packet switch.
- The packet switch looks at the headers sent by the customer node, makes a decision based on the address, and forwards the packet to the right destination on the WAN.
- The packet switch can queue packets if the outgoing link is busy.
- When a customer router sends no packets, the telco does not use any of the capacity on its trunks between telco sites.

AUTHOR'S NOTE: The term *packet switching* presents a small problem regarding the typical meaning of the word *packet*. The word *packet* generally implies "Layer 3 protocol." However, the term *packet switching* refers to a general class of protocols and offerings, some of which match Layer 2 and some of which match Layer 3. So just remember that the term *packet switching* is not meant to imply whether a particular packet-switching standard acts like Layer 3 of the OSI model.

Figure 7-42 shows a view of how packet switching works using an imaginary packet-switching protocol. The devices use the same TDM physical link types as with the T-carrier system. They use an imaginary data-link protocol, and the protocol identifies the destination address using a hex code (hex A2 in this example). The telco packet switches must know of the location of each destination, typically using a table as shown in the figure.

FIGURE 7-42

Packet-Switching Concept: Telco Node Receives, Queues, and Forwards Packets

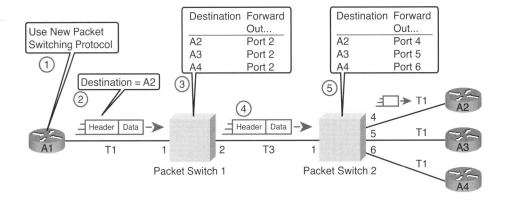

Following the steps in the figure:

1. Router A1 sends its next message over its T1 link and connects to Packet Switch 1.

2. The header of the packet identifies Router A2 as the destination.

3. Packet Switch 1 looks at the destination address and decides to send the packet out the T3 link (port 2) on the right.

4. The same packet crosses the T3 link.

5. The packet arrives at the second packet switch, which matches its forwarding table, sending the packet out port 4 toward Router A2.

With packet switching, the links between switches can be used as capacity to forward packets when they occur. The links between the switches do not have to be reserved for one customer or another. Most importantly, if one customer does not send packets for the next 10 minutes, that customer consumes none of the capacity on the links between the switches, so the telco can use that capacity for other customers.

Packet switching helps telcos waste less capacity on their trunks because experience shows that most customers' routers do sit idle on a regular basis. When a customer has a T1 leased line between sites, the load of bits sent over that line typically varies over time, and for short periods of time (for example, for a few seconds), the link sits idle. With TDM, the T1 channels that the telco reserved on its trunks are wasted. With packet switching, the telco packet switches only send packets over the trunks between switches when the customer sends them, so a temporarily silent customer link does not waste any capacity on the telco trunk.

Figure 7-43 shows a sample of how a telco can support twice as many customer T1 links—56 instead of 28—over the same T3 trunk between COs. Earlier, Figure 7-41 showed a TDM example with 28 T1 leased lines going over one T3 trunk, and that trunk being at capacity. Figure 7-43 shows a packet-switching example with twice that many customer T1s at the edge of the network. The telco, acting as a packet-switching service, expects that, over time, the total of all bits from all routers will not exceed a T3's worth of bits.

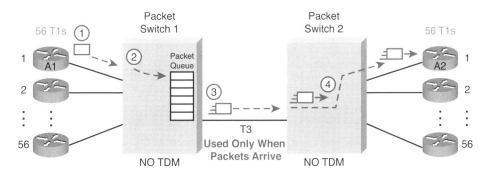

FIGURE 7-43

Packet-Switching Concept: Telco Node Receives, Queues, and Forwards Packets

The figure also shows what happens over short periods if the customer routers do collectively send more bits than the T3 can forward: The packet switches queue the packets in memory. Although voice bits would suffer from any kind of delay, if data experiences a few tenths of a second delay in the packet switch, it only causes a minor inconvenience for the user. Following the steps in the figure:

1. A router sends a packet, with the header for the packet-switching service, out the link to the packet-switching service.

2. Packet Switch 1 wants to send the packet to Packet Switch 2, but the T3 link is already busy with packets from other customers that arrived earlier. Packet Switch 1 puts the new packet at the end of the queue.

3. Each time the T3 has space to send another packet, Packet Switch 1 takes the next packet out of the queue and sends it, eventually sending the packet that arrived at Step 1.

4. Packet Switch 2 makes a decision to forward the packet to a particular router.

Frame Relay

The first widely popular packet-switching services used standards and technology called X.25. X.25 services started in the 1970s, with the services growing in the 1980s and with popularity starting to fall by the 1990s. Any device could connect to the X.25 service through a variety of links, mainly through switched analog circuits (dialup connections using modems) and digital leased lines.

Inside the world of packet-switching WAN services, the next major shift happened in the 1990s with the introduction of Frame Relay. **Frame Relay** began life as an effort from a small set of vendors that then formed a vendor consortium called the *Frame Relay Forum (FRF)*. The FRF defined Frame Relay standards in the 1990s

ON THE SIDE: The X.25 standards were defined by the CCITT, which later changed its name to the current name: ITU.

and into the 2000s. Eventually, the ITU took over the standardization of Frame Relay. The FRF eventually stopped doing its work because it finished the task—to help get Frame Relay established, standardized, and accepted in the market.

Like X.25, a Frame Relay network allows any device connected to the network to communicate with any other device. Figure 7-44 shows the typical type of drawing used to represent an enterprise Frame Relay network, when the details of the Frame Relay design do not matter. This type of figure just reminds us of what could happen in this network: All devices could send data directly to each other.

FIGURE 7-44

Typical Drawing of a Frame Relay Design, One Customer, Ignoring Details

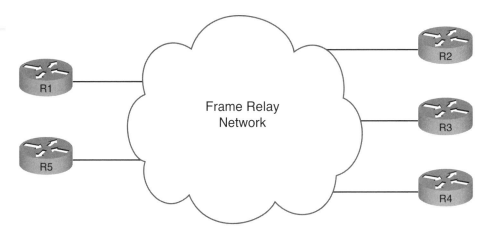

AUTHOR'S NOTE:
Frame Relay sends messages that are typically called *frames*, because Frame Relay technically looks more like a Layer 2 protocol, and the word *frame* refers to Layer 2 messages. However, for historical reasons, Frame Relay is called a packet-switching service as opposed to a frame-switching service.

This figure shows the type of figure often used to represent a packet-switching network, or to use the more modern term, a *multiaccess network*. Some networking technologies have a point-to-point technology, like leased lines; those links have exactly two devices. The term *multiaccess* refers to any link where more than two devices can communicate over the link, as is the case with packet-switching services. So, you might hear Frame Relay described as a packet-switching service or as a multiaccess network.

The rest of the Frame Relay discussion takes a closer look at what happens between the customer routers, the Frame Relay cloud, and inside the Frame Relay cloud.

Frame Relay Physical Access Links

First, focus on the edge of the Frame Relay network. The edge between the customer site and the Frame Relay network has many details and features with new terms, as follows:

- The telco office building, while usually called a central office (CO) in the voice world, is usually called a point of presence (POP) with Frame Relay and many later WAN services.

- As a generic term, Frame Relay standards refer to the customer device as a DTE (data terminal equipment).

- Again as a generic term, the standards refer to the device inside the Frame Relay network, which forwards the customer Frame Relay frames, as a *Frame Relay switch*. It is also called DCE (data communications equipment).

- The physical link between the DTE (the customer device) and the DCE (the telco Frame Relay switch) is called the *access link*.

Frame Relay networks often use the familiar T-carrier leased lines as the physical access links. Physically, no differences exist. You use the same router interface cards, the same cables (both inside the building and under the streets), the same CSU/DSU, and so on. The access link can be DS0, DS1, DS3, fractional DS1 or fractional DS3, or even some other types of links.

Figure 7-45 summarizes some of the Frame Relay terms with more detail shown for the Frame Relay network.

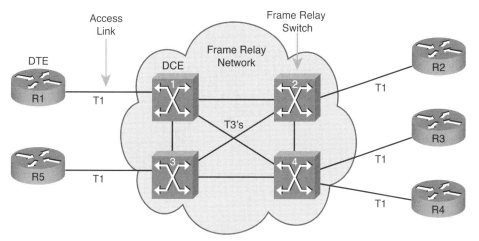

FIGURE 7-45

One Possible Telco Implementation of the Frame Relay Network

AUTHOR'S NOTE: Unfortunately, the world of networking has grown to use the DTE and DCE in two different but related contexts. In Frame Relay, and some other packet-switching services, the DCE is the switch inside the packet-switching service and the DTE is the customer device. On a leased line, the device that controls the clock rate is the DCE and the device being controlled is the DTE, as with a CSU/DSU and router, as seen earlier in Figure 7-33.

Frame Relay standards define what happens from the customer device (DTE) to the telco switch (DCE), but not what happens inside the telco network. Figure 7-45 happens to show the links as T3 links, just as a reminder of two facts—that there must be some connections between the switches and that the connections tend to be faster than the access links, to create enough capacity to forward frames for all customers. But the telco or service provider could use any technology that works, as long as it delivers the frames from one end to the other.

Frame Relay Virtual Circuit (VC) Concepts

The Frame Relay service uses a concept of a virtual circuit. First, think of the word *circuit* as a synonym for a leased line. To allow two routers to communicate over a WAN, you could order a leased line, or circuit, between the two routers. With Frame Relay, you do the same thing, except you connect the two routers with a virtual leased line called a *virtual circuit (VC)*. And because the telco has to permanently configure the VC, VCs are also called *permanent virtual circuits (PVC)*.

To better understand PVCs, start with the example in Figure 7-46. The figure shows Router R1 as the central site router. The network engineer has chosen to install physical leased lines from R1 to each of the other four routers in the network.

FIGURE 7-46

Four Physical Circuits Between Routers

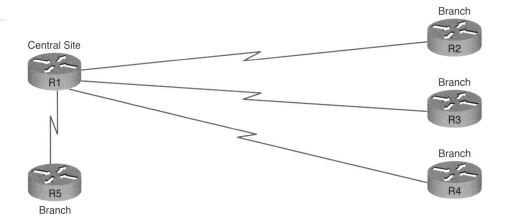

A Frame Relay network can mimic the design in Figure 7-46 using PVCs. Physically, all routers connect to the Frame Relay network with an access link. Logically, the Frame Relay network allows these pairs of routers to send frames over the network: R1-R2, R1-R3, R1-R4, and R1-R5. Figure 7-47 shows how you might draw the PVCs when using a Frame Relay design as an alternative.

FIGURE 7-47

Frame Relay Virtual Circuit (VC) Concept; Partial Mesh

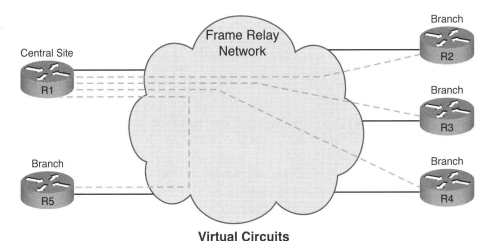

Virtual Circuits

Partial Mesh and Full Mesh

For a single Frame Relay customer, the customer can ask that all routers be able to send frames directly to all other routers, but he can also ask that only some routers be allowed to send frames directly to each other. Frame Relay networks do support the ability for every customer router to send a frame directly to any other customer router. If the Frame Relay network does allow it, why limit some routers from sending frames to each other? The simple answer: cost.

Service providers charge a monthly fee for the service, with part of that cost based on the number of PVCs. To allow two Frame Relay DTEs to send frames to each other, the provider must create a PVC between the DTEs. The more PVCs, the higher the cost.

A Frame Relay *partial mesh* design, as shown in Figure 7-47, makes sense when the traffic mostly flows to and from the main site. Packets between a branch site and the main site just use the PVC between those two sites. When branches need to send those rate IP packets to a remote branch, the packet just needs to cross two PVCs: one trip to the central site and then another back through the Frame Relay network to the other branch. That trip takes a little longer, but it keeps the cost down.

A Frame Relay *full-mesh* design makes more sense when most sites tend to send lots of IP packets to most every other site. A full mesh exists when the network engineer orders a PVC between every pair of Frame Relay routers, as shown in Figure 7-48. In this case, no matter where a router wants to forward an IP packet, the router can send the packet in a Frame Relay frame directly to the other router.

> **AUTHOR'S NOTE:**
> Many applications send packets from a user's device to a server, instead of sending packets between user devices. For example, if one branch user sends an email to a user at another branch, no IP packets flow directly between branches; they flow from the branch to the email servers, which probably sit at the main site anyway. As a result, partial mesh designs are common.

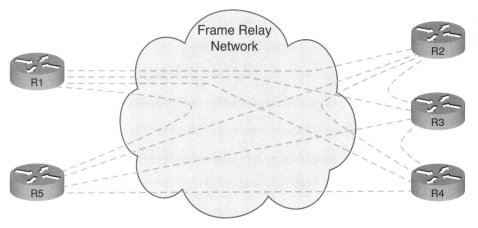

FIGURE 7-48

Full Mesh of Frame Relay PVCs

Frame Relay Forwarding with DLCIs

Every packet-switching technology defines protocols that the devices use to deliver data over the packet-switched service. With Frame Relay, most people just call the protocol *Frame Relay*, but the literal name is *Link Access Procedure Frame (LAPF)*. Among other details, LAPF defines a header and trailer, as shown in Figure 7-49. The header includes an LAPF address, called the *data-link connection identifier (DLCI)*.

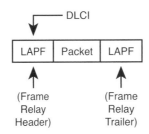

For this book's purposes, ignore the details of the LAPF header and trailer other than the DLCI. The LAPF header has one DLCI field, and that one DLCI field identifies the PVC. When a router sends a Frame Relay frame, the router encapsulates the IP packet inside an LAPF header and trailer. The router sets the DLCI to the number representing the PVC connected to the router that needs to receive the IP packet.

To piece the Frame Relay forwarding logic together with the DLCI concept, look at the example shown in Figure 7-50. The figure shows four routers. A central site Router R1, with a partial mesh of PVCs, connects with a PVC to each of the three remote routers on the right (R2, R3, and R4). The figure shows three DLCI values, each uniquely identifying the Frame Relay PVC.

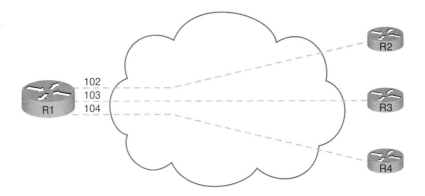

Continuing the example, R1 receives an IP packet from a LAN on the left (not shown) and decides to forward the IP packet to Router R2 next. (Chapter 8, "The Internet Protocol (IP)," discusses the IP forwarding logic in detail.) Figure 7-51 picks up the story at this point, with the focus on what happens in the Frame Relay network. Note that in this case, the figure shows some Frame Relay switches, just to provide a specific example.

> **ON THE SIDE:** Frame Relay DLCI values range from decimal 0 through 1023, with several of the low and high end of that range reserved for special purposes. The Frame Relay provider assigns the DLCI values.

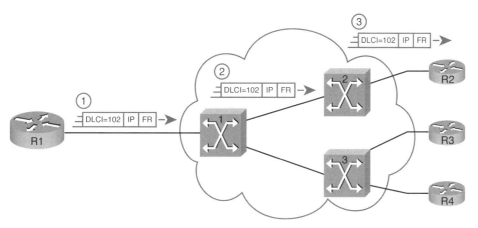

FIGURE 7-51

Example: Frame Relay Frame with DLCI 102 (R2)

Following the steps in the figure:

1. R1 encapsulates the IP packet into an LAPF frame, with DLCI = 102, which identifies this frame as being sent on the PVC connected to R2.

2. Frame Relay Switch 1 sees the frame, with DLCI 102. The switch has a table that tells it "If you get frames in this access link, with DLCI 102, send them to Switch 2." So, Switch 1 forwards the frame to Switch 2.

3. Frame Relay Switch 2 sees the incoming frame, with DLCI 102. Switch 2 has a table that tells it where to forward the frame, so Switch 2 sends it out the access link connected to Router R2.

Summary of Packet-Switching Services and Beyond

Frame Relay happened to emerge in the market in the early 1990s, at a time when DS0, fractional T1, and T1 lines were affordable; T3 lines tended to be noticeably more expensive at that time. Frame Relay became incredibly popular in the 1990s, and that continued into the 2000s, with most customers using DS0, DS1, and some DS3 access links.

Over time, the next major increase in WAN speeds came with the introduction of Synchronous Optical Network (SONET) technology in the 1990s. As briefly introduced back in Chapter 4's section, "Fiber Optics in the WAN," SONET defined a series of Layer 1 standards for much faster speeds using optical cabling. Note that the slowest of these speeds, OC-1, begins just a little faster than the T3 speeds discussed earlier in this chapter. Table 7-5 repeats the SONET speeds for reference.

TABLE 7-5

SONET Optical Carrier (OC) Names and (Rounded) Line Speeds

Name	(Rounded) Line Speed (Mbps)
OC-1	52
OC-3	155
OC-12	622
OC-24	1244
OC-48	2488
OC-96	4976
OC-192	9952

Also in the 1990s, another packet-switching technology came to the market—*Asynchronous Transfer Mode (ATM)*. As a WAN technology, ATM provided the same kinds of packet-switching benefits as Frame Relay, using the same concepts of access links and PVCs. However, ATM made a more natural fit with the new, faster SONET links. As the 1990s progressed, Frame Relay providers started offering ATM services, which were more popular when the customer needed much faster speeds. The service providers also offered packet-switching services that combined Frame Relay and ATM into a hybrid Frame Relay/ATM service.

The next big transition for WAN services, after ATM and SONET, happened with the introduction of multiprotocol label switching (MPLS). MPLS grew out of the TCP/IP community, using routers, the IP protocol, and quite a bit of its logic based on IP. MPLS could also use pretty much any physical and data link layer technology to forward the bits, including TDM links (T1, T3) SONET, or even Frame Relay and ATM. As a result, many WAN providers moved away from Frame Relay and ATM as WAN services, replacing those services with MPLS services in the 2000s.

The last big WAN movement mentioned in this chapter relates to Ethernet, and specifically, *Metro Ethernet (MetroE)*. In comparison, MPLS technology took some useful established technologies (IP and IP routers) and turned them into useful tools to create a great WAN service. Metro Ethernet does the same thing, taking Ethernet and Ethernet switching technology and turning them into a great WAN service as well. MetroE uses a physical Ethernet link as the WAN link between the customer and the service provider. The speeds run at those same speeds you read about back in Chapter 5 (under the heading "Ethernet Bit Rates (Speeds)") and the links often connect to LAN switches.

Going forward, MPLS and Metro Ethernet have the lead for private WAN services today. However, many options exist, including the fact that companies can use the Internet as a kind of WAN service. Chapter 9, "The Internet," which focuses on the Internet as an end to itself, discusses those options.

Figure 7-52 closes this summary by listing a timeline for the WAN technologies mentioned in this chapter. Note that the dates are general and meant to give you a way to compare some of the technologies. For all of these, there is no one useful date to remember, because it takes time, sometimes decades, to move from the research phase to having a useful operational service. However, the figure should give you a place to compare the wide range of WAN offerings over the years.

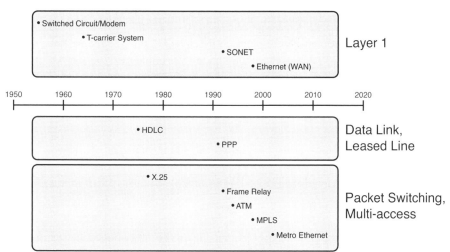

FIGURE 7-52

Comparison Timeline of WAN Technologies Mentioned in This Chapter

Chapter Summary

Wide-area networks (WAN) have a long history dating back to the early days of computing. Interestingly, WAN services have continued to progress over the years since the first analog modems in the 1950s allowed computers to send data over telco networks. Since that time, telcos have offered many WAN services, including digital circuits called leased lines and packet-switching services of several types.

In modern networks, whatever the WAN service, routers typically connect to both the WAN and LAN. The router takes IP packets off the LAN and forwards them over the WAN. Modern WANs also use several topologies, with routers sitting at the edges of the topology. The most common topologies include point-to-point, as with a leased line; hub-and-spoke, with leased lines connected to a central site; and multipoint, in which more than two devices can communicate directly, as with packet-switching services.

Leased lines can connect two routers over very long distances. Physically, the leased line uses 2-pair copper cabling that runs into the customer building on each end of the link. Each customer site needs a router, with a serial interface card and either an internal or external CSU/DSU. Inside the telco, the line connects to a switch that supports the T-carrier line types (DS0, DS1, and DS3); the rest of the telco network can use whatever technology the telco wants to use.

The T-carrier system breaks the DS1 and DS3 lines down from their simple serial bit rates into a series of physical layer frames and channels. DS3s contain 28 DS1 channels, and DS1s contain 24 DS0 channels. These channels allow the telco to offer leased-line rates at different speeds, other than the literal speeds of the DS0, DS1, and DS3 lines. Those different speeds just need to match a number of channels to use in one of these lines. To make the speeds and channels work, the customer CSU/DSU, along with the CO in the switch, must use the same channels.

Frame Relay acts as a packet-switching service. Routers connect to the Frame Relay service using a physical access link. The customer decides which pairs of routers need to send Frame Relay frames directly to each other, and orders a PVC for each pair. After the PVCs are installed, the routers can send Frame Relay frames that list the correct PVC address, called a DLCI, into the Frame Relay service. The Frame Relay switches then forward the frame over the correct logical PVC to the correct destination router.

Chapter Review Activities

Use the features in this section to study and review the topics in this chapter.

Answer These Questions

1. A user of a home telephone picks up her phone and makes a telephone call to a friend's home telephone in another part of town. Which of the following is likely to be true about this call?

   a. It uses a single pair of wires on the local loop at each end of the call.

   b. It uses a telco service called packet switching.

   c. It uses digital circuits at least on the part of the call from the CO to the phone that made the phone call.

   d. None of the answers is correct.

2. Which of the following are services that telcos have offered as WAN services over the years? (Choose two answers.)

   a. Switched analog circuits

   b. Dedicated digital circuits

   c. Partition switching

   d. Telekinetic-division multiplexing

3. This chapter claims that IP routers work well as devices that connect to many different types of interfaces, including LANs and WANs. Which of the following answers list the reasons why routers do well in this role? (Choose two answers.)

   a. Routers have much faster CPUs and can do the hard work to translate the incoming data-link header into the outgoing data-link header format.

   b. Router vendors sell many different types of physical interface cards, so the routers have the right physical connectors to connect to different types of networks.

   c. Routers use Layer 3 and ignore Layers 1 and 2.

   d. Routers discard old data-link headers and insert new data-link headers as part of their logic, which treats each interface's lower-layer details as independent from each other.

4. An enterprise network has many routers that connect to both a LAN as well as the WAN. Which one of the following statements best describes how routers typically use and think about their WAN connections?

   a. As a destination where end-user hosts reside

   b. As a transport service to deliver IP packets to the next IP router

   c. As nothing, because routers ignore Layers 1 and 2

   d. As an interesting and complex technology-filled network of its own, with such features as circuit switching, packet switching, SONET, ATM, and others

5. An enterprise builds a WAN design on paper. The main site, where all the servers sit, is shown in the center of a network diagram. The WAN has a leased line from that site to every remote site, with the remote sites drawn around the edges of the drawing in a big circle. None of the remote sites have a leased line directly between them. Which of the following terms is most typically used to describe this WAN topology?

     a. Multipoint

     b. Star

     c. Point-to-point

     d. Hub-and-spoke

6. A U.S.-based company wants to order a leased line between two sites, with the leased line using the traditional T-carrier DS0, DS1, and DS3 types of lines. Which of the following answers describe the available speeds and distances for the leased line? (Choose two answers.)

     a. No longer than 62 miles (100 kilometers) for up to T1 speed

     b. No faster than 43.736 Mbps (T3)

     c. 64 Kbps, 1.544 Mbps, and any speed in between

     d. No literal distance limitation

7. A telco customer has purchased a T1 leased line between two sites. The customer has already bought a router for one site, with a serial interface card with a built-in CSU/DSU. Which of the following answers lists other physical parts that the customer will need for that site's installation of the T1 leased line?

     a. A patch cable with RJ-48 connectors

     b. A serial cable

     c. An external CSU/DSU

     d. A demarc

8. A telco customer has a T1 leased line between two sites, called sites A and B. The telco has several switches between sites A and B that use T3 trunks. These switches use the T3 trunks along with time-division multiplexing (TDM) to create the leased line from site A to B. Which of the following answers is true about how TDM works in this design?

     a. The switches map the T1 customer lines to a T1 channel inside the T3 trunks.

     b. The switches interpret the customer bits as packets and forward the packets to the correct destination over the T3 trunks.

     c. The switches map the T1 customer lines to one of 28 different frequencies in the T3 trunks.

     d. The switches perform a digital-to-analog (D/A) conversion and send the bits over a unique analog frequency over the T3 trunks.

9. A telco network has TDM switches in the CO, ready to support T1 leased lines to customer sites. Two such switches have a single T3 trunk connecting the two switches, set aside to support T1s that run just between those two CO switches. Which of the following answers best describes the number of customer T1s the telco can support with these switches and the trunk?

   a. 20

   b. 24

   c. 28

   d. No exact number; it depends on how much time the customer T1s sit idle.

10. A customer ordered a full T1 leased line between two sites. The telco implemented that leased line in its network using the T-carrier technology discussed in this chapter, with DS1 and DS3 lines plus switches that use time-division multiplexing (TDM) logic. Into which of the following general WAN categories does this service fit?

   a. Ethernet switching

   b. Packet switching

   c. Label switching

   d. Circuit switching

11. A telco customer orders a leased line between sites A and B, with a requested speed of 1.024 Mbps. The customer plans to use an external CSU/DSU at each site. The telco uses only T-carrier technology and none of the more modern options like SONET, ATM, MPLS, or Metro Ethernet. Which of the following answers is true about the speeds used on this link?

   a. The physical line between the telco CO and site A uses a line speed of 1.024 Mbps + 8 Kbps for overhead.

   b. The physical line between the telco CO and site B uses a line speed of 1.544 Mbps.

   c. The telco rejects the request for the leased line because it is an unsupported speed.

   d. The CSU/DSU at site A uses a bit rate of 1.024 Mbps when sending data over the line toward the telco CO.

12. A telco customer orders a leased line between sites A and B, with a requested speed of 512 Kbps. The customer plans to use an external CSU/DSU at each site. The telco uses only T-carrier technology and none of the more modern options like SONET, ATM, MPLS, or Metro Ethernet. Which of the following answers is true about the speeds used between the router and the CSU/DSU?

   a. The CSU/DSU controls the router's sending and receiving speeds using clocking.

   b. The bit rate over the serial cable is 1.536 Mbps (T1 speed minus 8 Kbps overhead).

   c. There is no bit rate, because the telco rejects the order because of the speed not matching any of the T-carrier line speeds.

   d. The CSU/DSU and router are peers with regard to clocking, each sending at the speeds configured on each device, with the receiving device being slaved to the sending device's clocking.

13. Which of the following answers are true about DS1 framing and channels? (Choose two answers.)

    a. Each frame has 193 bits.

    b. The frame holds 24 bits, one per channel, plus overhead.

    c. The frame groups 8 bits together for each of 24 channels, plus overhead.

    d. If the customer ordered a leased line that ran at 768 Kbps (about half the T1 line rate) the number of frames per second would be about 4000.

14. Which of the following data-link protocols was created to be used on leased lines, with support for multiple Layer 3 protocols by including a Type field that identifies the type of packet inside the data-link frame?

    a. HDLC

    b. LAPF

    c. PPP

    d. SDLC

15. Which fields that exist in both the HDLC and PPP headers have such relatively small use in point-to-point leased lines today, to the point that the PPP standard actually allows the nodes to simply not bother to include these fields when sending PPP frames? (Choose two answers.)

    a. Flag

    b. Address

    c. Control

    d. FCS

16. Think about the differences in circuit switching using the T-carrier system (ignoring analog circuit switching) versus packet switching. Which of the following answers are true about packet switching, but not about circuit switching? (Choose two answers.)

    a. The telco physical links are digital circuits.

    b. The telco switch can queue the data waiting on the congested outgoing trunk to become available.

    c. The trunks between switches fit the bits into logical time channels on the trunk.

    d. The switches look at the bits to find an address, and use that address to make a choice of where to send the bits.

17. In a Frame Relay network, which of the following terms refers to the customer router that connects to the Frame Relay network?

    a. DCE

    b. POP

    c. DTE

    d. Access link

18. Which of the following answers is *not* true about a Frame Relay PVC?

   a. Identified by the LAPF header DLCI field

   b. Defined by the telco ahead of time, when the customer orders the service

   c. Must exist between two routers before the routers can send Frame Relay frames directly to each other

   d. Triggers the telco to create a telco leased circuit to support each corresponding PVC

19. A new Frame Relay customer is considering two competing Frame Relay designs for his WAN. One design uses a full-mesh topology of PVCs between the 20 routers. The second design uses a partial mesh that looks like a hub-and-spoke design. Assuming that all other technical details not mentioned in this question are the same when comparing the two designs, which of these answers are true about the partial-mesh design, but not true about the full-mesh design? (Choose two answers.)

   a. Not all routers can send a Frame Relay frame directly to each other.

   b. Frame Relay frames will be forwarded by the network based on the DLCI field in the Frame Relay header.

   c. The price should be lower.

   d. Users at spoke sites will not be able to send emails to each other.

20. Which two of the following WAN services make good use of protocols that enterprises have used for many years, with those protocols being expanded and enhanced to create new types of WAN services? (Choose two answers.)

   a. ATM

   b. MPLS

   c. Metro Ethernet

   d. PPP

Define the Key Terms

The following key terms include the ideas most important to the big ideas in this chapter. To review, without looking at the book or your notes, write a definition for each term, focusing on the meaning, not the wording. Then review your definition compared to your notes, this chapter, and the glossary.

Key Terms for Chapter 7

switched circuit	leased line	DS0
dedicated circuit	time-division multiplexing	DS1
circuit switching		Frame Relay
packet switching	T-carrier system	

List the Words Inside Acronyms

The following are the most common acronyms discussed in this chapter. As a way to review those terms, simply write down the words that each letter represents in each acronym.

Acronyms for Chapter 7

ATM	DTE	PTT
CO	ESS	PVC
DCE	FRF	SONET
demarc	HDLC	T1
DLCI	MetroE	T3
DS0	MPLS	TDM
DS1	POP	telco
DS3	PPP	WAN

Create Mind Maps

For this chapter, create two different mind maps. As usual, focus on using single words or short phrases, and do not try to leave longer notes.

Create a mind map for the T-carrier system. Include the three lines of the T-carrier system mentioned in this chapter, plus any concepts and terms that apply to each.

Create a mind map for Frame Relay. Mentally focus on all terms, but also try and organize these terms into categories inside the map.

Define Other Terms

Define the following additional terms from this chapter, and check your answers in the glossary:

Bell Operating Company	DTE	multiplex
channel	fractional T1	multipoint
circuit switch	Frame Relay Forum	multiprotocol label switching
data-link connection identifier	full mesh	packet switch
DCE	HDLC	partial mesh
demarc	hub-and-spoke	permanent virtual circuit
demultiplex	interface	point of presence
DS0	local loop	point-to-point
DS1	Metro Ethernet	PPP
DS3	modem	RJ-48
	multiaccess	

signaling	time channel	data-link connection
SONET	trunks	identifier
T1	virtual circuit	
T3	serial interface	

Complete the Tables and Lists from Memory

Print a copy of Appendix B, "Memory Tables" (which you can find online at www.pearsonitcertification.com/title/9780789748454), or at least the section for this chapter, and complete the tables and lists from memory. Appendix C, "Memory Tables Answer Key," also online, includes completed tables and lists to check your work.

Chapter | 8

The Internet Protocol (IP)

Chapter 3, "TCP/IP Networks," introduced the Internet Protocol (IP), as well as the rest of the major functions of a TCP/IP network. Chapter 3 introduced IP, and the TCP/IP model as a whole, to tell you about the major concepts of how a TCP/IP network delivers data from the sending device to the receiving device. Following Chapter 3, Chapters 4–7 then focused on the lower two layers of the five-layer TCP/IP model: the layers that create LANs and WANs.

This chapter moves the focus back to the topic of how TCP/IP networks deliver data from the sending device to the receiving device. The chapter begins that discussion by looking at the fundamentals of the TCP/IP network (Internet) layer, including the Internet Protocol (IP). This chapter also keeps the discussions in the context of a single corporate network. Chapter 9, "The Internet," continues the focus on how the TCP/IP network layer delivers data from end to end through a network, but in the context of the worldwide TCP/IP network called the Internet.

This chapter separates topics into four major sections:

■ The first section, "Introducing the Internet Protocol (IP)," introduces the functions at the TCP/IP network layer, both those defined by IP itself plus a few other related Layer 3 protocols.

■ The second section, "IP Addressing on User LANs," examines IP addresses. However, because IP addresses can be a difficult topic to learn the first time, this section limits the discussion to IP addressing from the user device perspective, specifically user devices connected to Ethernet and wireless LANs.

■ The third section, "IP Routing with Focus on Layer 3 Only," discusses IP routing, which defines how to deliver IP packets from end to end through a TCP/IP network. This section keeps the focus on Layer 3 rules, mostly ignoring the underlying LANs and WANs.

■ The last section, "IP Routing with Layer 1, 2, and 3 Interactions," also looks at IP routing, but focuses on how IP routing uses the LANs and WANs.

Chapter Outline

Objectives

- Describe the main functions of the TCP/IP network layer in regard to its focus on either physical or logical functions, and the focus on the network or endpoint hosts.

- List three major functions defined by IP.

- List common TCP/IP network layer functions in addition to IP.

- Examine a figure of an enterprise TCP/IP network and determine where IP address groups (IP networks or subnets) would be needed.

- Look at any IP version 4 address and determine its class, and if it is a unicast IP address, determine the class A, B, or C network ID of the network in which it resides.

- List the four IP settings typically set on IP hosts during static configuration.

- Describe the Layer 3 logic used by routers when routing IP packets.

- Describe an IP host's Layer 3 logic when routing IP packets.

- Explain the basic ideas of how the IP subnetting process subdivides a classful network into smaller groups.

- Predict the MAC and IP addresses used by two hosts on the same LAN subnet when they send IP packets to each other.

- Predict the MAC and IP addresses used throughout an IP packet's journey from a host in one subnet to a host in another subnet.

Key Terms

IP router

IP address

routing table

IP network

Dynamic Host Configuration Protocol

IP routing

IP route

IP subnetting

default router

Address Resolution Protocol

8

Introducing the Internet Protocol (IP)

The world of computer networking has used many networking models over the years, with the TCP/IP model being the most commonly used model today. As with any networking model, you can view each layer as providing services or as needing services. Each layer needs the services of the layer below it, and each layer provides services to the layer above it. The Internet Protocol (IP) sits in the middle of the five-layer TCP/IP model, so it both provides services to the layers above it and receives services from the layers below it.

AUTHOR'S NOTE:
As a reminder, the TCP/IP Internet layer is more commonly referenced as the network layer, using OSI terminology.

This first of four major sections looks at IP, and the TCP/IP network layer as a whole, using the entire TCP/IP model for perspective. The following sections begin by looking at the role of IP and the TCP/IP network layer in comparison to the other layers of the TCP/IP model. Then, these sections discuss the IP standard itself, along with three of its most fundamental functions: connecting LANs and WANs, addressing, and routing. Finally, these sections introduce other network layer protocols that help IP do its work.

IP and the TCP/IP Model

The next topic begins the introduction to IP by looking at IP in the context of the TCP/IP model and TCP/IP standards. First, this topic looks at the TCP/IP model as a whole, comparing the role of the TCP/IP network layer to the roles of other layers. Following that, the text introduces the specific TCP/IP standards for IP and other important TCP/IP network layer protocols.

Comparing the Roles of Different TCP/IP Layers

Almost every new term, standard, protocol, address, and idea discussed in any detail in Chapters 4 through 7 related to some physical layer or data link layer feature. Just as a brief reminder of a few of those, Figure 8-1 shows the five-layer TCP/IP model, with just a small number of those Layer 1 and 2 standards listed with their respective layers.

FIGURE 8-1

Example LAN/WAN Standards and Types in the TCP/IP Model

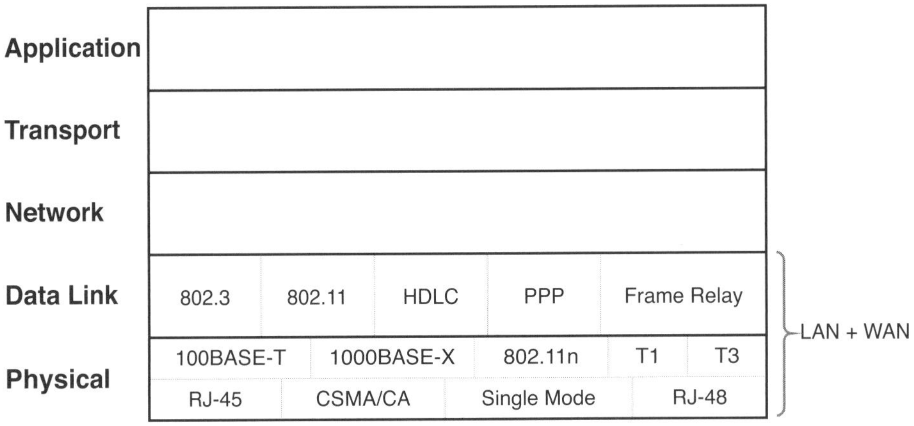

AUTHOR'S NOTE: As a reminder, TCP/IP uses the same names for its layers in the five-layer model as does the seven-layer OSI model, with one exception. TCP/IP's *Internet* layer matches the functions of OSI's *network* layer, and by convention, the networking world uses the OSI layer terms.

The lower two layers both focus on moving bits over a particular type of physical network. The physical layer standards obviously focus on the physical details. The data link layer defines the rules for how to move data over a particular type or family of physical standards. Simply put, TCP/IP Layers 1 and 2 focus on how to move data over a particular type of LAN or WAN.

In contrast to the focus on physical networking functions in the lower layers, the TCP/IP model's three upper layers define the nonphysical parts of the work, called *logical networking functions*. The left side of Figure 8-2 shows this physical versus logical perspective.

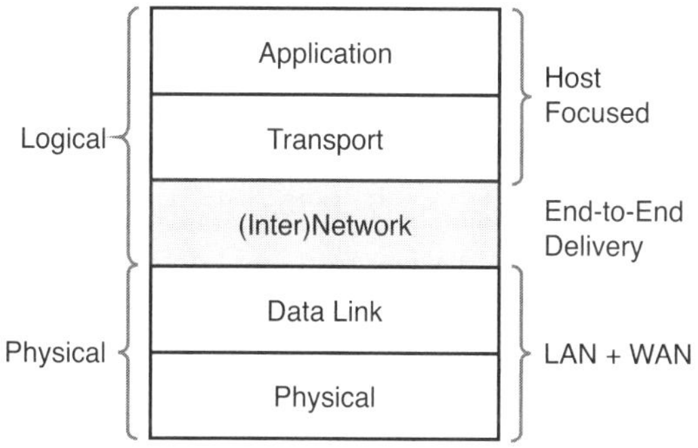

ON THE SIDE: The word *logical* in this case simply means *not physical*; it does not mean that some parts of TCP/IP are somehow illogical.

FIGURE 8-2

Various Perspectives on the TCP/IP Model and Roles

The right side of Figure 8-2 points out yet another perspective on the roles of the TCP/IP layers. The two uppermost layers, the application and transport layers, focus on the hosts (devices) that create, send, and process received data. In fact, all those IP routers that sit inside the TCP/IP network, between the hosts, ignore these upper two layers when forwarding IP packets between two hosts. In short, the two upper layers focus on the TCP/IP hosts—any end-user device, servers, or any other device that creates the data that needs to be sent through the TCP/IP network.

The TCP/IP network layer completes functions in a TCP/IP network by defining how to forward packets between any two hosts. The TCP/IP model's network layer includes the IP protocol. IP defines several important functions, including the idea of how to route (forward) data between any two devices that connect to the TCP/IP network.

To finish the comparison of roles as listed on the right side of Figure 8-2, the TCP/IP network layer delivers data from end to end through the network. The network layer provides this service to the upper TCP/IP layers, which focus on the work done on those endpoint hosts. And to meet its goals, the TCP/IP network layer must use various LANs and WANs, which create the physical networks that can forward bits.

The TCP/IP Network Layer

IP is the most important protocol defined by the TCP/IP network layer. IP plays a huge role in TCP/IP networks, which is not surprising, given that the name TCP/IP comes from two of TCP/IP's most important protocols—TCP and IP. Almost every computing device on the planet communicates in some way, and most of those use IP. Those devices might support only one type of LAN or WAN, or support only a few application protocols, but to be part of a TCP/IP network, the device needs to support IP.

Even though IP plays a huge role, the TCP/IP network layer also defines other protocols as well. You do not get to pick between using IP or using some alternative to IP; you always use IP to build a TCP/IP network. At the same time, some other TCP/IP network layer protocols help IP in some way by defining additional details not included in IP. Table 8-1 lists some of those protocols for reference; this chapter discusses most of these further.

TABLE 8-1

Other TCP/IP Network Layer Protocols

Short Name	Full Name	Comments
ICMP	Internet Control Message Protocol	Messages that hosts and routers use to manage and control the packet-forwarding process; used by the **ping** command.
ARP	Address Resolution Protocol	Used by LAN hosts to dynamically learn another LAN host's MAC address.
DHCP	Dynamic Host Configuration Protocol	Used by a host to dynamically learn an IP address (and other information) it can use.
DNS	Domain Name System	A protocol by which user hosts can use names, with a DNS server translating the name into a corresponding IP address, which is needed by the IP routing process.
RIP	Routing Information Protocol	An application that runs on routers so that routers dynamically learn IP routing tables, needed so that they can route IP packets correctly. An open routing protocol, defined in an RFC.
EIGRP	Enhanced Interior Gateway Routing Protocol	A proprietary routing protocol whose rights are owned by Cisco Systems.
OSPF	Open Shortest Path First	An open routing protocol, defined in an RFC.

ON THE SIDE: A great place to find RFCs is the RFC Editor website, www.rfc-editor.org.

IP exists as a standard, but because of its popularity and age, you can find a huge number of references explaining how IP works. First, IP exists as an Internet standard protocol, as defined in RFC 791. That RFC defines version 4 of the IP protocol, also called IPv4, although most people just refer to it as IP. Anyone can search the Internet, find the RFC, and read it to learn more about IP. You can also learn about IP by reading many different books (this book included), many websites, and documentation from many vendors.

Although the IPv4 RFC reached standard status back in 1980, IP's timeline stretches back to the 1970s. TCP/IP began its life as the result of research projects funded by the U.S. government, mainly the U.S. Department of Defense (DoD) through a group called the Advanced Research Projects Agency (ARPA). As you might guess from the version name, IP version 4 was part of a longer history of earlier versions of the protocol. These earlier protocols were used in the very early stages of the predecessor of the Internet, called ARPANET (the ARPA network). The core of IPv4 still works very well today, as proven by the fact that billions of people use it every day.

Although IPv4 has worked very well for many years, IP version 6 (IPv6) will eventually replace IPv4. IPv6 defines many of the same functions as does IPv4, with improvements in the details of how IPv6 implements those features. For example, IPv4 uses a 32-bit IP address, for a theoretical total of around 4 billion (4×10^9) IPv4 addresses. Interestingly enough, the world needs more IP addresses than IPv4 can supply, so IPv6 helps avoid the address crunch, using a 128-bit address, for a theoretical total of over 10^{38} addresses. This is just one example of one of the benefits of IPv4's replacement, IPv6.

> **ON THE SIDE:** IPv6 also exists as TCP/IP standards, in various RFCs, including RFC 2460.

Interestingly, the migration to IPv6 has already taken over a decade, and will likely take longer. Those of you using this book as part of your college curriculum will likely see the day when most computers use IPv6 instead of IPv4. However, the migration has been slow. IPv6 was defined back in the mid-1990s, and still today, far more end-user computers use IPv4 than IPv6. Figure 8-3 shows the timeline of IPv4 and IPv6 progress through history, with the date for IPv6 finally being a common mainstream protocol still out in the future.

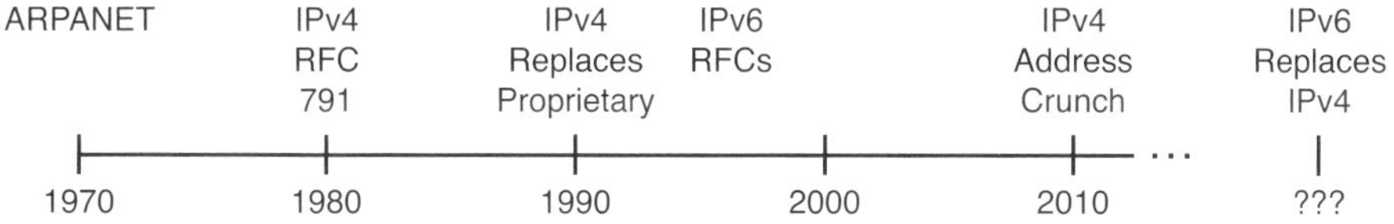

ARPANET	IPv4 RFC 791	IPv4 Replaces Proprietary	IPv6 RFCs	IPv4 Address Crunch	IPv6 Replaces IPv4
1970	1980	1990	2000	2010 ...	???

FIGURE 8-3

IPv4 Versus IPv6 Timeline

The rest of this first of four major sections of this chapter examines the TCP/IP network layer, looking at both IP and the other network layer protocols that help IP.

Functions of the IP Protocol

IP defines many functions that work together, with one ultimate goal—sending data from one IP host to another IP host through any TCP/IP network. Three IP functions stand out as the most important of those functions:

> **AUTHOR'S NOTE:** While IPv6 is an interesting topic, this book focuses on IPv4. When the text mentions *IP*, it refers to IPv4.

- Creating end-to-end physical paths through the TCP/IP network by interconnecting physical networks (LANs and WANs) using IP routers

- Identifying both the individual hosts, and groups of hosts, using IP addressing

- Routing (forwarding) IP packets to the right destination host based on the destination IP address

The next several pages discuss these three main functions of IP, but first, the next topic compares IP to something more familiar—the postal service.

IP and Analogy with the Postal Service

You write a letter, follow the rules, and put it in a post office drop box somewhere. Almost magically, the letter arrives at the correct destination, at least most of the time. The same thing happens with an IP host that sends an IP packet. This short topic makes more comparisons between the postal service and IP.

First, think about how the postal service physically moves its letters. Before the users can send letters, the postal service buys or leases many vehicles. It hires workers to operate the vehicles. It chooses where each and every vehicle should go and not go. It uses small trucks with the postal worker driving around neighborhoods, putting the mail into mailboxes next to the road. For densely packed places, like apartments and cities, the postal worker might park the truck and walk around to deliver the mail in a few buildings. The postal service also has planes that fly mail long distances, boats that move large volumes of mail (but much more slowly), and larger trucks to deliver mail between major cities.

The postal service must also plan the routes where the vehicles go. For example, if the post office has lots of trucks to drive around your town delivering mail, but it forgets to route a truck by your house or apartment every day, you will not get your mail. If it forgets to schedule a big truck to drive mail from one city to the next, for further distribution at that point, the postal service cannot meet its goal of delivering mail to all destinations.

So, how does that relate to IP? First, IP uses LANs and WANs like the postal service uses trucks, planes, and boats—to move things. IP defines the idea of a device called a router, which connects to LANs and WANs, relying on the LANs and WANs to physically move the IP packets throughout the TCP/IP network. And just like the postal service plans which vehicles take which mail delivery routes, IP defines the concept of routing IP packets, with the routers deciding which paths through the TCP/IP network, called *routes*, that each IP packet will take.

Moving back to the postal service again for a moment, the postal service requires letters to have a mailing address. First, the postal service had to define a standard for properly formatted postal mailing addresses. (Those standards vary from country to country.) To make the system work, the postal service has to make sure that every possible destination (house, apartment, and so on) has a unique address. If multiple locations use the same address, the postal workers would misdeliver some of the letters. And, the postal service had to train its workers, and even train the entire populace, to know how to address letters.

IP has the same general goal and same general purpose for IP addresses. IP requires each host that needs to receive IP packets to have a unique IP address. The IP RFC defines the format of those IP addresses.

The final postal service feature, called *sorting* in the postal service, defines how the postal service chooses where to send each letter next. For one letter, you can guess the general idea—someone (or some machine) looks at the address on the envelope. The person or machine decides on which small truck/large truck/plane to put the letter for the next leg of its trip. The logic: Look at the destination address, compare it to a list of possible outgoing vehicles leaving the building today, and put the letter on that vehicle.

For example, Figure 8-4 shows a person in the middle of the USA (in Ohio) sending a letter to someone in Hollywood, California (on the West Coast). The post office in Ohio has three options for where to send the letter today: a truck going to a post office in New York (on the East Cost), another truck going to Hollywood, and a plane flying to Hollywood as well. The postal sorting machine in Ohio, in the middle of the country, looks at the address, makes a sorting choice, and forwards the letter over route 1 to Hollywood using the plane.

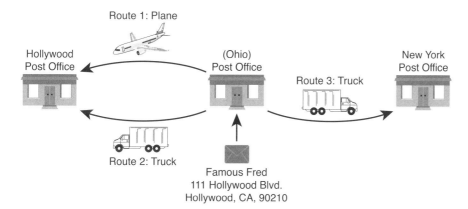

FIGURE 8-4

Example of a Post Office Sorting a Letter Sent to Hollywood, California

Figure 8-4 shows a single sorting choice at a single post office, but the entire postal system only works if the post office sites work together. One post office sorts the letter and delivers it to the next post office. That second post office does the same thing: sorts the letter and sends it to the next post office. The process continues at every post office until the last post office delivers the letter to the final destination.

IP routing works with the same overall logic and flow. A router looks at a packet's destination IP address and makes a choice of which LAN or WAN out which to forward the IP packet. As an entire IP network of multiple routers, the routers forward the packet from one router, to the next, to the next, until the last router forwards the IP packet to the destination host.

Now on with the specifics of IP.

Interconnecting Networks (LANs and WANs)

IP defines the jobs of an **IP router**, including the job to create an interconnected system of networks. In simple terms, routers use physical *interfaces* to connect to physical LANs and WANs. In fact, the word *Internet* actually comes from this idea of *interconnected networks*.

> **ON THE SIDE:** Note that the IP RFC uses the term *gateway* instead of *router*, but the industry as a whole uses the term *router* instead today.

To interconnect LANs and WANs, routers use physical connectors called *interfaces*. Figure 8-5 shows a few photos of a class of IP router commonly used in enterprise remote branch offices today. This particular model, from Cisco Systems, has two built-in Fast Ethernet interfaces with RJ-45 connectors. It also has two slots for removable small cards into which WAN interfaces can be installed.

FIGURE 8-5

Enterprise-Class Router, LAN Interfaces, and WAN Interfaces

Cisco Systems 1841 Router

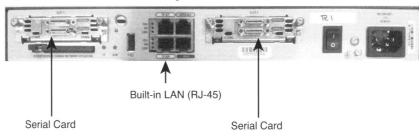

Built-in LAN (RJ-45)

Serial Card   Serial Card

When discussing IP routers, some documentation might require the details shown in Figure 8-5, but other documentation might require a lot less detail. For example, it might be important to know that a router connects to an Ethernet LAN and a leased line, but the specific interface card, connector type, and router model might not matter.

For example, Figure 8-6 shows a figure that omits specific details about router interfaces, but it implies quite a bit. The drawing implies LAN cabling on the left and right. It also shows a line with a jagged edge in the middle, which, by convention, means that the line represents a leased line. But it does not list the physical interface cards used by the routers, and it does not identify those cards by name or number.

FIGURE 8-6

Logical View of Interconnected LANs and WANs: Some LAN/ WAN Detail

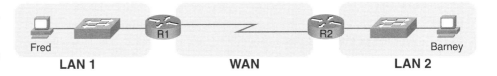

Fred   Barney

LAN 1   **WAN**   **LAN 2**

In some cases, the discussion might not even need to look at any details about the LANs and WANs. For example, when discussing the end-to-end path through a TCP/IP network, the logic might get no deeper than "use this LAN to reach Router X and this WAN to reach Router Y." For those discussions, any figures can hide all the LAN and WAN details, as in the example shown in Figure 8-7.

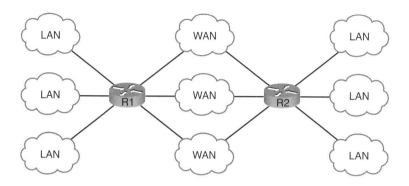

FIGURE 8-7

Interconnected LANs and WANs: Redundancy, But No LAN/WAN Detail

Identifying Hosts with 32-Bit IP Addresses

In addition to defining IP routers, the IP standard defines the details of IP addresses.

First and foremost, an **IP address** acts as a number to uniquely identify a host inside a TCP/IP network. Every device that wants to communicate inside a TCP/IP network must have an IP address, and the devices use that IP address when sending and receiving IP packets, much like we use mailing addresses to send letters through the postal service.

IP addresses exist both in binary and decimal form, with computers typically just using and storing the binary version. When IP hosts send data, they send IP packets, which begin with an IP header. The IP header holds both the source and destination IP addresses (binary) for the packet. Figure 8-8 shows the overall format of the 20-byte IP header for reference (note that this chapter ignores the rest of the IP header fields except for the source and destination IP addresses).

← 4 Bytes →			
Version	Header Length	DS Field	Packet Length
Identification		Flags (3 Bits)	Fragment Offset (13 Bits)
Time to Live		Protocol	Header Checksum
Source IP Address			
Destination IP Address			

FIGURE 8-8

IPv4 Header Format and Fields

AUTHOR'S NOTE:
The figure does not have space to show the entire 20-byte IP header from left to right. Instead, it shows 4 bytes per row, with five rows.

Most IP addresses act as *unicast IP addresses*, meaning that the IP address represents a single host. Each host must also know its own unicast IP address. To send a packet to another host, the sending host must know the other host's unicast IP address as well. (The upcoming section, "IP Addressing on User LANs," discusses how hosts know about their own IP addresses, and the upcoming section,

"Using Names That Correspond to IP Addresses," discusses how computers learn the IP addresses of the computers to which they want to send data.)

Although computers store IP addresses as binary numbers, humans typically work with IP addresses in *dotted-decimal notation (DDN)* format. To create an IP address in DDN format, based on the 32-bit binary IP address, you have to work through a conversion process, as follows:

1. Separate the 32 bits into four groups of 8.
2. Do the binary-to-decimal conversion of each 8-bit number; each decimal value will be between 0 and 255.
3. Put a period (dot) between each decimal number (hence the name *dotted-decimal*).

Figure 8-9 shows the same process in graphical form.

FIGURE 8-9

Generic View of Converting from a Binary IP Address to DDN Format

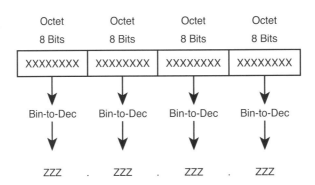

AUTHOR'S NOTE: IP actually calls each byte of the IP address an *octet* for historical reasons.

Next, just to show one example of the conversion process, imagine a computer whose IP address, in binary, is

    0000 1010   0000 0001   0000 0010   0000 0011

Figure 8-10 shows the conversion process again, with each of these specific bytes separated and converted into IP address 10.1.2.3.

FIGURE 8-10

Converting Binary IP Address to DDN 10.1.2.3

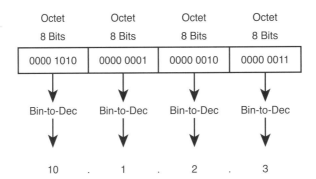

AUTHOR'S NOTE: If you do not know how to convert from binary to decimal numbers, just refer to Appendix A, "Numeric Reference Tables." This appendix lists a table of all 256 binary values for an 8-bit binary number and the decimal equivalent. You can just look up these four binary values and substitute the decimal values.

Routing IP Packets from Source to Destination Computer

As a brief review, IP defines how IP routers connect to LANs and WANs, resulting in physical end-to-end paths through a TCP/IP network. IP also defines IP addressing, which gives each and every device a unique number that identifies each device (each IP host) inside a TCP/IP network. With these first two functions of IP, the physical path exists between devices, and you can identify each device.

The third major function defined by IP, IP routing, defines how IP hosts and IP routers forward (route) IP packets through a TCP/IP network. The IP routing function relies heavily on the other two functions, using routers, the LANs and WANs connected to the routers, and the IP addresses that identify the hosts.

IP hosts play a small role with IP routing. When sending an IP packet, the host thinks about whether the destination address of the IP packet is on the same LAN as the sending host. If it is on the same LAN, the sender just sends the packet directly to the other host. If not, the sending host sends the IP packet to a router connected to the local LAN and lets the router deal with the question of where to send the IP packet next.

Compared to IP hosts, IP routers have much more IP routing work to do. The routers have the responsibility to know the locations of all the host IP addresses in the TCP/IP network. Each router must know, from its own perspective, how to forward IP packets so that the packets reach those destinations. Just like the postal service has to sort the mail, and put each letter on the right vehicle that will leave the post office sometime soon, a router must route each IP packet, meaning that the router must choose out which interface to forward each IP packet so that the packet reaches the right destination.

Interestingly, to fully understand IP routing, you have to think about IP addressing as well. IP addressing concepts help the IP routing process, by design.

The biggest help that IP addressing gives to IP routing is to group IP addresses. All IP addresses with the same value in the first parts of their addresses are considered to be in the same group of addresses. These addresses must be in the same location, for example, in the same LAN or in the same WAN. Figure 8-11 shows the idea, with three LANs and two WANs. The groups: all addresses that begin with 11, 12, 13, 14, or 15.

FIGURE 8-11

Example IP Address Groupings: All with the Same First Octet in the Same Group

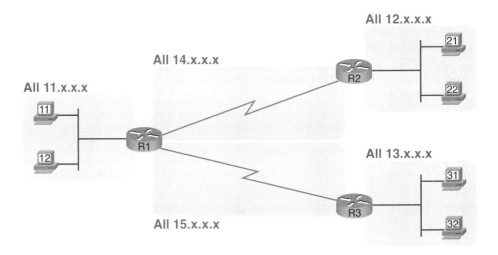

By requiring IP addresses be grouped in this way, IP routers can keep a shorter list of destinations in their routing tables. A router's **routing table** lists the possible destinations in the TCP/IP network, and the instructions about where to send the IP packet next so that it reaches that destination. If IP addressing did not group IP addresses together, each router would need a routing table entry for every single unicast IP address for every single IP host. With IP addresses in groups, each router can list one entry for the entire group. For example, keeping one routing table entry that means "all IP addresses that begin with 12" is much shorter than listing one entry for each of over 16,000,000 IP addresses that begin with 12.

Figure 8-12 shows an example of IP routing and IP routing tables, using the same address groupings shown in Figure 8-11. In this case, PC11, sitting on the LAN on the left of the figure, sends an IP packet to address 12.1.1.21, which sits in the LAN in the upper right of the figure.

Following the steps in the figure:

1. Host PC11, noticing that the destination is not on the same local LAN, sends the packet to the router on the same LAN as itself: R1.

2. R1 compares the IP packet's destination IP address (12.1.1.21) to R1's IP routing table, matching the entry for 12.x.x.x (which means "all addresses that begin with 12"). That routing table entry tells R1 to send the IP packet to R2 next.

3. R1 forwards the IP across the WAN from R1 to R2.

4. R2 compares the IP packet's destination IP address (12.1.1.21) to R2's IP routing table, matching its entry for 12.x.x.x. That routing table entry tells R2 to send the packet directly to PC21 over R2's LAN interface on the right.

5. R2 forwards the IP packet across the LAN from R2 to PC21.

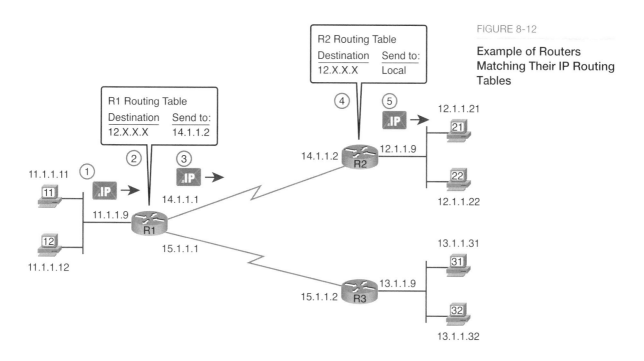

FIGURE 8-12

Example of Routers Matching Their IP Routing Tables

Other TCP/IP Layer 3 Functions

Besides the important functions of IP, the TCP/IP network layer needs to complete other tasks as well. The following sections introduce a few of those additional tasks and the protocols TCP/IP defines to help do those tasks.

Learning Routes with Routing Protocols

IP routers must have an IP routing table with useful routes for IP routing to work. For example, in Figure 8-12, R1 had a route for "all addresses that begin with 12," with instructions to forward those packets to Router R2 next. Without this route, Router R1 could not have forwarded the packet sent to host PC21.

Routers build their IP routing table in two ways: through *static configuration* or with *dynamic routing protocols*. Static configuration means that the network engineer remotely connects to the router's user interface and types in some commands to tell the router what to do, including the details of the routes to add to the IP routing table. The general process of making that remote connection, and typing commands to tell the router what to do, is called *configuration*. The term *static configuration* emphasizes the fact that the routes do not change, unless the engineer changes the configuration again. In this case, a network engineer could configure each router with the IP routes each router needs to know.

Alternately, the routers could use a type of application called a *dynamic routing protocol*. Most routing protocols exist as TCP/IP standards as defined in various RFCs. Each router runs a routing protocol application that implements the same routing protocol standard. The purpose of the routing protocol application is to talk to other routers to learn routing information from each other.

Routing protocols all use the same general idea of helping all routers learn routes by having all routers tell the other routers what they know. To do so, the routing protocol sends messages to other routers connected to the same LANs and WANs. These messages list routing information, like "I have a route for the group of all addresses that begin with 12." Other routers can learn about these groups of addresses and dynamically build their routing tables, instead of relying on static configuration.

Figure 8-13 shows how routers can use a routing protocol to learn routes. The figure focuses on the group of addresses on the LAN off Router R2, with addresses that begin with 12. R2 knows about this group because R2 connects directly to the LAN. The figure shows the messages sent by the routing protocols, listing the group of addresses as 12.x.x.x for shorthand.

FIGURE 8-13

Routing Protocols Advertising All Addresses That Begin with 12 as One Route

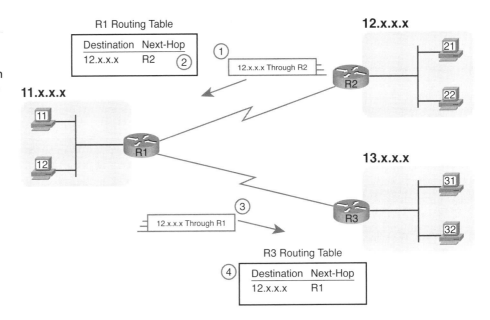

Following the steps in the figure:

1. R2 sends a routing protocol message listing an address grouping 12.x.x.x (all addresses that begin with 12).

2. R1 adds a route to its routing table, listing that group of addresses, and listing R2 as the next-hop router. For any packets R1 wants to send to addresses in this group, R1 will send the packets to R2 next.

3. R1 using the routing protocol messages to advertise a route for 12.x.x.x to Router R3.

4. R3 adds a route to its routing table, listing that group of addresses and listing R1 as the next-hop router.

AUTHOR'S NOTE:
Some of the commonly used routing protocols over the years have been Routing Information Protocol (RIP), Open Shortest Path First (OSPF), Enhanced Interior Gateway Routing Protocol (EIGRP), and Border Gateway Protocol (BGP).

Using Names That Correspond to IP Addresses

Most every computing device communicates using TCP/IP, so each device has an IP address; however, most people have no idea what an IP address is or what it looks like. Instead of using IP addresses, human users prefer to use text names to identify the other computers with which they communicate. Humans can simply remember the names more easily than the numbers.

The most obvious everyday example of using names to identify other computers is the web address. You have probably seen tons of advertisements that list the web address, the website, the place to find us on the web, or as it's technically known, the Universal (or Uniform) Resource Locator (URL). People might remember a URL like Certskills.com, but not the IP address used by that web server (173.227.251.150).

Humans use names, but IP packets use IP addresses, not names. In fact, if you go back and look at the IP header in Figure 8-8, you will see that the IP header has no place to list the name of any computer. The IP routing tables on routers do not list the *names* of the hosts, either; they list groups of IP addresses.

Users use names, and IP routing uses numbers, but it all still works. To make it all work, when a user uses a name, some function in the network must translate that name into its corresponding IP address so that IP packets can be sent to that IP address. And that something goes by the name of the *Domain Name System (DNS)*.

DNS exists as protocol standards defined in RFCs, with the user hosts and special DNS server implementing the DNS protocols. Like most protocols, DNS defines message formats as well as logic. With DNS, the servers keep a list of names and their corresponding IP addresses. (The networking staff at a company must do the administrative work to keep the list updated and accurate.) The DNS protocol then gives any IP host, acting as a DNS client, the capability to ask the DNS server to supply the IP address that goes with any given name.

Each IP host that refers to another host by name needs to act as a DNS client. The DNS client function simply sends a message to the DNS server and makes this statement: "Look in your list, find this name, and tell me its address." The DNS client sends a *DNS Request* message, with the server sending back a *DNS Reply*, as shown in Figure 8-14.

FIGURE 8-14

DNS Name Resolution Request, Reply, and Packet to Server1 IP Address

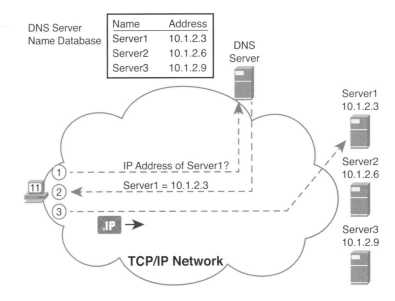

Following the steps in the figure:

1. The user at PC11 wants to connect to Server1, but PC11 does not know Server1's IP address. So, PC11 sends a DNS Request to the DNS server.

2. The DNS server finds that Server1 is 10.1.2.3 per its list, so it sends a DNS Reply to PC11 with that information.

3. PC11 can now send a packet with destination IP address 10.1.2.3 to Server1.

The figure shows how DNS works in one company, but it also works worldwide, as discussed in Chapter 9.

Other Network Layer Functions

TCP/IP defines other network layer functions as well. Some of those features, such as ICMP and Inverse ARP, simply did not fit into the scope of this book. Also, some of the network layer functions, like DHCP and ARP, are explained later in this chapter and in the next chapter. Figure 8-15 summarizes the main TCP/IP Layer 3 protocols as a reminder of their names.

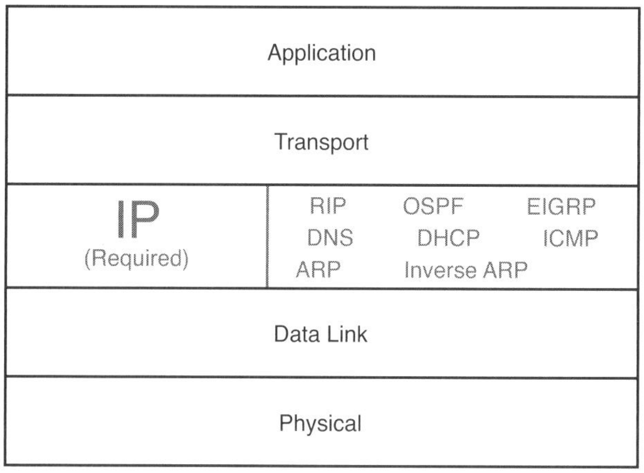

Application		
Transport		

IP (Required)	RIP OSPF EIGRP DNS DHCP ICMP ARP Inverse ARP

Data Link
Physical

FIGURE 8-15

IP with Its Support
Protocols

IP Addressing on User LANs

Every device that needs to send IP packets (called IP hosts) must have an IP address. Those IP hosts include every traditional PC, every phone, and every tablet computer. In fact, devices you would not think of as computers also act as IP hosts, needing an IP address with which to send and receive packets. For example, newer televisions can be used to access the Internet through wireless LANs; game consoles at home allow multiple players to reach each other through networks; modern point-of-sale cash registers use TCP/IP; even the little handheld computers retailers use to check inventory and prices can use TCP/IP, with the devices using an IP address.

For several reasons, IP addressing requires more thought and effort to learn as compared with data-link addressing. First, IP addressing has a lot more rules than data-link addressing. These rules give us many flexible options for IP addressing, which is good, but it also requires more effort to learn how it works. Second, IP addressing does not just happen automatically, but it must be planned, with a large variety of design choices to make. Finally, IP defines flexible options of how addresses must be grouped together. That flexibility gives engineers more options, but it also makes IP addressing concepts and math more complex, requiring more effort to learn.

This major section introduces IP addresses as an end to themselves, with the next (third) major section of this chapter discussing IP addressing within the context of IP routing. The following sections limit the discussion to the most fundamental IP addressing rules and focus on IP addressing with hosts on a LAN. By limiting the IP addressing topics, these sections hope to introduce the basics of IP addressing without overwhelming you with too many details at once.

The following sections break the topics into two parts. They first look at the IP address planning process, which includes the concept of grouping addresses together, much like the postal system groups mailing addresses based on the postal code (ZIP code in the United States). The rest of these sections show how a host on a LAN gets its IP address, either through static configuration or using a dynamic process using DHCP.

Planning LAN IP Addresses

Before thinking about IP addresses, think back to the other addresses you have learned about in this book, and how the devices know about those addresses. For example, you already know that every device gets a universal Ethernet MAC address when the manufacturer makes the NIC or other Ethernet device. You know that the MAC address (6 bytes, 12 hex digits) will be unique in the universe. You do not have to plan any Ethernet address details when buying and using new Ethernet gear; you just buy it, use it, and rely on the universal MAC addresses.

Most data-link addresses require little or no planning. Just for review and perspective, Figure 8-16 summarizes the various data-link addresses discussed so far in this book, with a note about who picks the data-link addresses in each case. Of all these, only the Frame Relay data-link connection identifiers (DLCI) might benefit from some prior planning. The customer and provider might discuss the literal values to use for DLCIs, even though the provider actually assigns the DLCI values to each PVC. For the rest of the data-link types in the figure, either the data-link addresses do not matter, or they happen as a side effect of the manufacturing process.

FIGURE 8-16

Data-Link Addresses: Not Chosen by Enterprise Network Engineers

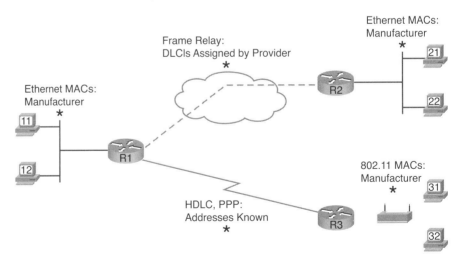

In contrast, IP addressing in an enterprise TCP/IP network requires planning. First, as mentioned before, every host has to have an IP address. Additionally, the manufacturer of the device cannot predict what IP address the device would need to use inside an enterprise. So the network engineers at a company have to think about IP addressing, its rules, the goals of the company, and so on and come up with a plan for what IP addresses to use.

Locations That Need IP Addresses

To plan what IP addresses to use, you need to follow some rules for IP addresses. IP addressing has several rules beyond just defining a 32-bit address. This topic does not work through the rules one by one, but rather it discusses the major concepts, mentioning the rules while talking about the concepts.

For example, IP requires that any device that sends or receives an IP packet on an interface must have an IP address assigned to that interface. As a result, any user device that connects to a TCP/IP network—a PC, tablet, smart phone, television, and so on—must have an IP address.

Another IP addressing rule states that IP addresses identify an interface connected to a LAN or WAN, as opposed to identifying the entire device. For example, routers typically have many interfaces, just as part of their job of connecting to different LANs and WANs. As a result, a router would have multiple IP addresses, one per interface. End-user hosts might have both a wired Ethernet and a wireless LAN adapter, so they have two interfaces. So, that end-user host would have two IP addresses, one per interface.

For example, consider the small corporate TCP/IP network topology shown in Figure 8-17. The figure shows an asterisk beside each LAN and WAN interface on hosts and on the routers, with an IP address needed for each of these devices.

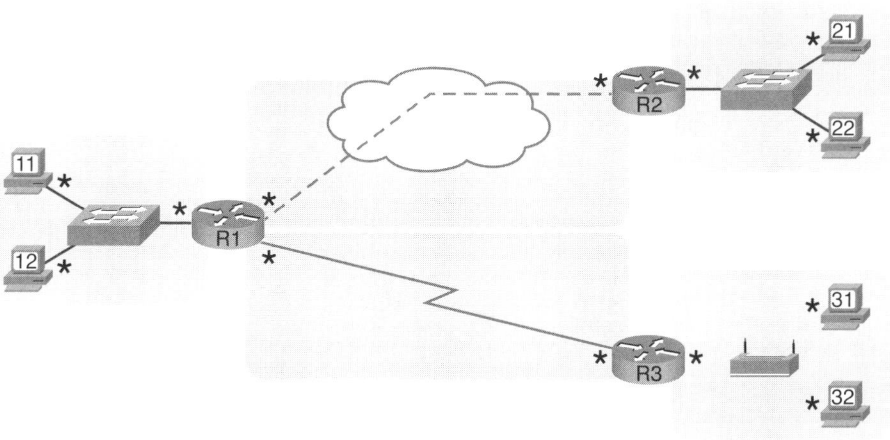

> **AUTHOR'S NOTE:**
> Reasonable IP addresses can be prechosen for small home-based networks that just connect to the Internet, because of a feature called Network Address Translation (NAT). This chapter ignores NAT, leaving it for Chapter 9. This chapter focuses more on larger corporate networks.

FIGURE 8-17

IP Addresses Used on Every LAN/WAN Interface

The figure not only shows what interfaces need IP addresses, but it also implies what devices do not need IP addresses. The figure does not show an asterisk beside the LAN switch or LAN AP, or their interfaces. It also does not show any asterisks inside the WAN sections that hide the WAN equipment. The only devices that truly need IP addresses are those that use IP logic, like the end-user devices (IP hosts) and routers. To do their Layer 1 and 2 work to forward data through the LANs and WANs, the LAN switches, access points, and WAN equipment inside the service provider networks do not need IP addresses.

However, although LAN devices do not need IP addresses, they often have IP addresses for network management purposes. LAN switches and access points can have an IP address and send/receive packets for their own purposes. For example, with an IP address on a LAN switch, an engineer could remotely connect to a switch to troubleshoot a problem, using the TCP/IP network to send packets to/ from the LAN switch. Without that IP configuration on the LAN switch, the engineer would have to go to the physical location of the switch.

IP Address Grouping Concepts

Another IP addressing rule, as mentioned earlier in this chapter, requires that IP addresses exist as groups. First, note that the word *group* is not the formal term, but just a description. Each group of IP addresses includes a range of consecutive numbers. For example, a group could be all IP address that begin with 11 in the first octet. That set of numbers would be consecutive, starting with 11.0.0.0, then 11.0.0.1, then 11.0.0.2, and so on, up through 11.255.255.255.

Not only must IP addresses exist as groups, but each LAN and WAN must also contain one group. That is, the set of IP hosts connected to one LAN must be in one IP address group. The IP hosts on a second LAN must be in some other IP address group.

The groupings of IP addresses allows IP routing to work better, with the IP routers listing one number to represent each address group in their routing tables, as seen earlier in Figure 8-12. Figure 8-18 repeats an earlier example of how IP addresses can be grouped, with five groups: three LANs and two WANs. In this example, the IP addresses in each group have the same first octet value. Note that the figure represents the idea of "all addresses that begin with 11" as 11.x.x.x, using the *x* as a wildcard.

FIGURE 8-18

IP Address Groupings: IP Networks

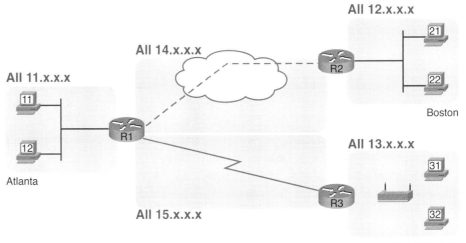

The idea of grouping IP addresses works a little like the postal service and postal codes (ZIP codes in the United States). People who live in the same apartment building, on the same street, and in the same town have the same postal code in their mailing addresses. When someone new moves into that town, his new mailing address uses the postal code for that new town. The mailing address of someone living on the other side of the country from you has a different postal code than your own postal code.

Now for the next rule of IP addressing: The prefix part of the IP addresses, the part that must be the same number for all addresses in a group, can be many sizes. By choice, the network engineer planning the IP addresses could decide to use any of the following choices. (Note that the list just shows three examples, but many others exist as well.)

First 2 octets (16 bits): All addresses in the same IP address group have the same value in the first 2 octets.

First 3 octets (16 bits): All addresses in the same IP address group have the same value in the first 3 octets.

First 20 bits: All addresses in the same IP address group have the same value in the first 20 bits, which spans all the first 2 octets and half of the third octet.

For example, the engineer that planned the TCP/IP network in the previous Figure 8-18 could have instead used a design like what is shown in Figure 8-19. In the revised design, one group of addresses bases the group on the first octet's value, namely all addresses that begin with 11 in the first octet. Two groups base the group on the value in the first 2 octets, as seen on the LANs on the right side of the figure. The two IP address groups on the WAN links base the groups on the value in the first 3 octets.

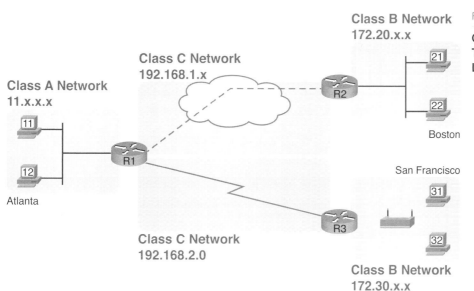

FIGURE 8-19

One-, Two-, and Three-Octet Prefix Lengths

This discussion has been referring to these groups of consecutive IP addresses as groups, to emphasize the concepts. However, you might have already heard of other terms for this idea of groups of IP addresses. Depending on many factors not yet discussed in this chapter, you might use one of many different terms to refer to a group of IP addresses. For now, this list introduces the common names for these groups of IP addresses. The rest of the chapter mentions how to use most of these terms at various points, beginning with the next topic:

- Classful IP network
- IP network
- Subnetwork
- Subnet
- Prefix

The First Tier: The Five IPv4 Address Classes

The original IPv4 RFC defined a way to group IPv4 addresses using a concept called *IP address classes*, or *classful IP addressing*. Classful IP addressing divides the entire 32-bit IP address space into large groups called classes. Inside the three largest address classes, the IP rules further divide the addresses into a number of IP networks, with each *IP network* being a group of predetermined IP addresses. In fact, the examples of the last two figures show IP address groups that match these classful IP addressing concepts.

The classful IP addressing idea begins by breaking down the entire universe of all IPv4 addresses. With 32 bits for the IPv4 address, that complete IPv4 address space includes 2^{32} addresses, or a little over 4 billion numbers. As written in DDN format, the numbers range from 0 to 255 in each octet: 0.0.0.0, 0.0.0.1, 0.0.0.2, and so on, up through 255.255.255.255.

Classful addressing first breaks down the entire IPv4 address space into five classes, referenced with a letter: A, B, C, D, and E. Every possible IPv4 address falls into a class, or into some range of reserved numbers, as listed in Table 8-2. The class is based on the value in the first octet of the DDN format IP address.

> **AUTHOR'S NOTE:** The terms *IP network* and *TCP/IP network* can refer to a collection of devices, cables, software, and so on that together allow hosts to communicate. However, when discussing IP addressing, the term *IP network* can also refer to one specific IP addressing concept, as discussed in this topic.

TABLE 8-2

Summary of IPv4 Address Classes Based on First-Octet Values

First Octet	Class	Purpose
0	A	Reserved
1–126	A	Unicast addresses, in class A networks
127	A	Reserved
128–191	B	Unicast addresses, in class B networks
192–223	C	Unicast addresses, in class C networks
224–239	D	Multicast addresses. Not used as unicast IP addresses
240–255	E	Experimental. Not used as unicast IP addresses

Of the five address classes, three classes (A, B, and C) define *unicast IP addresses*. The term *unicast* means that the address is used by a single interface only. In comparison, class D defines *multicast IP addresses*, which can be used to send one packet to many destination hosts at the same time. This chapter only examines unicast IP addresses, and otherwise ignores the multicast (class D), experimental (class E), and other reserved addresses.

The Second Tier: Classful IP Networks Inside Unicast Address Classes

IP breaks down classes A, B, and C further, into a number of IP address groups called **IP networks**. (Sometimes, to emphasize the fact that the IP network was defined by these class-oriented rules, the term *classful IP network* is used.) Each IP network can then be used as the group of addresses on a single LAN or WAN, just as in the examples shown in Figures 8-18 and 8-19.

IP divides each class using slightly different rules. The key differences: The groups (the IP networks) are large groups in class A, medium-sized groups in class B, and small groups of addresses in class C.

Class A rules take half of the entire IPv4 address space, with first octet values of 0 - 127, and creates 128 large IP networks. Specifically, those class A networks are the 128 sets of addresses that begin with a first octet of 0 through 127, respectively. However, the first and last class A network (the networks that begin with 0 and 127) are reserved, leaving 126 usable class A networks. Table 8-3 shows a sampling of the class A networks.

TABLE 8-3

Example Class A Networks

Network ID	Class A IP Network Concept	Size (Number of Addresses)
1.0.0.0	All addresses with a first octet equal to 1	> 16,000,000
2.0.0.0	All addresses with a first octet equal to 2	> 16,000,000
3.0.0.0	All addresses with a first octet equal to 3	> 16,000,000
4.0.0.0	All addresses with a first octet equal to 4	> 16,000,000
...	Skipping many...	> 16,000,000
126.0.0.0	All addresses with a first octet equal to 126	> 16,000,000

While humans might prefer to think about the concept like "all addresses that begin with 1," computers prefer to use a number to refer to the same idea. IP defines a network identifier, or *network ID*, for each classful IP network, with that number representing the IP network. The network ID cannot be used as a unicast IP address for any host in the network.

Each IP network's network ID has the same prefix part as the addresses in the IP network, but all 0s for the rest of the number. The prefix part is the beginning part of the IP address that must be in common among all addresses in the IP network, which for class A networks is the first octet. Each class A network ID then has the same value as the other addresses in the network as the first octet, and all 0s for the last three octets. For example, as shown in Table 8-3, the network ID for the class A network for "all addresses with a first octet of 1" begins with the prefix part (1), with the rest of the octets as 0, for a network ID of 1.0.0.0.

AUTHOR'S NOTE:
The terms *network number* and *network address* can be used as synonyms for *network id*.

Finally, although the class A rules create only 126 classful IP networks, each class A network includes over 16,000,000 IP addresses. For a given class A network, the addresses can use the entire last 3 octets to create unique IP addresses for hosts. With the 24 bits in those last 3 octets, each class A network supports 2^{24} IP addresses (minus 2, for two reserved numbers).

Class B includes one-fourth of the IPv4 address space, with a first octet value from 128 to 191 inclusive. However, IP breaks the class B address space into a medium number (2^{14}) of medium-sized IP networks ($2^{16} - 2$ addresses each, for a little more than 65,000 hosts per network). The grouping idea uses the first two octets. For example, the idea "all addresses that begin with 128.1" is the concept behind one class B network. Table 8-4 shows a few samples, for perspective.

TABLE 8-4

Example Class B Networks

Network ID	Concept	Size (Number of Addresses)
128.1.0.0	All with the first two octets equal to 128.1	> 65,000
128.2.0.0	All with the first two octets equal to 128.2	> 65,000
128.3.0.0	All with the first two octets equal to 128.3	> 65,000
150.48.0.0	All with the first two octets equal to 150.48	> 65,000
180.255.0.0	All with the first two octets equal to 180.255	> 65,000
191.200.0.0	All with the first two octets equal to 191.200	> 65,000

Class C includes one-eighth of the IPv4 address space, with all numbers whose first octet is between 192 and 223, inclusive. In this case, IP breaks down class C into a large number of small IP networks: over 2,000,000 IP networks, each with 254 IP addresses. After class A groups addresses based on one octet, and class B groups addresses based on two octets being the same, you could almost predict that for class C, IP groups addresses based on the first three octets.

For example, the concept of "all addresses that begin with 192.191.190" is a class C network concept. First, you can tell that it can only be a class C network, and not class A or B, because the first octet (192) sits within the class C range (192–223, inclusive). The class C rules also tell us that class C networks define the group using the first three octets. Table 8-5 lists a few sample class C networks.

TABLE 8-5

Example Class C Networks

Network ID	Concept	Size (Number of Addresses)
192.1.1.0	All with the first three octets equal to 192.1.1	254
192.1.2.0	All with the first three octets equal to 192.1.2	254
192.1.3.0	All with the first three octets equal to 192.1.3	254
200.200.200.0	All with the first three octets equal to 200.200.200	254
220.255.0.0	All with the first three octets equal to 220.255.0	254
223.1.1.0	All with the first three octets equal to 123.1.1	254

Summary of IP Addressing Rules

Summarizing, the classful IP addressing rules first break down the entire IP address space by class. Then, inside classes A, B, and C, where all the unicast IP addresses sit, IP subdivides each class into a number of IP networks. Inside the classes, IP creates a small number of large IP networks (class A), a medium number of medium-sized IP networks (class B), and a large number of small IP networks (class C). Figure 8-20 summarizes this breakdown of the entire IP address space.

FIGURE 8-20

Summary of How Class
Rules Break Down the
IPv4 Address Space

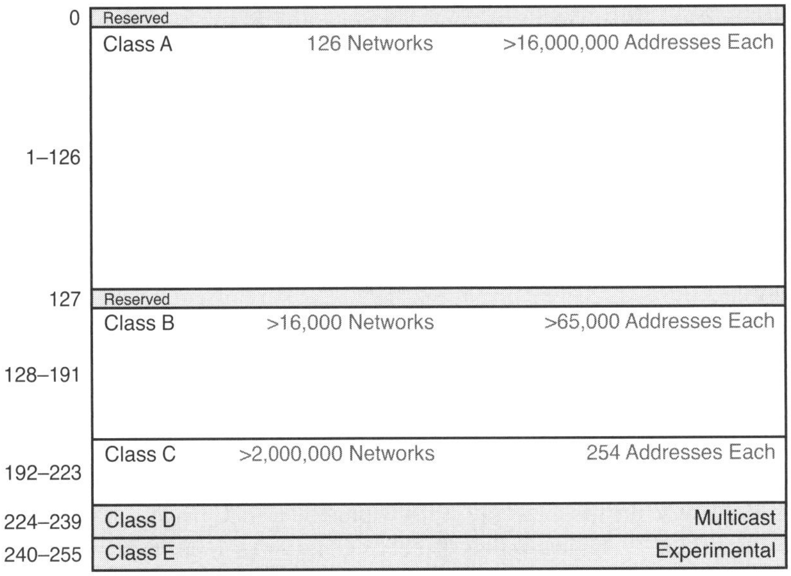

0	Reserved	
	Class A 126 Networks >16,000,000 Addresses Each	
1–126		
127	Reserved	
	Class B >16,000 Networks >65,000 Addresses Each	
128–191		
192–223	Class C >2,000,000 Networks 254 Addresses Each	
224–239	Class D Multicast	
240–255	Class E Experimental	

This topic introduced many IP addressing rules during the discussion, and there are even more than were mentioned here. As a study reference, the following list summarizes the IP addressing rules discussed so far in this chapter.

First, the basics:

■ An IP address is a 32-bit binary number.

■ An IP address is written in dotted-decimal notation (DDN) , with 8 bits converted to the decimal equivalent, with dots between the decimal numbers.

■ DDN numbers have values between decimal 0 and 255, inclusive.

Next, some design ideas:

■ Unicast addresses identify a single interface (as compared to multicast IP addresses).

■ Every interface connected to a LAN or WAN, over which IP packets flow when the device uses IP logic, must have a unicast IP address.

■ Addresses for interfaces on the same LAN or WAN must be in the same group of addresses.

Next, these points relate to the grouping concepts in IP:

- The IP addresses in a group have the same value in the first part of the addresses (the prefix).

- The length of the prefix part of an IP address, which is the same number for all IP addresses in the same group, can be different for different groups.

Finally, these ideas are about IP's class rules:

- Unicast IP addresses come from classes A, B, and C only.

- Classful IP addressing rules define class A, B, and C networks as one way to group addresses.

- A class A network includes all IP addresses with the same number in the first octet.

- A class B network includes all IP addresses with the same number in the first two octets.

- A class C network includes all IP addresses with the same number in the first three octets.

- The class for any unicast IP address can be determined by looking at the first octet and comparing it to the list of first-octet values shown in Table 8-2.

> **ON THE SIDE:** This section describes IP networks using class A, B, and C concepts, so this logic is called *classful addressing*. Alternately, *classless addressing* is another way to think about IP addresses, in which you ignore class A, B, and C rules.

Assigning LAN IP Addresses

Learning IP addressing can require a fair amount of work because of all the IP addressing concepts, rules, planning, and the math behind it all. On the other hand, the process of giving a user host its IP address, after you know what IP address to use, just takes a small amount of work.

Most hosts get their IP address from one of two sources: either through static configuration or through a dynamic process using the Dynamic Host Configuration Protocol (DHCP) . The following sections discuss a few details of each method.

Static IP Address Assignment

Host operating systems (OS) typically include some way for the user or IT administrator to type in the IP address that the device should use. Today, that generally means that you just have to find the right part of the graphical user interface (GUI) from which to set the IP address. Also, many OSs also let the user type a command to configure the IP address. Either way, after you know the right IP address to use, the process to configure or assign the IP address usually just takes a few clicks and a little typing.

For example, the Apple Mac OS provides a part of the user interface called *network preferences*, from which the user can set the IP address. The user can click the TCP/IP tab at the top of the first screen to display the TCP/IP settings. Then, to configure the IP address by just typing it in, the user must choose the Manually setting, meaning that the user wants to manually configure the IP address. Figure 8-21 shows a sample screen shot, with the IPv4 address of 11.1.1.11.

FIGURE 8-21

Static IP Address
Assignment on Mac OS X

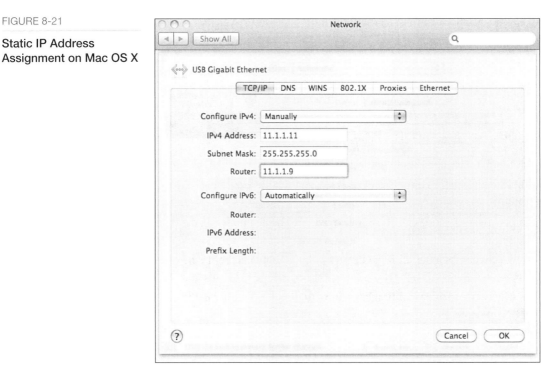

Besides the IP address, the host also needs to know other IP settings as well. The example screen in Figure 8-21 shows a couple of those additional items: the subnet mask and the router (also known as the default router, or default gateway). Also needed, but configured on another tab, are the IP addresses of the DNS server. On most OSs, the same GUI screens that let you configure the IP address also let you configure these other settings. Figure 8-22 summarizes those four key values.

FIGURE 8-22

Host IP Settings

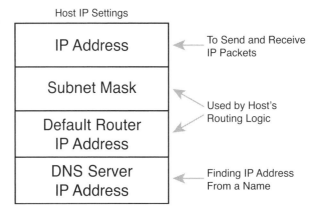

This chapter has already discussed the ideas behind an IP address and DNS server. The subnet mask, and the specific purpose of the default router IP address, are routing topics and are discussed in the upcoming section, "Host Routing Logic."

Dynamic Assignment with DHCP

The **Dynamic Host Configuration Protocol (DHCP)** defines a way in which hosts can borrow or lease an IP address for a period of time, usually over days, weeks, or months. DHCP also lets hosts learn the other key IP configuration settings, as listed in Figure 8-22. By choosing to let hosts use DHCP instead of static configuration, the network engineer avoids wasting time going to each device and setting the IP addresses.

ON THE SIDE: DHCP works very well as a way for most end-user devices; most corporate networks use DHCP for almost every user device.

DHCP operates on a client-and-server concept. DHCP exists as a protocol defined RFCs, and those RFCs define the role of a DHCP client and DHCP server as well. Most user hosts implement the *DHCP client* function, in which the host asks to learn an IP address it can use for some period of time.

The DHCP server function listens for requests from DHCP clients, telling them what IP address to use. Specialized DHCP server software creates the DHCP server function. The software can run on any computer, but most corporations set aside specific server hardware to act as the DHCP server. The network engineer then configures the DHCP server with a list of the IP addresses in each IP network that the server is allowed to give out, or lease, to DHCP clients.

This section shows how DHCP works using a couple of examples, both of which come from the network shown in Figure 8-23. This network has the same familiar three LANs and two WANs as shown in many other figures in this chapter. It uses a variety of class A, B, and C networks, with three remote locations: Atlanta, Boston, and San Francisco.

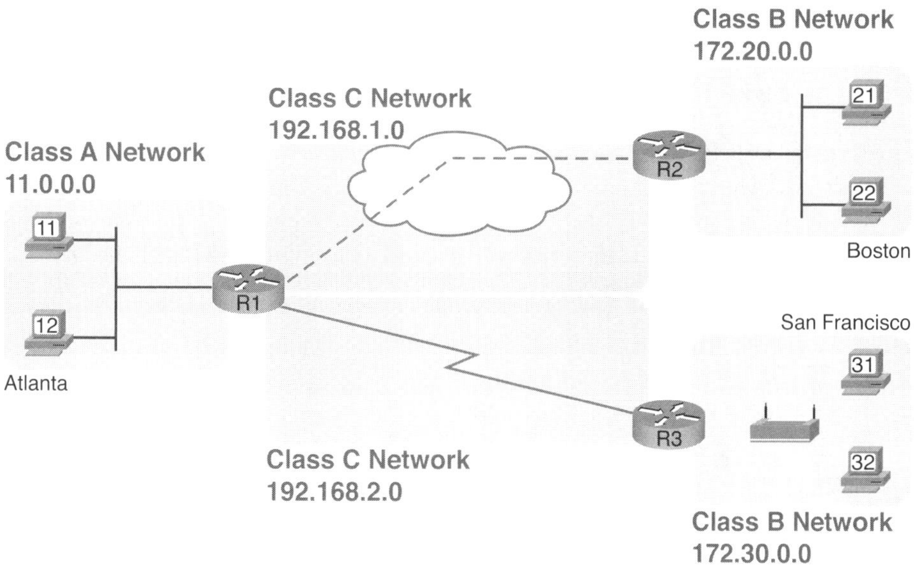

FIGURE 8-23

Sample Network for DHCP Discussions

When a device asks a DHCP server to let it lease an IP address, the DHCP server cannot give the DHCP client device just any IP address. Remember, IP addressing rules require that the IP addresses on one LAN all be from the same group. For example, if a new device were added to the Atlanta Ethernet LAN, that address should come from class A network 11.0.0.0.

Additionally, the DHCP server should avoid leasing out an IP address that the network engineer has already statically configured on some other device. For example, if PC12 were already configured with IP address 11.2.2.2, the DHCP server should avoid handing out that IP address.

To avoid having two devices try to use the same IP address, the IP addresses in each IP network must be divided based on whether they can be statically configured or assigned by DHCP. Additionally, the DHCP server must note which IP addresses it leases so that the server leases each IP address to only one DHCP client. For example, in the TCP/IP network shown in Figure 8-23, Table 8-6 shows a planning chart of how the IP addresses might be planned for DHCP and static assignment.

TABLE 8-6

Address Planning: Some Static, Some DHCP, for Every LAN

Location	Type	Range
Atlanta LAN	Static	11.1.1.1 – 11.1.1.254
	DHCP	11.1.2.1 – 11.1.2.254
Boston LAN	Static	172.20.1.1 – 172.20.1.254
	DHCP	172.20.2.1 – 172.20.2.254
San Fran LAN	Static	172.30.1.1 – 172.30.1.254
	DHCP	172.30.2.1 – 172.30.2.254

After the DHCP server exists in the network, and it has a configuration that tells the server which IP addresses the server can lease, the DHCP clients can request IP addresses. Figure 8-24 shows an example of the process. The figure shows only the devices connected to the Atlanta IP network from Figure 8-23, with the DHCP server located on that same LAN.

FIGURE 8-24

DHCP Lease Process Between a DHCP Client and Server

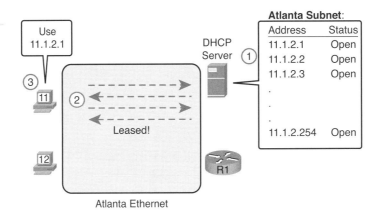

Following the steps in the figure:

1. The server begins with a configuration for the Atlanta subnet, listing the IP addresses it can lease and noting that all are open and available.

2. PC11 initiates the four-message DHCP exchange to lease an IP address, with the server leasing address 11.1.2.1 to the client.

3. PC11 now uses IP address 11.1.2.1.

The user can see the results of the DHCP process, typically from the same part of the OS user interface as where the manual IP address configuration happens. Figure 8-25 shows an example in which the same Apple Mac acted as a DHCP client to learn its IP address. (Note that the screen shot does not show an IP address from the subnet in the previous figure.)

FIGURE 8-25

DHCP Client Configuration on Mac OS X

The previous example showed the DHCP client and server on the same LAN, but DHCP also works with a centralized DHCP server and remote DHCP clients. In fact, most enterprise networks put the DHCP servers at a centralized site, with the majority of the users at remote sites. For example, Figure 8-26 shows the DHCP server still in Atlanta, but with a DHCP client on the Boston LAN.

FIGURE 8-26

Remote DHCP
Client in Boston

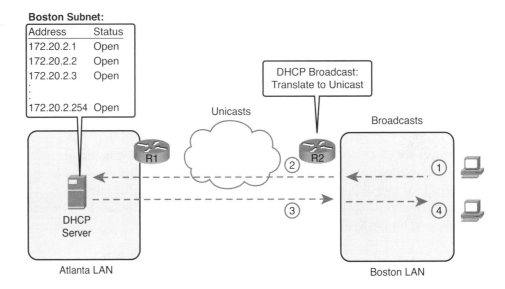

The local routers on a LAN have to help DHCP clients find the DHCP server
when the server is not on the same LAN. The messages sent by a DHCP client
cannot leave the local LAN on their own. So, the local router must know the DHCP
server's IP address and change the DHCP packet's destination IP address to point
to the DHCP server. That solves the problem and lets the messages flow from the
DHCP client, which does not yet have an IP address, and the DHCP server.

In Figure 8-26, the process runs as follows:

1. PC21 asks for a DHCP lease, sending a DHCP message that is broadcast on
   the local LAN.

2. R2 sees the DHCP message, changes the destination IP address to the address
   of the DHCP server, and forwards the IP packet to the DHCP server.

3. The DHCP server sends the next DHCP message back to the router (R2 in
   this case).

4. R2 forwards the DHCP message back out onto the LAN as a LAN broadcast.

IP Routing with Focus on Layer 3 Only

IP defines how to route packets across the entire TCP/IP network. Some of the
routing tasks focus on Layer 3, and Layer 3 only. Other routing tasks must use
logic from the two lower layers, as implemented by LANs and WANs, because the
network layer cannot physically send the bits. The network layer must rely on the
Layer 1 and 2 logic, as implemented in LANs and WANs, to move the bits from
one node to the next.

The section "IP Routing with Focus on Layer 3 Only" begins the third of four major sections in this chapter. This major section looks at the parts of IP routing that can ignore the LAN and WAN details, and focuses solely on Layer 3 details. In this section, while LANs and WANs exist, the hosts and routers connected to those LANs and WANs can ignore the details inside the LANs and WANs. Figure 8-27 shows the perspective used for this section of the chapter.

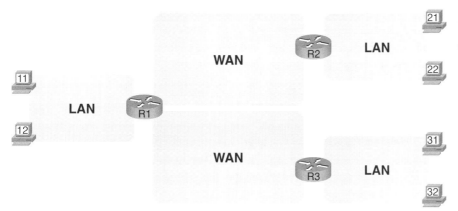

FIGURE 8-27

IP Routing Perspective, While Ignoring LAN/WAN Details

The following sections break the discussion down into three topics:

■ First, because you have already read about classful IP networks (class A, B, and C networks), these sections begin by discussing how IP routing works in a corporate network that uses classful IP networks.

■ The next topic looks at IP subnetting, which breaks classful IP networks into smaller parts, while also discussing how IP routing works when corporate networks use subnetting.

■ The final of the three topics in these sections looks at how end-user devices (IP hosts) think in regard to forwarding IP packets.

IP Routing with Classful IP Networks

IP routing defines how a router chooses where to send an IP packet next. A router has to look at each and every IP packet that comes in its interfaces. For each packet, the router first finds the true intended destination of the packet: the destination IP address as listed in the IP header. Then, the router compares that destination IP address to the router's IP routing table, finding the best route to use. That best route tells the router where to send the packet next by noting the interface out which the router should send the packet. And if every router does its job, the packet arrives at the correct destination IP host.

This topic looks at this routing process in detail, using examples with class A, B, and C networks.

Classful IP Networks and Network IDs

For a router to route IP packets, it must have an *IP routing table* with useful entries. The routing table lists multiple IP routes, with each IP route including several pieces of information.

Each IP route identifies a group of addresses, along with information about how to send IP packets to the addresses in that group. And instead of identifying the group as a long text description, like "all addresses that begin with 11," the route lists a number (or numbers). The number(s), along with some math, represent a group of IP addresses. For example, a route could list a classful network ID to identify the IP addresses in a classful IP network.

The idea of IP network IDs, and the fact that they represent groups of consecutive IP addresses, works a lot like postal codes in mailing addresses. Everyone in the same town has a unique mailing address, with each address having the same postal code (called the ZIP code in the United States). The same kind of idea works for the group of addresses in a class A, B, or C IP network—every host has a unique IP address, but the network ID is a number that identifies the entire group of all addresses in that IP network.

To route IP packets, routers need to look at the packets' destination IP address and compare that IP address to the list of class A, B, and C network IDs in the router's IP routing table. The goal of the comparison is to find the network ID whose range of addresses includes the destination address of the packet.

Finding a Classful Network ID Based on an IP Address

The router uses some math to make the comparison, but humans can make the same comparison in different ways. This topic reviews the class A, B, and C rules and network IDs so that the comparisons to the IP routing table make more sense. To begin the review, Table 8-7 lists the rules for class A, B, and C networks.

TABLE 8-7

Summary of IPv4 Address Classes Based on First-Octet Values

Class	First-Octet Values	Number of Network Octets	Grouping Concept
A	1–126	1	All addresses that begin with the same first octet
B	128–191	2	All addresses that begin with the same first two octets
C	192–223	3	All addresses that begin with the same first three octets

Routers can look at any IP address and find the classful IP network ID in which that IP address resides. The process uses some math, but for us humans, some easier logic can be paraphrased to the following:

1. Determine the class (A, B, or C) based on the first octet's value.
2. Determine the number of network octets based on the class.
3. To find the network ID:
   a. Copy the IP address's network octets.
   b. Write down 0 for the rest of the octets.

Table 8-8 shows four examples. The first column shows unicast destination IP addresses in some sample IP packets that arrive at a router. The router could use math to find the network ID, and humans can use the information in this section, to find the matching class A, B, or C network ID. Table 8-8 spells out the logic and resulting network IDs.

TABLE 8-8
Example Calculations: From Destination IP Address to Classful Network ID

IP Address in a Packet	Class	Concept	To Find the Network ID, Copy the First ___ Octets, and the Rest Are 0s	Network ID
11.1.1.11	A	All that begin with 11	1	11.0.0.0
172.20.1.21	B	All that begin with 172.20	2	172.20.0.0
172.30.1.31	B	All that begin with 172.30	2	172.30.0.0
192.168.1.1	C	All that begin with 192.168.1	3	192.168.1.0

After you know the class A, B, and C network IDs, you should now be able to determine the IP addresses allowed in each network. For example, the upcoming routing example will use the design shown in Figure 8-28. It lists five different classful IP network IDs. It also shows the IP addresses of the user hosts on the LANs, as well as the router interface IP addresses on those LANs. Based on the network IDs, you could be able to interpret those and determine the idea behind the network ID, for example, "all addresses that begin with 11" for class A network ID 11.0.0.0.

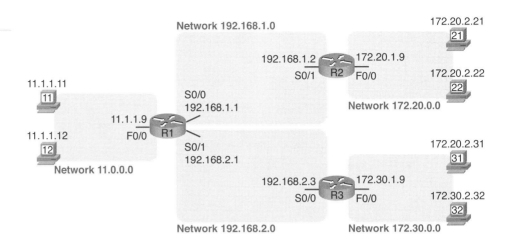

FIGURE 8-28

Five Classful Networks in a Small Corporate Network

IP Routing with Class A, B, and C Networks: Single Router

To better understand how routers route IP packets, you need a good understanding of the IP routing tables on routers. IP routing tables list IP routes. Each route lists information about how to match IP packets that the router needs to forward, as well as forwarding instructions that tell the router where to forward packets.

For example, Figure 8-29 shows a conceptual view of Router R1's IP routing table, based on the previous figure. That figure showed five classful IP network IDs. Either through static configuration or by using a dynamic IP routing protocol, Router R1 knows routes to all five classful network IDs, listed in five different IP routes.

FIGURE 8-29

R1 Routing Table with Routes for Five Classful Networks

Network ID	Local Outgoing Interface	Next Router
11.0.0.0	F0/0	(Local)
172.20.0.0	S0/0	R2
172.30.0.0	S0/1	R3
192.168.1.0	S0/0	(Local)
192.168.2.0	S0/1	(Local)

(Five Routes)

First, ignore the details in each route, but instead focus on the idea that a routing table is essentially a list of routes. Figure 8-29 shows five IP routes in this case. It has five routes, because the TCP/IP network shown in Figure 8-28 shows five classful IP networks. (Some large-enterprise IP routers might have tens of thousands of these routes.) When R1 receives an IP packet, it will need to search through all five routes, looking for the best match.

Next, think about the information inside each IP route in the table, but think about each router as two separate parts, as shown in Figure 8-30. Each route has information that the router uses to compare to the IP packet's destination address, to find which route best matches that packet. Each route also has forwarding information, which tells the router where to forward the IP packet if the packet matches that route.

FIGURE 8-30

How Router R1 Uses Its IP Routing Table: Match and Forward

.IP

① Compare Destination IP Address to List

② Forward Based on Matched Route

Network ID	Local Outgoing Interface	Next Router
11.0.0.0	F0/0	(Local)
172.20.0.0	S0/0	R2
172.30.0.0	S0/1	R3
192.168.1.0	S0/0	(Local)
192.168.2.0	S0/1	(Local)

The figure shows two steps in the routing process: to match the best route and then to forward the packet based on the matched route. For matching, when a new IP packet arrives at the router, the router makes a comparison. It compares the packet's destination IP address to the list of network IDs in all the routes. There will not be an exact match, because the IP routes list the network IDs that represent the entire network. However, the router looks for the class A, B, or C network in which the destination IP address resides. For example, a packet destined to 172.20.2.21 will match the second entry in the list, because 172.20.2.21 is in class B network 172.20.0.0.

The second part of the logic tells the router what action to take, specifically, where to send the packet next. Those directions include the *outgoing interface*, which tells the router out which of its local interfaces to forward the packet. For example, in the figure, S0/0 stands for serial interface number 0/0. Because the new packet matched the router for network ID 172.20.0.0, R1 sends the packet out R1's own S0/0 interface.

The IP route's forwarding instructions also list the next-hop router if the next device in the end-to-end path is a router, rather than the true destination. From a logic perspective, it means something like "send the packet out interface X, to the next router known as Y."

IP Routing with Class A, B, and C Networks: End-to-End Routing

The previous few figures focused on a single router making a single routing decision, but the end-to-end routing process relies on a series of routing decisions. Each router in between the source and destination host must make a routing decision, and together, they deliver the packet to the correct destination. In fact, not only do the routers have to work together, but the original host that created the IP packet also plays a role.

Each router in the end-to-end path through a TCP/IP network performs the same kind of routing logic as every other router; however, each router has its own forwarding instructions that tell it where to forward the IP packets next. With correct routes, each router moves the IP packet one step closer to reaching the true destination.

For example, Figure 8-31 shows the same TCP/IP network as the previous few figures, but with an end-to-end routing example. In this case, PC11 sends a packet to PC21 (172.20.2.21).

FIGURE 8-31

Routing from End to End: Multiple Cooperative Routing Decisions

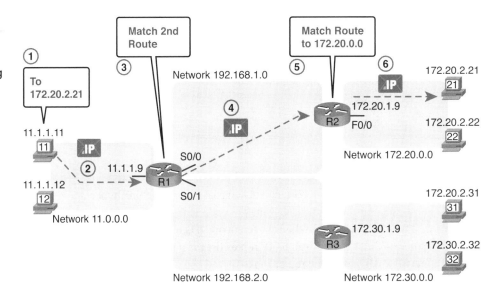

Following the steps in the figure:

1. PC11 decides to send a packet, destination 172.20.2.21, because of some user action (for example, the opening of a web page with PC21's name as the URL).

2. PC11, based on its host IP routing logic, sends the IP packet over the LAN to Router R1.

3. R1 performs IP routing, comparing the packet's destination IP address (172.20.2.21) to R1's IP routing table. R1 matches its route for class B network 172.20.0.0, because destination address 172.20.2.21 is in class B network 172.20.0.0.

4. R1 forwards the packet, per its routing table, out interface S0/0, toward R2.

5. R2 uses the same routing logic as R1, but R2 matches its own route for class B network 172.20.0.0.

6. R2's route for network 172.20.0.0 has different forwarding instructions. R2 forwards the packet out R2's local interface F0/0 (Fast Ethernet 0/0).

IP Routing with IP Subnets

As discussed earlier in this chapter, the IP RFCs define exactly how to subdivide the IPv4 address space for the entire universe. First, IP separates the IPv4 address space into address classes A, B, C, D, and E. Then, inside the three unicast address classes (A, B, and C), IP defines a number of classful network numbers.

In addition to those rules, IP defines additional rules that companies can use to take a single classful network and subdivide it further. The process of *subdividing* an IP *network* is called *subnetting*. Subnetting creates a number of smaller groups of consecutive IP addresses, with those smaller groups called *subnets* (short for *subdivided networks*).

While IP defines exactly how to subdivide IP addresses into classes, and how to subdivide classes A, B, and C into IP networks, subnetting gives the network engineer at a company some flexibility. The following sections introduce subnetting, giving the big concepts and a few examples, with a goal toward showing how IP routing works when a corporate network uses subnets.

Classful IP Networks and Wasted IP Addresses

Before looking at what subnetting does and how it works, first take a moment to think about one of the reasons why people use subnetting instead of just using classful IP networks.

Take a moment to ponder any class A network and its size. The size of a network can be defined as the number of IP addresses in the network. A single class A network has over 16,000,000 IP addresses. Those addresses can have any of 256 values (between 0 and 255) in each of the last three octets, as long as the first octet remains the same. That gives you 256 * 256 * 256 combinations, which comes out to more than 16,000,000 addresses. For example, 10.0.1.2, 10.255.44.199, and 10.194.0.88 are all addresses in class A network 10.0.0.0.

If you do the math to calculate the number of combinations of addresses in each type of network, you would notice that class A networks are huge and class B networks happen to be pretty large as well. Figure 8-32 shows the literal counts of the number of class A, B, and C networks, and the size of each.

FIGURE 8-32

Numbers of Classful
Networks and Their Sizes

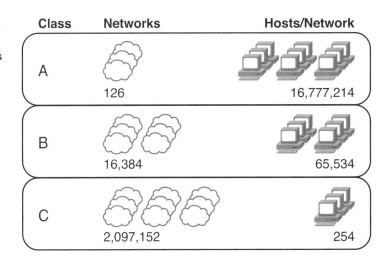

Class	Networks	Hosts/Network
A	126	16,777,214
B	16,384	65,534
C	2,097,152	254

ON THE SIDE: For those interested in the math, the number of addresses in a classful IP network can be calculated as 2 raised to the power of the number of nonnetwork bits (called host bits) minus 2. So, for class A, the calculation is $2^{24} - 2$; for class B, it is $2^{16} - 2$; and for class C, it is $2^8 - 2$.

Next, think about a design for a corporate IP network like the example seen earlier in Figure 8-31. The design uses a class A network 11.0.0.0 on one LAN (on the left). IP addressing rules allow addresses that begin with 11 to exist only on that one LAN. Can you imagine a single LAN with more than 2 million devices? It would be pretty ridiculous. In fact, the class B network 172.20.0.0, used in the upper right of the earlier figure, has over 65,000 IP addresses, which can only exist on that one LAN. In most corporate networks, a large LAN would include a few hundred devices. Network engineers would create multiple LANs to support larger groups of user devices, and each LAN would be a separate group of IP addresses.

Basically, engineers design individual LANs to have at most a few hundred devices in most cases, but class A and B IP networks have far more IP addresses than the typical LAN. And, because those IP addresses, if used, must be on a single LAN, most of the IP addresses would be wasted. The solution? IP subnetting.

Subnetting and IP Subnets

IP subnetting defines how to take a single classful network and break it into many smaller groups of IP addresses. Each smaller group, called a subnet, acts very much like an IP network. Each subnet contains a range of consecutive IP addresses. Each subnet has an identifying number, called a *subnet ID*, which is the lowest number in the subnet. And from a design perspective, the network engineer can use one subnet for each LAN and WAN, and avoid wasting so many IP addresses.

The IP subnetting rules give us many options for how to break up a classful network. You can break a classful network into a few large subnets. You can break it up into a large number of small subnets. You can even break it up into subnets of different sizes. However, that flexibility makes subnetting one of the more challenging IP addressing topics to learn.

Seeing an example can help to understand the basic idea. So, consider an example using class A network 10.0.0.0. First, to review the class A network by itself, as one group, the class A network 10.0.0.0 means this:

> All addresses that begin with 10

Subnetting allows the enterprise network engineer to make a different choice in how to group addresses. That choice lets the engineer decide how long the first part of the addresses should be—the part that has the same value in all addresses in the group. This beginning part defines the subnet.

For example, the network engineer could choose to group IP addresses as follows:

> All my subnets in network 10.0.0.0 will be defined by the first three octets.

The network engineer first does the subnetting by thinking, making notes, and drawing. To represent the idea in this example with network 10.0.0.0, Figure 8-33 shows several of the subnets created by the subnetting process. The figure shows a submarine icon just as a reminder that each line represents a subnet. Each line also lists a subnet ID and some text that explains the addresses in each subnet.

Subnet ID	Meaning	Subnet ID	Meaning
10.0.0.0	All that begin 10.0.0	10.1.0.0	All that begin 10.1.0
10.0.1.0	All that begin 10.0.1	10.1.1.0	All that begin 10.1.1
10.0.2.0	All that begin 10.0.2	10.1.2.0	All that begin 10.1.2
10.0.3.0	All that begin 10.0.3	10.1.3.0	All that begin 10.1.3
10.0.4.0	All that begin 10.0.4	10.1.4.0	All that begin 10.1.4
10.0.5.0	All that begin 10.0.5	10.1.5.0	All that begin 10.1.5
.	.	.	.
.	.	.	.
.	.	.	.

FIGURE 8-33

Subdividing (Subnetting) Class A Network 10.0.0.0

Subnets play the same role as classful IP networks in the overall design of a TCP/IP network. Without subnetting, the design required a classful network for every LAN and WAN. With subnetting, you can instead use a subnet for each LAN and WAN. Figure 8-34 continues the same example, using the same network topology as in the previous routing example. However, the IP addresses and IP networks have been replaced, now using five subnets of class A network 10.0.0.0.

FIGURE 8-34

Sample Corporate
Network Using Subnets
of Network 10.0.0.0

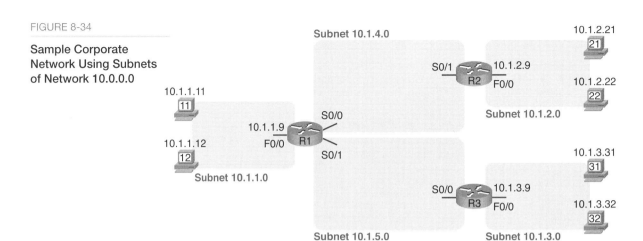

FIGURE 8-34

Sample Corporate
Network Using Subnets
of Network 10.0.0.0

Although a lot of the subnetting work happens on paper or in documentation, eventually the devices in the network need to know about subnetting as well. Somehow, the devices need to each know the subnetting rules the network engineer wrote in notes on paper at his desk. For example, in this example, the engineer must somehow communicate the fact that, in this TCP/IP network's IP subnetting plan, the first three octets of each address must be the same number to be in the same subnet.

IP subnetting RFCs define a number called a *subnet mask* as a numeric way to tell computers how much of the first part of the address must be in common to be in the same subnet. For example, the ongoing example from the last two figures states that the first three octets, or first 24 bits, must be equal. The subnet mask simply defines the number of bits in that first part of the addresses, or 24 bits in this example.

(This chapter does not go through the details of subnet masks, but it does at least show the subnet mask that would be used in the example that has been shown in the last two figures.)

To communicate the idea, the subnet mask can be written in one of two convenient formats. The following two subnet mask values represent the same idea, just using two different formats. Both represent the idea that the first three octets, or first 24 bits, define the common part in a subnet.

　　255.255.255.0

　　/24

In the first case, the subnet mask 255.255.255.0 lists 255's in the first three octets. The 255 means that the corresponding octet in the IP addresses must have the same value. The 0 means that octet is not part of the prefix that must be in common. (Note that other values besides 255 and 0 are allowed in the subnet mask; they are just not discussed here.)

In the second case, the /24 simply refers to the number of prefix bits (24) that must be in common for the addresses to be considered to be in the same subnet.

IP Routing with IP Subnets

IP routing works almost the same way whether the network design only uses classful networks or whether the design uses subnets. The hosts still send IP packets to a destination IP address. The routers still compare the destination IP address to their routing tables and forward the packet based on the matched entry. However, the routers must be able to figure out the range of addresses in each subnet, rather than in each classful network, to match the packets to the correct routing table entry.

Routers need a little more information when matching subnets in the IP routing tables: They need both the subnet ID and the subnet mask. With both numbers, any computer, routers included, can calculate the range of numbers in a subnet. Without the subnet mask, the router would not know which addresses are in the subnet and which ones are in a different subnet.

For an example of this change in how a router matches the routes in its routing table, consider an example based on the previous figure (Figure 8-34). PC11 again sends a packet to PC21, with destination IP address of 10.1.2.21. Focusing on Router R1's routing logic, R1 will have routes for all five subnets in the topology, including a route for PC21's subnet, whose subnet ID is 10.1.2.0. Figure 8-35 shows R1's routing table in this case, with each route listing the subnet ID and subnet mask.

> **AUTHOR'S NOTE:**
> For the examples in this chapter, you do not even need to know the math. All the example subnets in this chapter use the same logic, with the first three octets needing to have the same value to be in the same subnet.

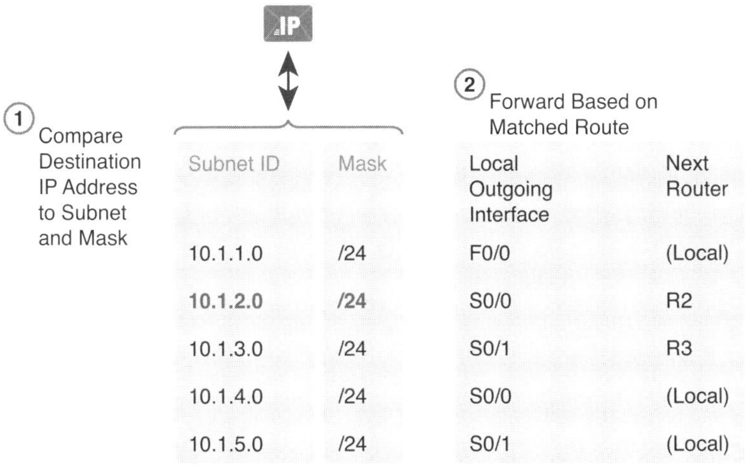

FIGURE 8-35

Routing Logic with Subnets and Masks

① Compare Destination IP Address to Subnet and Mask

② Forward Based on Matched Route

Subnet ID	Mask	Local Outgoing Interface	Next Router
10.1.1.0	/24	F0/0	(Local)
10.1.2.0	/24	S0/0	R2
10.1.3.0	/24	S0/1	R3
10.1.4.0	/24	S0/0	(Local)
10.1.5.0	/24	S0/1	(Local)

Host Routing Logic

The successful end-to-end routing of IP packets from one host to another relies on the routers between the hosts, but it also relies on the hosts themselves. This final short topic on routing from the Layer 3 perspective looks at the IP routing logic used on hosts.

> **ON THE SIDE:** In real routers, routes for classful networks and routes for subnets include a mask. The examples in this chapter just did not introduce the mask concept until the example that focused on subnetting.

Hosts need to make a simple two-part decision when sending an IP packet: to either send the IP packet directly to a destination on the same subnet or to send the packet to some nearby router and let the router deal with choosing a good route. The following sections focus on this simple two-option logic that most hosts use today.

Sending to Destinations on the Same Subnet/Network

The simple two-part host routing logic revolves around a single question:

> Is the destination address of the packet in the same IP address group (network or subnet) as I am?

A host answers that question based on its own IP address and subnet mask. While this chapter does not go through the math, any computer can calculate the range of IP addresses in a subnet based on an IP address and subnet mask. Each host knows its own IP address and subnet mask, so it can easily calculate the range of addresses in its own subnet. At that point, a simple comparison tells the host whether a packet's destination IP address is in the same subnet or a different subnet.

For example, consider how PC11 from the previous examples calculates the range of addresses in its own subnet. PC11 knows its own IP address of 10.1.1.11. It also needs to know its subnet mask, which would be /24 (255.255.255.0) in this case. Based on the recent discussions of subnetting, you know that this mask means that all the numbers in this subnet have the same value in the first three octets. So, this subnet includes the range of addresses from 10.1.1.0 through 10.1.1.255.

Next, consider what happens when PC11 sends an IP packet to PC12, which sits in the same IP subnet. PC11 (10.1.1.11) sends a packet to PC12 (10.1.1.12). As seen in Figure 8-36, PC11 first notes the destination IP address (10.1.1.12). Then, PC11 thinks about the range of addresses in its own subnet (10.1.1.0–10.1.1.255), which PC11 calculated based on its IP address and mask. Clearly, PC11 decides that the destination IP address is in PC11's subnet, so PC11 sends the IP packet directly to PC12, without sending the packet to Router R1.

FIGURE 8-36

IP Host Routing Logic: Local Destination

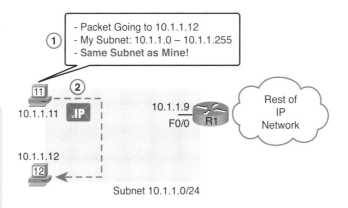

Sending to Destinations on Another Subnet/Network

When a host realizes that the destination is not on the same IP network or IP subnet, the basic host routing logic tells the host to send the packet to another device that should know more routes: a router on the same LAN.

A host's **default router** (or *default gateway*) setting tells the host where to send packets when they have a destination address in a different subnet. You might recall from the earlier section "Assigning LAN IP Addresses" that a host knows its own IP address, but it also knows its mask and its default router setting. This default router setting tells the host the IP address of a router that is attached to the same LAN.

Figure 8-37 shows an example of how a host uses it default router setting. In this case, PC11, IP address 10.1.1.11, sends an IP packet to PC21, IP address 10.1.2.21. PC11 realizes the destination is on another subnet, so PC11 sends the packet to the device at IP address 10.1.1.9 (PC11's default router setting), which is Router R1.

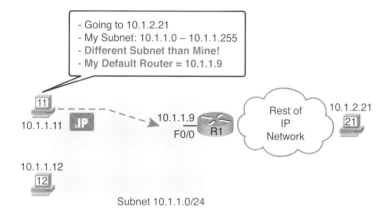

FIGURE 8-37

IP Host Routing Logic:
Remote Destination

IP Routing with Layer 1, 2, and 3 Interactions

When routing IP packets from the source host to the destination host, the Layer 3 logic focuses on the hosts and routers. Hosts send IP packets to their default routers, routers send the packet to other routers, and eventually, the last router forwards the packet to the destination host.

IP routing must also rely on the two lower layers, Layer 1 and Layer 2. Those layers, often combined together and referenced as either a LAN or a WAN, define what happens to move IP packets physically from host to router, router to router, and router to host.

This final major section of the chapter again looks at IP routing, but this time focusing on what happens with LANs and WANs. When a host sends an IP packet to its default gateway, what really happens? When a router sends an IP packet to another router, or to the destination host, what really happens? The following sections answer these questions.

These sections break the discussions into three main topics:

■ A review of encapsulation and deencapsulation, both on the sending host and on the routers that sit inside the IP network

■ IP routing logic when the destination host is in the same subnet (as compared to the sending host)

■ IP routing logic when the destination host is in a different subnet (as compared to the sending host)

Defining Encapsulation and Deencapsulation

The term *encapsulation* refers to action taken by a lower layer when it takes data from a higher layer and adds a header (and possibly a trailer) to the higher-layer's data.

While that previous short paragraph truly describes encapsulation, the idea makes more sense when seeing encapsulation happen. Figure 8-38 shows an example, in which a user at PC11 has opened a web browser and tried to connect to a URL at the web server on the right side of the figure. PC11 is now creating the bits that it will try to send toward Server S1, the web server in the figure.

FIGURE 8-38

Encapsulation Review: Application, Transport, and Network Layers

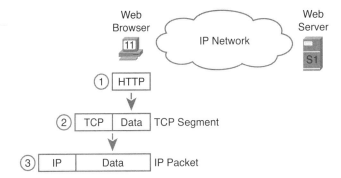

Following the steps in the figure from top to bottom:

1. The web browser creates the HTTP message, an *HTTP GET request*, with which the web client asks the web server to get a web page and return the web page to the client.

2. The TCP function on PC11 encapsulates the HTTP message into a *TCP segment* by adding the TCP header to the HTTP message.

3. The IP function on PC11 encapsulates the TCP segment into an IP packet by adding the IP header.

At this point in the process, PC11 wants to forward the IP packet at the lower left of Figure 8-38, but that IP packet cannot be sent out PC11's Ethernet NIC. PC11 has an Ethernet NIC, and Ethernet requires an Ethernet header/trailer as the first/last parts of what a device physically sends onto the physical link. So, PC11 has more encapsulation work to do before sending data. Figure 8-39 shows the idea, with PC11 encapsulating the IP packet into an Ethernet frame (Step 4) and then sending the bits over the LAN cable into the network (Step 5).

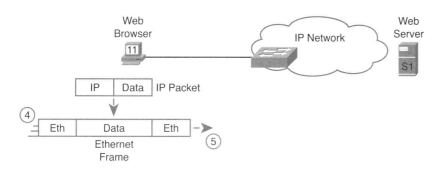

FIGURE 8-39

Encapsulation Review:
Data Link Layer

The rest of this section focuses on the issues and details of that last encapsulation process, as shown in Figure 8-39. However, before moving on to more details about IP routing and encapsulation, just as a brief review, the deencapsulation process also has to occur at some point. For example, if Server S1 happened to be on the same LAN as PC11, the frame would arrive at the server, and the server would then need to deencapsulate the data. That is, Server S1 would process each header (and trailer), starting at the outside, and working its way inward. Figure 8-40 shows the idea.

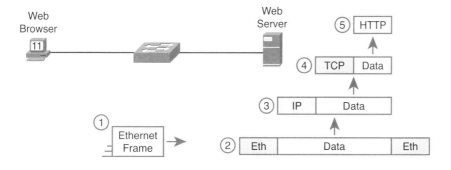

FIGURE 8-40

Deencapsulation on a
Receiving Host (S1)

Following the deencapsulation steps in the figure:

1. Server S1 physically receives the bits in this frame (Layer 1).

2. Server S1 processes the Ethernet header and trailer, and eventually discards them (Layer 2).

3. Server S1 processes the IP header and eventually discards it (Layer 3).

4. Server S1 processes the TCP header and eventually discards it (Layer 4).

5. Server S1 processes the HTTP message (Layer 7).

Routing Inside One Subnet

As discussed earlier in the section "Host Routing Logic," when an IP host sends an IP packet to another host in the same subnet, the sending host tries to send the IP packet directly to the destination IP host, without using a router. But how? This topic answers the specifics. To answer those questions, you have to look at the specific IP and MAC addresses used in the IP packet and Ethernet frame, as well as understand a new protocol—the Address Resolution Protocol (ARP).

Addressing Frames and Packets When Crossing One LAN/Subnet

When two hosts reside in the same IP subnet, the Layer 3 IP routing logic tells the sending host to simply send the IP packet directly to the destination. From a purely Layer 3 perspective, that means to encapsulate the higher-layer data in an IP packet and add the correct IP addresses to the IP header. The host sending the packet would put its own IP address as the source IP address, and the intended destination host's IP address as the destination address.

For example, in Figure 8-41, imagine that a user at PC11 has opened a web browser and tried to load a web page from Server S1. The two IP addresses (10.1.1.11 and 10.1.1.22) happen to be in the same subnet in this case. So, as seen in the figure, PC11 has built the IP packet, with source IP address 10.1.1.11 and destination IP address 10.1.1.22.

FIGURE 8-41

IP Addresses, PC11 to Server S1, Same Subnet

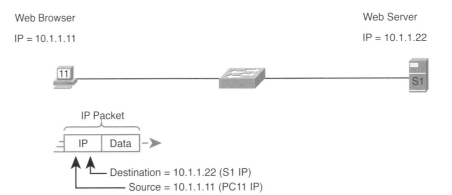

PC11 cannot just physically send the IP packet as shown in Figure 8-41; it must also add an Ethernet header. That Ethernet header must deliver the encapsulated IP packet to Server S1. How? The Ethernet header simply needs S1's MAC address as the destination MAC address, and as you might guess, PC11's MAC address as the source. Figure 8-42 shows both the MAC and IP addresses in the combined Ethernet frame and encapsulated IP packet.

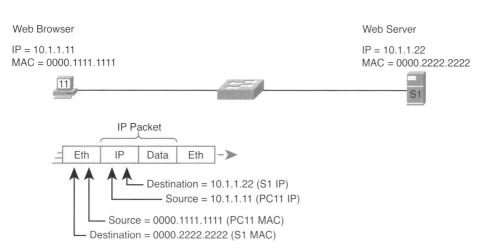

Web Browser

IP = 10.1.1.11
MAC = 0000.1111.1111

Web Server

IP = 10.1.1.22
MAC = 0000.2222.2222

FIGURE 8-42

IP and Ethernet Addresses, PC11 to Server S1, Same Subnet

IP Packet

| Eth | IP | Data | Eth |

Destination = 10.1.1.22 (S1 IP)
Source = 10.1.1.11 (PC11 IP)
Source = 0000.1111.1111 (PC11 MAC)
Destination = 0000.2222.2222 (S1 MAC)

Take a moment to stop and think about the Ethernet and IP headers in Figure 8-42, and the fact that the sender has to create these headers. How does the sender (PC11 in this case) know what addresses to use? It makes sense that the software on PC11 could know to create some IP header, and some Ethernet header, but how does PC11 know the specific address values?

As it turns out, the sender should know both source addresses (MAC and IP). The Ethernet NIC has a universal MAC address; the PC operating system can basically ask the NIC to supply it with that value. The PC also already knows its own IP address, either through static configuration or DHCP, as discusses earlier in this chapter.

The destination addresses require a little more thought. Starting with the destination IP address, the user has somehow identified the destination address. The user might have clicked a link, typed a name, or done something in an application that identified the destination host by name. Then, the sending host can use DNS to learn the IP address that corresponds to that name.

To learn the destination MAC address, the sending computer has to do some work using a new protocol: *Address Resolution Protocol (ARP)* . Table 8-9 summarizes how the sending host knows these four different addresses, with ARP explained following the table.

TABLE 8-9
How a Sending IP Host Knows What Addresses to Use

Address	Short Answer	Long Answer
Source MAC	On NIC	Given to the Ethernet NIC by the manufacturer; the sending host can find the MAC address on the NIC hardware.
Source IP	Configuration	Either through static configuration or DHCP, as discussed earlier in the section, "Assigning LAN IP Addresses."
Destination MAC	ARP	From its ARP table, or if not found, by using the ARP protocol, sending an ARP Request, and waiting for an ARP Reply.
Destination IP	User	User either typed or clicked the IP address, or a name, with DNS resolving the name to the corresponding destination IP address.

Discovering MAC Addresses Using the Address Resolution Protocol

The IP protocol sits at Layer 3 of the TCP/IP model, doing some of the most important Layer 3 work. However, other Layer 3 protocols have important but smaller roles, like DNS for name resolution and DHCP for the assignment of IP addresses and other configuration information. TCP/IP includes another protocol, called the **Address Resolution Protocol (ARP)**, to give hosts a way to learn the MAC address used by other devices on the same LAN.

ARP defines two messages to let hosts learn MAC addresses: the ARP Request and an ARP Reply. These messages allow a simple exchange, with the ARP Request as a question and the ARP Reply as an answer, like this:

> "Hey, if your IP address is X, tell me your MAC address."

> "I am IP address X, and my MAC address is Y."

The first message in this exchange goes by the formal name of ARP Request, or the less formal name of ARP Broadcast. The formal term, *ARP Request*, refers to the fact that it asks the other host to supply its MAC address. The informal term, *ARP Broadcast*, refers to the fact that the ARP message flows as a LAN broadcast frame. In other words, the LAN switches forward the ARP Broadcast to all devices in the LAN. By using a broadcast, the ARP Request reaches all devices on the LAN so that all devices at least think about answering with an ARP Reply.

Figure 8-43 shows the ARP Request process in action. In this case, PC11 wants to send an IP packet to Server S1 (10.1.1.22), a host in the same subnet as PC11. However, PC11 does not know S1's MAC address. So, PC11 sends the ARP Request shown in the figure.

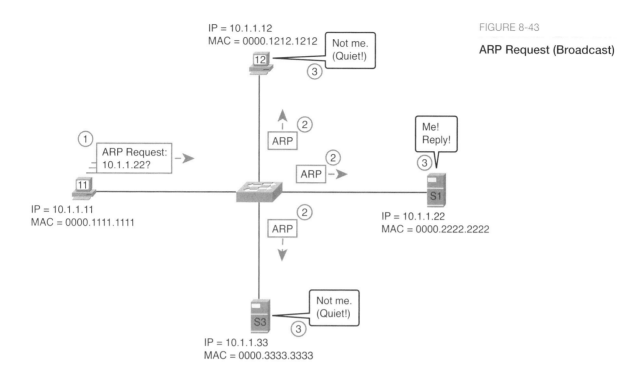

FIGURE 8-43

ARP Request (Broadcast)

Following the steps in the figure:

1. PC11 sends an ARP Request, a LAN broadcast, listing the IP address for the host that PC11 wants to reply with its MAC address: 10.1.1.22.

2. The LAN switch floods the LAN broadcast frame out all ports, because that is how LAN switches process all LAN broadcasts.

3. All three of the other IP hosts think about the request. The two hosts that do not use IP address 10.1.1.22 (PC12 and S3) silently ignore the ARP Request. S1 sees its own IP address (10.1.1.22) and decides to reply.

The host that sends the ARP Request does not learn anything from sending the ARP Request; it only learns from the ARP Reply. The ARP Reply simply lists the original IP address that the ARP Request asked about, along with the MAC address that host uses. Figure 8-44 shows the ARP Reply that Server S1 would make in response to PC11's ARP Request in the previous figure.

FIGURE 8-44

ARP Reply (Unicast)

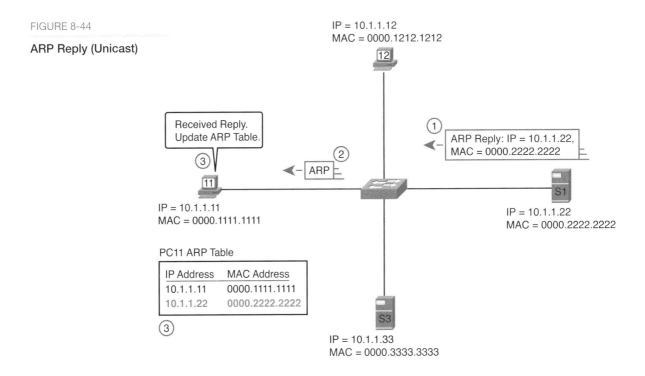

The figure shows a couple of other important points besides the fact that PC11 learned S1's MAC address. First, the ARP Reply is not a LAN broadcast; it is sent back to the MAC address of the device that sent the ARP Request. So, the figure shows the frame flowing from S1 to PC11, but not to the other two devices.

ON THE SIDE: You can see the ARP cache on many OSs using the **arp -a** command.

The figure also introduces the idea of an *ARP table*, or *ARP cache*. Each host keep a list of the IP addresses and matching MAC addresses that it learns using ARP (as well as its own IP address/MAC pair). Anytime a host needs to send an IP packet, the sender first checks its ARP table. The host needs to send an ARP Request only if it does not already have an ARP table entry for that IP address. In the example in Figure 8-44, the next time PC11 needs to send an IP packet to S1 (10.1.1.22), PC11 will not need to send an ARP Request. Instead, PC11 can first check its ARP table, and finding S1's MAC address, just use that value.

Routing Between Hosts in Different Subnets

Before diving into the details of IP routing once more, take a moment and think about someone who lives in Manhattan taking a trip to see a friend who lives in Los Angeles. For those of you not from the United States, Manhattan is a densely populated part of New York City, where most people do not own cars, but they instead use subways and taxis to get around. In Los Angeles (LA), another large city, but with a widely spread population, most people drive cars to get around.

To go from her Manhattan apartment to her friend's LA apartment, the person goes the entire distance, but none of the individual vehicles take the complete trip. For example, to get to the airport near Manhattan, this person probably takes a subway train. She hangs out at the airport, waiting on her flight, and then she gets on a plane for a cross-country flight to LA. Then she hang out in the airport in LA long enough to get her luggage and rent a car. Finally, she drives the rental car her friend's apartment in LA.

In this analogy, the subway train stayed in Manhattan. The rental car stayed in LA, on the other side of the country. And the airplane never went to this person's apartment, always staying either in the air or at the airports. None of the vehicles took the entire trip; only the person in the vehicles took the entire trip.

So, what does all this have to do with IP routing? The IP packets in a network act like the person who does travel through the full trip, while the data-link frame acts more like the individual vehicles that only matter for part of the trip. In IP routing, the IP packet goes from end to end, but the data-link header/trailer never leaves its own LAN or WAN.

Figure 8-45 shows the process, with PC11 sending an IP packet to PC21, which sits on the other side of a network. For reinforcement of the idea, the figure shows subway cars, a plane, and a car beside the different LANs and WANs.

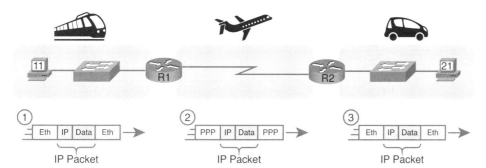

FIGURE 8-45

Example, IP Packet End to End, Data-Link Heads Stay on LAN or WAN (Subway, Plane, and Car Icons © Siarhei Pleshakou)

The next few pages look at IP routing between two hosts in different subnets. In particular, the discussion looks at the different data-link headers that must be added and removed by hosts and routers, making frames that act like different vehicles to move IP packets across the IP network.

Addressing Frames and Packets When Crossing Multiple Subnets

When routing IP packets between hosts in different subnets, the IP packet must pass through multiple LANs and WANs. The IP packet, particularly the source and destination IP address, does not change during that trip. The data-link headers and trailers do change, however, because routers discard and build new headers and trailers. That process also changes the data-link addresses in those headers.

First, look at the IP addresses in an example with Figure 8-46. In this case, PC11 (10.1.1.11) sends an IP packet to PC21 (10.1.2.21). The two hosts sit on different LANs, so they should be in different subnets. For this example, assume a subnetting plan like the earlier examples, with all addresses in a subnet having the same value in the first three octets.

FIGURE 8-46

**IP Addresses Stay
the Same Through
End-to-End Path**

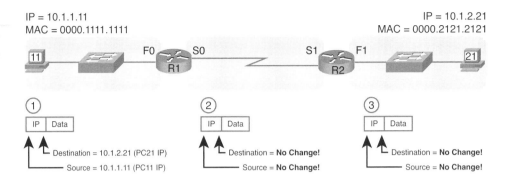

Following the steps in the figure:

1. PC11 puts its own IP address as the source IP (10.1.1.11), and PC21's IP address as the destination (10.1.2.21).

2. R1 does not change the IP addresses as part of the routing process.

3. R2 does not change the IP addresses as part of the routing process.

In contrast, not only do the data-link addresses change at each router, but each router also removes the entire data-link header and trailer of the incoming frame, and adds a new data-link header and trailer. The data-link frame has the job of moving the IP packet to the next router or host, and after the frame delivers the IP packet to the next router or host, the data-link header and trailer can be discarded.

To see how that works, take a look at the first data-link frame, using the same example started in Figure 8-46. In this example, PC11 sends an IP packet to PC21. PC11's IP logic tells it to send the IP packet to its default router, because the destination (PC21, 10.1.2.21) is in a different subnet than PC11. To make that happen, PC11 encapsulates the IP packet inside an Ethernet frame, with a destination MAC address of the MAC address on R1—namely, R1's MAC address on the same LAN as PC11. Figure 8-47 shows the specific details in this example.

FIGURE 8-47

**Ethernet Frames Use
MAC Addresses on
That LAN (Only)**

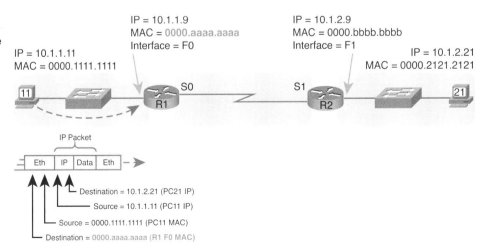

To learn R1's MAC address, specifically the MAC address on R1's F0 (Fast Ethernet 0) interface, PC11 uses ARP. ARP still lets the PC learn the MAC address of another device, but in this case, PC11 uses ARP to find a router's MAC address.

Removing and Adding Data-Link Headers at Each Router

After a frame delivers an IP packet to a router, the router no longer needs the data-link header and trailer. Think of the Ethernet frame as if you took the subway train to the airport—after you get to the airport, you get off the subway train and you do not need it anymore. With IP routing, the router removes the IP packet from the incoming data-link frame using deencapsulation, and then adds a new data-link header and trailer before sending the packet, using encapsulation. In fact, when a router routes an IP packet, it does several small tasks, including:

1. Deencapsulating the IP packet from inside a received data-link frame

2. Making a routing decision using the IP packet's destination IP address and the router's IP routing table, identifying the correct outgoing interface

3. Encapsulating the IP packet into a new data-link frame that works on the outgoing interface

Figure 8-48 shows an example of what happens on the two routers in the previous example, using the same numbers in the preceding list. In this case, when R1 receives an Ethernet frame, R1 extracts the IP packet, chooses its S0 interface as the outgoing interface, and adds a PPP header/trailer before sending the frame out interface S0. R2 receives the PPP frame, removes the IP packet, makes a routing decision to send the packet out R2's F1 interface, and encapsulates the IP packet inside a new Ethernet frame.

ON THE SIDE: Hosts use ARP to find the MAC address of other hosts in the same subnet. They do not need to use ARP to find MAC addresses in other subnets.

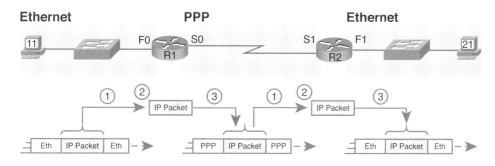

FIGURE 8-48

Routers Discard Old and Add New Data-Link Framing

Using ARP with Routers

When routers add the new data-link header and trailer, they have to choose what to put in the header/trailer, including the correct data-link addresses. With the PPP link in this example, R1 has little thinking to do, because PPP addressing requires no thought. Some data-link protocols, like Frame Relay and Ethernet, do require some thought, however. In those cases, the router needs to pick the right data-link addresses.

When routers need to forward IP packets out Ethernet interfaces, routers can use ARP to learn the correct destination MAC address. For example, on the right side of Figure 8-48, R2 needs to deliver the IP packet to host PC21. So, R2 builds an Ethernet header with PC21's MAC address as the destination. However, if R2 does not yet know PC21's MAC address, per R2's ARP table, R2 needs to use ARP to learn PC21's MAC address. Figure 8-49 shows an example, with R2 needing to use ARP, and then R2 sending the frame destined to PC21's MAC address.

FIGURE 8-49

Example of Router R2 Using ARP to Learn a Local Host's MAC Address

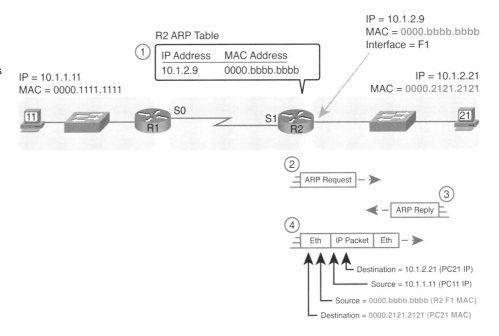

Following the steps in the figure:

1. R2 wants to forward an IP packet to PC21, but R2 does not see PC21's IP address (10.1.2.21) in R2's ARP table.

2. R2 sends an ARP Request looking for PC21's MAC address.

3. PC21 sends an ARP Reply, supplying its MAC address (0000.2121.2121).

4. R2 now forwards the IP packet, with destination MAC address 0000.2121.2121.

Chapter Summary

The Internet Protocol (IP), along with several other related network layer protocols, does the work to allow hosts to send IP packets to other hosts. IP defines several important jobs, including the IP routing process, by which routers make forwarding decisions of where to forward each IP packet. That forwarding logic relies on some of the IP addressing concepts defined by IP, particularly the idea of grouping IP addresses into predefined IP networks and flexibly defined IP subnets. IP also defines the role of IP routers in creating a physical end-to-end path through the TCP/IP network by having routers connect to LANs and WANs.

In an enterprise TCP/IP network, IP addresses must be planned. That planning requires knowledge of the two-tier classful structure of IP addresses A, B, C, D, and E, as well as the details of how IP breaks the three unicast address classes into multiple classful IP networks. The planning process requires understanding the rules, as well as choosing particular IP networks and subnets to use for each LAN and WAN. After they are chosen, each LAN and WAN interface that uses IP logic must be assigned an IP address, either through static configuration or by a dynamic process like DHCP.

The end-to-end routing of IP packets from one host to another relies on the sending host as well as the routers between the two hosts. The sending host must know when to send the packet directly to the destination host, when the destination is in the same subnet, or to the host's default router. Each router must make a routing decision for each packet by comparing the IP packet's destination IP address to the router's IP routes (as listed in the IP routing table). After the router finds a matching IP route, the router forwards the IP packet based on the matched route's forwarding instructions. With each router forwarding a packet correctly, the routers together deliver the packet to the correct destination host.

To physically forward the IP packets between hosts and routers, and between routers, these nodes use LANs and WANs. When forwarding the IP packets, the hosts and routers must encapsulate the IP packet inside a data-link frame that works on each LAN and WAN. As the IP packet passes through the TCP/IP network, routers must remove the IP packet from the incoming data-link frame, and encapsulate the IP packet in a new data-link frame, before sending it back out some other interface. On LANs, that means that hosts and routers alike will need to know the MAC addresses used by other hosts on the same LAN, so both use ARP to learn those MAC addresses.

Chapter Review Activities

Use the features in this section to study and review the topics in this chapter.

Answer These Questions

1. Which of the following answers describes the TCP/IP network layer?

    a. Provides end-to-end routing

    b. Focused on operations that occur on IP hosts

    c. Defines physical operations rather than logical

    d. Defines LAN and WAN operations

2. Which of the following answers are IP routing protocols that dynamically learn IP routes on behalf of IP routers? (Choose two answers.)

    a. DHCP

    b. EIGRP

    c. ARP

    d. OSPF

3. Which of the follow answers list a function related to TCP/IP network layer tasks, but the task is not defined as part of IP? (Choose two answers.)

    a. Discovering the IP address of another host based on that other host's text name

    b. Discovering the MAC address of another host based on the other host's IP address

    c. Connecting LANs and WANs using routers

    d. Defining a 32-bit address used to identify hosts in the network

4. Host 1, with IP address 1.2.3.4, sends an IP packet to Host 2, whose IP address is 5.6.7.8. Which of the following answers is true about the IP address information in the IP header of the packet?

    a. The IP header list Host 2's IP address, but not Host 1's IP address.

    b. The IP header lists the text character code for 5, 6, 7, and 8 to represent the destination IP address.

    c. The IP header lists the binary version of 1.2.3.4 as the source IP address.

    d. The header lists the text character code for the entire destination address 5.6.7.8, including the dots.

5. A user at PC1 opens a web browser and types in a URL that lists the name of a server (Server1). PC1 has never tried to send an IP packet to Server1. Which of the following protocols will PC1 need to use before PC1's browser can successfully see the web page from the server?

    a. DHCP

    b. DNS

    c. OSPF

    d. EIGRP

6. A user at PC1 opens a web browser and types in a URL that lists the IP address of a server to which PC1 wants to connect (address 1.1.1.1). The TCP/IP network has many IP routers, with many different physical paths. PC1 sits several routers away from the server with IP address 1.1.1.1. Which of the following protocols could impact which path the packets from PC1 to the server take? (Choose two answers.)

    a. DHCP

    b. OSPF

    c. ARP

    d. RIP

7. Which of the following answers are true about an IPv4 address class and the type of IPv4 addresses in that class? (Choose two answers.)

    a. Class B: Experimental IP addresses

    b. Class D: Multicast IP addresses

    c. Class E: Unicast IP addresses

    d. Class C: Unicast IP addresses

8. Which of the following answers lists a number that, based on the value in the first octet, fits into the address class listed in that same answer?

    a. 100.1.1.1, class A

    b. 128.1.1.1, class A

    c. 191.1.1.1, class C

    d. 192.1.1.1, class B

9. The size of a classful IP network can be defined as the number of IP addresses in the IP network. Which of the following answers lists a true statement about the sizes of class A, B, and C networks?

    a. Class A are smaller than class C.

    b. Class C are smaller than class B.

    c. Class B are larger than class A.

    d. Class B and C are the same size.

10. A user has configured the IP settings on his PC using static configuration. Which of the following answers lists something not typically set as part of the IP settings on a host?

    a. The MAC address of the default router

    b. The IP address(es) of the DNS server(s)

    c. The subnet mask

    d. The host's own IP address

11. PC1 and PC2 sit on the same LAN and subnet. The subnet ID is 1.1.1.0, and the subnet includes all numbers from 1.1.1.0 to 1.1.1.255. PC1 has been statically configured with IP address 1.1.1.1. PC2 now tries to lease an IP address using DHCP. What prevents PC2 from getting address 1.1.1.1 in the DHCP lease?

   a. The DHCP server uses DHCP messages to discover that PC1 has 1.1.1.1 as a statically configured IP address; then the DHCP server will not lease 1.1.1.1 to PC2.

   b. There is no guarantee possible; DHCP should not be used if static configuration is also allowed.

   c. The DHCP server should omit 1.1.1.1 from its list of addresses that it can consider for a DHCP lease.

   d. The DHCP server must be configured with the option to lease only even-numbered IP addresses.

12. The following answers each list one IP address and a possible IP network ID. Which answers show the correct network ID with its IP address? (Choose two answers.)

   a. 19.19.19.19: Network ID 19.0.0.0

   b. 200.200.200.200: Network ID 200.200.0.0

   c. 100.100.100.100: Network ID 100.100.0.0

   d. 192.192.192.192: Network ID 192.192.192.0

13. Host 1 sends an IP packet to Host 2. The IP packet passes through Routers R1, R2, and R3. When R1 forwards the IP packet, R1 matches a particular IP route in its routing table. Which parts of the route had something to do with the router's logic in matching this IP route? (Choose two answers.)

   a. Network/subnet ID

   b. Next-hop router

   c. Outgoing interface

   d. Subnet mask

14. A network engineer takes a class A network (10.0.0.0) and begins to create a subnetting plan. He chooses a plan in which all the subnets are the same size. Which of the following options would be allowed? (Choose two answers.)

   a. In each subnet, the first 2 octets of each address must have the same value.

   b. In each subnet, the last 2 octets of each address must have the same value.

   c. In each subnet, the first 22 bits of each address must have the same value.

   d. In each subnet, the last 22 bits of each address must have the same value.

15. PC1 connects to a LAN, listing Router R1 as its default router. PC1 wants to send an IP packet to 1.1.1.1. Which of the following answers is true about how PC1 chooses to forward this packet?

   a. PC1 always sends the packet to R1 (default router) next.

   b. PC1 runs a dynamic routing protocol and matches its IP routing table, much like a router.

    c. PC1 first determines whether the destination is on the same subnet as PC1 and only sends the packet to R1 if the destination is in another subnet.

    d. PC1 will ARP looking for 1.1.1.1's MAC address, no matter what.

16. In the following figure, PC12 sends an IP packet to PC22. The IP packet completes the trip from PC12 to PC22. Which of the following answers list the correct location and addresses used as this packet crosses the network from PC12 to PC22? (Choose two answers.)

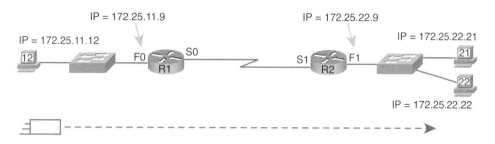

    a. On the LAN on the left, the source MAC address is PC12's MAC address.

    b. On the LAN on the right, the source MAC address is PC12's MAC address.

    c. On the LAN on the right, the destination IP address is 172.25.22.22.

    d. On the LAN on the left, the destination MAC address is PC22's MAC address.

17. In the following figure, PC12 sends an IP packet to PC22. The IP packet completes the trip from PC12 to PC22, and PC22 sends a reply packet back to PC21. Focusing on the packet from PC22 back to PC21, which of the following answers list the correct location and addresses used as this packet crosses the network? (Choose two answers.)

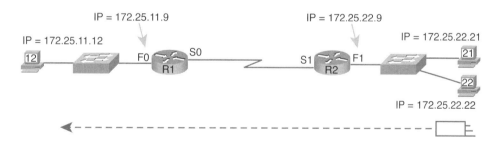

    a. On the LAN on the left, the source MAC address is PC22's MAC address.

    b. On the LAN on the right, the destination MAC address is R2's MAC address.

    c. On the LAN on the right, the destination IP address is 172.25.22.9.

    d. On the LAN on the left, the destination MAC address is PC12's MAC address.

18. Hosts PC1, PC2, PC3, and PC4 all sit on the same LAN subnet, along with Router R1. PC1 needs to send an IP packet to PC2. Imagine that none of the devices know any of the other device's MAC addresses yet. Which of the following messages will flow as a result of PC1 needing to send the packet to PC2?

   a. An ARP Broadcast from PC2

   b. An ARP Reply from R1

   c. An ARP Request from PC1

   d. An ARP Reply from all devices except PC1

19. PC1, PC2, and Router R1 all connect to the same LAN. PC1 and PC2 list R1 as their default router. PC1 sends an IP packet to PC2. PC1's ARP table was empty before starting this particular test. Which of the following would happen in this case? (Choose two answers.)

   a. PC1 would send the IP packet, inside an Ethernet frame, to R1 next.

   b. PC1 will send an ARP Request, looking for PC2's MAC address.

   c. PC1 would send the IP packet, inside an Ethernet frame, to PC2 next.

   d. PC1 will send an ARP Request, looking for R1's MAC address.

20. PC1 sends an IP packet to PC2. PC1 sits on a LAN. PC1 sends an Ethernet frame, with the IP packet for PC2 encapsulated inside the frame, to PC1's default router. Three routers, including PC1's default router, sit between PC1 and PC2. Which of the following statements is true about the data-link headers and trailers used during the trip from PC1 to PC2?

   a. The original Ethernet header will make the entire trip from PC1 to PC2.

   b. The original Ethernet header will be removed and later re-created with the same addresses.

   c. Four different data-link headers/trailers will be used, one for each different LAN and WAN.

   d. None of the answers is correct.

Define the Key Terms

The following key terms include the ideas most important to the big ideas in this chapter. To review, without looking at the book or your notes, write a definition for each term, focusing on the meaning, not the wording. Then review your definition compared to your notes, this chapter, and the glossary.

Key Terms for Chapter 8

IP router	Dynamic Host Configuration Protocol	IP subnetting
IP address		default router
routing table	IP routing	Address Resolution Protocol
IP network	IP route	

List the Words Inside Acronyms

The following are the most common acronyms discussed in this chapter. As a way to review those terms, simply write down the words that each letter represents in each acronym.

Acronyms for Chapter 8

IP	DDN
ARP	IPv4
DHCP	IPv6
DNS	

Create Mind Maps

Create a mind map for IP addressing rules. Use brief phrases, just enough to remind yourself of the ideas. At first, capture the ideas in any order. As you remember more and more rules about IP addressing, think about what rules seem to be about the same topics, and organize your IP addressing based on your categories.

Define Other Terms

Define the following additional terms from this chapter, and check your answers in the glossary:

router	classful IP network	deencapsulation
interface	DNS server	ARP Request
dotted-decimal notation	DNS client	ARP Reply
static configuration	DHCP server	ARP Broadcast
dynamic routing protocol	DHCP client	ARP table
routing protocol	DHCP lease	Internet Protocol
DNS Request	subnetting	Network ID
DNS Reply	IP subnet	IP version 4
IP address class	subnet mask	IP version 6
classful IP addressing	host routing	subnet ID
unicast IP address	encapsulation	

Complete the Tables and Lists from Memory

Print a copy of Appendix B, "Memory Tables" (which you can find online at www.pearsonitcertification.com/title/9780789748454), or at least the section for this chapter, and complete the tables and lists from memory. Appendix C, "Memory Tables Answer Key," also online, includes completed tables and lists to check your work.

Chapter 9

The Internet

The Internet touches the lives of most everyone on the planet today. Many of us use the Internet directly throughout the day. Some use it indirectly, for example, watching a news story when a reporter happened to learn some background information using the Internet. The Internet has an impact on political systems, economics, religion, human rights, and countless other parts of life.

While the impact of the Internet might be huge, it is basically a computer network. This chapter builds on what this book has already discussed about computer networking, and shows how we all collectively play a part in building the Internet.

In particular, this rather long chapter breaks down the topics into four parts, each about the same length:

- The first major section, "The Internet as a Network of Networks," explains how countless organizations work together to connect their TCP/IP networks together to create the network of networks that today we call the Internet.

- The second major section, "Internet Access Technologies," discusses how individuals and small businesses often connect to the Internet, focusing on three technologies: analog modems, digital subscriber line (DSL), and cable modems.

- The third major section, "Network Layer Concepts Before Scarce IP Addresses," examines the big three parts of the network layer (addressing, routing, and naming), with the simpler original rules of the Internet, when the Internet was not growing so fast.

- The fourth major section, "Network Layer Concepts with Scarce IPv4 Addresses," adds to the network layer discussion about the features required to deal with the fast growth of the Internet.

Chapter Outline

Objectives

- Explain how individual devices, some home-based TCP/IP networks, corporate TCP/IP networks, and ISP TCP/IP networks connect to create the global Internet.

- Show the typical devices and connections used in a connection from a corporate TCP/IP network and an ISP.

- Describe how ISPs work together to create the Internet core.

- Generally describe the Layer 1 and 2 features used when connecting to an ISP using analog modems, DSL modems, and cable modems.

- Compare and contrast analog modems, DSL, and cable as Internet access technologies.

- Explain IP routing in the Internet, in the direction from an enterprise toward the Internet and from the Internet toward an enterprise.

- List the typical steps that occur when a client needs to do name resolution for a host name that exists in a different DNS subdomain.

- Compare and contrast the public IP address assignment process that was used before IP address exhaustion, and after the introduction of CIDR.

- Explain the basic reasons why CIDR needed a route aggregation feature, and how route aggregation helped fill that need.

- Explain the fundamental concepts behind how NAT reduces the number of required public IP addresses.

Key Terms

the Internet

Internet edge

point of presence

Internet core

Internet access

analog modem

DSL

cable Internet

default route

host name

Domain Name System

subdomain

IPv4 address exhaustion

classless interdomain routing (CIDR)

Network Address Translation (NAT)

The Internet as a Network of Networks

The Internet is a network of networks that spans the globe. It connects corporate TCP/IP networks, small office networks, and individual users from home or from their mobile devices. It even includes the TCP/IP networks built by Internet service providers (ISP), who build their networks to help create the Internet.

Each part of the Internet exists as a network of some size by itself. For example, as discussed throughout Chapter 8, "The Internet Protocol (IP)," enterprise TCP/IP networks connect devices so that they can send data to one another. These enterprise networks use LANs and WANs, technologies from all layers of the TCP/IP model. Ultimately, inside that one company, the enterprise TCP/IP network moves IP packets from host to host.

To create the Internet, all these individual TCP/IP networks must connect to the Internet using some kind of Internet access technology. Internet access just refers to some kind of LAN or WAN link, usually a WAN, that connects one TCP/IP network to the Internet. It does not matter whether the network being connected is a huge enterprise TCP/IP network with hundreds of thousands of hosts, two hosts in a small office/home office (SOHO) network, or even a single mobile phone—the idea is that some access link gives that network access to the rest of the Internet, as shown in Figure 9-1.

FIGURE 9-1

Internet Access Links from TCP/IP Networks, Large and Small

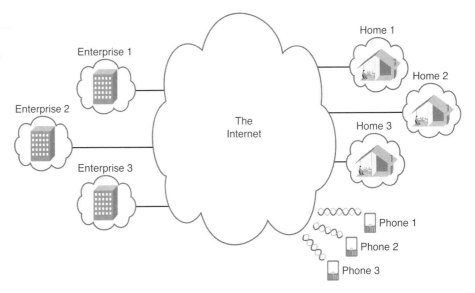

The figure shows just one of many perspectives on what the Internet looks like, focusing on the Internet edge and Internet access links. The middle of the Internet, the Internet core, includes many interesting parts as well. ISPs create the core of the Internet, which creates a physical network over which IP packets can flow between companies and individual uses, as seen in Figure 9-2.

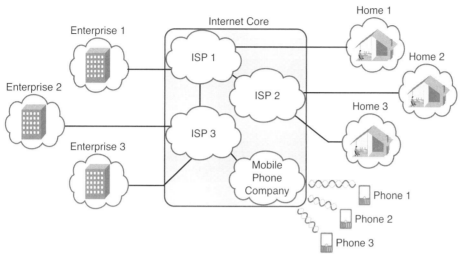

FIGURE 9-2

**The Internet Core,
with Multiple Service
Providers**

This first of four major sections of the chapter shows how smaller TCP/IP networks fit together to create the huge global worldwide Internet. The following sections begin with a look at how both companies and individuals connect to an ISP using some kind of Internet access link. The text then discusses how to create the Internet core by creating an ISP TCP/IP network and then connecting all the ISPs together. These sections close by looking at some other types of companies that help create the Internet by offering services for users of the Internet.

Connecting Enterprises to an ISP

Companies have many reasons to need to connect to the Internet. First, the company often wants to make its own information and services available. For example, if a company sells tires, it probably wants to make its website available on the Internet so that everyone else can learn about and buy its tires. Also, many companies want their employees to be able use functions from their computers that rely on the Internet. That could include letting employees use an Internet search engine like Google, or sending emails between the company and its suppliers and partners—both of which require connections to the Internet.

Some other organizations use the same network technology as companies, but have a completely different mission and reason for connecting to the Internet. Figure 9-3 shows a few of the types of organizations that have their own TCP/IP network, but different reasons for needing to be connected to the Internet.

FIGURE 9-3

Typical Organizations Whose TCP/IP Networks Connect to the Internet

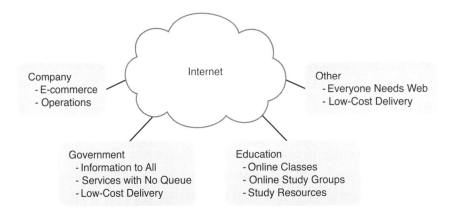

Although many types of organizations want to connect to and use the Internet, they all use the same kinds of TCP/IP networking technology. Because this chapter focuses on the technology, it just refers to all these organizations as if they were a company or enterprise.

Connecting to the Internet Edge

The term **Internet edge** refers to the part of the Internet topology between an ISP and the ISP customer. It sits at the edge of both an enterprise and ISP TCP/IP network, between them. Internet access links, like those seen earlier in Figure 9-1, connect the enterprise and ISP at the Internet edge.

For perspective, take just a moment, or at least a paragraph or three, to think about both a typical enterprise TCP/IP network and a typical ISP network. A company owns its own routers, LAN switches, LAN access points, PCs, laptops, cables, and so on. That company leases WAN services to use between company sites. And that company's TCP/IP network could work, standalone, without the Internet, to let all hosts in that company communicate with each other.

Ultimately, though, the company's motivation to build its TCP/IP network is to get the work done. That process usually involves the people who work at the company. So, an enterprise TCP/IP network typically has lots of end-user hosts, such as PCs, laptops, tablets, phones, and so on.

ISPs build their TCP/IP networks to do the work of the ISP as well; however, the ISP's work is to connect to customers and deliver their packets. Most of the people served by an ISP do not work for the ISP, but instead they work for the ISP's customers.

As a result of an ISP's business model, the ISP's TCP/IP network has many fewer end-user hosts, with much more focus on the parts of a TCP/IP network that forwards IP packets. The ISP network has lots of LAN and WAN links, with routers, but because the vast majority of the people sit in other (customer) TCP/IP networks, the ISP TCP/IP network has few user LANs.

Figure 9-4 shows this comparison between a typical enterprise and ISP network, with the enterprise showing many more user devices and the ISP showing primarily routers and links.

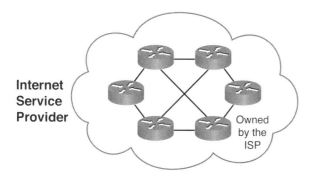

FIGURE 9-4

Comparing an Enterprise and ISP Network

Enterprise

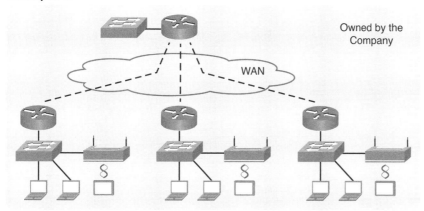

Companies physically connect to the Internet using an Internet access link. That access link can be any of the WAN technologies discussed in this book, or any other WAN technology. From a network layer perspective, the Internet access link acts like any other WAN link between routers, in that the two routers can send IP packets over the link. Figure 9-5 shows an example, with a leased line (T3) between the company's router and one of the ISP routers.

FIGURE 9-5

**T3 Serial Link Connection
to the Internet**

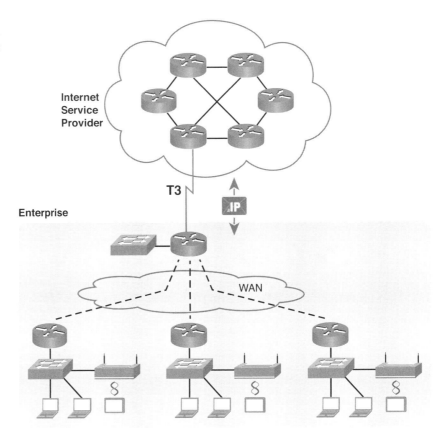

Securing the Internet Edge

The introduction of a connection to the Internet makes the enterprise TCP/IP
network much less secure. Simply put, any kind of cyberattack requires that the
attacker be able to send packets to the hosts being attacked, or read the traffic. If
the attacker sits in the Internet, and the company has no Internet connection, attacks
might never get started. With an Internet connection, the entire world can decide
to attack, including anyone from a smart-but-bored teenager to organized crime
syndicates.

Enterprises use many security measures and devices to make the Internet
connection more secure, including using both firewalls and intrusion prevention
systems (IPS). As usual, both functions can exist as either a standalone device or as
one function of an integrated single device. Both typically sit inside the enterprise,
near the Internet edge.

Many different options exist for how to approach network security for an Internet
connection. This section does not attempt to look at all the options, but the example
around Figure 9-6 shows one example just to give you a flavor of what happens.
In this case, as typical, the firewall sits inline, meaning that it sits in the path that
all packets take. The IPS sits outside the forwarding path for packets, so one of
the LAN switches forwards packets to the IPS. The IPS then sits back, analyzes
packets, and watches for signs of the bad guys trying to cause problems.

FIGURE 9-6

Example Case of Using an Enterprise Firewall and IPS

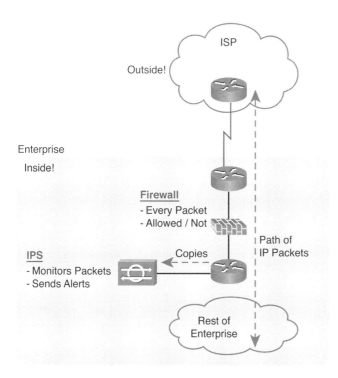

ON THE SIDE: This book uses only the term IPS, but the market uses several related terms, partly because of history and partly because of vendor product names. Other similar terms that refer to similar functions include intrusion detection system (IDS), intrusion detection and prevention (IDP), and intrusion detection and prevention system (IDPS).

AUTHOR'S NOTE: Intrusion detection systems (IDS) entered the market before IPSs; IPSs have replaced IDSs in the market. The early IDS devices typically sat outside the packet-forwarding path, as shown in Figure 9-6, resulting in some documentation referring to the IPS instead as an IDS in that case.

From a security perspective, the firewall separates a more trusted enterprise network from the less trusted Internet. As a result, the enterprise is sometimes called the *inside* network, and the Internet is called the *outside* network.

The single most common specific function of a firewall has to do with preventing access to servers inside the enterprise. To appreciate why a firewall might want to limit access to servers that sit inside the enterprise, take a moment to think about why an enterprise connects to the Internet in the first place. Most companies have the following types of goals:

- Allow users inside the company to connect to servers that sit outside in the Internet.

- Allow users outside the company (in the Internet) to connect to a small subset of servers inside the enterprise, like the company's public web server.

- Prevent users outside the company (in the Internet) from connecting to servers in the enterprise that are meant only for internal purposes (for example, a payroll server).

ON THE SIDE:
Adding rules to allow
some specific types
of traffic is often
called *punching a
hole* in the firewall.

Firewalls use a rule set that tells the firewall what packets to allow through and
what packets to discard. The most common beginning rule in the rule set is to
prevent outside clients from sending packets to inside servers. Then, the network
engineer can add rules that allow outside clients to reach some inside servers, but
only those specifically listed by the engineer.

Figure 9-7 shows a typical rule set for an enterprise firewall, with the following
rules:

A. (Default): Allow inside clients to reach outside servers in the Internet.

B. (Default): Prevent outside clients from sending packets to inside servers,
unless another rule allows the packet.

C. (New Rule): Allow outside clients to connect to the two public web servers in
the demilitarized zone (DMZ).

The figure shows two attempts from users in the Internet to connect to two different
servers in the enterprise. The first case, shown as Steps 1, 2, and 3 in the figure,
shows a user connecting to a public web server (rule C), which the firewall allows.
The second attempt, shown as Steps 4 and 5, shows an attempt to connect to
another server inside the enterprise, which is rejected because of rule B.

FIGURE 9-7

**Firewall Allowing
Connections to Public
Web Servers Only**

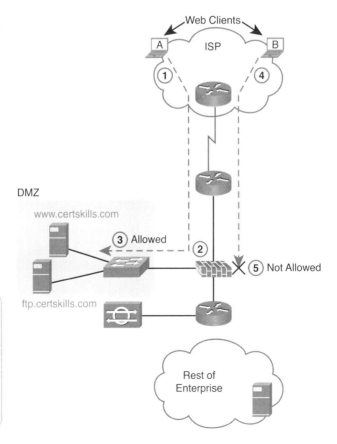

ON THE SIDE: The
security world refers
to the location of
publicly available
servers, like the
servers in Figure 9-7,
as a DMZ.

Following the steps in the figure:

1. Outside client A sends a packet to server www.certskills.com as part of its attempt to connect to the public web server of the enterprise.

2. The packet arrives at the firewall, because the firewall is in the forwarding path of packets.

3. The firewall allows the packet per rule C, and forwards it to the server (using routing logic).

4. Outside client B sends a packet to server payroll.certskills.com as part of its attempt to connect to the company payroll server.

5. The packet arrives at the firewall, because the firewall is in the forwarding path of packets. The firewall's rule B discards the packet.

Connecting Individuals to an ISP

While this chapter focuses mostly on the technology used to create the Internet, the biggest impact of the Internet might well be how it has changed individual lives on a daily basis. Just ask yourself what you did today that relied on the Internet. How many times today did you do something that used the Internet? What is the longest time today that you went without using the Internet? If the Internet were completely down for the next three days, what kind of impact would that have on your life?

Individuals have a variety of Internet access options from the home. Each of those technologies creates a WAN connection between the user's device and some ISP. That WAN connection might connect the user's device directly to the WAN, as shown in Figure 9-8, or the connection might use a router (not shown).

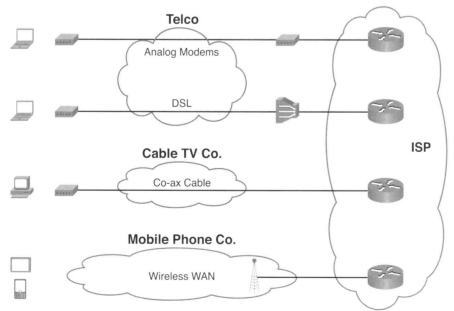

FIGURE 9-8

Four Main Options for Individual Internet Access

The second of the four major sections in this book, "Accessing the Internet," discusses each of these options, as well as some others.

Creating the Internet Core Using ISPs

Take a moment to think about an ISP as a business. The ISP offers a service, for which the ISP customer pays a fee, usually monthly. The ISP supplies these two fundamental services:

> **Internet access:** The legal right and the physical ability to connect to the ISP and send/receive bits at some rate; the actual rate might be a range of speeds, or it might be nonspecific.
>
> **Delivery to the entire Internet:** A commitment to deliver packets to hosts throughout the rest of the entire global Internet.

For the first service, this chapter has already discussed the idea of the Internet edge and Internet access links. For the second service, the ISP must create connectivity that allows packets to move from the sending host, at one customer site, all the way to the receiving host, at another customer site. And those hosts can even be located at customers of different ISPs.

To make it all work, each ISP has to create the following kinds of connections:

- Connections between that ISP's customers and an ISP point of presence (POP)
- Connections between all of that ISP's POPs, creating the ISP's own TCP/IP network, allowing all of that one ISP's customers to send packets to one another
- Connections to other ISP TCP/IP networks to form the Internet core, allowing all Internet hosts in the world to send packets to each other

The following sections look at each topic in this list, in order.

Connecting Customers to the ISP Point of Presence (POP)

To fill the need for the first item in the list, the ISP needs some equipment, including routers. To keep the cost down, the ISP typically tries to put its own equipment near to its customers, both for business and technical reasons. As you probably recall from Chapter 7, "Wide-Area Networks," some WAN services base their cost on the distance. Also, some WAN technologies, such as DSL, work best over short distances.

ISPs refer to a location near some set of customers as a **point of presence (POP)**. Just like a telco central office (CO) is a building where the telco keeps its equipment, the ISP POP is a building where the ISP keeps its networking equipment.

To create an effective Internet access service, an ISP needs to create a number of POPs in different locations. For example, if an ISP planned to advertise its services in six cities in a particular part of the world, it might create one POP in each city, as shown in Figure 9-9.

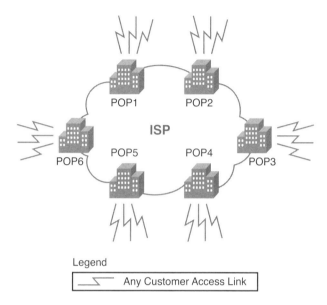

FIGURE 9-9

ISP Point of Presence (POP) Concept with Customer Access

The figure shows buildings for each POP, because they do physically exist in some building somewhere. However, the interesting technology part of the picture includes the real networking gear that the ISP installs in those buildings.

The POP typically holds many types of devices, and maybe a large volume of devices, depending on the number of customers the ISP expects to serve from the POP. Often, some routers serve as access routers, with connections directly to the customer's Internet access links. Other routers might be focused on connections to the rest of the ISP network, with high-speed WAN links to other sites. Within the POP, the routers need to connect to each other, usually using LAN links of some kind. Figure 9-10 shows a typical POP, with each access route using a direct LAN link to a distribution router, which in turn connects to the rest of that ISP's TCP/IP network.

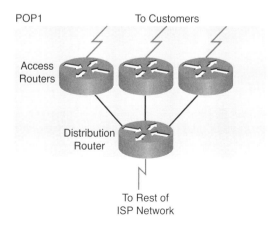

FIGURE 9-10

Example of Dividing Responsibilities Inside an ISP POP

Connecting POPs to Create an ISP TCP/IP Network

After creating POPs, an ISP needs to connect all its POPs together. Why? Well, the ISP commits to delivering IP packets to all other possible Internet destinations, and that includes destinations for other customers of the same ISP. For example, if an ISP has one customer connected to POP1, and another connected to POP2, but no ability to forward IP packets between these two POPs, the ISP has already failed.

While an ISP's own TCP/IP network needs to deliver IP packets between all the POPs, the details of how the ISP meets that goal are up to the individual ISP. Each ISP can build its network using any technology, devices, protocols, and so on, much like the telco can use any technology it wants to use to create WAN services. However, often today, ISPs use very powerful routers, which support large numbers of faster LAN and WAN optical links, with the ability to forward IP packets at high rates.

Figure 9-11 shows one example of how the ISP in the last few figures might complete its own TCP/IP network. It might put two more routers at a centralized site and use 10-Gbps Ethernet, or the Synchronous Optical Network (SONET) equivalent called OC-192, on all the links shown in the center of the figure.

FIGURE 9-11

Connecting All ISP POP Routers to Create an ISP TCP/IP Network

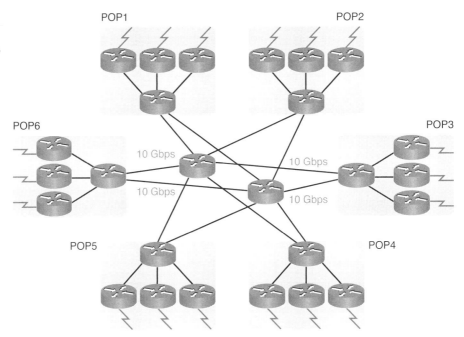

Connecting ISPs to Create the Internet Core

While creating a single ISP's TCP/IP network takes a lot of work, that work does not require the ISP to cooperate with other ISPs. One ISP can create its own POPs to support access links to its own Internet customers. That one ISP can choose what equipment to use, what WAN links to use, and what bit rates, and negotiate the costs for those links with WAN service providers. So, for that ISP's part of the Internet (that ISP's own TCP/IP network), that one ISP can work without talking with other ISPs.

However, to meet their commitment to deliver IP packets to hosts all over the Internet, ISPs must work together. Every ISP commits to delivering data to all destinations in the Internet. As long as competition exists, some customers will access the Internet through one ISP and some through another, and those two ISPs must somehow move packets between their own TCP/IP networks. In reality, hundreds of ISPs exist, maybe thousands, and they all commit to delivering packets to customers of all the other ISPs.

In short, ISPs work together to create the **Internet core**. The Internet core connects all ISPs to all other ISPs, sometimes directly and sometimes indirectly. As a result, all ISPs can then send packets to hosts connected to every other ISP.

Actual connections between ISPs often use technology already mentioned in this book as WAN technology. The links exist between routers, which lets the routers use the usual IP packet-forwarding logic, forwarding packets to the next IP router. The volumes of traffic can be relatively large, so the links commonly use the higher-end Ethernet speeds and higher-end SONET speeds. Figure 9-12 shows the idea.

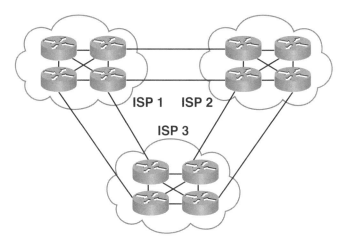

FIGURE 9-12

Creating the Internet Core: Connections Between Large ISPs

AUTHOR'S NOTE:
Tier 1 ISPs often cooperate to create less expensive high-speed interconnections in locations called *network access points (NAP)*. Each ISP puts one (or more) router into a NAP. All the ISPs use some high-speed LAN connections to a LAN switch, creating high-speed (but inexpensive) links between the ISPs.

The figure shows a couple of characteristics of Tier 1 ISPs. The term *Tier 1 ISP* refers to how the ISP operates and what its network topology looks like. Basically, Tier 1 ISPs invest heavily in their connections to other Tier 1 ISPs, usually with multiple links to each other Tier 1 ISP. Often, Tier 1 ISPs have connections in many different locations, often in different locations around the globe.

Tier 1 ISPs together create a high-volume, high-performance part of the Internet core. Figure 9-12 shows the main ideas, with each ISP using redundant links to each other ISP, with different routers. If any one link or router in that figure were to fail, the two ISPs would still have connections to each other. If multiple devices and links failed, in most combinations, connectivity between ISPs would still exist.

So, summarizing those Tier 1 features:

- Links to many other Tier 1 ISPs in the same geography
- Multiple links to one ISP, spread across different devices and locations for redundancy and performance reasons
- Often covers large geography—at least an entire country and often a continent, or global

Some ISPs simply do not have the same goals as a Tier 1 ISP, so they fall into a second general category, called (you guessed it) Tier 2. A Tier 2 ISP does not offer worse service to its customers, and it is not a second-class ISP. However, the terms *Tier 1* and *Tier 2* make many people automatically think that Tier 1 is better, so many ISPs might position themselves as Tier 1 ISPs, just for marketing purposes.

A *Tier 2 ISP* has goals that let it rely on the connections to the Tier 1 ISPs for some of its connections to the Internet. A Tier 2 ISP essentially connects to one, or a few, Tier 1 ISPs, instead of trying to connect to all the Tier 1 ISPs across the globe. Tier 2 ISPs can still have high-speed redundant links to their many connection points, and have many customers. For example, a Tier 2 ISP might have many connections inside one country or continent, and rely on connections to a few Tier 1 ISPs for connectivity to the rest of the world.

Figure 9-13 shows the idea of how Tier 1 and Tier 2 ISPs together create the Internet core, with Tier 2 ISPs in this case singly connected to one Tier 1 ISP, but with the Tier 1 ISPs more fully connected.

FIGURE 9-13

Connectivity Between Tier 1 and Tier 2 ISPs

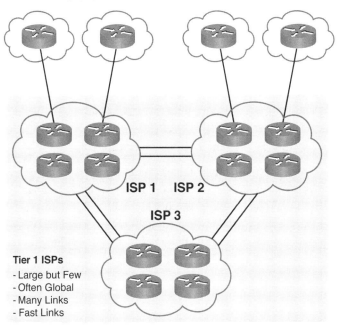

Tier 2 ISPs
- Fewer Locations
- Smaller Geography

ISP 1   ISP 2

ISP 3

Tier 1 ISPs
- Large but Few
- Often Global
- Many Links
- Fast Links

Adding Value with Other Providers of Service

The next topic completes this first major section of this chapter by looking at services in the Internet that have nothing to do with delivering IP packets from one Internet host to another. These services make the Internet much more useful.

For example, several companies offer a search engine service. You connect to that company's website and type in some text, and that company supplies a list of all the websites in the universe that the search engine company thinks match your search. Some of the more common search engines are Google, Bing, and Yahoo!.

If you take two minutes and stop reading, and think about what you do with the Internet, you can probably think of many services in the Internet. Some are useful for work, some for school, and some are just for fun. They might have nothing to do with moving an IP packet from host A to host B, but they make the Internet a useful place.

Regardless of the particular service provided, all these services use computers and TCP/IP networks to create their service. The company creating a service must follow a familiar story: It creates its own TCP/IP network with its own servers and routers. Then the service provider connects its network to the Internet. Then, when someone wants to use the company's service, the user can connect to the Internet and send packets to that service provider. Figure 9-14 shows the idea.

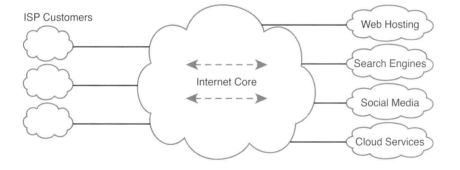

FIGURE 9-14

Other Service Providers Connected to the Internet

Many companies offer a large variety of services, but the figure shows four general types of services on the right just to give you some examples. The following list details some of the services each could supply:

- **Web hosting:** The customer picks a URL for his website, creates content for the website, and puts the files that make up that website onto servers that sit at the web-hosting company. The web-hosting company then acts as the web server for that customer. When any Internet user browses to the chosen URL, the packets go to/from the web-hosting company. (See the upcoming Figure 9-15.) Example companies include Google, Yahoo!, and Go Daddy.

- **Search engine:** Computers inside this company's network have programs that act like web browsers, systematically getting a copy of every web page they can find on the Internet. The programs then read the text, creating a huge index based on the words on each web page. Later, when a user connects to the search engine website, the search engine compares the user's search terms to the index, and lists the web pages that happen to have that same text. Example companies include Google and Bing.

- **Social media:** The company builds web servers that provide a framework for users to add their own content (text, photos, video, apps). Users sign up for an account and add their own content to the service provider's web pages. Later, others can look at those same pages to see what the individual users posted, interacting with friends through the site. Examples include Facebook, Twitter, and Google+.

- **Cloud services:** This term refers to a large variety of services available from the Internet. One example is file services, where a user creates and stores files in a folder that appears to be on her local computer, but the file actually exists on storage at the site of some service provider. The file can then be read by other authorized users from anywhere in the Internet. Examples include Dropbox.com and Box.net.

For example, many small and medium-sized businesses have a TCP/IP network and a website available for all the world to see. Some companies provide web-hosting services so that the company does not have to buy and install its own web servers; instead, it can use the web-hosting service.

Figure 9-15 shows an example of web hosting, using a company called Example Co. The Example Co website, www.example.com, exists on servers owned by a web-hosting company on the right side of the figure. When a user in the Internet browses to www.example.com, the packets flow to/from the servers at the web-hosting service. Example Co also connects its own enterprise TCP/IP network to the Internet for other reasons, such as to allow employees to look for information on the Internet.

FIGURE 9-15

Hosting a Website at a Web-Hosting Service, Not in the Enterprise's IP Network

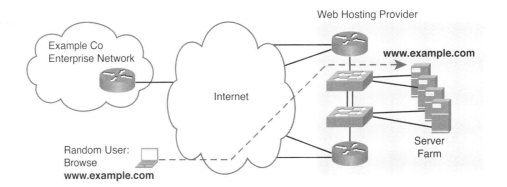

Internet Access Technologies

The term **Internet access** refers to the way that one device or network connects to an ISP so that the device or network can send packets between itself and the ISP. To physically access the Internet, some physical connection, typically a WAN, must exist between an ISP router and the ISP customer's router. After those two routers can send and receive IP packets from each other, that customer's site, whether it is a single PC or a huge corporate TCP/IP network, has a connection to the rest of the Internet.

Telcos typically offer different types of WAN links to homes and apartments than they offer for businesses, mainly for economic reasons. For example, one of the telco's biggest costs is the cabling that it installs between COs and from a CO to the business or customer. Consumers spend much less money than businesses, but business locations are typically located much more closely together than residential areas. So, the telco can spend relatively less money on cabling to the business areas of town, with much more expected income from those cables.

Of all the consumer Internet access technologies commonly found in houses and apartment buildings, most use existing cabling that has some other purpose. Two options use the two-wire (one-pair) local loop cabling from the telco, using the same analog phone circuit the telco has supported for many decades. Another option uses the coaxial cabling installed by the cable TV (CATV) company. Yet another option avoids the cabling issue altogether, using wireless WAN services, as discussed back in Chapter 7.

This second of four major sections in this chapter discusses Internet access technologies. However, because Chapter 7 has already discussed several WAN technologies that businesses would use to access the Internet, the following sections focus mostly on technologies that were originally meant for consumers. These sections, in order, look at analog modems, DSL, cable, and wireless WANs, with a few words on using business WAN technology as well.

A Phone Line and Analog Modem

In the original days of the public Internet, using analog phone lines with modems was the single most popular way for individuals to connect to the Internet. Both the telco phone network and analog modems existed and worked long before the Internet needed to use them. When the need for an inexpensive Internet access technology happened, analog modems and the telco were ready.

Layer 1 and 2 Analog Internet Access

Using analog modems for Internet access requires both the customer and ISP to work a little like they do when making a phone call over the local telephone system. They use the same local loop line from the home to a local CO. However, they remove the phone and add an **analog modem** on each end. One modem (usually at the ISP customer site) makes a phone call to the ISP site, creating an analog circuit. The two modems then modulate the digital signal into an analog signal to send over the analog circuit and demodulate it back into a digital signal.

If you step back and think about the big picture, an ISP POP might be set up to handle hundreds or thousands of customers dialed into the ISP at any one point in time. To make that work, the ISP works with the telco to create one phone number that rings through on any of thousands of phone lines coming into the ISP's POP, into a set of modems called a modem bank. The ISP publishes this one phone number, so the customer does not need to worry about different numbers to call. When a customer calls, the telco passes the call into the ISP POP over one of the phone lines that is not being used.

Figure 9-16 shows many of the parts for an ISP dial service. On the left, it shows two ISP customers, one with an external analog modem and one with an internal modem. It shows the one ISP phone number (555-1234), with the modem bank, and routers connected to the modem. If the ISP wants to support 1000 concurrent users in a POP, it needs 1000 modems (or equivalent) in that POP. After it is dialed in, the user's PCs can now send and receive bits with the ISP through Router R1.

FIGURE 9-16

Two ISP Customers Using Analog Modems and Analog Phone Lines

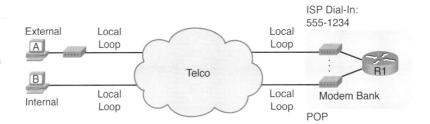

Although many data-link protocols have been used on analog modem links over the years, today the PC and router use the familiar Point-to-Point Protocol (PPP). As you will find out in this section of the chapter, PPP has many uses, including its original purpose as a data-link protocol to be used on any serial link. PPP gives both the PC and the router the ability to encapsulate and send their IP packets.

PPP also plays an important Layer 3 role on switched (dialup) serial links. With this model, the ISP does not assign IP address information to each customer, but instead, the ISP wants to give the customer IP address info to use just while the customer is connected to the ISP. When the customer hangs up the analog modem call, the ISP can use that IP address for a different customer.

The big question, which PPP helps answer, is this: How does the host learn its own IP address and other related IP configuration? The short answer is that both PPP and DHCP typically have a role. Together, they help the customer's PC learn its own IP address, the associated subnet mask, the default router IP address, and the IP addresses of any DNS servers. Figure 9-17 shows one example of how a PC can learn the information.

Following the steps in the figure:

1. PC A does not have an IP configuration, so it uses PPP and DHCP messages to request IP configuration.

2. Router R1, working with the DHCP server, finds and sends back the required IP configuration.

3. PC A can now send packets, using its assigned IP address (10.1.1.1) as the source IP address.

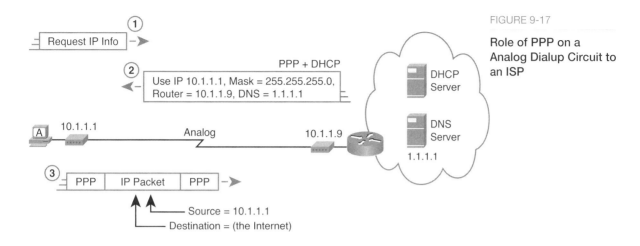

FIGURE 9-17

Role of PPP on a
Analog Dialup Circuit to
an ISP

Perspectives on Using Analog Phone Lines for Internet Access

As you work through the rest of the Internet access technologies, it can help to
pause to think a little about why ISP customers might choose one option over
another. This short topic, and a couple of others like it related to DSL and cable
modems, walks through some of those thoughts and comparisons.

First, analog modems run slowly but are typically a cheap option. Analog modems
use slower bit rates than all the other modern Internet access options. However,
most people already have home phone lines, and modems cost little. The cheapest
form of Internet access from the home today is to use analog modems.

Historically, analog modems have some big advantages that can also be useful to
think about before tackling the next topic (DSL). Think back to a world in which
the telco had a long-established voice network, with phones in every home, but the
Internet boom had not happened. When the Internet started growing so quickly,
ISPs could not afford to run cables to every home—the cost would have been too
high. It was an easy marriage between telcos, analog modems, and ISPs. More
importantly, it gave ISPs a potential customer base of anyone with a home phone
line, which in the developed part of the world, meant 99 percent of the homes.

Using analog modems for Internet access does have some negatives in addition
to the slow speed, however. To use it, the user must take an action, clicking a few
things on the screen to make the modem dial the ISP. That process takes some extra
time, usually 10–15 seconds to set up a call into the ISP. Additionally, you cannot
use the phone line to talk to someone while connected to the ISP; the phone line
can be used for one or the other, just not both at the same time. If you hang up the
call to the ISP, you cannot then use the Internet, so the Internet service is not on all
the time.

Finally, analog modems use symmetric speeds rather than asymmetric speeds. That
means that the upstream speed, the speed of sending bits from customer to ISP, is
the same speed as the downstream speed (the direction toward the customer). For
most Internet applications, many more bytes flow downstream than upstream, so an
asymmetric service with faster downstream speeds actually works better. Table 9-1
summarizes the key points.

TABLE 9-1

Comparison Points: Analog Modem

Name	Analog Modem
Physical link	Telco local loop
Always on?	No
Allows voice at the same time over the same medium?	No
Asymmetric? (Faster downlink possible)	No
Approximate real-life downlink speeds	56 Kbps

A Phone Line and Digital Subscriber Line (DSL) Modem

Using analog circuits for Internet access had many pros and cons, but two stand out in that they helped lead to the next Internet access technology. In most developed countries, telcos have installed local loops (in other words, phone lines) almost everywhere, both in businesses and homes. The negative: low speed, at least by today's standards.

Unsurprisingly, over the years, telcos have researched ways to keep the advantage of using local loop cabling to send data, but to send the data faster. One option was the development of faster modems, but that analog technology simply could not reach the speeds needed today. Telcos researched digital technology options as well, which resulted in a couple of technologies: first, Integrated Services Digital Network (ISDN), and later, digital subscriber line (DSL). This next topic looks at DSL.

Layer 1 and 2 DSL

First, think about voice on the local loop for a moment and ignore DSL. A home phone sends electrical signals with a range of frequencies that matched the human voice. The human voice makes sound waves from around 300 to 3400 hertz, and the analog electrical signals on the phone line use the same frequencies, to mimic the voice. When the analog electrical signal reaches the telco CO, it enters the telco switch, and the switch treats that electrical signal as what it is: a representation of someone's voice.

DSL works a little like a multilane highway going over that same local phone line. The voice travels over one lane and the data has several high-speed lanes, all on the same local loop cable.

In reality, **DSL** does still use the same telco local loop, but it creates the effect of having multiple lanes by sending multiple electrical frequencies over that one electrical circuit. DSL sends the data using digital electrical signals at frequencies outside the frequencies that humans speak or hear. (Those higher frequencies act like the extra data lanes in the multilane highway analogy.)

DSL also requires some changes to the devices on the end of the local loop cabling, including the device in the telco CO. A traditional voice switch expects that the entire electrical signal represents analog voice, but with DSL, the electrical signal has many frequencies that require some complex processing. A traditional CO voice switch would not know what to do with these higher frequencies. So, the CO needs a new type of device, called a *DSL access multiplexer (DSLAM)*, as shown in Figure 9-18.

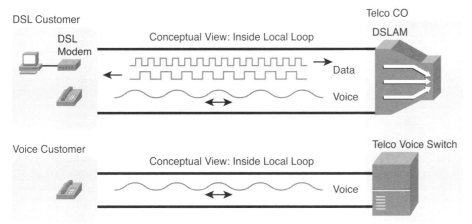

FIGURE 9-18

DSL Using Multiple Frequencies over a Single Local Loop

The consumer side of the DSL connection also requires a change. First, the telephone wiring into the home can be split so that the home has telephone extensions in different part of the house. All of those extensions connect to the same single electrical circuit. The following happens on the home side of the telco local loop:

- The telephone still connects to the same plug in the wall, still works the same way, and still sends the same analog electrical signal for voice.

- A *DSL modem* connects to another telephone extension in the house, and it sends and receives digital electrical signals at higher frequencies not used by the voice signal.

For example, Figure 9-19 shows three examples of the cabling in a home for a DSL connection. Only the top example shows the phone, with a telephone line splitter used so that, in the same room, an analog phone and the DSL modem can connect to the phone line. However, for all these connections, a phone could simply connect to a separate phone extension.

> **ON THE SIDE:** DSL providers often include little devices called *media filters* with their DSL modems, connected with the home telephone, to remove the sound caused by the data frequencies.

FIGURE 9-19

Home Cabling and Devices for DSL

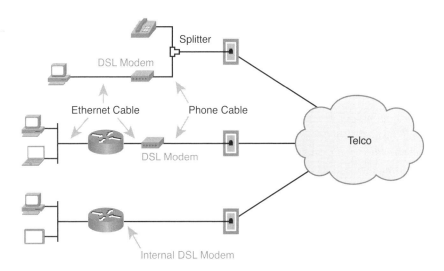

DSL includes many options, but the figure shows three just to show some of the options. The top option shows a case where the home has only one PC to connect to the ISP, so the PC can connect, without a router. The PC can use either an internal or external DSL modem (external shown). The middle and lower cases show a consumer router with a LAN, with the LAN connecting to DSL. Whatever device serves as the DSL modem needs to be plugged into a phone line, which often uses a phone Registered Jack 11 (RJ-11) connector, the same connector used in most home phone cables in the United States today.

Now that you have an idea about the physical setup and the concepts of multiple frequencies on the one circuit, next think about the job of the DSLAM. The DSLAM uses frequency-division multiplexing (FDM) to separate out the parts of the one electrical signal (remember, it is just one electrical circuit) into the voice and data frequencies. The DSLAM uses some frequencies to send data to the customer, some to receive data from the customer, and some for the analog voice signal to/from the customer's phone.

The DSLAM does not process the data or voice at the various frequencies; instead, it passes the data or voice off to the correct device. What device? The data goes to a router and the voice to a traditional voice switch, as seen in Figure 9-20.

To wrap up this section's discussion of how DSL works, next move up the TCP/IP architecture to the data link layer. If you take a step back, the DSL data-link protocols focus more on the following part of the puzzle, depending on whether a PC or a router connects to the DSL link:

> Move data-link frames from the home PC or home router to the ISP router.

DSL uses a couple of data-link protocols to reach this goal, but first and foremost, DSL connections use PPP. For example, a router at a home with a DSL line sends a PPP frame, with an encapsulated IP packet, toward the DSLAM, and that PPP frame arrives at the ISP router, as seen in Figure 9-21.

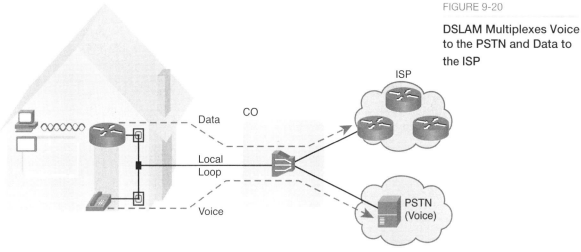

FIGURE 9-20

DSLAM Multiplexes Voice to the PSTN and Data to the ISP

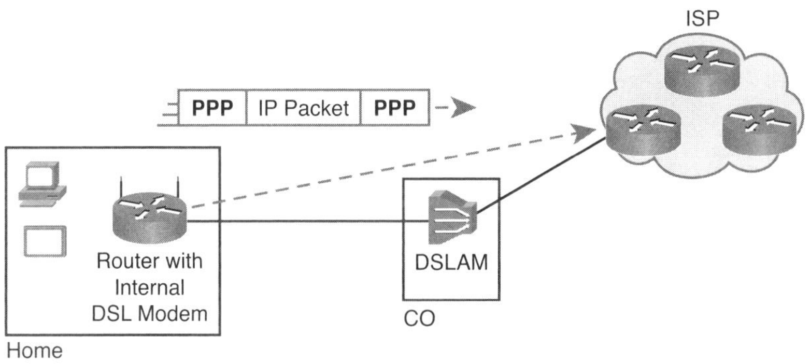

FIGURE 9-21

PPP-Encapsulated IP Packets Going from Home to ISP Router over DSL

Although the concept in Figure 9-21 is true from one perspective, it does not show the entire story. For example, with an external DSL modem, an Ethernet physical link exists from the PC or router and the DSL modem, so unsurprisingly, Ethernet data-link protocols are also used on that link. Also, inside the telco, the DSLAM uses another data-link protocol, ATM.

Interestingly, DSL still uses PPP, all the way from the home PC or home router to the ISP's router. How that works with Ethernet, and with ATM inside the ISP and telco, is beyond the scope of this chapter. However, just know that the DSL data-link story includes more detail.

ON THE SIDE: Some of the other data-link protocols that use PPP with DSL are called PPP over Ethernet (PPPoE) and PPP over ATM (PPPoA).

> **AUTHOR'S NOTE:** The router and IP hosts at the home still need IP addresses. The same IP concepts apply regardless of whether the home uses DSL or cable, so this chapter waits to discuss these IP details until you reach the section, "SOHO Address Assignment (Early Days)."

ON THE SIDE: For
a quick test, go find
the website of some
local DSL provider,
like your local telco,
type in your mailing
address, and see
whether it supports
DSL to your address.

DSL Versus Analog Modems

DSL does run faster than analog modems. But could there be any downside?
Are there other advantages, other than speed? This next topic looks at these two
questions.

First, DSL supports fewer customers, which is a negative from the ISP's
perspective at least. DSL has distance limitations based on the length of the local
loop, which affects whether it works at all and how fast it works.

For example, imagine three houses, located short, medium, and long distances from
the CO. DSL might not even work at the distance to the third house, removing that
potential customer from being able to buy DSL service. DSL might work at the two
nearer houses. However, after it is installed, the customer that sits a shorter distance
from the CO might get better bit rates than the customer at the medium distance.

But the big factor, of course, is speed. Pinning down one single speed for DSL can
be difficult. In fact, most companies that offer DSL do not even put a number on
their websites stating the speed. DSL has many standards, with different speeds and
with different ratios of the upstream and downstream speeds. And in practice, the
speed can be slower depending on the distance and quality of the local loop. That
said, if DSL works to your house, it will be faster than analog modems.

Table 9-2 summarizes these key comparison points.

TABLE 9-2

Internet Access Link Comparison Points: Analog and DSL

Name	Analog Circuit	DSL
Physical link	Telco local loop	Telco local loop
Always on?	No	Yes
Allows voice at the same time over the same medium?	No	Yes
Asymmetric? (Faster downlink possible)	No	Yes
Approximate real-life downlink speeds	56 Kbps	24 Mbps

AUTHOR'S NOTE:
Use the approximate
downlink speeds
for comparison
purposes. However,
note that the speeds
change over time and
differ based on many
factors, so do not use
the speed numbers
as absolute values.

A Cable TV Cable and Cable Modem

From a business perspective, analog modems and DSL both took advantage of
the already-installed telco local loop cabling. This kept the overall cost down,
increasing the number of customers who would pay for Internet service. And the
fact that the telco had so many phone lines installed in many countries increased the
size of the market.

Those big ideas beg the next question: What other utilities have a similar
arrangement, with some cable running into the homes of a large percentage of the
population? And could that be used for Internet services?

Cable television, also called CATV, does exactly that. Cable companies run a coaxial cable into each home or apartment. You can think of the cable as the equivalent of the phone company's local loop. The coaxial cable looks different and is round in shape, with a round connector. However, the cable has two conductors, which lets the CATV company create one electrical circuit from the CATV company to each customer. And of course, the original purpose for these connections was to offer quality television (TV) service.

This topic looks at the basics of how a CATV company can offer a cable Internet service. It starts by showing enough of the Layer 1 and 2 details of how the devices at home can send IP packets to and from a router at the cable company. This topic ends with a comparison of cable Internet service compared to analog modems and DSL.

Layer 1 and 2 Cable Internet

CATV companies began as businesses that delivered quality video signals to homes. To provide that service, these companies already used a lot of frequency-division multiplexing (FDM) technology. The CATV cable creates a single electrical circuit from the cable company to the home, but it supports a large number of TV channels. How does the CATV company do that? FDM.

A CATV company supports multiple TV channels by multiplexing the channels onto a single electrical circuit using FDM technology. Each TV channel can be thought of as a frequency channel, much like the different radio frequency channels on the radio in a car. One complex electrical signal comes over that one electrical circuit into the home from the cable company. To view a single channel on your TV, you choose a TV channel (actually a frequency channel). Your TV then knows to look at only one frequency range, or frequency channel, and ignore all the other frequencies coming over the cable.

To support the ability to send data, CATV researchers came up with a way to use some frequency channels for data instead of video. So, you can think of a **cable Internet** service as just another TV channel, but instead of video, the cable Internet channel sends your data, as shown in Figure 9-22.

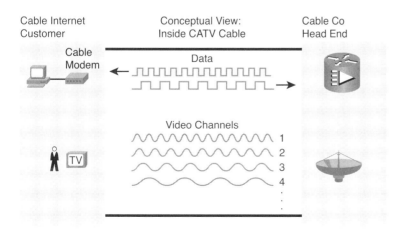

FIGURE 9-22

Cable Internet Using Multiple Frequencies over a Single Circuit on Coaxial Cable

The cabling at home follows the same basic structure as DSL and home phone cabling, except the cabling is CATV coaxial cabling instead of telephone cabling. The house might have several extensions with wall plates waiting for a coaxial cable and a TV to be connected; the cable modem can be connected to any of these. Also, the cabling can use a splitter. Figure 9-23 shows the cabling at the home that connects the cable modem function to the cable, whether internal or external. The cable modem must exist, but it can be a separate external device, an expansion card inside a PC, or an interface inside a router; the figure shows some examples.

FIGURE 9-23

Home Cabling and Devices for Cable Internet

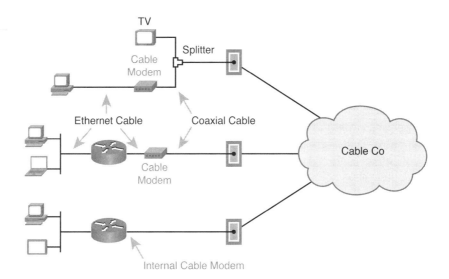

The cable company typically runs coaxial cable into the home, but in most cases, the physical cabling between the customer and the cable company uses a combination of coaxial and fiber cabling. Coaxial cables work well to support quality video, but they take up much more space than the thin copper wires used by telcos in their local loops. To keep the cost down, CATV companies use a combination of fiber and coaxial called *hybrid fiber coaxial (HFC)*.

HFC allows CATV companies to support many customers with just a few fiber cables, then using coaxial cables into each individual home, as shown in Figure 9-24. Depending on the particular part of town, the CATV company might have run the fiber part of the distance, or most of the distance, to the actual houses and apartments, using terms like these:

Fiber to the Neighborhood (FTTN): The fiber goes to the front of the neighborhood, with coaxial going the rest of the way to the houses.

Fiber to the Curb (FTTC): The fiber goes all the way into the neighborhood, and the fiber is buried at the curb that runs along the street where the houses sit.

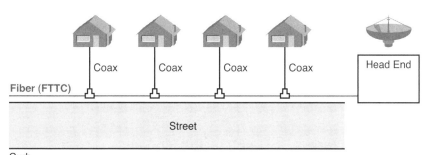

FIGURE 9-24

Hybrid Fiber Coax (HFC) and Fiber to the Curb (FTTC)

The CATV company calls its equivalent of the telco's central office (CO) a *head end*, as shown on the right side of Figure 9-24. The head end has space to hold various devices, including the devices that connect to the ends of the HFC cables shown in the figure. The head end also connects to the videos sources, like satellite dishes, multiplexers that multiplex the video signals, pay-per-view servers, and of course, IP routers to provide Internet services. Figure 9-25 shows a diagram, with a focus on how the head end routes the video and data traffic.

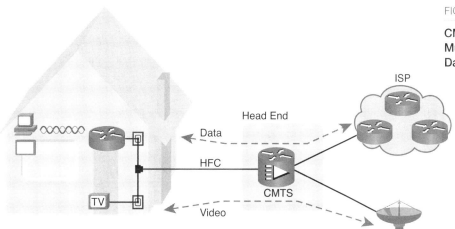

FIGURE 9-25

CMTS and Head End Multiplexes Video and Data

The head end uses a device called a cable modem termination system (CMTS) in the same role as the DSLAM with DSL. Basically, the CMTS looks for the data frequencies in the cabling, splits out the bits in those channels, and forwards those to/from the ISP router.

Finally, think about the end-to-end (left-to-right) physical connections in this figure. To support data, the cable modem encodes the data in the correct frequency channels to send to the CMTS device at the cable company head end. The cable modem also looks at the incoming electrical signal, uses FDM to look for only the data frequencies, and then decodes the data on those frequency channels. The CMTS at the head end does the same, using a specific set of frequencies to send data to and from the cable modems.

Finally, beyond these physical layer details, the cable modem also uses Layer 2 frames to encapsulate the packets. Several options and variations exist. Some options even use PPP, with similar concepts shown in the DSL section. Many use a data-link standard defined as part of DOCSIS (Data Over Cable Service Interface Specification), a cable-industry standard adopted and ratified by the ITU. However, the details of the data-link framing remain outside the scope of the book.

Cable Internet Versus DSL and Analog Modems

Cable Internet services follow a business model more similar to DSL than to analog modems. The cable company must provide the service between the head end and the customer, because the cable company owns a monopoly for the cabling. A separate company could act as the ISP, owning the router that sends data through the cable company. However, often today, the cable company can act as both the provider of data services and as the ISP.

Cable Internet has several other nice features as an Internet access technology. It has no distance limitations like DSL's limits. If the cable company has installed the cabling for TV service, it can support Internet service as well. The realistic actual bit rates (speeds) have increased over the years for both DSL and cable, but the cable data rates have remained faster than DSL over those years. Like DSL, cable Internet is an always-on Internet service, is asymmetric (faster downstream than upstream speed), and allows users to talk on the phone while using the Internet. Table 9-3 summarizes these key points.

TABLE 9-3

Internet Access Link Comparison Points

Name	Analog Circuit	DSL	Cable
Physical link	Telco local loop	Telco local loop	CATV cable
Always on?	No	Yes	Yes
Allows voice at the same time over the same medium?	No	Yes	Yes
Asymmetric? (Faster downlink possible)	No	Yes	Yes
Approximate real-life downlink speeds	56 Kbps	24 Mbps	50 Mbps

Other Internet Access Options

To complete this discussion about Internet access options, this final topic touches on a variety of other options.

The Wireless Telco and 4G

Chapter 4's section, "Wireless WANs," introduced the concept of a wireless WAN service. A wireless WAN service uses the technology that supports modern wireless phones, particularly the features that support a phone's ability to use data features, like web browsing, email, and a large number of customer data apps. Chapter 4 already spelled out the basics of how it works. This chapter reviews the details in the context of how it can be used as an Internet access option.

First, as a technology, wireless WAN technology supports many devices. Most obviously, wireless WANs support mobile phones, but they also support other devices, like tablets, laptops, or any other computer. These devices can have a built-in wireless WAN card—a popular option with tablets like Apple's iPad. Or, the device can just use a wireless WAN card in a spare expansion port. The example at the top of Figure 9-26 shows these first two options.

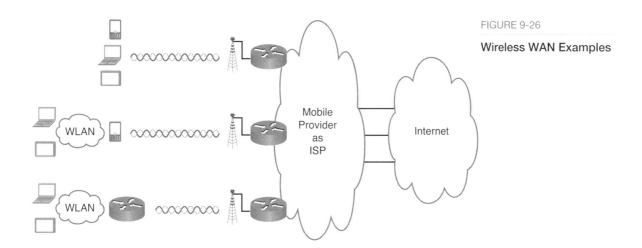

FIGURE 9-26

Wireless WAN Examples

The middle of the three examples on the left side of the figure shows another interesting Internet access option. In this case, a phone uses the wireless WAN to access the Internet. At the same time, the phone creates a small wireless LAN hotspot for a small number of devices, essentially acting as a WLAN access point. A businessperson could literally pull over by the side of the road, pull out his laptop or tablet, and connect to a WLAN created by his own mobile phone. The traffic from his laptop would flow into his phone using the WLAN and then out through the wireless WAN to the Internet.

The lower-left example in the figure shows one more option, this time with a router using wireless WAN technology instead of other WAN options. The router might be a typical integrated device, including a wireless AP and Ethernet switch, but for Internet access, the router could use a wireless WAN.

Wireless WANs give you one big and obvious advantage in being mobile. Wireless WANs can also compete based on speed with the more recent technology announcements of a fourth-generation (4G) technology called Long-Term Evolution (LTE). Although most wireless WAN providers do not publish their literal speeds, just saying that the speed is faster than the older technology, many user tests show speeds rivaling the faster cable modem speeds around 50 Mbps. As mobile providers keep expanding their 4G LTE coverage area, wireless WANs will become a very real option for high-speed Internet access for all users, not just those wanting mobile Internet access.

Any WAN Option, Consumer or Business

Most consumers access the Internet using analog modems, DSL, cable, or mobile WAN technology. However, consumers typically do not access the Internet using the WAN technologies discussed back in Chapter 7: time-division multiplexing (TDM) technologies like T1 and T3, Frame Relay, multiprotocol label switching (MPLS), Metro Ethernet, SONET, and ATM. Why? The answer mostly boils down to economics. The popular consumer Internet access technologies happen to use cabling that's already in most homes and apartments, which makes it inexpensive enough to be affordable.

However, consumers might be able to use traditional business WAN links to access an ISP. The issue of whether the ISP will or will not support a particular technology to your house or apartment has much more to do with economics rather than the technology. Depending on where you live, installing the service might require the telco to install new cabling under the ground, so using the service would require a large installation cost. However, if the telco already has cabling installed into your building, or nearby, the cost of Internet access using the WAN services listed in Chapter 7 might be the same as it would be for any business.

Regardless of the price, any of the WAN technologies discussed back in Chapter 7 can be used to access the Internet. Chapter 7 focused on connecting a pair of routers owned by the same enterprise using those WAN services. To connect to the Internet, a customer router just uses a WAN connection to an ISP router. Figure 9-27 shows a reminder of some of those WAN technologies from Chapter 7, with each of them used as an Internet access technology.

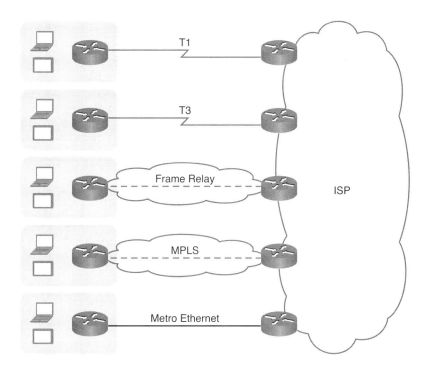

FIGURE 9-27

Enterprise WAN Options Used as Internet Access Technologies

Network Layer Concepts Before Scarce IP Addresses

You have reached the halfway point of this somewhat long chapter. This heading begins the third of the four major sections of the chapter, and at the same time, it moves the focus of the discussion from LAN and WAN topics to network layer topics. In fact, the rest of the chapter stays focused on the network layer of TCP/IP, namely the network layer issues that come up when building a global Internet.

Just to help you keep track of where you are in using this chapter, Figure 9-28 shows a little more context, with one box for each of the four major sections of the chapter. On the left, the first section looked at the Internet as a whole, walking through the pieces that connect together to create the Internet. The second section then focused completely on Internet access technologies, the WAN technologies used to access the Internet, mainly from small and home offices (SOHO).

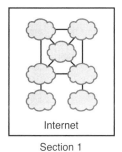
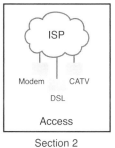
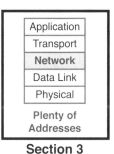
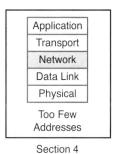

FIGURE 9-28

IANA-Assigned Classful IP Network Numbers

Both of the remaining two major sections focus on Layer 3 topics. The following sections look at the three main topics at the TCP/IP network layer: IP addressing, IP routing, and naming. Chapter 8 already discussed all three topics, but to build the global Internet, you have to think about some additional ideas related to each of these. These sections take what you learned from Chapter 8 and discuss how to use addressing, routing, and naming in a global network with billions of hosts.

This third major section also uses some original rules from TCP/IP, rules from the early days of the Internet. In those early days, the world had plenty of IP addresses. Eventually, the world started running out of IPv4 addresses, so the Internet community added some technologies to deal with that problem. This third section assumes a simpler world before IPv4 addresses became scarce. The fourth section adds more to the discussion, specifically the newer rules about features that deal with the fact that the world simply started to run out of IPv4 addresses.

This third major section sticks to the big three topics for the TCP/IP network layer, in this order: addressing, routing, and naming. For all three, the chapter focuses on what else you need to know about each topic beyond Chapter 8's information.

IP Address Assignments in the Global Internet

The Internet has a truly global reach. People from every continent, and most every country, use the Internet every day.

To make the Internet work globally, the people that build the Internet must agree to some administrative rules. Sure, the protocols defined by TCP/IP are essentially rules, so rules already exist. However, protocols define how the computing devices work, not the people. The world also needs a few specific rules for the people that build the Internet.

For example, just to make the point using an analogy, think about what cars can do versus what people actually choose to do with their cars. Most cars work best when riding on a road. If a road happens to be wide enough for four cars, if no other cars are around, a car probably rides just as smoothly on any part of the road. The car might be able to go 150 miles per hour, on any part of the road. However, we humans, being responsible drivers, follow the traffic laws: driving on the correct side of the road, not going 150 miles per hour, watching for traffic lights, and so on.

Similarly, while TCP/IP protocols define what computing devices can do, some additional rules define what we humans should do with those devices.

The topic on IP addressing focuses on one idea—the IP addresses used in the Internet must be unique among all IP addresses in the universe. The following sections first look at why the addresses need to be unique. They then discuss the administrative rules we humans must follow, both in enterprises and as individuals, to make sure that the IP addresses in the Internet are indeed unique.

IP Addressing Rules for a Global Internet

The Internet started as a small research network, researching the protocols that grew up to be TCP/IP. To test their new networking technology, the researchers built a network using that technology. So, when it came time to decide details like which node uses which address and what name, it could usually be settled by a quick phone call with some other researcher working on the same project to develop the protocols and devices to create TCP/IP.

As time passed, the research network grew, changed, and morphed into the Internet. To make this growing Internet work on a global scale, it had to meet the same basic requirements as the smaller earlier versions of the Internet had already met. The two main requirements that the world needed to follow in regard to IP addressing were

> **Individual IP addresses should be unique among all hosts connected to the Internet.** Every IP host must have a unicast IP address before it can send and receive IP packets. Among all hosts in the entire universe, at least those connected to the Internet, the IP addresses need to be unique.
>
> **Hosts should use IP addresses in groups, based on class A, B, and C networks, to aid routing.** Addresses could not be assigned randomly; instead, IP addresses had to be grouped together. Routers could then use routing tables that list one route for the entire group, making the routing tables shorter and making routing work more efficiently.

To make sure that all the companies whose TCP/IP networks connected to the Internet used unique IP addresses, all the companies had to agree to follow some administrative rules. The rules were essentially the same informal rules that the original researchers used:

- Before connecting to the Internet, ask for an assignment of a classful IP network (a class A, B, or C network).

- The Internet Assigned Numbers Authority (IANA) assigns the company a classful IP network.

- The only company in the universe that can use the addresses in that classful network is that one company.

By following these rules, every company gets its own class A, B, or C network, which can never be used by other companies.

Today, many different organizations, typically part of some not-for-profit organization, work together to assign IP addresses for the Internet worldwide. IANA, actually a part of a nonprofit called ICANN (Internet Corporation for Assigned Names and Numbers) works with five worldwide regional organizations to manage the address assignment process. This chapter ignores the details of the particular IANA partners, called Regional Internet Registries (RIR), referring to the entire group simply as IANA just to be brief.

Table 9-4 lists the five RIRs that work with IANA.

ON THE SIDE: IANA oversees the process of assigning IP addresses today. In the original Internet, the function was just done by one or a few people who volunteered to do the job, most notably a famous and respected pioneer of TCP/IP named Jon Postel.

TABLE 9-4

Regional Internet Registries (RIR)

Name	Locations Served
AfriNIC	Africa
APNIC	Asia Pacific
ARIN	North America
LACNIC	Latin America, Caribbean
RIPE NCC	Europe, Middle East, Central Asia

Enterprise IP Address Assignment (Early Days)

The original administrative rule for assigning addresses, so that no one used the same IP addresses worldwide, was for each company to use one classful IP network for its enterprise TCP/IP network. When a company wanted to connect to the Internet, it would apply to IANA and ask for an assignment of a classful network. IANA would then review the application and assign a network. Figure 9-29 shows the idea.

FIGURE 9-29

IANA-Assigned Classful IP Network Numbers

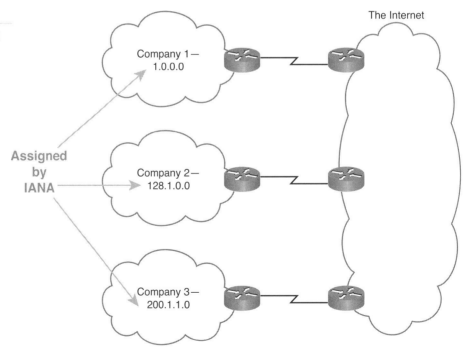

With these original rules for address assignment, IANA did not just hand out any IP networks. First, to ensure unique addresses, IANA only gave out IP networks that were not already assigned to some other company. Second, IANA only gave class A and B networks to companies that could justify the need for large numbers of IP addresses. For example, a company with ten employees did not need a class A network assignment.

So, the IANA IP network assignments followed these general rules:

- Only assign networks not assigned to another company yet.
- Assign the class of network just large enough to meet the need.

At the end of this administrative process, each company had a class A, B, or C IP address. Those IP addresses, called *public IP addresses* because they could be used in packets sent to the rest of humanity, should have been unique in the Internet.

At this point, the enterprise has an IP network to use. The rest of the story of IP addressing inside the enterprise follows the same rules as discussed back in Chapter 8. The enterprise network engineer plans subnets, one per LAN and WAN link. Then the various interfaces can be assigned with static IP addresses, and clients can use DHCP to dynamically learn their IP addresses. Figure 9-30 shows a conceptual view of the results of subnetting, with each company having multiple subnets of their respective class A, B, and C IP networks.

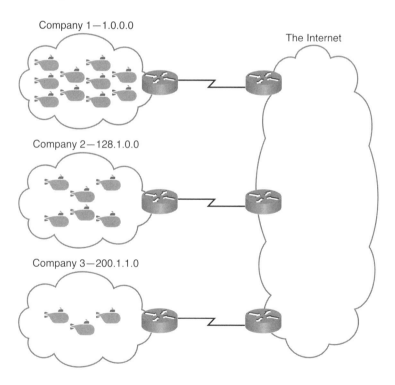

FIGURE 9-30

Enterprises Subnet Their One Classful IP Network

AUTHOR'S NOTE: The IP network assignment rules listed in this topic, for assigning a class A, B, or C network, was normal until around 1993. The final major section of this chapter discusses why the world started to run out of IP addresses, which then caused the rules for address assignment to change.

AUTHOR'S NOTE:
SOHO refers to small
office/home office.

SOHO Address Assignment (Early Days)

Back in the early days of the Internet, when IANA still gave each company a class A, B, or C network assignment, individual users could also connect to the Internet. However, in those days, most individual users connected using a single device, usually a PC with an analog modem. This short topic discusses how a single PC user could get a public IP address, unique in the Internet, to use when connected to the Internet.

To support users connecting to the Internet from their PCs with a modem, ISPs would register and receive some IP networks from IANA (or an RIR). The purpose: Dynamically assign each customer a public, globally unique IP address when he or she connects to the Internet.

Figure 9-31 shows an example. ISP1 reserved class C network 200.2.2.0. PC2 and PC3 have already connected, with ISP1 assigning them different IP addresses from network 200.2.2.0. PC1 just connected and wonders what IP address to use. The ISP router notices the new connection and sends a message to PC1, telling it to use IP address 200.2.2.4.

FIGURE 9-31

**Assigning IP Addresses
to SOHO PCs**

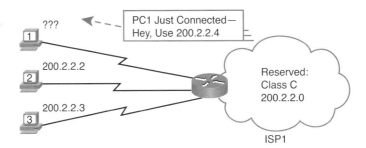

The most important difference between the SOHO user and the enterprise is that the SOHO user can completely ignore the administrative process to get a public, globally unique IP address. The ISP registers enough public IP addresses and assigns the addresses temporarily to the customer. Most SOHO customers do not even understand the concept of what a public IP address is.

IP Routing with the Internet

IP routing inside a single IP router works pretty much the same way, whether the router sits in a small corporate network or in the middle of the Internet. The router receives data-link frames and removes the IP packet. The router compares the destination IP address of the packet to the router's IP routing table, matching one entry in the table. The table tells the router out which interface to forward the IP packet, but first, the router adds a new data-link header and trailer around the packet.

However, as a network that connects other TCP/IP networks, the Internet does have many different routing issues as compared to an enterprise TCP/IP network. Some of those have to do with the packet-forwarding process (routing), and some have to do with how routers learn routes using routing protocols. The following sections look at a few of the basics of routing on a global scale, first looking at the core of the Internet, then from the enterprise perspective, and then from a home office perspective.

Internet IP Routing Protocols in the Internet Core

The Internet core contains many ISPs with many connections. The number of connections means that many possible routes exist between ISPs. Internet routers must choose the best route among many competing redundant IP routes, so the Internet core needs good dynamic routing protocols that can learn all routes, react to changes (for example, to a WAN link failure), and choose the best route among all the currently working routes.

And by the way, the routing protocol needs to work well with hundreds of thousands of destinations.

Besides needing a routing protocol to deal with large numbers of redundant routes, the routing protocol used in the Internet core needs to be able to think about which neighboring ISPs might be better from a business perspective. With an enterprise TCP/IP network, each route exists inside the enterprise, but with the Internet core, routes go from one ISP, to another, to another. Those ISPs typically have business contracts, called *peering agreements*, in which one ISP pays money to the other ISP for the right to send packets through its network. For example, often Tier 2 ISPs pay the Tier 1 ISP for the right to send packets to the better-connected Tier 1 ISP.

To support these needs for stronger and different functions in a routing protocol, Internet core routers use a different routing protocol: Border Gateway Protocol (BGP). BGP, by design, works well with relatively large numbers of routes. It also lets the ISP network engineers configure BGP to choose based on some business rules.

For example, Figure 9-32 shows ISP2, a Tier 2 ISP, with links to two Tier 1 ISPs. However, one connection has a high cost and one has a low cost. So, ISP2's BGP configuration tells it to prefer routes through the less expensive peering point.

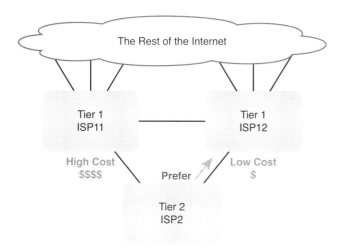

FIGURE 9-32

BGP: Choosing Routes (Indirectly) Based on Business Rules

BGP also has to battle with advertising much larger IP routing tables. For example, a very large enterprise might have 4000 IP routes, one for each of 4000 subnets. As shown in Figure 9-33, in the core of the Internet, the routing tables have grown to over 400,000 IP routes, even with a big effort to keep the size of the routing table from getting too large. So, the designers of the BGP protocol built BGP to be better able to handle the larger numbers of routes, as compared to routing protocols typically used inside enterprises.

FIGURE 9-33

Scale of Internet
Routing Tables:
Large Enterprise
Versus Internet Core
Routers

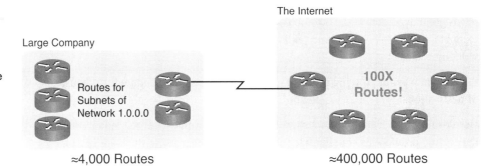

IP routing protocols can either be thought of as optimized for use inside an enterprise or optimized for use in the Internet. The routing protocols best used in enterprises, called *interior routing protocols*, include RIP, Enhanced Interior Gateway Routing Protocol (EIGRP) , and Open Shortest Path First (OSPF). Today, BGP acts as the only *exterior routing protocol*, most useful in the Internet.

IP Routing from the Internet to the Enterprise and SOHO

So, what routes do the Internet core routers need to advertise? Routes for all those class A, B, and C networks assigned by IANA to each company. After a classful network has been assigned to a company, all the routers in the Internet core need to know how to forward packets so that the packets eventually reach the ISP connected to that company, with that ISP finally forwarding the packets to the company.

For example, Figure 9-29 earlier showed an example with three companies receiving a different public class A, B, and C network. Figure 9-34 shows an updated version of that figure, with each company connected to some router in the Internet. Internet Router R4 has three routes, learned with BGP, one for each company's classful network.

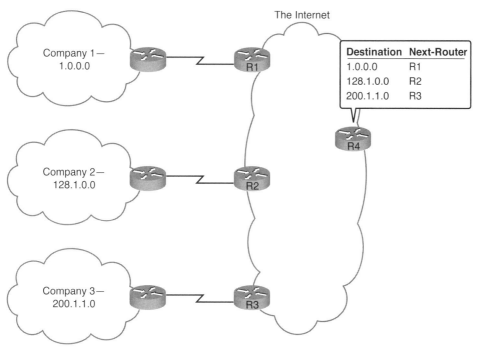

FIGURE 9-34

**Internet Routing:
IP Routes to Each
Classful IP Network**

The Internet core routers also need routes to reach SOHO users who have
connected through their ISPs. In that case, the ISP registered a class A, B, or C
network through IANA (or an RIR), which the ISP then uses for those customers.
In that case, the ISP would need to advertise that IP network using BGP, so routers
in the Internet would know how to forward IP packets to those SOHO customers.

IP Routing from Enterprise to the Internet

This next topic connects the idea of routing inside an enterprise, as discussed back
in Chapter 8, with the idea of routing inside the Internet.

First, think about the enterprise alone, as discussed throughout Chapter 8. Nothing
has changed. As a brief review, hosts still send packets to each other directly when
they sit in the same subnet. When the destination sits in a different subnet, a host
sends the IP packet to its default router, expecting the router to know what to do.
The enterprise's routers forward the packets to the correct destinations, based on IP
routes the routers probably learned with some interior routing protocol.

Next, think about an IP packet that begins in one company, goes out to an ISP,
through the Internet, and into a second company's TCP/IP network. When the
packet leaves the first enterprise network and reaches an ISP, routing still happens
as normal. The routers still receive IP packets, encapsulated inside data-link frames.
The routers in the Internet deencapsulate the IP packet, match the destination
IP address to their (large) IP routing table, match an entry, choose an outgoing
interface, encapsulate the packet in a new data-link frame, and forward the frame.

If you remove all the small steps in a router's routing logic, routers receive packets and then send them to the next router. Figure 9-35 shows the idea.

FIGURE 9-35

IP Forwarding
(Routing) on Several
ISP Routers

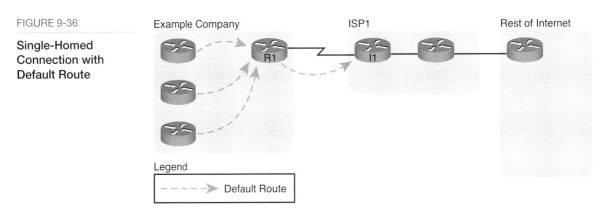

The next part of the routing puzzle begins at the beginning of the IP packet's journey, at the enterprise TCP/IP network where the packet is created. How does the enterprise know how to send packets to the Internet? This topic shows the basic answer to that question.

First, think about an enterprise with a single-homed connection to the Internet. A *single-homed* connection, as shown in Figure 9-36, means that the enterprise has only one WAN link connecting to some ISP.

FIGURE 9-36

Single-Homed
Connection with
Default Route

Enterprises typically use a default route when they have a single-homed Internet connection. A router's **default route** tells the router where to send packets when no other routes match the packet. The enterprise network engineer can set up a default route on every router so that all the routers in the enterprise deliver packets to the enterprise router connected to the Internet (R1 in Figure 9-36). The Internet edge router also uses a default route, this time to forward packets into the ISP (to router I1 in the figure).

Essentially, the default route option lets the enterprise worry about routing inside the enterprise, sending everything else to the ISP and letting the ISP worry about routing to destinations in the Internet.

A dual-homed Internet connection creates some great benefits, but the routing requires more thought. A *dual-homed* Internet connection means that the enterprise has two (or more) connections to the Internet. With two or more connections, the enterprise has a choice of where to send packets, so a default route might not work well. (This topic does not attempt to discuss all the different combinations of options, and pros and cons of each. However, it does show one option, just to give you a flavor of the choices.)

Using a default route with a dual-homed design can cause packets to take a longer-than-necessary route. For example, Figure 9-37 shows a dual-homed connection from an enterprise into two ISPs. ISP1 has customers who use IP networks 11.0.0.0 and 12.0.0.0, and ISP2 has customers who use networks 22.0.0.0 and 23.0.0.0. The enterprise network engineer for the example company (on the left of the figure) had set up default routing to prefer the route through ISP1. The figure shows the long route taken for packets going from the example company to network 22.0.0.0.

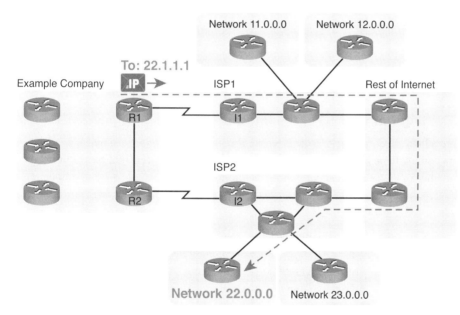

FIGURE 9-37

Inefficient Routes with Dual-Homed Internet Connections

Dual-homed designs can prevent some of the long routes from being used by using a routing protocol, usually BGP, between the enterprise routers and the ISP. For example, continuing the same example, the example company could use BGP between itself and both ISP1 and ISP2. ISP2's router would advertise routes for networks 22.0.0.0 and 23.0.0.0, and Routers R1 and R2 could be made to view the route directly through ISP2 as the better route for those IP networks, as shown in Figure 9-38.

FIGURE 9-38

Partial BGP Updates

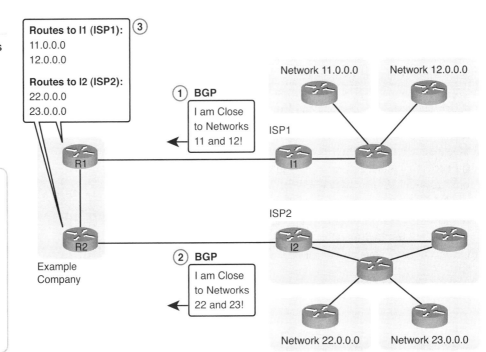

ON THE SIDE:
The idea of
having the ISP
routers advertise
only part of the
routes in the
large Internet
routing tables
is called *partial
BGP updates*.

IP Routing from SOHO to the Internet

When a home user connects to the Internet, the routing works like a single-homed connection with an enterprise. However, because the home user might connect directly from a host, rather than from a router, it can help to think about a few small points related to routing from the home toward the Internet; this short topic touches on these points.

First, consider the case in which the user device connects to the Internet, without using a small router, shown as SOHO1 at the top of Figure 9-39. The host has an OS, and the OS includes TCP/IP software. The IP software includes a concept of a default router. When connected to the Internet, the host's default router setting will refer to the ISP router (Router I1 in this case).

FIGURE 9-39

**Default Routers and
Default Routes**

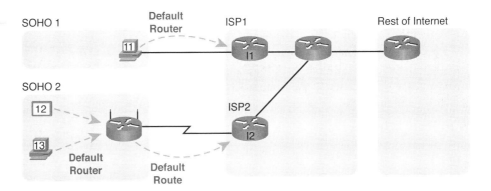

Unlike hosts, routers can have a *default route*. The terms *default route* (used on a router) and *default router* (used on a host) represent the same concept, but the terms are indeed slightly different. When a SOHO router connects to an ISP, as shown with SOHO2 in the figure, the SOHO router creates a default route pointing to the ISP router. So, two default routing concepts cause a packet from a host to arrive at the inbound ISP, as follows:

1. The sending host, like host PC13, sends the packet to its default router.

2. The router (R1) uses its default route to forward the packet to the ISP (Router I2).

3. At that point, the routers in the Internet have full routing tables and can send the packet to any destination in the Internet.

Name Resolution and the Global DNS System

Users almost always use names to identify the other computer to which they want to send data. For example, when you type in text to search the web using a search engine, and you click a web link listed in the search results, the link actually includes the name of another computer. When you send emails, you rely on some configuration for your email client that lists the name of the email server. And the TCP/IP world calls these names **host names**, in part because the generic term for a computer with an IP address is an *IP host* and the name identifies an IP host.

For IP routing to work correctly throughout the Internet, the Internet needs to follow some rules, as discussed earlier in the section "IP Address Assignments in the Global Internet." For the same reasons, the assignment of host names has some administrative rules to follow. Additionally, it relies on the **Domain Name System (DNS)**, which creates a globally distributed service that allows any user to find the IP address used by each unique host name, no matter where the host name exists in the Internet.

This topic breaks down the discussion into three areas:

- Creating globally unique host names
- Distributed administration of the lists of specific host names
- Distributed DNS name resolution

Creating Globally Unique Host Names

To create globally unique host names, the IANA follows an administrative process for how companies and individuals use host names in the Internet. It follows a process that works a little like what happens with IP addresses, as shown in Figure 9-40. In the figure, three companies of different sizes ask IANA (or a cooperating agency) for the assignment of some public IP addresses. In this case, the three companies get a class A, B, and C network. After they are assigned, only the companies that were assigned each IP network can use the addresses in each network.

FIGURE 9-40

Review: IANA Assigns IP
Networks

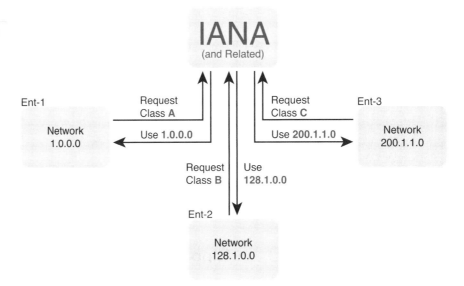

To create globally unique host names, those same companies need to follow a
similar process. The process relies on the format of TCP/IP host names as defined
for use with DNS, called *domain names*. With this format, the names exist as
characters, with some periods in between. The last part of the name, called a
subdomain, makes up the last part of the name. Figure 9-41 shows the format,
with a few examples.

FIGURE 9-41

Format and Examples
Using Domain Names

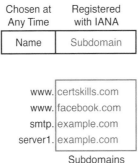

Chosen at Any Time	Registered with IANA
Name	Subdomain

www.	certskills.com
www.	facebook.com
smtp.	example.com
server1.	example.com

Subdomains

AUTHOR'S NOTE: The term *domain name* is used in several ways in
networking, and often two different people use this term to mean two different
ideas. For example, some people might call www.certskills.com a domain
name, but others might say the domain name is just the certskills.com part of
the name. When using this term, you need to be ready to figure out whether
these picky differences matter to the topic at hand, and if so, decide what the
other person really means.

To ensure unique host names throughout the Internet, a company or individual can register one (or more) subdomains with a domain name registrar. Similar to the process with IP address assignment, IANA oversees the process, working with many agencies and companies. A company that wants a new subdomain asks for the name, and if unused, the agency or company (authorized by IANA) registers the name so that no other company in the world can use the name. Figure 9-42 shows the overall process for three companies.

> **AUTHOR'S NOTE:** IANA oversees the process as shown in Figure 9-42. However, today, many companies offer domain name registration services, so the actual work shown in the figure as "IANA and Related" is done by a company.

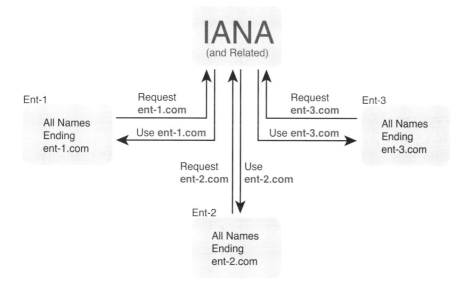

FIGURE 9-42

IANA/Others Approve
Subdomain Registrations

Distributed Administration of the Lists of Host Names

The use of host names that follow the domain name format, along with the administrative process, make sure that host names in two different companies will never be the same. For example, most every enterprise will have a public web server that uses the name *www*. That part of the name will be identical with other companies. However, the full name, which includes the subdomain that is unique to each company, will make the full host name unique.

For example, imagine that the three companies in the previous figure all have two servers with names www and Server1. The www servers happen to be the public web servers for each company, and the Server1 name happens to be used for some other service that only matters to people who work at the company. With the full domain names, as seen next to each server in Figure 9-43, each name is unique.

FIGURE 9-43

IANA/Others
Approve Subdomain
Registrations

Ent-1

WWW
(www.Ent-1.com)

Server1
(Server1.Ent-1.com)

Ent-3

WWW
(www.Ent-3.com)

Server1
(Server1.Ent-3.com)

Ent-2

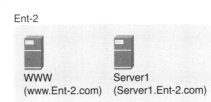

WWW   Server1
(www.Ent-2.com)   (Server1.Ent-2.com)

ON THE SIDE:
Domain names
can be listed in
mixed case, but
the names are not
case sensitive. For
example, the names
www.example.com and
www.ExAmPlE.com
are considered to be
the same name.

To keep all host names unique around the globe, each company must also not
duplicate names inside the company. For example, in Figure 9-43, now that a host
inside the company with subdomain ent-1.com has the name Server1, inside that
domain, the name Server1 cannot be used by another host.

To keep track of all the names inside a company, most companies keep a
centralized database of host names and their IP addresses as part of a DNS server.
Keeping all the names in one place helps the network administrators avoid giving
two hosts the same host name. Also, at some point, other hosts will want to ask
questions like "What is the IP address used by this host name," and the DNS server
will need to help answer that question. So, the DNS server configuration helps
prevent duplicate names, and it is ready to answer DNS name queries.

Figure 9-44 continues the example shown in the previous two figures, this time
showing a name server for companies Ent-1, Ent-2, and Ent-3. In each case, the
name server lists the short version of the name, along with the IP address used
by that host. (The name server will consider each short name to have the correct
subdomain at the end of the name.)

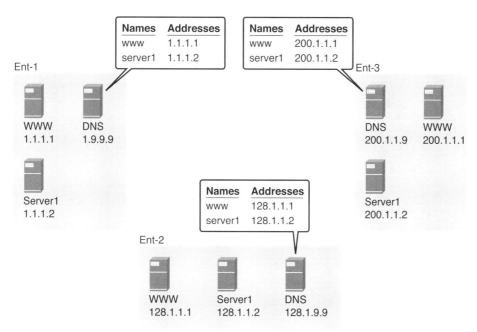

FIGURE 9-44

**DNS Servers and
Distributed Server
Configurations**

The figure shows that the configurations of the host names, and the corresponding
IP addresses for each, remain distributed. The next topic shows how the information
can remain distributed on different DNS servers and still answer users when they ask
to learn the IP address used by a host name.

Distributed DNS Name Resolution

The DNS system gives the world a way to create unique host names worldwide. The
sending host still needs to know the IP address of the destination host before sending
an IP packet, because IP packets use IP addresses, not host names, to identify the
sender and destination of each packet. However, as you can see in Figure 9-44, no
one DNS server knows all the host names.

DNS defines how the world creates a distributed database of host names and their
addresses. The DNS server for each subdomain knows all the host names and
matching IP addresses for that subdomain. Then, some special DNS servers inside
the Internet, called root DNS servers, know the IP addresses of all the DNS servers.
DNS also defines a protocol that the servers can use to basically ask around among
all the DNS servers, finding the DNS server for the right subdomain.

For example, imagine that a user at a host in Ent-2 wants to connect to www.ent-1.
com. That name exists in a different DNS subdomain, so the DNS for the sender's
subdomain, ent-2.com, will not know the IP address. But the sending host only
knows about the DNS servers in its own subdomain, so the process begins with the
sender asking the usual DNS server inside the same company, as seen in Figure 9-45.

FIGURE 9-45

**Finding the Right DNS
Server for a Domain
Name in Another
Company**

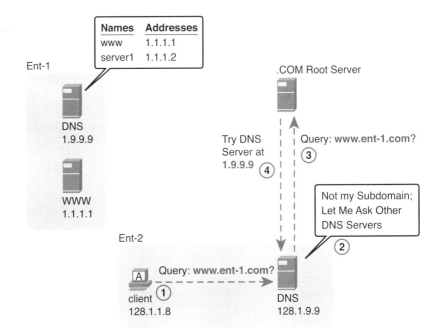

The figure shows the following steps:

1. Client A sends a DNS query to the DNS it knows, the DNS for subdomain
   ent-2.com, at 128.1.9.9.

2. The ent-2.com DNS server's logic is that it does not know the answer, so ask
   some other DNS. (Each DNS would be configured to know the IP address of
   other DNS servers.)

3. The ent-2.com DNS server asks a DNS root server to resolve www.ent-1.
   com.

4. The root server replies, not with the IP address of www.ent-1.com, because
   the root server does not know, either; it replies with the IP address of another
   DNS server, 1.1.9.9.

At this point, the client still does not know that www.ent-1.com's IP address is
1.1.1.1, but the name resolution process is almost complete. Figure 9-46 shows the
last few steps.

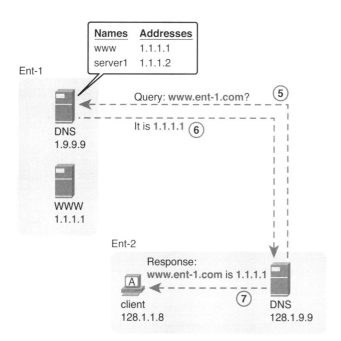

FIGURE 9-46

Getting a Response from the Authoritative DNS Server for Ent-1.com

Again, following the steps in the figure:

5. The ent-2.com DNS server next sends the name resolution request to the DNS for subdomain ent-1.com.

6. The DNS server for subdomain ent-1.com knows the name www.ent-1.com. In fact, it is the authoritative DNS for that subdomain, meaning that it has the authority to answer this query. So the ent-1.com DNS replies with the IP address of 1.1.1.1.

7. The ent-2.com DNS server replies to host A, so finally host A knows that www.ent-1.com resolves to IP address 1.1.1.1.

The process might seem to require a lot of work, given the need for two figures and seven steps. In reality, the process usually takes just a few seconds.

Network Layer Concepts with Scarce IPv4 Addresses

The world has too few IPv4 addresses. There are just not enough IPv4 addresses to give every host that needs an IP address its very own public, globally unique unicast IPv4 address. Take a look at some of the math:

- With 32 bits, IPv4 addresses create 2^{32} numbers, a little more than 4 billion addresses.

- Of those, about seven-eighths are unicast addresses (classes A, B, and C), for around 3.5 billion unicast addresses.

- The address assignment process, which keeps IPv4 addresses grouped by network, wastes some addresses, because each company might not use all the addresses.
- The world already has around 8 billion user devices connected to the Internet, even without waste.

In short, the world has too few IPv4 addresses, billions too few.

The Internet community saw this IPv4 address shortage happening by the late 1980s. It came up with a couple of good short-term solutions, meant to add a couple of years to the life of IPv4. The idea was to keep IPv4 working for a few more years, long enough for the long-term solution, IP version 6 (IPv6), to be defined, for vendors to write software to support it, and for everyone to migrate to IPv6.

This final of the four major sections tells the story of the two technologies that let the IPv4 Internet still work today, in spite of the IPv4 address shortage. The two short-term solutions, classless interdomain routing (CIDR) and Network Address Translation (NAT), not only extended IPv4's life by a few years but also extended it by a few decades. This final of four sections tells the story of the two technologies that let the IPv4 Internet still work today in spite of the IPv4 address shortage.

In particular, the following sections look at how CIDR changes two important ideas: how the IP address assignment process works and what routes are advertised inside the Internet core. Next, this section looks at NAT, focusing on the effect of how NAT greatly reduces the number of public IP addresses needed by each enterprise. The final topic in these sections looks at the changes to IP routing caused by CIDR and NAT. But first, these sections begin by looking at the original problem—too much need for too few IPv4 addresses.

IPv4 Address Exhaustion

As it turns out, by the late 1980s, it became clear that the world would run out of IPv4 addresses with the current plan. This problem became known as **IPv4 address exhaustion** (not that the addresses get tired, but that the world would use up its supply of this limited resource). There were many causes for address exhaustion, but two stand out: the inefficiency of assigning addresses based on classful IP networks and the growth of the Internet. This next topic looks at each of these two causes.

IPv4 Address Assignment Inefficiencies

Earlier in this chapter, the section "IP Address Assignments in the Global Internet" described the original plan for assigning public IP addresses. That plan gave every company a unique class A, B, or C network, and every host a globally unique unicast IP address, unique across the entire planet. The original public IP address assignment plan worked, but the process wasted addresses.

The original address assignment plan had problems in part because of the sizes of the classful IP networks and the number of each that existed. Table 9-5 shows a reminder of the sizes of each network class and the number of networks of each class.

TABLE 9-5

Number and Sizes of Classful IP Networks

Class	Number of Networks	Size (Number of Host Addresses)
A	126	$2^{24} - 2$ (>16,000,000)
B	16,384	$2^{16} - 2$ (>65,000)
C	2,097,192	$2^8 - 2$ (254)

With these three sizes, and only these three sizes, most every company wanted a class A or B network, and most did not want a class C network. Even if you worked at a small company, and 254 IP addresses met your needs, you thought that the company might grow, so you wanted a class B network at least. Using the same logic, medium-sized companies thought they might grow, so they wanted class A network numbers. So, compared to the number of companies and other organizations across the planet, the number of networks, particularly class A and B networks, began to look way too small.

> **ON THE SIDE:** Just for some perspective, according to the U.S. Census Bureau data for 2008, the United States alone in that year had around 110,000 companies with more than 100 employees. With the old rules of assigning one IP network per company, all these would have likely wanted a class B network, with only 16,384 class B networks available.

No matter the size of each class of network, most likely, a company actually needed fewer IP addresses than the number of IP addresses it received by getting a particular IP network assigned by IANA. For example, imagine a case in which a company really did need 500 host IP addresses, so it received an assignment of class B network 128.1.0.0. Every class B network supports more than 65,000 IP addresses—but this one company only needed 500. However, only that one company can use addresses in that one class B network, so as shown in Figure 9-47, most of the addresses in that class B network sit there, unused and wasted.

FIGURE 9-47

Wasted IP Addresses: Got 65,000, Need 500

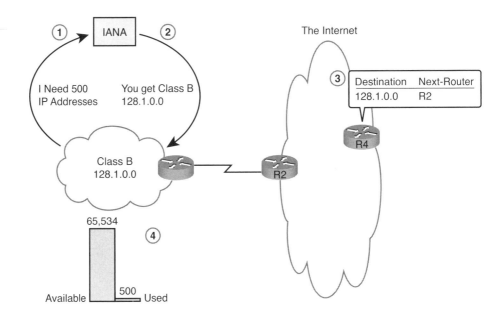

Following the steps in the figure:

1. The company asks for a class B network assignment from IANA.

2. IANA grants a class B network (128.1.0.0).

3. Internet routers update their routing tables with routes for all of class B network 128.1.0.0; the entire class B network must be in one place.

4. The graph shows the literal number of IP addresses in this class B network versus the number used.

Internet Growth Exhausts the IPv4 Address Space

The wasting of IP addresses meant that the world would run out of IPv4 addresses sooner, but the bigger challenge was the growth in the Internet. By the late 1980s, the Internet started growing fast. The Internet grew, and grew fast, for many years. Even without the waste caused by assigning entire classful networks, the world would still have run out of IPv4 addresses long before this second decade of the twenty-first century, just because of Internet growth.

To get a sense of the growth that the world was facing in the early days of the Internet that led to these short-term and long-terms solutions, look at the data in Figure 9-48. The figure shows the number of estimated Internet hosts over the years 1984–1992. The data in the graph shows approximations of data from a couple of sources, but mostly from RFC 1296, which collected the growth data in part because of the IP address exhaustion problem. And yes, the graph shows a huge growth rate, with the number of hosts increasing tenfold every two or three years.

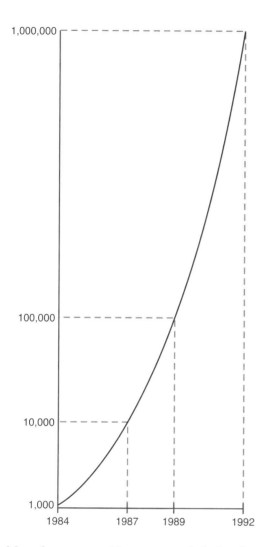

FIGURE 9-48

Approximate Number of Hosts Connected to the Internet, 1984–1992

AUTHOR'S NOTE:
The graph is not drawn to scale. The curve is actually much steeper.

Many factors caused Internet growth during the years shown in the figure. PCs went from being a curious toy for the tech-savvy hobbyist in the 1970s to mainstream business devices during the 1980s. Each of those new PCs, after being connected to the Internet, needed a public IP address. Most people did not have personal email accounts in the old days, but the Internet changed that equation, with many consumers connecting to the Internet just to have a personal email account. The Internet slowly added commercial features over the years, with the pace picking up significantly by the early 1990s, which led to a huge boom. And after the web browser and server were invented in the early 1990s, the Internet kept growing.

Classless Interdomain Routing

One of the two short-term solutions to the IPv4 address exhaustion problem, **classless interdomain routing (CIDR)**, attacks the waste problem. The old IP address assignment rules used three sizes of address blocks, based on class A, B, and C rules. CIDR allows the IANA to assign address blocks of many different sizes, so each company's block of addresses better matches the real need for addresses, avoiding the large amounts of waste that occurred in some cases, like in the example shown with Figure 9-48.

CIDR, originally created in 1993 in RFC 1338, actually defined two new types of rules. The first defines new address assignment rules that ignore class A, B, and C network rules. CIDR also defines route aggregation, which is a process to make the routing tables shorter in the core of the Internet. CIDR's address assignment rules actually increase the size of Internet routers' routing tables, so CIDR also defines route aggregation to help reduce the impact and keep those tables relatively smaller.

CIDR Address Assignment

With CIDR IP address assignment, two basic ideas change. First and most obvious, the size of the address block assigned by IANA (or a related agency) can be different than the original plan. However, the administrative process, and the players involved, often change as well. In fact, often, ISPs also play a role in the address-assignment process.

First, with CIDR, a new term must be used to define the addresses assign to a company by IANA. In the original plan, the terms *IP network* and *classful IP network* referred to the idea of a class A, B, or C network. With CIDR, the same idea goes by the names *address block*, *CIDR block*, or *CIDR address block*.

Next, each CIDR block must follow some basic rules. Like classful IP networks, a CIDR block is a set of consecutive IP addresses, unique in the Internet. However, a CIDR block can be any size that is a power of 2, for example, size 4, 8, 16, 32, 64, and so on. Just like with classful IP networks, the lowest and highest IP addresses in each CIDR block must be reserved and cannot be used as host IP addresses. (A few other rules exist as well, but they only impact what specific numbers IANA chooses, so those rules are not listed here.)

Finally, the administrative process with CIDR address assignment often includes the ISP. With this change, instead of the company dealing directly with IANA, the company deals with the ISP. The ISP gets a big block of addresses from IANA, and then the ISP assigns subsets of the address block to its customers. This administrative process actually works well to solve some routing problems in the global Internet as well.

To see how the pieces fit, consider the following example, as shown in Figure 9-49. First, ISP1, knowing that its customers will one day ask for CIDR blocks, receives an address block assignment from IANA. In this case, IANA assigns all of class B network 128.1.0.0, which includes all addresses from 128.1.0.0 to 128.1.255.255.

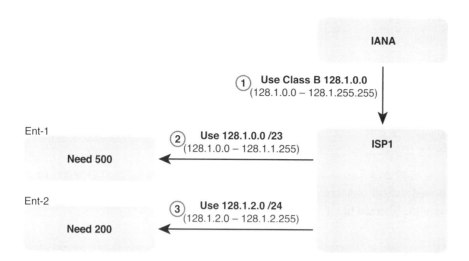

FIGURE 9-49

IANA Assigns to ISP; ISP Assigns Smaller CIDR Block to Customer

ISPs receive CIDR blocks from IANA for the purpose of then assigning subsets of that block to its customers. The figure shows that process, noted as three steps, as follows:

1. ISP1 had already requested a new CIDR block from IANA; the figure shows IANA assigning a new block, the entire class B network 128.1.0.0. Now ISP1 owns all addresses that begin 128.1, for the purpose of assigning CIDR blocks to ISP1's customers.

2. A company (Ent-1 in this case) wants to connect to the Internet, and it decides to use ISP1. The two companies talk, and Ent-1 submits paperwork that shows a need for 500 public IP addresses. ISP1 looks at the size of the request (500 addresses) as compared to the powers of 2 (64, 128, 256, 512, 1024, and so on). ISP1 chooses a CIDR block just large enough to meet the need, in this case of size 512 (2^9). (As a reminder, the first and last IP addresses in the block are reserved.) The CIDR block in the figure includes all addresses that begin with 128.1.0 and 128.1.1.

3. Another company (Ent-2) asks for a CIDR block with 200 public IP addresses. This time, the ISP can assign a block of 256 addresses (all addresses that begin 128.1.2) to reduce wasted addresses.

While the example shows the ISP assigning blocks that are a subset of a class B network, CIDR allows any grouping, as long as it aligns on boundaries based on powers of 2. For example, IANA could give an ISP all class C networks that begin with 200 (200.0.0.0, 200.0.1.0, 200.0.2.0, and so on, up through 200.255.255.0). Then, the ISP could assign CIDR blocks larger than a single class C network, as long as it lines up on a boundary of a power of 2.

CIDR Reduces Route Table Growth with Route Aggregation

The CIDR address assignment process, regardless of whether a company received its CIDR block from IANA or from an ISP, helped delay the day in which the world would finally run out of IPv4 addresses. However, if the CIDR RFCs had stopped here, without route aggregation, CIDR would have caused another problem: huge growth in the number of routes in the routing tables of Internet routers.

For perspective, think about the number of class A, B, and C networks, as listed back in Table 9-5. About 2.1 million such classful networks exist. With CIDR address assignment, each of those classful IP networks could be broken up and assigned as CIDR blocks to many different companies. Each CIDR block would need an IP route, making routing tables much larger.

Figure 9-50 shows an example, with ISP1 and three customers. The customers each received a CIDR block of public IP addresses from ISP1. Router R4, inside ISP1's part of the Internet, has three different IP routes, one for each CIDR block.

FIGURE 9-50

CIDR Address Assignment Creates Larger Routing Tables

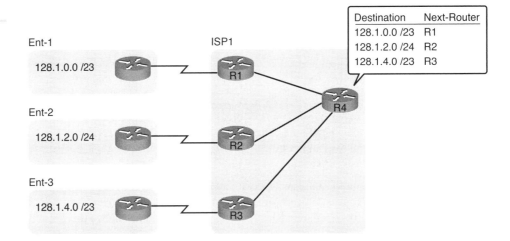

Destination	Next-Router
128.1.0.0 /23	R1
128.1.2.0 /24	R2
128.1.4.0 /23	R3

Ent-1

128.1.0.0 /23

Ent-2

128.1.2.0 /24

Ent-3

128.1.4.0 /23

ISP1

ON THE SIDE: Many people refer to route aggregation as *route summarization*, and the routes as *summary routes*.

AUTHOR'S NOTE: In the figure, the /23 notation lists a subnet mask that routers will use, along with the subnet ID that represents the CIDR block, to briefly represent the range of addresses in the block. For example, 128.1.4.0 /23 means 128.1.4.0–128.1.5.255; this book just does not get into the math.

The figure shows three routes, one for each CIDR block for the three companies on the left. Before CIDR address assignment, those same IP addresses would have been part of one classful network (class B network 128.1.0.0). That one group would have required only one route in the Internet routers.

CIDR defines a solution to this problem—*route aggregation*. With route aggregation, routers still advertise routes using dynamic routing protocols. However, they advertise one route, called an *aggregate route*, that includes the addresses in many smaller CIDR blocks.

Route aggregation requires that the worldwide IP address assignment process assign numbers in large consecutive groups. The large group is first assigned to a large organization, like an ISP. Then, the ISP assigns smaller CIDR blocks. That administrative process allows routers to create aggregate routes for the original large blocks.

This topic begs for an example, so the next example continues the example shown in the last two figures. ISP1 received from IANA the CIDR block that begins with 128.1, in other words, all of class B network 128.1.0.0. ISP1's routers need to know specific routes for every CIDR block ISP1 assigns. However, all the other ISPs in the Internet just need a route for class B network 128.1.0.0, sending those packets to ISP1. For example, Figure 9-51 shows how a router in ISP2's network has just one route for all the addresses in that class B network.

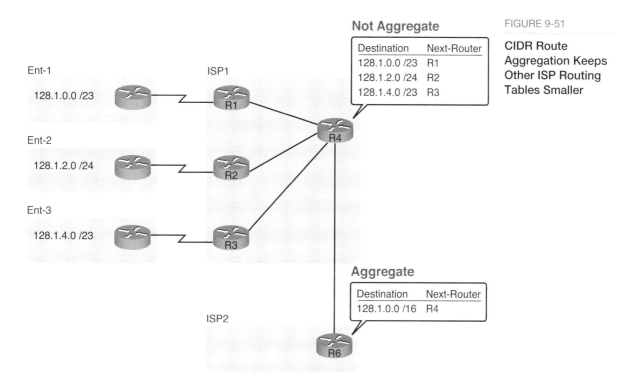

Not Aggregate

Destination	Next-Router
128.1.0.0 /23	R1
128.1.2.0 /24	R2
128.1.4.0 /23	R3

Aggregate

Destination	Next-Router
128.1.0.0 /16	R4

FIGURE 9-51

CIDR Route Aggregation Keeps Other ISP Routing Tables Smaller

In summary, CIDR helps solve the IPv4 address exhaustion problem by wasting fewer addresses, unfortunately increasing the number of IP routes, but also reducing the impact of the increase in routes by using route aggregation.

Network Address Translation

While CIDR attacked the IPv4 address exhaustion problem by reducing waste, **Network Address Translation (NAT)** attacked the problem by greatly reducing the number of unique IP addresses needed by each company or home network. Every device still needs an IP address, but NAT creates a way for multiple client hosts (hosts that act only as clients and not as servers) to share a unique public IP address. As a result, enterprises need fewer public IP addresses, and each enterprise can use a smaller CIDR block.

The following sections explain parts of how NAT works. They show some of the big ideas, as well as how NAT then requires the use of private IP networks and addresses.

NAT Perspectives on IP Addresses

NAT reduces the need for public IP addresses, that is, IPv4 addresses that must be unique among all hosts connected to and using the Internet. To begin breaking down how NAT helps with addressing, first think about the following analogy with the postal service.

Imagine where you live now, or in the past, where you lived with other people. Maybe you have roommates or a family, or think back to when you were a child and lived at home. For your apartment or house, how many postal addresses did the postal system have for your apartment or house? Only one address, of course. However, if you had four people living there, all four could receive mail at that one address; after the mail arrives, you just look at the envelope for the name on the front.

The same idea works at a business location. If a business has a ten-story building with 1000 employees, the postal service has only one postal address for the entire building. The postal service delivers mail to the building, and someone at that building sorts the mail and delivers it to the right desk. The person might look at the name or he might ask people to put some other identifying number on their letters (for example, 3rd floor, suite 104, or mail stop 3A) on the front of the letter. But the postal service just knows one postal address, with 1000 employees receiving their business mail at that one address.

NAT uses a similar principle, using one IP address as the globally unique address for hundreds or even thousands of real IP hosts. But to make that work, NAT changes the IP addressing rules slightly. So, take a moment to review a couple of the many rules about TCP/IP addressing:

- Every host needs an *IP address* on every network interface connected to a TCP/IP network.

- Additionally, to work connected to the Internet, each IP address must be a unique *public IP address*, which by definition is unique among all hosts connected to the Internet.

Keeping these rules in mind, next take a look at a simple example in Figure 9-52 that shows some client hosts, using public IP addresses. In this case, Company1 shows three client hosts, with addresses 128.1.1.1, 128.1.1.2, and 128.1.1.3. Each connects out to some web server in the Internet. The web server tracks the applications connects to each client, as noted in the thought bubble on the right.

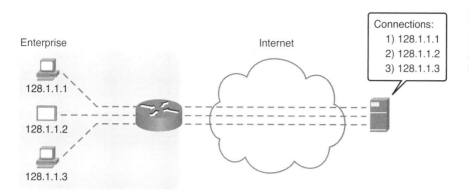

FIGURE 9-52

Hosts with Public IP Addresses Connected to Servers in the Internet

NAT relies on an important concept from the transport and application layers: The servers care very little about the actual IP addresses of the clients. Sure, the servers need to know the IP addresses of the clients, to send IP packets back to those clients. But a server does not care whether it has 1000 application connections with 1000 different hosts from 1000 different parts of the Internet, from 1000 hosts in the same single company, or even 1000 connections from one client computer.

For example, Figure 9-52 showed three different application connections from three clients. Figure 9-53 shows three different application connections from a single host. The server needs to know the IP address of the client in each connection, but otherwise, the server just views Figure 9-53 like it views Figure 9-52—as three client connections.

AUTHOR'S NOTE:
The examples in this section show all application connections made to a single server. The application connections could also have been to different servers, with no change in how NAT works.

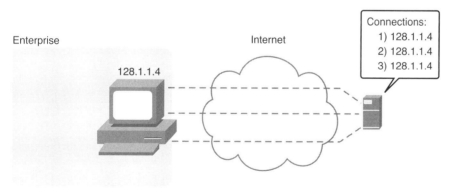

FIGURE 9-53

One Client Host with Three Application Connections

NAT works as a function on one device at the edge of an enterprise network, usually a router or firewall. That device's NAT function makes a number of real application connections from real clients in the enterprise and makes them appear to come from one or a few public IP addresses.

NAT reduces the need for public IP addresses—addresses that must be unique across the entire Internet—by combining the ideas shown in the previous two figures. Some device implements NAT. That NAT device makes application connections from large numbers of client hosts appear to be application connections from a single host. And, the only IP address that must be unique in the Internet is the one IP address used by the NAT function.

Figure 9-54 shows how NAT combines these ideas. In this case, the same three real devices each connect to the same real web server in the Internet. The router in the figure implements NAT, making all three connections look like they come from a host with IP address 128.1.1.4. Note that the server thinks it has three application connections from the same host.

FIGURE 9-54

NAT Function on a Router

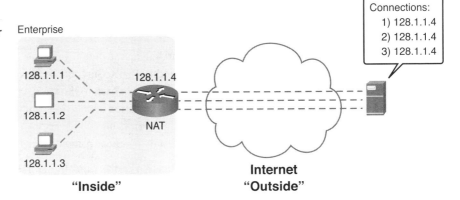

Public and Private IP Addresses

AUTHOR'S NOTE:
With NAT, the TCP/IP network whose clients are made to appear like one client with many connections is called the *inside* network, and the other side, typically the Internet, is called the *outside* network.

Public and Private IP Addresses

NAT does not reduce the number of required IP addresses, but it does reduce the required number of public IP addresses. All the hosts in the enterprise still must have an IP address per interface. However, those host addresses inside the enterprise can be reused from company to company. These host addresses inside the enterprise no longer have to be unique across the Internet, or to come from the public IP network or public CIDR block assigned to the company.

With NAT, the enterprise hosts use *private IP addresses*. RFC 1918 adds yet another rule to the IP addressing world, this time reserving a small set of class A, B, and C networks as private IP networks. IANA reserves these IP networks for use by any company or person inside his own TCP/IP network. The same private IP networks can be used by many different TCP/IP networks. And when combined with NAT, the hosts that reuse the same private IP network numbers, with the same private IP addresses, can all use the Internet.

When using NAT, an enterprise typically uses a private IP network for all the hosts inside the enterprise. At the same time, the enterprise can use a small number of public IP addresses for the NAT function: far fewer public IP addresses than the number of private IP addresses used, one per host interface, inside the enterprise network.

Figure 9-55 shows an example using private and public IP addresses. The figure shows three enterprise networks, each of which uses private class A network 10.0.0.0. That is, all three companies use IP addresses that begin with 10. The companies do not need to coordinate their IP addressing plans, and they can all use the same IP addresses from network 10.0.0.0, as shown. Each company uses a different public IP address block, as required; the figure shows one of each company's public IP addresses.

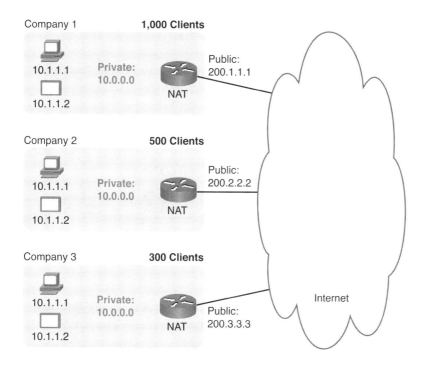

FIGURE 9-55

Three Enterprise Networks, Each Using Private Network 10.0.0.0

The figure shows some powerful concepts with NAT, as follows:

- Enterprises use a private IP network for host IP addresses throughout the enterprise TCP/IP network, in this case, private class A IP network 10.0.0.0.

- Two (or more) enterprises can use the same private IP networks, and the same IP addresses, with no problems in connecting to the Internet, with servers, and even with hosts in the other company.

- The device doing NAT, usually a router or firewall, uses some of the public CIDR block or IP network for NAT.

- The number of required public IP addresses is far lower than the number of necessary client IP addresses inside the enterprise. In this case, each company uses a single public IP address.

AUTHOR'S NOTE: So far, this section has been vague about how many addresses you can save. It varies based on applications and usage, so there is no one set answer. But just to give you a general idea, because of the fact that one user connection to a website can actually cause a few dozen application connections behind the scenes, you can usually support at least 1000 active client hosts with one public IP address.

While Figure 9-55 shows the use of one particular private IP network, RFC 1918 sets aside several private IP networks. Any company can just pick from the list, assign IP addresses from those networks, subnet those networks, and so on. In fact, because RFC 1918 reserves just one class A private network (10.0.0.0), many companies use exactly that: private class A network 10.0.0.0. Table 9-6 lists the private IP networks.

TABLE 9-6
Private IP Networks

Class	Number of Networks	Network IDs
A	1	10.0.0.0
B	16	172.16.0.0 – 172.31.0.0
C	256	All that begin with 192.168 (192.168.0.0, 192.168.1.0, 192.168.2.0, and so on, through 192.168.255.0)

Basic NAT Mechanics

So far, this NAT section has focused on the impact NAT has on reducing the need for public IP addresses. However, NAT uses some detailed steps of how to make large numbers of application connections appear to be coming from one device. This next topic looks at a few of those specifics.

The name itself says a lot about NAT's function: Network Address Translation. If fact, if you changed the name slightly to begin with *Network Layer* instead of just *Network*, the name would be an even better description. TCP/IP's network layer defines IP addresses. NAT translates (changes) the IP addresses inside IP headers as IP packets pass through the device doing NAT. What addresses does NAT translate between? Between the private IP address used by the real client host and the public IP address used by NAT.

To get a sense of the process, look at the example that includes the next two figures.

This next example shows host A, inside an enterprise network, opening a web browser and connecting to Internet-based server S1. At this point, host A has already completed name resolution and knows S1's public IP address of 9.9.9.9. Host A is now ready to send its first IP packet to public IP address 9.9.9.9.

Figure 9-56 picks up the story at this point, with Step 1 showing host A sending the IP packet. The figure shows four steps: A sends the packet, then two steps of how NAT works in the router, and the fourth step, which shows the packet after NAT has translated the packet.

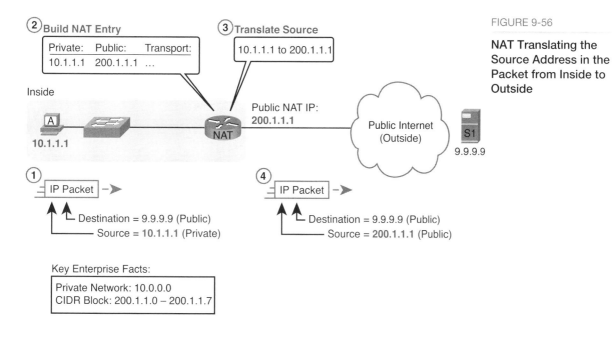

FIGURE 9-56

NAT Translating the Source Address in the Packet from Inside to Outside

Following the steps in the figure:

1. Host A sends an IP packet, with its own (private) IP address 10.1.1.1 as the source IP address, with the server's IP address (9.9.9.9) as the destination. The packet is routed normally through the enterprise until it arrives at the NAT router.

2. The NAT router decides to apply NAT to this packet (because of its NAT configuration). Because this is the first packet for a new application connection, the router creates a NAT table entry. This NAT table entry helps NAT translate the right parts of the packet header.

3. The NAT function on the router translates parts of the IP header, as well as the transport layer header (TCP or UDP). Specifically, the router changes the source IP from 10.1.1.1, host A's private IP address, to 200.1.1.1, a public address from the enterprise's CIDR block.

4. The router forwards the IP packet, source IP address 200.1.1.1, to server 9.9.9.9.

Note that the device doing the NAT hides the NAT function from both the client and server. As far as the server in the Internet is concerned, it just received a packet from a new client whose IP address is 200.1.1.1. As far as client PC11 is concerned, it has sent a packet to the server at IP address 9.9.9.9.

When the server wants to reply to the client, the server sends a packet to the IP address that the server thinks the client uses—but in reality, it is the IP address used by NAT. In this example, when the server replies to host A, in reality, the server sends a packet back to the NAT function at public IP address 200.1.1.1. Figure 9-57 picks up the story at that point, with Step 5 showing server S1's packet sent back to 200.1.1.1.

FIGURE 9-57

NAT Translating the Destination Address in the Packet from Outside to Inside

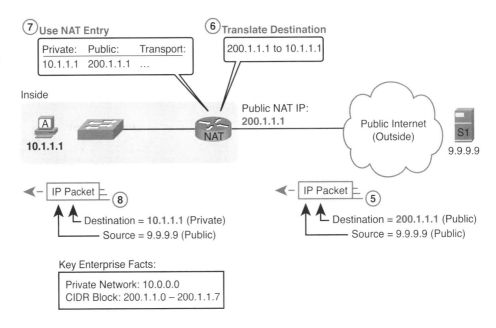

Again following the steps in the figure:

5. The server sends a reply to the client, with destination IP address 200.1.1.1. Routers in the Internet can forward this packet, because it is a public IP address, part of the enterprise's CIDR block.

6. Because NAT is configured to use IP address 200.1.1.1, the NAT router knows to translate this newly arrived IP packet destined to 200.1.1.1. The NAT router should now change the destination address to host A's IP address of 10.1.1.1.

7. Step 6 showed the result, but this step shows the NAT table entry that the router must have so that it knows the right address to use.

8. The NAT router forwards the IP packet to PC11's 10.1.1.1 private IP address 10.1.1.1.

> **AUTHOR'S NOTE:** The description of how NAT works in this section does leave out some details related to the TCP/IP transport layer.

IP Addressing with CIDR and NAT

> **AUTHOR'S NOTE:** This topic assumes that the company or SOHO site uses NAT.

The world today includes some sites that use the original IP address assignment rules using classful networks. Those sites typically do not have a need to use NAT. However, most companies and small office/home office (SOHO) sites use CIDR blocks and NAT. This chapter has already explained how addressing and routing work without CIDR and NAT; this next topic looks at the differences in how IP address assignment works with CIDR and NAT.

Changes to Enterprise IP Addressing

Before CIDR and NAT, the company first had to ask IANA or a member agency to assign the company a classful IP network. Then, the company could subnet that classful network and assign IP addresses from those subnets, as discussed earlier in the section, "IP Address Assignments in the Global Internet."

With CIDR and NAT, that process changes.

First, the enterprise network engineer picks and uses an RFC 1918 private IP network number. The engineer does not need to ask permission and does not need to contact IANA or the ISP. Many engineers pick class A network 10.0.0.0, because it is the only class A network among the private IP network numbers. Then, using the same subnetting logic, the engineer can subdivide the private IP network. She can assign some static IP addresses and use DHCP to allow clients to learn their IP addresses.

The enterprise still needs some public IP addresses, so it needs to request a CIDR block. The CIDR block supports two needs:

- Public addresses used by NAT for most client hosts
- Public addresses for hosts in the enterprise, typically servers, that need to bypass NAT and have static public IP addresses

For example, consider a medium-sized company that had a few thousand clients, plus several servers that need to be reachable from the Internet. The enterprise engineer decided to use one public IP address for every 1000 client hosts inside the enterprise. Knowing that the enterprise might grow to at most 3000 hosts one day, it might ask for at least three public IP addresses in its new CIDR block. Also, it might have a need for eight servers to be available from the Internet, with permanent static public IP addresses. So, when asking for a CIDR block, this company would ask for at least 11 IP addresses.

Figure 9-58 collects these main address planning concepts into one figure. It shows the two needs for public IP addresses at the top of the figure and a typical enterprise network with many client hosts at the bottom.

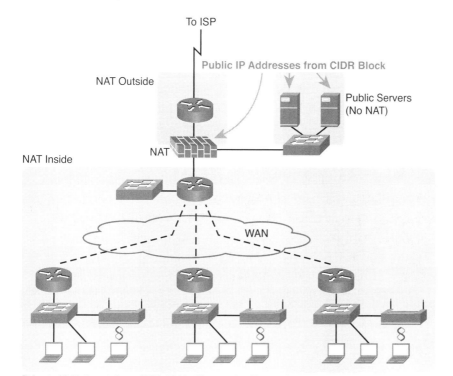

FIGURE 9-58

**Public and Private
IP Addresses in the
Enterprise**

Private IP Network from RFC 1918, Chosen by Enterprise Engineer

SOHO Address Assignment: With CIDR and NAT

In the early days of the Internet, a SOHO site typically had a single device (a PC), often with an analog modem connection to the Internet. To support that site, the ISP would dynamically assign a public IP address to the one SOHO PC for the duration of the connection to the Internet, as described earlier in the section, "SOHO Address Assignment (Early Days)."

Today, most SOHO connections to the Internet use a small consumer-grade router. Although it might be called a router on the retail package, these small devices typically combine many functions into one device. But no one wants a package that reads something like "combo router/switch/access point/DHCP server/NAT/firewall," so the world has come to call these devices *routers*. Figure 9-59 shows one such router, with its functions shown on the right side of the figure.

FIGURE 9-59

Various Roles of Consumer "Router"

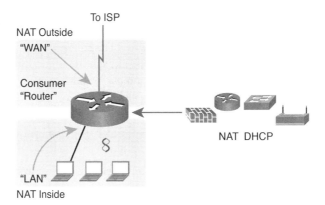

With routers meant for consumer use, the router vendors want the device to just work right out of the box. That is, the consumer cannot be expected to think about what private IP networks are, which one to use, what NAT is, and so on. So, these integrated routers, built for the consumer market, usually have one interface labeled WAN, with the others being WAN ports. Then, the router maker uses defaults like these:

- On the WAN port, it dynamically learns one public IP address from the ISP.
- It uses the one public IP for NAT.
- It makes the WAN port the outside port for NAT.
- Any traffic coming in from LAN ports will be processed by NAT.
- It picks one private IP network to use on the LAN (usually 192.168.1.0).
- It acts as a DHCP server on the LAN ports automatically, leasing IP addresses to all hosts on the LAN.
- It acts as a firewall, allowing clients to connect out to the Internet, but preventing clients in the Internet from connecting to servers in the home. (See the earlier section, "Securing the Internet Edge," for this concept.)

Figure 9-60 shows these same concepts, summarized into a diagram. Note that with all these defaults, the user can take the router out of the box and plug in the cables, and it works.

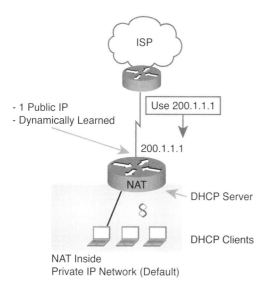

FIGURE 9-60

Default Settings on a Consumer-Grade Integrated Router

Chapter Summary

The Internet exists as a computer network made up of computer networks. The individual networks can range from the smallest TCP/IP networks in someone's home to both small and large corporate TCP/IP networks. Internet service providers (ISP) help make all the connections work by connecting to each individual or a corporate TCP/IP network, and then connecting to each other. Essentially, all the companies, individuals, and ISPs of the world cooperate, creating at least one path between each individual and network connected to the Internet.

The term *Internet access* refers to how one device or TCP/IP network connects to an ISP. Internet access can be done with WAN technologies that first existed as WAN services for enterprises, which were already discussed back in Chapter 7. This chapter looked at how SOHO users can connect to ISPs using analog modems, DSL, cable modems, and even wireless WANs. Each of these either uses existing cabling into the home or uses no cabling in the case of wireless WANs.

The Internet exists as a TCP/IP network, just a very large TCP/IP network. The sheer size of the Internet creates a need for some additional rules and functions that make this large TCP/IP network work well. The third major section of this chapter looked at the most basic changes to the core network layer functions of addressing, routing, and naming. In particular, it looked at the original IP address assignment process using classful IP networks, along with IP routing in the Internet core. It also showed how the Internet uses DNS, a distributed name database, to let hosts find the IP address used by a particular host name without the administrative burden of keeping a list of all host names on the planet.

Finally, the chapter ended with a section that showed the problems caused by huge Internet growth rates over many years, and described how both CIDR and NAT helped solve the problem for many years. CIDR changed the public IP address assignment rules, assigning address blocks that better match the real needs of the enterprise. NAT reduced the number of public IP addresses needed by a single company by using one public IP address to represent many real client IP hosts. Both helped delay the day when the world would run out of IPv4 addresses.

Chapter Review Activities

Use the features in this section to study and review the topics in this chapter.

Answer These Questions

1. IP hosts in two different company TCP/IP networks send IP packets to each other through the Internet. Which of the following is true about the Internet connections that must exist so that the packets can flow between the two companies?

   a. The two companies must connect directly to each other.

   b. The two companies must each have at least one Internet access link.

   c. The two companies must connect to the same ISP.

   d. The two companies must each connect to a Tier 1 ISP.

2. Which of the following standalone devices can be found near the Internet edge, with a primary purpose of providing some type of network security between an enterprise or SOHO TCP/IP network and the Internet? (Choose two answers.)

   a. LAN access point

   b. IPS

   c. Analog modem

   d. Firewall

3. Which of the following answers list a concept that is likely to be true about a single POP? (Choose two answers.)

   a. It is located near ISP customers.

   b. It contains many routers that work independently, without network connections to the other routers.

   c. It holds routers from multiple ISPs, allowing high-speed but inexpensive interconnects between ISPs.

   d. It connects to other ISP sites using some kind of WAN links.

4. Which of the following answers lists a fact that is true about a Tier 1 ISP, but not true about a Tier 2 ISP?

   a. Must have at least one network link to every other Tier 1 and Tier 2 ISP

   b. Has a network link to at least one other ISP

   c. Typically has many redundant high-speed links to other ISPs

   d. Most often, connects just to ISPs in the other tier

5. An enterprise network engineer wants to create a website for his company, Ent-1, with host name www.ent-1.com. Which of the following answers best describe a common place where the computer hardware for this website can be located? (Choose two answers.)

   a. In the Internet

   b. In the Ent-1 enterprise TCP/IP network

   c. At a web-hosting service

   d. In the IPS at the enterprise's Internet edge

6. A user has a PC and an analog modem. The user dials into her ISP, connects to the Internet, and surfs the web. The user then wants to make a phone call using her home telephone and the same telephone line. Which of the following answers is true in this case?

   a. The user must hang up the call to the ISP, and not surf, while talking on the phone.

   b. The call works, but the bit rate of the Internet connection reduces by 64 Kbps for the duration of the call.

   c. The call works, but the user can only send data when she is not talking, and receive data when the other person is not talking.

   d. The call works, with no change to the data speeds whether the voice call is happening or not.

7. A user migrates from using analog modems for Internet access to using DSL. The user sets up the DSL connection, using a PC, an Ethernet cable, an external DSL modem, and a phone line. The connection works, and the user surfs the web. The user also connects an analog home phone to another phone extension; the user then wants to make a phone call using his home telephone and the same telephone line used by DSL. Which of the following answers is true in this case?

   a. The user must hang up the call to the ISP, and not surf, while talking on the phone.

   b. The call works, but the bit rate of the Internet connection reduces by 64 Kbps for the duration of the call.

   c. The call works, but the user can only send data when he is not talking, and receive data when the other person is not talking.

   d. The call works, with no change to the data speeds whether the voice call is happening or not.

8. A user has lived at the same house for the last 30 years, using home phone services from the same local phone company. The user then calls an ISP and registers for DSL service to the home. The new customer is impatient, but the customer service rep tells the customer it will take a few days because a technician has do some work. Which one of the following answers is the most likely reason for the additional time required to install DSL service?

   a. The technician needs to connect the CO end of the local loop to a router.

   b. The technician needs to connect the CO end of the local loop to a CMTS.

   c. The technician needs to install HFC cabling.

   d. None of the answers is correct.

9. A user asks the cable company to install cable Internet service. The deal includes having a technician come and install all the equipment in the home. The equipment includes a consumer-grade router that performs several functions and an external cable modem. The cable company has equipment in its local head end offices as well. Which of the following devices, or functions inside the integrated router, plays a role in separating the data signals on the HFC cabling from the video signals?

    a. The router's firewall function

    b. The router's NAT function

    c. A cable modem

    d. The DSLAM at the head end

10. Which of the following Internet access technologies create an always-on Internet service, allow voice calls on the local telco's local loop while the Internet service still works, and use asymmetric speeds? (Choose two answers.)

    a. Cable Internet

    b. ADSL

    c. Analog modems

    d. T1

11. Imagine the early days of the Internet, before CIDR. A company wants to connect to the Internet, so it asks IANA or an associated RIR to assign the company some public IP addresses. Which of the following lists an approximate number of IP addresses that IANA or the RIR could possibly assign? (You can ignore rounding issues and the need to reserve any special cases.)

    a. 256

    b. 1024

    c. 8192

    d. 32,768

12. Imagine the early days of the Internet, before CIDR. A home user had one PC in the home, and she used an analog modem to access an ISP. Before she could send any packets into the public Internet, which of the following did the user have to do for her PC to have a public, globally unique IP address that allowed the PC to send and receive packets in the Internet?

    a. Register a class C network with IANA (or a related agency).

    b. Choose a private IP network and use NAT.

    c. No action is required, because the PC did not use TCP/IP.

    d. No action is required, because the ISP dynamically assigned a temporary public IP address to the PC.

13. Two Tier 1 ISPs use a dynamic IP routing protocol to exchange routing information about routes for their respective customers. Which of the following is the most likely routing protocol to be used in this case?

    a. BGP

    b. PPP

    c. NAT

    d. OSPF

14. A SOHO user connects a small office to the Internet using a cable modem. The small office has five PCs that connect to the consumer-grade router, which connects to a cable modem, which in turn connects to the cable company's coaxial cable. Call the five PCs PC A, B, C, D, and E, and the router R1. Which of the following answers is true about the routes used by the PCs and router for sending packets into the Internet?

    a. A's default router lists an IP address of one of the cable company's routers at the cable company head end.

    b. B's default router lists an IP address on R1.

    c. R1's default router entry lists an IP address of one of the cable company's routers at the cable company head end.

    d. R1 runs BGP to learn routes from a router in the cable company head end.

15. A company, Ent-1, uses the following URL to identify its public web server: www.ent-1.com. Ent-1 hosts its web server on a server inside the company's TCP/IP network, and with the company's own DNS server as the authoritative DNS server for this host name. A client in another part of the Internet opens a web browser and types in the www.ent-1.com name. Which of following must be true for the client to successfully learn the IP address used by host name www.ent-1.com?

    a. The client must know the IP address of the Ent-1 DNS server.

    b. The client must know the IP address of a .com root DNS server.

    c. The client must know the IP address of a DNS server that can in turn ask other DNS servers.

    d. The client must have a local file that lists this host name and its matching IP address.

16. Imagine the later days of the Internet, with CIDR. A company wants to connect to the Internet, so it asks IANA, an associated RIR, or an ISP to assign the company some public IP addresses. Which of the following list an approximate number of IP addresses IANA or the RIR could possibly assign? (You can ignore rounding issues and the need to reserve any special cases.) (Choose three answers.)

    a. 256

    b. 1024

    c. 8192

    d. 24,768

17. Which of the following are features defined by CIDR? (Choose two answers.)

    a. Public address assignment rules based on blocks of several sizes, based on powers of 2

    b. Host names that use a registered subdomain as the last part of the name, helping to create unique names across the Internet

    c. Reducing how many public IP addresses a company needs for its enterprise network by sharing public IP addresses

    d. Reducing the number of Internet routes using route aggregation

18. Which of the following were reasons why the world began to run out of IPv4 addresses back in the late 1990s and early 1990s? (Choose two answers.)

    a. Rate of growth of the worldwide population

    b. Growth of the Internet

    c. The introduction of tablet computers

    d. The waste in the IP address assignment process (by classful networks)

19. Which of the following is a private IP network?

    a. 1.0.0.0

    b. 192.168.68.0

    c. 172.32.0.0

    d. 200.1.1.0

20. A company builds its own TCP/IP network using class A network 10.0.0.0. The company then decides to connect to the Internet, so it asks an ISP for an Internet access link, and a CIDR block to support 111 public IP addresses. Which of the following answers lists the size of a CIDR block that the ISP would provide to this company?

    a. 111

    b. 128

    c. 150

    d. 200

Define the Key Terms

The following key terms include the ideas most important to the big ideas in this chapter. To review, without looking at the book or your notes, write a definition for each term, focusing on the meaning, not the wording. Then, review your definition compared to your notes, this chapter, and the glossary.

Key Terms for Chapter 9

the Internet	DSL	IPv4 address exhaustion
Internet edge	cable Internet	classless interdomain routing (CIDR)
point of presence	default route	
Internet core	host name	Network Address Translation (NAT)
Internet access	Domain Name System	
analog modem	subdomain	

List the Words Inside Acronyms

The following are the most common acronyms discussed in this chapter. As a way to review those terms, simply write down the words that each letter represents in each acronym.

Acronyms for Chapter 9

BGP	FTTC	POP
CATV	HFC	RIR
CIDR	IANA	RJ-11
CMTS	IPS	SOHO
DSL	ISP	
DSLAM	NAT	

Create Mind Maps

Create a mind map, or even a network diagram if you prefer, with five parts. Two parts focus on the customers of ISPs: one topic for Enterprise and the other for SOHO, with SOHO including individual users. For the next two categories, add Internet Edge and Internet Core. Then, add a fifth catch-all category.

Create a mind map that gathers all the terms and concepts from this chapter that matter to building the Internet. Only use terms of three words or less, or terms that have acronyms. For each term, place that term into one or more of the five categories, based on the category in which the concept gets used the most.

For example, NAT most often happens on a router or firewall at an enterprise, or at a SOHO site, so you could put NAT in both places. As another example, DSL is typically used as an Internet access technology, so place it in the Internet Edge category.

If your instructor has you do this exercise, ask the instructor whether you need to group the topics within each category.

Define Other Terms

Define the following additional terms from this chapter, and check your answers in the glossary:

Internet service provider

Internet core

firewall

DMZ

Tier 1 ISP

Tier 2 ISP

ISP dial service

upstream speed

downstream speed

asymmetric speed

symmetric speed

DSL access multiplexer

DSL modem

analog modem

cable television

coaxial cable

hybrid fiber coaxial (HFC)

head end

cable modem termination system (CMTS)

public IP address

private IP address

private IP network

public IP network

CIDR block

Internet Assigned Numbers Authority (IANA)

peering agreement

Border Gateway Protocol (BGP)

interior routing protocol

exterior routing protocol

single-homed

dual-homed

default route

default router

IP host

NAT table

NAT table entry

inline

DNS server

DNS query

root server

route aggregation

application connection

inside network

outside network

ISP

Tables and Lists from Memory

Print a copy of Appendix B, "Memory Tables" (which you can find online at www.pearsonitcertification.com/title/9780789748454), or at least the section for this chapter, and complete the tables and lists from memory. Appendix C, "Memory Tables Answer Key," also online, includes completed tables and lists to check your work.

Chapter 10

TCP/IP Transport

By this point in the book, you should have a good idea of how data moves from one computer to another in a TCP/IP network. Chapter 4, "Transmitting Bits," through Chapter 7, "Wide-Area Networks," focused on LANs and WANs, which define how to move the bits over a single link, or across links of the same general type. Chapter 8, "The Internet Protocol (IP)," and Chapter 9, "The Internet," moved up the TCP/IP stack to define how TCP/IP delivers IP packets between any two hosts, no matter what kinds of LANs and WANs exist in the TCP/IP network.

This final chapter in this book completes the story of the network's job: to move data from one application on one host to another application on another host. The TCP/IP model's two upper layers, the transport and application layers, define how these applications can communicate, as well as describe other important features of what the application can do over the TCP/IP network. As shown in Figure 10-1, these two upper layers of the TCP/IP model focus on the hosts in the TCP/IP network, as opposed to the three lower layers, which focus on delivering data across the TCP/IP network.

FIGURE 10-1

Scope of Impact for TCP/IP Layers

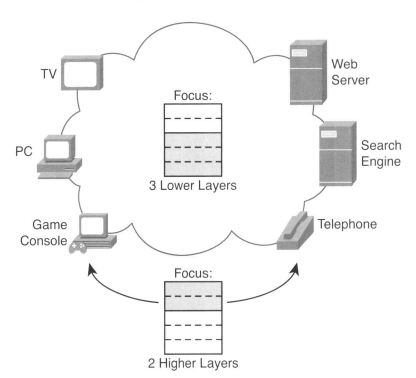

This chapter discusses some of the more important features of these two higher layers of TCP/IP:

- The first major section, "Providing Services with Transport and Application Protocols," shows how applications, application layer protocols, and transport layer protocols work together.

- The second major section, "Connecting Apps Using Transport Layer Port Numbers," looks at the most important transport layer function: how the transport layer identifies the correct sending and receiving application process on each host by using port numbers.

- The last major section, "Comparing Other TCP and UDP Functions," then looks at several other transport layer functions while comparing TCP and UDP.

Chapter Outline

Providing Services with Transport and Application Protocols

Connecting Apps Using Transport Layer Port Numbers

Comparing Other TCP and UDP Functions

Chapter Summary

Chapter Review Activities

Objectives

- Explain the relationship between network applications, application protocols, and transport protocols.

- Give examples of where application and transport layer protocols are implemented in a typical TCP/IP host.

- Sketch the concept of an application flow occurring over a TCP/IP network.

- Explain why servers often use well-known ports.

- Give examples of TCP flows using port numbers, listing the source and destination ports used.

- Explain why clients often use dynamic ports.

- Sketch the concepts of IP MTU and TCP MSS and their relationship.

- Explain how a sending TCP host segments data.

- Describe the basics of how TCP acknowledges data and performs error recovery.

Key Terms

Transmission Control Protocol

User Datagram Protocol

flow

TCP segment

UDP datagram

source port

destination port

well-known port number

dynamic port

TCP segmentation

guaranteed delivery

error recovery

Providing Services with Transport and Application Protocols

Every TCP/IP network creates a basic IP packet delivery service, created by the functions of the lower three layers in the TCP/IP model. If all that the applications in the world needed to do was to deliver packets from host to host, with no other logic, no other functions, and no other needs, the TCP/IP model would just have those lower three layers.

This first major section of this chapter introduces how TCP/IP's two upper layers provide some other functions beyond the basic IP packet delivery service. These functions occur mostly on the endpoint hosts themselves, with the networking devices between the hosts focusing only on the lower three layers of TCP/IP.

This first major section of the chapter looks at the upper layers from three perspectives:

- The first topic takes the viewpoint of the host computer, where most of the application and transport layer work happens.

- The second section looks at topics related to the TCP/IP network that sits between the two hosts.

- The final topic discusses how IT workers and users choose application and transport protocols.

Host Perspectives on the Upper Layers

Most of the transport and application layer work that happens in a TCP/IP network happens on the hosts themselves. This first topic looks at the hosts from two perspectives: the software that implements the TCP/IP protocols and how those protocols work together.

Software Architecture on the Endpoint Hosts

First, think about the software on a typical desktop computer. It has an operating system (OS), oftentimes one of the Microsoft Windows OSs, maybe a Mac with MAC OS, or Linux. If the host happens to be a tablet computer, the OS might be Apple's iOS or Google's Android OS.

Although the OS plays a huge role, the user mostly spends time using the applications (apps). These include text messaging, email, voice calling, word processing, web browsers, and many specialized apps for mobile devices—and the list could go on.

The OS and the apps that run on the OS, even without the existence of a network, work together. The OS's job is to provide a good place to run apps. The apps assume that the OS will be there to provide that environment.

With those purely software concepts in mind, now think about the upper layers of the TCP/IP protocol model, from the perspective of a host. Protocols exist as ideas recorded in some document, like the Hypertext Transfer Protocol (HTTP) in RFC 2616. In general, product vendors read the protocol documents and then write software and build hardware that implements those protocols.

On TCP/IP hosts, the upper-layer protocols exist in both the application and OS software. Typically, the application developer includes the application layer protocol within the app. The OS vendor typically includes the transport protocol (and network layer protocols as well) inside the OS. For example, when a user installs a web browser on his computer, he installs one software package, but it includes the functions of HTTP. Figure 10-2 shows this relationship between the protocols, using a web browser as an example.

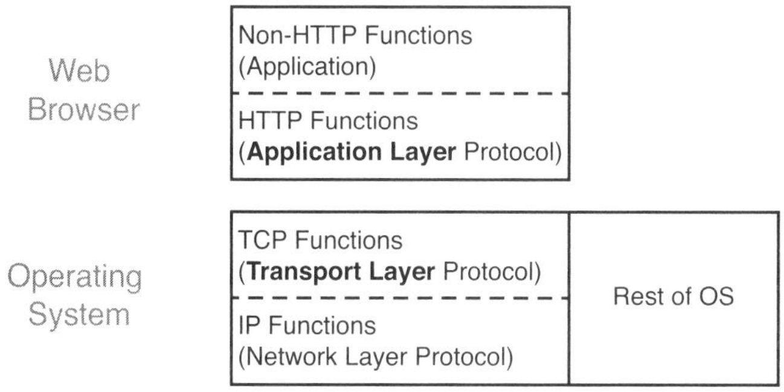

FIGURE 10-2

Software Architecture of the Application and Transport Layers

Serving the Needs of the Next-Higher Layer

To better understand the roles of the two upper layers of TCP/IP, however, it helps to mentally separate the application software into two parts: the part that implements the application layer protocol and the rest of the app. Think of a typical app, and ask yourself, what else does it do besides send and receive data? For example, a web browser has to have a user interface. It has menu options, where users can customize such features as the size of the text, the security settings, the home page, and so on.

On each host, each function both has needs and supplies the answer to the needs of other functions. For example, consider a web browser—as two parts, the HTTP part and the rest of the application—plus the OS's TCP and IP functions. The application needs to get a web page; the application protocol can do that. When the browser application needs to get a web page, HTTP serves that need by using the HTTP GET command to get the web objects that make up a web page. Figure 10-3 shows the idea of how each part needs something and has that need supplied.

FIGURE 10-3

**Needing and Supplying
Services in TCP/IP Upper
Layers**

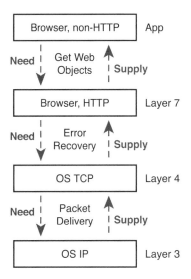

The figure shows just one example, with one service supplied by each layer, but it does show the point. Different applications need different services, so the services supplied by the application protocols vary quite a bit. However, the two main transport layer protocols, **Transport Control Protocol (TCP)** and **User Datagram Protocol (UDP)**, supply a very specific small set of services.

Network Perspectives on TCP/IP Upper Layers

Most of the application and transport layer work happens on the endpoint hosts. Some discussions of these upper layers can completely ignore the TCP/IP network that exists between the hosts. When learning about these upper layers, however, it helps to take some time to think about these upper layers while also thinking about a typical TCP/IP network existing between the endpoint hosts.

The following sections take a look at a few short topics, including encapsulation across TCP/IP networks and how the IP forwarding process mostly ignores the upper layers.

Encapsulation and Headers

Like any other networking protocols, the application and transport layer protocols use headers to do their work. The application protocol on the sending host adds an application protocol header, expecting that the receiving host's application layer protocol will read and react to the contents of that header. The transport layer also adds headers to do its work as well.

This chapter does not look at the application headers, but it does discuss several parts of both the TCP and UDP header. The goal is to understand the functions created by the headers, more so than just memorizing the fields in the header.

Figures 10-4 and 10-5 show the TCP and UDP headers, respectively, for reference. Note that both figures show 4 bytes of the header across, with multiple rows, for the 20-byte TCP and 8-byte UDP header.

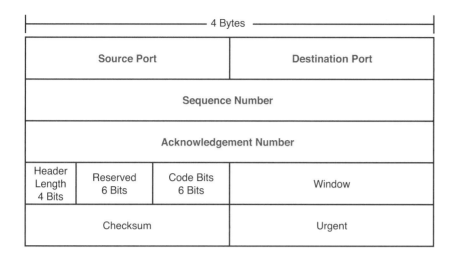

FIGURE 10-4

TCP Header Reference

FIGURE 10-5

UDP Header Reference

First, think about the network from the sending host's perspective, from the transport layer and up. The sending host adds the original application and transport layer header to the end-user data to create a message. These upper-layer messages remain mostly unchanged as they pass through the network. And the upper layers just want the message delivered to the matching application on the other side of the network.

Figure 10-6 shows an example of this process, with the upper-layer headers and data highlighted. This example shows a message from the web server on the left going to the web browser on the right. The message shows the TCP and HTTP headers, plus user data, going through the complete route from host to host. It also shows the data-link and IP headers, with the data-link header/trailer changing at each router, as usual.

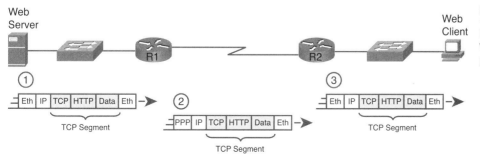

FIGURE 10-6

Encapsulation with Web Traffic, All Layers

The figure also introduces a new term: TCP segment. A **TCP segment** is the part of a message in the network that begins with the TCP header, through the encapsulated data, but ignoring the lower-layer headers and trailers. UDP has a similar concept and term (**UDP datagram**). The transport layer's goal is to deliver these messages—TCP segments and UDP datagrams—from the sending app to the receiving app.

IP Versus Transport Perspectives on Encapsulation

Anytime you think about or discuss the work done by one layer in the TCP/IP model, you can choose to ignore some details about the lower layers. To compare TCP/IP's transport layer to the network layer, this next topic first reviews how you might discuss IP forwarding as an end to itself, and then it describes a similar process using TCP.

Network layer IP forwarding logic, ignoring the lower layers, follows a hop-by-hop process between hosts and routers. Earlier, Figure 10-6 shows the LAN switches and the telco leased line, with all the headers shown. A purely IP view of that same process, as shown at the top of Figure 10-7, shows each LAN and WAN as a simple line. The figure shows the packet flowing from source to destination as three steps, because this example has three major steps in the IP routing logic. Also, the encapsulation just shows the IP header, ignoring the headers and trailers for any lower layers.

FIGURE 10-7

IP Versus Transport
Perspective on
Encapsulation

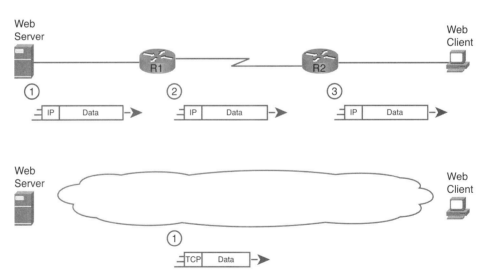

The lower half of the figure shows how the transport layer, TCP in this example, sees the entire TCP/IP network as a single step of sending the TCP segment to the other host. Just like the network layer view ignores the data-link details, the purely transport layer view can ignore parts of the network layer and other lower layers. It does not show the three IP routing steps shown at the top of the figure, because from TCP's perspective, the entire TCP/IP network, shown as a cloud, acts as a simple IP packet delivery service. The TCP/IP network hidden by the cloud could be two hosts connected by a single LAN cable, or it could be two hosts on different continents that use the Internet to communicate. In either case, the transport layer processes work the same.

Choosing Application and Transport Protocols

When choosing the technologies in the lower three layers, the choices do have some impact on what protocols that particular TCP/IP network uses. For example, if the network uses leased lines between routers, the data-link protocol will likely be either High-Level Data Link Control (HDLC) or Point-to-Point Protocol (PPP). If instead the network uses Frame Relay, the data-link protocol would be Frame Relay.

Neither the IT worker nor the user chooses an application or transport layer protocol directly. Instead, the people who create the idea for the application create the application protocol (or choose an existing application protocol). When they create that application layer protocol, they also choose which transport layer protocol to use. So, the IT worker does not sit back and choose to use TCP, to use UDP, or to use HTTP; he chooses apps, and the apps use whatever the application creators chose.

For example, web browsers and servers were first created in the early 1990s. When this new app was created, HTTP did not exist, so the creators of web browsers created HTTP as the communications part of the app, doing functions like getting web objects. When creating HTTP, they looked at the two commonly used transport layer protocols at the time, TCP and UDP, and chose to use TCP. That happened 20 years ago, and as a result, when you use a web browser today, you use HTTP and TCP.

As you read through the chapter, you will learn more about the services provided by both TCP and UDP. For now, Figure 10-8 shows this concept of how each app uses one transport layer protocol. It shows four apps that have been mentioned at some point in the book, two of which use TCP and two of which use UDP.

ON THE SIDE: Domain Name System (DNS) uses UDP for the name resolution requests discussed in Chapters 8 and 9, but it also uses TCP for some other functions that this book does not discuss.

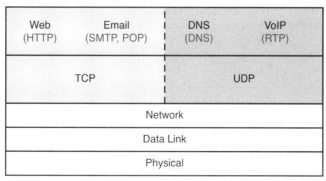

FIGURE 10-8

Some Apps Using TCP and Some Using UDP

Connecting Apps Using Transport Layer Port Numbers

TCP and UDP provide a different set of functions to applications. However, both provide one very important function—they connect the right application process on the sending host to the right application process on the receiving host.

This second of three major sections in this chapter looks at how these transport layer protocols connect application processes. The following sections begin by discussing the basic concept of a connection or flow between two application processes, and describe how both TCP and UDP use a concept called a port number to identify each process. This topic then closes with a discussion of how both TCP and UDP know which port numbers to use.

Application Connections and Flows

Most host operating systems (OS) allow *multiprocessing*, during which more than one program can be active at the same time. A multiprocessing OS gives each active program a share of the CPU and RAM, with each program taking turns. Each active program, when running as one of the many programs that each get a share of the CPU, is typically called a *process*.

Both the TCP and UDP transport layer protocols offer the following service to any computer process:

> Delivering data between that process and some matching process on another computer

The transport layer protocol makes this commitment to the computer process, while relying on the lower layers to do some of the work. As seen back in Figure 10-3, the network layer provides an IP packet delivery service to the transport layer, which takes care of the movement of the data from host to host. That process, of course, uses the LANs and WANs as defined by Layers 1 and 2.

So, what work is left for the transport layer to do? One function is to identify the correct application process on the destination host, as shown in Figure 10-9.

FIGURE 10-9

Concept of App-to-App Flows Between Two Apps

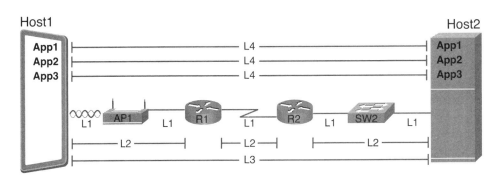

Two commonly used terms, *connection* and *flow*, both refer to this single idea of two application processes sending data to each other, as shown at the top of the figure. The transport layer protocols must create these connections and flows, and be able to identify data for each, to deliver the data to the correct application process. The top of the figure represents three flows.

Using Port Numbers to Identify the Application Process

Both TCP and UDP use port numbers to identify the application processes in each flow. By assigning each process a port number, and including that number in the TCP or UDP header, the transport protocols can identify the specific computer process that either sent the data (**source port**) or needs to receive the data (**destination port**).

The port numbers for both TCP and UDP range from 0 through 65,535, because they exist in the headers as 16-bit binary numbers. With 16 bits, 2^{16} (65,536) possible values exist, with decimal equivalents from 0 through 65,535. Most of the time, people use the decimal equivalent values.

> **AUTHOR'S NOTE:** Although the numbers use the same range, TCP port numbers are a different set of numbers than UDP. Just to cut down on repeating facts and clarifying at every turn, the rest of this section uses TCP examples. However, the port number concepts apply to both TCP and UDP.

Like all the other numbering plans with TCP/IP, the numbers must follow some rules. The rules can be summarized as follows:

- On a single host, all TCP port numbers must be unique.
- Among all hosts, TCP port numbers can be reused.

For example, Figure 10-10 shows the same two hosts as in Figure 10-9, with three TCP flows, but now with TCP port numbers shown. In this case, both hosts use TCP port 1024, and that is allowed. However, Host1 has three TCP port numbers that are unique on Host1, and Host2 also has three TCP port numbers that are unique on Host2.

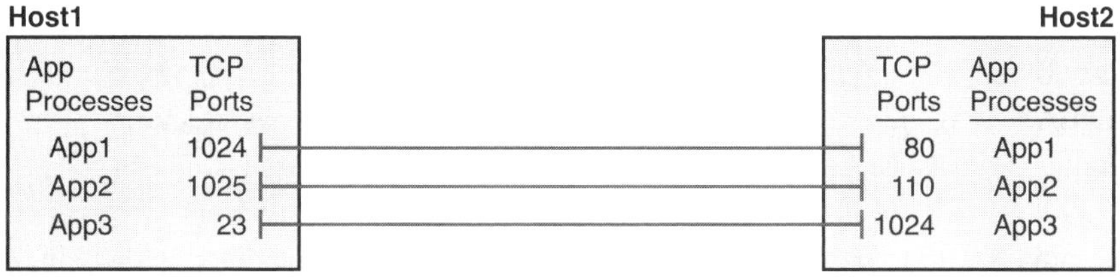

> **AUTHOR'S NOTE:**
> The rest of this chapter uses the term *flow*, rather than always repeating "*connection* or *flow*," as the general term for the concept at the top of Figure 10-9. The term *flow* generally applies to this idea for both TCP and UDP, while the term *connection* typically refers to only TCP flows.

Host1					Host2
App Processes	TCP Ports			TCP Ports	App Processes
App1	1024			80	App1
App2	1025			110	App2
App3	23			1024	App3

FIGURE 10-10

Three TCP Flows with Unique TCP Ports per Host

10

The port numbers only need to be unique on each host, without the need to be unique across all hosts, because of how TCP uses the destination port number. As shown back in Figure 10-4, the TCP header has both a source and destination port number field. When the destination host receives a TCP segment, the TCP software compares the destination TCP port to a list of all currently used TCP ports (and their matching computer processes). TCP then gives the data to the process that uses that port.

It can help to see a full example or two that shows both the source and destination port. Figure 10-11 shows two examples. The first example, at the top of the figure, shows the source and destination ports for a segment, going from left to right, over the top flow in the figure. The second example, at the bottom of the figure, shows the ports for a segment also going from left to right, but for the bottom of the three flows in the figure.

FIGURE 10-11

Destination Host Chooses the Right Destination App Based on the Destination Port

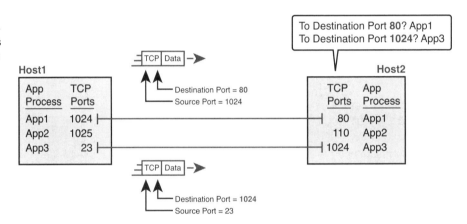

The right side of Figure 10-11 shows the logic on the destination host's TCP software. When the top segment arrives, with destination port 80, Host2 looks at its list of active TCP ports, finding port 80. TCP also keeps track of which computer process has opened each TCP port, so TCP knows which process gets the data. In the same way, when the segment with destination port 1024 arrives, Host2 looks at the same list, finds the process named App3, and gives the data to that process.

Note that when choosing the app process to which to give the data, the destination host ignores the source TCP port number.

Choosing the Port Numbers to Use for Each App

This book has already discussed a couple types of numbers that need to be unique. With LAN MAC addresses, the IEEE uses a process by which manufacturers give a unique universal MAC address on every network interface card (NIC) or LAN interface. With IP addresses, IANA gives each company an IP network or classless interdomain routing (CIDR) block, with that company assigning numbers within that network or block.

With TCP (and UDP), the port numbers need to be unique only on the local host. Because the port numbers only have to be unique on each host, each host's TCP software has control. TCP acts as a traffic cop, preventing more than one process from using the same TCP port number.

To use a port to communicate, an application must ask TCP for permission to use that port with a process called *opening a port*. When opening a port, an application process basically makes a request in one of two ways:

- The app tells TCP the port number that the app wants to use, and TCP agrees only if no other process already uses that port number.

- The application asks TCP to give the application any port number to use, one that no other process currently uses.

This topic looks at the small differences in both approaches, and discusses how these approaches help clients connect to servers.

Initializing Servers with a Well-Known Port

Many applications in the TCP/IP world follow a client/server model. In that model, the server must make itself available to clients. The server application (web server, email server, and so on) must start, and be ready to receive, requests for any client. Clients, on the other hand, can just work when they want to work and then go away. For example, you can open a web browser, surf the web, and close the browser. The web servers, on the other hand, must always be up and running, waiting for potential clients to ask for content.

For the client/server model to work, the server's computer process must start and open a TCP port, waiting on TCP segments to arrive into that TCP port. That one opening sentence has a lot of meaning behind it. The physical server must be started. The OS running at that server must be working. The server software must be started and running on the OS. And the server software must open that TCP port, with TCP agreeing. All those steps must happen before the server can accept the first message from the first client.

To show the initialization steps, take a look at a new example, using the real port numbers that would be used by both a web server and email server using *Post Office Protocol version 3* (POP3). Figure 10-12 shows the server host on the right. Two server software processes have just started: a web server and an email server. The web server, which uses HTTP as the application protocol, uses port 80, and the email server, which uses POP3 as the application protocol, uses port 110.

10

FIGURE 10-12

Two Servers with Well-Known Ports Open and Listening for New Connections

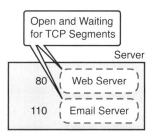

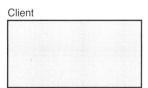

No Apps Yet!

> **ON THE SIDE:** The need to first open a server port before clients can connect is a little like needing to open a restaurant before you can ever expect to have any customers eat at the restaurant. You open the restaurant and hope that enough people (clients) want what you're serving.

When a server comes up and initializes, it opens the TCP port as the way to tell TCP that the server intends to use that particular port number. By opening (registering) with the TCP software, an application essentially tells the TCP software that it is claiming the right to use that port number on that host. And, to prevent more than one application from using the same port number on that host, the TCP software simply rejects any attempt to open a TCP port that is already open.

Figure 10-13 shows the steps that happen on the server host when the server software registers to use a specific port number. This example shows web server software. That software uses its default setting to use the well-known port for HTTP: TCP port 80. (More details on the well-known port concept after the figure.)

FIGURE 10-13

Server Initializing Well-Known Port 80 for HTTP

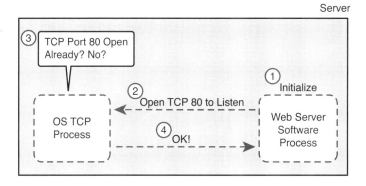

Following the steps in the figure:

1. The web server software starts running.

2. The web server sends a notice to the OS's TCP process, stating that the web server software wants to use TCP port 80 and listen for incoming TCP segments going to port 80.

3. The TCP software in the OS checks to make sure that TCP port 80 is not open by any other application on that host, to prevent two applications from using the same port.

4. The TCP software informs the web server software that no other application was using port 80, so the web server can use it.

At this point, the servers are ready, but no clients have tried to connect. The servers (software) sit waiting. The TCP software on the server knows which process to give segments sent to both TCP port 80 (web server) and 110 (email server).

Figures 10-11 and 10-12 have actually been building concepts to discuss an important concept related to which port numbers servers usually use. Think to the future, when the client on the left opens a web browser and email client, connecting to the servers on the right. The segments will flow to the server on the right. How does the client host know that the web server on the right uses port 80? Or that the POP3 server uses port 110?

The answer: **well-known port numbers**. The people who created the related application layer protocols, HTTP and POP3, asked IANA to reserve a unique TCP port number that should be used only by that application layer protocol. As it turns out, HTTP reserved port 80, and POP3 reserved port 110. Web browser software knows that web servers should use port 80 by default, and email client software knows that POP3 servers use TCP port 110 by default. Figure 10-14 shows the result of clients connecting to the two servers, with port numbers shown.

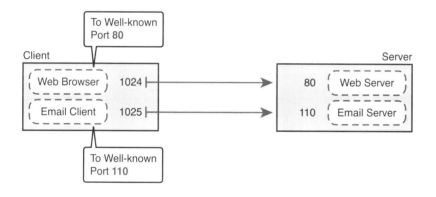

FIGURE 10-14

Clients Send TCP Segments to Correct Well-Known Port Numbers

TCP defines the concept of a well-known port number as a port number reserved for use by servers that use a particular application layer protocol. If someone creates a new application layer protocol, he can ask IANA for a well-known port number, one not assigned to any other application protocol. For example, before POP3 existed, IANA had not assigned TCP port 110 to any other application layer protocol, so IANA then assigned 110 to POP3. Similarly, before HTTP existed, no other application layer protocol used port 80, so IANA assigned port 80 to HTTP.

Table 10-1 lists some of the common TCP/IP application protocols, along with the transport protocol, well-known port numbers used, and a brief description of the purpose of the protocol.

AUTHOR'S NOTE:
IANA reserves the first 1024 TCP and UDP ports numbers (0–1023) as well-known ports. You can find the list of well-known port number assignments with a simple Internet search.

10

TABLE 10-1

Common Application Protocols and Their Well-Known Port Numbers

Application Protocol	Transport Protocol	Port Number	Description
HTTP	TCP	80	Used by web browsers and web servers
Telnet	TCP	23	Used for terminal emulation
SSH	TCP	22	Used for secure terminal emulation
FTP	TCP	20, 21	Used for file transfer
DNS	UDP	53	Used for name resolution
SMTP	TCP	25	Used to send and receive email
POP3	TCP	110	Another email protocol
IMAP	TCP	143	Another email protocol
SSL	TCP	443	Used to encrypt data for secure transactions
SNMP	UDP	161, 162	Used to manage TCP/IP networks

Initializing Clients with a Dynamically Allocated Port

Clients and servers have several differences, but one basic difference matters a lot to the discussion of TCP (and UDP) ports. Simply put, clients send the first message in a flow.

First, think about the client, which sends the first message in a flow. Because clients send the first message, they need a way to know the server's TCP port number, so the well-known port number concept solves that problem. The client's application process still needs a port number to use, but it does not matter much what port number. Why? Because the server can learn the client's port number from the source port number field in the first message.

Figure 10-15 shows an example, using the same port numbers as the previous figure. In this case, the first TCP segment, from the client on the left to the server on the right, goes to destination port 80. The steps in the figure are explained after the figure.

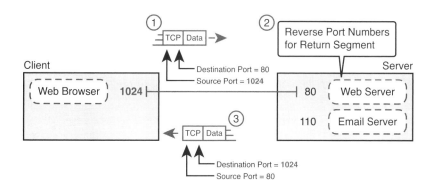

FIGURE 10-15

Client Initializing a Dynamic Port Number Assigned by the OS (TCP)

Following the steps in the figure:

1. The client sends a TCP segment, from source port 1024 to destination (well-known HTTP port) 80 on the server.

2. The server's TCP software, when building the TCP segment to send back to the client, simply reverses the TCP source and destination port numbers.

3. The TCP segment from the web server to the web browser lists a destination port of 1024, matching the port number used on the client.

The client does not need to use a well-known port number. The client, because it sends the first message in a flow, can just pick any currently unused port number. The server then learns the client application process's port number from that first message.

Instead of opening a specific TCP well-known port number, the client application processes ask TCP for a **dynamic port number**. In this type of a request, the client asks TCP to find an unused port number—any unused port number on that host. The application can use it, and then release it back to TCP, letting some other application process use it later.

Figure 10-16 shows what happens on a client computer. In this case, the user opens a web browser, probably in preparation to connect to the web server shown in the last few figures.

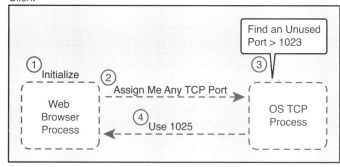

FIGURE 10-16

Client Initializing a Dynamic Port Number Assigned by the OS (TCP)

10

Following the steps in the figure:

1. The user starts the web browser software.

2. The web browser asks TCP to assign a TCP port number.

3. The TCP software in the OS chooses a port number that is a) >1023 and b) currently unused.

4. The TCP software informs the web browser of the port number to use.

IANA regulates the range of numbers the world should use for well-known ports and dynamic ports. IANA also defines a third class of port numbers called registered ports. These ranges apply to both TCP and UDP port numbers, and are summarized in Table 10-2.

TABLE 10-2

Well-Known, Registered, and Dynamic Port Numbers

Type	Port Number Range
Well-known	0 – 1023
Registered	1,024 – 49,151
Dynamic	49,153 – 65,535

You might have noticed that many examples in this chapter show dynamic port numbers just above 1024, but the table lists those numbers at the low end of the range of registered port numbers. As it turns out, in practice, many OSs use parts or all the registered port number ranges for dynamic port number assignments. Over time, the OSs of the world might finally use only the dynamic port numbers as listed in Table 10-2. OSs do indeed avoid using the well-known port number range as dynamic ports.

From Initializing Ports to Creating Flows

To finish this discussion of TCP port numbers, this last topic pulls the client and server concepts together into a cohesive story.

As mentioned earlier in the chapter, both TCP and UDP make the promise of delivering data from one application process to the correct application process on another computer. To do that, TCP needs to encapsulate the data inside a TCP segment. That TCP segment will list the sending application's port number as the source port and the receiving application's port number as the destination port.

To begin that process, any servers must first initialize and start listening for new flows from clients. For example, a web server would initialize and use well-known port 80, because web servers use HTTP, and HTTP has been assigned well-known TCP port 80. In the same way, an email server that used POP3 would use well-known port 110.

Figure 10-17 shows that specific example, after the servers have initialized but before any clients have connected to any servers.

Clients

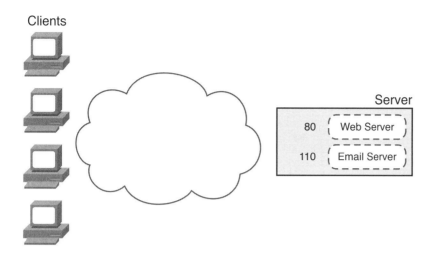

FIGURE 10-17

Email and Web Servers Waiting for Flows

When any of the clients on the left decide to connect to one of the servers on the right, the clients need to decide what source and destination port numbers to use. For the destination port numbers, the client application would be programmed to know the well-known port used by servers. For example, all web browser software has been programmed to know that HTTP uses well-known port 80. For the source port, the client just has to ask the OS for a unique dynamic port number, as shown back in Figure 10-16.

For example, imagine that the client on the left of Figure 10-18 opened a web browser to connect to the web server on the right. As it turns out, downloading one web page often creates multiple TCP flows, so imagine that three flows were created in this case. The client (Host A) would need three TCP port numbers, one per flow. The user at Host A also checked his email with POP3, creating a fourth flow, as also shown in Figure 10-18.

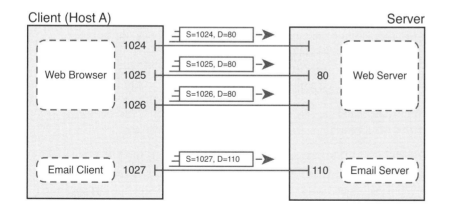

Legend

S = Source Port
D = Destination Port

FIGURE 10-18

Four Flows with (Dynamic) Source Ports and Well-Known Destination Ports

When the web server and email server respond, they already know what port numbers to use when responding for each flow. When responding to messages over any flow, the return message just reverses the source and destination port numbers. Figure 10-19 shows the values, with four messages sent from right to left in the figure, showing the port number values reversed as compared to Figure 10-18.

FIGURE 10-19

Port Numbers Reversed for TCP Segments in the Opposite Direction

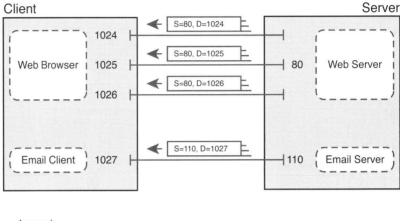

Legend

S = Source Port
D = Destination Port

Comparing Other TCP and UDP Functions

TCP and UDP both deliver data between applications on different hosts using port numbers to identify the application processes. However, if TCP and UDP performed exactly the same functions, in the same way, the world would not need both TCP and UDP. This final major section of the chapter compares TCP and UDP.

First, if you compare the functions of TCP and UDP, and count the number of functions, TCP wins. TCP simply does more. It segments large data into smaller chunks. It guarantees delivery of data using error recovery. It controls the flow of data in a TCP connection. UDP? None of the above.

UDP, on the other hand, has none of the extra overhead of TCP. UDP uses fewer bytes, uses less processing on the hosts, and typically runs faster.

Comparing TCP and UDP might be a bit like comparing a luxury car to a dirt bike. Both work, and both work well for their intended purpose. You certainly don't want to drag your spouse and kids on a trip to Grandma's using the dirt bike. And you don't want to go off-road through the mountains with the luxury car. They were just designed for different jobs.

The following sections look at two of TCP's features that UDP does not do: segmentation and guaranteed delivery. For these topics, these sections discuss not only how TCP does these functions but also the effects of UDP's not doing those same functions. These sections end with an overall comparison of TCP and UDP.

Segmentation

The amount of data an application needs to send varies. One application might need to send a single byte at a time. Another application might send the same amount of data every time, small or large. Another application might send small amounts of data one time and huge amounts just a moment later.

When an application thinks about sending data, the application tends to think of the data as a large chunk of data. For example, the data might be the entire contents of a graphics file for a website, an email attachment, or the text of an email. However, the network has some size restrictions on how much data can be sent in a single IP packet. Something must be done to deal with the fact that applications might want to send data in larger chunks than the network can forward.

This next topic looks at how hosts deal with the fact that applications might want to send a large block of data. First, the text looks at the network's rules to limit the size of data going through the TCP/IP network. Then the text looks at how TCP and UDP each solve this problem.

Size Restrictions for Messages in a TCP/IP Network

Imagine that you need to send a book to a friend, a friend who lives so far away that you need to mail the book. The job is simple, right? You find a box that's a little bigger than the book, put the book inside, tape it shut, write the address on the box, and send it through the postal service or some other shipping company. During its trip, the box ends up on several different trucks, riding over the roads, and eventually arrives at the home of your friend. One box, one book, no problem.

Now imagine that you work for a road construction company, and your company happens to be building a bridge. The project engineer tells you that he wants you to ship a part to the bridge construction site. You start looking around for a box to use for the part, just like you did for the book, and he starts laughing. The steel beam he wants to have shipped is 200 feet long, is 20 feet wide, and weighs 100 tons. As it turns out, the project engineer was trying to be funny—that part is too long, too wide, and too heavy to be shipped over the roads.

> **ON THE SIDE:** Big parts like the beam for the bridge are often made as smaller parts that can be sent over the roads and then assembled on-site.

Similar to the road rules about the maximum length, width, and weight for what you can carry over the public roadways, many data-link protocols have rules about the maximum length of the data inside a data-link frame. For any data-link protocol that limits the size of the data field, devices that use that data-link protocol should simply avoid sending too-long frames. If it ever happens, the receiving device typically discards the frame.

> **ON THE SIDE:** In Ethernet, a too-long frame is called a *giant*.

The maximum allowed length of data-link frame's data field defines the maximum size of an IP packet encapsulated in a data-link frame. Most data-link frames encapsulate an IP packet in the Data field. As an example, Ethernet limits the Ethernet Data field to 1500 bytes. So, IP packets that are sent over Ethernet must be limited to 1500 bytes.

Other data-link protocols support other sizes, but the common data-link protocols support sizes either larger than 1500, or they have no restrictions.

> **ON THE SIDE:** Some switch and server Ethernet NICs support a feature called Jumbo frames, which allow a larger Ethernet frame size, but in general, assume that Ethernet supports 1500 bytes of data, making the IP maximum transmission unit (MTU) 1500 bytes.

IP uses the term *maximum transmission unit (IP MTU)* to refer to the maximum size of an IP packet that can be sent out a given interface, based on that interface's data-link protocol. Figure 10-20 shows the idea, based on Ethernet. It shows an IP MTU of 1500, in a packet that has an IP and TCP header (each 20 bytes).

FIGURE 10-20

IP MTU Concept on Ethernet Links

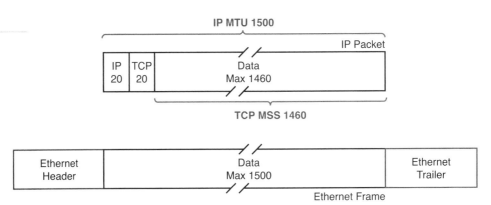

TCP defines a similar concept, called the *maximum segment size (MSS)*. MSS defines the maximum size of the data field in a TCP segment, not including the TCP header. (Note that the IP MTU concept includes the entire IP packet, including the IP header.) Because the IP and TCP header both require 20 bytes of space, the MSS = MTU – 40, making the MSS for data crossing an Ethernet be 1460.

TCP Segmentation

Next, think about the problem again. Applications sometimes want to send large amounts of data, far more than can fit in a single IP packet or TCP segment, based on the MTU and MSS math just discussed. But somehow, the data crosses the TCP/IP network. For example, probably even today, you have surfed to some web page, and that web page showed some graphical images. That data crossed at least one Ethernet most likely, and those image files were far larger than the IP MTU of 1500 and TCP MSS of 1460 expected on an Ethernet interface—yet they still managed to cross the Internet.

As it turns out, both IP and TCP define a way to deal with the problem:

IP fragmentation: When a router needs to forward an IP packet out an interface, if the packet is longer than the IP MTU of the outgoing interface, the router breaks (fragments) the IP packet into several smaller IP packets and sends those instead.

TCP segmentation: TCP on the sending host breaks the larger data into pieces of a size of TCP MSS (or smaller) when creating the original TCP segments.

Both IP fragmentation and TCP segmentation play an important role in TCP/IP networks today. IP fragmentation gives routers a way to deal with the problem after the IP packet gets into the TCP/IP network. The IP MTU concept applies per interface, so as a packet flows over some route, it might reach a router whose outgoing interface MTU happens to be smaller than the size of the IP packet. IP fragmentation lets the router make sure that the data gets to the destination by breaking the IP packet into smaller packets, packets that do not get reassembled until they reach the destination host.

TCP segmentation takes a totally different approach. First, only the sending host thinks about segmentation (breaking the larger data into smaller pieces), with the receiving host putting the chunks back together into the original large chunk of data. The routers in between do not think about TCP segmentation.

Combining the two ideas, the sending host's TCP software segments the data based on MSS, but if at some point the IP packets happen to be too large for some link, the routers in the TCP/IP network can still deliver the packet to the right destination.

Figure 10-21 shows an example of TCP segmentation. The figure shows the internals of what happens inside a web server, when the web server needs to send a web object called picture.jpg. The file has a convenient 14,600 bytes, exactly ten times the MSS on the server's Ethernet interface.

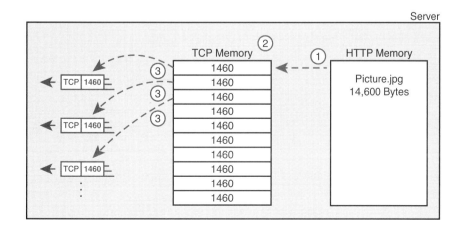

FIGURE 10-21

Web Server Sends Web Object; TCP Segments

10

Following the steps in the figure:

1. The web server software has an entire object, picture.jpg, size 14,600 bytes, in memory, ready to send to a client, so its HTTP function gives the data to the TCP software.

2. The TCP software on the server puts the data in memory, but TCP also breaks the data into MSS-sized segments (10 segments of 1460 bytes each).

3. TCP puts each of the 10 separate TCP segments of data into 10 different TCP messages (also called segments) and sends them to the web client.

On the receiving host, TCP also provides the service of reassembling the segments into the correct order. The TCP segments, traveling inside IP packets, could arrive out of order. TCP headers use a sequence number field to label each segment so that the receiver can reassemble the segments back into the correct order before handing them off to the receiving app.

UDP and the Need to Segment Data

UDP does not have an equivalent term like TCP's MSS, but it has a similar concept. The term *UDP datagram* refers to UDP messages that include a UDP header and its encapsulated data, as shown in Figure 10-22. The size of the UDP data field is potentially limited to some maximum size on each link, based on that link's IP MTU. For example, the figure shows the maximum size of the UDP datagram's data field as 1472 on an Ethernet link.

FIGURE 10-22

UDP Datagram Maximum Data Size on Ethernet Links

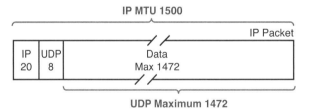

Unlike TCP, UDP does not segment larger data to fit inside the UDP datagram's Data field. An application that uses UDP cannot give UDP a big chunk of data, expecting UDP to break the data into segments. When using UDP, the application must segment the data into smaller sizes before passing the data off to UDP.

In some cases, UDP-based applications do not send large data. In other cases, the UDP-based application protocol creators simply preferred to segment the data inside the application.

For example, Voice over IP (VoIP) applications use an application protocol called Real-Time Transport Protocol (RTP). RTP uses UDP, not TCP. RTP does not send large chunks of data, instead sending lots of small UDP datagrams, typically 200 bytes or less. RTP creates many of these small UDP datagrams per call (typically about 50 per second per direction in a phone call).

Guaranteed Delivery and Error Recovery

Sometimes, the application designer wants his applications to know with certainty that the data arrives at the other end of the flow. In other cases, the application designer might look at the needs of an application and decide that the app really does not need to know for sure whether the data was delivered.

TCP provides a **guaranteed delivery** service to all applications that use TCP, whereas UDP does not. Essentially, the app passes the data to TCP, expecting that TCP will definitely deliver the data to the other end of the flow. TCP commits to delivering the data to the app on the other end of the flow—or if it fails, letting the app know that it failed.

TCP cannot literally guarantee delivery of any single TCP segment. For example, when devices transmit bits, bit errors can occur, so much so that the Layer 1 transmission fails. In some cases, the Layer 1 transmission works, but some bits might have changed in transit. So the data link layer notices the error and discards the received frame. Sometimes IP routers receive IP packets, and because of congestion, the router discards the IP packet.

TCP uses a mechanism called TCP error recovery to resend lost TCP segments. No matter the reason why a TCP segment does not arrive at the destination host, TCP notices that the data did not arrive. TCP then recovers from these losses by resending the lost data.

This topic looks at how TCP can guarantee that data gets delivered, first by looking at how TCP acknowledges that the data arrives and then seeing how TCP reacts when the data does not arrive.

Confirming Receipt of TCP Data

As part of the TCP error recovery process, TCP must know when data arrives at the destination host correctly. If it arrives without error, great; the TCP sender can continue as normal. If not, the TCP sender can use TCP error recovery to recover from the error.

To confirm that the destination received the data without error, TCP must have a way to notice errors and a way to signal which data was received without error. When the destination host receives a TCP segment, TCP looks at the header checksum. The TCP header Checksum field has the same basic purpose as the Frame Check Sequence (FCS) field in many data-link protocol trailers—to recognize when the data was changed during transmission. With TCP, the checksum applies to the entire TCP segment. If the destination host does the math with the TCP checksum, and errors occurred, the destination host discards the TCP segment.

For any segments that arrive at the destination host for which the TCP checksum shows no errors, the receiving host must somehow tell the sender that the segment arrived. TCP uses a concept of identifying each TCP segment's data using a *sequence number*. Then, the receiving host's TCP code sends back a TCP message

10

acknowledging that the segments were received, using the same numbers to identify the received segments.

Figure 10-23 shows an example of TCP acknowledging data that arrives with no errors. In this example, a web server, on the right, sends three TCP segments to a web browser on the left. The server labels the TCP headers in the three segments as SEQ (sequence number) 1, 2, and 3, respectively. The client sends a message back to the server essentially stating that the browser received all three TCP segments, and needs to get number 4 next.

FIGURE 10-23

TCP Sequence Numbers and Acknowledgment Concepts

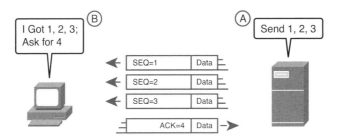

The TCP software on the two hosts cooperates to identify each TCP segment (sender's job) and to acknowledge the receipt of the segments (receiver's job). To make that work, the hosts use two fields in the TCP header: the *sequence number* field (abbreviated as SEQ) and the *acknowledgment number* (abbreviated ACK).

The receiving host acknowledges segments by stating the sequence number of the next TCP segment the receiver expects to get, using a concept called a *forward acknowledgment*. Instead of acknowledging the sequence number of the last received segment, the acknowledgment (based on the ACK field in the header) lists the next sequence number expected. In a way, the receiver is looking forward to receiving the next segment.

For example, in Figure 10-23, to acknowledge receipt of the segment with sequence number 3, the client PC on the left sends a TCP segment with an ACK of 4. This forward acknowledgment value of 4 implies that the client got segment 3 and expects to receive 4 next.

> **AUTHOR'S NOTE:** The examples in this section show the sequence and acknowledgment numbers as numbering TCP segments. In reality, these numbers identify the byte number of the first byte in each segment. This section uses this general description, which does not match exactly what happens with TCP, to keep the focus on the concept behind the process.

TCP Error Recovery Using SEQ and ACK

The TCP **error recovery** process uses the same SEQ and ACK fields that hosts use to confirm that TCP segments arrive. When TCP segments do not arrive at the destination host, or they arrive but that have errors (so they fail the TCP checksum math), the sender needs to know so it can resend that segment. The receiving host sends back a different acknowledgment value, implying that something wrong happened, allowing the sender to resend TCP segments.

Thinking like the host sending the data, the TCP error recovery process uses these main concepts:

1. Send data in TCP segments with sequence numbers.
2. Expect to receive an ACK with the next sequence number.
3. If the sender does not receive an ACK with the expected value, or receives no ACK in a reasonable time, resend TCP segments.

When the receiving host gets some of the TCP segments, but not all, the receiving host can send back an ACK—but with a value that tells the sender to recover some of the data.

For example, imagine the same set of three TCP segments as in Figure 10-24, but now, the second TCP segment happens to have bit errors during its trip through the TCP/IP network. As a result, some router discards that TCP segment. Figure 10-24 shows the idea, with SEQ and ACK fields.

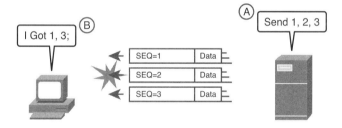

FIGURE 10-24

Example with an Error; the Recovery Happens Later

This figure mostly sets up the scenario so that you can first think about what should happen. The client on the left got the segments with sequence numbers 1 and 3, but not the one with sequence number 2. What should the host do? As it turns out, TCP hosts do the following:

> Acknowledge only the data up to the point at which a segment is missing.

In this example, that means the client acts as if it received the segment with sequence number 1. So, the client sends back a TCP segment with ACK=2.

Now think about the server, on the right. The server sent 1, 2, and 3, but it gets a TCP segment with ACK=2. What should the server on the right do? The server realizes that the client's ACK=2 means that the client did not receive the segment with sequence number 2. The server reacts by resending segments starting with segment 2, as shown in Figure 10-25.

10

FIGURE 10-25

Receiver Confirms What Was Received and Implies What Was Not

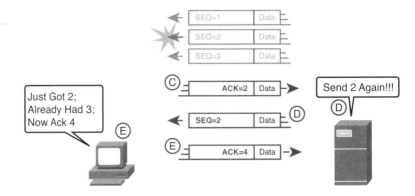

Following the steps in the figure:

C. The client (on the left) sends back a TCP segment, ACK=2, meaning that a) the client received the segment with SEQ=1 and b) the client did not receive the TCP segment with SEQ=2.

D. The server (on the right) chooses to resend the segment that the client had not yet received, the TCP segment with SEQ=2.

E. The client now has both the segment with SEQ=2 and SEQ=3, so the client confirms that it has both, with a segment showing ACK=4.

UDP and Nonguaranteed Delivery

UDP does not offer a guaranteed delivery service to applications. As a result, UDP does not need to do any error recovery. But is that a bad idea?

First off, some applications simply do not need error recovery. For example, Voice over IP (VoIP), using the RTP application layer protocol, does not need error recovery, which is one reason that RTP uses UDP. As it turns out, in the time it takes TCP to recover the data, too much time would pass for the lost voice bits to be useful. TCP error recovery would be useless for a live voice call. So, application protocols like RTP that do not need guaranteed delivery need a reasonable transport layer option, and UDP supplies that option.

UDP also gives application protocol designers an option for less overhead than TCP. The TCP Sequence and Acknowledgment fields are 4 bytes each, and UDP needs neither of these fields, making the UDP header smaller than the TCP header. Also, some of the TCP error recovery features (not discussed here) actually make the sending host stop and wait before sending more data. UDP has no reason to stop and wait. So UDP uses less overhead bytes and can send data faster than TCP.

UDP and TCP Compared

TCP and UDP both have some important features in common. Both connect applications. Both provide a service by which an application can send data, not just to another host but to the correct application on the destination host, using the port numbers in the TCP and UDP headers.

Beyond the use of port numbers, the comparisons of the two can be summarized as follows:

TCP: More functions, but slower as a result

UDP: Faster because of less overhead, but with fewer functions

Table 10-3 summarizes some of the common comparison points for TCP and UDP. The first two items in the table relate to the use of port numbers, which both TCP and UDP use. The rest of the functions exist only with TCP.

TABLE 10-3
TCP and UDP Comparisons

Feature	TCP	UDP
Delivering data between two applications	Yes	Yes
Identifying servers using well-known ports	Yes	Yes
Segmenting data	Yes	No
Guaranteed delivery through error recovery	Yes	No
In-order delivery	Yes	No
Flow control	Yes	No

Chapter Summary

While the lower three layers of the five-layer TCP/IP model focus more on what happens between two hosts, the two upper layers focus on what happens on the endpoint hosts. Hosts not only need the IP service of delivering the data to the right destination host but also the transport layer service of delivering data to the correct destination application process. Different applications also need different services from the network, so the TCP/IP model's protocols include a large number of application protocols to meet those different needs.

The core function of the transport layer protocols, common to both TCP and UDP, is to deliver data to the correct destination application process. TCP and UDP both use port numbers to identify an application process. Both protocols include a source port and destination port field in their headers, which allows each message in a particular application-to-application flow to identify both the sending process and receiving process. And both use the well-known port concept to identify servers.

TCP provides many more services than UDP; however, UDP provides its basic service with much less overhead. TCP segments large data into smaller chunks, guarantees delivery of data by using error recovery, and delivers the data in order, plus a few other functions that UDP does not do. However, UDP can run faster with less overhead bytes in each message.

10

Chapter Review Activities

Use the features in this section to study and review the topics in this chapter.

Answer These Questions

1. Which of the following answers lists a need of transport layer protocols that can be met by the TCP/IP network layer protocols?

    a. A delivery service that recovers and resends lost data

    b. Segmenting data into smaller chunks of a size that can be sent through the TCP/IP network

    c. Delivering data to the correct destination application process on the destination host

    d. Delivering data to the correct destination host

    e. Providing communications functions to application software

2. Which of the following answers list a need of application layer protocols that can be met by the TCP/IP transport layer protocols? (Choose three answers.)

    a. A delivery service that recovers and resends lost data

    b. Segmenting data into smaller chunks of a size that can be sent through the TCP/IP network

    c. Delivering data to the correct destination application process on the destination host

    d. Delivering data to the correct destination host

    e. Providing communications functions to application software

3. Which of the following answers lists a service provided by an application layer protocol to the application?

    a. The ability to identify the correct destination application process on the other end of an application flow

    b. The ability to communicate using a TCP/IP network

    c. Encoding data over a cable

    d. Encapsulating data between a header and trailer

4. A user opens email client software on her tablet computer after connecting to the Internet. The user successfully downloads her latest email. Another student happens by and starts spouting off about how the first student has been using email, POP3, IP, TCP, HTTP, 802.11, and other acronyms all just to check email. The first student just stares at this second student, but it does cause the first student to wonder: Which of the following answers accurately describes where some of these features are implemented on the tablet?

    a. POP3 in the email application software

    b. HTTP in the email application software

    c. TCP in the email application software

    d. UDP in the OS

5. A user of a tablet computer goes to a coffee shop and connects to the Internet through a wireless LAN. The user then connects to a web server somewhere far away in the Internet. Which of the following statements are true about the messages that flow from the tablet's web browser toward the web server? (Choose two answers.)

   a. The 802.11 frame sent by the tablet arrives at the web server.

   b. The IP packet sent by the tablet arrives at the web server.

   c. The TCP segment sent by the tablet arrives at the web server.

   d. The UDP segment sent by the tablet arrives at the web server.

6. Which of the following answers accurately describe the size of the TCP, UDP, and IP headers, assuming that the headers include no additional optional fields? (Choose three answers.)

   a. IP: 20

   b. TCP: 8

   c. UDP: 8

   d. TCP: 20

   e. UDP: 12

7. When thinking about the messages that flow inside a TCP/IP network, you can think about the header for a particular layer and its encapsulated data, ignoring any lower-layer headers and trailers. Which of the following answers list a protocol with the correct matching term for the name of the message that includes that protocol's header plus its encapsulated data? (Choose two answers.)

   a. UDP: Packet

   b. TCP: Connection

   c. UDP: Datagram

   d. TCP: Segment

   e. UDP: Flow

8. An application running on a user's device is currently sending data to/from an application on some server inside an enterprise TCP/IP network. According to this chapter, which of the following terms are the most common terms that refer to the idea of these two application processes communicating with each other? (Choose two answers.)

   a. Connection

   b. Pipe

   c. Circuit

   d. Flow

10

9. Which of the following answers describes a commitment that both TCP and UDP make to the application protocols that use them?

   a. Delivering data to the correct destination host

   b. Delivering data in the same order in which it was sent

   c. Delivering data to the correct destination application process

   d. Segmenting large data into sizes that flow over the network

10. Which of the following answers lists a transport protocol with the correct size, in bits, of that protocol's destination port field in its header?

   a. UDP: 8

   b. TCP: 12

   c. UDP: 16

   d. TCP: 32

11. A user of a tablet computer has three browser tabs open, with those tabs currently using TCP port numbers 55555, 55556, and 55557. The user opens another browser tab. Which of the following port numbers could the browser use?

   a. 55555

   b. 55558

   c. 80

   d. 77777

12. A user of a tablet computer has three browser tabs open, with those tabs currently using TCP port numbers 55555, 55556, and 55557. The user opens an application that uses UDP. Which of the following port numbers could the new application use? (Choose two answers.)

   a. 55555

   b. 55558

   c. 80

   d. 77777

13. The user of host A opens a web browser and successfully loads a web page hosted on web server B. Host A's browser uses TCP port 55555, and web server B uses the well-known HTTP port for web servers. In the messages that contain the contents of the web page that appeared in the web browser's window, which of the following answers is true?

   a. The source port = 80.

   b. The source port = 55555.

   c. The destination port = 80.

   d. The question gives too little information to determine whether the other answers are correct.

14. The user of host A opens a web browser and successfully loads a web page hosted on web server B. Host A's browser uses TCP port 55555, and web server B uses the well-known HTTP port for web servers. Which of the following terms refers to the category or type of port number used by the web browser (55555 in this case)?

   a. Plain old port

   b. Registered port

   c. Simple port

   d. Dynamic port

15. Which of the following answers lists the correct transport protocol and well-known port number used by each application protocol listed?

   a. DNS–UDP: 53

   b. HTTP–UDP: 80

   c. Telnet–TCP: 110

   d. POP3–UDP: 53

16. Which of the following statements are true regarding MTU? (Choose two answers.)

   a. Defines the maximum size of an IP packet that can flow from host to host over the entire IP route.

   b. The MTU value describes the size of the entire IP packet.

   c. Defines the maximum size of an IP packet that can be sent out a particular interface.

   d. The value describes the size of the entire IP packet's data field.

17. Which of the following statements are true regarding MSS? (Choose two answers.)

   a. Defines the maximum size of a TCP segment that can flow from host to host over the entire IP route.

   b. The MSS value describes the size of the entire TCP segment.

   c. Defines the maximum size of a TCP segment that can be sent out the interface on the source host.

   d. The value describes the size of the entire TCP segment's data field.

18. A web server hosts a web page. Part of that web page includes a graphics image, in a file named fred.jpg, that shows a photo of Fred. The file size is 300 KB. The web server's Ethernet interface has an IP MTU of 1500. Which of the following answers is true about the process that moves the contents of fred.jpg from the web server to the web browser?

   a. HTTP on the web server breaks the data mostly into 1500-byte chunks.

   b. TCP on the web server breaks the data mostly into 1480-byte chunks.

   c. IP on the web server breaks the data into mostly 1480-byte chunks.

   d. TCP on the web server breaks the data into mostly 1460-byte chunks.

19. Which of the following answers best describes how TCP guarantees delivery of data over a TCP connection?

   a. By sending two copies of every TCP segment

   b. By sending a TCP checksum that allows the receiving host to correct any errors that occur during transmission

   c. By noticing when data is lost and then resending the lost TCP segments

   d. By routing packets over links that have the fewest number of errors

20. Which of the following answers list a feature that TCP offers but that UDP does not? (Choose two answers.)

   a. In-order delivery of data

   b. Identifying servers using well-known ports

   c. Delivering data to the correct application processes

   d. Error recovery

Define the Key Terms

The following key terms include the ideas most important to the big ideas in this chapter. To review, without looking at the book or your notes, write a definition for each term, focusing on the meaning, not the wording. Then review your definition compared to your notes, this chapter, and the glossary.

Key Terms for Chapter 10

Transmission Control Protocol	UDP datagram	dynamic port
	source port	TCP segmentation
User Datagram Protocol	destination port	guaranteed delivery
flow	well-known port number	error recovery
TCP segment		

List the Words Inside Acronyms

The following are the most common acronyms discussed in this chapter. As a way to review those terms, simply write down the words that each letter represents in each acronym.

Acronyms for Chapter 10

TCP	HTTP	ACK
UDP	RTP	IP MTU
SEQ	MSS	
POP3	MTU	

Create Mind Maps

Build a mind map to compare TCP and UDP functions and header fields. List TCP on one side and UDP on the other, leaving more space for TCP. List the functions by name, in your own words, using as few words as possible just to remind you of the function. Then, in the next level down, list the header fields used to make the function work, plus any terms that you can think of that relate to that function.

Define Other Terms

Define the following additional terms from this chapter, and check your answers in the glossary:

application process	port	maximum segment size
TCP header	TCP port	maximum transmission unit
UDP header	UDP port	
sequence number	Post Office Protocol	IP fragmentation
acknowledgment number	Real-Time Transfer Protocol	in-order delivery
connection		flow control
TCP connection	registered port number	

Complete the Tables and Lists from Memory

Print a copy of Appendix B, "Memory Tables" (which you can find online at www.pearsonitcertification.com/title/9780789748454), or at least the section for this chapter, and complete the tables and lists from memory. Appendix C, "Memory Tables Answer Key," also online, includes completed tables and lists to check your work.

Appendix A

Numeric Reference Tables

This appendix provides several useful reference tables that list numbers used throughout this book. Specifically:

Table A-1: A decimal-binary cross reference, useful when converting from decimal to binary and vice versa.

TABLE A-1

Decimal-Binary Cross Reference, Decimal Values 0–255

Decimal Value	Binary Value	Decimal Value	Binary Value	Decimal Value	Binary Value	Decimal Value	Binary Value
0	00000000	32	00100000	64	01000000	96	01100000
1	00000001	33	00100001	65	01000001	97	01100001
2	00000010	34	00100010	66	01000010	98	01100010
3	00000011	35	00100011	67	01000011	99	01100011
4	00000100	36	00100100	68	01000100	100	01100100
5	00000101	37	00100101	69	01000101	101	01100101
6	00000110	38	00100110	70	01000110	102	01100110
7	00000111	39	00100111	71	01000111	103	01100111
8	00001000	40	00101000	72	01001000	104	01101000
9	00001001	41	00101001	73	01001001	105	01101001
10	00001010	42	00101010	74	01001010	106	01101010
11	00001011	43	00101011	75	01001011	107	01101011
12	00001100	44	00101100	76	01001100	108	01101100
13	00001101	45	00101101	77	01001101	109	01101101
14	00001110	46	00101110	78	01001110	110	01101110
15	00001111	47	00101111	79	01001111	111	01101111
16	00010000	48	00110000	80	01010000	112	01110000
17	00010001	49	00110001	81	01010001	113	01110001
18	00010010	50	00110010	82	01010010	114	01110010
19	00010011	51	00110011	83	01010011	115	01110011
20	00010100	52	00110100	84	01010100	116	01110100
21	00010101	53	00110101	85	01010101	117	01110101
22	00010110	54	00110110	86	01010110	118	01110110
23	00010111	55	00110111	87	01010111	119	01110111
24	00011000	56	00111000	88	01011000	120	01111000
25	00011001	57	00111001	89	01011001	121	01111001
26	00011010	58	00111010	90	01011010	122	01111010
27	00011011	59	00111011	91	01011011	123	01111011
28	00011100	60	00111100	92	01011100	124	01111100
29	00011101	61	00111101	93	01011101	125	01111101
30	00011110	62	00111110	94	01011110	126	01111110
31	00011111	63	00111111	95	01011111	127	01111111

TABLE A-1

Continued

Decimal Value	Binary Value	Decimal Value	Binary Value	Decimal Value	Binary Value	Decimal Value	Binary Value
128	10000000	160	10100000	192	11000000	224	11100000
129	10000001	161	10100001	193	11000001	225	11100001
130	10000010	162	10100010	194	11000010	226	11100010
131	10000011	163	10100011	195	11000011	227	11100011
132	10000100	164	10100100	196	11000100	228	11100100
133	10000101	165	10100101	197	11000101	229	11100101
134	10000110	166	10100110	198	11000110	230	11100110
135	10000111	167	10100111	199	11000111	231	11100111
136	10001000	168	10101000	200	11001000	232	11101000
137	10001001	169	10101001	201	11001001	233	11101001
138	10001010	170	10101010	202	11001010	234	11101010
139	10001011	171	10101011	203	11001011	235	11101011
140	10001100	172	10101100	204	11001100	236	11101100
141	10001101	173	10101101	205	11001101	237	11101101
142	10001110	174	10101110	206	11001110	238	11101110
143	10001111	175	10101111	207	11001111	239	11101111
144	10010000	176	10110000	208	11010000	240	11110000
145	10010001	177	10110001	209	11010001	241	11110001
146	10010010	178	10110010	210	11010010	242	11110010
147	10010011	179	10110011	211	11010011	243	11110011
148	10010100	180	10110100	212	11010100	244	11110100
149	10010101	181	10110101	213	11010101	245	11110101
150	10010110	182	10110110	214	11010110	246	11110110
151	10010111	183	10110111	215	11010111	247	11110111
152	10011000	184	10111000	216	11011000	248	11111000
153	10011001	185	10111001	217	11011001	249	11111001
154	10011010	186	10111010	218	11011010	250	11111010
155	10011011	187	10111011	219	11011011	251	11111011
156	10011100	188	10111100	220	11011100	252	11111100
157	10011101	189	10111101	221	11011101	253	11111101
158	10011110	190	10111110	222	11011110	254	11111110
159	10011111	191	10111111	223	11011111	255	11111111

Table A-2: A hexadecimal-binary cross reference, useful when converting from hex to binary and vice versa.

TABLE A-2

Hex-Binary Cross Reference

Hex	4-Bit Binary
0	0000
1	0001
2	0010
3	0011
4	0100
5	0101
6	0110
7	0111
8	1000
9	1001
A	1010
B	1011
C	1100
D	1101
E	1110
F	1111

Table A-3: Powers of 2, from 2^1 through 2^{32}.

TABLE A-3

Powers of 2

X	2^x	X	2^x
1	2	17	131,072
2	4	18	262,144
3	8	19	524,288
4	16	20	1,048,576
5	32	21	2,097,152
6	64	22	4,194,304
7	128	23	8,388,608
8	256	24	16,777,216
9	512	25	33,554,432
10	1024	26	67,108,864
11	2048	27	134,217,728
12	4096	28	268,435,456
13	8192	29	536,870,912
14	16,384	30	1,073,741,824
15	32,768	31	2,147,483,648
16	65,536	32	4,294,967,296

Table A-4: Table of all 33 possible subnet masks, in all three formats.

TABLE A-4

All Subnet Masks

Decimal	Prefix	Binary
0.0.0.0	/0	00000000 00000000 00000000 00000000
128.0.0.0	/1	10000000 00000000 00000000 00000000
192.0.0.0	/2	11000000 00000000 00000000 00000000
224.0.0.0	/3	11100000 00000000 00000000 00000000
240.0.0.0	/4	11110000 00000000 00000000 00000000
248.0.0.0	/5	11111000 00000000 00000000 00000000
252.0.0.0	/6	11111100 00000000 00000000 00000000
254.0.0.0	/7	11111110 00000000 00000000 00000000
255.0.0.0	/8	11111111 00000000 00000000 00000000
255.128.0.0	/9	11111111 10000000 00000000 00000000
255.192.0.0	/10	11111111 11000000 00000000 00000000
255.224.0.0	/11	11111111 11100000 00000000 00000000
255.240.0.0	/12	11111111 11110000 00000000 00000000
255.248.0.0	/13	11111111 11111000 00000000 00000000
255.252.0.0	/14	11111111 11111100 00000000 00000000
255.254.0.0	/15	11111111 11111110 00000000 00000000
255.255.0.0	/16	11111111 11111111 00000000 00000000
255.255.128.0	/17	11111111 11111111 10000000 00000000
255.255.192.0	/18	11111111 11111111 11000000 00000000
255.255.224.0	/19	11111111 11111111 11100000 00000000
255.255.240.0	/20	11111111 11111111 11110000 00000000
255.255.248.0	/21	11111111 11111111 11111000 00000000
255.255.252.0	/22	11111111 11111111 11111100 00000000
255.255.254.0	/23	11111111 11111111 11111110 00000000
255.255.255.0	/24	11111111 11111111 11111111 00000000
255.255.255.128	/25	11111111 11111111 11111111 10000000
255.255.255.192	/26	11111111 11111111 11111111 11000000
255.255.255.224	/27	11111111 11111111 11111111 11100000
255.255.255.240	/28	11111111 11111111 11111111 11110000
255.255.255.248	/29	11111111 11111111 11111111 11111000
255.255.255.252	/30	11111111 11111111 11111111 11111100
255.255.255.254	/31	11111111 11111111 11111111 11111110
255.255.255.255	/32	11111111 11111111 11111111 11111111

Glossary

Numerics

1000BASE-T A particular Ethernet standard shortcut name, also known by the formal standard 802.3ab, which defines 1000-Mbps (1-Gbps) operation, star topology, using four-pair UTP cabling.

100BASE-T A term that refers to all Fast Ethernet standards, including 100BASE-Tx, which refers to the one Fast Ethernet standard that uses two pairs in a UTP cable.

100BASE-Tx The common name for one of several standards that are part of the IEEE Fast Ethernet 802.3u standard. This standard uses two twisted pairs in a UTP cable, with a bit rate of 100 Mbps.

10BASE-T The common name for one of several standards that are part of the IEEE Ethernet 802.3i standard. This standard uses two twisted pairs in a UTP cable, with a bit rate of 10 Mbps.

10GBASE-T A particular Ethernet standard shortcut name, also known by the formal standard 802.3an, that defines 10-Gbps operation, star topology, using four-pair UTP cabling.

2G A mobile phone (wireless WAN) term that refers to the second major generation of mobile phone technology.

3G A mobile phone (wireless WAN) term that refers to the third major generation of mobile phone technology.

4G A mobile phone (wireless WAN) term that refers to the fourth major generation of mobile phone technology. This is the most recent generation as of the publication of this book.

802.11 The original IEEE wireless LAN standard; also the base name of the IEEE working group for wireless LANs.

802.11a An IEEE wireless LAN standard, ratified in 1999, using OFDM encoding, the 5-GHz UNII frequency band, and a maximum data rate of 54 Mbps.

802.11b An IEEE wireless LAN standard, ratified in 1999, using DSSS encoding, the 2.4-GHz ISM frequency band, and a maximum data rate of 11 Mbps.

802.11g An IEEE wireless LAN standard, ratified in 2003, using DSSS encoding, the 2.4-GHz ISM frequency band, and a maximum data rate of 54 Mbps.

802.11n An IEEE wireless LAN standard, ratified in 2009, using OFDM encoding, both the ISM and UNII frequency bands, a maximum bit rate for a single stream of 150 Mbps, and other options related to using multiple antennas to achieve bit rates that theoretically approach 600 Mbps.

802.3 The name of the original IEEE Ethernet standard, as well as the overall base name of all IEEE Ethernet LAN working committees.

802.3a An IEEE Ethernet LAN standard, first approved in 1985, for 10-Mbps operation over a type of coaxial cable that was thinner than the previous standard; hence it was called Thinnet.

802.3ab Also known as Gigabit Ethernet, an IEEE Ethernet LAN standard, first approved in 1999, for 1-Gbps operation using UTP.

802.3ae Also known as 10GBASE-X, an IEEE Ethernet LAN standard, first approved in 2002, for 10-Gbps operation using fiber.

802.3an Also known as 10GBASE-T, an IEEE Ethernet LAN standard, first approved in 2006, for 10-Gbps operation using UTP.

802.3ba An IEEE standard for both 40-Gbps and 100-Gbps speeds, first approved in 2010, for operation on fiber and other cabling (but not UTP).

802.3i Also known as 10BASE-T, an IEEE Ethernet LAN standard, first approved in 1990, for 10-Mbps operation over UTP cable, using a centralized cabling device called a hub.

802.3u Also known as Fast Ethernet, an IEEE Ethernet LAN standard, first approved in 1995, for 100-Mbps operation using UTP and fiber cabling.

802.3z Also known as Gigabit Ethernet, an IEEE Ethernet LAN standard, first approved in 1998, for 1-Gbps operation using fiber.

A

A/D See *analog to digital*.

AC See *alternating current*.

access layer When thinking of a campus LAN design, if you place the end-user devices at the bottom of a drawing, and put the more centralized devices at the top of the drawing, the drawing can be viewed as layers. The access layer is the lowest layer, connected to the end users, and is called *access* because it is where the user devices access the LAN.

access point (AP) A wireless LAN device that plays two important roles: connecting the wireless LAN to other networks through a wired (cabled) connection to a LAN, and communicating using radio waves with all the devices in that wireless LAN.

ACK See *acknowledgment number*.

acknowledgment number A field in the TCP header that the a host uses, after receiving data on a TCP connection, to signal back to the original sender about which segments the receiver received without error.

actuator arm In a hard disk drive, the stick-like part that moves up/down and in/out to place the read/write head (at the end of the arm) over/under a particular platter/track.

address block See *CIDR block*.

Address Resolution Protocol (ARP) A protocol that allows an IP host on a LAN to discover the MAC address of another host on the same LAN.

aggregate route A single route that includes multiple CIDR blocks.

alternating current (AC) A type of electrical circuit in which the power source alternates the direction of the electrical current in the circuit over time.

AM See *amplitude modulation*.

amplitude When describing energy that acts like waves, when graphing the waveform centered on the X axis, and graphing some kind of power (for example, voltage) on the Y axis, the amplitude is the maximum height of the curve over the X axis.

amplitude modulation (AM) A term referring to the process of changing (modulating) an energy wave over time by changing its amplitude.

Amplitude Shift Keying (ASK) The formal term for a class of networking encoding schemes that shift (change) the amplitude of the energy signal to encode different bit values.

analog A description of a technology that means that some concept or action the device uses attempts to be similar to—to be an analog to—something that happens in the real world. Today, it is also used to simply mean "not digital."

analog electrical signal Electricity whose current, when graphed over time, changes gradually, making for a smooth curve, which allows the graph to be similar to other waves that exist in nature, like sound waves.

analog modem A device at the customer and ISP end of an analog circuit, created when one modem calls the phone number of the other modem, with the two modems sending data using the analog circuit.

analog to digital (A/D) A type of electronic device that converts an analog electrical signal to a digital signal that represents bits or vice versa.

antenna   A radio device that generates different radio waves based on the electrical signal passing through the antenna, and can convert sensed radio waves back into an electrical signal.

AP   See *access point.*

app   A common shortened alternative to the word *application.*

application   Generally, a function on any kind of computer or electronic device that is useful to the user, which can give the user a reason to want to own and use the device. More specifically, software that performs some useful function for a user.

application connection   The concept that goes beyond just getting an IP packet from one host to another, but extends that concept to the application on each end.

application process   In a computer operating system, an application program that the operating system (OS) has starting running or executing, giving that program memory to use and access to the CPU, so that the program can actively do its work.

ARP   See *Address Resolution Protocol.*

ARP Broadcast   Another term for *ARP Request*, with emphasis on the fact that ARP Request messages use a broadcast destination address, so all nodes on the LAN should receive a copy of the message.

ARP cache   Another term for *ARP table.*

ARP Reply   A message defined by the ARP protocol sent in response to seeing its own IP address listed in an ARP Request message, listing its own IP address and MAC address.

ARP Request   A message defined by the ARP protocol in which one host lists the IP address of another host on the same LAN, with the message asking that host to supply its MAC address in an ARP Reply message.

ARP table   A table on a host, with matched sets of IP and MAC addresses of hosts on the same LAN, typically as learned by the ARP protocol.

ASCII   American Standard Code for Information Interchange. An early standard text character set that originally used a 7-bit code per character.

ASK   See *Amplitude Shift Keying.*

associate   A process in wireless LANs in which a wireless client sends frames with an AP, and if successful, the client and AP agree that the AP will send frames to the client and process frames received from the client.

Associate (Request and Response)   The names of 802.11 management and control frames that a client uses to signal with an access point during the association process.

association process   The process by which a wireless client and an AP send management and control frames so that by the end of the process, the AP agrees to send frames to the client and process frames received from the client.

asymmetric speed   A characteristic of some transmission technologies in which the speeds in opposite directions can be different.

Asynchronous Transfer Mode (ATM)   A series of networking standards for both LANs and WANs, which for WANs is used to create a type of packet-switching service that happens to also work well with SONET physical links.

authenticate   The name of both the process, and of specific 802.11 management and control frames, that wireless clients and APs use for the AP to confirm that the wireless client passes security checks and is allowed to use a particular AP to connect to a particular wireless LAN.

authoritative name server   A DNS server that is the trusted source of name-to-address mapping information about a particular DNS subdomain.

autonegotiation   A process defined by the IEEE so that nodes on the same Ethernet link can exchange messages for the purpose of choosing the best speed and duplex option that both nodes support.

B

bandwidth   This term has two common meanings in the world of networking. 1) The bit rate or speed at which bits pass over some networking link. 2) The width, or number of frequencies, in a consecutive range of frequencies (often called a frequency band).

Basic Service Set (BSS)   In wireless LANs, a single wireless access point (AP) and the client devices that send data to/from that AP.

Beacon   An 802.11 management and control frame used by wireless access points to announce their presence, as well as to announce the name of the wireless LAN they help create.

Bell operating company   A term that refers to one of the many companies in North America that grew from, and were affiliated with, the companies that Alexander Graham Bell and his partners started after Bell invented the telephone.

Bell System   A term referring to the entire group of Bell operating companies.

BGP   See *Border Gateway Protocol*.

BIA   Burned-in address. A common term for universal MAC address. See *universal MAC address*.

binary digit   A numeral 0 or 1 in base 2 number.

bit   The smallest unit of data stored in a computing device, representing a single binary digit of value 0 or 1.

bit rate   The number of bits sent in a second over some link.

bit time   In an encoding scheme, the time period during which the encoding scheme sends an energy signal to represent 1 bit.

Border Gateway Protocol (BGP)   An exterior routing protocol, used mostly between ISPs in the Internet core and between ISPs and customers with dual-homed connections to ISPs, with which the routers can exchange large volumes of routing information, as well as choose the best routes through the Internet using a variety of criteria.

Broadcast frame   From the perspective of a single Ethernet LAN switch, a frame whose destination MAC address is not known to the switch, in that the switch's MAC address table does not list the frame's destination MAC address.

BSS   See *Basic Service Set*.

bus   In computing, a bus exists as some physical pathway over which bits can be transmitted between components. The pathways often exist as electrical circuits, sometimes as metal sitting on a plastic circuit board and sometimes using cabling.

byte   A unit of data in a computer: 8 bits.

C

cable   A rope-like collection of plastic coating around copper wires that networking devices can use to send bits from one device to another.

cable Internet   A term referring to Internet access services provided by a cable company, using many components, including a cable modem, coaxial cable, and a CMTS at the cable company head end.

cable modem termination system (CMTS)   A general term for a type of computing device that sits in the cable company head end, connected to the HFC cable plant, for the purpose of encoding and decoding the data signals sent to/from customer cable modems.

cable television (CATV)   A type of high-quality television service in which a company (the cable TV company) receives the TV signals, placing them onto cables that run into the home, rather than requiring each home to have a TV antenna to receive the TV signals.

CD   Compact disc. A digital permanent storage technology, originally used for audio but also used to store bits that represent any digital data, that uses light (typically lasers) to write and read data on removable discs.

cell phone   An old term for *mobile phone*.

central office   The term that refers to a telco office space where the telco keeps its equipment. Leased lines physically connect from a telco customer office building into the CO.

central processing unit (CPU)   The microprocessor in a computer that performs the primary job of processing data for the computer.

channel   A subset of the capacity of a physical link in the T-carrier system, created by using time-division multiplexing (TDM) technology to separate the links bits into different time slots.

character encoding scheme   A synonym for character set. See *character set.*

character set   A list of the characters that can be used in a given language or languages, mapped to corresponding unique binary codes and published as a convention or standard so that computers can use a consistent set of binary values to represent text values. Examples include ASCII, ANSI, and Unicode.

CIDR   See *classless interdomain routing.*

CIDR address block   See *CIDR block.*

CIDR block   With the IANA address assignment strategy after the creation of CIDR, a block of IP addresses whose size is some power of the number 2, assigned to a company by IANA or an associated agency.

circuit board   A plastic board onto which lines of metal have been placed, along with other computer components like microchips and buses, that together allow the components to send data to each other using the electrical circuits on the board. The motherboard is one example of a circuit board.

circuit switch   A generic term for the device in the telco offices that creates an end-to-end circuit by connecting two physical ports (and possibly time-division multiplexing channels inside the links on those ports) and forwarding bits between each port as long as the circuits are considered to be up.

circuit switching   The overall process by which a series of telco devices called circuit switches connect a circuit from one customer device to the other, with the device's logic taking incoming bits on one segment in the link and forwarding those bits out the matching outgoing segment, without storing the bits.

Cisco Systems   A technology company that is generally known to have the largest market share when selling the routers and switches discussed in this book.

cladding   In a fiber-optic cable, the material around the core that helps direct light back into the core.

class 5 switch   A telco term from the Bell System referring to a type of circuit-switching device called a 5ESS.

classful IP addressing   A way to think about IP version 4 addressing in which the person uses IP address classes to classify addresses. See also *classless IP addressing.*

classful IP network   Another term for *IP network,* with emphasis on the fact that the IP network concept is based on classful IP addressing rules.

classless interdomain routing (CIDR)   One of the short-term solutions to the IPv4 address exhaustion problem that actually helped solve the problem for a much longer time frame. CIDR allows more flexibility in how many addresses IANA assigns to a company, and it helps reduce Internet routing table sizes through route aggregation.

classless IP addressing   A way to think about IP version 4 addressing in which the person does not use IP address classes to classify addresses. See also *classful IP addressing.*

client-server   A model for how many networked applications work, in which one device asks for some information (the client) and the server supplies the information.

cloud services   A term for services of many kinds in which the service provider's service exists somewhere in the Internet and the customer sits elsewhere in the Internet.

CMTS   See *cable modem termination system.*

CO   See *central office.*

coaxial cable   A type of cable with many uses in electronics, including sending video and data.

codec   Short for coder/decoder. A device that converts analog voice into digital voice (coding) and vice versa (decoding). Another term for analog-to-digital conversion.

coder   See *encoder*.

coding rule   A synonym for *encoding rule*.

commercial business   A synonym for *small/medium business*.

compression   Generally in computing, the process of taking some digital item (something made of bits) and using fewer bits to represent the same item. For video files, the process of taking a video and representing the video as fewer bits.

computer   A device that processes—receives in, thinks about, changes, stores, sends out, displays, and prints—data in the form of bits.

computer network   A combination of many components that work together so that many different devices can communicate.

computer networking   The gerund form of the term *computer network*.

conductor   In electrical circuits, a conductor is any material that works well at the molecular level to allow electricity to flow through the material.

configure/configuration   For a networking device, the process through which a network engineer types information about what the device should do, or what the device should know, so that the device knows specifically how the network engineer wants the device to work.

connection   With TCP, another term for a flow that happens to use TCP.

core   In a fiber-optic cable, the glass fiber in the center of the cable over which light can pass.

coverage area   The space in which the wireless radio signals in one wireless LAN can effectively reach and be used to send and receive data between the WLAN's APs and its clients.

CPU   See *central processing unit*.

crossover cable   A UTP cabling pinout in which the wires in a wire pair connect to different pins on opposite ends so that one node's send logic connects to the other node's receive logic. In Ethernet, pins 1,2 connect to 3,6, and pins 4,5 connect to 7,8.

CSMA/CA   Carrier sense multiple access collision avoidance. The process wireless LANs use to take turns sending in a wireless LAN.

CSU/DSU   (Channel Service Unit/Data Service Unit) A device that synchronizes the transmission speeds on a leased line in the T-carrier system by matching the T-carrier line speed on one side and the bit rate used by the customer device on the other.

current   In an electrical circuit, the flow of electrical energy in a given direction. Current can also be thought of as the flow of electrons in the circuit, but more literally, it is the flow of the energy of the electrons as they leave their molecular shells and rest again in another molecule.

Cyber Monday   A business term in the United States that refers to the Monday after the Thanksgiving Day national holiday that is traditionally the largest single online shopping day of the year.

D

dark fiber   A fiber that has been installed but has not yet been connected to any node, so the fiber has no light in the middle.

data communications (datacom)   A long-standing term that refers to the entire networking industry, with particular emphasis on the use of networks for traditional data applications between computers, in contrast to telecom.

data frame   A type of 802.11 frame that carries data from the upper layers on behalf of users.

data-link connection identifier   The term defined by Frame Relay, particularly the LAPF protocol, for the LAPF header field used as an address field to identify a Frame Relay virtual circuit.

data processing   An somewhat older term used to refer to the computer industry as a whole.

DC   Data center or direct current.

DCE   Data communications equipment. This term has two uses in networking: 1) In packet-switched networks, the node (device) that sits in the telco network at the edge of the network, on the other side of the physical access link that connects to the customer device (the DTE). 2) A reference to a device that provides clocking on physical cabling that uses clock pin leads, such as on a leased line, in which the CSU/DSU controls the speed a router sends/receives bits by providing clocking to the router.

DDN   See *dotted-decimal notation*.

de facto standard   A standard that exists because it is what already happens.

DEC   Digital Equipment Corporation. A (former) technology company that no longer exists because of various mergers and acquisitions, whose vendor networking model (DECnet) was popular during the years when vendor networking models were common in corporate networks.

DECnet   The proprietary networking model developed and used by Digital Equipment Corporation (DEC).

decode   The process of receiving bits by sensing an energy signal over time, as transmitted by an encoder, and interpreting the incoming signal back into the original binary numbers that existed on the sending device.

decoder   The electronics that decode the energy signal. See *decode*.

dedicated bandwidth   A term referring to how some networks allow each node to send whenever they want, without the need to coordinate with other devices that do not happen to sit on the same physical link, resulting in a total network capacity that is the sum of the bit rates of all links added together.

dedicated circuit   An electrical circuit created by a telco on behalf of a customer, with the circuit staying up all the time, dedicated for use by the one customer that ordered the circuit. Also known as a leased line, leased circuit, and point-to-point line.

deencapsulation   The act of discarding a networking header or trailer after it is no longer needed, typically by a networking device or host after receiving a message in the network.

default gateway   Another term for *default router*, typically an older, more traditional term, because the IP protocol originally used the word *gateway* instead of *router*.

default route   In a router, a concept in which the router has a special route, the default route, so that when a router tries to route a packet, but the packet's destination does not match any other route, the router routes the packet based on the default route.

default router   A host IP setting that refers to the IP address of some router, on the same subnet as the host, to which the host sends IP packets when the destination is on some other subnet.

demarc   Short for *demarcation*, a legal and business term used by telcos to specify the physical dividing line in the cabling and equipment for a telco service in a customer building, where the customer is responsible for the cabling and devices to one side of the demarc, and the telco is responsible for the cabling and equipment on the other side of the line.

demodulate   The opposite of modulate. For modems, the process of taking the incoming analog electrical signal that was originally created by the modem on the other end of the analog circuit and interpreting the changing (modulating) incoming analog electricity as binary digits (bits).

demultiplex   The opposite of multiplex. For a multiplexer, the process of taking an incoming digital serial bit stream on one link; finding the logical frames and channels inside that bit stream based on line standards like DS0, DS1, and DS3; and splitting out (demultiplexing) the channels in the one bit stream into multiple streams that the multiplexer sends out different ports.

desktop   The term used in most personal computer operating systems (OS) to refer to the entire display image. The OS creates the desktop so that the user can interact and control the computer by using the desktop.

destination MAC address   A field in the Ethernet header that lists the MAC address of the device to which the Ethernet frame should be delivered.

destination port   In a TCP or UDP header, a 16-bit field that lists the port number of the application process to which the TCP segment or UDP datagram should be delivered.

DHCP   See *Dynamic Host Configuration Protocol.*

DHCP client   Any computer whose software includes the DHCP client function, which includes most computer operating systems today, with which the client asks a DHCP server for the use of an IP address for some period of time.

DHCP lease   The result of a successful DHCP Request, in which the DHCP client holds the rights (the lease) to use an IP address, as identified by the DHCP server, for some period of time.

DHCP server   Software running on some computer that acts in the DHCP server role, per the DHCP protocol, which means that the server keeps a list of IP addresses in each subnet that can be loaned or leased to DHCP clients. The server waits for DHCP messages requesting the use of an address and leases an unused address to the client.

dialup   An Internet access option in which the user uses an analog modem to call (dial) the phone number of the ISP.

direct current   A type of electrical circuit in which the power source keeps the direction of the electrical current in a single direction over time.

directional antenna   A type of wireless antenna that does not send its wireless radio signal in equal strength in all directions, but instead directs the signal in a particular direction.

directory   An inverted tree, or hierarchy, of directories (folders) and files, with the information stored on each disk drive media, that identifies and organizes the files stored on that media. A part of the file system.

disk (disc) drive   This term refers to a device that has several internal parts, but as a whole, the device provides permanent storage.

display   A computer output device that contains many small lights called pixels. By lighting the lights with the correct combinations of colors, the computer can display text, display images, and simulate movement. Also called a screen or monitor.

display adapter   A function in a computer, often implemented in separate hardware (and sometimes on a separate circuit card).

distribution layer   When thinking of a campus LAN design, if you place the end-user devices at the bottom of a drawing, and put the more centralized devices at the top of the drawing, the drawing can be viewed as layers. The distribution layer is the layer above the access layer, connecting the access layer switches and distributing frames between the access layer devices.

DIX Ethernet   The name of the originally published Ethernet prestandard documents as created by three companies working together: DEC, Intel, and Xerox.

DLCI   See *data-link connection identifier.*

DMZ   A networking term borrowed from the real world, a demilitarized zone (DMZ) in a network is a part of a company's TCP/IP network that hosts outside the company can access, with less restrictive security rules as compared to other hosts inside the company.

DNS   See *Domain Name System.*

DNS client   Any computer whose software includes the DNS client function, which includes most computer operating systems today, with which the client can take the text name identified by the user and send a request to a DNS server, in an attempt to discover the other host's IP address.

DNS query   A synonym for *DNS Request.*

DNS Reply   The name of a message defined by the DNS protocol in which a DNS server sends back the IP address used by a host, in response to a DNS Request message received from some DNS client.

DNS Request   The name of a message defined by the DNS protocol in which a DNS client lists the name of an IP host and a request for the DNS server to send back a DNS Reply with that host's IP address.

GL

DNS server   Software running on some computer that acts in the DNS server role, per the DNS protocol, which means that the server keeps a list of names and corresponding IP addresses, ready to reply with that information to a DNS Request from any DNS client.

DOCSIS   Data Over Cable Service Interface Specification. A broad standard, now ratified by the ITU, that defines many standards for sending data over cable systems, including a data-link protocol used between the cable modem and CMTS.

Domain Name System   The name of both a protocol and the system of actual DNS servers that exist in the world. In practice, DNS provides a way for the world to distribute the list of matching host name/IP address pair information, letting each company maintain its own naming information, but allowing the entire world to discover the IP address used by a particular host name, dynamically, using DNS protocols, so that any client can refer to a destination by name and send IP packets to that host.

dots per inch   For printers that print by essentially placing ink or toner on a large number of individual dots on the page, this term references the density of the number of dots the printer can attempt to mark in an inch of space.

dotted-decimal notation (DDN)   The decimal format used for IP addresses, in which each set of 8 bits is represented by its decimal equivalent, with each of the four decimal numbers separated by a period (dot). The format used to write 32-bit IP addresses as decimal numbers.

double word   Two words of computer memory, or 32 bits.

download   A common term that refers to most any application process in which the user copies a file from a remote site to his or her local computer using a network.

downstream speed   For some transmission media, particularly those used for Internet access, the speeds can be different for each direction. The downstream speed refers to the bit rate from the ISP toward the customer.

DPI   See *dots per inch*.

drive letter   Defined as part of the file system, the drive letter identifies a permanent storage device, or drive, using a letter of the alphabet.

DS0   Digital Signal Level 0. One of the physical line standards in the T-carrier system, as originally created by the companies of the Bell System in the United States. DS0 runs at 64 Kbps.

DS1   Digital Signal Level 1. One of the physical line standards in the T-carrier system, as originally created by the companies of the Bell System in the United States. DS1 runs at 1.544 Mbps, with a 193-bit frame, 24 DS0 channels, and an 8-Kbps overhead channel.

DS3   Digital Signal Level 3. One of the physical line standards in the T-carrier system, as originally created by the companies of the Bell System in the United States. DS3 runs at 44.736 Mbps, with 28 DS1 channels and additional overhead.

DSL   Digital subscriber line. A type of Internet access service in which the data flows over the local loop cable from the home to the telco central office, where a DSLAM uses FDM technology to split out the data and send it to a router, and split out the voice frequencies and send them to a traditional voice switch.

DSL access multiplexer   A general category for a type of networking device that sits inside a telco CO and connects to the ends of two-wire local loop cables, using FDM technology to split out the analog voice signals and digital data signals for a line that supports both analog voice and DSL data.

DSL modem   A device at the customer end of a DSL local loop that encodes and decodes the data on the local loop cable in a DSL connection.

DSLAM   See *DSL access multiplexer*.

DTE   Data terminal equipment, or data circuit-terminating equipment. This term has two uses in networking: 1) In packet-switched networks, the node (device) that sits in the customer site, connected by a physical access link to a node in the telco (the DCE). 2) A reference to a device that slaves its rate of sending and receiving bits to a device on the other end of the cable by watching for changes in the state of the clocking pin leads on a serial cable. This occurs on a leased line, in which a router connected to an external CSU/DSU receives clocking from the CSU/DSU (the DCE), with the router acting as the DTE.

dual-homed   A general category that describes the topology of the connections from a company to the Internet in which the company has two or more connections to the Internet, which gives the company more outbound routing options (routing toward the Internet).

duplex   A networking link that allows bits to be sent in both directions.

DVD   Digital video disc. A digital permanent storage technology, originally used for video but also used to store bits that represent any digital data, that uses light (typically lasers) to write and read data on removable discs.

Dynamic Host Configuration Protocol (DHCP)   A TCP/IP protocol that uses a client-and-server model of communication, with messages that allow a client to ask the server to loan or lease to the client the use of an IP address for some period of time.

dynamic port   A port number from inside a range set aside by IANA, from 49,153 to 65,535, that a host can choose at any time to assign to any application process, as long as that one host is not using that same port number for some other application process.

dynamic routing protocol   Any protocol that defines the process and messages by which routers learn IP routing information over time, changing its routes based on changes to the network.

E

edge switch   In a campus Ethernet LAN design, this term refers to the Ethernet LAN switch to which the end-user devices connect.

EGP   See *exterior gateway protocol*.

EIGRP   Enhanced Interior Gateway Routing Protocol.

electrical circuit   A complete loop of material that conducts electricity.

electromagnetic interference (EMI)   A term that refers to all effects that hinder electronics devices and networking links as a result of how electrical circuits create electromagnetic energy, and how that energy also creates additional electrical current, making it appear that electricity moves from one circuit to another.

electromagnetic radiation   A term that refers to a broad class of types of energy, all of which move as waveforms through space. These include radio waves, X-rays, microwaves, and visible light.

electromagnetic spectrum   The standard list that identifies all types of electromagnetic energy, placing different types into different categories based on their frequency and wavelengths.

email   Electronic mail. An application in which the user can type text and attach other files to create the electronic equivalent of a postal letter, and send the email to another person using his or her email address.

email server   Software that sits inside the network to provide some function that is important to how email works, particularly the service to accept outgoing mail and to hold incoming mail for a user until he or she can check the email.

email system   The entire process plus all the components that work together so that users can send emails to each other.

EMI   See *electromagnetic interference*.

encapsulation   The act of adding a networking header or trailer as part of the work done by a protocol, typically by a networking device or host, before sending a message in the network.

encode   The process of transmitting bits by varying an energy signal over time to represent different binary values, with a matching device on the other end of the link decoding the energy signal back into the original bits.

encoder   The electronics that encode the energy signal. See *encode*.

encoding   The process of varying the energy signal on a link so that after the signal is decoded on the receiving device, bits have been communicated over the link.

encoding scheme   A set of rules that define how to change the pattern of the waveforms of energy to represent binary 0s and 1s.

enterprise   A category of businesses that refers to a relatively large business (or possibly large government institution) that builds its network for its own purposes, rather than selling network services to other companies.

enterprise network   A network owned and operated by a company, with that company being somewhat larger than typical, generally (but not exactly) with more than 1000 employees.

error detection   In networking, the process by which a node determines whether a received message was changed by the process of sending the data.

error recovery   In computer networking, the process of both noticing an error and taking action, so that the data that was lost in the network (the error) is resent successfully.

ESS   Electronic Switching System. See also *Extended Service Set.*

Ethernet   A family of LAN standards from the IEEE that use either copper or fiber cabling.

Ethernet broadcast address   A special Ethernet address, FFFF.FFFF.FFFF, used to send frames to all devices in the same Ethernet LAN.

Ethernet frame   The bytes of data that flow in an Ethernet LAN, which begins with the Ethernet header, followed by data (which actually holds headers from other layers as well as end-user data) and ends with the Ethernet trailer. Ethernet LANs deliver Ethernet frames from one Ethernet device to another.

Ethernet header   A data structure that an Ethernet node adds in front of data supplied by the next higher layer to create an Ethernet frame. The header holds these important fields: Preamble, SFD, Destination Address, Source Address, and Type.

Ethernet LANs   A collection of devices, including user devices, LAN switches, routers, old hubs, and cables, all of which use IEEE Ethernet standards at the physical and data link layers, so that the devices can send Ethernet frames to each other.

Ethernet multicast address   One of three categories of an Ethernet MAC address (the others being unicast and broadcast). Ethernet multicast MAC addresses can be used to send one frame to a group of NICs on the LAN, without having to send a separate copy of a unicast frame to every device in the group.

Ethernet trailer   A data structure that an Ethernet node adds after the data supplied by the next higher layer to create an Ethernet frame; the trailer holds one field, the FCS field.

Ethernet Type   A 2-byte field in the Ethernet header, following the Source Address field, that lists a code. The code identifies the type of data that follows in the Data field, typically a type of Layer 2 packet, often an IP version 4 packet.

Extended Service Set (ESS)   A wireless LAN in which all devices communicate through one wireless access point at a time, but the wireless LAN has at least two access points that cooperate to create the single wireless LAN.

exterior gateway protocol (EGP)   A synonym for *exterior routing protocol.*

exterior routing protocol   Any IP routing protocol designed to be most useful between multiple TCP/IP networks of different companies or organizations. BGP is the only modern exterior routing protocol.

F

Fast Ethernet   The informal name for one particular Ethernet standard, originally defined formally as 802.3u, which was the first Ethernet standard to surpass the original 10-Mbps speed to run at 100 Mbps.

FCC   See *Federal Communications Commission.*

FCS   Frame Check Sequence. A 4-byte field in an Ethernet trailer, used as part of the process by which a receiving Ethernet node performs error detection.

FDDI   Fiber Distributed Data Interface. A type of LAN technology, popular in the 1990s, which ran at 100 Mbps before Ethernet supported 100 Mbps and used fiber cabling. It was a popular option for the core of campus networks in the 1990s because of its speed and fiber cabling.

Federal Communications Commission   The organization appointed by the U.S. government to regulate emissions of EM energy in the United States.

fiber-optic cable   A type of cable that uses glass fibers in the center of the cable as a path over which to shine light for the purpose of transmitting data in a network.

Fiber to the Curb   A cable plant implementation, particularly in HFC cable plants with a cable company, in which the company runs fiber cable from the head end to the curb on the side of the road that passes by houses and apartment buildings.

Fiber to the Neighborhood   A cable plant implementation, particularly in HFC cable plants with a cable company, in which the company runs fiber cable from the head end to the front of a neighborhood, and then coaxial cable from that point to the rest of the way to homes and apartments.

file   A collection of bytes, assigned a name for easy reference by the file system and grouped together for storage on a permanent storage device.

file system   The term that refers to a combination of features that together let the OS manage data as files, identify permanent storage drives using drive letters, organize files on each drive using directories, and track important file information, including file locations on disks, using directories and pointers.

firewall   A networking function, implemented either as a standalone device or as part of an integrated device, that performs network security functions at the edge of a network.

flooding   Part of an Ethernet LAN switch's forwarding logic in which the switch forwards a frame out all ports, except the port in which the frame arrived.

flow   A term referring to the concept of the exchange of data between an application process on one computer and a matching application process on another computer, with each process identified by its TCP or UDP port number.

flow control   A feature of TCP in which the TCP sender speeds up and slows down its rate of sending data.

FM   See *frequency modulation.*

folder   In file systems, another term for directory. See *directory.*

forwarding   Part of an Ethernet LAN switch's forwarding logic that refers to the choice a switch makes to take a received frame and send it out a single outgoing port, because the frame has a destination MAC address known to the switch (as listed in the switch's MAC address table).

fps   Frames per second.

fractional T1   A leased line that supports less than T1 speed between the two customer routers, using a fraction of the capacity of the T1.

frame   The specific term referring to the data link layer header and trailer, plus all headers and data encapsulated between the data-link header and trailer.

frame buffer   A synonym for pixel map. See *pixel map.*

Frame Relay   A widely popular packet-switching technology and service that emerged in the market in the 1990s, using permanent virtual circuits (PVC) between pairs of routers that can send frames to each other, and data-link connection identifiers (DLCI) to address and identify each PVC.

Frame Relay Forum   A vendor consortium created to help make Frame Relay standards and product interoperability happen.

GL

framing bit   In a T1 frame, the first of the 193 bits, used collectively by the devices on a T1 to identify the frame in the serial bit stream and for some other purposes as well.

frequency   When describing energy that acts like waves, the number of times that the entire waveform repeats per second.

frequency band   A range of consecutive frequencies set aside by a regulatory agency like the FCC for a specific type of communications.

frequency channel   A subset of a frequency band, used by one device or service to transmit information.

frequency modulation (FM)   A term referring to the process of changing (modulating) an energy wave over time by changing its frequency.

Frequency Shift Keying (FSK)   The formal term for a class of networking encoding schemes that shift (change) the frequency of the energy signal to encode different bit values.

FRF   See *Frame Relay Forum.*

FSK   See *Frequency Shift Keying.*

FTTC   See *Fiber to the Curb.*

FTTN   See *Fiber to the Neighborhood.*

full duplex   A networking link that allows bits to be sent in both directions and at the same time.

full mesh   In Frame Relay and other multiaccess networks that use a virtual circuit (VC) concept, a topology in which all devices connect to all others with a VC.

G

gain   A reference to the amount of power added to a transmitted radio signal.

game console   A consumer device that allows the user to run video game software.

GB   Gigabytes. See *gigabyte.*

GBps   Gigabytes per second.

Gbps   Gigabits per second.

Gigabit Ethernet   The informal name for one particular Ethernet standard, defined formally in 802.3z (for fiber) and 802.3ab (for UTP), with a speed of 1 Gbps.

gigabyte   1,073,741,824 bytes, or if rounding, 1,000,000,000 (1 billion) bytes.

global MAC address   Another term for *universal MAC address.*

guaranteed delivery   A TCP function in which the TCP software on a host provides the application protocol the service of making sure that all data arrives at the destination host, or if it simply cannot be delivered, of notifying the application protocol that the data was not delivered.

H

half duplex   A networking link that allows bits to be sent in both directions, but only one direction at a time.

hard disk drive   A device that stores files, as directed by a computer's CPU, typically using stacked round magnetic platters to record the bits as differing magnetic fields on different locations on the platters' surfaces.

hardware spec   Short for hardware specification. Hardware specs, oftentimes also standards (but not always), define the physical details that must be known by a manufacturing company so that it can build networking products correctly.

HDD   See *hard disk drive.*

HDLC   High-Level Data Link Control. An early data-link protocol used on many early variations of WAN services, mainly used today on leased lines.

head end   A term that refers to the facility where a cable company keeps the equipment that connects to one end of the HFC cable plant, with the other end sitting in the cable company customers' homes, apartments, and offices.

header   Bytes of data, defined by some standard or protocol, and added in front of the user data that needs to be sent. Protocols use headers to store information that the protocol needs to communicate with other devices.

hertz   A unit of measurement for the number of events that happen per second; in networking, it usually refers to the number of waveforms that occur per second.

HFC   See *hybrid fiber coaxial*.

host name   A name made up of alphabetic, numeric, and some special characters, used to identify a specific IP host. Host names that follow the convention for domain names in the DNS system use a hierarchical design, with periods separating parts of the name.

host routing   The forwarding (routing) logic used by IP hosts, which typically reduces to two choices: Send the IP packet directly to the other host on the same subnet, or send the IP packet to the default router if the destination is on a different subnet.

HTTP   See *Hypertext Transfer Protocol*.

HTTP GET Reply   A message defined by the HTTP protocol that allows a web server to reply to an HTTP GET Request.

HTTP GET Request   A message defined by the HTTP protocol that allows a web browser to request a web object from a web server by listing the web address of the object.

hub-and-spoke   A term used for WAN topologies in which one central site (the hub) connects to many remote sites (spokes), but the remote sites do not connect directly to each other.

hybrid fiber coaxial (HFC)   A general term for the cable plant installed between the cable company offices (head end) and the homes and apartments of its potential customers, with the cable plant including a mix (hybrid) of fiber and coaxial cable.

hyperlink   In a web browser, a hidden connection between text or an image to a hidden web address, so that when the user clicks the text or image, the web browser loads the web page as listed in the web address.

Hypertext Transfer Protocol (HTTP)   The protocol used by web browsers and web servers to define the format of URLs (web addresses) and the messages used to exchange web objects.

I

I/O   See *input and output*.

IANA   See *Internet Assigned Numbers Authority*.

IBM   International Business Machines. A technology company whose vendor networking model (SNA) was very popular during the years when vendor networking models were common in corporate networks.

IBSS   See *Independent Basic Service Set*.

ICANN   See *Internet Corporation for Assigned Names and Numbers*.

ICMP   See *Internet Control Message Protocol*.

IEEE   See *Institute of Electrical and Electronic Engineers*.

IEEE working group   The name of a group of people (mostly volunteers) who work together to develop new IEEE standards.

IGP   See *interior gateway protocol*.

incoming email server   An email server that waits for, receives, and holds emails addressed to a particular email address, keeping the emails until the user downloads the emails from the incoming mail server.

Independent Basic Service Set (IBSS)   Also known as an ad hoc wireless LAN, a WLAN service in which each user device sends frames directly to the other devices in the WLAN, without the need for a wireless access point.

Industrial, Scientific, and Medical (ISM)   The formal name of one of the wireless unlicensed frequency bands reserved for use by the FCC and other national regulators in other countries.

information technology   A common term used to refer to the computer industry as a whole.

GL

informational RF   A type of RFC, published by the IETF, but not as a standard. Informational RFCs allow a working group to publish information in cases where the details do not require a standard, or for which the standardization process has no benefit.

inline   In networking, a reference to the location of some networking devices in which they receive and forward packets, like a router, but usually for some other purpose, like performing NAT or firewall functions.

in-order delivery   A feature of TCP in which the TCP makes sure that the data it gives to the destination host's application is in the same order in which the sender sent the data.

input and output (I/O)   This term refers to the process of adding bits into a computer (input), and receiving the bits out of the computer (output), in forms meaningful to the user. Examples include typing on a keyboard (input) and looking at images on a display (output).

inside network   For several networking functions, including both firewalls and NAT, the idea that the device or function separates parts of the network, with one part being the more trusted part of the network (the inside).

Institute of Electrical and Electronic Engineers (IEEE)   A professional association based in the United States that standardizes many important networking technologies, including Ethernet (wired) LANs and wireless LANs.

insulator   In electrical circuits, an insulator is any material that resists the molecular process that occurs when electricity flows through the material.

integrated networking device   A single networking device that performs the roles of more than one networking device.

Integrated Services Digital Network   A type of switched (dial) service from telcos that transmits data using digital signals instead of the analog signals used with traditional phone calls or circuits that use analog modems.

interface   A generic word, usually used when also speaking of network layer topics and IP, that refers to a device's connection (interface) to the TCP/IP network. Logically, IP expects that an interface has an assigned IP address. The most common term used to describe the physical connectors on an IP router.

interior gateway protocol (IGP)   A synonym for *interior routing protocol.*

interior routing protocol   Any IP routing protocol designed to be most useful inside the TCP/IP network of a single company or organization. These include RIP, EIGRP, and OSPF.

International Organization for Standardization (ISO)   The standards organization that developed the OSI model. Also called ISO.

international standard   A standard approved by a group of nations. It is the same idea as a national standard, except the approval process includes many countries. The standards typically relate to functions that benefit from being consistent among countries.

International Telecommunications Union (ITU)   An agency of the United Nations whose mission is to develop and certify international communications standards. For TCP/IP, the ITU publishes standards that mostly act as WAN data-link and physical standards in the TCP/IP model.

Internet/The Internet   The global network formed by interconnecting most of the networks on the planet, with each home and company network connecting to an Internet service provider (ISP), which in turn connects to other ISPs.

Internet access   A broad term for the many technologies that can be used to connect to an ISP so that the device or network can send packets between itself and the ISP.

Internet Assigned Numbers Authority (IANA)   A part of the Internet Corporation for Assigned Names and Numbers (ICANN), with specific authority to manage the assignment of host names, IP address blocks, and other numbers that must be coordinated to help make the Internet work smoothly.

Internet Control Message Protocol   A TCP/IP Layer 3 protocol that defines many functions that allow for better management of TCP/IP, with focus on TCP/IP network layer functions, including the ability to test network connections using the **ping** command.

Internet core   The part of the Internet created through network links between ISPs that creates the ability of the ISPs to send IP packets to the customers of the ISPs that connect to the core.

Internet Corporation for Assigned Names and Numbers   The nonprofit company that oversees the worldwide process of number and name assignments, including the IP address space and domain names.

Internet edge   The part of the Internet between an ISP and the ISP customer, whether the customer is a company or organization with a large private TCP/IP network, or whether the customer is a single individual.

Internet Protocol (IP)   The main TCP/IP network layer protocol. IP defines addressing, considered logical because it works independently from the physical networks, and routing, which defines how to forward packets from one host to the other.

Internet service provider (ISP)   A company that provides Internet services, typically with two major parts: the ability for customers to access the Internet through the ISP, and the commitment by the ISP to maintain connections to all possible destinations in the Internet, either directly or indirectly.

interoperable   The result of two (or more) devices or software working together correctly because they use the same standard.

intrusion prevention system (IPS)   A type of networking security device that monitors for complex types of attacks, comparing traffic patterns versus known attack profiles, logging and alerting engineers when attacks happen, and possibly acting to disable users and connections to prevent problems when attacks occur.

IP   See *Internet Protocol*.

IP address   A 32-bit binary number, often written in the DDN format, that hosts use as their unique identifier in a TCP/IP network, much like a postal mailing address in the postal system.

IP address class   One of the five classes defined by the IP version 4 addressing rules, namely, class A, B, C, D, or E.

IP fragmentation   A function of IP, typically done on routers, in which a router has an IP packet in memory and the router needs to forward the packet, but the packet is longer than the allowed IP MTU of the outgoing interface. In this case, the router fragments the packet—breaks it into smaller IP packets—and then forwards the smaller IP packets.

IP host   Any device that has an IP address.

IP MTU   See *maximum transmission unit*.

IP network   When discussing IP addressing, this term refers to a group of IP addresses as defined by class A, B, or C rules. Also called a classful network ID.

IP network ID   Another term for *network ID*.

IP packet   The term referring to the message that flows through a network from sending IP host to receiving IP host, including the IP header plus all higher-layer headers and user data, but also not including the data link layer header/trailer.

IP route   One entry in an IP routing table that lists some potential destination (usually a network ID or subnet ID) as forwarding instructions, including the interface out which the router should forward the IP packet.

IP router   A device that performs IP routing. A physical device with roles defined by the IP protocol, including to connect LANs and WANs using its physical interfaces, and to route (forward) IP packets that come in any interface out the correct outgoing interface.

IP routing   The process of forwarding an IP packet from end to end through a TCP/IP network, as well as the logic used on an individual host or router as its part of the forwarding of the packet to its end destination.

GL

IP routing table   Another term for *routing table*.

IP routing table   A list of information in an IP router that the router uses to make IP routing decisions.

IP subnet   A group of consecutive IP addresses that can be used as the set of IP addresses on a single LAN or WAN, created when a classful IP network was subdivided into smaller groups through subnetting.

IP subnet ID   Another term for *subnet ID*.

IP subnetting   The process of taking a class A, B, or C IP network and subdividing it into a number of smaller groups of addresses (subnets).

IP version 4   The most commonly used version of the Internet Protocol, standardized since 1980 and used throughout the world and the Internet.

IP version 6   The protocol that is likely to replace IP version 4 over time, notable for its long IP address (128 bits).

IPS   See *intrusion prevention system*.

IPv4   See *IP version 4*.

IPv4 address exhaustion   A term referring to the very real problem in the worldwide Internet, which first presented itself in the late 1980s, in which the world appeared to be running out of the available IPv4 address space.

IPv6   See *IP version 6*.

ISDN   See *Integrated Services Digital Network*.

ISM   See *Industrial, Scientific, and Medical*.

ISP   See *Internet service provider*.

ISP dialup service   An Internet access service offered by any ISP in which the Internet access happens using analog modems over switched (dialed) analog phone circuits.

ITU   See *International Telecommunications Union*.

J–K

jacket   In a cable, the outer part of the cable that holds the rest of the cable's parts.

KB   Kilobytes.

KBps   Kilobytes per second.

kbps   Kilobits per second.

keyboard map   Information that matches the key (or key combination) that exists on a keyboard to some matching binary code so that the keyboard can tell the computer specifically what key(s) were just pressed.

kilobyte   1024 bytes, or if rounding, 1000 bytes.

known unicast frame   From the perspective of a single Ethernet LAN switch, a frame whose destination MAC address is known to the switch, in that the switch's MAC address table lists the frame's destination MAC address.

L

LAN   See *local-area network*.

LAN capacity   The concept of the sum of all bits sendable in a LAN.

LAN edge   A reference to the part of the campus LAN with the end-user devices and the switches to which they connect, through an Ethernet switch or a wireless LAN access point, that contains the largest number of physical links.

LAN switch   A networking device that has multiple physical sockets into which LAN cabling can be connected, for the purpose of providing a centralized device to connect the devices in a LAN.

laser   An optical device that generates a precise beam of light, usually in a very narrow direction at a very specific frequency, used for many purposes, including to send data over fiber-optic links and to read and write CDs and DVDs.

layer   In a networking model, a subset of the model that helps divide the functions of the entire model for easier understanding, to allow modular engineering and make discussions about networks much easier.

learning   Part of an Ethernet switch's logic related to the forwarding process by which the switch learns MAC addresses and their associated port numbers.

leased circuit   Another term for *dedicated circuit*.

leased line   A physical link between two locations, provided by a telco, that allows two-way communication between sites. Because the customer does not own the physical line between sites, but rather pays a monthly fee for the service, it is called a leased service or leased line. Also known as a dedicated circuit, leased circuit, and point-to-point line.

LED   Light-emitting diode. An optical device that generates a broad light that can be used for many purposes, including to send data over fiber-optic links.

licensed frequency band   A set of consecutive frequencies reserved by national regulators (like the FCC in the United States), with the regulations requiring that a company purchase a license for the right to send information using a small subset of the frequency band. The regulations prevent other companies from using the licensed frequencies so that only the company that owns the license can use those frequencies.

link   A generic term for any network cable or wireless communications path between two devices over which bits can be transmitted.

link speed   A synonym for *bit rate*.

local-area network (LAN)   A network typically owned by a company, so it exists typically within the space occupied by that company and is therefore closer together than wide-area networks. See *wide-area network*.

local loop   The cabling that runs from a telco central office (CO) to a customer home or business to support analog phone calls.

LTE   Long-Term Evolution.

M

MAC   See *Media Access Control*.

MAC address   A data link layer address, 48 bits in length, usually written as 12 hexadecimal digits and used to represent different devices connected to LANs.

MAC address table   On a LAN switch, a table of MAC addresses and local switch ports that the switch uses when making its decision of where to forward Ethernet frames that arrive at the switch.

MAC header   Another name for *Ethernet header*.

MAC trailer   Another name for *Ethernet trailer*.

management and control frames   802.11 frames defined for some overhead function in 802.11, instead of being a data frame, which carries upper-layer information.

Manchester encoding   A specific encoding scheme, used in the original 10BASE-T standard, in which a bit value is not encoded by the state of the signal but by whether the signal moves from high to low state, or low to high state, in the middle of the bit time.

maximum segment size   With TCP, the maximum number of bytes allowed in the TCP segment's data field, which is derived from the sending host's outgoing interface IP MTU setting.

maximum transmission unit   With IP, the maximum size in bytes of an IP packet allowed to be forwarded out a given interface.

MB   Megabytes.

MBps   Megabytes per second.

mbps   Megabits per second.

mechanical mouse   A mouse that uses mechanisms, such a mouse ball and internal wheels that rotate when the mouse ball rolls, to recognize mouse movement and translate that into measured movements in an X,Y coordinate system.

Media Access Control (MAC)   The formal IEEE 802.3 Ethernet term for the data link layer, data-link header, and other data-link features, including addresses.

GL

medium (media) A generic reference to one physical networking link (medium) or multiple links (media).

megabyte 1,048,576 bytes, or if rounding, 1,000,000 (1 million) bytes.

megahertz Millions of hertz.

memory module A plastic card that contains RAM microchips and other electronics so that it can be connected to a computer, usually on the motherboard, making the RAM available to the CPU of the computer.

Metro Ethernet (MetroE) A type of multiaccess WAN service that uses Ethernet as the physical access link and usually uses an Ethernet switch as the customer site device, with the customer sending Ethernet frames from one customer site to the other.

mobile phone Also known as a cell phone, a mobile phone is a device that can make voice calls, and do other functions, using wireless radio signals, allowing the user to move around with the device.

mobile phone network The network created by a mobile phone company to allow phones (and other devices) to communicate with the phone company, to other subscribers of that phone company, and with the other phones in the world.

modem A term for the device placed on the end of a telephone line, and connected to computers on each end, so that the computers can call each other and send data over the analog circuit.

modem bank In an ISP dialup service, a large set of modems sitting in a room, connected to a large number of phone lines, waiting for incoming calls from Internet dialup customers.

modulate The opposite of demodulate. For modems, the process of taking the incoming digits (bits) from a computer and encoding them on an analog voice circuit, for the purpose of communicating the bits to a matching modem and computer on the other end of the link.

monitor Another word for a computer display. See *display*.

motherboard A plastic card that contains a large variety of electronic components that together make up many of the core functions of a computer. The components attached to the motherboard typically include the CPU, RAM, buses, and expansion slots, plus the input/output electronics for keyboards, displays, printers, and mouse.

mouse A computer input and control device that mimics the user's movement of the mouse by moving a mouse pointer on the screen, so that the user can then take an appropriate action (like clicking a mouse button), telling the computer to take some action on the item to which the mouse pointer is pointing.

mouse pointer An icon that the computer displays on the screen that mirrors the movement of the mouse.

MPLS See *multiprotocol label switching*.

MSS See *maximum segment size*.

MTU See *maximum transmission unit*.

multiaccess A network service that allows more than two devices to connect to the service.

multiaccess network A more common term today for a packet-switched network, with this term drawing attention to the fact that more than two devices connect to the service.

multicast IP address An IP address not meant for use as a unicast address, but instead as a way to send one packet to multiple IP hosts, reducing overhead in the network for applications that need to send the same packet to many hosts.

multimode fiber A type of fiber-optic cabling that has a larger core, for the purpose of accepting light at multiple angles, typically from LED transmitters.

multiplex The opposite of demultiplex. For a multiplexer, the process of taking multiple incoming digital serial bit streams and putting all of them into different channels on a single line that has time channels, like DS1 and DS3 lines.

multipoint A WAN topology in which more than two devices can communicate directly over the WAN.

multiprotocol label switching (MPLS)   A type of WAN service, and the related protocol standards, that acts as a packet-switching service that operates in part based on the IP protocol.

N

NAT   See *Network Address Translation*.

NAT table   A list of NAT table entries, maintained by the NAT function on a device.

NAT table entry   One item in the NAT table that lists all the information NAT needs to translate the correct headers to support one application connection passing through the NAT function. The entry includes the private IP address and public IP address.

national standard   A standard approved by a nation. In practice, a nation's government typically creates or appoints some organization to oversee standards for the nation.

network address   Another term for *network ID*.

Network Address Translation (NAT)   One of the short-term solutions to the IPv4 address exhaustion problem that actually helped solve the problem for a much longer time frame. NAT reduces the number of public IP addresses needed by one ISP customer by using one public IP address for the traffic from many real client hosts.

network ID   A number used to identify a class A, B, or C network that has the same value in the network part of the number as all the IP addresses in the network, and 0 in the rest.

network number   Another term for *network ID*.

network server   A computer and/or software that provides some service in a network that helps make the network do its job.

network topology   A diagram or concept of a network that shows the network as nodes, which represent various networking devices, and links, which represent the cables or wireless links between the devices.

networking device   A specialized computer created for the purpose of doing some task to create a network.

network interface card   A computer expansion card, or simply a function included in a computing device, that physically connects to a network.

networking model   An organized collection of networking standards from which vendors can build products, and engineers at companies can follow the standards when implementing their networks, so that after all the products have been implemented, the network works correctly.

networking standard   A document that details information about some technology or protocol related to networking, and that document has been passed through a review and approval process that certifies the document as a standard.

NIC   See *network interface card*.

node   A generic term for any networking device that sits on the end of links, for the purpose of both connecting links to create physical paths and to make decisions about how to forward data through the network.

noise   In networking, energy, typically electrical or radio, that makes it more difficult for the receiving node to understand the received electrical or radio signal. In wireless communications, any radio signal that is not part of the signal that a wireless node is either sending or receiving.

nonoverlapping channels   In wireless LANs, channels (frequency ranges) used for sending data for which the frequencies do not overlap, which allows multiple devices to send data at the same time in the same space.

O

ODD   See *optical disc drive*.

omnidirectional antenna   An antenna that transmits its radio signal in all directions, with equal signal strength in all directions, resulting in a circular coverage area.

open networking model   A networking model whose standards can been read and used to create products without payment to any one company.

open shortest path first   A TCP/IP standardized IP routing protocol.

Open Systems Interconnection (OSI) model   An open networking model developed by ISO over the same time frame as TCP/IP.

operating system   The software on any computing device that controls the hardware and creates the environment on which the user of the device can run applications useful to the user.

optical disc drive   A disc drive that uses light (usually a laser) to store bits, by changing the surface of the disc to reflect light differently for a binary 0 as compared to a binary 1. ODDs include CD and DVD drives.

optical mouse   A mouse that uses optics, such as shining a light and using light sensors to sense the angle of reflection, to recognize mouse movement and translate that into measured movements in an X,Y coordinate system.

optical receiver   A receiver that receives data by sensing incoming light.

optical transmitter   A transmitter that sends data using light.

optics   A description of any technology that uses light to do some function.

OS   See *operating system.*

OSI   See *Open Systems Interconnection model.*

OSPF   See *open shortest path first.*

outer jacket   See *jacket.*

outgoing email server   An email server that waits for a user to send outgoing emails, and after they are received, the outgoing email server finds the incoming email server that holds emails for the recipient of the email and forwards the email.

outside network   For several networking functions, including both firewalls and NAT, the idea that the device or function separates parts of the network, with one part being the less trusted part of the network (the outside).

P

packet   The specific term referring to the network layer header, plus any headers that follow, up through the user data. Specifically, this term omits the data link layer header and trailer.

packet switch   A telco device that works with other like devices to create a packet-switching service, with each device forwarding customer packets based on the address in the header of the packet sent by the customer device.

packet switching   The process of forwarding customer data in a WAN by looking at the header of the messages sent into the WAN by the customer and making a per-message (per-packet) decision as to where to forward each message.

partial mesh   In packet-switched networks that use a virtual circuit (VC) concept, a design in which a VC exists between a subset of the router pairs, but not all pairs.

peering agreement   A legal contract between two ISPs that lists business and technical details related to networking links between the two ISPs, including the possibility that one ISP might have to pay the other ISP for the right to send IP packets over the link.

period   In a waveform, the time it takes for one complete cycle of the waveform to complete; 1/frequency.

permanent virtual circuit (PVC)   In packet-switched networks, a logical connection between two customer devices, typically routers, that allows the routers to send messages directly to each other, and specifically the case in which the connection is predefined and never goes away.

phase   When describing energy that acts like waves, in a sine wave, the specific point or place in the repeating continuous wave.

Phase Shift Keying (PSK)   The formal term for a class of networking encoding schemes that shift (change) the phase of the energy signal to encode different bit values.

photodiode   An optical device that senses incoming light and converts that light into electricity. Used as part of an optical receiver in networking.

pin position   In any connector attached to the end of a networking cable, a place in the connector, usually identified by a number, into which an individual wire can be placed.

pinout   The wiring details in a cable with connectors that identify each wire and the pin position of each wire on both connectors on both ends of the cable.

pixel grid   The rectangular set of pixels that physically exist in a computer display.

pixel map   A mapping between each pixel on a computer display and a binary code. The binary code represents the color that the pixel should display.

plastic coating   For copper wires user in networking cables, the plastic added to the wires to give them strength.

platter   In a hard disk drive, the round discs that can be magnetized to hold bits.

point of presence (POP)   A term used by service providers, particularly for WAN or Internet service providers instead of traditional telcos, that refers to the building where the provider keeps its equipment. Access links that connect the customer device to the WAN service physically connect into the POP.

pointer   Generally, a pointer in computing is some value that identifies (points to) some other value. In this book, one example includes a pointer associated with a file that identifies the hard disk drive's sectors that hold the contents of the file.

point-to-point   A topology in which two devices sit on the ends of a communications link.

POP   See *point of presence* and *Post Office Protocol*.

POP3   Post Office Protocol (version 3).

port   A much-used term in networking; most often used to refer to the socket or place in a switch into which a cable can be inserted into the switch. With TCP and UDP, a number, from 0 to 65,535, that a host can use to identify an application process.

Post Office Protocol (POP)   An application protocol commonly used on email client software to retrieve incoming email.

postal telephone and telegraph   A term referring to parts of government organizations that provided some major communications function for the company—typically postal service, telephone services, and telegraph services. Telephone companies that happened to be part of the government, rather than a private company, were referenced by this name.

PPP   Point-to-Point Protocol. A data-link protocol used on physical and logical point-to-point communications links.

PPP over ATM (PPPoA)   A combination of data link layer protocols that can be used in some cases with Internet access technologies, which allows PPP frames to flow from the customer router to the ISP router when only part of the overall path uses ATM.

PPP over Ethernet (PPPoE)   A combination of data link layer protocols that can be used in some cases with Internet access technologies, which allows PPP frames to flow from the customer router to the ISP router when only part of the overall path uses Ethernet.

Preamble   A field in the Ethernet header that has alternating binary 1s and 0s, which the receiving node should recognize to mean that a new frame is being transmitted on the link.

prefix   In an IP network or IP subnet, a number of bits at the beginning of all addresses must have the same value for the address to be in that network or subnet. The term *prefix* refers to this beginning part that must be the same value for all addresses in the group.

GL

prestandard   A document that acts like a standard in that it documents details that many people can choose to follow to make their products interoperable. However, the document has not passed through the entire formal standards process (and might never), so the prefix ("pre") reminds us of the fact that the document is not finalized as a standard.

printer driver   Software that adapts the content held by the application (text or image) into information that tells the printer how to make the image appear on the printer.

private IP address   An IP address in a small set of specific class A, B, and C networks as defined in RFC 1918. Specifically, any IP address in class A network 10.0.0.0, class B networks from 172.16.0.0 through 172.31.0.0, and addresses in all class C networks that begin with 192.168.

private IP network   An IP network as defined in RFC 1918 that can be used by any company, at any time, for any purpose, but being particularly useful for a company that also uses NAT. Specifically, class A network 10.0.0.0, class B networks from 172.16.0.0 through 172.31.0.0, and class C networks that begin with 192.168.

probe   In 802.11 wireless LANs, the name of a process and the name of some management and control messages used by a process, through which a wireless client can query all access points in a wireless LAN to find out which access point is the best access point for that client to use right now.

project number (IEEE)   The name of the IEEE identifier for a working group, which for Ethernet starts with IEEE.

protocol   A set of rules that different devices and/ or software must follow so that the network works correctly.

PSK   See *Phase Shift Keying*.

PSTN   See *public switched telephone network*.

PTT   See *postal telephone and telegraph*.

public IP address   An IP address in the unicast class A, B, and C range that also sits inside the range of addresses IANA is allowed to assign to a company to use as globally unique IP addresses in the public Internet.

public IP network   All class A, B, and C networks, except for a small set of reserved IP networks, including the reserved private IP networks. IANA (and its member agencies) can then assign IP addresses from the public IP networks as part of the effort to keep all public IP addresses unique in the Internet.

public switched telephone network (PSTN)   The formal term for the combined worldwide telephone network.

PVC   See *permanent virtual circuit*.

Q–R

quad word   Four words of computer memory, or 64 bits.

queuing   A general term for the process in a networking node in which the node uses RAM to store messages (frames, packets, and so on), waiting for the node's outgoing interface to be available for sending the next message.

radio antenna   See *antenna*.

radio waves   Electromagnetic energy in a particular range of frequencies (per the electromagnetic spectrum), useful for encoding data in networks.

random-access memory (RAM)   A type of short-term computer memory (storage) used by computers, primarily used as temporary working memory by the CPU.

range   In wireless LANs, a synonym for *coverage area*.

read/write head   In a hard disk drive, the component at the end of the actuator arm that writes bits by setting the magnetic charge and reads bits by sensing the push/ pull from existing magnetic charges.

Real-Time Transfer Protocol (RTP)   An application protocol commonly used by Voice over IP (VoIP) applications to send voice as bits insides IP packets over a TCP/IP network.

receiver   A device that receives an energy signal, examines what the energy signal looks like, and makes a choice (per the encoding rules) as to what bits the energy signal represents.

Regional Internet Registry (RIR)   The term for the class of organization that manages domain name registration processes for major geographies around the globe, as authorized by IANA.

registered port number   A TCP or UDP port number reserved with IANA for a particular application protocol, but outside the well-known port range.

removable media   A reference to a feature of some permanent storage devices in which the media that stores the bits can be removed from the storage device. Examples include CD and DVD drives.

Request for Comments   The official term for a document created by the IETF to detail a particular technology or protocol. An RFC can also be a standard, or it might not be.

RFC   See *Request for Comments*.

RIP   See *routing information protocol*.

RIR   See *Regional Internet Registry*.

RJ-11   Registered Jack Type 11.

RJ-48   The name of the connector used on many leased-line connections for the cabling inside the customer site.

root server   A special type of DNS server, located in the Internet, that keeps lists of trustworthy (authoritative) DNS servers for the DNS subdomains of the world.

route aggregation   A function defined by CIDR that allows routers to advertise and use routes to collect multiple CIDR blocks into a single route, called an aggregate route, thereby reducing the size of the IP routing tables in the Internet.

route summarization   A synonym for *route aggregation*.

router   Another term for IP router. See *IP router*.

routing information protocol   A TCP/IP standardized IP routing protocol.

routing protocol   A shorter term for *dynamic routing protocol*.

routing table   A list of IP routes used by an IP router when making routing decisions about where to forward an IP packet.

RTP   See *Real-Time Transfer Protocol*.

S

screen   Another term for a computer display. See *display*.

screen resolution   A reference to the number of pixels currently in use by a display, shown as two numbers in a rectangular grid called a pixel grid: width x height.

SDLC   Synchronous Data Link Control. An older serial data-link protocol, defined by IBM, from which HDLC was derived.

search engine   A service provided by some service provider in which the provider, in the background, finds keywords from every web page it can find in the Internet, building an index. Users can then enter search terms and ask the search engine provider to list links to all web pages that match those search terms.

sector   In a hard disk drive, the location that can store bits as concentric circles; a sector is one part of one these complete concentric circles. In other words, it is a part of a track.

SEQ   Sequence number. A field in the TCP header that the sending TCP host uses to label the first byte of data in the segment so that the receiving host can signal whether the receiving host successfully received the segment.

serial interface   A router physical interface that, like many interfaces, sends bits one after the other (serially), used to connect to leased lines by connecting the interface to a CSU/DSU using a serial cable.

Service Set Identifier (SSID)   The formal term for the name of a wireless LAN, as advertised in Beacon frames.

SFD   Start Frame Delimiter. A 1-byte field in the Ethernet header, following the Preamble field, that continues the Preamble, but ends in a slightly different bit pattern (11), signaling to the receiving node that the next field is the Destination Address.

shared bandwidth   A term referring to how some networks must share the right to send data by taking turns, which limits the total number of bits sent by all devices (the network's total capacity).

shielded twisted-pair (STP)   A type of cabling that uses pairs of copper wires, twisted together, with extra shielding from the effects of EMI.

shorthand name (IEEE)   The term for a type of name for IEEE standards. These names begin with a speed, list "BASE-" in the middle, and end with a suffix, for example, 10BASE-T.

signaling   The process of telling the phone company what telephone number you want to connect with by tapping keys on the telephone keypad, or doing the equivalent with a modem.

sine wave   A waveform that matches the mathematic sine function, found in many types of natural energy, with a continuous change over time from the high point, down to a low point, and back to the same high point.

single-homed   A general category that describes the topology of the connections from a company to the Internet in which the company has a single connection to a single ISP, in which case the company can use default routing toward the Internet.

single-mode fiber   A type of fiber-optic cabling that has a smaller core, useful for accepting narrow bands of light from laser transmitters.

site survey   A process by which a network engineer walks around a site, performing tests and looking for sources of interference and radio noise, all with the goal of making a wireless LAN installation work better.

Skype   A voice service created with an application on a computer in which the application acts as a phone, using the Internet to transmit the voice call's bits.

small office/home office (SOHO)   A networking term used to refer to a size of remote office that can and often does use small integrated network devices, with the network device doing all the functions needed by the site: routing, switching, access point, and so on. Literally, a small business office with either one person, or just a few, at someone's home or at a small office location.

small/medium business   A category of businesses that refers to a relatively small business (or possibly smaller government institutions) that build their networks for their own purposes, rather than selling network services to other companies.

SNA   Systems Network Architecture. IBM's vendor networking model, popular from the 1970s into the 1990s.

social media   A service in which the provider creates web pages in which the user can easily customize and add content, sharing that content with others, so that the website becomes a way to share with friends and associates.

SOHO   See *small office/home office*.

solid state   A description of some types of electronics that means that the device or component does not have any moving parts.

SONET   Synchronous Optical Network. A series of physical standards for progressively faster line rates that begin with a base rate called OC-1, which runs at 51.84 Mbps, up through OC-768, which runs at roughly 10 Gbps.

sound wave   The wave of movement of air as a sound passes through the air, which shows a slight change in wave height when graphed over time, similar to a graph of analog electrical signals.

source MAC address   A field in the Ethernet header that lists the MAC address of the device that originally sent the Ethernet frame.

source port   In a TCP or UDP header, a 16-bit field that lists the port number of the application process that sent the data in the TCP segment or UDP datagram.

speaker   An electronic component that takes in analog electricity and creates sound waves.

SSID   See *Service Set Identifier*.

standard   An agreement as to how different devices should work together to perform a task, with emphasis on the fact that the parties that care—businesses, governments, and so on—have agreed to use the same standard.

standard RFC   A type of RFC that has passed through the IETF's formal standardization process, called the standards track, and passed.

standards body   An organization involved in developing or certifying standards.

standards group   A synonym for *standards body*.

standards organization   A synonym for *standards body*.

star topology   A network topology in which links extend outward from a central node, somewhat like rays of light going out from a star/sun.

static configuration   When working with networking devices, the process of connecting from a network engineer's computer to the network node and typing instructions that tell the node what to do.

STP   See *shielded twisted-pair*.

straight-through cable   A UTP cabling pinout in which the wire at pin x on one end of the cable connects to pin x on the other end of the cable.

stream   In wireless LANs, a function introduced with 802.11n in which a single device could use multiple antennas to send and receive bits at the same time (multiple streams).

subdomain   With DNS naming terminology, this term refers to a part of a host name (or domain name). That smaller part can be the part that a company registers through IANA or some authorized agency to identify all hosts inside that company.

subnet   Another term for *IP subnet*.

subnet address   Another term for *subnet ID*.

subnet ID   A number used to identify a subnet.

subnet mask   A 32-bit number, often written in other formats, that defines how many bits must be in common for the IP addresses inside one subnet.

subnet number   Another term for *subnet ID*.

subnetting   Another term for *IP subnetting*.

summary route   A synonym for *aggregate route*.

switch   A networking device used as a node in a networking topology, most often used to connect nearby user devices that need to use a cable to connect to the network.

switched circuit   A circuit created by the phone company in reaction to signaling (the user tapping telephone keys or a modem sending in the same digits), with the telco tearing down the circuit when the user is finished.

symmetric speed   A characteristic of some transmission technology in which the speeds in opposite directions are identical.

Synchronous Optical Network (SONET)   A series of physical layer standards that run over optical links, with each standard using a bit rate that is a multiple of the lowest base rate (OC-1, 51.84 Mbps), plus overhead.

system unit   A case, usually made of light metal or hard plastic, that encloses all the internal components of a personal computer, typically including the motherboard, expansion slots, connectors (for example, USB ports), slots for drives that have removable media, a power supply, and so on. It is sometimes referred to as an enclosure, desktop, or simply the computer.

T

T1   T-carrier Level 1.

T3   T-carrier Level 3.

T-carrier system   The name of the combination of different physical line standards (DS0, DS1, DS3, and others), plus circuit switches that use time-division multiplexing (TDM) features, that together allowed the phone company to create digital circuits from end to end and create leased-line services for customers.

TB   Terabytes.

TCP   See *Transmission Control Protocol*.

TCP connection   With TCP, another term for a flow that happens to use TCP.

TCP header   The 20-byte data structure that the TCP protocol adds to messages for the purpose of doing TCP's work.

TCP port   A port used by TCP.

TCP segment   The term referring to the message that flows through a network from sending IP host to receiving IP host, including the TCP header plus all higher-layer headers and user data, but also not including the network layer header or the data link layer header/trailer.

TCP segmentation   The process of the TCP software on a host accepting data to be sent by an application, and breaking the data into smaller sets of size MSS or smaller, so that the data fits into the TCP segments that are allowed to be sent out that host's interface.

TCP/IP   Transmission Control Protocol/Internet Protocol.

TCP/IP model   An open collection of standards related to all parts of networking, grouped together purposefully, so that if a company builds a network using these standards and using products that use these standards, the different network components will work together correctly.

TCP/IP network   A computer network that uses the standards defined and referenced by the TCP/IP model.

TDM   See *time-division multiplexing*.

telco   See *telephone company*.

telecom   Short for telecommunications, a term that refers to computer networking but with emphasis on the traditional roles played by telephone companies.

telephone   A device with a microphone and speaker that can create a voice call with another phone so that one phone converts voice into electricity and sends it over the telephone network, with the other telephone converting the electricity back to sound.

telephone company   A company whose business is to create a telephone network and offer telephone services to customers.

terabyte   1,099,511,627,776 bytes, or if rounding, 1,000,000,000 (1 trillion) bytes.

The Internet   See *Internet/The Internet*.

the web   A common slang word for the Internet, with emphasis on the entire collection of web servers accessible through the Internet.

TIA   Telecommunications Industry Association.

Tier 1 ISP   A general category for an ISP in which the ISP has more connections to other ISPs, often with a wider geographic reach, often a global reach, with higher-speed redundant links to other Tier 1 ISPs.

Tier 2 ISP   A general category for an ISP in which the ISP has fewer connections to other ISPs, and typically a smaller geographic reach than Tier 1 ISPs, generally relying on the better connections of a Tier 1 ISP to forward IP packets throughout the Internet.

time channel   In the T-carrier system, many of the physical lines can be separated conceptually for the purposes of time-division multiplexing by using some bits for one channel, some for the next, and so on. For example, a DS3 has 28 DS1 channels inside it.

time-division multiplexing   A type of logic used by some networking devices, including circuit switches in the telco, in which the switch divides a faster-speed line into time channels. The TDM logic takes the bits off slower-speed lines and forwards those bits inside the time channels in the higher-speed line (multiplexing), and when receiving bits on a higher-speed line, finds the bits in each time channel and splits those back out to the correct slower-speed line (demultiplexing).

Token Ring   An old LAN technology, popularized by IBM and standardized by IEEE as standard 802.5, that competed with Ethernet LANs in the 1980s and 1990s.

topology   A view of a network, either in concept or in a drawing, that represents the network as a series of nodes and links.

track   In a hard disk drive, the locations that can store bits exist as concentric circles; a track is one of these complete concentric circles.

trailer   Bytes of data, defined by some standard or protocol, and added after the user data that needs to be sent. Used almost exclusively by data link layer protocols.

transceiver   A word that combines the terms *transmitter* and *receiver*, useful to refer to a single device that plays both roles.

Transmission Control Protocol   One of two commonly used transport layer protocols in TCP/IP, with many useful features, including the delivery of data to the correct application process using port numbers, guaranteed delivery of data, in-order delivery of data, segmentation of large application data blocks, and flow control.

transmitter   A device that creates an energy signal, using an encoding scheme, to send bits over some networking link.

trunks   Links between telco switches.

twisted pair   A pair of wires used to create an electrical circuit, but when manufactured, the wires are twisted together, for the purpose of reducing the amount of EMI created by the wires.

U

UDP   See *User Datagram Protocol.*

UDP datagram   The term referring to the message that flows through a network from sending IP host to receiving IP host, including the UDP header plus all higher-layer headers and user data, but also not including the network layer header or the data link layer header/trailer.

UDP header   The 8-byte data structure that the UDP protocol adds to messages for the purpose of doing TCP's work.

UDP port   A port used by UDP.

unicast IP address   An IP address that represents a single interface connected to a TCP/IP network, which by definition comes from a class A, B, or C network.

Uniform Resource Locator (URL)   The formal term for *web address* as defined by HTTP. Also called a Uniform Resource Indicator (URI), and commonly also referenced as Universal Resource Locator.

UNII   See *Unlicensed National Information Infrastructure.*

universal MAC address   A MAC address assigned to an Ethernet device (NIC, switch port, and so on) by the manufacturer, following rules defined by the IEEE, so that the device's universal MAC address is unique among all other universal MAC addresses in the universe.

Universal Serial Bus   A common bus technology in personal computers that standardizes the sizes of connectors, speeds, and other rules, allowing devices of many kinds of external devices to connect to a computer.

unknown unicast frame   An Ethernet frame with destination MAC address FFFF.FFFF.FFFF.

unlicensed frequency band   A set of consecutive frequencies reserved by national regulators (like the FCC in the United States), with the regulations allowing anyone's devices to use the frequencies, although all must follow certain rules (like limiting power) so that all can get along when using the same frequencies.

Unlicensed National Information Infrastructure   The formal name of one of the wireless unlicensed frequency bands reserved for use by the FCC and other national regulators in other countries.

GL

unshielded twisted-pair (UTP)   A type of cabling that uses pairs of copper wires, twisted together, with no additional shielding from the effects of EMI.

upstream speed   For some transmission media, particularly those used for Internet access, the speeds can be different for each direction. The upstream speed refers to the bit rate from the ISP customer toward the ISP.

URL   See *Uniform Resource Locator*.

USB   See *Universal Serial Bus*.

USB flash drive   A device used as a permanent storage device that uses flash memory to store data, sits external to the computer so that it can be easily removed and shared, and uses a USB connector to connect to a computer's system unit.

User Datagram Protocol   One of two commonly used transport layer protocols in TCP/IP, with few features but with little overhead as a result. UDP's main feature is the delivery of data to the correct application process using port numbers.

UTP   See *unshielded twisted-pair*.

V

vendor group standard   A standard (or arguably prestandard) document, approved by a group of vendors, often to get compatible products to market more quickly than would otherwise happen, but also with a long-term goal of working toward standards with an appropriate standards group.

vendor group/vendor consortium   An organization created by a group of vendors so that they can work together on some goal. These goals can include creating a standard to be used by the vendors in the group, allowing those vendors to bring products to market more quickly, even before a more formal standards group creates a similar standard.

vendor networking model   Also called a proprietary networking model, any networking model owned and developed by a single product vendor.

vendor standard   Also called a proprietary standard, a standard approved by a single vendor so that the vendor keeps control.

video compression   A process by which a video file is changed and saved as a new smaller file, possibly with the cost of making the video be a little less clear.

video frame   A grid of pixel locations of a chosen width by height that contains the lights/colors to be shown in a video at a single point in time.

virtual circuit   See *permanent virtual circuit*.

voice call   A more modern term for a telephone call that does not use the word *telephone*, instead emphasizing the fact that the traffic that flows between the endpoints is voice.

Voice over IP   Voice traffic that happens to pass over a computer network that follows the rules defined by the TCP/IP network model.

voltage   The measure of the difference in electrical force between two points; electromotive force.

VPLS   Virtual Private LAN Service.

VPWS   Virtual Private Wire Service.

W

WAN   See *wide-area network*.

wavelength   For an energy wave, the distance between the leading and ending edge of one complete waveform; it can be calculated from the frequency and the speed at which the energy travels.

web address   Text that identifies details about one object in a network so that a client can request that object from a server. An informal term for *URL*.

web browser   Literally, software controlled directly by a user that requests web pages from a web server, and after receiving a page, displays the web page in a window. More generally, this term refers to both the software and the hardware on which it executes.

web client   A synonym for *web browser* that in a small way emphasizes the client-server relationship with web servers.

web hosting   A service provided by some service provider in which a company puts its web server content on a web server (hardware and software) owned by the web-hosting company so that the hosting company essentially runs the web server site as a service.

web link   A synonym for *hyperlink*.

web object   A single file, identified by a web address, that can be pulled by a web browser from a web server using HTTP. Web pages typically contain multiple web objects.

web page   In a web browser, all the text, images, video, and sound that fill the window of the browser when the user opens a link to some web address.

web server   Literally, software that stores web pages and web objects, listens for requests for those pages, and sends the contents of those pages/objects to clients. More generally, this term refers to both the software and the hardware on which it executes.

well-known port number   The reserved port number, inside the range 0–1023, set aside for use by a particular application layer protocol.

wide-area network (WAN)   A network typically leased from a service provider, often from a telco, because the company using the network cannot legally or cost-effectively create the network because it would pass through public land or land owned by other people. This term also refers to longer networks, because they are more likely to need to pass through other people's land. See also *local-area network*.

Wi-Fi   A term created by the Wi-Fi Alliance as part of its overall wireless LAN branding and marketing strategy; this term has become somewhat synonymous with *wireless LAN* over time.

Wi-Fi Alliance   A very successful vendor alliance that works to make the wireless LAN industry a success, including work to push for new wireless LAN standards, wireless LAN product testing, and product certification.

Wi-Fi hotspot   Another term for *WLAN hotspot*.

wired keyboard   A keyboard that communicates with the computer through a cable; the cable holds wires that the computer and keyboard use to transmit bits.

wired LAN   A local-area network (LAN) that uses cables/wires; the word *wired* refers to the wires inside UTP cables.

wired mouse   A mouse that communicates with the computer through a cable; the cable holds wires that the computer and mouse use to transmit bits.

wired/wireless LAN edge   A campus LAN design term referring to campus LANs, with the edge of the LAN having both wireless connections plus wired Ethernet LAN connections.

wireless client   The generic term for any device that uses wireless LAN technology to communicate through an access point.

wireless hotspot   An informal term for a location where a wireless LAN exists for the purpose of letting anyone connect to the LAN and then to the Internet.

wireless keyboard   A keyboard that communicates with the computer through radio waves; the keyboard transmits bits to a wireless receiver that connects through a cable to the system unit.

wireless LAN   A group of wireless clients, plus one or more wireless access points, with the access points all using a common SSID (wireless LAN name).

wireless mouse   A mouse that communicates with the computer through radio waves; the mouse transmits bits to a wireless receiver that connects through a cable to the system unit.

wireless router   An integrated networking device, often used in SOHO locations, with the device usually acting as an IP router, wireless AP, and Ethernet LAN switch.

wireless WAN   A type of network that uses no wires (cables), instead using radio waves, with a wide-area network (WAN) business model of longer distances, a service provider (usually a mobile phone company), and a fee structure in which the customer pays a monthly fee to the mobile phone company.

GL

wireless-only LAN edge   A campus LAN design term referring to campus LANs with only wireless connections between end-user devices and APs, and no wired Ethernet LAN connections at the edge.

wiring closet   A room in an office building, often one (or more) per floor, with LAN cables running from each user location into the closet. Typically, the network's LAN switches also sit in the wiring closet.

WLAN   See *wireless LAN*.

WLAN hotspot   A location, typically in a business like a retailer or restaurant, where customers can come and go and where the company offers a wireless LAN plus Internet access to its customers, often for free.

WLAN name   An informal term for *Service Set Identifier (SSID)*.

word   Two bytes of computer memory, or 16 bits.

working group   The term for an IETF committee of people working on developing a technology for eventual publication as an RFC.

World Wide Web   The formal name of the collection of websites throughout the Internet, and a synonym for *the web*.

WWW   See *World Wide Web*.

X–Z

X.25   A packet-switching service based on ITU standards that was the first popular packet-switching service.

Index